PEOPLE PATTERN POWER

PEOPLE PATTERN POWER:

P³

THE NINE KEYS TO BUSINESS SUCCESS

BY

MARILYNE WOODSMALL

AND

WYATT WOODSMALL

OF THE

THE INTERNATIONAL

RESEARCH INSTITUTE

FOR HUMAN TYPOLOGICAL STUDIES

ISBN: 1-892876-00-0

This publication is designed to provide accurate and authoritative information with regard to the subject matter covered. It is sold with the understanding that the publisher is not engaged in rendering legal, accounting, or other professional advice. If legal advice or other expert assistance is required, the services of a competent professional person should be sought.

From a *Declaration of Principles* jointly adopted by a Committee of the American Bar Association and a Committee of Publishers and Associations.

This book is available at quantity discounts for bulk purchases.
For information on instruments, tapes, and trainings
call 703 757-7945 or fax to 703 757-7946.

Visit our web page at http://www.peoplepatterns.com

TABLE OF CONTENTS

TRADEMARK AND SERVICE MARK NOTIFICATION

The terms People Pattern, People Patterns, People Pattern Power, People Pattern People, People Pattern Profile, People Pattern Pledge, People Pattern Creed, People Pattern Prayer, Value Culture, Value Culture Model, Value Culture Profile, Userware, the Yin/Yang of Values, the Yin/Yang of Management, the Yin/Yang of Sales, the Yin/Yang of Negotiations, the Yin/Yang of Training, the Yin/Yang of Personnel Selection, Advanced Behavioral Modeling, Advanced Learning Technologies and Mind Coach are trademarks and service marks of Marilyne Woodsmall and Wyatt Woodsmall.

The terms People Pattern, People Patterns, People Pattern Power, People Pattern People, People Pattern Profile, People Pattern Pledge, People Pattern Creed, People Pattern Prayer, Value Culture, Value Culture Model, Value Culture Profile, Userware, the Yin/Yang of Values, the Yin/Yang of Management, the Yin/Yang of Sales, the Yin/Yang of Negotiations, the Yin/Yang of Training, the Yin/Yang of Personnel Selection, Advanced Behavioral Modeling, Advanced Learning Technologies and Mind Coach may not be used in connection with the sale, promotion, description, name, or advertisement of any person, product, or service whatsoever without the prior written consent of Marilyne Woodsmall and Wyatt Woodsmall.

Any use of the terms People Pattern, People Patterns, People Pattern Power, People Pattern People, People Pattern Profile, People Pattern Pledge, People Pattern Creed, People Pattern Prayer, Value Culture, Value Culture Model, Value Culture Profile, Userware, the Yin/Yang of Values, the Yin/Yang of Management, the Yin/Yang of Sales, the Yin/Yang of Negotiations, the Yin/Yang of Training, the Yin/Yang of Personnel Selection, Advanced Behavioral Modeling, Advanced Learning Technologies and Mind Coach in critical essays, articles, or reviews must include the phrase People Pattern, People Patterns, People Pattern Power, People Pattern People, People Pattern Profile, People Pattern Pledge, People Pattern Creed, Value Culture, People Pattern Prayer, Value Culture Model, Value Culture Profile, Userware, the Yin/Yang of Values, the Yin/Yang of Management, the Yin/Yang of Sales, the Yin/Yang of Negotiations, the Yin/Yang of Training, the Yin/Yang of Personnel Selection, Advanced Behavioral Modeling, Advanced Learning Technologies and Mind Coach are trademarks and service marks of Marilyne Woodsmall and Wyatt Woodsmall.

*This book is dedicated to our wonderful parents,
both living and deceased.*

THE NINE KEYS TO BUSINESS SUCCESS

PROLOGUE

I am a highly successful manager. This book is about how I came to be that way. I had the good fortune to go to work for an incredible company called Success, Incorporated where they taught me the nine keys to business success. These keys are called *People Patterns*^{SM}. They have been the foundation of my accomplishments, achievements and expertise. These nine keys are nine different People Patterns that occur in all people. I learned how to identify these patterns in myself and in other people as well. Most important of all, I learned how to relate differently to a given individual based on that person's People Patterns. This has allowed me to be a highly effective communicator. It has also allowed me to have a far greater impact and influence on other people than I would have ever imagined being possible. This book is the story of how I first came to be exposed to these patterns.

SUCCESS, INCORPORATED

I remember well my first day on the job at Success, Incorporated That day was to mark a whole new chapter in my life. At the time, little did I realize just how much a change was in store for me. After four years of college followed by an MBA from a prestigious university, I had the opportunity to pursue my intended career in the real world. I remember that I was ready to leave the books and theories of academia behind me and to start applying all that I had learned. For a period of time I worked for several different companies, and I was not satisfied with any of them. Although I was a good manager, it always seemed like there was something missing that I could not quite put my finger on. I finally interviewed for a position as a middle manager at Success, Incorporated

There I found the missing piece, and it was there that my real education as a manager began.

I still clearly remember that day long ago which was my very first day on the job here at Success, Incorporated. As I was riding to work that morning, I remember reviewing in my mind what I knew about my new employer and what had initially attracted me to this company. Of all the companies for which I had worked, Success, Incorporated was the most successful from several points of view. First, it was an industry leader in sales. Second, it had one of the highest customers' satisfaction ratings in the industry. Third, it was known for its quality products and services. Fourth, it was particularly respected and known for its highly innovative approach to managing people. Last, but certainly not least, it was rated by its own employees as one of the most desirable companies in the country to work for.

THE INTERVIEW

I must admit, however, that there was something else that had intrigued me about this company from the start. This was its unique interview process. Every other employment interview that I had ever had was basically a carbon copy of all of the others. They all focused on my education, my work experience, and my overall appearance. These factors obviously represent the traditional criteria used to evaluate a job candidate. At Success, Incorporated they asked me, instead, a series of what I thought at the time were strange and unusual questions. I remember that some of the questions they asked me were the following:

"What do you want in a career?"

"What will having that do for you?"

"Why did you choose your current job?"

"Do you prefer to live your life spontaneously or to live it according to a plan?"

"How do you know when you've done a good job?"

Another thing they did was to show me several pictures. One was of a group of people on a boardwalk at the shore. Another was a scene of a crowded park. Then they asked me to describe at length what I saw in these pictures. They also asked me to imagine that I was about to walk through a door into my ideal career, and that I should describe to them what I imagined. Next, they placed three chairs in front of me and asked me to tell them what the relationship was among the three chairs. I had no clue as to what they were trying to find out about me from these questions, but I must have answered them satisfactorily, because I got a job offer from them soon afterwards.

P³ - P CUBED

Well, here I was a new employee of Success, Incorporated. I had just finished filling out the usual requisite forms in the Personnel Department. I was scheduled to begin an intensive ten-day, one-on-one orientation and training program with my new mentor. Little did I know what new and fascinating learnings were in store for me! The secretary showed me into my new mentor's office, said that I should make myself comfortable and that Shana would join me in a minute. Shana's office was very interesting. As I glanced around her office, I noticed an unusual transparent cube on her desk with the letter "P" inside it. I also observed several plaques on the wall. One of them had the following slogan:

People Pattern Power
is the key
to business success.

I also noticed that the bookshelf behind her desk contained not only many of the latest management books, but a few books on golf and tennis as well.

At that point, I heard a pleasant "Hello" and turned around to meet my new mentor. Her eyes sparkled with enthusiasm and she was full of energy. She surveyed me with a look that seemed to see all. She greeted me with a rather firm handshake that was not unlike my own. Then she asked me to be seated and sat opposite me rather than behind her desk. Somehow, she made me feel comfortable and at ease, so I had no qualms about asking her what that weird cube was on her desk with the letter "P" inside it.

"How appropriate of you to ask." She said. "Since that cube is the basis of our company's success. It also happens to be what you will be learning about during your orientation and training program with me over the next two weeks. We call this P^3 *(P cubed)* which stands for *People Pattern Power*[SM] . This is what you get from using People Patterns effectively at work and in your life. It also stands for *People Pattern Person*[SM] which is what you are about to become as a result of our special training program to make you a *People Pattern Manager*[SM] ."

"Oh, that is what that plaque on the wall is about." I said.

"Yes" she responded. "In fact, that is the best place to begin. First, let us begin by defining *People Patterns*[SM]. People Patterns are simply the patterns in human behavior. Although we are all unique, each of us behaves in set ways. Each of us has our own set of patterns, and we share different patterns in our set with other people. These patterns represent the different perceptual filters through which we take in information about the world around us, through which we evaluate that information, through which we are motivated, and through which we take action. These patterns are like putting on a special pair of glasses with changeable lenses. Each lens brings certain aspects of our environment into a sharp focus, while distorting other aspects or causing them to disappear. Each lens or filter represents a different People Pattern. We will be examining a small number of these patterns that are most significant. What makes each of us unique is our particular combination of these patterns. We summarize what we have learned about these patterns and how to use them in what we call the People Pattern Creed. Here is a copy of it for you."

I looked at the piece of paper that Shana had handed me. It read:

THE PEOPLE PATTERN CREED
All human beings are creatures of habit.
These habits lead to consistent patterns of behavior.
These patterns are called People Patterns.
All of our language and our actions reflect these People Patterns.
People Patterns are readily detectable by a trained observer.
People Patterns can be utilized to enhance communication.
People Patterns can also be used to increase influence.
A wise person will use them to do so.
To do anything less is to fail to respect another person's uniqueness.

"So now you are familiar with the principles of the People Pattern Creed. Next we need to talk about how to apply these principles. In order to utilize them effectively, you must be willing and able to change what you are doing in order to get other people to change what they are doing. This brings me to an important corollary of the People Pattern Creed."

People think their own way
and not our way.

"To get another person to change what he is doing or his way of thinking, it is necessary to tailor your communication to the way that he thinks and behaves. What may cause you to change is often quite different from what will cause him to change." Shana continued.

"The form and not the contents of the ways that people think is reflected in their People Patterns. It is necessary to match their set of People Patterns (i.e., their model of the world) in order for them to be influenced by your communication. In order to accomplish this, you need to do four things which are to focus, observe, communicate and verify."

Focus
Observe
Communicate
Verify

"To *focus* simply means knowing what your specific outcome is for that specific communication. All of your communications need to be purposive. Do not just do things arbitrarily and impulsively, but always have an outcome in mind for everything that you do and say. I cannot stress this enough. Effective communicators always operate from well-formed outcomes. Without outcomes clearly in mind, communication is simply a chance activity. Your outcome should include how you want the other person to think or to behave. Once you have this clearly in mind you can tailor your communication to get the response that you want."

"To *observe* means that you need to pay attention to and observe the person with whom you are communicating until you understand his or her model of the world. In other words, observe his or her particular set of People Patterns. Observe until you can think the way that the person with whom you are communicating does. Observe until the structure of his way of thinking becomes your way of thinking. Only then will you be able to match your communication to that person's model of the world."

"To *observe*, also, means something else. It means that you must observe the person with whom you are communicating to see how they are responding to you. You have to see if what you are doing is working or not. The only way that you can know this is by continually observing the verbal and non verbal responses of the person with whom you are communicating. Here at Success, Incorporated we have a highly pragmatic approach to communication. It is based on a simple principle which is that:

The meaning of a communication is the response that you get.

In other words, it is not what you intend to communicate, or what you think that you communicate, but what the other person perceives you as communicating that matters. For practical purposes, the meaning of your communication is determined by the way in which the other person responds to you. If his response is what you intended, then you are successful. If his response is not what you intended, then your communication has not succeeded in getting you your outcome. In this case, you need to do something else. Anything else certainly has a higher probability of success than what doesn't work. If you are not getting the response that you want, then repeating yourself louder and more emphatically is not likely to lead to success either. You have to change your communication and to continue to observe and monitor the response until you are successful." Shana motioned for me to hold my questions and went on.

"To *communicate* means to engage in the interaction with a person using his particular People Patterns so that the change that you want the person to make will make sense to him in terms of his model of the world. It is critical to communicate with a person by matching the form of his thought processes. Remember that it is the *form* of what you say rather than the *content* of what you say that is important. It would be like speaking a foreign language. The content is what you want to communicate, and the form is the language in which you express what you want to communicate. If the person does not understand your language, you can repeat the content until you are blue in the face, and he will still not understand you. If you speak that person's language, however, then he will understand what you are saying immediately. Usually, people get caught up in content, and forget that the content has to be expressed in the other person's language before he can understand it. This means matching a person's People Patterns in your communication with him. To do this, you have to have enough behavioral flexibility to transcend your own patterns. You have to have enough behavioral flexibility so that you can take on the patterns of the person with whom you are communicating. Remember, too that things get better by change and seldom do they improve by chance. For other people to change, you have to change the way that you communicate with them."

"To *verify* means to check to see that the change that you want has indeed occurred. If it has not, then you have failed in one of the above steps. In that case, repeat the process until you are successful in achieving your outcome. To summarize, you need to focus on your outcome, you need to observe their patterns and how they are responding to you, you need to vary your communication until you get the response that you want, and you need to continually verify to make sure that you are successful."

"P^3 (People Pattern Power or People Pattern Person) is the key to our company's success. P^3 summarizes the principles upon which our company is built. These principles represent the various perceptual filters through which human beings see the world. The People Pattern Person (alias '*P cubed*') is one who can easily identify these different filters in others. He is one who can modify his own behavior and language to fit the People Patterns of the person with whom he is communicating. He is a person who effectively understands and uses the four step change process. When he does this, the other person will not only understand him better, but he will also have a greater likelihood of influencing that person, and of getting that person to change."

PEOPLE PATTERN POWER TRAINING PROGRAM

Since this was my first interaction with Shana, I thought it would be appropriate to simply listen for the time being, so she proceeded to explain more about my orientation training program at Success, Incorporated.

"This one-on-one training program that you are about to begin deals with your putting on a special pair of glasses in order to identify both your own People Patterns and those of the people with whom you are communicating. This training program is about you learning to change the filters in your own glasses in order to match the filters of those people with whom you would like to communicate more effectively. Remember that each of us wears our own customized glasses with our own set of particular filters. It is this personal blend of filters which becomes our personal model of the world. It is this unique blend of People Patterns or filters that become a significant part of our behavioral profile. To the extent that our model overlaps somehow with that of another person, we will be able to enhance communication with that person."

"Over the next two weeks, during the course of this initial training and orientation program, you will begin to discover the basic People Patterns that guard the doorways of our perceptions. Once you identify these patterns, you will know what elements of experience are filtered in and what elements are filtered out. Once you know this, you can match one or more filters of the other person's model of the world. You can begin to see the world the way that the other person does. Moreover, you can begin to speak his language and walk in his shoes. You can chart the boundaries of his experience. In short, you can communicate effectively and efficiently with anyone, because you are matching that person's experience."

"Our internal behavioral profile or model of the world serves not only as a standard guideline in our daily interactions with others, but also reflects a particular set of language patterns through which we communicate verbally. It should not be any surprise to you that a mismatch of language patterns can result in many a disastrous interaction. This training, then, will not only teach you how to see the world through another person's filters, but will also teach you how to customize your language patterns to match the People Patterns of the person with whom you would like to communicate more effectively. Our goal is to enable you to enter the other person's reality and to share his People Patterns even if only temporarily for the purposes of the interaction. It does no good to talk about your experience if it does not match that of the other person with whom you are communicating. The person simply would not understand you. He would understand what you say, i.e., the content. But it is the form of your communication that matters. *How* you say it is as important as *what* you say. We live in a society that is asleep when it comes to form. Effective communicators know that content is secondary. What really counts is matching the model of the world of the person with whom you are communicating, and when you do this well, it occurs totally outside of the other person's conscious awareness."

"Well, if I understand what you have said thus far" I chimed in, "my training program will enable me to understand what makes myself and others tick. I'll be able to put the filters of others into my own glasses, and in so doing, I'll be able to enhance my communication with them and thus have a far better chance of influencing and changing them. Right?"

"Yes" Shana smiled, and then she quickly added: "You'll also develop more compassion for those around you with different People Patterns than your own. You will begin to understand why we often think so negatively of other people who behave differently from us. We often think that people are going out of their way just to make our lives difficult. With People Patterns we can see that it is not meant personally. People are simply following their own patterns. Once we realize this, we can feel better about ourselves and about others. This brings me to another corollary of the People Pattern Creed which is: *We seek less stress and conflict in the company and in ourselves.*"

PUTTING PEOPLE IN BOXES

"This all sounds great." I said. "But I have a question. Will not some people consider People Patterns to be just another way of putting people in boxes?"

"That is a good question." She replied "None of us likes to be put into a box ourselves, yet we all categorize other people every day. Whenever we describe another person or put a label on him, we are putting him or her into boxes. In fact, bureaucracies do this all the time with distinctions of race, nationality, religion, marital status and the like on forms and questionnaires. Quite frankly, much of the bureaucratic yet culturally accepted categorization in these areas ends up putting females into boxes more than men. Just think about it. Women are forced to specify their personal status of Ms. or Mrs. or Miss, which immediately categorizes them with all the connotations each form of address has in the minds of different people. Men, on the other hand, are universally known as Mr. and that is all. Anyway, that is another topic entirely, for another time perhaps."

"In any case, the important and relevant question should be:

How good a job do we do of sorting people into boxes in terms of enhancing human interaction rather than detracting from it?

And also, what are the consequences of doing so? This is what the People Pattern Power Training Program is all about. Only by becoming a People Pattern Person with People Pattern Power can one enter another person's model of the world. Then, and only then, can we begin to experience and feel any compassion for our fellow workers and customers with whom we share this space forty hours or more a week, fifty two weeks of the year. By seeing the world through the People Pattern filters of others, only then can we begin to understand why their behaviors, their reactions, their language are not like ours."

Our goal is not to box ourselves in the darkness of ignorance, but rather to light the path to an understanding of our colleagues, managers, family, friends and fellow man in an increasingly hostile and difficult world.

"I could not agree with you more." I interjected.

"One more thing about the way that we communicate here at Success, Incorporated before I go on. We have found that highly effective communicators know a secret. They know that man is a creature of habit, and that all human beings follow patterns in their thinking, talking, walking, eating, working, in short, in all of their daily behaviors. They know that habits are not just physical, but are also mental and emotional. Among the mental habits, the most important is that of using our People Patterns or perceptual filters. These People Patterns determine what a person will and will not experience about the world. In short, these People Patterns determine how we live our lives personally and professionally. These People Patterns determine how we interact with our colleagues here on the job - be they managers, peers, employees, or customers. In fact, they determine how we interact with our fellow members of society, but that will be the subject for another discussion."

"Once you know this secret about a person, you then know how to communicate with him and how to go about persuading him to change. Once you identify a person's People Patterns, then you suddenly become privy to a whole new world view as seen through his glasses. As we've already mentioned, there is a fundamental principle of human behavior."

People think their own way and not our way. To get them to change, we have to communicate with them by utilizing patterns from inside and not from outside their model of the world. We have to communicate with them using patterns that match their perceptual reality.

QUESTION OF MANIPULATION

I thought for a minute and a question occurred to me. "I accept what you are saying, but wouldn't some people consider this to be manipulative?"

Shana smiled. "That is an excellent question, and I am glad that you brought it up. It is a reflection of the integrity with which you interact with other people. There are several ways to answer your question, and they all revolve around what you mean by manipulation. If you look in a dictionary, you will find several meanings for the word 'manipulation'. One meaning defines manipulation simply as 'skillful or artful management'. I doubt that you would object to this. Another meaning, however, defines manipulation as 'adapting or changing a person or situation to suit one's purpose or advantage'. This is the use of manipulation with which you and most people are concerned." I nodded in agreement as she continued.

"You can't help but influence other people both positively and negatively. Everything that you do, or don't do for that matter, will have an effect on the people with whom you are dealing. The only real question is whether your influence on other people will be conscious and skillful or whether it will be unconscious and a matter of chance. In this sense, you can't help but manipulate. Everything that you do is manipulation. The question is whether it is intentional or unintentional, and if it is intentional the question is whether you are skillful and artful at it or not. Some of the most manipulative people whom I know do not view themselves as manipulative at all. This is because they do it unconsciously and without awareness. In their minds, it is not manipulation, because it is not conscious or intentional. But, in fact, it is."

The only real question is whether your influence on other people will be conscious and skillful or whether it will be unconscious and a matter of chance.

"So the real question ultimately has to do with how you are going to manipulate other people. If you do it in such a way that you gain at their expense, which is often called a win/lose, then they will be anxious to return the favor by getting back at you at the first opportunity. If a person feels that they have been taken advantage of, a common reaction is a desire for revenge. This can quickly escalate. Obviously, such a situation is totally unacceptable in any personal or professional context. The alternative is to manipulate people in such a way that you both gain. This is commonly called a win/win. You don't take advantage of them, and they don't take advantage of you. People Patterns, like any other valid personality typology, is a powerful tool. It can be used for a win/win or it can be misused for a win/lose. My council to you is to always use this tool wisely and responsibly and to always seek a win/win in all of your personal and professional interactions. It simply doesn't make sense to do otherwise, nor is it worth it in the grand scheme."

Always seek a win/win in all of your interactions.

"There is another way to view what People Patterns are all about. Every individual filters the world to fit his internal model. People Patterns give you a knowledge of this filtering process. You can communicate with people in one of two ways. The first way is to communicate according to your patterns. To make sense of your communication, the other person will translate it through his filters. In other words, he will delete, generalize and distort what you say according to his model of the world. This often leads to misinterpretations and misunderstandings. The other way to communicate with other people is to translate your message into their language. You do this by stating what you want to communicate using their patterns. In this way, the other person does not have to translate your message through his filters, because you stated it in terms of his filters in the first place. This does several things. First, it lessens the likelihood of miscommunication and misunderstanding. Second, it speeds up the communication process, because it reduces the translation time. Third, it pays the other person the ultimate compliment, which is that you are willing to tailor your communication to make it as easy as possible for him to understand you. This builds bridges between people instead of walls." Shana did not pause so I continued to listen attentively.

"Last let us talk for a minute about how you can persuade or influence another person. It is certainly possible to do this in several ways. You can threaten, cajole, or plead with someone. Or you can take a different approach. In this approach you understand that people do things for their reasons and not for your reasons. Since this is the case, then your reasons will be of little use in persuading them. So if your reasons don't help, then what does? The answer is obvious. People do things for their reasons. In order to persuade or influence another person, the most effective way is to understand his reasons and his model of the world and to present what you want him to do in terms of his reasons and his model of the world. In general people do things for reasons. Very little behavior is arbitrary. So if it makes sense to someone in terms of his model, then he will do it. If it doesn't make sense in terms of his model, then the person won't do it. People Patterns help you to understand other people's models of the world."

"This doesn't mean that you will automatically be able to influence or persuade another person?" I asked.

"No. Not at all." Shana replied. "You will only be able to do this if you can present your position so that it makes sense to the other person. Your ability to do this will be determined by your creativity and by your understanding of the other person's world. It is obviously far easier to persuade people to do things that benefit them, than it is to persuade people to do things that do not benefit them. So we come back to win/win. If what you want is a win/win and if you can present it in terms of their model so that it makes sense to them, then they will do it. If what you want is a win/lose, then it will be very difficult to present it in terms of their model so that it makes sense to them. You may get them to do it by forcing them or tricking them or deceiving them or confusing them. All of these approaches are manipulative in the worst sense. In your business and personal relations, I strongly council you to always work for a win/win and to communicate this in the other person's model so that it makes sense to him. If you do this, then you will embody the essence of what People Patterns are all about. The great sales trainer Zig Ziglar likes to say that 'you can get anything in the world that you want, if you help someone else to get something that they want'. Life is about win/win and fair exchanges. People Patterns make it easier to give people what they want, and in so doing you can get what you want. That is what People Patterns are all about."

If what you want is a win/win and if you can present it in terms of the other person's model of the world so that it makes sense to him, then he will do it.

"It sounds like you and Success, Incorporated have certainly done an excellent analysis of communication. It is about time other companies got on the band wagon, don't you think?" I stated enthusiastically.

"It is interesting that you should say that, because you bring me to my next point, and, in fact, to the first People Pattern Lesson which explains why some people have difficulty with change. When something new appears, there are always going to be those who want to maintain the status quo. These individuals are quite comfortable with things staying the same, and getting them to change is always a challenge."

PEOPLE PATTERN OVERVIEW

"The last thing that I want to do today is to give you a brief overview of the People Pattern Power Training Program that you will be experiencing during the next two weeks with a follow-on session in several months. During this time you will learn nine People Patterns. For each pattern you will learn what the distinction is, how to identify it in yourself and others, and how to utilize it in five different business contexts. These are management, sales, negotiations, training and personnel selection and placement. I will begin each day by teaching you the pattern and how to identify it in yourself and others. Then you will visit one of our top managers in each of the five areas. They will personally mentor you in specific applications in their area."

"It sounds like a great program. I can hardly wait to begin."

"You already have. Let me give you a brief overview of the nine People Patterns that you will master during the next two weeks. When you analyze human beings, you will find that they engage in four primary activities. First, they take in data from the world. We call this the perceptual activity. They then respond to that data in light of the data that they have previously stored in their memory. They respond in three ways. One, is that they think about it. We call this cognitive activity. Two, is that they respond to it emotionally. We call this affective activity. And three, they take action. We call this conative activity. Each of these four activities has certain People Patterns associated with it."

FOUR HUMAN ACTIVITIES
Perceptual -Sensing
Cognitive -Thinking
Affective - Feeling
Conative - Doing

"You will learn three People Patterns relating to perception. These are the Change People Pattern which relates to our perception of sameness and difference, the Primary Interest Pattern which relates to the kinds of content in which people are interested, and the Information Pattern which relates to how we take in data from the world and store it in memory. There are two People Patterns related to cognition. These are the Evaluation Pattern which relates to the locus of our judgements about the world and the Decision Pattern which relates to the basis of all of our decisions. The affective realm has to do with emotions and feelings. This is also the realm of our values. There are two People Patterns relating to emotions. These are the Motivation Pattern which relates to how people are motivated and the Motive Pattern which relates to why people are motivated. Last, there are two People Patterns relating to doing. These are the Activity Pattern which relates to how people perform any activity and the Organization Pattern which relates to how people manage time and space."

THE NINE PEOPLE PATTERNS
Change
Primary Interest
Information
Evaluation
Decision
Motivation
Motive
Activity
Organization

"In any case, I think you now have a good overview for the moment, so we'll start bright and early tomorrow with our first People Pattern. Do you have any questions before we end for today?"

PEOPLE PATTERN PROFILE

It occurred to me that I had a couple of questions. The first related to my initial hiring interview.

"When I interviewed for the position here at Success, Incorporated I took some kind of a test called the People Pattern Profile. Will I be learning about that test?"

Shana smiled. "That is a good question, and I am pleased that you asked it. You will be learning to master the People Patterns that serve as the basis for the People Pattern Profile. Obviously you cannot give everyone in the world a test to determine their People Patterns. You will be learning to identify the patterns in the context of your daily business activities. More important, you will be learning how to utilize the patterns to create change. There are an infinite number of ways to classify people. The ultimate test of any classification system is its utility. It doesn't do any good just to be able to identify nine People Patterns in two minutes. The importance of People Patterns lies in their utilization to create change. That is what you will be mastering."

"With respect to the People Pattern Profile itself, it is a valuable instrument that can be used in a variety of ways. It is an excellent instrument for personnel screening. It can also be used in team building and as a way to appreciate diversity and develop cooperation. An organization effectiveness specialist can also use it as a diagnostic instrument to assist in determining what intervention would be most appropriate. And there are many other possible uses that I will not go into now. As you know, we use the People Pattern Profile in-house and license it to other companies and to individual consultants. In order to be eligible to purchase and use the instrument we require that clients take a training program from us which teaches them the People Patterns and how to interpret and utilize the People Pattern Profile."

COMPETENCY MODELING

I had one final question. "I am curious about one of the things that you do here which you call modeling. What is it and how does it relate to job competencies and to People Patterns?"

Shana thought for a moment. "What you have asked covers a broad area. Later you will receive an in-house training in modeling. For the moment I will give you a general answer to this question. It will make more sense once you have been trained in People Patterns."

"First, let me start with modeling which is perhaps the main key to our company's success. Modeling is a process of capturing, encoding, replicating and transferring expertise. It begins with experts who are able to perform at an exceptionally high skill level. Modeling addresses the question 'How is it possible?'. How is it possible that one person can produce amazing results while other people can only produce mediocre results? The answers are twofold. They are *what they do* and *how they do it*. A lot of people claim to do behavioral modeling. Usually all that they end up doing is listing what the expert does. What we do here goes much deeper. We have all been in the position of knowing what we want to do, being highly motivated to do it, and still not being able to do it. This is because we either don't know how to organize ourselves to do it or because there is something in our mind that is preventing us from doing it. Our approach to modeling captures not only *what* the expert does but *how* he does it. It also focuses on assisting the individual who wants to acquire the skill to remove any blockages that are preventing him from doing so. Trainings that we design are model based. We model the experts in an area and design a training to transfer the expert skills to other suitably selected trainees. This requires a special kind of training that focuses on behavioral modification. It is not enough to know what to do or to know about how to do it. It is necessary to actually be able to do it. That is the focus of our modeling process and of our trainings."

"Modeling can have three major by-products. First, it can reduce training times and increase skill levels over conventional trainings. Second, it can help to design the man-machine interface of equipment. We call this *psycho-ergonometrics*. This is the science of designing human machine interfaces that are optimally user friendly. Third, it can help in personnel selection. Preselection is always more important than training. We live in a world in which many people believe that you can train anyone to do anything. That is simply not the case. It is important to select the right people and to train them properly. The best way to select the right people is to select people who have the same talent and innate abilities as people who are already successful at that job. This is where modeling comes in. Traditional methods of hiring rely on education and job experience. Neither one of these is correlated with job success. Other more sophisticated approaches rely on complex psychological inventories. Unfortunately, these inventories leave out key factors that are essential to success and that can only be determined by modeling people who are already successful." Shana continued to answer my question.

"You also asked about job competencies. Many companies have found that traditional selection and training processes have failed to meet their needs. In attempting to identify the cause of the deficiency they have realized that although they had been able to identify the required skills needed for high performance, they had been unable to identify whether or not people would be able to perform these skills. This fueled the search for so-called 'competencies'. A 'competency' is an underlying characteristic of an individual that is causally connected to superior job performance. The search for job competencies is based on the belief that what prevents people from performing at a high level is a lack of ability or competence. This is an important insight. The problem lies in the implementation of the program. Armed with this basic insight, companies set off to try to identify the basic competencies. Here is where the problem arises. Many efforts in this area identify characteristics that are so vague and general that they are of little value. More sophisticated approaches divide competencies into more basic categories. These include such things as attitudes, beliefs, values, self identities, motives, traits, cognitive and behavioral skills, and content knowledge. This approach is more precise and more difficult to do well. A modeling approach has the greatest chance of success in identifying competencies that are actually related to job performance. This is because it extracts the characteristics of people who have demonstrated superior performance in the actual job. *All too often competency models are based on someone's theory of what works rather than on what expert performers actually do.* Our modeling approach is the most sophisticated approach to competencies currently available, because it operates at the process level and distinguishes those characteristics that are actually causally connected to expert performance. Furthermore it identifies not only 'what', but more critically 'how' and it incorporates this knowledge into a training program which is designed to modify behavior and to produce superior performance."

"Last, where do People Patterns fit in? People Patterns are one component of both the modeling and the competency process. They enable us to understand how a person filters the world. Expertise is based on a number of factors among which are: 1) A set of beliefs that support superior performance. 2) A set of values that motivate one to expend the time, energy and resources required to acquire expertise. 3) A set of perceptual filters and sorting patterns that enable one to acquire the necessary data from one's environment. 4) The ability to make highly refined discriminations about that environment in one or more of the representational systems which are visual, auditory, kinesthetic, olfactory, gustatory, and digital (which relates to meanings). 5) An optimal strategy or sequence of representational system accesses. 6) A means of decomposing tasks and a set of heuristics for focusing choices. People Patterns are directly related to the third factor. People Patterns are only part of the modeling puzzle. They are necessary, but they are not sufficient for a complete model. During the next two weeks you will be learning about People Patterns. If in the future you are interested in modeling, then there will be opportunities to pursue that interest. In the meantime I think that you have had enough for one day. I will see you tomorrow morning. Be prepared to put on a new set of lenses with different filters so that you can have a whole new world open up to you. Also, be prepared for discoveries about yourself and other people. Most of all, be prepared to begin the process of becoming a master of People Patterns, a P^3 Manager^{SM}."

KEY 1:

THE CHANGE PEOPLE PATTERN

INTRODUCTION

I was waiting for my car pool while my kids were getting ready for school. One of the younger ones was upset, because her dress was in the wash. I heard my wife say with exasperation: "But you can't wear the same dress every day." And my daughter replied: "Why not? I like that dress, and I want to wear it all of the time." I was reflecting on my daughter's answer and then my son came in. My wife took one look at him and said: "You can't wear that." "Why not?" he insisted. "Because it doesn't match and looks outrageous." she said with great frustration. Then she added: "Why do you always have to be so different?" "I like to be different." he responded. My wife gave me a knowing look and said "I wonder who you got that from." At this point my car pool arrived, and I quickly escaped. When I arrived at work I had to stop by Personnel to drop off a form. I handed it to the receptionist and noticed that Karen was in her office conducting an employment interview. As I hurried on to Shana's office, I was thinking of my own recent job interview. At least I was now beginning to understand what some of the questions were all about. Perhaps I was getting more of a sense of what I didn't know about the intricacies of human interaction in spite of all the schooling and the standard theories I had learned about how people behave. In any case, my curiosity had peaked concerning the rather unique interview process I had experienced. I mentioned this to Shana when I arrived at her office.

"I will bet that you thought that I was probably from another galaxy based on the types of questions I asked you during my initial interview with you!" exclaimed Shana with a gleam of satisfaction in her eyes.

"Well, I do admit that I has wondering what an unusual line of questioning I was experiencing, and especially because this whole time you were completely businesslike and speaking in a rather matter of fact tonality as though this was the norm rather than the exception."

"I could tell by your physiology and eye movements that the gears were going at full speed in your mind; and more important, I knew by your reactions to my questions that the change from more typical interview questions was a welcome one."

"Was it that obvious?" I asked a bit embarrassed as though my inner being had been totally exposed.

Shana grinned with satisfaction. "In fact, I knew then that anything different and atypical served as a magnet drawing your attention. So I realized that you were a person out of my own mold, and that you and I would get along just fine from that perspective."

"What could have told you all that so quickly?", I asked with what I am sure was a puzzled look on my face.

"That is precisely what today's lesson is all about. Do you remember the three chairs I placed in front of you during the initial interview? I specifically asked you a target indicator question about the relationship among the three chairs."

"Yes, and I remember saying that they were all different from each other."

"I kind of knew what your answer would be based on several other things that you had said prior to that question and also by the rather unconventional tie that you had on that day (and another unique one today, I might add). More on that later, though. Let's get back to the chairs."

I must admit that I was really beginning to wonder how Shana was getting this information about me so quickly.

"Have you ever wondered why some people stay at the same job for years on end and, in many cases, for the duration of their entire professional lives?" I would bet that you could never stand for that, right!"

"Well, uh, no I couldn't. How do you know that?", I asked, getting a little annoyed in a non-confrontive manner.

"Alas! The secrets of change are about to be revealed to you, my friend. A bit more patience while I continue a bit. For example, have you ever wondered why some people always eat at the same restaurant whenever they go out to dinner, while others constantly vary their choice of eating spots? Or what about the individual who ends up buying the same car year in and year out, or buys from the same dealer every time, while others simply have to change the make of their automobile every time they are due for a new one? What is the relationship between what you are doing now and what you were doing a month ago at work? Why do some people react so negatively to anything that deviates from their normal routine, yet others seem to thrive on variety?"

"How is such diversity of behavior possible?" I chimed in. "This is a question I had been asking myself for a long time, and nothing and no one in my past studies and experiences had ever been able to answer the question."

"Diversity! What a great word. It fits your pattern to the tee! In any case, the answer to your question lies in another basic People Pattern called the Change Pattern. The Change People Pattern tells us so much about a person. First, it reveals how a person will be able to deal with change or not deal with it, as the case may be. The Change People Pattern also reveals how a person associates elements of his present experience to his past experience."

"You can get this information from three ordinary chairs," I reluctantly asked as though I already knew the obvious.

"This pattern reflects the four different ways in which individuals view the world around them based on the particular perceptual filters we use when taking in the thousands of sensory stimuli which bombard us at every minute of every day. The distinct perceptual filter through which we see the world personalizes our experience. They also clearly explain why we often take many of our own behaviors for granted as the norm for others, when in actuality, they are merely actions or conduct expressing our personal models of the world. So what is our reaction when we come across someone who does not see eye to eye with us, who does not react to a seemingly identical scenario or set of conditions in the same manner as we do?"

"I would rather not utter the expletives I use to describe those who don't think in the way that I do."

"Most of us automatically categorize any person with a different model of the world than ours as a complete and utter idiot, to put it rather mildly!" Shana laughingly revealed.

THE CHANGE TEST

"Bear with me now as we delve into the dynamics of change for the rest of the day. So what is the Change People Pattern, and how do we identify it in ourselves and in others? Just what are those perceptual filters which refine and customize our particular experience? Briefly, in any given life experience or situation, a person will focus his attention on one of four elements. The one he chooses determines his Change People Pattern. We use the following simple test to determine quickly this People Pattern: take three quarters, (or any three coins of the same denomination) and place them all heads up on a flat surface, with two of the coins facing in one direction, and the third rotated 90 degrees from the other two. Try this first on yourself, and then on a spouse, friend or colleague. Ask the person the following target indicator question ' What is the relationship among these three coins?' Pay close attention to the way you word the instructions. Make sure you say ' What is the *relationship among* these three coins?.'

Also, pay close attention to whatever they say. We are not looking for long involved philosophical responses, but simply for whatever spontaneously comes to mind when the person is asked this simple question."

"So the coins can be used in place of chairs or any grouping of three similar items. I hesitate to use the word similar because that goes against everything I believe in." For the first time, the word 'similar' began to take on a very new meaning in my mind, I realized.

"You will be amazed to find completely different responses from different people. With this coin scenario as with any situation in life, a person will notice one of four things: 1) Some people will notice only similarities (i.e. that the coins are all quarters, are all on the table, are all the same color, and are all basically the same). They may even repeat back the question paraphrasing it as 'what is the similarity among these three coins?' Often they will unconsciously reach out and, without any thought, turn the coin that is rotated 90 degrees back so that it is aligned with the others. These are people who notice only the similarities, and who are totally oblivious to any variations among the coins. They either don't see them or just feel that they are irrelevant. They are called *sameness* people. People who wear the Sameness People Pattern exclusively will not even notice that one coin is rotated 90 degrees to the other two. 2) Some seeing the coins, will notice similarities first and then differences (i.e. they would say that the coins are basically the same with one or two differences. A person may notice that one is rotated 90 degrees, or that one is shinier than the others, or that they have different dates. This second category is that of *qualified sameness* people. Although they have a balanced view in that they notice both sameness and difference, qualified sameness people notice the similarities first and then any obvious differences. 3) The third type of person will see only differences among the coins (i.e. the coins are in fact all different, with different dates, different degrees of shininess, and are positioned in different ways, etc.). In fact, they will not even mention that they are all quarters. These individuals are called *difference* people, because their perceptual filters allow them to exclusively see differences and no similarities at all. 4) The fourth type of response will be from a person who notices differences first, and then mentions the similarities in passing (that the coins are basically different, with some similarities, such as all being placed on the table, or all being quarters). These individuals are called *qualified difference* people since their perceptual filters first target the elements of distinction and uniqueness in any situation and only then notice obvious similarities."

CHANGE PEOPLE PATTERN
Sameness
Qualified Sameness
Difference
Qualified Difference

"Are you with me thus far?" Shana asked.

"Please do continue. If I don't interrupt to ask any questions, it's because I am so intrigued by all of this. I would like to know what the responses to this simple question about the coins reveal about a person's customized filters and their significance as manifested in his behaviors. I also would like to know if the types are evenly distributed in society."

It was obvious that Shana really appreciated my questions.

"I will answer your last question first. The types are not evenly distributed. In the modern industrialized world the breakdown is as follows. About 5% to 10% of the population is sameness. The proportion is higher in developing countries and among rural people. About 55% of the population is qualified sameness. This sameness and qualified sameness people make up about two thirds of the world. Qualified difference people make up about 25% of the population. And difference people make up about 5% to 10% of the population. There are more difference people in industrialized countries and among urban and highly educated people. So sameness and difference people are about equally distributed. The big disparity is due to the fact that the qualified sameness people outnumber the qualified difference people by more than two to one. These percentages will prove to be important in many areas, and you will hear more about them from your teachers in the different departments that you will visit after we finish. Now with respect to your second question." Shana paused for a minute and continued.

PERCENTAGES
Sameness - 5% to 10%
Qualified Sameness - 55%
Difference - 5% to 10%
Qualified Difference - 25%

"The way in which you answer the question about the three coins or three chairs indicates first and foremost how well you deal with change. It reveals the way in which you react to new experiences and to new situations and reveals a great deal about your lifestyle . It will also explain how it is possible for your colleague, spouse, friend, or whomever, to be such an idiot so much of the time! Remember if others do not have the same perceptual filters that we do, they will necessarily take in the world differently and will act differently from us. And it is usually quite difficult to understand how another person can react in a way totally alien to ours when faced with a seemingly identical situation. We have done this simple test time and time again, both one on one, as well as in front of large groups of people. Without fail, the sameness and qualified sameness people simply cannot believe the reactions of the difference and qualified difference people, and vice versa. The reaction of the sameness person is always 'What is wrong with him? Doesn't he see that all of the coins are the same?'. Likewise, the difference person will go nuts, because he cannot understand how anyone could fail to see what to him are so obviously three totally different, distinctive and unique things. Each group has difficulty understanding how the other groups can have such a completely different and outrageous (based on their perceptual filters) view of what appears to be the same situation in front of everyone."

"Are you ready to learn about each of the four aspects of the Change People Pattern?"

"Let's go for it."

SAMENESS

"Great! Let us now consider the implications of this People Pattern by discussing one by one the four aspects of the Change People Pattern: *sameness, qualified sameness, difference* and *qualified difference,* and see how and where they each manifest in today's society and in your particular lifestyle."

"The first way of viewing the world is through the eyes of a person who filters the world by sameness. A person operating out of a Sameness People Pattern does not tolerate change well and prefers to maintain a great deal of continuity in his lifestyle, whether it be in a personal and/or professional context. This is the individual who does a job from fifteen years to life with no variety whatsoever. Run of the mill routine is the road taken by a sameness person. He expects to live in a status quo world, and ends up angry and even occasionally out of touch when change does creep in. This individual stays in the same job, often lives in the same house for years, and stays married to the same person. Divorce is quite rare among couples who are both heavily into sameness. Even if marital problems do arise, people with sameness filters either ignore them or go out of their way to find solutions which will prevent a change of circumstances."

"Excuse me for interrupting. Does this mean that difference people can never stay married to the same person forever?"

"On the contrary. First, you have forgotten the contextuality factor. When it comes to true love, not infatuation, the Change People Pattern, although there, manifests in other ways. The chances for success, however, are directly related to both mates having Difference People Patterns in their approach to everyday living. In fact, there are some very happy difference couples out there. These are marriages in which both mates are heavily difference oriented and naturally make difference an important factor in their relationship. What I mean is that they end up having quite fulfilling relationships, because they really do enjoy playing the difference game of life together. They end up sharing difference rather than sameness (except for themselves). In the context of everyday life they both encourage changes in activity and scenery. For example they would both enjoy changes in things such as where and what and when they eat. More than sameness couples, they really do spice up life and their own relationships. And, besides, we all know that in some special relationships there are other factors at work which have nothing to do with earthly matters."

"I bet that sameness couples would go nuts with such diversity of activity and interest." I interjected.

"Yes, and it is extremely difficult for them to cope with surprises in life, because unexpected occurrences are new elements which do not fit into their habitual mold. In such situations, they will continue to look for similarities, and pretend that difference simply does not exist. For example, if a sameness person ends up divorced for whatever reason, he/she is most likely to look for another mate with the same qualities as his previous spouse, or someone who reminds him in some, even small way of him/her. Failure in this domain of relationships can lead to extreme depression. Much of the growing depression in our society can be directly linked to loneliness. The worst case is people who end up alone after the breakup of a significant relationship. If they are sameness in orientation, and suddenly find themselves separate from their significant other who had provided the foundation of commonality and similarity, then they end up at the deep end of mental despondence and gloom. In a therapeutic context it would be helpful to know the person's Change People Pattern, which could, in some instances, explain the extreme despair."

"Similarly, when faced with a forced job relocation, a sameness person is more likely to view it as a traumatic experience, since it means moving from a comfortable, known situation into a new and strange working and living environment. The results can be devastating in some cases, and these people often end up seeking therapy. This is why the current job market with many companies downsizing is so traumatic. Difference people will anticipate what is going to happen and look for another job. It is the loyal sameness people who remain in place and then get laid off. When the world stops being what it always was, they often don't know how to cope. This results in a great deal of personal tragedy. It is no small wonder that the corporate world is taking so much heat. What in essence it is doing is sacrificing loyal sameness employees on the alter of corporate greed. Many systems thinkers are arguing that full employment should be a corporate responsibility."

"In any case, when faced with a novel situation, the sameness person will necessarily see elements of the new experience which are similar to things with which he is already familiar. For sameness people, this is their way of understanding and dealing with reality. They will constantly look for similarities. They abhor change in general and will go out of their way to make certain that their lives stay the same. If moving into a new home is unavoidable because of job relocation, for example, then the sameness person will try to make the new living quarters resemble as closely as possible the former home. This may be by choosing the same style house with the same room layout if possible or by keeping all of the same furniture. Often the house they live in is similar to the one in which they grew up. Holding on to remnants of the past will provide their security blanket to deal with the uncertainty of the new environment, and will make the job transition a little more palatable. People with Sameness People Patterns look only for similarities, and in some extreme cases, so much so, that they end up ignoring or actually deleting from awareness everything that is different. They may end up living in a fantasy world of their own making, where time stands still. This, of course, does represent a major distortion of reality."

"You know, I had never really thought about all of this as a distortion of reality, and in essence, each type does, indeed, distort reality by taking only what they want to take and what fits into their comfort zone."

"And there is more. True sameness people are really quite good at ignoring and even obliterating all elements of difference in order to maintain the status quo. As long as they continue to look through their sameness colored glasses, they are quite content to float through life that way. Their sameness view of the world cuts them off from the multi-faceted aspects of reality, but they do not seem to mind. Often, they will get quite upset when someone tries to rock their sameness boat by inserting some element of difference into their lives. How many times have sameness parents with difference adolescents thrown up their arms in total disgust and frustration at their children's attempts to change their lifestyles? Sound familiar?"

"Oh my God! I just realized that my youngest daughter is sameness. No wonder why I perceive her to be the difficult one."

"Sameness people certainly do not want things that are new and different. Absolutely not! There could be nothing more loathsome and unpleasant than change to one who lives in sameness. This type of individual is most at ease with everything the same. By the way, they also tend to be politically and morally conservative. I should note in passing that there are some extreme sameness people who seek out difference in order to eliminate it and leave behind only sameness. They are the true reactionaries of society. As I already mentioned sameness people make up about five to ten per cent of the population."

Shana still had more.

"Have you ever either in the context of work or when eating with family or friends tried to change dinner time or lunchtime? If you notice that the reaction is particularly negative, you are dealing with a sameness person. Someone who is in the habit of eating his lunch every day at noon is not going to be pleased with having his routine upset. Likewise with the couple who always eats dinner at six o'clock. Changing this locked in schedule would be a major scandal in such a household! By the way, I bet you can name many a colleague who ends up eating at the same place for lunch every day, not out of convenience, but out of sameness. Doing so fits into their sameness comfort zone. Sameness people usually end up with the same routine every day, and rarely will they deviate from it of their own volition. Even a sameness person who works out of his home, where he is free is organize his day as he wishes, will tend to engage in the same activities at the same time every day. I have a friend who fits this bill. For example, he may go jogging at seven every morning, get phone calls made between nine and ten, work at the computer from ten to twelve, take a lunch break from noon to two, and engage in the same work activity all afternoon. Outside appointments will be made to fit into his regimented work style, and anyone who disturbs this will certainly not be appreciated. Try asking a sameness friend sometime to do you a simple little favor in the middle of his tightly organized schedule, and you will understand what I mean from the reaction you will get. Heaven forbid that it should disrupt his daily routine! Now you'll understand why you thought he was so difficult and inconsiderate!"

QUALIFIED SAMENESS

"I will continue to allude to the Sameness People Pattern throughout our discussion, and will now turn to, and examine more closely, the second aspect of the Change People Pattern, Qualified Sameness. As I mentioned earlier, people who filter the world through Qualified Sameness People Patterns first see similarities in a new situation, and then obvious differences. In the case of the three coins, they would first notice that the coins were all the same denomination, all turned with the same side up, and all on the table in a row (not necessarily in that order), and then they would notice one or two obvious differences (that one is turned in another direction or that one is scratched)"

"As I mentioned previously, the qualified sameness person represents the majority of society. This individual is balanced in the sense that he can perceive both sameness and difference, but simply sees the similarities first. Qualified sameness people tend to stay in their jobs from seven to nine years, are more likely to stray in their marriages than pure sameness people (although it will probably happen only once, if at all), and will have a little less trouble dealing with change in their lives than pure sameness people. In general, qualified sameness people are basically sameness oriented in their lives, but do occasionally need an element of diversity injected here and there. This provides the bit of variety that they need in life to break up the eventual monotony of the pure Sameness People Pattern. In some ways, the Qualified Sameness People Pattern is healthier than the pure sameness one, since the former do not ignore or delete great portions of reality as do the latter. They are more likely to lead balanced lives, and they do not end up in therapy as often as those one sided individuals who are ruled exclusively by the Sameness People Pattern."

"Many of the people I have dealt with in my corporate work seem to exhibit this pattern." I added.

"That is an excellent point. In fact, the average business person comes out of the Qualified Sameness People Pattern. People who filter by qualified sameness are interested in improved versions of what they already have. Improvement is the essence of capitalism and also forms the basis for Total Quality Management. Qualified sameness people like things to be basically the same, although a bit better. For example, with car buying, these people will buy new cars more often than sameness people in order to get some element of variation, yet may buy the same brand to maintain the similarity. The way in which the element of sameness is preserved will vary from one person to another, as will the way in which variety is manifested. For example, the qualified sameness car buyer may purchase the same make car each time, but he may change the color. There will always be some primary criterion of similarity in their choice of car (or other item purchased) with the element of difference secondary. Of course, the element chosen to maintain sameness will vary from one person to another as a function of his personality and personal tastes and habits."

"The typical life pattern of a qualified sameness individual would be the following: one who stays in the same job for seven to nine years and who will then make a change. If he happens to stay at the same job longer, it usually means that there is some element of difference interjected now and then to satisfy his need for occasional change. He may, for example, be involved in doing the same tasks every day, and may find the variety in the form of different people he meets in the course of a day on the job. Changes in daily routine, although not particularly desired on a frequent basis, are welcome from time to time. The qualified sameness person will live in the same house until some uncontrollable or unforeseeable circumstance forces him to make a change (children exceeding the number of available bedrooms, a job move, etc.). Moving is not as traumatic as for the total sameness person. There are, of course, qualified sameness people who will have a case of the seven year itch to move simply because they feel like moving. Often this coincides with their so-called middle age crisis."

I didn't feel like interrupting, so Shana continued.

"We recently had an interesting qualified sameness experience here at Success, Incorporated with an employee who was told by outside psychologists that he was going through a mid life crisis. Although he loved his job, he, for some inexplicable reason, felt he needed a change of sorts. We realized what was happening so we merely changed various aspects of his assignments as well as the people with whom he would interact. Perhaps the so-called middle age crisis is not really what it has been written up to be after all. It may simply be symptomatic of one's Change People Pattern. Is it the sameness or difference people who will end up having a difficult time dealing with this supposedly delicate time in life? Generally speaking, those with a pure Sameness People Pattern appear to be able to cope less with all of the changes, both hormonal and other, brought on by mid life. These changes represent a forced new way of seeing oneself which is often totally alien to one's previous self image. It is precisely this perceived difference that is so troublesome for a pure sameness individual. And, if one is qualified sameness, the degree to which the element of difference crops up determines to a large extent the amount of difficulty the person will have in dealing with the changes brought on in mid life."

DIFFERENCE

"May I venture to say that you will find this People Pattern to be of particular interest to you!" beamed Shana.

"You know, I can honestly say that I am beginning to see and understand these differences." I responded jokingly.

"Differences you say. Such an unexpected word from someone like you." she added with just a bit of irony and sarcasm in her tonality.

"The next aspect of the Change People Pattern corresponds to a third way of viewing the world. It is called the Difference People Pattern. Difference people thrive on life constantly providing elements of variety. Surprise is the spice of life. When looking at the three coins, people of this pattern will see only differences (i.e. that the coins have a slightly different coloration, that they have different dates, that they are ever so slightly out of line, etc.). Sound familiar?"

"That's exactly what I did when you asked me the question about the quarters." I quickly realized.

"Pure difference people will not even mention that the coins all happen to be of the same denomination! In fact, they consider those who talk about similarity to be outright bores. Difference people are superb at making distinctions of all kinds, and at times they make surprisingly nuanced ones".

"Like the pure sameness people who delete all that is different, difference people also end up distorting reality in their own way, by deleting everything that is the same. Whenever they walk into a room, they will immediately see everything that is different or out of place. In their mind, whatever is distinctive or different stands out from the rest. Who always notices the picture frame that is a little off center? Or that books are not evenly aligned on a bookshelf? Why, your devoted difference person (or qualified difference person), of course. Things that stick out like a sore thumb to a difference person most often go totally unnoticed to the sameness person. In a way, the difference person is the exact opposite of the sameness person, also reducing reality to one element, only in this case, instead of sameness it is difference. Their world view is necessarily a warped one as well. The dynamics of a couple in which one person is sameness and the other difference becomes quite lively and has the potential of creating major rifts in a relationship. The sameness person will tend to want to stay at home more often, engaging in the same activity, whether it be snuggling up with a good book, sprawling in front of the television with a bag of chips, or playing cards. The difference person will want to vary his activities all the time. He will loathe the idea of sitting at home every evening engaged in some monotonous habitual regime of whatever activity. The sameness person will want to engage in the same tasks in his job, while the difference person will seek out variety in different forms."

"I see and understand now how you pegged me immediately. What a terrific and fun way of discovering the Change People Pattern!" I was really excited to learn more, and I was not disappointed.

DIFFERENCES AMONG DIFFERENCE PEOPLE

"Being the good difference person that you are, you must realize that the world of difference cannot simply be reduced to one category with no distinctions within itself. There, of course, needs to be difference within difference. That difference manifests in that there are basically two kinds of difference people: 1) mismatchers or counter-examplers, and 2) polarity responders. Most of us have run into people who are always pointing out exceptions to everything. They are the mismatchers of the world. Their favorite words are 'yes but'. They are experts at finding exceptions and counter examples and at figuring out why things won't work. I am certain that you may know some of these type people within your personal circle of friends and close colleagues, aren't I right?"

KINDS OF DIFFERENCE PEOPLE
Mismatchers/Counter-examplers
Polarity responders

"Obviously, there are always exceptions to everything, Shana, and yes, I can now understand why some may find me to be a pain at times!" I explained.

She continued with this fascinating portrayal of difference people which I absorbed like a sponge with, might I add, a tinge of great subjective satisfaction.

"There really aren't people around who will always go out of their way to explain why something can't or doesn't work, are there?" I realized that I should maintain a respectful demeanor, so I stopped there.

"When another person comes up with a suggestion, the mismatcher will be there to show why it won`t work. Haven`t you ever been in a meeting where one person always seems to provide counter examples to all the suggestions put on the table? Whatever you say or do, the mismatcher is up and ready with his arguments against it. This type of person can drive others up a wall with his exceptions to the rules. He is often perceived by others as an out and out pain in the you know where!"

"It isn't all bad with the mismatcher, however, since they are those occasionally necessary individuals who best serve the role of troubleshooters in our society. The ideal is to have the mismatchers know at what point in a discussion to provide the counter-example. That would make most meetings more pleasant and, moreover, more productive. It is best when the mismatcher waits until a plan has been put on the table and its advantages outlined, before he sets out to show its weak points. Premature mismatching discourages people, and over time they stop contributing. They even begin to despair that nothing will work. Balance again is the name of the game. On a personal level, imagine being married to a mismatcher or having a mismatcher as a boss. That means that every time the husband/wife or boss presents an argument or plan, the mismatcher spouse/boss will be all too ready to provide all of the reasons why it won`t work. How frustrating that must be over and over again! In those cases, it would be helpful to mention the behavior to the mismatcher spouse/boss so that he/she knows that you are aware of this pattern. Putting this behavior in front of him/her may ease the situation, and eventually lead to a more accepting reaction from the mismatcher. Be forewarned, though, that his initial reaction will be something like 'No, that is not true!'. In no matter what context the mismatcher appears, understanding the reason behind his behavior perhaps takes him out of the realm of nuisance into the realm of simply someone with a different model of the world."

"Fortunately for me, it was I who always came out of the difference mold; and I now understand why at times people thought that I was acting so disruptively!"

POLES APART

Shana went on.

"The second type of difference person is the polarity responder. The polarity responder will always do the opposite of what you tell him to do. It is almost as though you automatically trigger a negative reaction, a contrary reaction in him that provokes a behavior exactly the opposite of what you tell him to do. Anyone with children can easily identify with this kind of behavior. Just think of every time you have told your child to behave in a certain way or to perform a certain task and they have done just the opposite. When a child is going through his polarity responder period or phase of growing up, he will tend to do the opposite of whatever you tell him to do. Traditionally, over the years, parents have developed a special way of dealing with such behavior. It is, of course, called reverse psychology. As they become adults, most, but not all people somehow outgrow polarity responses. There are, however, some individuals who retain this rather dubious distinction throughout their entire adult lives. They are considered real pains by the people who have to deal with them on a regular basis. Polarity responders and mismatchers often end up in the strangest of places. They show up in our very own homes, at the office, at the local grocer's, and even in positions of government. Perhaps some of the people you considered to be terribly stubborn or difficult, are merely manifesting their polarity responder behavior."

"Now I understand why it is no wonder that difference people, particularly this kind, have so many problems with relationships. They become so ensconced in difference that they omit the other half of reality. Imagine living or working with someone who is forever picking apart everything you say or do? Imagine the tedium of putting up with constant opposition and complaining? 'That is wrong.' or 'Don't you ever do things right?' or 'That is not going to work.' or 'Do not do it that way.' Whether they are mismatchers or polarity responders, difference people are the nitpickers in society. They are the people who are habitually mismatching either ideas, whole plans, and/or small details. As you probably have experienced at some point in you life, having to put up with people who tear apart notions for what appear to be stupid reasons can be both tedious and quite annoying. Once you understand these patterns, it becomes easier to deal with people like this. Once you know for example, that a person is a polarity responder, you simply tell them the opposite of what you would like them to do. This can be helpful in any life context, whether in business or personal life. It would be helpful to show these people how to create more balance in their lives rather than letting them continue to walk through the world with their distorted way of perceiving reality."

QUALIFIED DIFFERENCE

"Last, and certainly not least, we move on to the fourth and final aspect of the Change People Pattern, i.e. Qualified Difference. Remember the coins or the chairs. These are people who first see difference in a situation. They focus on these differences, and only once they have observed the differences will they then notice any obvious similarities. Qualified difference people tend to stay in their jobs from twelve months to several years. If they do end up keeping their jobs for a longer period of time, it is because they have found the needed diversity to spark their continued interest. If not, their tolerance level for sameness is low, and they move on to something different. Like the qualified sameness group, those characterized by this People Pattern are also balanced in that they can perceive both difference and similarity. They do not delete huge portions of reality like their total difference brethren. Like the pure difference people, they like change, but it does not have to be revolutionary, just as long as it does occur. They represent the opposite side of the coin of qualified sameness. Qualified difference people comprise approximately 25% of the population."

"Just for a change could you give an example of how the Qualified Difference People Pattern translates into everyday life?" I politely asked.

"I cannot imagine you ever asking for a change! How dare you!" she amusingly retorted. "This kind of person will still prefer variety to sameness, yet occasionally will reveal a desire for repetition, for some expression of something familiar, albeit minimal and secondary. People of this type will, for example, like to dine out at different spots, but may eat the same dish at each restaurant. Remember, this pattern is the flip side of qualified sameness, so that the examples of the former we discussed earlier would apply to this pattern, but with an emphasis on the difference element rather than on the sameness element. A qualified difference person needs a great deal of variety in his life. In the context of a relationship with his mate, this may be expressed as a desire to share an interest in several dissimilar activities or hobbies to balance out the sameness of being with the same individual. Divorce is not as prevalent in this category as among the pure difference people, but the rate is much higher than among pure sameness and qualified sameness people. In dating, the qualified difference person could be content having a relationship with only one person, provided that they share varied interests. Does that answer your question?"

"Yes and would the same apply to employer/employee relations?" I asked.

"Certainly. Remember that the context may always change, and often does in the natural course of daily activity, while the patterns will always apply to human behavior in its varied forms."

"Because you are such a good difference person", she added, I know that you are not on overload with all of the distinctions that I have been making this morning. In fact, I'll bet that you have welcomed each and every one of them."

"I really have undergone an incredible awakening as far as my own Change People Pattern, and it has helped me to understand my interactions with colleagues, family and friends over my entire life. In fact, I kind of like where I am."

"I see that today will be a most enlightening day for me for different reasons." I added.

"Of course, for different reasons!" she chuckled.

PRAYERS

"Before you go, let me tell you the prayers. Each People Pattern has prayers associated with it. There are always prayers." Shana chuckled. "In fact sometimes prayers are all that we have. Here are the ones for today. The Sameness Prayer is:"

O Eternal and Unchanging One, give me this day my daily routines. Provide me with endless continuity and the comfort of the status quo. Lead me not into change of any kind or into new and different circumstances of life. Let this day be filled with the peace of constancy and the serenity of sameness. Deliver me from those who would dare change Thy stable and perfect world, and in particular the way I live. And please make sure that those who would seek change, keep far away from me and my family. For Thine is the same, constant, infinite, perpetual Force that leads me to stay on the path of uniformity in all that I do. Amen.

"And the Difference Prayer is:"

God Almighty, Creator of all the wonderful and different manifestations of life in Thy ever changing Universe, give me this day the joy of diversity and the novelty of change in all of its splendor. Lead me not into the torture of tedium and into the drudgery of sameness. Let this day be complete with new and innovative ways of dealing with the different activities and challenges of daily life. Deliver me, please, oh Lord, from the monotony of routine and from the boredom of consistency, and especially from those who would stifle my creativity and who would inflict their dull, boring sameness ways upon me. Provide me with the joys of unique and exciting opportunities in a Universe which reflects Thine own diversity and ingenuity. Amen.

"Now it is time for you to go see Marvin in Management to learn more about this marvelous People Pattern."

MANAGEMENT

Marvin greeted me enthusiastically. "I understand that you have been quite impressed with the way in which we run things around here."

"Yes" I said "I am really looking forward to my lesson in management regarding the Change People Pattern, because over the years I have found myself quite frustrated in dealing with certain of my colleagues. With the little that I now understand about the Change People Pattern, I have already begun to understand how it could apply to managing different types of people."

"First there is a correlation between a person's Change People Pattern and how long that he is likely to remain in a job. A sameness person will stay in a job fifteen years to life unless he is forced to leave or unless the job involves so much change that the stress level is too high. A qualified sameness person given the same qualifications will stay in a job from seven to nine years. A qualified difference person will stay in a job from one to two years unless the routine level is too high. A difference person will want constant variety and change. They will change jobs every six months to a year unless the job that they are in provides constant change. So one man's meat is another man's poison. Let us discuss each type in turn."

JOB LENGTH
Sameness - 15 years to life
Qualified sameness - 7 to 9 years
Qualified difference - 1 to 2 years
Difference - 6 months to 1 year

"Even though you are not exactly sameness in orientation, I thought we would begin our lesson with that aspect of the Change People Pattern."

"First in the work place, if you have a manager who is a sameness person, and employees who are not, there will necessarily be friction between them. The sameness managers will want his employees to carry out tasks in the same way all the time, i.e. the way that he wants it to be done. His mottos are 'if it isn't broken, then don't fix it' and 'leave well enough alone.'. If the employee shows any innovation or initiative to change the way he is performing his job, this is interpreted through the sameness filters of his employer as representing a deviation from the one standard, set, recognized way of doing things. And this of course is not acceptable. The sameness boss will think that the difference employees are simply trying to be clever by coming up with new ways of doing things. You will hear comments such as 'What is the matter with you? Why can't you do the job the way I've told you, the same way everyone else manages to get things done?'"

"Excuse me for interrupting. I've had someone constantly say to me: 'Do you think you are being smart in doing it a different way? Why can't you do things the same way that I do? Is something wrong with you?'"

"That is an excellent point. The reverse situation with a difference boss and sameness employee can also create a strain in a work relationship. I will discuss that in a minute."

"So what do managers need to do with sameness employees?"

"As a general rule of thumb: if you get the workers to learn the job well, they will end up doing it forever. Remember that a sameness person will stay at his job from fifteen years to life, changing only due to outside factors which necessitate the move. A sameness person will want to remain in his comfort zone of a job as long as he can. Also, sameness people seem to mind red tape less than the other pattern types. What they do mind however is change. With their 'not broken, don't fix it attitudes' they will not like any kind of reorganization. For them change is a sign that management did not get it right to start with. From their perspective, there is one best way to do things, and it is management's job to find and maintain it. If management wants to change, this means that they didn't get things right in the first place. Several changes are evidence that management is totally incompetent and does not have a clue as to what is going on. In short, management's job is to set up the right system at the beginning and to never change it. Anything less is unacceptable and means that employees are just being used as guinea pigs by management."

"As for managing a qualified sameness person, make sure you emphasize the 8 to 5 work schedule, or whatever regularly scheduled work period is involved. A change in schedule is acceptable as in the case of overtime, as long as it does not disrupt the normal routine too often. Expect the workers to take their lunch breaks at the same time each day, with only occasional change. Also, qualified sameness workers often like to take their vacations at the same time each year, if at all possible. They will interject the element of variety by perhaps going off to a different place each time, or doing something different."

"I imagine that the element of variety will differ from one person to the next, and as I have been already told, there is always the contextuality factor which comes into play." I must admit that I was really proud of myself for having picked up on these nuances so readily. I knew that my facility was in part based on the fact that I am a difference person!

"You are indeed learning well. In any case, with 55% of the world falling into the category of qualified sameness, and 5% to 10% part of the sameness category, they represent a huge portion of the global work force. They are the very souls who have struggled for over two centuries to make this country what it is today. And they are certainly a group to be taken seriously by government as a potentially powerful force. Not to mention their incredible buying power. They are certainly there to be acknowledged in marketing, advertising and related fields. Not doing so spells disaster for most companies out there. I know that Michael will brief you on the marketing applications of the Change People Pattern, so I will not be redundant."

"Thanks to all of you I have come to understand why people with opposite Change People Patterns working together can result in some fascinating dynamics". I was trying to be polite for I knew all too well how nasty interactions between different types do actually play out in the real world of business."

"You are so right. For example, watch out if a boss is a difference person with sameness employees. The boss's mottos are 'if it isn't broken, then break it and make it better' and 'never leave well enough alone'. It is guaranteed he is going to be constantly frustrated by the lack of initiative and creativity on the part of his subordinates. 'can't you be more creative?' or 'Why can't you come up with a different way of doing that? You've been in this same dead end job for twenty years and haven't shown a spark of creativity or any desire to change and improve!' may be some of the typical comments of a difference boss to his sameness employees. If a difference employee is stuck with a sameness boss, the former is going to get pretty tired of doing things the same way all the time, and will be fast to get out of a dead end situation, and change departments or his job for that matter. 'I'm fed up with this same nonsense every day.' 'What an absolute bore!' Not to mention a few other terms of which idiot is the most polite is a common reaction."

"Ah yes! We somehow tend to think of others who do not think or act like us as complete idiots, and it has become more than just a figure of speech." I said that I could remember many instances in my own career where I felt those very sentiments and had those very opinions of certain of my colleagues."

"You will have no problem dealing with difference employees. Just what would you do with them?" Marvin inquired.

"If I happened to have difference employees, I would have them do different things if at all possible. If other difference workers are anything like me, they will have the urge to go on to something else once they learn a given job or task."

"Exactly. Difference employees quickly get bored at doing the same job or the same task day in and day out, even if it seems like a short period of time to others."

"Before we move on to the realm of Qualified Difference, I would like to discuss one type of businessperson who lies at the core of creativity in businesses. This type of businessperson who is always out creating new and exciting things is the entrepreneur. Interestingly, although most business people are sameness or qualified sameness, the typical entrepreneur is a person who sorts by difference. He is the one who makes distinctions and who is capable of creating new and innovative things and of taking on interesting new projects that represent a break from tradition. By the very nature of his job, he is constantly re-organizing, re-structuring and synthesizing, whether it be on the level of individuals, ideas, or entire organizations. This is both a strength and a weakness. It is a strength in that it creates innovation and new products and ways of doing things. It is a weakness in that the entrepreneur may create a better way, but he may be unsuccessful in marketing it or in managing a company. When you get to sales, Michael will warn you about how difficult it is to sell something that is new and totally different. There are many great ideas that are genuine improvements that never make it because the vast majority of people are perfectly content with the status quo. Also, entrepreneurs often make poor managers. They are constantly changing systems and employees, and neither one of these helps to build a viable organization. For entrepreneurs to be successful they need to hire a good marketer and qualified sameness managers to handle daily operations; and they need to leave them alone to do their jobs. This seldom happens and many innovative companies sired by truly creative geniuses fail to make it in the business world."

As Marvin continued in his discussion of entrepreneurs, I began to understand why I always fit in really well with the entrepreneurial spirit.

"It's like when something works, a sameness person will want to maintain the status quo, whereas the difference person will want to encourage change, and go on to the next thing. Why do you think that there is often so much discord within organizations? They are just a microcosm of society where sameness people butt heads against difference people, with each thinking that the other side is a jerk? One side thinks constantly in terms of change and more change. These people are looked upon as radicals by the sameness contingent."

"My wife would immediately bring up some of the women who were instrumental in catalyzing the women's movements - like Susan B.

Anthony in her time and the present day Gloria Steinem. They are probably difference people flowing against a strong tide of sameness."

"History has shown that it usually takes what is considered (at the time of its emergence) to be a radical or revolutionary action and idea to get the gears rolling toward any effective and lasting change in anything whether legislation, mores or outlook on things, people or events. If you read the book by the two co-founders of this company about People Patterns in Society, you will find a plethora of references to all facets of present day culture. Right now, however, let's literally get back down to business."

"As a difference person, I think that I am usually quite flexible when it comes to daily schedules." I wanted to make this fact known, and Marvin couldn't agree more.

"Difference people may have a particular time of day they like to have a certain meal, but they are much more open to variety and actually prefer frequent change. If they happen to be stuck in a 8 to 5 job situation, they will usually vary, for example their lunch hour, and may try to perform required tasks at different times each day, or week. By creating novelty in such a work situation, they can stay at that job a bit longer than they ordinarily would. Otherwise they will be changing positions with the seasons, almost."

"I can certainly second that thought wholeheartedly!"

"I guess that here at Success, Incorporated we will have to make sure that your tasks and interactions do vary as much as possible!" Marvin underlined with a change in his intonation.

"In a job situation, it is important if you are a manager with a qualified difference employee or employees, to vary the tasks in order to provide constant variety. If possible, change the way in which something is done, and/or change the time of day which certain tasks are performed. Above all, try to inject elements of variety into the job. Remember that qualified difference people yearn for change and dislike static situations. If there is some repetition of tasks, management needs to play them down. Instead, management should emphasize improvements that can be made. Stress the different ways in which a task can be performed. The pure difference person will want to do something new and different each time. Once he learns a task well, the difference person will want to move on to something else to challenge him. The sameness person, once he knows a job, will stick to it and have no desire to change, while the qualified sameness or difference person will tend to do the same thing, gradually improving upon it, evolving as he goes along."

"As you are talking, Marvin, I have been observing the people walking by this glass enclosure, and I have been noticing the way that they dress. Won't the manner of office attire reflect the Change People Pattern of an individual?"

"That is an excellent observation. Leave it to our friendly difference person to notice such a thing. In fact, often difference and qualified difference people will have a unique style of dress, to lesser degrees depending upon whether they are deeply into the former or the latter. A pure difference person is more likely to dress uniquely, or sport a one-of-a-kind tie or an unusual outfit. Qualified difference people prefer unique apparel or else tend to dress in a classic manner with unique accessories, for example."

"I can say that as a pure difference person, I will often vary my colors and styles from day to day. Different ties are a must for me."

"At the office, you can tell a lot about a man from his selection of ties from day to day. In any case, a qualified difference person will always vary some ingredient in his dress, either style or color, or accessories, and at the same time maintain an element of similarity from one outfit to another. For example, he may wear a different outfit each day, yet keep within the same color scheme, such as variations of black and grey, or red and white. Even though the outfits change all the time, the colors are similar. Or perhaps, the accessories stay the same, and the styles change. Again, the nuances and combinations of what is sameness and what is difference will vary from one person to another depending on his personal tastes, resources and personality. They will change contextually as well. Also, a person's choice of dress is also affected by the Evaluation People Pattern which you will learn about later this week."

"I, a true blooded difference person, am still amazed by the number of distinctions constantly being made in relation to the Change People Pattern regarding the various aspects of business. I have thoroughly enjoyed learning about managing the four types from you; and I am certain to have questions come up as I learn the ropes here at Success, Incorporated. Thank you for your time"

"I always enjoy going through this material, because I know how helpful and insightful it is in dealing with people and situations in the workplace. Do have fun with Michael as he takes you through the ins and outs of the Change People Patterns as it relates to sales."

SALES

Michael had obviously been expecting me, as he gave a me warm but firm handshake as he personally greeted me at the door.

"Welcome to the world of the Change People Pattern in Sales", he smiled. I understand that you have already had some training elsewhere in sales, and I am certain that what you will be learning here will go far beyond what you have studied thus far."

"In fact, every day at this company has been totally different from any work experience I have had prior to now." I said.

"Totally different. I am not surprised", he responded with that knowing look in his eyes which I had already become accustomed to seeing in the various managers training me thus far.

"It would appear to be quite appropriate for a change, that we vary the order of the different aspects of the Change People Pattern in our discussion of sales. Right up front, I will tell you that the implications of the Change People Pattern are far reaching in the domain of sales," Michael uttered in a very precise, matter of fact tonality.

"Before I discuss the specific tactics of selling to each pattern, let me make a few general remarks. As I will continuously emphasize, every salesperson will close a certain percentage of the people that they contact. This depends on the nature of their presentation and the demographics of the market. Given this fact there are only two ways to increase sales. One is to see more prospects, and the other is to increase one's closing ratio. The first is called 'working hard' and the second is called 'working smart'. Which would you prefer?"

Working Hard
versus
Working Smart

"Working smart, of course."

"I thought that. The question is how does a salesperson increase his closing ratio. Most salespeople have a set presentation format with either one or several closes. If their presentation is good, then this sameness approach may be successful. If it is not good, then they will starve. The point is that any fixed approach will only be successful with a certain percentage of the market. Some approaches are better than others. Many companies use what are called script books. These are transcripts of the more successful presentations and closes. In telemarketing, someone has written a set presentation and the telemarketers are expected to follow it. They are monitored for script compliance, and they are not allowed to deviate or improvise. This is a straight sameness game."

"That is one of the reasons that I cannot stand telemarketers." I said.

"You are not alone." Michael said emphatically. "For a sameness salesperson to increase sales he is forced to work hard. To work smart, one has to vary his approach with each prospect. One has to have a variety of approaches and to match them with each prospect. This is a difference approach. It requires having a variety of ways to present a product and a variety of closes readily available. It also requires the ability to rapidly access each prospect and to determine which particular approach to use with that prospect."

"It sounds like hard work." I said.

Michael smiled. "Yes hard but in a different sense of hard. What it does require is inspiration and not perspiration. It requires the ability to detect differences in others and to tailor one's approach accordingly. There are many courses and books on sales that list hundreds of closes, and there are books full of different lines to handle objections. I have already mentioned script books. If done correctly they are compilations of the best presentation lines, closes, and objection responses of the most successful salespeople in an organization. A good script book is a valuable resource. It should be carefully prepared and carefully guarded. We, of course, help our clients to prepare and use script books. A good script book is important, but it does not guarantee sales. Salespeople need to be trained in how to use it. That is the critical factor. The key is matching the script book to the prospect. This involves more than just memorizing a bunch of lines. It involves knowing the lines, but more important it involves being able to detect and utilize the patterns of your prospect. *That is the essence of sales - tailoring the presentation to the prospect.* That is what I will be teaching you to do with respect to the People Patterns."

I kept quiet and Michael continued.

"In sales there is what is called the 'itch cycle.' This is the period of time before a customer will be ready to purchase your product again. This is very important. Repeat business is an important aspect of sales success. Most people buy a new car on a regular basis. Real estate salespeople know that families move up as they expand in numbers and income. This People Pattern gives us a key to these time frames. Sameness people will usually have longer time frames and difference people will have shorter ones. Sameness buyers are more numerous and have more brand loyalty than difference buyers."

Whatever you are selling, it is important to determine the 'itch cycle' for that particular item for each of the Change People Patterns. Once you know this, you will know how long to wait before contacting each customer to sell to him again.

"That is right about trading up to a bigger and better house as your family and income expands. We moved three times in six years as the size of our family grew and as my wife and I got promoted." I reflected.

Michael smiled. "Now let us discuss how to sell to each pattern. Let's go right to the tactics of selling to a difference person, rather than beginning with sameness."

"You know that I'll second that motion anytime." I exclaimed.

"Okay. If you are face to face with a difference person, make sure you talk about the uniqueness of your product. Stress how it is different from those of your competitors. If you start talking about its being just like everything else, you might as well forget the sale. That translates into instant rejection on the part of the difference filterer."

"That sounds like a reaction I would have." I interjected.

"No surprise," Michael said. "In any case, we will later touch upon marketing and advertising strategies that appeal to the different types of Change People Patterns; and now we continue on with selling to difference people."

"If you are dealing with a difference person, your tactic will be totally opposite than that of the sameness scenario. Instead of mentioning the similarities between your product and your competition's product (as I will demonstrate later), you emphasize the unique character of the service or product and that it is new and exciting and maybe even revolutionary. For the ultimate difference person, the more out of the ordinary, the more original and atypical the product or service, the greater the attraction to it. Depending on what you are selling, if it is a one of a kind item, your chances of selling it are incredibly enhanced. Mention that the product is state-of-the art, and a complete break with tradition. Remember that a difference buyer does not always buy based on need. Also, when dealing with pure difference buyers, avoid talking about aspects of the product that have remained the same."

"That is me to the tee." I exclaimed.

"The difference buyer wants a product because it is something different from what he already has or from what his friends or acquaintances have. For example, he may have a perfectly good fax machine in his office, but ends up buying another one, not because it is better than the model he has, but because it is different. Distinction is the magic word when dealing with people of this pattern. A word of caution as well, particularly if you come up against mismatchers and polarity responders. Prepare yourself in advance with answers to possible 'why it won't work' statements on the part of the mismatcher, and use reverse psychology on the polarity responder."

"Now I can see why it would be such a painful experience for a sameness salesperson to have to sell products to a customer who was difference in orientation." I realized just how much of a challenge that could be to some unknowing salesperson who had no clue whatsoever about the Change People Pattern.

"Let's talk about how you would approach a sales interaction with a qualified difference person. If you are selling to a qualified difference person, talk about what makes your product or service different from others. Unlike the approach with the pure difference person, you do not need to accentuate the unprecedented nature of the product. It does not have to be revolutionary, just different. Highlight any features or aspects of the product or service that are unlike anything your competitor's products or services provide. Then, casually in passing, mention a feature or one particular characteristic of the product that is similar to what they have or know about other products, but without dwelling too long on its sameness aspect."

"Then the key here is to show them that they are getting the best of two worlds. With your product or service they are getting the best from the past and the latest technology from the present and beyond." I gladly added.

"Indeed. And there is a whole series of language patterns and ways of influencing people in the various People Pattern groups and various other techniques which we teach in the context of our in-house trainings on sales and marketing".

"What if you want to sell a product to the average business person?", I wanted to know.

"That was my next area. Now we move into the realm of selling to qualified sameness buyers. If you want to sell a product to the average business person, who, remember from what Shana told you, happens to be qualified sameness, then you will want to present the product as an improved version of what he already has. Remember that improving upon a product is not the same as changing it outright. And after all, isn't improvement what business is all about? Avoid saying that the product is new and different. Doing so will simply alienate the prospective buyer. He's not interested in buying something with which he is totally unfamiliar. The qualified sameness buyer is looking for a product that hits home, that relates in some way to something he already has or uses, even if it isn't the identical product. For this reason, you need to stress the similarities between your product or service and the old one, and underscore that the new item is a better improved version of the previous one. Also, be sure to talk about the background or history of your product, emphasizing how over the years it has gradually improved on its way to becoming the great product or service that it is today. It helps to mention the durability of the product, and the fact that the user will not have to change it often. Remember that the continuity factor is important in the eyes of the qualified sameness consumer."

"This explanation reminds me of the Japanese mentality." I said.

"Yes, in more ways than one. The Japanese for years have been masters of imitation. In other words, they have perfected the art of improving upon already existing products to make them better. This translates pure and simply into a qualified sameness mind set."

"What would your sales presentation be to a pure sameness person?" I pondered.

"In some ways, this is the easiest approach to use of the four. Remember that sameness people prefer to live life in the status quo, so that buying anything 'new' is on one level, an oxymoron. They will buy something new in the sense that it is in its pristine, unused state upon purchase. But it is certainly not new in the sense of being innovative or different in type or style from what they previously had, unless of course, their original model was discontinued and is no longer available on the market. In that case, they are forced to deal with the element of unfamiliarity which makes them quite uncomfortable. Pure sameness people want their products and services to remain the same."

"Although it may seem strange, does this mean that sameness buyers do not even care about new and improved versions?" I asked with great curiosity.

"You are so right. In fact, if you mention that your product or service is better than before, you will more likely turn off the potential sameness buyer rather then make a sale. Have you have ever been in a situation where you were selling an improved product line to a customer, and they reacted rather negatively, even to the point of rejecting the advancement or amelioration?   You were unknowingly dealing with a pure sameness person. In such cases, even if the product has new features, do not mention them. This is because on an unconscious level the sameness buyer will reject anything that is new."

"That must really be a stretch for a difference person like me selling a product to such a sameness buyer!"

MARKETING AND ADVERTISING AND THE NEW COKE

"One of the most valuable and immediate applications of the Change People Pattern is in the field of marketing and advertising. A company really needs to understand the nuances and implications of this paramount People Pattern. Ignorance of it can literally break an organization or company. Let us take some specific examples."

"Do you remember what Coke did a while back?" Michael asked.

"I'm not sure to what you are referring." I answered.

"Several years ago, the Coca Cola Company made the rather dubious decision to change the formula for Coke, a drink which not only had become a national institution, but a worldwide phenomenon as well. Now that you know that over 65% of the population is sameness or qualified sameness, how do you think they are going to react when their favorite drink - their liquid lifeline, the taste that they had taken for granted would never change, the drink they had served for decades - suddenly was modified?"

"I know now why the new Coke failed so miserably," I chimed in.

"Is the general public going to be thrilled to have their Coke change its taste? Far from it. Spending mega bucks in advertising for the new Coke would be to no avail. If only the corporate decision makers had considered the Change People Pattern before they decided to change the formula for the most famous drink on the planet! Would masses of sameness and qualified sameness consumers appreciate having the classic taste modified, or having something disappear that had become so much a part of their life? No way. One of the few things they had begun to count on to remain unchanged suddenly had been unpardonably transformed!   Would the sameness and qualified sameness crowd beam with joy at the taste of the new Coke? Of course not. They are not going to want a product that is new and different. The new Coke represented a catastrophic deviation from sameness in the minds of the millions of consumers who had been in the habit of drinking the same formula for so long."

"Given what I know now, it all suddenly makes great sense to me. Sameness people want both their products and their services, for that matter, to remain the same. In fact, they expect them to remain unaltered," I added.

"Precisely. And they will be adamant in their resistance to change of any kind. So the new Coke proved to be a harsh lesson in marketing at the least. Of course the Coca Cola Company responded to the public outrage and brought back the original coke. They even relabeled it 'classic'. So the lesson is when marketing for a sameness constituency, keep in mind that some things do not change. If you've got something going for you, stick with it. They would love to see the good old times remain forever."

Michael continued on. "The lesson not only applies to products but to packaging. What happens when a company that for years has successfully packaged a product a certain way, suddenly decides to change the way it`s presented. A decision made by a difference or qualified difference person. Obviously the change can draw a negative reaction from the sameness world. You may ask why not target the difference world instead. Two simple reasons. First the sameness market is twice as large as the difference market. And two is that difference people lack brand loyalty. Difference people are going to change brands frequently for variety. In short, the company is losing on two scores if they fail to appeal to the majority of consumers."

"All this is so obvious to me now that I have learned about the Change People Pattern."

"The bottom line is to know the make up of the market that you are after and to manage your advertising accordingly. Also, package your product to match the pattern of your market. I'll give you some more examples. Several years ago, there were a few companies, Nestles among them, which decided to run excerpts of old TV advertisements from several decades ago. Remember the Nestles Quick Chocolate dog? He came back and appealed to all the sameness and qualified sameness baby boomers, who nowadays seem to be quite a lucrative market for many products. Then there was the Speedy Alka Seltzer kid and Tony the Tiger who reappeared for awhile, media ghosts from the past who help sales by reconnecting the present with times of yore. Procter and Gamble, America's largest purveyor of household and personal care products obviously understands (even if by marketing goofs) the need to give its consumers exactly what they want. The company at one point decided to reintroduce the original green version of its revered Prell shampoo, which had been replaced in 1991 by a blue rendition of the product that bombed in the marketplace. They have learned their lesson well from the Coke blunder. It went a step farther. Now Procter and Gamble also launched a campaign to bring back its old shampoo color exclaiming 'Green is back! The original formula you've always loved'. Following Coke's footsteps, P&G is selling blue Prell along with the traditional green, in the same way Coke sells both Classic and New versions of their drink. In this way, they appeal to both the sameness and qualified sameness customers."

"I suppose that means that the difference crowd would be attracted if they changed the names of the new products to something totally different." I wanted to know.

"That's exactly right. Marketing managers with difference People Patterns need to position their products based on the Change People Pattern in response to respective groups they are targeting. If they have a product that is outrageously different, they need to realize that it will be appreciated by only a small segment of the population. That usually does not translate into mega bucks. Maybe you remember a car called the Edsel. It had a vertical rather than a horizontal grill. It sure looked different, and it sure did not sell. Up until now, advertising companies and marketing consulting firms have been coming up with their explanations of these marketing fiascos. They have mentioned everything from betrayal of customer loyalty to the breaking of an emotional bond between a customer and a product. These explanations clearly do not touch the heart of the issue at stake here."

"So you are saying that the real crux of the matter deals with the Change People Pattern." I asserted.

"You have obviously learned your lesson well. People react to change in four different ways and in order to market effectively to these various types one needs to have a precise understanding why some of us abhor change and others of us accept it with open arms. There are lots of marketing executives around itching to make a name for themselves by bringing in something boldly new and different. These difference filterers would do better to realize that the average person is sameness and qualified sameness and target these groups appropriately."

Michael went on. "Almost every time we pick up a magazine or happen to see commercials on TV, it never ceases to amaze us how many times advertisers end up estranging themselves from a large portion of their market, because they are using the wrong approach for what is the predominant Change People Pattern of their desired market. Just think of products for a typically sameness or qualified sameness following being advertised as 'totally unique and revolutionary'! Or else you'll see 'so different from everything else out there'. These tactics work wonders with difference and qualified difference buyers, but will only serve to alienate the typical sameness and qualified sameness person."

"There is one whole industry, however, that is based on difference."

I was curious as to what that could be.

"It is called the high fashion industry. What is fashion? Fashion is figuring out some new way to be different. Fashion designers make their living by coming up with differences in men's and women's clothing. How many ways can you change a shirt or a tie? You can change the collar, or the pockets or the buttons on a shirt. With a tie you can change the width and the patterns and the colors. Most of the public are not into high fashion. From their perspective, the designs are weird, and they wouldn't be caught dead in them. For the difference person however, difference fashions are where it is at. Most of the public, which is sameness, continue to buy the same styles, which to the fashion conscious are dull and tasteless. Most corporate business people continue to wear the same blue or grey suits with white shirts. Even their ties all look alike. This does not deter the *haute couture* industry, however. They go on coming up with their new designs. Often the more different they are the more they cost. And there are enough difference people that keep buying them to keep them in business. It is a strange world."

Michael reflected and went on. "The sales world in general is largely built on gradual improvements. Products have things called features. Every new model has new features to make life easier. The question is if the feature was so helpful, then why didn't they put it in to begin with. Every year there are new features. It is as if there were a great storehouse of features in the sky, and every year the poor buyer is blessed with a few more of them. Why didn't someone think these things up from the start and put them all in? What would it be like to just once own a product that already had all the features built in at the beginning?"

"Have you ever heard of planned obsolescence?" I quipped.

Michael laughed and switched topics.

"Think about the four aspects of the Change People Pattern as used in stores when you go shopping. Whether by common sense or by chance, department stores and chain stores are stroking the feathers of the sameness and qualified sameness consumer by maintaining a similar decor and structure to their stores."

"I know what you mean. When I go into a Neiman Marcus, I can easily distinguish it from Saks, or Bloomingdale's, or Macy's."

"Indeed. Each chain has its individual flooring, counters, lighting, etc. which are particular to each. These motifs are carried throughout all the stores in the various locations so that the habitual shopper feels at home in the same ambience and decor in each one. In fact, some of the stores have even maintained the same layout where space permitted, so that the make-up counters, the jewelry counters, the men`s wear, shoe department, etc. are not only always on the same floor, but also occupy the same location on that floor. Subconsciously, that makes the sameness shopper feel comfortable and relaxed to be in a familiar place."

"I realize that we are running out of time for this session, so if you have any more questions, feel free to ask me whenever you get the chance." Michael said with enthusiasm. "Now it's time to move on to the world of negotiations. Have fun!"

"Thank you so much for your valuable insights into the applications of the Change People Pattern relating to sales and to marketing." I really did appreciate the time and information that Michael shared with me so willingly.

NEGOTIATIONS

As it turned out, Beverly was just finishing a negotiating session. She waved at me to be seated. In listening to the interaction, I could already begin to identify the four aspects of the Change People Pattern. Needless to say, I was quite pleased with myself. I also realized how incredibly helpful it would be to me in the context of both my professional and private life.

"Are you ready for a rather different approach to negotiations?" she laughed after finishing.

It was obvious that news of my patterns was common knowledge among the department managers. Now at least, I could actually see that how they were communicating with me was different from how they talked to others.

"Wouldn't it be helpful to have the Change Pattern at your disposal when in the middle of some major negotiation?" she added. In the framework of the Change People Pattern, many of the approaches discussed for sales apply as well in the domain of negotiations. There is rarely a day that goes by when we do not get involved in some level of negotiating, whether with a spouse or kids, a car dealer, or with a major corporate client."

"I can certainly use this information in dealing with my own children for sure." I said with a sigh of welcome relief, knowing that everything I was learning would help me immensely in my personal life interactions as well as in my professional ones.

"I can relate to that, too. A knowledge of this People Pattern would greatly enhance your ability to achieve your desired goal in any negotiation. Each of the Change People Patterns has a particular approach which proves to be most effective when negotiating with that type of person."

"Let's discuss sameness first. Remember that a sameness person discerns only that which is similar to his past experience, so that in any negotiating situation, you must emphasize the aspects of the present circumstances that are identical or at least parallel to the previous set of circumstances. In other words, stress continuity with the past. At all times you should underline the areas of mutual consensus. If anywhere you do agree on something, make sure that those conditions are brought out up front. Go out of your way to indicate that you are both in this negotiation for basically the same end result - a win /win situation for the two of you. If the two sides represent eye catching major differences in point of view and position, try your best to avoid discussing these disparities."

"Is that because sameness people detest change and often have an excruciating time dealing with it," I guessed.

"Precisely. So your best bet is to be ready to handle resistance to change on the part of the sameness and qualified sameness person. They will be most resistant to any kind of change that involves 'give backs.' Once a sameness person becomes accustomed to something favorable, he will certainly not want to give it up. Certainly do not expect significant upheavals in his position or, for that matter, much desire to change at all," she added with a knowing smile, saying that I would probably find this situation to be the most challenging for me, given my personal orientation.

"Some other advice when negotiating with sameness people. Make an extra effort to match and mirror their body posture, gestures, and voice volume, tone, and tempo. Also, stress any commonality, and avoid any surprises. Make sure that the negotiating sessions are at the same time and place every day."

"With the qualified sameness person, you will find him a bit more amenable to discussing a change of position, provided that he views the change as an improvement of his current situation. *Better* is the key word when negotiating with qualified sameness people. Your goal should be to demonstrate how the final agreement will be an improved version of what already is, and that it is preferable and better for both of you. Again, first and foremost, emphasize the ways in which the new conditions resemble those of the original scenario. Even if the terms seem obvious to you, and even if it seems like an utter waste of time, carefully go over the similarities between previous and current or desired conditions. Only when the qualified sameness person acknowledges the similarities and feels comfortable with the discussion, do you begin to allude to the aspects of the situation that have more or less been modified."

"Great!" I exclaimed. Now we move into my realm, that of difference."

"This is where the fun begins. The approach with a difference person will take on a totally different shape, of course. Your ultimate goal is to make the difference person realize that the final agreement is totally different from the conditions set forth at the start of the negotiating process."

"That's what I would look for in any negotiation." I chimed in.

"Remember that simply on principle, the difference person will want to make changes in the terms of the agreement. Sometimes, these may represent major shifts of position. So you need to be prepared in advance for such demands, and have ready some conditions (unimportant for you), that you would be willing to change when asked to do so by the difference person. Be prepared to deal with one who will mismatch and disagree with what you say."

"That's crazy! That doesn't work." I said jokingly.

"Right on! You must know your position thoroughly and have already prepared responses in advance to challenges like 'That will not work.'. Also, beware of the person who will want to do the opposite of what you say, the polarity responder. In that case, use time worn reverse psychology to deal with him. Your bottom line goal should be to convince the difference person that the final form of the mutual agreement embodies and represents all that is new and even unique to your previous accords with him or with others."

"Last but certainly not least, we move to the qualified difference person. He too, will be interested in understanding how the final agreement differs from previous ones. Make a point from the start of the negotiation of emphasizing the differences between the past and currently proposed terms of the agreement. Only when you know that the other person has acknowledged that, do you proceed with mentioning in passing the similarities between the two. The accent still needs to be on divergence. The more you show how the current terms are dissimilar to prior ones, the quicker you will arrive at a mutual agreement."

"Does that mean that if the new terms represent a totally opposite point of view, I should say so?" I responded with a contented look on my face.

"Precisely. And there is more. Also, as with the difference person, expect this People Pattern type to demand changes. Decide ahead of time which conditions are insignificant to you in the overall scheme of things, and then propose them as your modifications to the accord. Finally, stress that your goal is to come up with creative solutions and novel and interesting twists in the agreement."

"I would guess that these recommendations for negotiating with the various types of change People Patterns are simply basic guidelines to help me in my negotiations."

"These are suggestions that will help with any negotiations, no matter what they are and with whomever you have to negotiate. These guidelines merely scratch the surface, and do not, because of time requirements, cover the scores of possible scenarios in which you may find yourself in real life. There exists an entire other level of subtleties which may come into play in negotiations, which you will learn in the future from our in-house manual on negotiations, as well as in the negotiating skill shops we give within the company."

"I certainly have a lot to study and mull over. The good part is that there are so many different possibilities with which to work, and that is always a lot of fun."

"Next you will be heading to Frank in Training who will be showing you how the Change People Pattern applies to the realm of training and education. With what you have already learned here, the rest will be much easier."

"I'm sure it will be still different in some way from what I have heard thus far."

"Please feel free to ask me questions any time something comes up. I'd be more than happy to provide you with more guidelines and specific insights into different negotiation situations. Remember that every negotiation will have different elements involved, which makes the interaction all the more interesting."

Beverly was quite pleased with the way in which I received and processed the information.

"Thank you, Beverly. I will certainly take you up on your offer as new and different negotiations arise." I really was very grateful for the valuable information.

TRAINING

"Welcome to the Training Department." Frank said. "I'm certain that by now you are used to having things presented to you from a new and different perspective."

Frank was quite relaxed and of all the sessions today, I had the feeling that this one would be the most laid-back of all.

"This is your next to last session of the day, so I thought that we would relax and have some fun with the information. Also, I think that it is important in training to enjoy oneself to the fullest, since a relaxed mind and body really do enhance the learning process. More on that later. Right now, though, before we get into the facets of training in relation to the Change People Pattern, I thought we would discuss how this pattern fits into education in general. I will make the distinction between training and education clearer as we go on."

"I'm glad that you will explain the difference to me, since this is not a distinction that I would have made." I politely said.

"I will refer frequently to the current 'dis-educational system' in our country, and today we will position it in terms of the Change People Pattern. The system is basically qualified sameness, as are most bureaucratic institutions. So unless you come out of this pattern, you will not fit in very well. Think about when you were in school. If you or any of your classmates did not 'learn' your lesson well, it was assumed that it was the fault of the student. This is one of the major fallacious premises upon which our 'dis-educational system' is based."

"What you are saying certainly takes me back to my school days. Tell me more." I asked, curious about the distinctions being made.

"The learning process should be the responsibility of the teacher, and when a child or student does not assimilate material, it really signifies that the teacher simply does not understand one fundamental principle upon which all learning, with no exception is based. This one underlying principle is that each of us learns in different ways."

I remained quiet so that Frank could continue uninterrupted.

"So what do you think happens when our 'dis-educational system' creates and sustains a self enhancing cycle of sameness and qualified sameness teachers who expect their students to duplicate exactly what is thrown out at them? We end up with sameness and qualified sameness students doing well, because they succeed at regurgitating material given to them by their instructors. Meanwhile, difference and qualified difference students get caught in the quandary, because they do not relate to sameness at all."

"Now I know why I constantly got into arguments with many of my teachers who were pure sameness. They really must have thought that I was going off the deep end with my comments and questions," I stated with a satisfied smile.

"We are talking here about two diametrically opposed approaches to learning. Remember that people with the sameness People Pattern see only similarities in any situation. So in the learning context, they will learn best by seeing and understanding how the new material (that which they are to learn) is similar or like that which they already know. Sameness people much prefer simplicity over complexity. They like to simplify things as much as possible."

"This is so incredibly right. Every time that I attempted to make one of my infamous distinctions, forget it! The sameness teacher would go crazy!"

Frank laughed as he continued to explain these so important distinctions.

"The minute you begin to make distinctions or talk about contrast or differentiation, you quickly lose the sameness person. They constantly filter difference out of their reality, out of their experience, so if you present contrast and dissimilarity within the framework of your teaching, you might as well be talking to a brick wall. Therefore, in your teaching or training, present material in a simple way. If you discuss things in the form of general principles, you are in safe territory. Sameness people are uncomfortable with exceptions to the rule. In fact, even if you spend time on anomalies or discrepancies, they will probably remain oblivious to them. To teach or to train sameness students effectively, continue to stress how what you are teaching them relates to what they already know and is merely a progression of it."

Sameness - Looks for commonalities
Difference - Makes distinctions

There was still so much more that Frank wanted to say, so I basically sit still and listened attentively.

"As far as the ambiance of the classroom is concerned, sameness students, just like their compatriot sameness workers, prefer routine. Avoid changing schedules on them, or regularly scheduled events. They like to do things at the same time each day. Recess at the same time, lunch breaks, study breaks, etc. need to remain constant. Notice which kids get upset most when their routine is interrupted for whatever reason. We guarantee it will not be the difference student. Also, study habits for sameness kids follow a rather uniform routine. They are the ones who get annoyed when parents change the habitual dinner time, or break time for whatever reason."

"I hadn't really thought about that with my own kids until now. Thanks for the insight. I know that I will have to change a few things in our household now that I have learned this information." I was quite pleased once again that what I was learning was applicable to my personal life.

"The teaching approach with qualified sameness students is similar to that of pure sameness in that the former also learn by noticing the similarities between what they already know and what they are learning. But that is where the affinity ends. Remember that qualified sameness people are balanced in that they see both similarity and difference in situations. The same holds true in the learning context. They first see similarity and then begin observing difference. They initially notice elements of sameness and then determine what exceptions exist." Frank stopped a second to see if I had any questions. I made a sign that I was still in pure listening mode, so he went on. He probably thought that my silence was due to end of the day fatigue.

"Unlike pure sameness, qualified sameness students are capable of handling complexity, although they, too, prefer generalizations. As far as the classroom is concerned, routine is still endorsed over erratic scheduling. The same applies to study habits at home, although qualified sameness kids can deal with interruption and change more easily than pure sameness kids. All those sameness and qualified sameness teachers and lecturers out there, particularly on the elementary and junior high levels, are probably quite popular with students (since a majority are of the same People Pattern), because they are quite skilled at throwing out great generalizations about things. This is precisely the way to present subject material to effectively reach them."

"Otherwise, learning is an outright failure. Right?" I asked.

"You took the words out of my mouth. So what happens to the few difference and qualified difference students around? They are the ones who like to make distinctions rather than collapse them as do sameness people, and are usually reprimanded or scorned for being the class troublemakers and nitpickers. They are the ones who appear to ask complicated questions or to make off the wall remarks, when in fact, they are merely making distinctions that the sameness students simply do not see."

"Sure sounds like me!" I announced.

"And there is more. The difference and qualified difference people are the types who go on to higher education, to graduate school or law school by choice, rather than by requirement. They are the ones who seek out difference, look for exceptions to the rule. They learn best by seeing how things differ from what they already know, and pointing out those distinctions to the rest of the world. Qualified difference students are the reverse of qualified sameness. Although the former first notices disparities, they also take in similarities, albeit secondarily. Their outright preference is still difference, and they still opt for complexity over simplistic generalizations. Have you had enough?" Frank asked.

"No please go on. This is fascinating material which has enlightened me on more than one aspect of my educational experiences."

"Difference people are those who go out of their way to find disparity. They prefer elaborate models and theories to simplistic statements. Unlike the sameness crowd, those with Difference People Patterns thrive on complexity. They consider general principles and axioms to be overly simplistic and gross generalizations to be meaningless to reality.

Remember difference people are constantly looking to see what does not or will not work, and are coming up with new models to explain the distinctions they make."

"Excuse me. Are researchers often the difference people of the world?" I wanted to know.

"Precisely. Scholars, scientists, researchers, and erudite types usually come out of the Difference People Pattern. They are the ones who constantly provide counter-examples to arguments and try to explain why something does not work. They seem to find complexity in everything. What often appears to be quite a simple scenario, ends up an incredible imbroglio to the difference mind."

"Think back to your earlier school days." Frank asked. "Who was considered to be the class pain? Who was always the one who disagreed with the general opinion? Who was constantly making distinctions that went over the heads of many of the students? The difference person, who else! Once this difference student gets to graduate school, he is right in his milieu in the company of more difference classmates, and more often than not, a difference professor."

"As I look back on my school days and relive some of my interactions with teachers and students, I must have seemed to be a real pain to them. Quite intolerable in fact."

"And I'm sure that you had a fantastic time being a pain!" chuckled Frank.

"As we move up the learning ladder," he continued, "we are expected to make more refined distinctions in an attempt to explain existence. After all, what are most programs of higher learning all about? Making distinctions, concocting theories, finding exceptions and then codifying all these into what becomes accepted laws. Remember our prior discussion about scientists and creative people in general?"

"Please refresh my memory." I asked.

"Let us discuss the growth of knowledge. It involves a rhythm of sameness and difference. What do scientists do in reality? They first look into the chaos of the world and search for regularity. They look for correlations which are invariant and which they can quantify in laws. Once these laws are in place, then the next or difference phase begins. They now look for exceptions to the laws. They categorize and classify and catalog and measure to test the general laws. They find out where the law is either limited or does not work. In short, they search for exceptions and counter examples. Once they find them, however, they do not rest there. The next step is to go back to the sameness side and to find the regularities in the exceptions. The goal here is to build a more sophisticated theory where the counter-examples and exceptions at the previous level are now seen as special cases of the still greater and more complex regularity. And the cycle repeats. The bottom line is that scientists, researchers and related occupations are literally professional matchers and mismatchers who codify their mismatches into more complex matches. This, in essence, is the basis of the progression and evolution of knowledge."

GROWTH OF KNOWLEDGE
Sameness - Search for correlations
Difference - Search for exceptions

"Last, but certainly not least, I would like to briefly touch upon the notion of creativity. So what is creativity? By its very nature creativity entails the introduction of some new or novel element. In short, something different from what exists already. And if our current 'dis-educational system', particularly at primary and secondary levels, bolsters sameness and continuity of the status quo, what do you think that does to promoting difference or the creative spark? Here at Success, Incorporated we teach an entire course on creativity. In this we explore the notion of genius in great detail. Today is not the day to go into this. I will explore this with you one day in the future when you learn about the social and cultural applications of People Patterns."

"There is so much that I didn't know!" I blurted out with a sigh.

"Are you ready to move on to personnel applications?" Frank inquired, sensing that I had already had a rather chock full day of insights.

PERSONNEL : HIRING THE RIGHT PERSON FOR THE RIGHT JOB

"Do come in." Karen was quite polite and obviously ready to take on the task of teaching me all about the applications of the Change People Pattern in personnel selection and placement.

"I know that you have received a great deal of information today, so I will do my best to make this session brief yet informative. All I ask is that you maintain an open mind and also that you remember the factors which determined whether or not you were hired to join our work force here at Success, Incorporated."

"How could I ever forget that unique experience? And to say that I have been inundated with information is a welcome understatement. There is so much to learn. The bright side is that I think I now have a feel for the nuances of the Change People Pattern, although I still need to hear specifics from you before the information becomes encoded in my brain."

"From your first interview, you must have realized that we do not rely on resumes and appearance in making hiring decisions around here. From the rest of your sessions today about the various business applications of the Change People Pattern, you have probably come to realize that when it comes to the workplace and jobs, there are certain factors which need to be addressed for each of the four types. For example, when it comes to sameness workers, they fit best into particular kinds of jobs. There are obviously certain jobs that are perfect for the sameness person. They thrive on routine. Jobs that require constant repetition of tasks, such as assembly line work would be ideal for a sameness person who is absolutely in heaven doing the same thing day in and day out, even for a lifetime. People who filter by sameness would be happiest and most productive in such positions. They will stay in these jobs from fifteen years to a lifetime unless they are forced to change due to circumstances beyond their control or unless so much variety is introduced into the job that they can no longer tolerate the stress."

"No variety is the spice of life! That is their slogan! Right?"

"What the others have said is true. You are really learning this material quite well. In hiring people for jobs that demand routine, stress job security and continuity, both of which are of paramount importance to the sameness worker. Emphasize the work schedule, whatever shift it is, stress that it probably will not change. Talk about pride in workmanship, that your firm really does take pride in the end product. It is no coincidence that the major automobile manufacturing plants are located where they are."

"I had never really thought about why the people of the Mid West would be such good candidates for that type of work. It all makes great sense now." I announced.

"Think about the reasons why. Any job requiring a person to perform a task the identical way each time is well suited for those who filter by sameness. This is crucial on assembly lines, because deviating from the routine results in defects and poor quality end products. Also important to sameness workers is the security of knowing that the conditions in which they work will not change. They do not respond well to frequent changes in management and in their superiors. Moreover, when the actual structure of an organization is modified, particularly one in which they have worked for years, the result is chaotic discontent. In some cases change is inevitable for reasons beyond control, and if management does not understand how to facilitate and present this transformation, you've got serious problems with your sameness employees. Here is the perfect example of what I mean. We at Success, Incorporated were working on a project several years ago modeling machine operators at different plants for a company that manufactures label paper. In one plant, the workers were quite fortunate to have a bright innovative young manager who understood the importance of these and other behavioral components when dealing with employees both in hiring and in general managerial contexts. In the plants where management had no knowledge of and moreover, no interest in learning about the human typologies, the overall ambiance of the plants was extremely negative and workers were always dissatisfied with what they perceived to be the apathetic 'higher than mighty attitude' of their managers."

"It must be so frustrating to be dealing with people who have no interest in learning new information to help them make changes for the better! Speaking of a sameness orientation."

"Actually there was more to it. Moreover, management had been ordered to introduce a new methodology and structure and impose it upon a work force that was for the most part sameness and qualified sameness (which makes sense since they work best in assembly line jobs.) This new structure known as HPO or High Performance Organization, although a valid and quite effective concept in itself when appropriately implemented, was poorly received by the workers. In fact, at first it was utterly rejected by them, because management refused to acknowledge certain verities about the workers' values and behavioral traits which got in the way of their acceptance of the new organizational arrangement. Ironically, at those plants where the few selected expert workers (those modeled and some new hirees) were taught the different behavioral patterns and values, they not only began to understand themselves and their fellow workers for the first time, but also began to understand why there was so much resistance to the High Performance Organization. Their newly acquired knowledge allowed them to accept, if only a little more, the new structure being imposed on them after years of routinely doing the same thing day in and day out. Moreover, they suddenly realized why management would continue to have problems with the workers' endorsement of the new structure if they did not resort to an appropriate method of implementation. Of course, due to particular personality issues of some of the management team, certain people felt threatened by the workers suddenly seeing through them and realizing that management was not doing all it could."

"That boils down to politics as usual in the workplace. Right?"

"Yes, and meanwhile, the sameness members of management, who themselves do not like drastic change, let alone having to implement it, tried to find scapegoats wherever they could to explain their inability to master the situation. The threatened ones refused to acknowledge the sameness mentality, because their own hands had been called."

"It is so critical to remember that sameness people are much better suited to hold 8 to 5 jobs, or any job that requires a daily time schedule, since routine is what they can cope with best. The bottom line in this discussion is the fact that companies would be saving money and increasing productivity if they hired prospective employees based on this particular People Pattern when it is a crucial component of potential success at the job. If a company needs workers for a job that requires constant repetition, the personnel office would be well advised to hire new employees whose Change People Pattern is sameness or qualified sameness. In most assembly line work hierarchies, there is usually a supervisor, or at least one individual on each shift who is responsible for correcting breakdowns. Repairing the machine entails adding an element to the normal, habitual task of smoothly running the machine. Varying the basic task a little, then, corresponds to injecting a trace of difference into similarity, therefore, suiting the qualified sameness person to a tee. It would be helpful, then, for management to put into such supervisory positions that require occasional variety within an otherwise routine job, a person with a Qualified Sameness People Pattern. More on this later."

"I meant to ask this question during my session on management with Marvin, and then we got into another discussion, and I forgot until now. What about a bureaucracy? I really have a horrible time dealing with bureaucratic nonsense? Could that be a sameness system of sorts?"

"How perceptive of you! And you have touched on one of my nemeses of sorts. Dealing with red tape has always been a bone of contention for me. And you are right on. Bureaucracy in all of its manifestations, in all domains, on all levels of society is first and foremost a sameness and qualified sameness institution. Think about the Postal Service, Medicare Offices, Social Security, the Military, the IRS, or take the public educational system as a case in point. Organizations such as your local school board are comprised primarily of sameness or qualified sameness minds which do not look well on innovative changes in the educational system. For them it is important to guarantee that things remain the same, or at least do not change too much."

"If a new idea is proposed to a sameness person, watch out! Right?"

"You know the pattern. He will probably react by saying that things have never been done that way in the past, so why should they begin now to break with what is a solid and accepted tradition. A few years ago a highly effective and innovative Superintendent of Schools in New York City was dismissed because his forward looking ideas were not accepted by a traditional sameness and qualified sameness school board. So what if the number of dropouts had not increased and illiteracy had decreased under Joseph Hernandez? What he espoused was too different for this sameness and qualified sameness institution to handle. Such bureaucracies seem to be locked eternally into the status quo. And anyone who has the courage to implement something different within the system, even if proven effective, unfortunately gets shot down. There is also the issue of a clash of values at work in this instance. But that is a topic for another time."

"What about the military?" I asked.

"The government bureaucratic machine, particularly the military, is but another example among many in our world in which sameness appears to take the upper hand. Just think about all those young men and women who go off to join the Army, Navy, Air Force or Marines. These recruits have to be prepared to live by routine during months of training, a sameness agenda day in and day out, until (if and when) a situation arises which requires military intervention. This kind of regime better fits the mold of a sameness or qualified sameness person than one who sorts by difference. Moreover, a career in the standard military is more likely to be chosen by someone from the former group, although life among the ranks of something like the French Foreign Legion lends itself more to the mentality of the difference person."

"What kinds of jobs then, fit the mold of the qualified sameness person? The qualified sameness person will do well in positions in which there is a large amount of repetition of task, but where elements of variety will be introduced from time to time. If you are managing a qualified sameness person, expect him to enjoy routine, but also expect him to want a change of pace from time to time in his habitual performance. Secretarial jobs in which there is a particular daily routine of tasks to be completed i.e. sorting of mail, answering of calls, typing of letters, combined with occasional novel assignments such as receiving out of town visitors, planning a business luncheon, etc. are ideal."

"That makes sense, since those types of positions afford the qualified sameness person with the right amount of sameness and difference to maintain his interest."

"Expect a qualified sameness person to stay at his job from seven to nine years, depending on how much variety is interjected in the context of his job. He will stay at his job until he learns how to do it well, and then will want to learn new skills. By doing so he improves his status or position and moves up the corporate ladder or up in the bureaucratic hierarchy. As long as there is room for improvement and learning new skills, the qualified sameness person will probably stay at the same job. If, however, he finds himself at a dead end with nothing new to learn, he will begin getting bored. At that point, he will want to move on to a more fulfilling job. Most of the jobs in the corporate world that involve gradual professional growth and upward mobility suit the qualified sameness person to a tee."

"I remember that the average businessperson is coming out of a qualified sameness mind set."

"Now on to your realm - that of difference. If you think about yourself it will be easy to figure out the kinds of jobs that would appeal to a pure difference person."

"Difference people are likely to stay working in a job from six months to a year. If they are lucky enough to find employment which involves a great amount of variety, then they may remain in that job an entire lifetime."

"Like any relationship, the difference person will stay on if there is a constant stream of variety coming into play. Right?"

"That kind of job is more the exception than the rule, though, unless custom created for the difference person. If, however, the job entails anything routine that demands repetition of any kind on a long term basis, you had better not count on hiring them for longer than the year period mentioned above, if you can keep them interested that long. The amount of change built into the job and the person's tolerance level for sameness will usually determine the period of time at which the difference person will stay on the job. More than any other type, the pure difference person feeds on constant diversity and some type of contrast interjected in the context of his work. In hiring the difference employee, tell him that things are constantly undergoing change in the context of the job (provided it is true). I can usually spot a difference person from their resume. They will be constantly switching jobs or work assignments. Their resumes go on forever. When I see a resume like that I know that they are involved in the constant search for difference in the workplace. Unless they are carefully placed, they will be moving on very soon. Often difference people can be the very best at certain jobs. The tragedy is that even though they are doing a job extremely well, they are quickly ready to move on to something else with a new challenge to master."

"Qualified difference workers like a balance of difference and sameness. As you have already learned, there needs to be some elements of variety interspersed with some baseline of sameness in the context of the job. As long as there is a juggling of both elements, things different and things similar, they will be happy campers. Also, remember that contextuality comes into play here as well."

"Qualified difference employees will stay on a job longer than a pure difference person, and will also change jobs more frequently than a pure sameness person. On the average they will stay in a job one to four years. Always beware when you have a resume with frequent job changes, particularly when they occur over a relatively short period of time. Of course, the duration will be more or less significant depending on the type of job involved."

"I promised that I would not keep you in here too long, so if you do not have any questions now, I will send you back to Shana for your end of the day debriefing. I hope that this brief time we spent together has given you helpful insights. Obviously, there is so much more and whenever there arises a specific situation or question about whom to hire for what, I would rather personalize and customize the interview or interaction to fit the task at hand. We at Success, Incorporated pride ourselves on the People Pattern Profile^{SM} we have created to help other businesses in their personnel and hiring needs."

SUMMARY

Shana was happy to see me. "Do you have any questions?"

"A couple." I said. "I was wondering when these People Patterns begin to develop. I can observe them even in my young kids. Are we born with them or do we develop them? If we develop them, then at what age?"

"Excellent questions." Shana responded. "You have touched on an age old debate between nature and nurture. Some people believe that personality patterns are innate and others believe that they are developed in childhood. Sameness people prefer to believe that they are innate and that they cannot be changed. Difference people prefer to think that man is a product of his environment, and that as the environment changes, then man changes. This view holds that the People Patterns develop in childhood as arbitrary coping mechanisms. They quickly become perceptual habits. Some may change as we grow older and some may remain pretty much fixed. Also, traumatic events in childhood or adulthood may force us to readjust these coping mechanisms. So I leave it to you to choose which explanation that you think most adequately fits the facts. Of course, I do know which you will choose."

We both laughed.

"I have one more question."

Shana listened attentively.

"It seems to me that only a difference person could fully appreciate and utilize People Patterns."

"That is an excellent point, and it needs a few qualifications." Shana answered. "Obviously distinctions are created by difference people. But People Patterns are a special kind of distinctions. They are about regularities or patterns in the behavior of people. They simply codify the different ways that people habitually act and think. Sameness people view all people as the same and just like them. They will be looking for sameness and not difference. They may be comfortable with one distinction, but by the time that they are taught several People Patterns they start saying 'But isn't that like this?' and 'Isn't that just a special case of this?' Their goal is to reduce all of the distinctions to just one distinction. That, of course, misses the point. As for utilization, as I emphasized yesterday, to be successful with using People Patterns, a person needs to be able to do several things. These are. 1) understand the distinction. 2) be able to identify the pattern in themselves and others. 3) know how to utilize the pattern to influence other people. 4) have enough flexibility of behavior that they can vary their behavior as appropriate to get the desired response. Difference and qualified difference people will find these tasks easier than qualified sameness people and total sameness people may find them very difficult."

KEY 2:

THE PRIMARY INTEREST PEOPLE PATTERN

INTRODUCTION

Now that I was learning to be a People Pattern Manager, the conversations in the car pool were becoming more interesting to me. Before I had been bored most of the time. Now I was beginning to look for patterns in the conversations of different people in the car pool. It occurred to me that I did not have a lot in common with most of the people in my car pool. For instance, all Tom ever seemed to talk about was what his family was doing. They went here and did this, and then they went there and did that. I really was not interested in all the running around that his family seemed to do. Bill was not much better. All he ever seemed to talk about was people whom I didn't know and could care less about. Today it was on his cousin's best friend's sister who had met the grandmother of his next door neighbor by accident at a shopping mall in Berlin. Sue and her husband liked to travel, and she was always describing some exotic place that they had been to or were going to visit. Some of the places seemed interesting, but I thought that it might be easier and cheaper just to watch a travel video than to actually go there. At least Dave was usually interesting. He was into equipment big time. He was especially knowledgeable on computers, video equipment, cars and sports equipment. He could always be counted on to know what the newest features were and which brands were the best buys. Dave's only problem was that he would often go into too much detail. I was interested in technological advance in general, but I really didn't need to know all of the numbers and fine points of every brand. Today Tom was talking about his family's latest outing. Sue interrupted to find out exactly where they were on the outing. Then Bill was confused about which one of Tom's kids was involved. They were all focused on the story, and I was thinking of the ramifications of children growing up in Tom's household. The children had gotten into a problem.

Everyone seemed interested in exactly how this happened. To me it was obvious how it happened, and I could not understand why this did not seem to occur to Tom or to his wife. By the time we got to my drop off point I was exasperated. I was early for once and leisurely walked to Shana's office. She had not arrived yet, so I set down and picked up the P³ cube on her desk. I thought about People Pattern Power and becoming a People Pattern Person and wondered if this would make life more interesting.

INFORMATION

Shana arrived and asked me what I was thinking about at that moment. I said that I was wondering if People Patterns would make life more interesting and if they could help to spice up the conversations in my car pool. Shana laughed and said that she didn't know if anything could do that, but if anything could, then what we were going to talk about today might. So she began.

"Today we are going to talk about information. One of the prime functions of managers is to manage information. A manager has to gather information about what is happening and to compare what is happening to what should be happening. If there is a discrepancy between the two, then the manager has to figure out what corrective action to take. Then he has to communicate that information to the necessary people so that the corrective action actually happens as the manager envisions. He then needs to continue to monitor the situation. Okay so far?"

I nodded, and Shana continued.

"The success of any manager is largely dependent on his ability to manage information. No manager can know everything. The key is for the manager to know only what he needs to know and no more. He needs to be able to quickly and efficiently find out what he needs to know in order to manage well. He also needs to avoid devoting time and energy on information which is interesting but not necessary for him to manage. We call this the difference between the need to know and the need to not know. Too much information is just as bad as not enough information. The key is the right amount. No more, but no less either."

Need to know
Need to not know

"This is interesting." I said. "It had not occurred to me that there could be too much information."

"I wonder how that could be." Shana chuckled and went on.

"There are several People Patterns which all have to do with information. The first, which we will cover today, is called the Primary Interest People Pattern, and it has to do with the content of the information.

"It sounds complicated." I said. Shana looked at me and continued.

"Everything is complicated until you understand it. Actually, it is quiet simple. Let us begin."

"Then I guess I'm ready to jump in." I said, hopefully with enthusiasm in my voice. "Just what is a Primary Interest Pattern?" I asked.

COMMONALITY OF INTERESTS OR WHAT MAKES THE WORLD GO ROUND

"This People Pattern deals with what people have (or do not have) in common. It deals with the glue that bonds people together and which, when absent, leaves them permanently estranged. It deals with why we find some people interesting and why we can hardly stand to be around other people. All of us have known people with whom we just seemed to mesh. We have also had experiences of being stuck listening to a relative or a stranger when we were bored to death and could hardly wait to escape at the first opportunity. I'm sure you have been in these situations before." Shana said with a slight smile.

"More recently than you realize." I responded.

"Our Primary Interest Pattern is just what it says. It is that area of life in which we are most interested. It is the focal point of our interest and attention. We pay attention to things that interest us, and we could care less about things that do not interest us. We enjoy being around people who share our interests, and we find it torture to endure the company of people whose interests are not the same as ours. Our interests determine how we run our lives. They determine where we go, what we do, and with whom we do it. They determine what we spend our money on and how we spend our time. Any questions just yet?"

"Only that I'll bet that this pattern has a great effect on our culture." I said.

"Yes, indeed. Our combined Interest Patterns determine what is popular and what is not. They determine which movies and TV shows are watched and which lose money or are canceled due to poor attendance or low ratings. They determine what books, magazines and newspapers we read. They determine what becomes a best seller and what bombs. Also, they determine what sells and what does not. They determine what we collectively spend our money on and, hence, what things are popular and profitable and what things remain on the shelves. They determine what stores and restaurants are successful and which go out of business."

RELATIONSHIPS

"This pattern also has a major effect on relationships." she continued. When you first meet someone, it is usually fairly obvious after some initial conversation whether or not you share common interests. This mutual link, that interest which puts you at ease with that person because you seem to be walking on common ground, is the Primary Interest Pattern. This People Pattern is quite important, because it represents an easy and effective way to break the ice between two people and to establish rapport. The Primary Interest Pattern is so powerful that it can make or break a relationship."

"At least I am already aware of the fact that sharing another person's main interests will certainly facilitate communication with that person." I added. That seemed fairly logical.

"If your interests differ, then by learning something about their interests, you will be able to open a channel of communication with them. This is one of Dale Carnegie's powerful strategies for developing relationships in his now classic book *How To Win Friends And Influence People*."

Shana continued. "If you have been wondering why you do not feel comfortable with a particular person, it may very well be that the two of you do not share the same interests. How many of us have been forced to put up with hours of inescapable, sheer boredom in the company of an acquaintance, colleague, or maybe even a relative who does not share any interests in common with us? What downright drudgery! Alas! We can now shed light on those endless moments of misery with an understanding of this all important People Pattern."

"And the opposite is true with people you like." I said even though it seemed so obvious.

"Of course. You may be in a new situation with new acquaintances, and realize that the reason you are getting on so well is because you have the same interests as the other person or persons. You may have been wondering for years why it is that you mesh so easily with someone and why being with that person seems to be so effortless. On occasions you have had the feeling that you have known someone for years, even though you had literally just met that person. Conversations seemed to glide along with such ease; you could move from one topic to another, with enthusiasm and keen interest overflowing all around. Little did you know that your common Primary Interest Pattern was at work bringing you together."

"Maybe it is time to bring on the Twilight Zone music." I jumped in to say while I began to hum the familiar tune."

"Not necessary. This is the stuff of real world communication: men, women, whites, people of color, Orientals, Native Americans - no distinctions - a world in which each individual no matter what race, religion or nationality, has his own bag of personalized elements which either opens a channel of communication or does not."

"So is that why so many relationships fail or break down?" I wanted to know.

"Precisely. After whatever initial pleasantry and attraction there is, if the two individuals do not share either Primary or Secondary Interest Patterns, then the chances are that their relationship will be short lived. How many times have you either said or heard someone else say 'We simply do not enjoy the same things. We seem to have nothing in common'? What is being revealed is that the two people do not share a common Primary or at least Secondary Interest Pattern. It is certainly no accident or stroke of destiny that some couples seem to get on so much better than others. You can bet that in most of these cases, there exists a common Primary Interest Pattern between them."

PRIMARY INTEREST PATTERN

By now I have learned that there is always more. Just when I think that we can move on to the next phase, there are always more refinements and distinctions to be made. And so Shana proceeded to talk more about this all important People Pattern.

"As you know, we all have many different interests. (After all, being the good difference person that you are, you are more than aware of this fact.) People we know or know of have many more different interests. Aren't there as many different interests as there are people? There are many different interests, but they all fall into one of five categories. So just what are these five categories of interest which we either share or do not share with our fellow human beings? They correspond to the Primary Interest Patterns."

"How can we identify them? Are there target indicator questions? What are they?" I wanted to know everything.

PRIMARY INTEREST PEOPLE PATTERN
People - Who?
Things - What?
Activity - When? and How?
Place - Where?
Information - All of above and Why?

"The five Primary Interest Patterns are: 1) people, 2) things, 3) activity, 4) place, and 5) information. People who filter by people will always ask the question 'who'; people who filter by things will want to know 'what'; those who filter by activity will be interested in 'how' and 'when';

individuals who filter by place will want to know 'where'; and those who filter by information will want to know all of the above and 'why' as well."

In a louder tone of voice, Shana recited a little poem: "The great poet Rudyard Kipling who served as a writer and journalist in India wrote in a little poem in his book of *Just So Stories*:

I keep six honest serving-men
(They taught me all I know);
Their names are What and Why and When
And How and Where and Who.

You may be asking how come there are five Primary Interest Patterns and not ten or twenty. The Primary Interest Patterns are deeply rooted in the language that we speak. If you look in a good grammar book, you will find that a 'noun' is the name of a person, place, thing, activity, quality, concept, or condition. Person is people, place is place, thing is things, activity is activity, and quality, concept, and condition are information. In short, the Primary Interest Patterns are the classes of names of what exists in the world."

"To come to think of it. That is true. They all correspond to the classes of nouns." I chimed in.

"Yes, and these patterns are also connected to the ways in which we process information through our senses. Our interaction with people is primarily auditory and secondarily visual and kinesthetic. Our interaction with place is primarily visual and secondarily in terms of feelings. Activity is primarily kinesthetic and secondarily visual. Our interaction with things is primarily visual or kinesthetic. We process information digitally through symbols."

I was listening attentively, so Shana went on. "When we say that each of us has a Primary Interest Pattern we do not mean that this is all that is of interest to us in our lives. It simply means that this area is the one in which we are most interested. All of us have a Primary Interest Pattern, and many of us also have a Secondary and even a Tertiary Interest Pattern as well. There are also one or more categories in which we have little if any interest."

"Could you give me an example." I asked.

"For example, I may filter primarily by people and secondarily by place. This means that I am most interested in people and particularly in where they are. We will go into this in more detail later in our discussion. To say that each of us has a Primary Interest Pattern is the first cut. It is also important to know the Secondary and even Tertiary Pattern as well. It is also important to know what the categories are in which we have little or no interest."

"I assume that when you talk to a person you will quickly find out his Primary Interest Pattern." I asked.

"Certainly, and then you can begin to observe how his Secondary and Tertiary Patterns begin to blend in with the Primary one. It is one's Primary Pattern, though, which will usually be the principal ingredient in their personalized blend of interests. Often people reveal their primary interest by the questions that they ask. Some people are even unable to interpret what you are telling them until they can place your information in the context of their filters."

"We will now consider each of the Primary Interest Patterns and see how they may manifest in our lives and in the lives of others. I will also give examples of how a Secondary or Tertiary Pattern may affect the Primary Interest Pattern."

"And I'll be able to confirm my own Primary Interest Pattern, of which you are already aware." I said, and then a question occurred to me. "Are these types equally divided?"

Shana paused. "No she said. People, activity and things are much more prominent than place and information."

PRIMARY INTEREST PEOPLE PATTERN
People - 30%
Activity - 30%
Things - 30%
Place - 5%
Information - 5%

PEOPLE

"First, as I have mentioned earlier, a person may filter by people. This means that his primary interest in life is other people. What he enjoys most doing, then, relates to people, whether they be family members, distant relatives, acquaintances, complete and utter strangers, colleagues or whomever. This may be expressed in his always liking to talk about people, or else in his constantly wanting to be with other people. In conversations with people filterers, you will notice that they will always mention the names of people, even though the name is totally unnecessary to the conversation at hand. Also their preference may even be expressed in their choice of profession which will be marked by a constant need for interaction with other people."

"I can think of a close friend who has the gift of gab when it comes to telling you about other people." I said the moment I realized the connection.

"Yes, and they are the gossips of the world (their Secondary Pattern is information), and usually every family has several. Try listening (if you can bear it for a period of time) to your family gossip at your next holiday dinner or family event. No matter what the occasion, no matter where the event, even at a funeral, the person who filters by people is simply going to be engaged in conversation about other people. They will always be curious to know about and talk about Mr. and Mrs. So and So, and they will be mentioning name after name even though the names mean nothing to those listening."

"If your Primary Interest Pattern does not coincide with a people person's Primary Interest Pattern, then conversations with that person can be tediously boring. After all, who in the world cares that your cousin's brother-in-law's niece enjoyed her trip to Spain, where she ran into your neighbor's daughter's best friend's dentist at a museum? Do you have friends or relatives whose conversations with you are always geared toward their children or parents or other family members? You may not want to hear about so and so, but a people filterer will fill you in on all the people in his world, whether you like it or not, and worse, whether you know those people in his world or not. And you will end up hearing a list of names which will never ever be meaningful to you."

"It is so boring when they go out of their way to mention specifically the name of the individual or individuals in question, even though their names have no relevance whatsoever to the point of the conversation! My sister has an in-law who does that, and it is so annoying!" I said.

"And they are probably people you have never heard of and will never meet! Any time of day, any time of the year, anywhere in the world, the person who filters by people thrives on news about other people and/or on simply telling you about people."

"I notice these people types all the time, because it annoys me so much." I interrupted.

"I'll bet, since this pattern is not your Primary Interest Pattern. Notice the next time that you are in the company of a person who filters by people. Ask a question relating to activity - let's say a vacation. Instead of telling you what they did, notice how the brunt of the conversation revolves around whom they saw (either people they know or simply a description of the types of people they encountered on their trip). To the amazement and dismay of a non-people person, this can be an outrageous bore!"

"Yes, and it usually is!" I said.

"It is astonishing just how excited and thrilled people who filter by people can become when they really get into it! This type of person is precisely the one you will find perusing a copy of what else but People Magazine! Also, who do you think is buying up all those copies of the Star or National Enquirer at the local grocery store? Or else who is perusing with great interest the magazines that are lined up at the grocery checkouts. Who else but a people person would care about the nonsense gossip headlines strewn across the pages of these tabloids!"

As Shana laughed, she continued. "Beware of the people filterer who goes around incognito! He is the one who wants to avoid being seen picking up a copy of a tabloid newspaper while he is standing in the supermarket checkout line. He very stealthily sets his gaze upon the entire rack, pretending all the while that he is bored stiff or that he is carrying on a conversation with you! You know, and we know that he can't fool us! A person with a different Primary Interest Pattern really has a difficult time understanding how anyone could waste his time reading such seemingly insignificant articles, and, moreover, often false stories about whatever star happens to be in the limelight at any given point in time."

"Why bother about the lives of other people when your own life is already so complicated?" I asked.

"As one whose Primary Interest Pattern (or secondary one, for that matter) is not people, yours is a typical reaction. Who cares that Mr. X gained thirty pounds, or that Mr. & Mrs. Z are getting a divorce? Or that Superstar A was recently seen having a cozy dinner with Superstar B? After all, there are enough cases of all of the above in the average person's own life to keep him busy. So who would have the time to worry about the people who are the subject of these gossip magazines? Who cares! Such would be the reaction of a person whose Primary Interest Pattern is not people."

"I've never understood how some people could be taken in by this nonsense garbage. It's like those people who watch the gossip shows like Entertainment Tonight and Show Biz Today among others. I could never understand how they could be so bored by their own lives to have to be interested in what these celebrities are doing. I couldn't care less! Even if I don't agree with such proclivities, at least I know the reasons behind this behavior." I said with contentment.

"You couldn't care less, because you do not filter by people. To someone like you, doing so is a waste of time. Remember that everyone is different. By the way, office parties are seventh heaven for the gossip people filterers Gossip columnists would be out of business were it not for the people filterers of the world. Not to mention the major big city tabloid newspapers! Next time you hear a gossip columnists talking about the names in the news and what they are doing, you will know that he or she primarily filters by people, and secondarily by information. These filters obviously match those of a lot of other people who rank among their loyal viewers. They too, filter primarily by people and secondarily by information. Even if some gossip magazines publish incorrect stories and/or exaggerated headlines, it does not matter as long as the readers who sort by people can get information to quench their Secondary Information Pattern with stories and more stories about what else - people!" Even Shana seemed exasperated by all of this, although she maintained an outwardly objective viewpoint.

"Of course, the extent to which a people person accepts the information will vary a great deal from one person to the next. TV programs such as *Entertainment Tonight*, *Hard Copy* and *A Current Affair* also have as their main subject matter people, in some cases celebrity stories, in others, average Americans with scandalous intrigue or unusual incidents in their lives. It seems all these shows are trying to outdo each other in providing the raunchiest and most scandalous and provocative material. Healthy people filtering is fine, but when taken to depths of the lowest of the low in exploitation, it raises a whole series of ethical questions about which we will talk at a later time. Not to mention that these programs are often simply a poor excuse for 'sexploitation' and exposing flesh. More on that when we discuss Value Cultures in our other training."

SECONDARY FILTER

"I mentioned before that a person's Primary Interest Pattern is tinted with nuances of his Secondary and/or Tertiary Patterns. Let us take the case of the individual who filters by people. Obviously, no two people will be interested in the same aspect of other people. There are different characteristics by which a person will filter other people."

"Does that maybe have to do with the different combinations of patterns?" I asked.

"As the good difference person that you are, it is not surprising that you realized that pretty quickly." Shana was obviously pleased as she answered my question.

"Yes, it does. For example, a person whose Primary Interest Pattern is people and whose Secondary Pattern is things is going to be interested in the material aspects of the person being talked about. What kind of house does he live in? How does he dress? What does he collect? Does he have the latest in video equipment? What kind of car does he own? Etc., etc."

"Moreover," she went on, "if you have ever been to a luncheon of status conscious men and women, all gabbing about so and so and each outdoing the other as far as wearing the accepted status symbols of the day, you will be in the company of individuals who filter by people and by things. This type of person will necessarily talk about the worldly possessions of the people who are the subject of their conversations. This type of individual loves to hang out at cocktail parties and receptions sporting the latest look in power ties or evening wear, meeting as many people as possible, and chatting about the other guests and particularly concentrating on things and objects in relation to these people. The society and social pages of any city's newspaper is the in print reflection of this particular People Pattern."

"That doesn't sound like me at all." I volunteered.

"You are right there. Meanwhile, if the person who filters by people is most interested in places where the people go, or places where they are seen, their Secondary Interest Pattern is that of place. For them, it is important to be with people, and at the same time, the place where they meet them matters as well. Not only are the people with whom they associate important, but also where they meet these people, and where they live and/or work. The Le Cirque 2000 crowd in Manhattan or the Spago clique in LA or the Taillevant crowd in Paris are great examples of this Primary and Secondary People Pattern combination. For the *habitués* of one of these 'in' eating places or any other, for that matter, it is absolutely crucial to be seen with certain people, and moreover, be seated at a particular table in the exclusive restaurant. More often than not, the place where you are seated reflects your status in the hierarchy of that particular establishment. If a people/place person is describing, for example, a friend's vacation, he will emphasize people seen and places visited."

"That still doesn't reflect my Primary Interest Patterns". I again chimed in.

"If a person who filters by people concentrates on what the other people are doing, then their Secondary Interest Pattern is activity. Simply talking about the people is not enough in such cases. It is also crucial to discuss the activities in which these people are engaging. For example, if they are telling you about someone's vacation, they will necessarily talk about the person with an emphasis on what he/she did on that vacation, whether it be sunbathing, reading, shopping, visiting museums, etc. If he is talking about a person's profession, he will stress the tasks he performs as part of his job, and the kinds of people with whom he works." Shana gave me a glance that asked if I had any questions.

"What about the amount of details involved in the descriptions given by the person?" I was curious to know.

"The degree of detail that a person gives relating to his Primary and Secondary Patterns varies form one individual to another, and is determined by the Chunk Size People Pattern which we will get to tomorrow. It explains why, when people tell stories and /or give information, some provide incredible amounts of detail and data, while others simply want to get to the bottom line as quickly as possible."

"I hear a lot of people filtering whenever I go to get my hair cut." I said.

"That's a perfect example. One of the most common places to experience people filtering is at your hair salon or barber! Think about it. Salons are prime territory for everyday people filtering since they lend themselves so well to the exchange of information about what else -

people! Stylists, colorists and barbers spend their lives working on people and often could probably publish tomes about their clients. Have you ever sat in one of these places and not heard a conversation between the professional and client or between clients themselves which wasn't about some person or persons?"   Shana was thinking about the salon she frequents as she continued on.

"Begin to notice what factors are emphasized, and this will be your indication of the Secondary Pattern. 'I saw Jim while skiing in Aspen.' (people and activity), or 'Have you heard about Sue dining out with George in Tribecca?' (people and place), or 'Have you seen Scotty's ring?' (people and things). More often than not, topics seem to revolve around 'who is with whom', or 'who is doing what', or 'who has purchased what', or 'who is where'."

"God! There can be so many different combinations!" I exclaimed.

"That's what makes it so interesting." Shana replied. "The possible combinations are really intriguing and will determine the 'color' of a particular conversation. If you happen to be a person who filters primarily by something else, do not be surprised if you have found traditional 'salon' conversations to be superficial or outright boring, and maybe even uncomfortable. Then there is the other side of the coin as well. Maybe you are a so called 'hair professional', and never quite understood why you get on better with certain clients, and find others totally uninteresting. Chances are you simply do not share the same Primary Interest Pattern with them. Remember that *we are most at ease with those whom we perceive to be most like us.* Consequently, people who filter by people will feel most at home with other people filterers, and even more so with those whose Secondary Interest Pattern matches theirs."

THINGS

"The second type of Primary Interest Pattern is the person who filters by things. His life centers on the material aspects of the world. 'What' is the key word for people who filter by things? These things and objects may be useful, functional, enriching, healthy, spiritually significant, aesthetic, personally meaningful, status symbols, idiosyncratic objects of admiration, and /or simply useless junk. The collectors of the world are the primary embodiments of this People Pattern. Their creed is simple. It is 'whoever dies with the most unique and limited edition toys wins'. They believe that if some is good, then more is better. They also believe that too much is just barely enough and that way too much is just right. Depending on one's values, bigger, brighter, newer, and more are better. In some cases older, scarcer and rarer are also better. And still in other cases, the more useful and functional the better. Our values determine which toys attract us."

"I wonder if, in the same way that people filterers can affect the popularity of people, so can people who filter by things affect the popularity of items?!" I said, thinking out loud that I was probably right.

"Yes, of course. Collectively, the people of the world who filter by things determine what things sell and what things do not. They also determine what things are worth based on what price they are willing to sell them at or what price they will pay to buy them. They purchase things not because they need them but because they just want to have them. They enjoy buying, owning, possessing, collecting and exchanging things. They flock to the stores that contain the things that they want. If the stores are not readily available, then they thrive on specialty catalogs for equipment, jewelry, videos, etc. or on the advertisements in specialized magazines. They also like to visit museums and galleries where things are on display. The Smithsonian Institute is one of the world's largest collectors of things, but every large town has some kind of museum that collects something."

"I think that part of me reflects this Pattern, but I think that it is my Secondary one." I declared, waiting for a response.

"That remains to be seen. For the time being, though, whether they be philatelists who amass hundreds of stamps, or people who collect myriad kinds of shells, or avid collectors of rare coins or classic cars, this type of person shares the same Primary Interest Pattern: things. People who do not share their interests in things often find their prize collections totally boring. The classic stereotypes of thing filterers are women whose major interest revolve around clothes, jewelry, and fashion and men whose primary interest revolve around stereo, video, computer, auto or sports equipment. Today's lifestyles have come to reveal that these 'things' formerly associated with either male or female consumption have now clearly crossed any gender lines. Women are interested in computer equipment, fitness and sports while men are interested in clothing and fashion and even skin care."

"You can say that again. The male speçies is beginning to rival women more and more when it comes to clothing. I see it more and more. Just look around this office." I said.

"It is certainly true that men are more style and quality conscious than ever before. Obviously, not all men are into the same 'things'. How many gentlemen are into ties and rush off to their favorite shop to buy the newest in patterns or colors? Or perhaps they have bought a collector's Jerry Garcia tie? Or perhaps they prefer to collect suspenders, cufflinks, belts, socks or hats? Nowadays t-shirts appear to be the big thing. Both men and women of all ages are buying them in different styles and themes. In fact, one can get a t-shirt to advertise any occasion, event, personality, slogan, product, country, city, etc. You name it. If something is part of tangible or even intangible reality, you can bet that there is probably a t-shirt somewhere in the world announcing or confirming its existence. If you can't manage to find one to meet your fancy, you can always go out and have one made up 'custom' to your personal tastes and whims at the local shopping mall. (You can even get a People Pattern Power T-Shirt or a P³ Manager T-Shirt.) Some men even have their own collection of custom, initialed dress shirts."

THE DEMOGRAPHICS OF THE THING WORLD

"Who filters by things?" I wanted to know.

"There is no general rule, since people of all sexes, races, religions, and nationalities fit into the Interest People Pattern of people whose primary pattern is things. Those who concentrate on very specific things often make hobbies and even professions of amassing them. These are the avid collectors of the world who are usually also experts on the items that they collect. They narrow down their interest in things to such a degree that they become quite knowledgeable about that one thing, whether it be birds, 45 RPM records, basketball cards, heirloom jewelry, pocket watches, Elvis memorabilia, fourteenth century Italian prints, Lalique crystal, coins, autographs of historical figures, stamps, antique cars, rare books, fine English china tea cups, Frederick Remington sculptures, autographs, sports memorabilia, Beany Babies, or whatever."

I did not interrupt, so Shana finished her train of thought.

"As I indicated, children at a very early age can often begin to show interest in one kind of toy or item because of their parents' interest, and this penchant can be carried through into adulthood. Filtering by things may vary from minimal interest to exaggerated attraction to them, and the items by which people filter will be even more varied, including cars, ceramics, stamps, rocks, clothing, jewelry, antiques, stereo equipment, computers, perfumes, books, hats, pets, flowers, and the list goes on and on."

"Would I be right to guess that Imelda Marcos filters by things?" I asked with a wry tone of voice.

"Actually, that is perhaps one of the more amusing examples of someone who filters by things to the nth degree! Marcos and her extraordinarily huge collection of shoes rumored to number in the thousands probably sets the record for someone who sorts by shoes!. Of course, most thing filterers usually do not go to this extreme, and probably could not afford to do so."

Shana went on to explain the types of thoughts that go through the mind of a person who filters by things.

"What are the kinds of questions in the minds of people who filter primarily by things? In discussions with friends the main focus of their conversations will center on things and finding out about the kinds of 'things' in the lives of their friends. They might, for example be concerned about the kind of car owned by their friends, for example, or the type of stereo equipment bought by them, the kind of furniture in their house, what kind of tie does the man in the house wear, what brand of perfume/cologne does the friend wear, etc. etc. Does the friend have the latest in computer hardware? Items bought in the past, family heirlooms, recently purchased merchandise, objects in the house, art work, golf clubs and sports gear in general, chocolate, gourmet dishes (there are people who do filter by food!), hair accessories, orchids, picture frames, Toby mugs, cufflinks - the list is endless, although the principle behind each item is the same. The person who filters primarily by things will be interested in always talking about 'things' of importance in his life and seeks to find out about those things in the lives of others."

"I keep on asking about detail. Does the same thing apply here as with describing people?" I was again revealing this other pattern of mine.

"Yes, of course. The amount of detail the person will need about these things will vary depending on the People Pattern that we will get to in a minute. The People Pattern of filtering by things knows no socioeconomic barriers, although the cultural and economic level of the individual will to a large degree determine the kinds of things by which the person will filter."

IDENTIFYING CHARACTERISTICS

"OK. So how would I recognize a person who filters by things?" I asked.

"Identifying a person who filters by things is easy. If you have ever been invited to someone's house, and they immediately begin talking about the plethora of objects and things arranged around the room, chances are that you are in the company of a person who filters by things. These individuals are often quite obvious about the things they covet, and go out of their way to make certain that these items somehow enter into the conversation. Or else, the highly prized 'things' will be out in the open, made quite apparent even to a neophyte's eye. The reason that a certain type of item is collected is a bit deeper to find. That deals with Value Cultures, a subject which we will touch upon next week and that you will learn more about in a future training. In fact, the reason for collecting particular items may be much more profound than you would imagine."

"A person's office is also a reliable indicator of one's thing filter." Shana went on to say. "Any ardent and serious thing filterer is bound to display in a subtle manner or not so subtle manner, the array of 'things' by which he filters. Think of the desk top or office of a friend (or your own if you filter by things), and notice that the 'things' that meet their fancy are in one way or another visible. It is quite amusing to be talking with someone who filters exclusively by things, because no matter how one tries to talk about let's say, people or places, if their Secondary Pattern is neither of these, the conversation will revolve around things the entire time. The person even gets a bit annoyed when others attempt to switch the conversation to another Pattern. In such cases, their tolerance for other topics of conversation is bounded and nuanced by the Secondary Pattern that blends into their Primary Pattern, things."

SECONDARY FILTERS

"People who filter primarily by things will be secondarily interested in others types of Interest Patterns. For example, a person whose Primary Interest Pattern is things, may filter secondarily by people. This means he will want to know who is associated with the things by which he filters. For example, if he is into classic European cars, he will certainly find much more in common with those who partake in the same diversion. He will obviously have a tendency to prefer the company of those who share the same interests, and will tend to want to know who those individuals are and what they have in the way of classic cars. Star Trek aficionados who amass incredible numbers of trinkets and other items of memorabilia from the ever popular show are in seventh heaven at their conventions, where thing filterers can meet thousands of fellow Trekkies (people filtering). If a person collects Biedermeyer furniture or Russian Regency chairs, he will want to know who else shares this interest and what pieces the person has. For him, meeting other people at antique shows and indulging in conversations with them about their mutual pastime will be more important than the location of the show."

"I collect things, but so far I am not totally at home with the description fitting me exactly." I declared.

"There is a reason for your reaction which will become apparent by the end of the session. In any case, if a thing filterer filters secondarily by place, the whereabouts of the show rather than who is there will take precedence. Also, eventual placement of the objects will matter a lot. Where will they be placed? In an office or a residential setting?" Shana did not want me to interrupt again while she finished up her explanation.

"Meanwhile, someone who filters secondarily by activity will be interested in how the things are used. Will they be used primarily for entertaining guests and in what context - entertaining business associates at the club or on the golf course, at dinner parties, brunches, buffets, lunches, etc.? Will the things serve the family first? Are the things for use in the context of family activity, i.e. watching TV, reading the newspaper, lounging around and the like? Are they equipment that are used in some sport or hobby or are used to do something. Or are they used in the context of business meetings or general office work?"

"If this same person filters secondarily by information he is going to want to have the maximum amount of detail concerning the things, and he will expect lengthy descriptions of them."

"That sounds like me to some extent." I declared.

"Almost, but not quite. Back to this example. If a person who filters by things is buying a new chair, he will want to get as much background information as possible on it. Where is it manufactured and by whom? How does the price compare to comparable items on the market today? Is it a durable material? If an antique, how old is it and to whom did it belong? The list goes on and on. He will consult catalogs and reference material and may frequent museums, galleries and trade shows where he can learn more. He may even seek the ideal vocation for a thing/information filterer - that of a museum curator or cataloger."

PLACE

"The third type of Primary Interest Pattern is that of place. People who filter by place are most interested in location, that is, where it is that they are located at any given time. In their lives, place takes priority over activity, people, things, and information. What matters most to these folks is where they are or go; whether it be their place of work, where they shop, where they live, where they conduct business meetings, or where they have lunch and dinner. Where they are is always of paramount importance. In short, where they carry on the business of living their daily life and all that it entails matters most."

"So how do I recognize this type of person?" I again asked.

"It is relatively easy to identify someone who fits into this People Pattern, since in the course of conversation, he will almost always emphasize the place where something occurred rather than the activity or people involved. Nuances of the latter may become secondarily significant, depending again on the mélange of the other filters with the primary one. If you have ever walked into someone's office with posters of various locations scattered on the walls, or with pictures of places set out on a desk or table, chances are that you have come face to face with a person who filters primarily by place. These may take the form of their favorite spot (their home, special vacation spot, preferred city, etc.) or of a place they dream of visiting someday."

"I can immediately think of some colleagues here who fit the bill." I said.

"Let's not mention names. I know exactly to whom you are referring." Shana replied. "Perhaps in your circle of friends or family members you know someone who often dwells either on places they have visited over time or on one particular location (for example, their home). For them, place somehow manages always to be the main topic of discourse. It is for them that the cliché 'There's no place like home' applies most appropriately."

"What about secondary filters?" I asked.

"If the secondary filter is people, then they will discuss the people that are in the various locations that they are telling you about. If the secondary filter is activity, then they will tell you about what goes on in that place. If the secondary filter is things, then they will tell you about the things that are present in that location. And if their secondary filter is information, then they will tell information about the place such as its exact location, its history, its geology, its structure, its economic value, etc."

"A good example of secondary place filters will be found in travel posters and literature. When people go on vacation to a certain spot, then what is important about that spot? Let us take, for instance, the Bavarian Alps or the Loire Valley. Why do people go there? For the Bavarian Alps it may be the beauty of the mountains themselves. Or it may be the activities that you can do there such as skiing or hiking. Or it may be the people that are there with whom it is fun to be. Or it may be some of the Castles there such as Neuschwanstein which are unique in and of themselves. For the Loire Valley, it may be to go biking and hiking or to have country picnics. Or it may be to visit the historic and lovely *chateaux* such as Blois, Cheverny, Chambord, Amboise or Chenonceaux. These secondary filters will determine how one relates to that place. Travel guides and travel agents often filter by place."

ACTIVITY

"The fourth type of Primary Interest Pattern is that of activity. Individuals who filter by activity are mainly interested in what is happening, in activities and in what is going on. These activities may occur at home, at the office, at vacation spots, at school, or anywhere. What matters here is not first the place, but rather, what is happening. *How* and *when* are the key words for the person who filters by activity. He may secondarily be concerned with people, i.e. who is engaging in the particular activity; or with place, i.e. where is the activity taking place; or with things, i.e. what objects or equipment or materials are being used in the activity; or last but not least, with information in general about the activity, i.e. with detailed descriptions of the activity that provide the greatest amount of information relating to it."

"It is obvious that the activity person likes to move, right?" I asked.

"Indeed. The activity person is in love with motion. They want to be engaged in movement themselves or to watch other people or things move. They need to sense their bodies in motion, and this is part of their identity. Sensations are of primary importance to them. The need for movement can become like an addiction. They are used to their heart beating at a certain rate and the feeling of blood coursing through their body. They are full of energy, and this energy finds expression in movement. They may find it difficult, if not impossible, to be still. When this happens to children we call this hyperactivity. This usually isn't hyperactivity at all but an activity child's natural need to move. Parents and educators want to suppress or destroy this natural desire. In their minds what is needed is self discipline and education. A more accurate name for it is 'torture'. Many adults share this same need, and without parents and educators to handicap them, they find ways to move at work and at play."

"That is an entire other discussion which I would like to pursue sometime." I announced.

"Definitely, but after your training sessions are over. In any case, life involves movement. Some people enjoy the journey and others only want to reach the destination. We all have to move to earn a living and to get from place to place. Some people want to minimize the motion. We often say that they are lazy. They prefer to sit or lie rather than to stand and move. Other people require movement. They can't stand to just sit or lie around. They want to be up and about. Meanwhile, there are some careers that involve more movement than others. At one extreme are those jobs that require gross motor skills such as construction work. Other jobs require fine motor skills. These vary from the craftsmanship of an artisan or an artist to the delicate movements of a neurosurgeon. Still other jobs require primarily verbal or intellectual skills. Desk bound jobs traditionally require less activity."

"Whatever one is doing can be viewed as activity." I declared.

"Yes." Shana replied. "Whatever one is doing can involve motion in it or one can try to minimize the movement. Activity filterers have energy that has to be discharged through direct or vicarious movement. Even if they are forced to do a desk job, they will need to move around. They may get up and pace or be restless at their desk. During lunch or breaks they will exercise or move around. After being forced to be still for extended periods, they will need to compensate by working out or dancing the night away. They will prefer jobs involving opportunities for movement and action."

"The nature itself of all activities necessarily entails the notion of time, so 'when' may often be a question asked regarding them. Whatever the activity in which we are involved, it has to happen at a certain time and over a certain period of time. Everything from eating dinner, reading the newspaper, putting in an average workday, making photocopies, dictating a letter, to sleeping at night is in some way delineated by hours, minutes, and seconds! Activity filterers view life as one big macro activity set within one's time clock on earth, which in turn, is made up of thousands of micro activities which fill up the days and years within it. In business, the Type A personality who is constantly doing without a moment's respite is one who often filters by activity." Shana continued.

"There are some activity filterers who live by the clock and for whom 'when' is the critical question. These people appear to filter totally by time. For them the emphasis is not so much on what they are going to be doing but on when they are going to be doing it. These are the people that keep schedule books. It is not so much activities, but how the activities fit into their time schedule that matters. Everything has to have a time, and their whole life revolves around their time schedule."

"That certainly is a new and different way of looking at it!" I said.

SPORTS

"Athletes must filter by activity. That would make sense." I said.

"Indeed. For many people what comes to mind first when they think of activities is sports. After all, sports of all kinds do involve activity, whether we be participants or observers. This leads us to an important point regarding those who filter primarily by activity. Within this context, we have two kinds of activity: 1) participatory or dynamic activity, and 2) non participatory or static activity. Filtering by activity does not necessarily mean actually engaging in the particular action or endeavor. It may simply involve observing the activity either directly or on television. Being a spectator or fan can and usually does involve yelling and jumping around and can be both physically and emotionally taxing."

"So what you are saying is that many people who filter primarily by activity are in some way involved in athletics, whether it be participative or spectator sports." I added my two cents.

"Yes. Professional and amateur athletes are more often than not amid the ranks of those who filter primarily by activity, and obviously participatory activity for that matter. For them, a particular form of activity is so important and so much enjoyed that it becomes their chosen profession in life and a way of earning a living. When it comes to retirement, many professional athletes have a difficult time adjusting to the state of non-activity. It is not surprising then, that so many former professional athletes end up getting involved in some other activity relating to their respective sport, whether it be scouting, coaching, managing, broadcasting, etc. Although they are no longer physically playing the game, they take on a non participatory participating role in the event, with a surefire influence on the end result from a different point of view. Nowadays, they also have the lucrative option of maintaining an association with the game in a more direct non participatory role in the form of TV/radio broadcasting. What is the so called 'jock'? It is simply a person who filters primarily by sports activities."

Before I could say anything Shana picked up her pace.

"People who are into activity but not into sports will find other outlets for their energies. They may like to go dancing in the evenings and on weekends. They may like to go out to dine or to shop simply because of a need for activity. As spectators they may attend movies, plays, and concerts. Or they may stay home and work out while watching action movies on television. Also, they may like outdoor activities such as hiking, camping, boating, skating, jogging, caving or bird watching. They may actually enjoy mowing the lawn or weeding the flower bed. They may not sleep well unless they have expended their excess energy, and when they have, they may sleep like a log. They are the types who fall asleep easily once they have released their excess energy through some kind of activity."

IDENTIFICATION

"Again, identifying people who filter by activity is fairly easy, because they are usually involved in *doing*. And if you happen to catch them during a moment of respite, notice that they will be talking about *doing*. They tend, more often than not, to talk about what they are doing or about what others are engaged in doing. The time the event occurred or is occurring is usually mentioned in passing as well. If you ever ask an activity filterer about his vacation, certainly do not be surprised to hear exclusively about what he did. Rarely will he describe the things he saw during the trip, or the people who accompanied him, or the place he was, but rather he will emphasize the events of the trip: 'We went to Buckingham Palace and saw the changing of the Guard, then took a cab to the Carlton Tower to have afternoon tea, then raced off to browse around Pimlico, bought a couple of things, and to top the day, rushed to the theater for a fabulous performance of Cats. The actors did such a phenomenal job! Afterwards, we grabbed a bite and had a lovely walk about.' The way an activity filterer describes his vacation makes you wonder if it really was a period of relaxation after all, or simply a non stop unraveling of ordered or spontaneous activities to fill up each day. Ask an activity filterer about what he is doing or what he did, and you'll find that getting along with him will be much easier than if you start asking about people in his life (unless you specifically talk about what those people are doing), or about places (unless they are the places where the activities occur) or things (unless they are used in the activities)."

"What are some tell tale signs of an activity filterer?" I asked.

Shana smiled. "They will talk about activities and what they are doing. Also, often walking into a person's office is a good barometer of the activity filter," she said, as she looked around the very office in which we were having this discussion take place. "Look for pictures on their desks or on the wall of them engaged in their favorite activities. Or look for equipment such as a tennis racket or golf putter. Or look for sports memorabilia or for sports related office equipment such as pens, paper weights, telephones, etc."

INFORMATION

"The fifth type of Primary Interest Pattern is that of information. People who filter by information are interested precisely in that — information. This means both the obtaining and the giving of information. They want to know it all and often do. They have a need to know 'what', 'when', 'where', 'how', 'who' and 'why'."

"I guess I've found my niche, so to speak, haven't I?" I declared.

"You'll know that very soon. Information filterers will want to know everything that could possibly be known about these, including all of the circumstances, qualities, notions, characteristics and data associated with them. They also often have a need to tell it all whether you want to hear it or not. About them it can truly be said 'unhappy is he who knows it all and finds someone with whom to share his information, only to find out that that person is not interested!'. Information filterers are often perceived by others to be either the 'walking encyclopedias' or 'the know-it-alls' of the world. They are easy to spot, for they are the bookworms of society, the curiously curious who thirst for data and facts, although some information filterers can be quite subtle in the revealing of the information. They may be more discrete and selective in terms of with whom they will share information. The more information for them the merrier."

"So their offices tend to be stuffed to the hilt with papers?" I asked.

"If you happen to walk into the office or home of an information filterer, do not be surprised to stumble upon tons of papers and documents and books and more books. They will amass many kinds of magazines and written material, even hoarding it until they find the time to get to any specific piece. Book shops and libraries are paradise to the information filterer. Whereas chatting meaninglessly about people seems like an utter waste to them, spending hours browsing through books is both worthy and enjoyable to them. Information filterers are the least common of any of the Primary Interest Patterns. They make up less than 5% of the population."

"Please let me go on before you ask more questions. Whereas people who filter by people or even by activity enjoy the company of others and do not mind mingling with lots of other people, primary information filterers tend to be loners and to dislike crowds. The one exception is in a teaching context where they do not mind sharing their information with large numbers of people. Some information filterers prefer to be selective as far as to whom they are giving information, so that even teaching is not desirable because they have no control over who is getting what information. When transferring of information does occur, this may happen in seminars or classroom situations."

"So scholars filter by information, I would presume?" I asked.

"Yes. Some stereotypical information filterers include scholars, the 'archetypical academic living his ivory tower existence', and those who devote their lives to computer science and forget about life. In fact, the arrival of the computer age is a dream come true for information filterers, who can now readily have access to literally millions if not billions of bits of data at the push of a button. The great challenge of this new era of information is to learn how to keep up with the onslaught of data gushing forth at a rate that surpasses the brain`s capacity at any given time to absorb the data explosion and to turn it into intelligence. This is another realm of study which we will consider at another time. Those who filter by information will be well equipped to deal with this challenge. and certainly welcome it."

Shana continued on.

"Meanwhile, the mad scientists and researchers who spend their days analyzing any bit of data that happens to come through their hands are also particularly representative of this facet of the Primary Interest Pattern. They thrive on problem solving and tend to live solitary lives (or with a limited amount of interaction with the outside world). As with all of the other People Patterns, balance is the spice of life."

"Information is great if it is useful." I added.

"I would agree. Theories and models are fine and dandy and are an indispensable part of knowledge; but one needs to know how to utilize them. Perhaps the ultimate question is 'So what?' Concepts may or may not be useful. Theories need implementation. The key is understanding how to use information. Without utility, information falls into the intellectual garbage heaps of history or quietly gathers dust on musty shelves. The true information junkie does not care if knowledge is useful. All that is required is that he finds it interesting. The rest of the world is usually less charitable."

"Like the other types of Primary Interest Patterns, the Information Pattern is also tinged by whatever Secondary Pattern is combined with it. For example, an information filterer who is secondarily interested in people will tend to be interested in observing people in an attempt to gather information about them. He may have more facility in dealing with others socially than an information filterer who filters secondarily by things or place. Information filterers with secondary people filters are not usually into gossip per se, a rather fine distinction which sets them apart from those who filter primarily by people and secondarily by information. The bottom line for information filterers is information, that is, learning something about a person or people, rather than arbitrarily talking about them for the sake of chatter. Also, the kind of information about people of interest to him will be on a different level than mere gossip dealing with people's private lives. These people become the biographers and not the tabloid journalists of the world."

"What if the Secondary Pattern is things?" There was an obvious reason why I was asking this question now. Shana knew it and laughed out loud as she began to explain this type of person.

"If an information filterer secondarily filters by things, he will want information about objects and things. This translates into a desire for more and more data. It may be relevant to him but to no one else. This type will often have subscriptions to and be on the mailing list of many different magazines and catalogues relating to his fields of interest. He will often be found on the telephone or Internet getting information about the particular items or things in which he is most interested. He will inevitably send for a catalogue and additional information about a new item he happens to see in a store, hear about from a friend or colleague, or come across in an advertisement. If he collects a particular thing, you can bet that he will be an authority on the subject, and always avid to learn more and more about it. Information/thing filterers make good authors for specialized books on things, since they will be thorough and comprehensive and since they are usually experts on that particular thing."

"I wonder who fits that description?" I muttered.

"If only we could tell...." Shana again laughed and proceeded to place. "If an information filterer filters secondarily by place, then he is going to have a plethora of travel guides, maps and photographs about places he likes or about which he is curious. He may write travel articles or guides. His ideal occupation is as a travel consultant or travel guide. He may be an interesting travel companion."

"Walk into the office or home of an information person who filters secondarily by activity, and you will come across shelf after shelf of 'how to' guides and manuals. Each of these explains in detail how to do some particular thing or to engage in some activity. He will probably have a preferred place in his home in which he stores his piles of information, whether it be a library or home office. This becomes his data storing castle in which he is king. His ideal occupation is as a teacher, instructor or writer on the activity about which he is an expert. He is the one who writes the 'how to manuals' that are found in abundance in every bookstore."

"Finally, a person who filters primarily by information and also secondarily by information is the ultimate ivory tower intellectual of the world. He usually knows nothing about anything except his particular area of expertise, but he usually knows all that there is to know about it. He will surround himself with huge tomes and with reference books of all kinds. He will be into all forms of getting and retaining information, from computer software, to videos, to audio tapes, and most of all to books. His magazine subscription list will usually be quite extensive and span several areas of interest. You can bet that whatever the particular special interest that the information filterer has, he will possess every book, catalog, video, brochure, etc. on the market describing, analyzing, reviewing, commenting on, explaining, in short, anything that gives information about the interest in question."

"Most of the world will find this type of individual to be dry, boring, insipid, dull and stale. Renaissance type minds are the exception. They have a wealth of interesting information on many topics and fields. One who filters primarily and secondarily by information has a harder time connecting with the world of people than any other type. He is definitely viewed by others who do not share his filter as weird and myopic. It is as though he is living in a world of his own with no concern or interest in the trials and tribulations of those around him. He is much more comfortable with data, theories, computer software, conclusions, findings, reports, results, statistics, etc. Anything that will enhance his knowledge base is his oyster. Needless to say there are not too many of this type of animal roaming the earth."

"How can one identify a person who filters by information?"

"If you have the opportunity to drop in the home of one who filters by information, you are definitely going to be overwhelmed by the quantity of reading material in the form of books, catalogs and the like, and/or audio cassettes, or visual material. Massive libraries are usually the domain of the information filterer. The kinds of books, videos, etc, that he has will be indicative of his secondary filter."

"For example, if he has an extensive library with books on general fields such as art history, the martial arts, yoga, linguistics, philosophy, semiotics, management, English, Italian, French, and American literature, meditation, athletics, etc, then you are more than likely face to face with a person who filters both primarily and secondarily by information. He will want to have the most complete and comprehensive editions out there on those subjects. Moreover, if there is one particular field or topic that captures his fancy, he will definitely want to include all intelligent material available on the subject within his reach. The information may be neatly organized or sloppily scattered everywhere, depending on other personality traits as we shall find out later in this training program. As long as the information filterer knows that his data is close to him, and accessible in one way or another, he will take comfort in being surrounded by it."

"There is another way to recognize the information filterer, even if he attempts to walk around incognito. A person who filters by information will ultimately let it sneak out in the context of everyday conversation. Think about it a minute. What is it that the information filterer wants in a conversation? Obviously, information, of course. He indulges in the giving and obtaining of data. And, since we all naturally assume that other people share our same model of the world, the information filterer speculates that other people seek information as well. So the next time that you are talking to a suspected information filterer, notice that he is either asking you endless questions to find out details that you can't remember or he is giving you unnecessary information which is inconsequential or extraneous to the discussion at hand. You end up thinking, why is he asking all of these questions or why is he adding these tidbits of information which are immaterial to the conversation and totally besides the point!"

"In short, you will know, because he will always be giving you information or asking for information from you. He will always be telling you things or giving you things to read. When you ask him why he is telling you, he will say that he just thought that you ought to know."

"For example, take the following scenario. You are setting up an appointment with someone to meet at a certain time. Not only do you end up settling on a time, but in the course of the conversation you find out that the person is leaving on a trip, and is being driven to let's say JFK airport for a flight on United to Chicago for a three day business trip. None of the above information has anything to do with the meeting in question, so why is the person giving you all this extra information?   It is the information filterer at work doing what he does ever so well - giving information, because he assumes that the rest of the world thrives on it just as he does!"

"The information filterer is utterly driven to provide as many facts as he can. If you have a close friend, spouse, or associate who fits this mold, you know what I mean. It is quite amusing. You will find that the person who filters by information is usually at a loss when told that what he is saying is not particularly relevant to the conversation, and he can get incredibly frustrated when others do not appear to appreciate the data coming out of his mouth."

"Whenever one who has another Primary Interest Filter encounters one who filters heavily by information, you really do get the feeling that the person is from another planet. Once again, how is it possible for him to be such an bore? Your reaction is 'Why is he giving me all this trivial or unnecessary data?'. 'Why is he telling me all this when it really doesn't have any bearing on the gist of our conversation?'. The other scenario is usually one in which the information presented by the information filterer is relevant, but it is simply more than needed, so that the non information filterer listener ends up confused and asking himself what he is supposed to do with the information. Unless your spouse or mate shares the information filter with you, either primary or secondary, preferably primary, it will be a real challenge to maintain an interesting and absorbing relationship with him. Even banal everyday conversation will eventually be tedious and difficult if the two of you do not share in some way the information filter. In short, boredom will set in quite quickly."

I had another question. "Is there any other quick way to tell people's primary interest?"

Shana looked at me and continued. "One very reliable indication is how they spend their discretionary income. Do they spend it on people, or on activities, or on buying things, or on travel, or on books? This is a real good indicator."

"There is always so much to know. I'll have a great deal of work ahead of me." I said.

"At least it will be different each time and will provide interesting challenges." Shana responded.

HIGH VERSUS LOW CONTEXT

Shana thought for a moment and continued. "I am always emphasizing that everything is context dependent. This is particularly true when it comes to information. In fact, the meaning of any information is context dependent. By this I mean that the meaning of the information changes as the context changes. In order to understand the meaning of any communication it is necessary to determine the specific context in which the communication is happening. That will provide the specific meaning."

"Context also plays another role in communication that applies specifically to the Primary Interest People Pattern. This has to do with the fact that different people require different degrees of context to understand the meaning of a communication. There are people who are high context people and people who are low context people. People who are high context need a certain amount of information about where, when, who and what is going on. For instance, if you were having a conversation with a high context person about an altercation, they might interrupt you to find what street corner in Manhattan this altercation occurred on. A low context person could care less about what street corner in Manhattan it occurred on, because that is not relevant to the information that they want to extract from the event."

"In general, when you tell a story or you pass on information, normally you will be talking about activity people or activity things. You may be telling a story, and the listener may become very frustrated and interrupt you because he needs more context in order to understand what you are saying. In order to understand the story, he may have to know when it happened, or where it happened or who was involved in it. High context people need some or all of this information in order to make sense of any communication. If they do not have that information, they can't make sense of the story."

"Low context people do not need or want a lot of information. They are less concerned about context. All they are concerned about is the bottom line. When they tell a story and people interrupt them, they get very frustrated, because they feel that the setting and cast of characters are not relevant to their point."

"High context people are often perceived by low context people as being slow, boring, irrelevant and never able to get on with it. Low context people, on the other hand, are perceived by high context people as abrupt, rude, callous, and insensitive, because all they want is the bottom line."

PRAYERS

"Here are the prayers. The People Prayer is as follows."

O God Almighty, Creator of man and woman in his own image, allow me to personify those good qualities which others will appreciate on a grand scale. Give me this day my daily dose of many, fun people whose company I will enjoy and who will like spending time with me as well. Please provide me with bountiful opportunities throughout life to share my experiences with the people I love and who, in turn, will tell me about themselves and their circles of friends and acquaintances. Deliver me from boring people who don't bother to talk about others in their daily conversations and especially from those who refuse to name drop. Please provide me with great gossip and TV shows that tell me what celebrities are doing what with whom. And, yes, dear God, please give me good friends galore whom I can rejoin when I die and with whom I can continue to have a grand time in Heaven in the afterlife. Amen.

"The Place Prayer is:"

O Omnipresent God, Maker of Heaven and Earth, Whose love is everywhere in the Universe, please provide me the chance to visit many of the wondrous sites around the planet created by Thy Hand. Give me this day a beautiful place to ponder the direction of the rest of my life. Allow me to have the perfect place to live and to work and from which to learn from life's experiences. Deliver me from those who might seek to confine me and to prevent me from experiencing the places I love so much in this life.

Please, dear Lord, whose Presence is evident in all places, allow me to experience this joy of Thy Being wherever I venture, until that time when I am admitted to the greatest of all Places, your home in Heaven. Until then, please make my life in the here and now close to being like Heaven on Earth. Amen.

"The Thing Prayer is:"

O Awesome God, Divine Being of Miraculous Powers, Creator of all creatures big and small, Maker of all entities, animate and inanimate in this grand universe, please provide me with those things which will bring me happiness in this world. Give me this day the privilege of appreciating the beauty of all those things that Thou have made manifest on earth, in all of their myriad forms. Please provide me with the objects, trinkets and toys that I deem necessary to make my stay in this realm as pleasant and as fulfilling as possible. Deliver me from those who might get in the way of my conspicuous consumption. Also, please, Wondrous Being, allow me to collect any of those things which will facilitate my entrance into the Magical Realm of Paradise where I will be able to experience directly the things most pure and precious in all of the Universe. Amen.

"The Activity Prayer is:"

O Animated Being Most Holy, Whose Divine Breath put into motion the entire workings of the glorious Universe in seven days, please give me the strength to complete the tasks I have been asked to accomplish during my time in this earthly life. Give me this day the energy and courage to carry out my personal mission as I engage in the various activities which make up my daily life. Please deliver me from a life of tedious torpor and boring inactivity and especially from those who might bind me to a role of passive observation instead of active participation. Provide me, too, with interesting projects and challenging ventures which will keep my days both busy and captivating. And, dear Lord, I do know how busy Thou are, but please remember to keep me out of trouble and from engaging in activities that might prevent me from someday coming into Thy World where I may experience in person the wonder of Thy Gestures which eternally give life to the motion of the Heavens. Amen.

"And last the Information Prayer is:"

Understanding God, Keeper of Eternal Wisdom, Who comprehends all there is to know in the Universe and beyond, allow me to have the intelligence to survive on this ever changing planet . Give me this day all the information I need to keep up with an increasingly complex world in which knowledge is in a constant state of flux and where wisdom is power. Please provide me with all the meaningful data, facts, statistics, books and resources that I will need to allow my mind to be healthy and alert, to grow and to prosper. Deliver me from the ignorant masses who don't care or are too blind to know, and especially from those who might get in the way of my personal enlightenment. Deliver me, too, from the state of confusion and please provide constant clarity of thought to allow me to function in this chaotic world. And please, dear Lord, give me the good sense and wisdom to evolve my being now and throughout eternity so that I may transition fully aware and prepared to experience directly Thy Essence and Divine Intelligence. Amen.

MANAGEMENT

Marvin was happy to see me as always. After a firm hand shake, he said that we had a lot to cover and should get started.

"You have spent a lot of time discussing the Primary Interest Filters with Shana. Let us discuss some basic applications. In any human interaction, it is crucial to establish rapport to facilitate communication. With rapport, we create a bond or a sense of harmony between two people. Tied into this bond is a sense of trust that develops between them. The key to establishing rapport with a person is commonality. *We are most comfortable with those whom we perceive to be most like us.* We are going to be most comfortable with those whose interests match ours and who do the same things that we do. We will be least comfortable with those who are least like us. If we have no interest in common we will find little to talk about."

"It sure makes sense to me." I added. Marvin smiled and continued.

"In a business context it may be necessary at times to establish rapport with someone with whom we have little in common, or even with someone whom we do not like very much. In this case we would be well advised to find out what the person's interests are from somebody who knows him. If the contact is important and we have different interests, it may be necessary for us to do some research so that we can talk intelligibly on the things that interest the person with whom we want to establish rapport. This will go a long way to make him feel comfortable with us. If the person is into activities, then it helps to know which ones he enjoys and what he does in his spare time. Once we know this, we may arrange to meet with the person while participating in the activities which he enjoys. We may also want to meet in one of the person's favorite places if place is important to him. If his primary interest is people, then it is wise to find some mutual acquaintance whom both can talk about. If the person is into things, then we should find out his hobbies and interests in an attempt to learn something about him, so that we can talk intelligibly and excitedly about those things that interest him. Last, if he filters by information, then he will be excited if we can tell him something that he doesn't know or provide him with some data that he doesn't have. All of these efforts on our part will go a long way to establishing rapport with the person in question."

"This sounds like a lot of work. Is it worth it?" I said with a grin. Marvin looked straight at me.

"That depends on how important it is for you to establish rapport with the person with whom you are doing business. In an important business situation one needs to do one's homework. Chance favors the prepared mind. Here, as in most areas of life, the Boy Scout Motto is good advice - Be Prepared. Business is work. The question is whether you want your work to produce results are not. Results come from both hard work and smart work. Here at Success, Incorporated we do both. We want to succeed and build relationships that last over time. That is why rapport is worth any extra effort that it takes."

"I was just kidding." I said. Marvin went on.

"The Primary Interest People Pattern is also important in other aspects of management. As a manager you manage information. You have a Primary Interest Pattern and the people reporting to you have a Primary Interest Pattern. The information that you receive from them will be filtered by their Primary Interest Pattern. You need to take this into account as a manager. It may be necessary to hear from several people or to do some extra research to get the information that you need to manage successfully."

"Managers, like everyone else, have Primary Interest Filters. If they are too strong they can bias a manager's judgements. That is why it is so important that you know your own People Patterns. It helps you to avoid projecting them on to other people and it helps you to know your own blind spots. A manager who filters too much by people may get so heavily involved in the lives of his people that he loses perspective. On the other hand, a manager who does not filter by people may lose touch with employee morale and with the legitimate needs of his work force. Balance, as always, is key. The same applies to other People Patterns. A manager who filters too much by activities may spend so much time running around that he never gets anything done. It is critical not to confuse activity with productivity. One can exhaust oneself and accomplish nothing. Only productive activity counts. On the other hand, a manager who does not sort by activity may not participate sufficiently to know what is actually going on."

Marvin looked at me. "I know, I know. Balance, balance, balance." I said.

Marvin smiled and continued. "The manager who filters too much by things may get so caught up in the things that he loses touch with what the things are there for. Equipment is important in business, but it is not an end in itself. On the other hand, a manager who does not filter by things may not pay proper attention to preventive maintenance and quality control. A manager who filters too much by place may be so involved with the location that he loses touch with what is going on there. Also, he may spend all of his time in his favorite places and never make the necessary visits to other places where his attention may be needed as well. Still, a manager who does not filter by place may ignore the critical connection between environment and productivity. It is not only naive but stupid to assume that high productivity can occur in a degraded environment. Moreover, with today's spiraling health costs the quality of the work environment is taking on an increased dimension. What is left?" Marvin said with a chuckle.

"I was wondering about information." I said.

Marvin continued. "I can't imagine why. The manager who filters too much by information may get so caught up in his facts and figures that he becomes disconnected from actual reality. An organization is not just production figures on paper. These figures are important, but they must be weighed against other factors. On the other hand, the manager who does not filter by information may not heed the warning signs of oncoming problems. He may also make poor decisions that are hampered by his inability to assemble the necessary information. So to summarize, all of these factors are important. To ignore any is to blind oneself to critical success factors. Ignorance of these parameters can come either through lack of interest on one's own part or through the inadvertent filtering of one's subordinates. A People Pattern Power Manager takes all of this into account. He is aware of his own interests and limitations and takes the necessary steps to overcome them. He is also aware of the interests and limitations of his subordinates and takes these into account in assessing the value and completeness of their reports. Are you with me so far?" Marvin asked. I said that I was and he moved on.

"One final comment on the Primary Interest People Pattern. It will obviously effect where people focus on a job. If needs in this area are not met, then it may become a source of job dissatisfaction. With a little skillful care it can, instead, be made a source of job satisfaction. All it requires is common sense and a manager's attention. With people people, take time to build a relationship with them. They will do things for you if they like you. They will want to work around others and will like to talk. With place people, where they work will be important to them. They will modify their work area. They will only want to travel to certain places. Be cognizant of this. With thing people, they want money to buy things, because he who dies with the most toys wins. They will want the latest equipment and office furniture. With activity people, what they do will be important to them. They will not like inactivity. They will want to do things rather than reflect and stand still. Give them a job that involves action. And last with information filterers, they will always want information. Tell them everything. They will like to ponder and think. Also, they probably will prefer a quiet, secluded place. Give them problems to solve and leave them alone."

"That sounds like a great plan." I chimed in. I looked at the clock and realized that it was time to move on to sales.

SALES

Michael was just coming from a sales meeting, brimming with enthusiasm.

"If a salesperson keeps doing what he has always done, then he will keep getting the same results that he has always gotten. And if he works on commission, then he will keep making what he has always made. To change this situation, he has to stop doing what he has always done and do something else that works better. Things don't get better by chance, they get better by change. And for things to change, the salesperson has to change. People Patterns can help a salesperson to work smart as well as hard. People Patterns assist the salesperson to change his approach with each prospect. That allows him to close a higher percentage of prospects, and that is the most effective way to work smart." Michael was on a role and I did not want to interrupt.

"In addition to helping establish rapport, which I am sure Marvin emphasized, a person's Primary Interest People Pattern can help a salesperson know what to emphasize. Sales are often lost because the salesperson talks about the wrong things or gives too little or too much information. A strong mismatch of the Primary Interest People Pattern between seller and buyer may often end up in the loss of a sale. For example, people who filter by information will expect a salesperson to be highly knowledgeable. They are constantly lamenting the implacable ignorance of all salespeople. A more common problem is the salesperson who filters by information. He is an expert on his products, and his greatest joy is telling customers all about them. Unfortunately, this joy is often not shared by his customers. Most customers have a low tolerance for information, and many sales are lost by salespeople with a compulsive need to show off their product knowledge."

"As you know, people are interested in different things. Let me take the case of a real estate salesperson. If he is selling to a people person, he would do well to talk about other people who like the house and about the family that lives there and about interesting people whom he knows. This will make the people filterer feel at ease. If the agent is selling to an activity filterer the situation is different. He should find out what activities the prospect enjoys and stress their availability in the area. He should make house buying into an activity so that the buyer feels comfortable. If the person filters by things, then the salesperson should stress the features of the house. He should talk about the fixtures and the names of the appliances. He should get into a discussion about china or crystal or silverware or jewelry or whatever things interest the buyer. He could also talk about the kinds of furniture that would work in the house."

"If the buyer filters by place, then the agent needs to find out what kind of places the prospect likes and feels most comfortable in. Also, it helps to know what kind of places he does not like. The agent should try to show the prospect houses that match the description of what he likes and avoid those that would not please him. If the person feels most comfortable in a particular place, then the agent should go with him to that place if possible and close the sale there. In addition, the agent should find out the kinds of restaurants the prospective buyer likes, and be ready to tell him about the similar ones in the area where he is buying the home. Talk to him about places he likes and where he goes on vacation and make him feel comfortable."

"If the buyer filters by information, then the sales agent will be asked a lot of questions. If the sales agent does not know something, then he would be well advised to find out the required information and to get back to the prospective buyer with it. The buyer will appreciate this; and if he does not get his questions answered he will probably go to an agent who can answer them. Never demean or belittle the questions of an information filterer."

"So if a salesperson invests a few minutes at the beginning in eliciting a prospect's Primary Interest Filters, this will pay off big in dividends down the road." I said.

"Exactly." Michael said and continued. "Professional sales agents often develop diverse interests so that they can establish some commonality with almost anyone. If a sales agent is stuck in only one filter, then he will have great difficulty selling to prospects who do not share this filter."

"There are a few more tips when dealing with prospects with different Primary Interest People Patterns. If the prospect is a people person, then his relationship with you will be of great importance to him. He will buy from people whom he likes or who know someone whom he likes. He will certainly not buy from you if you don't fit the bill. He will want a salesperson to take the necessary time to build a relationship. And rapport is more important to this type of person than with any other type."

"If the prospect is a place person, then the setting of the sale will be important to him. He will go to stores if he likes the place and avoid stores if he dislikes the place and/or the area. With thing people, what they are buying will be very important to them. They like and collect things. So respect and be enthusiastic about the things that you are selling. Activity people will buy things that support their activities. Functionality will be important. Shopping itself may become an enjoyable activity for them or it may interfere with other activities that they have planned. They will have to fit it into their schedule. Respect their time and make the process enjoyable. Last, with information people, you can bet that they will want a lot of information on what they are buying. They expect a salesperson to have product knowledge. In fact, often they are more knowledgeable than the salesperson with whom they are dealing. Be knowledgeable, and don't try to fake it if you don't know something. Find out and get back to the client. I could go on, but this should give you the general idea." Michael smiled and I realized that it was time to visit Beverly in negotiations.

NEGOTIATIONS

Beverly was preparing for an upcoming negotiation. She was going over her intelligence report on the other party. She showed it to me. It included information on the other side's interests and on their most likely proposals. It also included a lot of detailed information on the other side's negotiators. This included the names and ages of spouses and children, their addresses, their hobbies and activities, where they go on vacation, and what their People Patterns were. I was impressed and also curious where she got all of this information. She said that it came from good research and from talking to people who knew the other parties.

"A lot of what I can say about the Primary Interest People Pattern in negotiations has already been covered by Marvin and Michael. And a lot of it is obvious to anyone who thinks about the pattern. I know that you have learned a great deal already, so I will only cover some highlights."

"That is fine with me." I said. Beverly went on.

"With people people, relationships are obviously very important to them in negotiations. Be nice to them and go out of your way to get rapport with them. Ask about their families, friends, and colleagues. In the negotiation stress the consequences for the people involved. Talk about what impact the agreement will have on the people involved. Tell a lot of people stories. Say things like 'any caring person would' or 'no one who cares about people could possibly'."

I laughed. Beverly looked at me and said "It works. Don't knock it until you try it."

"With place people, the setting of the negotiation will be particularly important to them. They will be comfortable in certain settings and not in others. Try to go where they are comfortable. Pay particular attention to the ambiance. Lights, colors, sounds, smells, and temperature may prove very important. Talk to them about their favorite places and how nice that it will be to finish the negotiation so that they can go there."

"With thing people, they may be concerned about dress or that you have the right pen or briefcase. They will be concerned with tangibles. Surround them with nice things. Talk about their favorite things. Offer them gifts if it is appropriate to do so. Talk about what money can buy. Use thing analogies and stories."

"Activity people will view the negotiation as an activity. The schedule will be important to them. They may view negotiations as a challenge. Keep them involved. Get them moving if possible. Move around yourself. Walk with them or if possible engage in activities with them. There are an amazing number of deals that are made on the golf course, and particularly if the clients are winning."

"Finally, information people will do their homework in advance and will want a great deal of information from the other side. Be prepared to inundate them with data. Ask them for data. Refer to data. Quote data. Stress that the agreement needs to take into account all of the relevant information that is available. Also stress reasonableness and fairness."

"We could go on." Beverly said. "But this in addition to what you have already learned should get you started. I am sure that Frank will be waiting with some more interesting applications for you."

TRAINING

Frank was looking at a stack of overhead transparencies when I arrived at his office. He turned off the projector and motioned for me to set down. He studied me carefully and began.

"Education and training involve information transference as a critical component. Education and training is where information comes to the floor, but the information needs to be about something. A lot of people have an activity sort. This is particularly true of males during their primary school years. Play or activity is fun, and everything else is evaluated against this standard. When people with an Activity Primary Interest People Pattern come into a classroom situation, they are not particularly interested in information. The only information that they are interested in is information about activities. One of the best ways that you, as a teacher/trainer, can begin to get their interest and attention is to engage them in activities. Try to tie information to activities, and use activities as a vehicle to transmit the information to be taught."

"There are other people who are interested, instead, in things, and to reach them give them things to look at or with which to interact. Talk to them about things or give them information that relates to things of interest to them. In school these people are often attracted to shop or home economics. People who sort by place will want the training to be related to place. Also, they will be easily influenced by their surroundings. If they are turned off by the place and if they do not want to be present in the room where the training is occurring, then they will be adversely affected in their ability to learn. Environmental orchestration is critical in any training or educational environment. There is a whole science connected with arranging an environment for optimal learning. In addition, there is an ancient art of placement called Feng Shui, which we have been applying for over ten years in our work. You will learn more about this in the future when you attend our course on training. There is also a problem with what is called 'state dependent learning'. What this means is that the student is only able to access the learning in the same state and space in which he learned the information initially. In the first place, it is important in training, that skills and learnings be available not just in the classroom but in the real world back on the job. To prevent 'state dependent learning' it is important to future pace or connect the skills and learnings to the contexts and environments where they are required. This must be a critical component of the training design."

"Many people come out of a People Primary Interest Pattern. For them school is an opportunity to socialize and to gossip. Both of these activities involve talk. It is difficult to talk and listen at the same time. These students are happiest when the trainer or teacher provides opportunities for social interaction and group collaboration. This is particularly important at the beginning. People people may be dying to talk to or meet fellow classmates. Until this opportunity is provided, their attention span may be very limited. In training talk about people. Connect the information to be presented to people. Tell stories about how the information impacts people and how it directly affects their lives. This will make information interesting to people people. For instance in teaching history, make it biographical and talk about events in terms of the people involved."

"Okay, so far." Frank said. I started to talk but Frank continued.

"I know, I know. What about people who sort by information?" I smiled.

"Very few people's Primary Interest People Pattern is information. Usually information is a secondary or tertiary sort for people. The trainer will usually have to link information to something else. Trainers and teachers tend to be low context people, and education itself tends to go toward low context. A lot of students may have difficulty understanding simply because they haven't been provided the necessary context. There are students that need to know when, where, why, and who was involved as well as what it is."

"Training and education tend to abstract knowledge that is cross-contextual. A lot of people who have high context needs have trouble with education, because they need a context to be provided. Trainers need to understand the needs of these people. Their need for context will become evident, because they will interrupt initially to ask for it. Unfortunately, trainers and teachers often beat them into a baleful silence so that they are afraid to ask anything. It is important to find out their need for context before this happens. If the trainer finds out their need for context and provides it, he will be able to communicate with them a lot more effectively."

"Also, training design needs to balance information with activity. We use two basic models in our skill development training design. The first is a four quadrant model based on four different learning styles. The first quadrant begins by motivating the students to learn. This answers the basic question 'why should I learn it?' in the sense of 'for what purpose.' The second quadrant presents the necessary information to be able to understand and to apply the skill. This answers the question 'what do I need to know to in order to perform the skill'. The third quadrant involves the student in actually doing the skill. This answers the question 'how do I actually do it?' The fourth and final quadrant has to do with generalizing the skill and applying it in the real world. It answers the question 'what can I do with the skill'. People filterers are more comfortable in the first and fourth quadrants which involve discussion and interaction. Information filterers are more comfortable in the second quadrant where they are taught directly. Activity filterers are more comfortable in the third quadrant where they do things. Thing filterers are more comfortable in the third and fourth quadrants which involve applications, and place filterers may be most comfortable in the fourth quadrant where learnings are transferred to the outside world."

SKILL DEVELOPMENT TRAINING DESIGN
Motivation - Why?
Information - What?
Practice - How to?
Application - What if?

"The second model we use for training design involves the way that we present information in the second quadrant. We call it the CP^3 Model. CP^3 stands for concepts, principles, processes and procedures. All of these are necessary for the mastery of any skill. Most training designs leave out one or more of these principle components. This is a highly sophisticated design model, and you will learn more about it when you take our in house Train the Trainer Course."

CP³ MODEL
Concepts
Principles
Processes
Procedures

I would like to have learned more, but Frank smiled and I realized that I had to move on.

PERSONNEL SELECTION

Karen was just finishing up an interview, and then she joined me.

"As I keep emphasizing, *preselection always buys more than training.* Hire people with People Patterns for positions for which they are best suited. For jobs involving continuous interactions with large numbers of people, people filterers are going to be best suited. The receptionist who filters by people may be a bit of a gossip, but he has an ability to put large numbers of people at ease that people with other filters lack. Hotel jobs (particularly concierges, desk clerks, etc.) which entail constant mingling with people from all over the world would best suit people filterers, as would any job involving a lot of one on one personal interaction. Imagine having to deal with flight attendants who are not people filterers. Any well seasoned traveler knows how unpleasant that can be. Do not hire people filterers for solo jobs involving little if any human interaction, since they will go absolutely nuts."

I nodded and Karen continued.

"Hire people with a Thing Primary Interest filter for jobs involving equipment. They are good at building and fixing things. They relate better to things and equipment than to people. The best typists and mechanics are often thing people. Give them a computer or a wrench and leave them alone with it. In today's business world we rely more and more on high technology equipment. Thing people are naturally attracted to jobs as technicians and operators and their success often impacts the overall business more than is realized."

"Hire activity people for jobs involving movement and action. These may vary from jobs requiring gross motor skills to jobs requiring fine motor skills. Any job that requires a lot of movement will appeal to an activity person. Do not hire activity people for jobs that require them to sit still for extended periods of time. They will go stir crazy. The more an activity person is able to move, the happier he will be."

"People who filter by place will be comfortable in some locations and not in others. In hiring them make sure that they will feel comfortable in the surroundings in which they will work. They may prefer to work indoors or outdoors. For example, they may go crazy indoors without a window. All of these things are highly individualistic and have to be taken into account. They may be willing to work only in certain areas or in certain parts of the country. They may or may not be ideal for jobs requiring travel, depending on their personal tastes and quirks."

"People who filter by information are obviously useful in a variety of contexts. They are in demand wherever information management is required. The challenge is often to translate their knowledge into a form that is useful to other people in the organization and to the business in general. This may require intermediaries. Do not hire information people for action jobs. Knowing and doing are two different things. Businesses are always complaining about how little education prepares people for the work force. 'Knowing about' is not necessarily 'knowing how'. Action may be required to make rapid choices based on limited information. Information filterers frequently do not do well in such situations. Action requires practicality and pragmatism, and these are not emphasized in the theoretical world of information. Also, information people may go nuts if you surround them with people people. They require peace and quiet and are adversely affected by disruptions and constant chit chat, which they consider to be a waste of time."

"Once again the key is to hire people based upon their People Patterns. People who are well suited to their jobs will not only do their job better, but they will also have less stress and enjoy the job more. People who like their jobs and the environments in which they work are going to work better at what they do. That adds up in the long run to higher productivity and profits. People who are not suited for a job may be able to cope or compensate. However, they will often either be bored or stressed out. They will not enjoy the job, and over time their performance will suffer. Everyone wants to work with people who enjoy their job and who perform well. Believe it or not, they are out there. With a knowledge of People Patterns, one has a better chance of finding them and placing them in the right position. Fit is what personnel selection and placement is all about. In these training sessions, I am giving you a brief overview of how these People Patterns will help in the hiring of personnel. In our Profiling Plus^{SM} Training Program, I go into a lot more detail about the use of People Patterns and Value Cultures in hiring."

SUMMARY

I returned to Shana's office after a long and interesting day. She greeted me and asked for questions or observations. I thought for a moment and then spoke. " People Patterns are really interesting, but are people really either one or the other?"

"I am glad that you asked that question." Shana answered. "I cannot emphasize enough what I told you the first day. People Patterns are always a continuum. People are never either one or the other. People are always both/and, and they are never either/or. In teaching the People Patterns we will emphasize the ends so that you can understand the difference between them and the strengths and liabilities of each extreme. In reality, people are somewhere along a continuum between the two ends. People who are closer to the ends tend to fit one pattern more than the other. People who are in the middle are balanced. They can go both ways as appropriate; and they have the flexibility that people who are trapped at the ends lack. I have constantly emphasized that balance is critical. The ideal is to be able to vary one's People Patterns so that one can match one's behavior to the present conditions of the environment. No People Pattern is good or bad, but some People Patterns are more effective than others under certain circumstances. Each pattern has strengths and liabilities. The goal is to reap the strengths and to avoid the liabilities. To do this, one must be able to change with context. This requires balance which is the key to all success in life."

KEY 3:

THE INFORMATION PEOPLE PATTERNS

INTRODUCTION

I was having a conversation with my wife and kids while I was waiting for my car pool which was late. I was asking my daughter about her youth league soccer game. She said that it went okay and that her team did well. This was frustratingly uninformative, so I kept asking her questions to find out who won, what the score was, how long she played, how many goals she made, if there were any problems for her, and how she felt about it. Whenever I asked a question she would give some broad general answer. I was getting exasperated at having to pull information out of her, and she was getting frustrated that I kept asking so many questions.

Then my other two children started arguing with each other about something one of them had done. One kept asking the other why he did it. The other said that he did it, because it was obvious to him that it was the right thing to do. This was far from obvious, though, to my other son. He kept asking the other whether he had tried it before, whether he knew anyone else who had tried it, whether he had read somewhere that it would work. In short, he wanted my other son to prove to him that what he had done was the right thing under the circumstances. I could tell that my son was getting agitated about this third degree. For him it was obvious that he had done the right thing, and it was inconceivable to him that his brother was questioning him about it.

At this point my car pool arrived, and I escaped from the family feud to the continuous wrangling of the car pool. Fortunately most people were relatively quiet, and I arrived at my drop off point right on time.

INFORMATION PEOPLE PATTERNS

Shana was waiting for me. She smiled and motioned for me to sit down.

"Today you should be happy, because we are going to talk more about something that is very important to you."

"What is that?" I asked.

"Information!" she revealed. "Yesterday you learned that information was one of the five Primary Interest People Patterns. These have to do with the content of any communication. Today you will learn about the Information People Patterns. There are two different patterns. Both have to do with the form or structure of the information." Shana continued.

"The first of the Information People Patterns is called the Perceptual Source People Pattern. It has to do with how we take in information from the world. The second Information People Pattern has to do with the structure of the information itself and the form in which it is presented. This concerns the quantity or amount of information and the level of specificity of the information. We call this the Chunk Size People Pattern."

INFORMATION PEOPLE PATTERNS
Perceptual source - Where it comes from
Chunk size - How much of it is there

PERCEPTUAL SOURCE

"Yesterday we talked about the content of any information exchange." Shana went on to say. "There are several other important People Patterns having to do with information. The first has to do with how we take in information from the world and how we represent it to ourselves internally. We call this the Perceptual Source People Pattern. Perception is the process through which a human being forms an internal representation of the external world. The Perceptual Source People Pattern has to do with how we form that internal representation. Our internal representation is determined by what we pay attention to in the outside world. Do we focus on the elements of our experience or on the interconnections between the elements? Do we focus our attention on the sensory components of our experience or do we see beneath the surface world of appearances? The key distinction is whether the information comes into you through your five senses or seemingly from somewhere else. We call information that comes through our five senses of sight, hearing, touch, taste and smell *tangible* information. It is tangible, because we can, so to speak, put our finger on where it comes from. We call information that comes from somewhere else *intangible*, because we can't directly connect it with any direct sensory input. It seems to come from a combination of all of the senses and yet to go beyond them in some mysterious way. We usually say that such information comes from some 'sixth sense' or that it comes from our insights or our intuitions."

PERCEPTUAL SOURCE OF INFORMATION
Tangible - From five senses
Intangible - From intuition

"Tangibles take in information about the world through their senses. They want things to be tangible. They focus on what they can see, hear, feel, taste or smell. These individuals focus on the concrete and on the factual. They also focus on immediate facts and experiences as well as on concrete data and information. Tangibles focus on the present and on the now. They want proof, and this proof has to derive from sensory evidence that anyone else can verify. Nothing is intuitively obvious to them. They see the world in terms of the real, immediate and practical facts of experience and life. They are empiricists and pragmatists. If it can't be proven on the basis of sensory evidence, then they do not believe it." Shana saw that I had no comments so she continued.

"Intangibles, on the other hand, get information about the world through non-sensory means. They have a sixth sense and intuit things. They focus on the possibilities and the meaning of each situation. Intangibles look for the relationships, meanings and possibilities between and among and behind the various elements present in a situation. They see the interconnections and the whole, and, as a result, they approach things abstractly and holistically. These types of individuals focus on the future. They are rationalists and visionaries. To them the sensory is obvious and mundane. For these people, the most interesting insights in life are not sensory based, but come from direct insight or intuition which goes beneath the surface of mere appearance. In fact, intangibles do not deny their senses, but they feel that they are not limited by them. They believe in the evidence of their senses, but they believe that they can know things equally well by other means. Intangibles are frustrated by the fact that other people seem to be locked into the mundane, and, moreover, that others are so pedestrian in their insights."

Shana paused. "How do you recognize each?" I said.

"That is easy." Shana said. "Pay attention to the information that they give you and ask yourself how they are getting it. Is it something that comes through the senses or is it some insight or intuition that they have that can't be directly connected to any one or combination of sensory experiences? Ask yourself what facts, data or proof do they have of what they are saying. If the person wants to offer you facts, data or proof, then he is a tangible. If, on the other hand, the person has no need or desire to offer you facts, data and proof, then he is an intangible. Also, pay close attention to what the person asks for. If he is always asking you for evidence and proof, then he is a tangible. If the person doesn't ask for evidence or proof and seems bored when you provide it, then he is an intangible."

"Are there any target indicator questions?" I asked.

"Yes." Shana said. "You could ask them some of the following questions: 'Do you want proof or is it obvious?' 'Do you make decisions on the basis of the real, practical and concrete or on the basis of abstract possibilities?' 'Which is more important to you - the actual or the possible?' or 'How was your day?' Tangibles will want proof that is concrete and tangible. They will focus on the actual and on the now. Nothing will be obvious to them. They will give sensory details and will provide you a minute to minute description of their day." Shana went on.

"Intangibles, on the other hand, will find things obvious, and they won't need or want proof. They will focus on possibilities and on the future. Contrary to their tangible counterparts, intangibles will be bored by sensory details. They will either give you a general conceptual answer about their day or they will give you a dissertation on life."

I reflected a moment and noted. "I bet that there are more tangibles than intangibles."

Shana smiled. "Good intuition. As a matter of fact, tangibles outnumber intangibles about three to one. The typical businessman or businesswoman is a tangible."

"How do the two groups view each other?" I asked.

PERCEPTUAL SOURCE PEOPLE PATTERN
Tangibles - 75%
Intangibles - 25%

Shana's answer did not surprise me. "Tangibles are usually viewed by intangibles as slow, stubborn, fact and detail oriented, concerned with the here and now, lacking in insight, and unable to make obvious leaps in logic. Tangibles consider intangibles to be space cases, flakes, airheads and scatter brains, and believe that they have their heads in the clouds. Also, tangibles think that intangibles are totally out of touch with the harsher realities of life."

"It sounds delightful." I quipped. Shana chuckled and said "It is." Then she continued.

"So far we have talked about the content of all communication and about how we take in information from the world. Now let us talk about the form or structure of the information that we actually communicate."

CHUNKING

"To do this I need to introduce a new concept to you. It is called *chunking*, and it refers both to the amount of and to the specificity of the information that we communicate. It also relates to the place of that information in the knowledge hierarchy. Chunking is a very powerful notion. Chunking relates to how we break information down into communication units. Normally, we can only pay attention to seven plus or minus two chunks of information at once. If we are presented with more information than we can handle, or if information is presented in greater detail than we can handle, then we become confused and overwhelmed. If, on the other hand, we are presented with too little information or too few details, then we may lack sufficient information upon which to make decisions. Also, we may become bored and distracted. The amount and the depth of information are critical to any communication."

The key to effective communication is
providing a person with
the amount of information that he needs
to the depth that he needs it.

"It sounds fascinating." I said. "I can hardly wait to get the details."

Shana laughed. "Why does that not surprise me?" And then she continued.

"Information flow can be measured in terms of quantity and quality. The amount of information that is presented in any situation is what we call the information quantity. Notice whether the information quantity is large, where a person presents a lot of information, or whether it is small, where a person presents hardly any information at all. Some people cannot wait to tell it all, and other people are famous for being unwilling to tell other people anything. They believe that information should be hoarded and only handed out, if at all, in small amounts, a little at a time. Obviously, people who sort by information become highly frustrated when they are dealing with someone who intentionally withholds information from them. Some information needs to be kept secret, because its general dissemination could result in personal or financial loss. What we are talking about here, however, is ordinary information that is being withheld. Often people think that knowledge is power and that they can use it to control other people. They withhold it or exchange it for a price. Obviously a restricted flow of information can result in poor decisions. There is a standard joke in many organizations where important information is routinely withheld and where what little information that is given out, is distorted. People in organizations like this say that they are treated like mushrooms, because they are kept in the dark and fed distortions. The success of any organization depends on the flow of the best information possible to the decision makers who need it." When I remained silent, Shana went on.

INFORMATION PARAMETERS
Quantity
Quality

"With respect to whatever information is transmitted, however, it is important to notice its quality. Part of the quality is determined by its veracity. Another part of the quality is determined by its timeliness. These are factors that we will not go into further at this point. There is a third factor involved in information quality, however, which will concern us. This has to do with the scope and the depth of the information. The scope of the information is determined by how many different aspects are included. The depth of the information is measured by how much detail is presented on any given aspect. If the quantity of information is held constant, then scope and depth are inversely proportional. In other words, you can either say a little about a lot or a lot about a little. In communication, people show a preference for either scope or depth. We call people who prefer scope *global*. They prefer to communicate the overview or the big picture. We call people who prefer depth *specific*. They prefer to communicate the details and specifics."

INFORMATION QUALITY
Veracity - Truthfulness
Timeliness - When needed
Scope - A little about a lot
Depth - A lot about a little

"People with a Specific People Pattern prefer the specifics and the small details. We call this process 'chunking down'. It means to go into more and more detail or to go into greater depth and less scope. Specific people prefer depth to scope. They actually think in terms of details, and they also communicate to others in such a manner. Specific people like to communicate all of the small details, and they are comfortable with and able to understand small pieces of data. They also want other people to communicate to them at the same detailed chunk level at which they communicate. Specific people also usually prefer that the specifics in any communication to them be arranged in some kind of hierarchical order. When they are presented with the big picture, they immediately start asking questions to fill in the details." Shana continued.

"Specific people are often so lost in the details that they are not able to make sense of the larger picture. They often can't see the forest for the trees. They can't see the big picture because of all of the details. Also, they often have difficulty with setting priorities. This is due to the fact that they are unable to weigh various options against each other, because they lack the ability to chunk up to the big picture."

"People operating out of a Global People Pattern prefer scope over depth." Shana went on to say. "They prefer the big picture and the broad overview. They are most comfortable with large chunks of information, and they make sense of the world in terms of the overall framework of a situation. Global people see the whole project at once. They communicate this way, because they think in this way. We call this process 'chunking up'. It means to go into less and less detail or inversely to consider greater scope and less depth. Global people are aware that details exist, but they consider them to be either trivial or irrelevant. They are most comfortable with the big picture. They also want other people to communicate with them the same way. When global people are presented with details, they will endeavor to extract the big picture from them. Also, they may talk at such a global level that specific people either have difficulty understanding them or think that they are not saying anything at all. They often can't see the trees for the forest."

CHUNK SIZE
Global - Big picture
(Prefer scope to depth)
Specific - Details
(Prefer depth to scope)
Balanced
(Can provide both scope and depth)

"How do you tell which someone is? Are there target indicator questions?" I wanted to know.

"Yes." Shana continued. "You could ask some of the following questions: 'Tell me what you want?' 'If we were going to do a project together which would you want me to give you first the big picture or the details?' 'Do you need the other?' or 'What do you want to know about the project?' Or simply listen to the amount of detail that the person gives you. You can also pay attention to whether they ask you for more detail or if they seem bored by the detail that you are giving." Shana proceeded to explain this important distinction even more.

"Specific people will give you all sorts of details and may chunk down several levels in answering you. They will present their answers in terms of hierarchical orders or layers of detail. When they describe what they want, they will give you specific details. They will use lots of proper nouns and extra modifiers. They will want the details of the project and will not need or care about the big picture."

"Global people, on the other hand," she went on to say, "will give you an overview without any of the details. They will tell you what they want in a general way without going into detail. They are more interested in knowing about the big picture first and couldn't care less about the details. Global people will describe the project in general without using proper nouns or extra modifiers. They will tend to speak in simple sentences with few prepositional phrases. If you give specifics they will ask you to chunk up. If you insist on specifics they will get bored very quickly."

"Does balance exist with this distinction?" I wanted to know.

"Most certainly." Shana replied. "Many people are balanced. They will want both the big picture and the details. They will usually, however, have a preference to start with one or the other. Specific people may just want the details and not care about the big picture, and global people will often just want the big picture and will not care about the details. Balanced people will want both. They will have the ability to chunk up and down as required."

"The two types are not evenly distributed. Specific people who prefer depth are about 15% of the population, while global people who prefer scope are about 60% of the population. Also, about 25% of people are balanced in this area. They are balanced with respect to scope and depth, and they can provide you with both the overview and the details."

CHUNK SIZE
Specific - 15%
Global - 60%
Balanced - 25%

CHUNKING UP, DOWN, AND LATERALLY

"Information must always be understood in context." Shana went on to explain. "In fact, all meaning is context dependent. As the context changes, then the meaning of any communication changes. When we examine any context we can focus our exploration in several directions. First, we can investigate the context further and explore it in greater depth. We call this chunking down. Second, we can increase the scope to include the surrounding contexts. We call this chunking laterally. Last, we can look for a larger context which encompasses both the context that we are in and other parallel contexts. We call this process 'chunking up'. So in any situation we can move in three directions which are down, lateral, and up respectively. One of the functions of General Systems Theory is to study the nature of these relationships." Shana continued without interruption from me.

"We can chunk down in several ways. One is to simply give more details or to describe the situation more specifically in greater depth. We can also chunk down by considering the components of whatever we are investigating. Reality comes hierarchically organized into wholes and parts. The parts at one level are wholes at a lower level, which are made up of still further parts at an even lower level. We can also chunk up in two ways. One is to give a less detailed description of the situation. The second is to realize that whatever we are studying is itself a part of a larger whole. We can chunk up by considering the larger whole of which whatever we are studying is a smaller part. We can also chunk laterally in several ways. One would be to explore whatever surrounds whatever we are studying. The other would be to study other parts parallel to the one that we are investigating. To do this, we first have to chunk up to a larger whole and then chunk back down to a different part of the whole than the one that we started with."

"Is there an easy test to determine which way that you are chunking?" I asked.

"Yes, if we confine chunking to wholes and parts or to classes and class members. This is the domain of Systems Theory. Systems Theory studies the relationship between the wholes and parts of any system. If we confine ourselves to the relationship between wholes and parts, then we can identify what direction that we are chunking in as follows. Take any two things. They can have one of three relationships to each other. The first is that one is part of the other. In this case, if we move from the part to the whole, then we are chunking up. On the other hand, if we move from the whole to the part, then we are chunking down. It may also be the case that both things are part of a larger whole. If both things are parts at the same level of the same larger whole, then we are chunking laterally. The third situation is when the two things under consideration are both parts of different wholes. In this case, they have no whole part relation to each other. And, in such a case, when we move from one to the other we are not chunking up, down or laterally. Instead we are simply changing chunks. Is this clear?"

I indicated that it was and Shana continued.

"It is more difficult to be precise in our chunking when we confine our exploration to descriptions of a situation. As I have said, we can distinguish between global and specific chunks. This designation is always relative to one another. It is not absolute."

"There are also some combinations of chunking moves that lead to problems. For instance, there are people who consistently chunk down and mismatch. This is called nitpicking, and these people are often unpopular. There are certain other people that chunk up, chunk laterally, and then chunk down into another universe. That is the structure of confusion. And if the pattern is constant, then such people are usually labeled as 'insane'."

Chunking
Up
Lateral
Down

RELATIONSHIP BETWEEN CHUNK SIZE AND PERCEPTUAL SOURCE

"How does chunk size relate to perceptual source?" I asked.

"That is an excellent question." Shana said. "The difference between the perceptual source and the chunk size in any communication is really critical. The perceptual source has to do with where the information comes from, and the chunk size has to do with the quantity and quality of the information. The perceptual source relates to whether the information is tangible or intangible or whether it is concrete and tangible or abstract and intangible. The chunk size has to do with whether the information is detailed and specific or global. There are four possible combinations. Some people are specific and tangible while others are specific and intangible. The former give highly detailed descriptions of concrete things and the latter give highly detailed descriptions of abstract ideas. Also, there are some people who are global and tangible while others are global and intangible. The former give general descriptions of concrete things and the latter give general descriptions of abstract ideas."

COMBINATIONS OF CHUNK SIZE AND PERCEPTUAL SOURCE
Global and tangible
Global and intangible
Specific and tangible
Specific and intangible

RELATION TO PHILOSOPHY OF KNOWLEDGE

"What does all of this have to do with analysis and synthesis and induction and deduction and a priori and a posteriori?" I asked.

"Where did you learn those terms?" Shana asked. I said that I had taken a philosophy course in college and that I was never able to quite figure out how all of these distinctions were related. I was not sure whether Shana was going to answer the question or even if she could. She paused a minute and continued.

"I will answer your question at two levels. First, let us consider the way the words are normally used in a business context. Then I will consider their use in philosophy. The structure of synthesis is taking a large number of assorted facts and then finding the pattern in them. It involves being able to chunk up from a variety of seemingly unrelated things to find that there really is a connecting pattern. The structure of analysis is breaking something down into its constituent parts. This involves chunking a whole down into its parts."

Analysis - Taking things apart
Synthesis - Putting things together

"Induction is a logical process of building up and deduction is a logical process of breaking down. Deduction is starting with a statement and determining its consequences and continuing to work down from any given statement. Thus, it is a process of chunking down to the consequences. Induction is a process of taking a number of things and working up from there to come to some kind of a general conclusion. It is a process of chunking up from several instances to a larger generalization. A priori means that you can figure something out ahead of time before you experience it and a posteriori means that you have to wait until you experience it in order to figure it out."

Deduction - From the general to the particular
Induction - From the particular to the general

"Managers need to be able to both deduce and induce. Deduction is going from general to specific and induction is going from specific to general. Managers also need to be able to do both analysis and synthesis. Analysts who specialize in taking things apart are quite prevalent in the business world. People who can do good synthesis are far less common. Synthesis is one of the rarest activities in our society and perhaps one of the most difficult things to do well. It is a process of combining things together in a certain way. However, it involves more than just combining things together. It is not purely induction. It is a process of combining things together and then seeing what the larger whole is, of which the combination is a specific part and also seeing what function or role that part plays in the larger whole. Synthesis is a process of combining a group of disparate things, coming to a conclusion about them, and then taking that conclusion as an isolated point and determining what larger whole it is a part of and what its function is in that whole. This requires a special talent. Are you with me so far?"

A priori - Before experience
A posteriori - After experience

I nodded and Shana continued.

"You also asked a philosophical question. As you will recall, the analytic synthetic distinction was introduced into philosophy by Kant and it referred to two classes of propositions. In an analytic proposition, the subject is merely explicated by the predicate in which it is already contained. It does not convey any new information but merely clarifies a term further. A synthetic proposition, on the other hand, does give new information and adds something new. Kant also distinguished between a priori propositions which arise before experience and a posteriori propositions which arise after experience. These two distinctions led him to a four fold classification of propositions. These are analytic a priori which are true or false as a matter of logic alone, synthetic a posteriori which are true or false from empirical observation, analytic a priori which are generally believed to not exist, and synthetic a priori which are preconditions of experience, but tell us something new about the world. The existence of this last class of the synthetic a priori is argued among philosophers to this day."

"Induction and deduction are far less controversial. Deduction is the logical process by which one derives conclusions from premises. If the premises are true, then the conclusion must be true. The truth of the deduction is determined by logic. The truth of the premises must be determined, however, by inspecting the world. An argument may be valid, that is logically correct, but the conclusion may be false because one of the premises turns out to be false rather than true. Every good manager knows that false premises may lead by perfectly valid arguments to fallacious conclusions."

"Last, induction is a process of moving from the particular to the general. An inductive argument does not prove its conclusions like a deductive argument does. Instead, the conclusion is only probable based on the instances from which the generalization is made. Every good manager has to be on guard against conclusions based on incomplete or invalid samples. Induction deals with statistical probabilities and not with certainties. Every manager needs some training in understanding probabilities and statistics. It is amazing how many seemingly plausible probabilistic conclusions are invalid or how many seemingly implausible probabilistic conclusions are valid. But that is a discussion for another day. It is time to move on."

PRAYERS

"Here are the prayers. The Tangible Prayer is:"

O Lord Almighty, Who reveals His Glory on this Earth, allow me to see, hear, feel, taste and touch Thy Essence through the myriad manifestations created by Thy Hand. Give me this day the real and concrete evidence of your Wondrous Being through the beauty of those things which surround me in my daily life. Deliver me from those who might complicate my life with abstractions and theories which would take me away from the reality of existence. Please, dear Lord, make things obvious to me, and deliver me from all that is not evident and conspicuous. Provide me with enough data, proof and evidence to facilitate my thinking which will make my life on this planet a lot more pleasant. Deliver me too, from those who might force or coerce me to trade the vicissitudes of an uncertain future for the verities of the here and now. Amen.

"The Intangible Prayer is:"

O Ethereal Lord, Insightful Master, in Whom I believe without ever having seen Thy Image or touched Thy Presence, give me this day the freedom to seek all that is theoretical and speculative. Allow me to experience the joy of knowing without reliance on my eyes and ears. Allow me to understand without seeing, touching, hearing, tasting or smelling that which is somehow and somewhere present (or not) in my earthbound environs. Deliver me from those who might confine me with their concrete facts, data and proof of manifestation. Allow me, also, to intuit all that is invisible and shrouded to unseeing eyes. And dear, Incorporeal God, deliver me from the ennui of present moment fixations and allow me to focus on the interesting and fascinating possibilities of an unpredictable and unforeseeable tomorrow. Amen.

"The Global Prayer is:"

O All Seeing, All Knowing and All Powerful God, give me this day a clear overview of what my journey is to be upon this earth. Allow me to always and everywhere see the forest and to ignore the trees. Deliver me from those who might complicate my life with details and clutter my world with unnecessary information. Please, Omnipresent God, deliver me especially from people who might obscure my thinking by forcing specificity upon my unwilling mind. Please remove the chains of superfluous and useless information in an already complicated world of excess so that I may live freely and unencumbered by detail. And, dear Lord, remember to surround me with friends, like me, who thrive on the big picture as opposed to those who have gone astray and who are forever lost in trivial minutia. Amen

"And the Specific Prayer is:"

O Precise and Exact God, Who has created every single creature and entity, animate and inanimate, in the Universe from the tiniest of protozoa, to the grandest of dinosaurs, Who has counted the zillions of sparkling stars whose shimmer lights up the night sky and the myriad star systems that support a multitude of life forms, Wondrous Being of Endless Wisdom and minute distinctions, give me this day enough information and details to deal with this ever changing, complex, intricately interrelated, multifaceted and multifarious universe. Allow me to revel in the lovely, unending, fascinating flow of parts rather than be taken down by the monotony and frivolity of the irrelevant whole. Allow me to always see the trees in the forest. Please deliver me from those who might trivialize the trivia. And please remember, explicit Lord, to provide a detailed plan of specificity for me to follow Thy Will to the tee. Amen.

MANAGEMENT
"Both tangibles and intangibles have important roles to play in any business. The challenge is that they have difficulty communicating with each other, and that they perform well in different jobs." I motioned for Marvin to continue.

"The primary difference has to do with the nature of the obvious. A main characteristic of tangibles is that nothing is obvious to them. They do not make intuitive leaps. On the other hand, intangibles find many things to be obvious, because they are able to leap beyond the given to come up with something else. Things that are obvious to the intangibles are definitely not obvious to the tangible. If you want to tell tangibles things, you must be absolutely explicit. Nothing is obvious to the tangible. You have to tell them exactly what you want them to do. You have to give them a set of procedures to follow, and you have to give them a set of evidence criteria that they can see, hear, taste, feel and touch."

Tangible - Nothing is obvious
Intangible - Intuitions are obvious

"This sounds all to familiar." I chimed in. Marvin smiled and continued.

"The typical businessperson is a tangible. The tangibles are the empiricists of the world. In fact, empiricism was developed by tangibles.

Empiricism wants proof, evidence, facts, and data. These are things that are near and dear to the heart of tangibles. Tangibles always want you to prove it. When you try to market anything in business, the tangibles that comprise the majority of the business community want to know what facts, what data, what proof, what evidence there is that it works. Anecdotal evidence to the businessperson is interesting, but it does not prove anything. It is inconclusive. They want tests conducted by rigorous scientific standards using control groups. In trying to market intuitive ideas to the typical businessperson, assume that nothing is intuitively obvious to him. When you go in and say that you know it works, he is not interested in that. This has been one of the big challenges in marketing many great ideas to the business world. There are many great ideas that can be used in a business context to get great results, but unless they are based on facts, data and proof, then selling them to the typical tangible manager can be a real challenge. The challenge is to learn to enter the reality of the tangible and to think in those terms."

I did not interrupt with questions so Marvin continued.

"Intangibles also play a vital role in business. The tangibles are the administrators that keep the business going on a day to day basis. The intangibles are the ones that provide the ideas and the strategic planning. There must be a system in which the intangibles pass on ideas to the tangibles. It is the tangibles that grind through the process of making it, manufacturing it, administering it, and getting it out."

"And, of course, a balance is needed." he went on to say. "An organization comprised of all intangibles may just be a space factory. They may have a tremendous number of incredibly great ideas, but nothing ever gets done. On the other hand, there may be an organization comprised totally of tangibles. They may get a lot done, and there may be a lot of activity. Unfortunately, they may never have a creative idea or make any changes in their products."

"So how does one manage tangibles?" I asked.

"In managing tangibles, tell them exactly what to do and why to do it that way. Assure them that the way you suggest has been proven to work. Be concrete and tangible with them. Don't expect them to do long range planning or abstract thinking. They will be good at administration and handling concrete details."

"In managing intangibles, give them the big picture and tell them how what they need to do fits into that picture. They will be good at long range planning and abstract thinking but will probably not be good at managing routine day to day activities. Intangibles will be bored with sensory specifics and with concrete details."

CHUNK SIZE PEOPLE PATTERN IN MANAGEMENT

Marvin paused and indicated he was ready to move on to another area. I nodded and he continued.

"Perhaps the greatest challenge in any communication is knowing when enough is enough. This involves knowing at what level of detail to begin and end the communication. In any communication between people there comes a point when each party is satisfied that they understand what the other person is trying to communicate. If the conversation continues beyond that point, then interest begins to wane. When you know, then you know; and it is time to move on."

*The greatest challenge in any communication
is knowing when enough is enough.*

"To get the other side in a communication to the point where they are satisfied that they understand all that they want or need to understand may require anything from a broad overview to a detailed account. People can be dissatisfied in two ways. The first is that they don't know enough. They want to be told more. We call this wanting more details or chunking down. The second is that they know enough. They are satisfied and don't want to be told anymore. We call this getting the big picture or chunking up. The key to any communication is knowing what level will satisfy the other party or at what level to chunk the communication."

*SOURCE OF DISSATISFACTION
Told too much
Not told enough*

"Tell me more." I said and laughed. Marvin laughed and continued.

"Each person has a preference for chunk size. Some people just want the broad overview. We call them global people. Other people want all of the details. We call these specific people. Obviously these two extremes of the continuum have challenges in communicating with each other. As a manager you manage information. You have to both receive and communicate information. In doing this, it is necessary to continually monitor the chunk size of your communication. In most organizations the higher you are in the management of the organization, the more you are concerned with the big picture. The lower that you are in management, the more you are concerned with details. Of course, some people are always concerned with details even when this is unnecessary to what they need to do. When a manager is concerned with more details than necessary, he is usually accused of micro-managing."

"This is really interesting." I said.

Marvin smiled. "Don't worry, there is more. Let us take a typical relation between a manager and those who report to him. There are two ways that communication can break down. Suppose that the manager is a specific chunker and that the employee is a global chunker. The manager will give detailed and specific instructions as to what he wants done. The global employee will chunk these specifics up and get a big picture. He will then operate out of this global instruction to himself. Inevitably, he will not do the specifics that the manager asks for. The manager will be frustrated that the employee never does what he tells him while the employee will believe that he is doing what he was told. He will feel that the manager is nit-picking and micro-managing him. So both sides will be frustrated. What the manager needs to do is realize that the employee will chunk the specifics up to a global overview. The manager needs to start with a global overview and then give only the critical specifics. The manager will need to continually monitor the situation and to understand that the employee will not be able to deal with the same specifics that the manager can."

"What about the reverse situation?" I asked.

Marvin chuckled. "I am coming to that. What if the manager is global and the employee is specific? Then the manager will provide a global overview of what to do. The employee will be looking for details. His constant complaint will be that the manager never tells him what the manager wants from him or what he is supposed to do. This is because the manager simply gives him global generalities, and for him being told what he needs to do is to have it broken down into small chunks. The manager will be frustrated because the employee will always be looking for more specifics and will always be trying to get the manager to chunk things down further. The manager will feel that his instructions are adequate and will feel that the employee is either stupid or contrary. Neither situation is satisfactory. What the manager needs to do is to be able to chunk down when necessary."

"So the situation is that every manager needs to be able to manage chunk size. He needs to be able to chunk up or down as necessary for the person with whom he is communicating. The ability to do this is critical in management. When communicating with a specific person, a manager needs to tell the person the specific details of what to do in a logical sequence. He needs to use extra modifiers and proper nouns. Also, he should not expect the specific person to read between the lines or to see or understand the big picture. When communicating with a global person, a manager needs to tell the person the broad overview of what to do and skip the details. He should avoid using too many extra modifiers or going into too many details or the global person will get bored. The manager should anticipate that the global person may fill in the details for himself in a different way than the manager would. The specific manager must guard against micro-managing global people."

I nodded and Marvin continued.

"There is an area in which almost every manager has experienced frustration at one time or another. This occurs when a senior manager assigns a junior manager to study and report on a situation. The junior manager does a lot of work and prepares a highly detailed and specific report. Frequently this report is a work of art. The junior manager expects the senior manager to read and appreciate all of the nuances of the report. What happens is just the opposite. The senior manager listens until he is assured that the junior manager has indeed done his homework. Then he asks for the bottom line conclusion. The junior manager is devastated. His response is 'But don't you want to know how I got to the conclusion?'. The senior manager's response is 'no'. The senior manager only wants to know the bottom line and that it was based on adequate analysis. He does not want to have to go through the whole analysis. That was the junior manager's responsibility. Does this sound familiar?"

"All too much so." I said.

"There is another management challenge that arises from chunk size. It is directly related to the potential for a person to either over or underestimate things. People who are large chunkers tend to overestimate or underestimate and to be less accurate in their estimations than small chunkers. Because the large chunkers have bigger increments, they may err on either side by a larger amount. Small chunkers are more likely to be accurate."

"People who are large chunkers have more difficulty giving accurate estimates of time; because they do not have any idea how long it is going to take to do something, and they assume that they can get a lot more done in that time than they actually can. People who are small chunkers throw up their hands in despair, because there is never enough time to do what needs to be done."

"It sounds all too familiar." I said

ANALYSIS AND SYNTHESIS IN MANAGEMENT

Marvin continued. "There is another area which is critically important in management. This has to do with analysis and synthesis. Most managers are good at analysis, but unfortunately they are usually not equally good at synthesis. Synthesis is what enables an organization to go beyond the given and to come up with new and creative solutions to business challenges."

"Probably the greatest advance in management theory in this century is as a result of cybernetics, operations research, and systems theory. Unfortunately, most managers, who are stuck in their analytic mind set, do not understand the critical implications that systems theory has for business. Analysts like to take things apart. They think that the way to build a better product is to improve the parts. And they reason that if you are going to build a better product, the way to do so is by building it out of all of the best parts. Let me give you an analogy popularized by Russell Ackoff who is perhaps the leading systems thinker in business today. Ackoff poses the question 'how can we build a better car?'. Remember, the analysts say to build it of all of the best parts. So we take the best motor from one car, and the best brakes from another, and the best carburetor from still another, and the best left tail light from still another. We bring all of the best car parts in the world and lay them out on the floor. And what do we have? Do we have the best car in the world? No, what we have is a heap of junk, because none of the parts fits together!"

"What systems theory emphasizes is that:

The performance of a system is not the sum of the performance of its parts taken separately but is the product of their interactions.

To build a better car we have to design it so that the parts work together better. This is particularly important in management. Managers all too often think that they can improve performance in an organization by focusing on improving each of the units in the organization. This approach is limited. It is important to improve each of the units, but it is more important to coordinate and integrate the interactions of the units. It is a manager's job to manage and optimize the interaction between units. This is the path to a high performance organization."

"How does bench marking which we hear so much about lately fit into what you are saying?" I asked.

Marvin smiled and continued. "An excellent question. Bench marking is often disaster. As you know, the idea behind bench marking is that the way to improve is to study your more successful competition and incorporate their best methods into your process. The problem is that it may work for them but not for you. You just can't take the best parts of your competition and put them together. To do so is like the car made of the best parts. It wouldn't run. It is the coordination of the interactions that creates the performance. Unless you benchmark this, which seldom happens, you will be falling into the trap of believing that productivity comes from the optimization of parts. Once again, it is the integration of parts that is critical. If you take the best components of how your competitors do business and put them together, then you will find that they do not fit together and you will be worse off. In any system there are tradeoffs. When you optimize one part it will adversely effect other parts. It is the design of the interaction of the parts that is critical. The key is to optimize the performance of the whole and not of the parts. You could put a helicopter engine on a lawn mower, but this does not mean that it will cut grass better. In fact it will be impossible to control. Do you get the point?"

"Loud and clear." I said.

Marvin looked at his watch and said that it was time for me to move on to Michael in sales. I thanked him and left.

SALES

"In sales tangibles and intangibles are looking for different information." Michael began enthusiastically. "Tangibles want products that they can see, touch and feel. Make sure that you have samples available. Let them handle the product. If possible let them use it. Often giving the product to them for a period of time on approval is a good strategy. When selling to them, it is important to be concrete and factual. The salesperson needs to be sensory specific and matter of fact. It is important with tangibles to not make claims that you can't back up. It is important to provide evidence or proof as to the value of your product. Tell tangibles what your product can do for them now and not what it can do for them in the future. Emphasize practicality. Focus on immediate benefits. Sell them."

I nodded and Michael continued.

"Selling to intangibles is quiet different. They are much more likely to buy products based on abstract ideas which are intuitive to them. With them it is okay for the salesperson to be abstract and to emphasize possibilities. In fact avoid making your product seem mundane and ordinary. Be original. Make leaps in logic. Do not dwell on or state the obvious. Also, tell what your product can do for them both now and in the future. Emphasize the possibilities of your product. And make sure not to bore them with concrete details. Focus on how your product fits into the overall frame of their life."

"There is a big difference between selling to tangibles and selling to intangibles." Michael went on to say. "Salespeople who are good at selling to one may not be good at selling to the other. In general it is more difficult to sell intangibles than to sell tangibles. They involve two different approaches. Also, it makes a big difference if the product that you are selling is tangible or intangible."

CHUNK SIZE PEOPLE PATTERN IN SALES

"Chunk size is critical in sales. Salespeople either tend to give too many or too few details. Some salespeople who have a lot of product knowledge can't wait to tell the prospect all about their product. This will make the specific person happy but will turn off the global person. On the other hand, if a salesperson lacks product knowledge, then he will turn off the prospect with a specific orientation. The prospect will view a global sales presentation as fluff and will feel that the salesperson does not know what he is talking about. In sales, specific product knowledge is critical, but the salesperson must know to whom to give it, how much to give, and most important of all, when to shut up. It is critical that the salesperson be able to recognize where the prospect is at, and to provide him accordingly whatever specifics he requires but no more."

The greatest challenge about
product knowledge
is knowing when
to shut up and ask for the order.

"When selling to specifics, it is important to present the details of your product in a sequential fashion. Give the prospect a lot of details and use proper nouns. Make sure that your presentation is sequential and avoid using simple sentences. Do not use fluff or generalize. Specific people may want specific colors, sizes, or other variations. Be prepared to handle specific objection. Also, be sure that your close is explicit and that the prospect understands that you are asking for his order."

With no comments from me, Michael continued.

"When selling to a global buyer, provide an overview of your product and skip the details. Use generalities. Avoid sequences. Be prepared to handle general objections. Keep your close general."

"Today is the age of consultative selling. Each salesperson must query the prospect to find out what he needs and wants. Specific people will have specific needs and expect specific products tailored to those needs. Global people will have global needs and expect that their needs will be best fulfilled by a combination of products. They want global solutions that will work across the board and not just in specific instances. These two extremes place an extra burden on any product provider. The provider will need to have a variety of products that will fit highly specific needs on the one extreme and which, at the same time, will be versatile enough to fit a variety of needs on the other extreme. Usually products are optimized one way or the other. Some product providers choose to specialize and go after a small niche with a superior product. Other product providers choose to generalize and go after prospects who want multi-functionality. The essence of consultative selling is knowing what you are providing and going after that market. If you provide one, and the prospect wants the other, then the ethical consultative salesperson will refer the prospect elsewhere." Michael continued with his train of thought with no comment from me.

"Every salesperson wants to build referrals and product champions. Specific buyers will like specific features of your product that are well matched to their needs. Global buyers may be more satisfied with the overall product. In using referrals and product champions, make sure that you match global to global and specific to specific. With specific buyers try to make sure that they share interest in the same specific. On the reverse side, specific buyers will have highly specific complaints about features of the product that they do not like and global buyers are more likely to dislike the product in general. It is important to be able to deal with both types of remorse before it spreads."

Michael asked if I had any questions and when I said no, then sent me on to negotiations.

NEGOTIATIONS

Beverly was happy to see me. She launched right in.

"The Information People Patterns are important in negotiations. As always, one has to modify one's negotiating approach to fit the circumstances of those with whom you are negotiating. Tangibles and intangibles are about as far apart as you can get. When negotiating with a tangible, it is critical to emphasize the concrete and practical. Give the tangible person concrete proof. Use visual aids. Quote data and statistics. Tangibles will always want to pin you down. Be prepared to defend your position. Do not speculate or make claims that cannot be substantiated. Be literal and do not get abstract on them. Moreover, do not expect them to extrapolate or read between the lines. Be extremely explicit about your position and about their position. If they use tactics they will usually be fairly blatant. The danger is that they may be so blatant that the intangible fails to recognize them."

"On the other hand," Beverly proceeded to explain, "when negotiating with intangibles, it is okay to emphasize the abstract and the possible. Do not waste their time with data, statistics and proof. Focus on how things fit into the overall framework. Intangibles are quite capable of reading between the lines and will have an intuitive grasp of where the negotiation is going. They will jump around a lot more that tangibles. In fact, they may pursue multiple objectives simultaneously. With them it is more important to be on your toes. They are more likely to surprise you, and if they use tactics, you may find their tactics to be more subtle than those used by a tangible."

"When tangibles negotiate with intangibles, the tangibles will often have difficulty figuring out what the intangibles want, because it is seldom explicit. The intangibles, on the other hand, may distrust the explicit proposals of the tangibles. With the two sides there is a high probability of misunderstanding and miscommunication."

CHUNK SIZE PEOPLE PATTERN IN NEGOTIATIONS

"Chunk size is as important in negotiations as in any other area of communication. It is one of the most common causes of failure to reach an agreement in any negotiation. One of the fundamental challenges in negotiations is to know how the other side chunks. If you are negotiating with someone, it is important to find out if the person wants the big picture or the details. If you are negotiating and all the person cares about is the big picture, and you are giving him the specifics, then the person will end up bored and frustrated. He will feel that you are in general agreement, but that for some reason you are being a nitpicker. And beware when the person gets bored, he may become hostile."

"On the other hand, if the person is someone who wants the details and all you are doing is giving him the big picture, he will think that you are simply providing him with fluff. You are not communicating what the person needs. And it follows that if the person is not getting what he needs, then he, too, will become hostile." Beverly continued on since we were running short of time.

"In any negotiation where you are working to reach agreement, it is critical to know the chunk size of the person with whom you are negotiating. A global person believes that general agreement is all that is necessary and that the specifics are irrelevant. A specific person will be just the opposite. For him there is no agreement until all of the specifics are decided on. This attitude, in turn, will really upset the global person who will view the specific person as a nitpicker who is negotiating in bad faith. Many a negotiation has deadlocked because of a failure to take the Chunk Size People Pattern into account."

Global - Want agreement on generalities
Specific - Want agreement on specifics

"So it is critical how you communicate with people and how you and they chunk information. What you need to find out is whether or not they want the big picture or the specifics. Which do they want first and do they need or want the other one? Frequently, you can get a good idea from the questions your opponent asks and from his approach as to whether he wants more or less information than you are giving him. A good barometer is that you can often tell from your own frustration whether you need to provide more or less information."

"When you are negotiating with specific people, it is critical to break things down into specifics and to stress the details. You should use a lot of modifiers and proper nouns. It is also important to make your presentation in a logical sequence. Avoid generalities and vagueness. Emphasize the trees. With global people the situation is reversed. With them, present the big picture and avoid the details. Avoid logical sequences. Also avoid extra modifiers and proper nouns. Emphasize the forest."

"One of the all time classic mismatches of chunk size in international negotiations was between the American President Ronald Reagan and the Israeli Prime Minister Menachem Begin. They were at two opposite extremes. Reagan was a mega-global chunker. As far as he was concerned, all that mattered was that the Arabs and Israelis wanted peace. From Reagan's perspective, all that remained was to work out the irrelevant details. Begin, on the other hand, believed that there were no irrelevant details. From his perspective there could be no lasting peace until all of the details were worked out. This drove President Reagan crazy. From Reagan's point of view, Begin was derailing the peace process over irrelevancies. From Begin's perspective Reagan was being unbelievably naive, and all pressure by the United States for Israel to reach an accord with its Arab neighbors was misguided."

Beverly smiled and said that it was time for me to see Frank in Training. I thanked her for giving me an entirely new perspective on negotiating.

TRAINING

Frank was excited to see me and immediately began his explanation without my saying anything.

"The Information People Patterns are very important in training design and delivery. There is a big difference between whether you are training students who are tangibles or intangibles. One of the first lessons that trainers need to learn themselves is that nothing is intuitively obvious to tangibles. Most trainers assume that since it is intuitive to them, then it is intuitive to their students. It isn't if their students are tangibles. Trainers need to understand this. They also need to understand that when their students are tangibles, they will need more facts and more data and more evidence than the trainer would normally give. To intangible trainers, teaching tangibles is like pulling teeth. You have to lead them carefully, and you can't leave any steps out. You have to explain everything explicitly. Tangibles are not going to be able to make any jumps in logic or reasoning. They have to have it all laid out for them, and they will challenge you unless you can offer them facts, data, and proof."

"In the traditional school system this is one of the ways in which a science education differs from a liberal arts education. In a physics class everything is proven, and the teacher feels it is his obligation to derive everything from the basic axioms. The people who are going to do well in the liberal arts are the people who are intuitive, and the more intuitive the students are, the more that they will be rewarded. The people who do best in practical subjects like science and engineering are the tangibles."

"In any training there will be at least a few people in the class who are intangibles. They are the ones who are going to be able to make leaps in logic. They are probably the ones in the class to whom the trainer, if he or she is an intangible, is going to be directing most of his or her energy. This is because the trainer knows that they are the ones who are developing in precisely the way in which the trainer would like them to develop." Frank was really into it, so I did not interrupt.

"Tangibles get bored rather easily. They are more interested in activity and have a need to move around. Also, tangibles need excitement and motion and are into doing and activity. Tangibles have a hard time sitting still and tuning in to theory and abstract principles and ideas which they do not think are particularly important anyway." Frank went on.

"Intangibles are future oriented, and tangibles live in the now. Tangibles have the best sense of time because they are living most in the now. The intangibles, since they spend their time out in the future, often can't make realistic estimates of how long it takes to transfer the future into the present."

"In the training room, tangibles want concrete facts, evidence and proof. They do not like theories or abstractions. This means that they will be good at history and concrete sciences like biology and physical chemistry. In addition, tangibles will do well on short answer and true false tests. They will not be strong in originality and creativity. Meanwhile, they will focus on the now and do assignments in advance. Given this, it is a good idea to lay out the course schedule and reading assignments for them at the beginning."

"In the training room intangibles want theories and original ideas. They are bored by the concrete and the practical. They will not like history or biology. Instead, they will be attracted to creative writing, theoretical science and philosophy. Intangibles will focus on the future. They will do best on essay tests and on projects that require creativity and originality."

CHUNK SIZE PEOPLE PATTERN IN TRAINING

"Education is frequently involved in filling in the details. There are certain students who are not interested in the details, and they are never going to remember them. In our educational system, students are usually rewarded for remembering the small details. The fact that the details are not known to a student does not mean that he is any worse off or that he knows less than any other person. It just means that detail is less important to this type of student. There are certain people, on the other hand, who need the details. Some teachers only present global information, and students who want details are frustrated. As I have emphasized, students come to trainings for a variety of reasons. Some are interested in the people there and some come for activities. Others come because they want information, and if they are not getting enough information they get angry."

"So a trainer needs to know that specific people learn by remembering details. They will be good on short answer and fill-in-the-blank type tests. They do not like generalizations. On the other hand, global people learn by abstracting the big picture from the details. They do not like to memorize details. They will do best on general essay type questions."

"From what you are saying then, students understand in different ways." I said with a question in my voice.

"Precisely." Frank replied. "Students understand information in two different ways. Specific students like to start with the specifics and build up to the big picture. If you only provide them with the big picture they will get frustrated. Global students, on the other hand, need to start with the big picture so that they can see where the details fit in. If you just provide them with details then they get lost from the beginning. In any training design, it is imperative to take these two different needs into account. Every training needs a rhythm of moving from the global to the specific and then back to the global. It is important to begin with a brief overview to orient the global students. It needs to be brief so that the specific chunkers do not tune out. Then the trainer should descend into the details and slowly build back up to the big picture. This way when you get to the big picture, the specific chunkers will be ready for it and the global chunkers will be comfortable. So there needs to be a continuous rhythm of moving from the overview to the specifics and back to the overview. In this way every student's needs are taken into account."

"What happens if a trainer doesn't do this?" I asked.

Frank reflected a minute and answered. "If you don't follow this rhythm, then half the class will be lost and confused. The worst thing that you can do is to start in the middle and chunk down. This loses all of the global students and many of the specific students. Without the overview, the global students are lost and without the overview at the end once the specifics are covered, the specific students will not be able to generalize."

"This is why we use the CP³ Model to present information. I mentioned it to you yesterday. It begins with the concepts and definitions. Unless students understand these, they will have no idea what you are talking about. It next moves to the general principles which provide an orienting overview. Also, the general principles provide the explanatory framework for what follows. Next is the process flow. This describes how the system changes over time and describes the stages that it goes through as well. Last are the specific procedures for taking action in the world. Many trainings just provide procedures. We call this short transfer training. It is short transfer because students are only able to apply specific procedures in specific cases. When things change, the students have to be retrained. In contrast to short transfer trainings which only provide procedures, we emphasize long transfer training. This results from understanding the principles and the process. This understanding enables the students to expand and generalize the procedures to fit different contexts. In this way, students can adapt to gradual change, and it avoids the necessity of continually retraining them. Believe me, in an age of increasingly tight training budgets this is the only approach that is viable."

"I believe it." I said. Frank continued.

MISUNDERSTANDING

"Students get lost and confused for one of two reasons. When a student is stuck and does not know how to proceed it can be for one of two reasons, and it is important to know which it is. The student is either lost because he doesn't know where he is and how he got there in the first place. Or else the student is lost because he doesn't know where to go next. In the first case, the student needs orienting generalizations, and in the second case he needs specifics on how to proceed. So there are two approaches to answering any question that a student may ask. Most trainers respond to any question by providing more details. This is often the wrong approach. Once again, students ask *why* questions for two reasons. The first is that they are lost because they cannot figure out how they initially got to where they are. Chunking down will only confuse them further. Instead, the trainer needs to chunk back up so that they can see how what they know fits into the overall picture. Once they orient themselves, then they will be ready to chunk down again. The second reason that students ask questions is because they don't know where to go from where they are. In this case, they need to chunk down. Chunking up will not help them because they already know where they are. So a trainer must always be alert to questions and avoid chunking down as a matter of course. Often, the better approach is to back up and present the bigger picture so students can see where they are. Only then is it appropriate to chunk down."

It occurred to me that I had a question. I had recently taken some computer training for a new software product, and I had been amazed how much trouble people in the class seemed to be having. So I asked Frank about software training. As usual he had a ready answer.

"Software training is often really bad, because the trainers know about the features of the software but know nothing about training. Also, it is often designed by the software companies to showcase the features of their product. In any software, the eighty/twenty rule is in effect. This is that you use twenty percent of the commands eighty percent of the time, and you only use the other eighty percent of the command twenty percent of the time. Since this is the case, the majority of the training should be devoted to the most used commands. But the software companies want you to know all of the features of their product, so you spend large amounts of time on features that you rarely or never use. This is a chunking problem par excellence. Besides, most computer training involves learning one procedure after another. People get lost in procedures. What is needed but not provided is a map of procedures. Accordingly, this would say that if you want to do this, then use this procedure and if you want to do that, then use that procedure. Providing this would mean that people would know what the procedures are for and where they fit into the overall program. Instead, what happens is that people get lost in procedures. Somewhere on the eighth step of the procedure for a mail merge they get lost, and then they throw up their hands in despair. What they fail to realize is that each procedure is separate. They are used to each piece building on and requiring the previous piece. If you get lost on one procedure, that simply means that you will not be able to do that procedure. It does not mean that you will not be able to do other procedures. Also, students are expected to learn detailed procedures by doing them once. This represents a naive view about the power of human memory. The training should focus, instead, on how to use a procedures manual or the on-line documentation. I could go on and on about bad computer software training design, but the bottom line is the chunking problem. It is all chunking down and no chunking up."

I reflected that Frank's analysis was an accurate account of what I had observed. Then I realized that Karen was waiting for me and moved on.

PERSONNEL

Karen was busy talking to one of her associates and waved for me to sit down.

"The Information People Patterns are important in personnel selection and placement. They come into play in all jobs that involve information processing and communication; and, quite frankly, this is just about all jobs. Let us begin with the Perceptual Source People Pattern. Every organization needs a good balance of tangible and intangible people and also needs people who are balanced in this Pattern. Tangibles form the front line in any organization. They are the ones who are responsible for day to day operations. They are the ones who focus best on the many concrete daily tasks involved in any business operation. Intangibles are also important. They are most critical in strategic planning and in design.

They are best at creating systems for the tangibles. Moreover, they are the future eyes and ears of any business. The intangibles are the ones who see possibilities instead of necessities. Likewise, they are the ones who intuit what is happening. They form the creative vanguard that can go beyond the given. So both are critical to any business. The key is to have the right person in the right place within the organization. Some jobs are best done by tangible people and other jobs call for intangible people. Many critical jobs require someone who is balanced and has the flexibility to do both." Karen continued.

"So in summary, hire tangibles for jobs requiring a focus on the present. They make good administrators. Hire them for jobs that do not require originality. Likewise, hire tangibles for mundane service jobs. In hiring, be concrete and specific as to what the job entails. Mention salary and concrete benefits."

"Hire intangibles for jobs requiring originality, creativity or future focus. These people make good planners and strategists. Do not hire them for jobs requiring the accomplishment of something in the present. In hiring, be sure to stress future development. Do not bore them with sensory details about the present."

CHUNK SIZE PEOPLE PATTERN IN PERSONNEL

Karen paused and continued.

"Chunk size is also important in personnel selection and placement. Different positions require different chunk sizes, and it is important to match the two. I am sure that Shana and Marvin stressed that the higher in an organization that you go, the greater the need for people who can chunk up. This does not mean that they should not be able to chunk down when appropriate. In general, leadership positions require balance and the ability to chunk both up and down. Line workers often need to handle the specifics of day to day operations. They will need to be able to chunk down. This is both a blessing and a curse. The blessing is that they can handle the specific requirements of any day to day operation. The curse is that they will always be complaining about the way things are run, because they are unable to chunk up to see how things all fit together. These type of people are focused on their particular area and are unaware that the needs of their particular area must be balanced against the needs of the organization as a whole. The needs of the few must always be balanced against the needs of the many, but in such a way as to honor both sets of needs. That is what management is all about."

"So in general, hire specific people for jobs requiring attention to detail. Be specific in advertising for and describing the job. Specific people may have difficulty transitioning up the ladder to jobs that require more general thinking unless they can develop balance in this area. Hire global people for jobs where attention to details in not required. In most businesses, the higher one goes in the business, the more global the chunk size at which one needs to operate. In hiring global people, present the broad overview and ignore the details. Many critical positions require a balance in this People Pattern. These positions require someone who can chunk up, down, and laterally as circumstances demand. These people are often hard to find."

Karen paused a minute. "I could go on but these are the basics. Do you need more details?"

I laughed and said that what she had presented was sufficient. She smiled and I returned to find Shana.

SUMMARY

I returned to Shana's office to find her reading a report. She greeted me and asked how the day had gone and if I had any questions. One question had occurred to me.

"How does one develop balance in this or in any other People Pattern for that matter?"

Shana paused as usual to reflect for a minute. Then she answered.

"You always ask the difficult questions. To develop balance, you first have to understand what your People Patterns are. You also have to understand how they are both strengths and weaknesses. Most people spend their lives focusing on increasing their strengths. Balance involves focusing on your weaknesses as well. Part of understanding your People Patterns is to acknowledge and to understand your weaknesses and blind spots. Once you understand what they are, then you have to do something about them. People Patterns are learned behaviors. You don't have to unlearn what you can already do. What you do have to do, is learn something else. This is the key to flexibility and balance. In learning other People Patterns, you must learn to focus attention on things in which you are not normally interested and to which you do not normally pay attention. To understand what it is like to do this, it would be very helpful to model or study other people who have those People Patterns. Put yourself in their shoes and imagine what it is like to see the world through their filters. Practice being them until you can do both your pattern and their pattern. That is how you develop balance."

KEY 4:

THE EVALUATION PEOPLE PATTERN

Shana was conducting a meeting on an on-going project, and I sat in. I could not help but notice how eager some of the participants seemed to be for feedback on their roles in the project. Several seemed to be taking copious notes on exactly what was said about them. If nothing was said about certain parts of the project, then they would even interrupt to also ask for feedback on that part. At first I thought that they were just looking for a pat on the back, but not all of the feedback was positive. So, I abandoned that hypothesis. In any case, I was puzzled about their need for so much feedback. I also noticed that some other participants seemed to have the attitude that they knew that the project was going well regardless of what other people thought. They would argue with criticism, and they did not seem to take it to heart. It was my impression that they were going to do what they pleased and that they really didn't care what the others thought about them. This puzzled me also. After the meeting I could hardly wait for everyone to leave so that I could share my observations with Shana and find out what was going on.

Shana greeted me with a welcome smile after the meeting and wished me well on my fourth day of immersion in People Patterns. It was obvious that she realized just how much I had been learning and was pleased that I was taking it in so enthusiastically. Before sending me off to my respective managers for the day, she began by asking me for my reaction to the meeting. Then she began asking some relevant questions to begin the training session of the day.

"Have you ever wondered why some people always seem to be dependent on other people to know what to do or think in any situation while other people seemingly could care less what other people think or do and insist on doing their own thing in spite of everybody else? Have you ever noticed how some people seem to be always asking for and taking advice while other people never ask for advice and even ignore it when it is given?"

"It's strange that you should ask that, since these are the exact questions that I wanted to ask you about what went on at the meeting." I retorted.

"Have you ever paid rapt attention to a TV commercial with some celebrity endorsing a product and thought that you would try it? Or have you wondered who would be dumb enough to buy the product just because the celebrity endorsed it?"

"It seems that every time I see some silly commercial like that either myself or my wife will make that very comment!" I added.

"Have you ever asked someone why they did something and been told that other people are doing it so that it must be okay? Or else have you been told that this person just knew that it was the right thing for them to do? Have you ever tried in vain to convince someone of something or been amazed when they were convinced by someone else? Have you ever wished that your children would think for themselves or have you ever wished that they weren't so stubbornly independent? We will discover the reasons behind these behaviors in the Evaluation People Pattern. If you don't have any questions yet, I will go on." she added.

INTERNAL AND EXTERNAL REFERENTIAL PEOPLE PATTERN

"One of the most basic human activities is making judgements. We make hundreds of judgements every day. These are reflected in what we think and in how we behave. We can approach these judgements in two ways. We can ask the question 'why' or we can ask the question 'how'. If we ask someone why he is doing something, then he will give us explanations, justifications and excuses or he will tell us a story. More on this at the end of next week. If we ask the person how does he know that what he is doing or thinking or saying is right, then he will either tell us that he just knows it is right or he will justify it by pointing to others who think or behave in a similar fashion."

"There's more to this than meets the eye." Shana went on. "The question as to how one justifies conduct is fundamental. It lies at the base of all morality and ethics. What is morality? Morality has to do with the fundamental question 'What should I do?'. In deciding what we ought to do, we base our decisions either on what we know is right inside or on what others say is right. The others may be an intellectual system (such as a philosophy), an organized group (such as a religion or political party) or just our peers. Who is to say what is right? This question poses an age old quandary."

"I had a question. What is the correct balance between the personal freedom of the individual and social pressure for conformity by the group?" I asked.

"Great question. In other words, how do we find the point of equilibrium between the need for independence by the individual and the need for conformity by the group? We will find that the dynamics of history is driven by a tension between these two poles. A good example is the heated battle over abortion that is going on in many parts of the world today. On one hand we have liberal politicians and citizens standing up for what they internally believe is right. On the other hand we have conservative politicians and the religious right insisting that others conform to some external criteria such as a religious or a social doctrine which they think is right." I kept quiet so as not to break Shana's train of thought.

"Some people base their decisions on internal criteria while others base their decisions on external criteria. We call the criteria that a person uses to make judgements their 'referential filters'. If people make decisions based on internal criteria we say that they have an Internal Evaluation People Pattern. If, instead, people make decisions based on external criteria, then we say that they have an External Evaluation People Pattern. If people do what seems right inside and also check to see what effect their decisions and actions have on others, then we say that they have an internal pattern with an external check. If, on the other hand, people base their actions and decisions primarily on what others think and then combine it with an internal verification, then we say that they have an external pattern with an internal check."

EVALUATION PEOPLE PATTERN
Internal referential frame
External referential frame

"Can a person be both?" I wanted to know.

"Yes, certainly. There are some people, although they are few in number, who are balanced between the two. Again, balance is the ideal because there are times when an Internal Evaluation People Pattern would be preferable to an external one and vice versa."

"A person with an Internal Evaluation People Pattern bases his decisions and actions on what he knows inside to be the right choice. When faced with a situation calling for choice or action, he goes inside and evaluates the various options based on his internal experience. This experience may take the form of pictures, feelings, internal dialogue or logic. I will go into this more tomorrow when I discuss the Sense People Pattern. We sometimes refer to this inner knowing as intuition or conscience. This may take the form of a feeling or of a vision or of a voice in the head telling us what to do."

"That sounds like the way my mind works." I added quietly.

"You continue to make the connections really well. That is good." Shana replied as she continued. "A person with an External Evaluation Pattern bases his decisions and actions on people, events, beliefs and ideas which are outside of him in the world. These are people whose sense of self is based to a large degree on what other people say and think about them. F. Scott Fitzgerald once said that the great 'American disease' was wanting to be liked. He did not know it at the time, but he was referring to people with an External Evaluation People Pattern. When faced with a situation calling for action or a decision, they go outside and evaluate the various options based either on what other people think or what they learn from external data. We call the external source that they refer to, the 'external referent' for their decision. This external referent may take several forms of which the principle ones are people, systems, and information. When the external source is other people, a person does things because other people tell him that this is what he should do. These other people may be a parent, a spouse, a friend, a teacher, a boss, a business associate, or a peer group."

"Can that evaluation also be based on what some system says is right or wrong?" I queried.

"Definitely. Other people base their evaluations on some system. This may take the form of a religion or a movement or a political party or a philosophical system. In making decisions these people determine what is correct in terms of the guidance provided by that system. Still other people with External Evaluation Patterns rely on data or information about their progress in the world. They base their decisions on results or on performance figures. They know that they are doing the right things, because data or statistics (such as monthly sales figures) verify that what they are doing is working."

INDICATORS

Now I was ready to learn how to identify the two types of Evaluation patterns. "How do you determine if you are dealing with someone with an Internal or an External Evaluation Pattern?   Are there target indicator questions?" I asked.

"Fortunately, this is very easy to determine. All you have to do is ask a simple question: 'How do you know that what you are doing or propose to do is right?' An alternative question to ask is: 'How do you know when you have done a good job?' Pay close attention to their answers and to their behavior." I wanted her to continue, so I did not interrupt.

INDICATOR QUESTION
How do you know when you have done a good job?

"Do they decide for themselves or do they need to rely on the opinions of others? Are they their own judge of things or do they look to others for approval? People with Internal Evaluation People Patterns will give answers like 'I just know' or 'It just feels right'. People with external filters will give answers like 'My boss told me' or 'The church says' or 'My friends do it' or 'The monthly sales results were above quota'. They will give you answers based on what other people think or on what others believe or on external data."

She went on.

"In addition to listening to their answers to the above questions pay close attention to their behaviors. Are they always telling you what other people think? This is indicative of an External Evaluation People Pattern. If, instead, when you or other people tell a person what other people think and the reaction is 'I could not care less', this is indicative of an Internal Evaluation People Pattern. Also, do they need constant re-enforcement of their feelings from others or are they self assured and confident about their conduct? The former reveals an External Evaluation People Pattern and the latter an internal one."

"I now know that I have an Internal Evaluation People Pattern, because I just know when I have done a good job." I remarked in passing.

"That was one of the qualities we were looking for in hiring you, as a matter of fact. With an Internal Evaluation People Pattern we knew that you yourself make this type of judgement. You know when you have done a good job. As with others like you, you do not have to ask anyone else or check out outside data. Instead you have some kind of personal, internal way of knowing when you have done a good job. You will say things like: 'It just feels right' or 'I just know'. You have your own internal barometer to evaluate anything you do. This includes any of your behaviors as well as your very being. This internal check may take several forms. It could take the form of a feeling inside you that indicates to you that you have done something well or that a specific behavior is acceptable. It could also take the form of an internal voice which approves of what you have done or a personal vision in which it looks right."

"I noticed that some of the people attending the meeting needed specific feedback from their supervisors for them to feel good." I said.

"What you witnessed was the External Evaluation People Pattern in action. With an External Evaluation Pattern, you know that you have done a good job either because people tell you or because of feedback from the world in terms of data or statistics. To determine whether you have done a good job you need to know what other people think. This may be your boss or peers or your spouse or parents or even a stranger. Or you may need to look at your monthly sales figures or some kind of objective data about your performance. Without some kind of feedback either from people or data you will have no way to evaluate your performance. This may lead to an unduly stressful situation and a great deal of discomfort. We will go into this shortly."

"Okay, so if I ask the following question: ' How do you know when you have done a good job?' I will be able to determine the Evaluation People Pattern of the person or persons. Right?"

"Yes." she said. "What is the answer? The person either knows that he has done a good job because there is something internally that tells him so (such as a feeling) or because of some kind of external information (such as someone or some data is telling him)."

"If he has an Internal Evaluation People Pattern, then he will often say 'I just know'."

"What if everyone else thinks differently?" I inquired.

"That doesn't matter with a person who has an Internal Evaluation People Pattern. In fact, everybody else might think differently, and it would not effect that person's beliefs or decisions. If, on the other hand, a person has an external pattern, then the only way that he will know that he has done a good job is when his boss or spouse or someone else tells him. If the person doesn't get any feedback, then he has no way of knowing whether he has done a good job or not. If he has an external pattern, then he will value feedback either from other people or from external data such as statistics or monthly sales figures."

"I know for certain that I have a strong Internal Evaluation People Pattern, because I always decide for myself. I always know internally whether I have done something well or not. And I certainly don't need to be told and will often ignore the feedback when I am told. I do, however, pay attention to the responses of those whom I respect and note when their evaluations do not meet my own." I asserted with great confidence.

"You are right, and there is more. In fact, you are fortunate to be contextually balanced in that you have an Internal Evaluation People Pattern with an external check. There are others who are balanced in a different way in that they may have an External Evaluation People Pattern with an internal check." Shana explained.

"There exists an interesting dynamic with this Evaluation People Pattern of which you need to be aware. It is that if you have an internal pattern, then you often project that other people have internal ones as well, and so you tend not to give other people feedback or if you do, you give them only negative feedback. You know when you are right and assume that everyone else should know also, and that they shouldn't have to be told by you or anyone else. If, on the other hand, you have an external pattern, then you need to be told how you are doing. And if you are not told, then you become anxious and worried about how you are doing. You feel that you are not getting the necessary feedback from others and that they are leaving you in a vacuum as to how you are doing."

PRAYERS

"The prayer for a person with an Internal Referential People Pattern is:"

O Lord, all knowing God, please let me make my own decisions. Give me this day the inner certainty to know when I am right. Lead me not into dependency upon other's opinions and grant me the courage and self reliance to steer my own course in life. When the multitudes go one way, grant me the certainty to march to my own drummer, no matter how contrary the tides. Let me decide for 'moi'. Deliver me from bad decisions which are based on the false values imposed by society. Also, deliver me from the tempter whose voice may lead me astray even when I am right. Please shine upon me the light of clarity to decide wisely and to hear my inner voice which is the best of all except for Thine own. Amen.

"And the prayer for a person with an External Referential People Pattern is:"

Almighty God, all knowing, the true Source of all guidance and counsel, provide me with my life's instruction. Lord, Ultimate Source of right and wrong, give me this day the necessary direction to conduct my life in accordance with Thy Will. Please answer my prayers for advice and counsel before I make any decisions. Deliver me from those who would expect me to make decisions on my own and especially from situations where I cannot get feedback about what I am doing. Deliver me too, from false counsel. Provide me with wise counselors who can give advice and make recommendations that help me to sort through the trials and tribulations on the journey of life. Amen.

"I don't have any questions right now, so I guess that I am ready to go off to my session on management in relation to the Evaluation Pattern."

MANAGEMENT

As usual Marvin was very anxious to get going, since I was a few minutes late in arriving at his office. And when I later learned about the Organization People Pattern on day nine, I understood why he did not appreciate my being late.

"Let's get right down to business. Shana has already gone through the basics of the Evaluation Pattern, so I will begin to explain its applications in management. The dynamics of the internal/external polarity has important consequences in the business world. Think about the relationship between a manager and the employees that he manages. Imagine how often communication breaks down between managers and their employees, because one happens to have one pattern and the other the opposite pattern."

"Yes. I can remember that happening in past positions more often than I would have liked." I commented.

"Let us consider a manager who has an internal pattern and an employee who has an external pattern. The employee will need constant feedback to know if he is performing correctly. He will need both praise and/or blame whichever is appropriate in the situation. In a situation where the manager has a strong internal evaluation pattern, he is certainly going to have a hard time understanding his employee's need for constant feedback. The manager will think that it a waste of his precious time to be constantly patting workers on the back or chastising them for their performance. From the manager's perspective, if the employees are doing their jobs well, then they should know how they are doing and they should not have to be told. He will assume that his employees have his identical model of the world, so that they do not need feedback. And if his employees are like him, then they will not need or want feedback either. Meanwhile, those employees who are not like him will be frustrated, because he never tells them how they are doing. The manager may yell at them occasionally but will almost never give them any positive feedback."

EXTERNAL FRAME
Needs feedback
INTERNAL FRAME
Ignores feedback

"I can certainly recall many a situation in which former managers refused to give feedback to us. That suited me just fine, but some of my colleagues were totally lost and felt rejected at some level."

"Yes, and the consequences are often deadly to the morale of those who need feedback and are not getting it; and this often leads to declines in productivity. If, on the other hand, the manager has an external pattern and his employees have an internal one, then the situation will be quite different. The manager will assume that the employees are like him, and he will be constantly giving the employees positive and negative feedback on how they are doing. The problem is that the employees will neither need nor welcome any kind of feedback. They will only care what their boss thinks concerning their work if it results in rewards or punishments for them. Employees with an internal pattern know inside when they are doing well at their jobs, and they do not want or require their manager's confirmation. In fact, feedback from the manager is often taken either as interference or as a bother."

"I have had that reaction, especially when I felt that my manager did not know as much as I did." I remarked.

"The person with an internal pattern views any evaluation of his performance by his manager as an evaluation of the manager's ability to make evaluations rather then an actual evaluation of his (the employee's) performance. If the manager's evaluation agrees with his, then he believes that the manager is capable of evaluating his performance correctly but nevertheless wonders why he would bother to do so. If, on the other hand, the manager's evaluation of his performance differs from his own, then the person assumes that his evaluation is correct and that the manager either is uninformed or simply wrong. He may even go so far as to believe that his manager is virtually incompetent, as demonstrated by his incorrect evaluation of the employee's performance."

"And the manager, of course, will be frustrated by the employee's unwillingness to listen to or accept his performance appraisal." I chimed in.

"You can see, then, how helpful it would be to understand this People Pattern distinction in a work context. Imagine trying to manage a group of employees with strong Internal Evaluation People Patterns. As far as they`re concerned, there is no need for management evaluations, since they are the ones who make evaluations on themselves. A way of dealing with these people is to determine what motivates them, threats or incentives, and then to provide the appropriate motivator. We will discuss this another day when we deal with motivation."

I was so intrigued that I didn't interrupt to ask any questions.

"The implications of this distinction for management is very important." Marvin went on to say. One of the best selling popular books on management is Kenneth Blanchard and Spencer Johnson's *The One Minute Manager*. This book is based on three principles. Two of these are relevant here. The 'one minute manager' does one minute goal settings and gives one minute praisings and one minute reprimands. When he finds an employee doing something wrong, then he takes a minute to reprimand him; and when he catches him doing something right, then he also takes a minute to praise him. This approach works extremely well for managing people with External Evaluation People Patterns. They will really appreciate the feedback, particularly the positive feedback. We live in a world in which it is common to hear when people are displeased with us but, unfortunately, far less common to hear when they are pleased. The 'one minute manager's' one minute praisings are an act too often neglected, and this is a critical part of productive management."

"Whereas the 'one minute manager' will do very well with people with external patterns, he may be less successful with those with internal filters.

His advantage is that he provides both positive and negative feedback and that he keeps it short. One minute praisings and reprimands will provide necessary feedback to people with internal filters and will do so in a form that is minimally distasteful. It turns out that the 'one minute manager' is pretty savvy about people, and this accounts for his success."

"I think that I have said enough for the present time about managing employees with different Evaluation Patterns. Now it is time you move on to the realm of sales."

SALES

In sales Michael greeted me with a warm smile. "Today we will consider sales with a new twist - from the perspective of the Evaluation Pattern. Another area within the business context where the Internal/External People Pattern distinction is particularly important is in the realm of sales. It makes a major difference whether you are selling to someone with an internal or an external pattern. If they have an internal pattern, then they would not care what you or other people think about your product. From their perspective, most other people including the public at large are absolutely lacking in discrimination. If, on the other hand, they have an external pattern, then what other people think about your product will be critical. Any questions or comments thus far?" Michael inquired.

"No. More distinctions, though." I responded.

EXTERNAL FRAME
Cares what others think
INTERNAL FRAME
Does not want to hear what others think

"Let us elaborate on this crucial distinction between internal and external patterns which may make or break any salesperson. If you are trying to sell a product to a person with a strong Internal Evaluation People Pattern, then it is he who must decide whether your product is worth purchasing or not. Do not trouble him with what you or others think. Instead find out how he makes evaluations. On what does he base his decisions? Is it a feeling, a picture or an internal voice? Try to get him to fit your product into his internal representation."

"So what you are saying is that part of selling a prospect is finding out what his internal pattern is." I said.

"Precisely." Michael responded. "If it is a feeling, then you must generate that feeling in him. If it is a picture, then you must give him the right picture. You will use language not about what other people think but about what he thinks. For example you might say: 'I think that when you consider this inside and think about all the options, then you will undoubtedly decide or undoubtedly realize (or you will feel or see it) this way.' You are trying to get him to focus inside and to have that feeling you want him to have or to see that picture you want him to see or to talk to himself in that certain tone of voice. We will go into this in more detail tomorrow when we discuss the Sense Sort."

Michael went on to say: "In any case, make sure that you use language that emphasizes the fact that the prospect is the one who will ultimately decide whether or not to buy your product. You can emphasize the fact that you know that you really cannot sell him on the product, and that you know that ultimately he will make the decision for himself. This will be aligned with his model of the world. Tell the prospect that you know it is he who will personally evaluate the merits of the product and then decide whether or not to buy it. Telling him about other people who have used and liked the product is useless. A person with an internal pattern could not care less about what other people think, and moreover, will think less of you for telling him. From his perspective, if he doesn't like the product and other people buy it, then this is not an endorsement of the product, but rather a tragic commentary on the poor tastes of other people."

"If, on the other hand," Michael went on to say, "you are dealing with a person with an external pattern, then there are two possible strategies. The first, if at all possible, is to position yourself as his external referent. To do this you have to present yourself credibly as someone knowledgeable on the subject, who is trustworthy and who has his best interests at heart. If you can do this, you will be highly successful selling to people with external patterns. The keys, once again, are competence, trustworthiness and sincerity. In the facetious words of one well known sales trainer 'When you can fake these, you will have it made'."

"The other strategy is to appeal to other external referents besides, or in addition to, yourself. To do this tell the prospect about other people whom they admire or respect, who, in fact, buy or use your product (as with celebrity endorsements). Take the time to talk to your prospects to find out who these significant people are and, if possible, connect those people to your product. If you provide examples of people whom they don't like or don't respect, you had might as well close the door shut to selling them anything. This will turn them off, so do your homework carefully."

"Michael, while you have been explaining this to me, what suddenly came to mind was the approach used on the TV shopping channels like QVC and the Home Shopping Network and on infomercials. It never ceases to amaze me how many millions of people buy products because of the testimonial calls by supposed buyers. I have no problem with at home shopping, but what irks me is the nonsense you hear from the hosts who, I now understand, are selling to the consumers with strong External

Evaluation Patterns when they utilize testimonial calls. I will buy a product not because of some testimonial phone call, or because of the host's lauding of the product, but rather because I want to buy it for a particular reason of my own."

"You would be amazed at how gullible people with strong External Evaluation Patterns can be!" Michael added. "And some of these hosts have learned their trade quite well. They constantly put a counter on the screen that indicates the quantity of items being sold, saying cleverly, 'while supplies last' so as to instill a fear of being left out into the customers if they do not immediately jump onto the band wagon by purchasing the item. If you cannot connect your product to specific endorsements then give them statistics to show that your product is the best selling product in some relevant market. TV show hosts do this well. If you are not the number one product in the market, then find some relevant market segment in which you shine and tell the prospect about that. Above all be honest. Honesty is truly the best policy."

"What if the prospect filters by external data?" I wanted to know.

"Then provide him with as much information and data as possible. The more data the better. Also, because people with external patterns are so influenced by others' opinions, it would be to your advantage to set up a group demonstration or presentation. When they see or hear other people's reactions (hopefully good ones), then they will react accordingly to fit in with the rest. Again, TV shopping hosts and even auctioneers use this tactic quite successfully. Be careful, though, since it is a common tactic to seed the audience with shills who will place phony bids at auctions."

I suddenly had a thought about con artists, so I asked: "What about the sundry con artists working across the country?"

"Who do you think is going to be more susceptible to their clever techniques of luring in the poor, unsuspecting consumer by appearing to be honest and caring? A person with an external pattern is more likely to fall victim to these manipulative criminals. These guys are incredibly creative with their illegal schemes to rip off their fellow man. A person with an internal pattern views them as a bunch of crooks, and believes that anyone who is dumb enough to buy into their game deserves what he gets. Then there is the congruent salesperson or even the guru type who, although he is legally selling his products and is legitimate, could not care less about the consumer he is successfully targeting."

I thought that this last comment was a bit harsh, and at the same time I knew inside (Ha! Ha!) that Michael was indeed right.

"One problem in selling to people with external patterns is that significant others may quickly reverse their buying decisions. This is a common problem in door to door sales. Impressionable housewives or house husbands fall pray to door to door salespeople only to have their decisions reversed later by their spouses."

"I am happy to say that both myself and my spouse have strong Internal Evaluation People Patterns, which actually can create another type of problem." I interjected.

"I won't go into details on the consequences of this on couples. In any case, since decision reversals are a common problem among couples, salespeople for large ticket items will want to have both parties present if the two of them are going to have a say in the decision. Another problem with selling to people with strong external filters is that they are influenced by the last persuasive person to whom they have spoken. A salesperson may sell them quite easily only to have the sale taken away by another salesperson who comes along right after him."

I found this material elucidating to many of the interactions I had had over a period of many years in my previous places of employment. "So every salesperson would be wise to determine his prospects' People Patterns." I said.

"Salespeople usually close a fixed percentage of the prospects on whom they call. As every salesperson knows, there are only two ways to increase sales. One is to see more prospects and the other is to close a higher percentage of those that they do see. The first way is called 'working hard' and the second way is called 'working smart'. Which would you rather do? To work smart, a salesperson has to have the flexibility to vary his presentation to fit the needs of the prospect. The first thing any smart salesperson needs to do to be more successful is to develop an in depth knowledge of these People Patterns and to use them to alter his presentation to match the People Patterns of his prospect. When this happens it is called 'sales success'. Now perhaps the name of our company makes more sense to you. I should remind you that we do conduct a whole series of People Pattern Workshops for different types of companies."

"What happens if you are making a general proposal, and you are not sure with whom you are dealing?" I inquired.

"In that case, you should cover both options. This way you play it safe. As you get more skilled in diagnosing people and you are fairly sure what someone is, then you simply tailor your proposal to fit them. Covering both options is better than just covering the one that does not work. Ideally you will be able to detect the relevant pattern/s of your prospect and then effectively utilize them. Always be on guard against the tendency to project your own patterns on to other people."

I was glad Michael mentioned that last point, because over the course of my several days here I began to notice that there were some, including myself, who at times, would project their own patterns on to others.

CELEBRITY ENDORSEMENTS

"I would like to talk a bit now about celebrity endorsements, which, are, by the way, a great example in our present day culture of External Evaluation behavior. If Liz Taylor (who has been labeled a world institution) or Michael Jordan (who has been called the greatest athlete of all time) creates a new fragrance, then the person with the external pattern is going to run out to purchase it. Whether it smells good or not becomes a secondary issue. What counts is that the person is wearing the scent of a legendary Hollywood star or an NBA super star. This is an important point which promoters and ad agencies need to understand."

"I am relieved that both my spouse and I have internal patterns!" I chuckled.

"In the case of Liz Taylor, we are dealing with a Hollywood actress who has remained in the hearts of her fans for decades. And in the case of Michael Jordan, we are dealing with the most recognizable face on the planet. It is unlikely that either will fall from grace due to some front page story in The National Enquirer. People with external patterns can identity with a person who has lasting star power, whereas they may not be as impressed by some lesser actress who appears on some hit situation comedy for a year and then disappears into oblivion or with some trash talking NBA want-to-be. The external pattern fan's identification with Liz or Michael may in some cases be a lifelong association."

"Moreover, with all the external evaluation people flocking to fragrance counters world-wide, the new perfume or cologne inevitably becomes a huge success, re-enforcing all the more the external's need to be associated with it. If the majority is wearing the scent, this translates into acceptance by the public at large in the mind of the person with the External Evaluation Pattern. After all, in their eyes, splashing a star's scent on yourself will allow you to share in the star's power, even if vicariously, and that means acceptance. The same principle applies to all other products endorsed by celebrities in the media. Marketing moguls would do well to bank on lasting idols rather than on fly by night newcomers whose success is trendy and short-lived."

"The car company adds come to mind with their celebrity endorsements. General Motors and Oldsmobile and then Ford capitalized on the star power of children of famous entertainment celebrities. If William Shatner's and Harry Belafonte's and Susan Lucci's siblings can drive these automobiles, then surely this bestows a certain glamour and again acceptance upon the average John or Mary Doe's or their kids with their strong external patterns."

"Now that I am aware of the Evaluation People Pattern, I think that the marketing strategies of these companies are brilliant. And these guys don't even know why what they are doing is working so well from a behavioral perspective."

"Ironically, they don't. And by magnifying celebrity endorsements these firms are planting fertile seeds into the malleable minds of the consumers with an external pattern. The big movers at the top realize full well that if giant superstars like Michael Jordan or Tiger Woods are seen wearing Nike apparel on nationwide or even worldwide television, then all the external pattern people of all ages are certainly going to want to get on the bandwagon as well. Bill Cosby (another legend in his own right) has done wonders for JELL-O pudding and desserts. It is terrific when such positive, family oriented individuals can indirectly influence children in such a positive fashion. Imagine all the little mouths at home pulling at their mother's or father's apron strings for a serving of one of these products. The impact of this approach is twofold. One, the kids get approval via the television screen from their idol for buying the product that he recommends, and two, the product is a success, so that everyone on the block has to get in the picture, with a resulting mutual admiration society that is created, not to mention the millions in the bank for the company whose product is advertised."

"Marketing guys are getting even more clever or shall I say subtle in that now they are using famous voices (like Lauren Bacall for Fancy Feast and Tom Selleck for AT&T) rather then images of the actors to promote their products."

"Now that you mention it, I knew that certain voices sounded familiar, and I simply could not place them until now. That really is sneaky on the part of the advertiser." I complained.

"It may be sneaky, but it works quite effectively for reasons which we will not delve into at the present time." Michael retorted.

"Obviously celebrity endorsements have little, if any, effect on buyers with strong internal patterns." He went on to say. "Usually they are just amused by the situation or see it as a negative reflection on the gullibility of humanity. People with strong Internal Evaluation People Patterns are oblivious to most advertisements anyway, so advertisers should write them off and focus on the people with external patterns, whom they can influence successfully. Strong Internal Referential People Pattern people usually throw up their hands in despair at the stupidity (according to their model of the world) of present day advertisements. In fact, they consider most advertising as an insult to their intelligence."

"I am constantly complaining about the stupidity of TV and magazine adds. The advertisers really must think the entire public at large is dumb. My spouse and I are constantly amazed at what advertisers do get away with in their commercials." I said not at all facetiously.

"There is a lot more to be said about the negative impact of today's advertisements on children and even on gullible adults, but that would require another week long training session on values. That will be for another time."

"I don't have any more questions now, and I am sure that this evening I will be watching the commercials during the nightly news with an entirely new perspective thanks to you, Michael."

"Have fun with the material. That's part of the learning process."

NEGOTIATIONS

As usual, Beverly was quite cordial when I arrived. I now recognized her having used the Internal Evaluation People Pattern with me when we first met.

She began by telling me how the Internal/External People Pattern relates to the field of negotiating. Her first question was: "What type of person would you like to have on the other side of the negotiating table, a person with an internal filter or one with an external one?" And she gave me no time to answer.

"In most cases," she said, "it would be to your advantage to have someone whose Evaluation Pattern is external, because he will be concerned with what you and other people think of him and of what he proposes. If you can get him to respect you, then he will go out of his way to please you and to make sure that, if possible, you are satisfied. He would certainly prefer not to upset you, and will go out of his way to maintain good relations."

"So how would I influence someone with an external pattern?" I wanted to know.

"To exert maximum influence on a person with an external pattern, find people whom he respects and admires who happen to agree with your position. Also, quote statistics to justify your position. The person with an external pattern is more likely to be influenced by precedent and tradition and common practice."

She continued. "Negotiating with a person with an external pattern is far from being a piece of cake, but it is usually easier than negotiating with an internal pattern person. Remember that his focus will be on the outside. As strange as it may seem, you may even occasionally find an external pattern person actually asking you how he is doing during the course of the negotiations. Be sure to provide him with plenty of feedback, both positive and negative."

"I have actually had that happen to me, and I was quite astonished, to say the least, although I remember hiding my reaction well." I said.

"So if you are dealing with a person who has an external pattern, be prepared to have data and statistics reflecting the opinions of those he respects or admires. It even helps to pay him compliments and to constantly reassure him that he is doing the right thing. Be sure to tell him what you think. If you are skillful enough, you can reach the point of telling the other person what they actually need to decide in the negotiation. The more external references that you can give him the better."

"I have had blocks occur when other people suddenly appeared in the middle of a negotiation." I added.

"That is an excellent point which I was just going to address," responded Beverly. "One problem area in negotiating with a person with an external pattern arises when they have access to other people who influence them during the negotiation. This is particularly a problem if these people are also at the table. The external pattern person will very probably be influenced by them and may become even more stubborn and recalcitrant. The external pattern negotiator may also be representing other people's interests and feel strongly obligated to those people. In this case, the best approach is to fall back on standard negotiating tactics and frame your position as best you can so that there is something in it for them."

"Meanwhile, I had better count on some tough negotiating if I am dealing with a person who has an Internal Evaluation Pattern, right?" I asked.

"You mean like you!" Beverly chuckled. "He is not going to be worried at all about what you think of him. All he cares about is making his points well and ending up with a win. You might be able to express your opinion at some point, but his ideas will take priority for him. Just think how a grasp of this People Pattern will help you in any negotiation you have, whether at the office, at a major board meeting or at home with your spouse or kids (where some of the most sophisticated skills are required)."

"Yes, with my kids in particular." I chimed in.

"If dealing with a person with an internal pattern, the language you use should indicate your acknowledgment of his internal knowing, i.e. that you know that he will not be influenced by others and that, no matter what, the decision will be made ultimately by him. When you acknowledge to the internal pattern person that you are indeed aware of this, this will get his respect and, hopefully, also his cooperation. Rattling on about what other people think does no good with a person with an Internal Evaluation Pattern. In fact, it usually annoys the person. Instead, you need to talk about his thoughts on the subject and to present your side in terms of his frames."

"If you have no questions thus far, I will continue," she added.

"I will go into this in detail next week, but for now I will tell you that there are three basic approaches to negotiations. These are hardball, softball and principled. People with strong internal patterns may tend to be hardball players. People with strong external patterns are usually softball players, if you are the focus of their external filter. If someone else whose interests conflict with yours is their external filter, then they may become stubborn hardball players."

"Principled negotiations is an interesting approach to negotiating." I declared.

"Actually, you are more correct than you probably realize at this point. What it suggests is that both sides use an external pattern and that the pattern be fair, objective, external criteria. Principled negotiations will be practiced most easily by people whose frame of reference is external data. If the person's reference frame is external to other's opinions, then he will play hardball or softball to satisfy those opinions. The person with an internal pattern may not be willing to engage in principled negotiations if he thinks that he can get a better deal playing hardball. Principled negotiations appeals to notions of fairness and equality. These notions will have more influence on a person with an external pattern than a person with a strong internal one."

"I'll bet that the person with a strong internal pattern will not consider the notion of fair, objective criteria as valid." I added.

"Precisely." Beverly confirmed. "Of course, principled negotiators are aware of this and learn tactics which allow them to remain principled even when the other side insists on playing hardball."

"I have tried to capsulize a lot of information into a short presentation for you on the Evaluation People Pattern and how it relates to negotiating. I hope that this session was helpful." Beverly said as she guided me to my next session.

TRAINING

Frank started off the session immediately. "The Evaluation People Pattern also has vast implications in the field of education.

The greatest enemy of learning is the belief that one already knows something.

A person learns best when he believes both that he does not already know something and that the person from whom he is learning the material does know it and can teach it to him. We learn new things by trusting the expertise of others. As we become more and more proficient, however, we begin to develop confidence in our own abilities in a given area. In time we may come to believe that we know as much if not more than our teacher."

"Yes, I see this attitude among managers time and time again in corporations," I said.

"And such an attitude does and will effect learning in a negative manner. So learning occurs best when we start with an external pattern and then develop our own internal one. This is what learning and education are all about - developing our own expertise through learning from others. Problems can arise, however, as we will see."

Frank continued since I had no questions for the moment. "Take, for example, the street kid who has no choice but to develop an internal pattern in order to survive on the streets. It is generally difficult for him to trust others, which makes learning almost impossible. This is a very important point. If the kid with the internal pattern thinks he already knows everything he needs to know, that he will learn new things on his own without the help of other people, in this case teachers. Then the learning process will come to a standstill in the classroom and elsewhere."

"That explains what is happening in our schools at this very moment. Parents and teachers keep on complaining about the lack of learning in the classroom, but they really don't have a clue as to the reasons why." I added.

"The problem is quite widespread and no one understands the root cause of the problem. In order for any student to take part in the learning process, he must go external in relation to the teacher, otherwise there will be major problems. If he believes the teacher does not know what he is talking about, and that the information disseminated is not valid, then he is obviously not in a position to be learning effectively, if at all. The teachers, meanwhile, have an extremely difficult time handling students with this type of attitude, whether it be the tough guy with the internal pattern, or the whiz kid who thinks he knows more than the teacher. If the teacher tries to deal with them, the result is often disastrous, because he has no knowledge of the type of language to be used with impossible internal pattern kids. Obviously the same applies to learning in a corporate setting." Frank paused looking to see if I had questions or comments.

"If it's alright with you, I will continue," Frank said.

"If the teacher happens to be dedicated and creative, it helps to have kids with external patterns who look up to him. On the other hand, difficulties arise when an alcoholic or addict teacher ends up with a classroom full of kids with an external pattern. Several news items of late have reported certain teachers caught using drugs and also selling them to their students. Some role models they are! The poor external pattern kids think that suddenly drugs are OK since the authoritarian figure they respect indulges in them, so that taking drugs somehow takes on an air of legitimacy. No matter what, the high external pattern person will fall prey to his overwhelming desire to win the approval of his peers. In our schools today this very scenario is played out time and time again. Such a tragedy!"

"The bottom line is that a child or manager or whoever, should have an external pattern in the classroom." I added.

"Whether a manager attending a seminar, or a child in the classroom, a person in learning mode ideally demonstrates an external pattern in the context of learning. In summary, within the educational system it is important that a learner start with an external pattern with respect to the teacher, because if learning is to take place at all, it can only happen in the presence of an external pattern early on. The student needs to assume that his teachers know what they are talking about and that the information they are giving is valid."

"I have seen the problems resulting in seminars when some of the students (arrogant managers, for example) think that they know it all when they have obviously never been exposed to the material." I added.

"If a student does not have an external pattern with respect to education, then there are bound to be problems. A lot of students in the educational system do not have external evaluation patterns. They think to themselves: 'What does the teacher know?'. At that point it is very easy for them to close down and to drop completely out of the educational process, which is usually the case. This is perhaps one of the most difficult things for a teacher to deal with in his profession. They have to get these students to come back out of their shells and to develop an external filter with respect to learning. The teacher has to convince the students that he, the teacher, has something to teach them that they do not already know and that learning is to their advantage."

"I can see where that is a huge problem in classrooms whether in the corporate setting or in our schools." I said.

"Yes. In fact, this is one of the most fundamental problems of education. It is learning how to get students to shift back once they go into an internal pattern which is frequently a rebellion against something or someone. In many cases, students who grow up on the streets are forced into an internal evaluation pattern."

"I guess the opposite is true for students (managers, kids, whoever) with external patterns." I added.

"Yes, students with external patterns make their peer group the focus of their external pattern. What usually occurs is a we/them attitude in which the students think that they know what is right and that the teachers are wrong. This may also seriously curtail learning in a classroom. Competent teachers in this country strive on a daily basis to get students to pay attention to them and to go against the peer pressure for rebellion against the educational system. Thus, internal and external patterns are so very important in a learning context. The way in which we deal with them may well determine the future of education in the world in the 21st century."

"I assume that we begin life with an external pattern. Right?" I asked.

"Yes, of course. We all start off in life with an external pattern. Some of us develop an internal one along the way. In learning, it is helpful if we develop an external pattern, to also have an internal check. If the teacher has something to teach us, then there is something we can learn. We need to evaluate it, however, and see how we can use it ourselves. Maturity is often a process of moving from an external pattern to an internal one. Learning is a state of moving from an external pattern with respect to the material to a place where one develops an internal knowing that it is true."

"How does this work with my own kids?" I asked.

"Children start life with external filters. As they grow older, one of two things happens. Either they keep the external filter and shift the referent from their parents to their peer group, or they develop an internal filter of their own. It is rare today to find children who continue to maintain an external filter with respect to their parents as they grow older. In general, parents get squeezed out. This is why it is so important to instill values into your children while they are young and you can still have an influence on them. If you wait until they begin to grow up, it will probably be too late."

"Frank, this session has been particularly enlightening for me and I can now apply the information not only in corporate settings but at home as well with my own children and with their friends. Thank you so very much."

PERSONNEL

Karen greeted me warmly and immediately began our session. "The implications of the Evaluation Pattern in hiring are quite significant. More often than not, companies end up hiring the person with the Evaluation Pattern that does not fit the bill for the type of job involved."

Karen went on. "The Internal/External Pattern comes down to one thing:

Does the job require someone who can be a team player or someone who wants to be a loner? For the task at hand to be done well, does it require someone who can take feedback and who needs it, or rather does it require someone who can do it alone without constant pats on the back?

This may seem like a trivial point, but if the Evaluation Pattern does not fit the job or task, the results can be quite negative."

I did not interrupt so Karen continued. "A person with an External Evaluation People Pattern will be best in a job in which there is interaction with others. He will fit in much more readily in a position that involves team work of some kind. Also, an external pattern person will need some kind of feedback during the course of his doing the job. This type of person simply cannot work at a job in which there is no one to guide him and to tell him whether or not he is doing a good job. A person with an external pattern definitely needs a job where he is often told how he is doing."

"Meanwhile, a person with an Internal Evaluation People Pattern does best in a job in which he is left to do his own thing. The one thing that annoys this type of person the most is when someone else, whether a colleague or manager, tells him how he is doing. The internal pattern person knows inside whether or not he is doing a job well. He certainly does not need anyone else telling him how he is doing, and definitely does not need or want anyone else telling him what he is to do. The internal pattern individual wants to be left alone when it comes to doing his job. He is not well suited to team work jobs, and would much prefer to do things alone, his way. Team work jobs involve a great deal of interaction and mutual discussion of performance. This type of situation does not work well with a person who has an internal pattern."

"Let me make one more point. If you want to appeal to a person with an internal pattern, what you do is tell the person that he is in charge of his own decisions. Tell him that he probably knows when he is doing something well, and that you realize that he works well on his own, without pats on the back and accolades from arbitrary individuals. Now, if you want to appeal to one with an external pattern, make the person feel at home. Reassure him that some form of feedback is part of the job, and that people are often congratulated for a job well done. The approach for the two patterns is totally different, and once you understand the difference between the two, life in the office becomes a lot easier. It really does facilitate interactions, since you can understand why some people constantly need reassurance about how they are doing, and why others simply couldn't care less."

"That insight really does explain so many of the situations in which I have found myself with co-workers who were always expecting me to applaud them. I could never understand why they needed constant words of encouragement."

"This is a scenario that gets repeated time and time again in the workplace all over the world." Karen added.

"The patterns are obvious in attitudes during interviews, aren't they?" I asked.

"Indeed. The person with an external pattern often looks to the interviewer for feedback of some sort, whether it be in the body language or in the actual comments of the interviewer. An interviewer with a poker face usually makes the external pattern interviewee quite uncomfortable, to say the least. Also, the individual with an external pattern tends to look at the interviewer much more often than a person with an internal pattern."

"I rarely do."

"Now you know one of the reasons why. The person with an internal pattern such as yourself tends to be his own person. He is not looking for feedback from the interviewer to see how he is doing, because he knows inside whether or not the interaction is going well. And, as strange as it may seem, given the context of job seeking, the person with the internal pattern really does not care what the person asking the questions thinks. If he does not get the job, he simply tells himself that the interviewer was probably an idiot."

"That sounds familiar."

SUMMARY

Shana looked up and asked me how the day had gone. I smiled and said "I don't know. I was hoping that you would be able to tell me." We both laughed. Then Shana became philosophical for a moment. "We live in challenging times in which more and more people have access to powerful weapons of mass destruction whether they be words or bombs. I don't know which to fear most. Is it the demagogue who is willing to sacrifice others for what he is sure is right or is it the mindless masses who are only too eager to follow anyone who claims to represent the majority."

KEY 5:

THE DECISION PEOPLE PATTERN

INTRODUCTION

The car pool was on time, and the usual arguments were in full swing. A debate was raging about a city council plan to build a mall on land that had been dedicated for a park, and everyone seemed to have an opinion. Dave was in favor of the mall and was presenting all sorts of logical arguments for it based on tax revenues and projected growth curves. Tom was against the mall and wanted the park. He kept saying that it just didn't feel right to build a mall where there was supposed to be a park. Sue was more concerned about what the mall would look like. She said that she could see a park, but she wasn't sure that she could see a mall. And Bill said that neither of the options sounded right to him. He was afraid that either one would adversely effect the peace and quiet of the neighborhood. Nobody seemed to be convincing anyone. The volume kept getting louder and louder, and tempers were beginning to flare. Fortunately we arrived at my drop off point, and it was none too soon as far as I was concerned.

TYPING YOURSELF

Shana began the session with her usual trigger indicator questions that were pertinent to the People Pattern for the day.

"Please listen to the following questions. When was the last time that you bought a new or used car? How did you decide that a particular model was the right one for you? Do you remember when you decided to marry? Why did you choose your special mate? How did you know that this person was the right person to be your spouse? Or perhaps you recall selecting one particular computer over another? What made you choose the one that you did? Why do you watch one particular news program or news anchor among the various news programs available to you? Are you aware of why you made these various decisions? We all make hundreds of decisions every day. Some of them involve choosing between multiple alternatives, and some are simply go/no go decisions. The basis of these decision making strategies is the People Pattern called the Decision People Pattern."

"I could answer these questions, but I would rather continue listening to find out more about what I am supposed to be looking for." I said.

"Have you ever asked someone why he did something, and the answer that he gave you made no sense to you at all? When you ask your spouse, kids, boss, or friends why they did something or why they think something, do they ever give you answers that make you begin to believe that they are complete idiots? Have you ever argued with someone and given him valid reasons as to why he is wrong and had him not change his mind? What can you conclude from all this? The other person was wrong, you pointed out to him that he was wrong, and he still ignored you. What was his problem? Was he hard of hearing or just plain stupid?"

"Sometimes I do, in fact, think that very thought!" I jokingly uttered.

"Do you agree with what goes on in the world? Do you ever read the newspaper or watch the news on television and wonder to yourself what the world is coming to? Do you ever wonder how the politicians who are supposed to be running things could be so stupid? You could straighten out the mess in a hurry, but no one will listen to you."

"Sometimes I actually get quite discouraged when I begin to really ponder those types of questions. I feel like I am a voice of reason crying in the wilderness." I responded.

"I'm sure that you feel that you are a prophet without honor in your own country and frequently in your own home or office. What is to be done? In a recent off Broadway play in New York a priest in a ghetto community proclaims that there are only three fundamental questions. These are: 'Who made the world?' 'How did it get so screwed up?' and 'What can we do about it?' All of us are well too aware at times that things are all screwed up, and we often wonder what can be done about it. If people would only listen to the voice of common sense. Why is communication so difficult? Really now, why are things so screwed up? To understand 'why' we need to understand the Decision People Pattern."

THE REAL DYNAMICS OF THE DECISION MAKING PROCESS

Shana noticed that I was anxiously awaiting more information, so she proceeded.

"Most people think that they make decisions based on logical reasons. If you ask people why they do things, they will tell you that they do things because they make sense to them. If you ask yourself 'Why you do what you do?', the answer will probably be 'because it makes sense'. People think that they are reasonable and that what they do makes sense. It does - to them. As we have seen, it may not make sense to someone else and certainly not to a philosopher or logician."

"How do we in fact make the hundreds of decisions that confront us daily?" I wanted to know.

WE DO THINGS FOR FOUR REASONS
It looks right
It sounds right
It feels right
It makes sense

"And why do we think that what we do makes sense? We have very little awareness of our decision making process. As we have said, in reality, we decide to do things on the basis of one and only one of four reasons: either it 1) looks right, 2) sounds right, 3) feels right, or 4) makes sense. When we do things because they look, sound or feel right, this makes sense to us. Sense to us, however, is not necessarily sense to someone else. Sense to the world is giving a deductive argument based on valid premises that lead to a necessary conclusion. There are some individuals in the world who indeed make decisions this way. They comprise less than 5% of the population, and they make some of the dumbest decisions imaginable."

People with makes sense filters do things in the name of sense that less reasonable people have the common sense not to do.

"Are you saying, then, that most people decide to do things because they either look right, sound right or feel right?" I queried.

"Exactly. But these people think that they are making sense. Why is this? It is because when things look right, sound right or feel right, they seem to be right, so we assume that they must indeed make sense. And they do, but not in the sense of logic and reason. Now bear with me as I go through the logical argument."

"That's what I have been waiting for." I said.

"As every logician knows, logic has to do with the formal structure of argument and not with the nature of the world. Logic says that if premises A and B are true, then it necessarily follows that C is true (or false). Logic has no way of determining whether A and B are true, however. The truth of A and B has to do with the way that the world is, and not with logic. It is possible for a statement to be logically true and experientially false, because it was based on a false premise that was assumed to be true. It is also possible for a statement to be logically false and experientially true, because it was based on the incorrect assumption that some premise was true or false. So logic is limited to the formal structure of argument. We still have to check to see if the premises are true. How do we do this? The most common way is to use a method of correspondence. Do you follow me thus far?"

"Yes. Please go on."

"We say that a statement is true if it corresponds to the way that the world is. And how do we know this? Because it looks right, feels right, sounds right or makes sense. The end result is that in our minds we often translate these sensory representations into the notion of making sense. What is 'sense' in this sense? It is a remembered feeling."

"So what do we actually mean when we say that we decide things or do things, because they look right, sound right, feel right or make sense?" I wanted to know.

"We call the process through which a person goes about deciding something a *'strategy'*. Deciding is a process of generating possible alternatives, gathering data on these alternatives and evaluating them to decide which one is best. Fortunately, this whole process occurs outside of our conscious awareness, so we do not have to think about it. A decision strategy has five parts."

PARTS OF A STRATEGY
Trigger
Operation
Test
Decision point
Outcome

" First, is the trigger which is some internal or external event that tells us that we have a decision facing us. Second is the operation through which we generate various possible solutions and gather data about these possibilities. We represent the various possibilities either as a picture or a sound or a feeling or a list of criteria."

"The third and most critical part of a decision making strategy is the test. The test is always a comparison. We compare the picture, sound, feeling, or list that we are using to represent the alternatives to some internal picture, feeling, sound or list that we already have in our head. These internal pictures, sounds, feelings, and lists are constructed by us and represent what is most uniquely us. These differ from one person to another and change as our experience changes over time. We call these ideal pictures, sounds, feelings, and lists *values*. Are you with me thus far?" Shana asked.

"So far so good. This is great stuff". I wanted more.

"When we say that something looks right, sounds right, feels right or makes sense, what we actually mean is that the way in which we are representing it, matches some ideal picture, sound, feeling, or list we have in our head. The fourth part of a decision strategy is the decision point which tells us whether we have a match or not. If we have a match then we make the decision. If we do not have a match, then we generate another alternative or gather more data about the one we are considering or in some cases, we simply lower our standards and settle for less. The fifth and final part of the strategy is the outcome which is the decision that you have just made."

"Where do our senses fit into all of this?" I asked.

"The only data that we can gather about the world comes in through our senses. Our primary senses are visual, auditory, kinesthetic, olfactory and gustatory. We store the data that we gather about the world as pictures, sounds, feelings, smells and tastes. We also have the ability to construct pictures, sounds and to a lesser extent feelings, smells, and tastes (at least in Western cultures). These constructions may be made up of combinations of remembered elements or they may represent something new. They are the source of all creativity. Some of the most important of these constructions are the ones that we use to generate possibilities."

"So a looks right decision corresponds to a visual picture in our heads?" I asked.

"Yes. If we happen to have a looks right decision making strategy, what we are doing, in essence, is creating a visual representation in our minds of each of the alternatives, and then comparing those pictures to the ideal picture in our mind of the thing about which we are deciding. When they match, we in turn, experience an internal sensation which we translate as making sense, even though in reality it is a feeling. Actually, the situation is slightly more complicated, and what we actually compare are certain characteristics of the pictures. We will go into this in greater detail in another training session."

"What about a sounds right person?" I asked.

"If you are a sounds right person, the principle is the same, except that in this case, you make an internal or external auditory representation of what each alternative sounds like and compare this to an ideal sound in your head. If the two match, the sounds right person also ends up with an internal sensation of making sense." Shana went on.

"Remember that the particular internal sensation created by the match, i.e. by the decision making sense, is experienced differently from one individual to another. The end result, however, is always the same: the person translates the decision as making sense. Likewise with the feels right person. He, in fact, compares an ideal internal representation of what feels right to the feeling associated with each of the alternatives. This can be a slow and cumbersome process if there are several alternatives to evaluate. If they match, once again the makes sense feeling confirms the decision as a right one."

"I guess what's left is a person who actually makes decisions on something making sense. Now that will seem the exception rather than the rule to me." I declared.

"Yes, finally, the person who really does make decisions based on sense, sidesteps the internal sensations, pictures, and sounds. Instead of dealing with experience directly they deal with it derivatively through words and symbols. First is the outside event. Second is the impact of that event on the nervous system via the senses. This is experienced visually, auditorially, kinesthetically, olfactorily and gustatorily. Third is the linguistic response in which we translate the experience into words. The makes sense decision maker focuses on the linguistic response rather than on the direct experience. In making decisions he constructs a list of linguistic criteria. He then compares the various alternatives to his ideal list. Whichever of the alternatives best matches his ideal list is the one that he says makes sense."

"All of this really does make sense to me now." I said, not deliberately trying to be clever.

"In each of the four cases, though, we end up with a match. When this match occurs we say that the decision makes sense. Although this feeling of a match is an internal sensation, the exact nature of that internal sensation will vary from one person to another. The end result is still the experienced feeling of something making sense."   Shana continued without waiting for comments or questions.

"Ironically, although we have successfully encoded the various sensory representations internally, allowing for easy and direct access, somehow along the way, we inadvertently bypass the direct link and use an intermediary interpreter in its place to decode the message. That final message relayed to us is that of making sense."

IMPORTANCE OF DECISION PATTERN - INFLUENCING OTHERS

"At least now I understand the meaning of the name 'Decision Pattern'." I declared.

"Yes. Quite an appropriate name for this People Pattern, the Decision Pattern. Why is an understanding of the Decision People Pattern so helpful? In all facets of our daily experience in the course of our multitudinous interactions with people, it is critically important to know whether a person is doing something because it looks right, sounds right, feels right or makes sense, because this provides us with the key as to how to influence that person. A grasp of this People Pattern will be a great step on the road to understanding others, and in so doing, facilitating communication with that individual. Knowing how a person makes decisions enables us to better persuade that person by entering into his reality and providing the necessary sensory stimulus that is required to impact his world view. Thus, a mastery of this People Pattern will help you influence others in their decisions in all contexts of life."

UNIVERSAL MISCONCEPTION ABOUT DECISION MAKING

"As I keep emphasizing, in general, people do not make sense; they simply think that they do. We have been programmed in society to think that what we do makes sense. Either something makes sense, or it doesn't How many times have you heard the catch all phrase 'That doesn't make sense' in response to something you are saying or doing? More often than not, the person, outside of his conscious awareness is making the remark not because it actually makes sense, but because it looks right, sounds right or feels right. Most people do not realize the drawbacks and limitations of the notion 'makes sense'".

"And making sense has become such an acceptable practice and part of institutionalized convention," I said.

"Yes, and because of this fact we assume that decisions are always made based on their making sense. In actuality, we usually make decisions based on looks right, sounds right, and feels right, and in our need to justify these decisions to others, whether to a spouse, boss, colleague, or whomever, we then attempt to make sense of the sensory representations we create. Think about it. Unless they've had this explained to them, the average person will think you are absolutely insane or else totally off the wall if you tell them, for example, that you just bought a new home because it felt right or sounded right!" Shana was again anxious to finish up this topic, so I did not interrupt.

"If the decision somehow does not meet the criterion of making sense as deemed admissible by convention, somehow it simply cannot be a valid decision. Imagine an important leader deciding to pass major legislation, or deciding to deploy troops in one of the many political hot spots of the world today, and specifically upholding and justifying his decision based on it looking right, sounding right or feeling right. Public reaction would put him in the loony bin. The decision may be brilliant and absolutely the right thing to do, but the decision maker will be attacked for his reasons. It would be far better to focus on the decision than arguing over the reasoning behind it."

"Come to think about it, if a decision cannot be justified and explained with logical reasons, it will not be readily accepted as rational and sound." I said.

"You are so right. In other words, it does not make sense, and therefore cannot be a valid, sensible decision. We make decisions based on looks right, sounds right, feels right, and in our need to justify these decisions to others, whether to a spouse, boss, colleague, or whomever, we then attempt to make sense of them. We have already seen where this approach leads."

"We need to understand the dynamics of decision making. Whenever someone makes a decision we first need to find out if it looks right, feels right, sounds right, or makes sense, and then we need to find out what picture, sound or feeling they are using as a basis of evaluation. Great leaders make brilliant decisions and order that they be carried out. It is when the leader is asked to justify them that the problem arises."

We would be better off evaluating a person's track record than their after-the-fact rationalizations. This will provide us a far better measure of their decision making ability than an analysis of their reasoning. It is far more important to do the right thing for the wrong reasons than to do the wrong thing for the right reasons."

THE FOUR DECISION PATTERNS

"So if people make decisions based on looks right, sounds right, feels right or makes sense, how do they know that they are doing this?" I wanted to know.

"What they are in fact doing is creating an internal sensory representation corresponding to one of the Decision Patterns, and encoded accordingly. Whatever the internal representation, it is usually outside of the person's conscious awareness. This applies to both the encoding and decoding of the final message. As you know, we have special people here at Success, Incorporated called behavioral modelers who specialize in the encoding and decoding of these internal messages. Just what are the sensory representations comprising the Decision People Pattern which are the foundation of all of our decisions? They will either be pictures, sounds or feelings used as our personal gauge in making the decision. This personal gauge acts as a customized decoder of the stimuli coming in from all around us."

"For the looks right people, it takes the form of a *picture*: People who make decisions based on the 'looks right' principle are actually creating a picture or image in their minds which literally looks right to them. The key for looks right people will be the visual aspects of a situation or thing that will be most important to them. They will be attracted to how things look, and will like to have graphic material that they can see. They will make decisions based on the external picture corresponding as closely as possible to their ideal internal image or representation. If there is a match between the internal picture created in the mind and the visible external picture, we are on track and the decision is go. If the two pictures for whatever reason do not correspond, than we put up the red light." I simply had to interrupt here to let her know that I was aware of my own pattern.

"That's me isn't it?" I queried.

"In fact, yes it is. It didn't take you long to grasp this." Shana was obviously pleased as she continued to explain the pattern.

"For the sounds right person, the internal representation takes the form of a *sound*: Those who decide to do things based on the 'sounds right' principle are, in fact, making an internal auditory representation in the form of sounds or words which literally sound right to them. Sounds right people will be focusing their attention on the auditory components of any situation. They will be interested in hearing about things and how things sound. The various characteristics of voice, whether pitch, volume, tone, timbre, and tempo will be the elements the sounds right person literally tunes into. The way things sound will be the crucial factor in leading them to making a decision. The auditory component may be their own voice, or that of someone else, or a song or even a particular sound, all of which will depend on what decision they are making and what elements are involved in that decision. In any case, the way things sound will be the crucial factor in leading them to making a decision."

"This sounds great!" I said, this time trying to be funny with no success.

"For the feels right person, the internal sensory representation takes the form of a *feeling*. This feeling is a sensation in a given part of their body which literally feels right to them. Feels right people will be into doing things, moving around, experiencing movement and sensation in their bodies and literally feeling comfortable with their decisions. Making physical contact with others such as a tap on the shoulder or handshake will be important to them. They like to experience things and will want to move around and do and touch things."

"Here we are back to making sense again." I really was not trying to be annoying.

"Last but not least, for the makes sense person, the internal sensory representation takes the form of an internal remembered feeling which they call 'making sense'. These make sense people live in a decision world of reasons and data. They will usually have a checklist of criteria to be met before a choice is made. If the pre-conditions or standards are not met, you end up with a no go decision. It is as though the person has a simultaneous double checklist from which he can compare the corresponding elements for a fit or mismatch. How things look, sound or feel could not be farther from a make sense person's reality. All of his decisions are based solely on this internal remembered feeling which bypasses all of the other internal sensory circuits (if they have ever been encoded in the first place) and results in the feeling of something making sense."

IMPLICATIONS

"The implications of the Decision People Pattern are far reaching. If you think about the number of decisions both conscious and unconscious, trivial and significant, one makes on any given day, you can begin to understand and appreciate the importance of this People Pattern. Everything involves decisions from what time to get up in the morning, what coffee mug to use, what clothing to wear on any given day, what newspaper to read, what appointments to make, what to have for dinner, what recreation to engage in after work, what TV programs to watch, to what snacks to nibble on, and the list goes on and on."

"Obviously, like the other People Patterns discussed thus far, the Decision Pattern affects us in all aspects of our daily living, both personal and professional." I added.

"Yes, in everything from job choice to choice of spouse or mate, to sales and marketing, negotiations, hygiene and health, religion, politics, education, domestic issues and social issues."

DO YOU MAKE SENSE?

"In this day and age we are constantly bombarded with the written word in the form of newspaper articles, magazine articles, press releases, faxes, e-mail, web sites, and the like, all of which supposedly make sense. But do they really? Not particularly. What we have in reality are internal sensory representations in the form of pictures, sounds and feelings, all induced by the various guises of the written word." Shana proceeded to ask the following questions as guidelines for me to figure out my own strategies.

"Think a moment about reading the morning newspaper at breakfast or during your commute. First, upon reading this sentence, did you create a picture in your mind, or perhaps a sound or maybe you felt a particular sensation associated with reading the newspaper. The fact that you are doing any of this may very well be outside of your conscious awareness. Most of us are simply not accustomed to thinking along these lines." She continued to guide me with other questions.

"Now, think about reading a particular front page story today. Did what you read make sense (in your customary way) to you? How do you know that it made sense? Begin to notice whether you made an internal visual representation, an internal auditory representation, or an internal feeling or kinesthetic representation all of which lead within their particular circuit, to a remembered feeling of making sense. Or did you simply have a list of criteria or logical reasons which end up triggering the remembered feeling of making sense? Your answer to this question will open the door to a whole new level of understanding your decision making strategies."

DECISION
Picture
Sound
Feeling
List of reasons

"I know that I made an internal picture of that story." I responded.

"Good. Let us now zero in on some of the ways in which to identify a person's Decision People Pattern."

INDICATORS

I was anxious to know how to determine a person's Decision Pattern and to find out the target indicator questions. Shana continued.

"There are certain indicators of what a person's patterns are. The most important one is to listen to his language."

"What about his language?" I said. Shana smiled and continued.

"It is necessary to listen to the words that the person uses to describe his experience and particularly to the verbs, adjectives and adverbs. These refer to what in grammar is called the 'predicate' of a sentence. Looks right people in describing their decision use visual words like see, look, appear, view, watch, bright, clear, and focused. Sounds right people use auditory words like hear, tell, say, talk, speak, discuss, sing, tone, chime, and ring. Feels right people use kinesthetic words like feel, grasp, balance, resist, warm, smooth, soft, hard and firm. And makes sense people use unspecified predicates like think, understand, experience, learn, process, decide, motivate, conceive and demonstrate. By listening carefully to the words a person uses to describe his experience, you can learn how he represents that experience to himself internally. Also, listen to his tonality and rate of speech. Visual people tend to speak rapidly with a high tonality. At the opposite extreme kinesthetic people tend to talk slowly in lower tones. Auditory people speak with a rhythm and vary their tone. Makes sense people will tend to talk at a constant rate in a monotone. There are other indicators, but you need to master these first."

"I can see that I have my work cut out for me. What about the prayers for each type."

PRAYERS

"The prayers are as follows. The Looks Right Prayer is:"

O God of Splendorous Beauty Who sees all, Creator of the wondrous Universe, Father of the sparkling stars, Master of the Radiant Dawn, please make this day full of light and beauty. Give me this day the sight to appreciate the glory of nature's grandeur. Allow me to perceive the shimmering rays from Heaven above to guide me through hours of darkness, come they may. Deliver me from all that is unpleasant to behold or from that which is drab and dismal. And please allow me to live in beautiful surroundings that will always inspire me to make the appropriate decisions in life. Most of all, allow me to see beauty in all of Thy Creations. Amen.

"The Sounds Right Prayer is:"

Almighty God, All Powerful Voice, Orchestrator of the Universe and Harmonious Source of the Eternal Music of the Spheres, allow me to hear the sounds of Thy grandiose creations. Give me this day the ears to hear the melodious chords of Thy comforting Voice and to discern the sounds of right from wrong. Deliver me from the discordant clamor of man, and particularly from those who would make my day miserable by yelling and screaming or by blasting their loud music in front of my delicate ears. And please, dear Lord, please allow me to hear always a positive inner voice along with Thy inspirational tones to guide me along the road of life. Amen.

"The Feels Right Prayer is:"

O Loving God, All Forgiving of man, please allow me to feel deep within myself the glory of all Thy creations. Give me this day the positive and uplifting feelings which will carry me through the daily trials of life. Allow me to feel at all times the intensity of Thy Love. Deliver me from those who are unfeeling and who lack compassion toward others. Surround me with those who might touch my deepest feelings and who will share the joy of the human connection. And please, sensitive Lord, please make my life as comfortable as possible. Fill my life with caring people and let me live in soothing, supporting surroundings so that I can be steered in the right direction. Amen.

"And the Makes Sense Prayer is:"

O All Knowing God, Divine Intelligence, please give me the knowledge to make decisions which make sense. Give me this day the information I need to know how to proceed whenever I need to make a decision. Please share Thy Divine Wisdom with the unenlightened here on earth. Give me the awareness to know the consequences of what I do. Deliver me from the ignorant and from those who reject learning. Provide me always with enough data and statistics about relevant matters so that I will always know what and why throughout life. And, please, Brilliant Divine Creator, pass on some of Thy Erudition to some of us down below who need quality information to make the right decisions. Amen.

MANAGEMENT : WHY EVERYONE THINKS THAT HIS BOSS IS AN IDIOT

Marvin was in rare form when I arrived. He began with an intriguing question.

"First, let's get something straight. Have you ever thought that your boss (present or past) was an idiot? Be honest now."

"With all that I'm learning I could hardly think that!" I responded with great enthusiasm in my voice.

"Then what about your spouse, your kids or your parents? Have you ever thought that they were idiots? Yes, you have. How is it possible that you have a friend who is an idiot, or that you raised your kid to be an idiot or that you work for a boss who is an idiot? The reason is simple. You are about to learn the single most important lesson that you will ever learn in your entire life about communication. It will explain why 99% of all attempts to persuade someone else to do something are a total and absolute waste of time!"

"All of this is really quite amusing when put that way?" I said.

"Every human being on the planet does what he does for one and only one of four reasons. They do things because they: 1) look right, 2) sound right, 3) feel right, or 4) make sense. Almost everybody does things for the first three reasons, and almost no one does things for the last reason! Yet, an amazing thing has happened. The make sense people have managed to take over control of communication in the world, and they did it with one simple word. That word is 'why'. Let us see how this works."

"Suppose your boss or spouse decides to do something. Being a conscientious and dedicated employee or spouse, you are never content to do something just because someone tells you to do it, so, of course, you use the magic word and ask 'why'. This is where the fun begins. 'Why?' is a request for what? It is a request for reasons and logic. But, of course, people do not normally do things for reasons or logic. Everyone knows that most people are neither logical nor reasonable! Most people do things because they either look, sound or feel right. But they cannot tell you that why they did what they did is because it just looked right or felt right or sounded right. After all, you might think that they were an idiot."

"So why did they do it?" I asked, at least now knowing the response.

"They did it because it looked, sounded or felt right, but they cannot tell you this. So what do they do? They make up reasons, of course! These reasons have nothing to do with why they actually did it. They are rationalizations after the fact. They are an attempt to make sense out of something that never made sense in the first place. They are an effort to get you to stop asking that annoying (and, as we will see, stupid) question 'why'."

"So what do you do when they give you their reasons in response to your question?" I said.

"You certainly don't say 'wonderful' and let it go at that. Not a chance. Their reasons were unreasonable. Their rationale did not make sense. Any idiot can see that. So being a conscientious and dedicated employee or spouse, what do you do? You point out the errors in their reasons, of course. You explain patiently why what they just said makes no sense. After all, you have their best interest at heart. You merely want to lend a helping hand, because you really care about them and want them to avoid making a stupid mistake that they will later regret."

"And what inevitably happens. Does the person thank you for pointing out the errors in his reasoning? Not a chance! He insists on being right. Or if he is particularly generous, he may give you another reason. If the first reason was no good, the odds are that the second reason will be even worse. So, in exasperation, you point out the errors in his second set of reasons. At this point, even the most magnanimous boss or spouse throws up his or her hands in despair and says that he or she is the boss and that is the way that it is. So, what conclusion are you left to draw? The only possible logical conclusion that you can draw is that your boss or spouse is an idiot. Because not once, but twice, you pointed out the error in his or her reasoning, and he or she insisted that he or she was right anyway."

I fortunately understood and appreciated Marvin's great sense of humor, so I found this entire argument about idiots quite amusing and appropriate given the nature of the explanation. I am sure that some people would not grasp the humor at all, however.

"It's not that bad. Listen well. This is the second most important lesson that you will learn in your entire life about communication. What I am about to say may seem strange."

If you really want to get people to change their minds, then you have to get them to change the pictures in their heads, or the way in which they talk to themselves or the feelings in their bodies!

"Moreover, the way you do this does not involve logic and reason. Most people do things because they either look right, sound right or feel right. So to actually get them to change, it is necessary to get them to change their pictures, sounds or feelings."

"How do I do this?" I asked.

"To appeal to the looks right person, paint a word picture. Tell visual stories and use visual metaphors. Use graphic visual language and speak rapidly. Describe how you think that things should look and observe the person's response. Looks right people make pictures by looking up or by defocusing their eyes. Invite them to picture what you are describing, and keep adjusting the picture until you get the response that you want. Have the person change both the form and the content of his picture.   He can change the content by making another picture with different content. He can change the form of his picture by maintaining the same content but changing some parameters of the picture such as its size, distance, focus or brightness."

"To appeal to a sounds right person, speak to him in a pleasant tonality and make your voice sound like music to his ears. Describe how you think that things should sound. Be poetic and allow your voice to sing. The person will listen to himself with his eyes on a level to the left or to the right. Vary your voice and your verbal description until you get the response that you want."

"To appeal to the feels right person, get his emotions involved. Speak to him slowly and appeal to his feelings. Tell stories or use metaphors that are designed to elicit a feeling response. Feels right people will look down to the side when accessing their feelings. Tell the person how you want him to feel. Feels right people are slower to reach decisions, because it takes time for feelings to grow. Let the feels right person take whatever time he needs while you continue to work to steer him to the desired state which produces the response that you want."

"Of course! Why didn't I think of that?" I said.

"Master communicators have always known this. There has always been a conflict between rhetoric and logic. Plato attacked the sophists who had the ears of the people. The logicians have always complained about human gullibility. They have always known that most human beings are, according to the logicians' own standards, unreasonable. Philosophers even coined a special name for the masses of humanity. They referred to them simply as 'the vulgar'. The 'vulgar' are simply those who did not share the philosophers love of reason. The logicians have always lamented the fact that human beings were swayed more by sentiment than by reason. They saw this as the greatest human failing."

"That's the story of mankind." I interjected.

"They chose to be, in their eyes, right rather than to be effective. They failed to appreciate the glory of man. They failed to understand the true wonder of the human intellect. By focusing on a narrow corner of man's capabilities, they blinded themselves to the incredible scope of the human intellect. In their intellectual arrogance and desire to be right, they ignored the fact that there are many paths to truth and that reason is but only one of them. They understood that there was something greater than reason. They called it wisdom. Unfortunately, in their love affair with words, they failed to grasp that true wisdom and insight more often comes in the form of a vision or a voice or a feeling than in the form of a tedious and involved argument."

"Reason is important, however." I said with conviction.

"Indeed. Make no mistake - reason is very important. But it is not all that it is made out to be. There are other paths to wisdom, and the truly effective communicator is the master of all paths. Let us explore these other paths more fully and see how they apply in all that we do. In doing so, we will discover that the only real idiots are those who lack the flexibility to vary their communication until they get the response that they want. The only real idiots are those who insist that reason is the only path to truth. The only real idiots are those who lack the wisdom to sway the human heart. The only real idiots are those who fail to see the vision, or to hear the truth resonating deep inside, or to feel the feeling of certitude coursing through their bodies."

Marvin finished his soliloquy and sent me off to sales.

BUYING STRATEGIES

Michael was excited to see me and greeted me warmly.

"As we both know, we live in a consumer oriented society even though recessionary years can put a damper on big spending from time to time. If people can't afford large ticket items, they still can afford smaller ticket items. In addition, in order to function in life we all need to buy staple items on a regular basis, such as food and toiletry items. In short, we all buy things at some point. The question is how do we decide what to buy? Why do we buy one brand rather than another?" Before I could attempt to answer the question, Michael's voice resumed in an authoritative tonality.

"Let us now consider buying strategies in light of the Decision Pattern. As we've said, a large portion of our everyday living revolves around consumerism. How is it that we decide to buy whatever it is we need or want or fancy? Each one of us ends up buying some items fairly regularly, such as a loaf of bread or quart of milk, and buying other items less often such as large ticket items like a car or even a house. No matter what the item purchased, we all have our own personalized means of making the decision to buy the product or item in question."

"Given how many decisions we need to make on a daily basis nowadays, knowing this is so incredibly helpful and enlightening!" I said, thinking out loud.

"Yes, for sure. You often hear that times have changed, that in the good old days everything seemed so much easier and less complex. Even going out to the grocery store and buying edibles and provisions nowadays can be somewhat perplexing. It used to be that buying a simple quart of orange juice or milk was a relatively uncomplicated matter. These days, with the variety of different brands as well as different kinds of milk and juice which cater to the various dietary needs and the whims of our fellow citizens, more factors enter into play than ever before when it comes to making the final decision as to what to buy." Michael was right on my wave length every time I made a comment. It is as though he could literally see my thoughts. I came to realize that a solid knowledge of these People Patterns allowed one a special look into another person's world.

"How, in fact, do we make the decision as to what to buy?" he went on. "Like all other decisions, we make it by means of our particular Decision Pattern. Even with banal things, we each nevertheless make buying decisions in one, and only one of four ways: it either looks right, sounds right, feels right or makes sense. The same applies to everything, whether valuable, extravagant, costly items, or basic, inexpensive, trivial or bargain articles."

"What about buying something of great import in one's life?" I was curious to know.

"All right. Let us consider something on the high end of the shopping scale. Most people have been in the market to buy a home at some point in their lives. How do you think people end up writing a check for one particular home among the many they have looked at? Unbeknownst to them, this choice of where to spend their life is based on one, and only one thing - the decision is based on their Decision Pattern." I wanted him to continue so I did not say anything.

"Those with looks right strategies end up purchasing one house or apartment over another based literally on a pictorial representation made in their minds of what that house should look like. Does it look right? If it fits their visual expectation, their personal ideal of what the right house looks like, they will buy that house. The mental picture of the house that looks right triggers their decision to buy it. If the mental representation does not coincide with the close to perfect image, chances are the deal will fall through."

"That sounds like me again." I said.

"You've got it. For visual buyers the aesthetic aspect, i.e., the visual components, will take precedence over other factors. If the prospective buyer has a looks right Decision People Pattern, he probably will have a fairly clear picture in his mind of the ideal house. He may, for example, have his heart set on a sprawling red brick, four bedroom ranch with a three car garage, and a particularly large family room off the eating area. If the homes on the market do not look right, i.e. do not literally fit the picture, the looks right buyer will probably not want to waste time looking at them. If the realtor shows him houses that do not match the picture (as with fewer than four bedrooms or a two car garage), the chances are much slimmer that the prospective buyer will take the property."

"When I think about my looks right strategies, I now realize just how important first impressions are to me. That is precisely what happened when we bought our first house." I was delighted that I could picture all of this in terms of my own buying strategies.

"That first impression really does leave its mark. Remember that the initial visual impression takes on even more significance with a looks right person. If he drives up to a white colonial house with columns and expects to see a brick ranch, you had might as well forget it. The looks right person will be immediately turned off by what he first sees if it does not correspond at the outset to his internal picture of what the house is to look like. The picture in front of his eyes, i.e. the house he sees simply does not look right. If upon entering, the inside matches his expectation, then there is still a chance for a sale. The sounds right, feels right, or makes sense person will at least be interested in other factors besides the initial visual impression. The latter will enter the home with an open mind (unless other things relating to their Decision People Pattern get in the way, and we will touch on these later)."

"I am sure that appearance really counts for me." I quickly interjected.

"I am not surprised." Michael responded. "The first thing that the looks right buyer will consider will be the overall appearance (inside and out) of the house. Cleanliness will be particularly important to them. They want the house to look good. A looks right buyer will want the house to be neat and clean. Remember appearances mean a lot to the looks right person, so if a looks right buyer walks into a messy, disorderly home that is for sale, it is highly unlikely that he will leave with a good impression of that home, or of the seller for that matter."

As he smiled at me he confirmed exactly what I had been thinking about my own reactions to home buying. "The looks right buyer", he said, "is more likely to do the finger test for dust than the other Decision Patterns, and will also pay more attention to the layout and decor, always with the thought in mind that it does or does not 'look right'! Are the rooms laid out in a way that corresponds to that internal visual picture? Does the kitchen fit the picture? What about the backyard? (Remember that one's Primary Interest Pattern will determine what things the buyer will pay most attention to in this picture, and in general will affect what elements take precedence within the sounds right, feels right and makes sense Decision Patterns as well.) The physical appearance and layout of the house is literally only part of the picture."

"The person showing the property, whether the seller or the realtor, had better make sure that he, too, has a 'good presentation'." he added. "He had better 'look right' to the seller. If either of them appears unkempt, closing the deal becomes even more of a challenge. To someone with another Decision Pattern, such details will appear to be totally ludicrous. Again, how is it possible to be such an idiot when it comes to buying such an important thing as a house! Since about 40% of the population makes decisions based on the looks right Decision People Pattern, realtors and sellers need to take heed, and begin targeting the buyer market appropriately. The likelihood of increasing one's sales will be measurably enhanced when this knowledge is put to proper use."

"I can't believe all that goes on in my head as a looks right decision maker. I'll certainly be noticing a lot more about how I make decisions. Here all of this time, I fell into the trap of thinking that my decisions were made on the basis of them making sense. What did I know?" I uttered with welcome relief.

"Let us now turn to the sounds right pattern. The sounds right person is a far cry from a dime a dozen, although there are some albeit rare individuals who will buy based on this people pattern. Approximately 5% to 10% of society fits into this category. When it comes to buying a home, the person with a sounds right buying strategy will be more in tune with the sounds, noises, and voices associated with the purchase of a particular home. Does it literally sound right? His focus will be on how things sound, rather than on what they look like. The tone of voice of the realtor or of the seller and anyone related to the deal will take on great significance, factors which seem totally incomprehensible to those without a sounds right decision strategy."

"So what does one need to know if selling to someone like that?" I queried.

"If you are selling a house to a sounds right person, what could you do to play up to his particular strategy? First, make sure you (the realtor or seller) speak to the buyer in a pleasant tone of voice. Avoid yelling or shouting, or whispering, since sounds right people are particularly sensitive to extreme volume levels on both ends of the scale. Sounds right people also often have a seemingly uncanny ability to detect deception and they will pick up on any incongruity on the part of the agent or seller."

Michael then talked about music, which is something I would not have considered. "Also, playing pleasant music in the background could enhance chances of selling a particular property. Try to find out what their favorite piece of music is, and discretely play it in the background. If your kids are fond of blasting the stereo or TV at an ear shattering volume, have them refrain from doing so during the buyer's visit. And the sounds (traffic noise, air conditioning units humming, birds chirping, trees swaying, etc.) in and around the house will bear heavily on the decision of the sounds right buyer, since he will pick up on sounds that are normally ignored by others. If you have noisy neighbors, pray that they will be gone during the visit."

"So if there are creaks in the house, that would turn off the sounds right person?" I asked now knowing what the response would be.

" For certain. Do not count on a sale if the doors stick or slam shut, or if there is any disruptive sound that starts up. That noise gets recorded in stereophonic sound in the sounds right buyer's mind, and he will not forget it! If the prospective sounds right buyer happens to turn on a faucet which creates a clamor in the pipes, he may well decide against a house which otherwise may have appealed to him. Make sure that the bedrooms are quiet. A sounds right person will be more susceptible than most to even what seems to be imperceptible sounds such as traffic. Moreover, if you live near a highway, make a point of blotting out somehow the clamor of passing vehicles. Leave the clock radio on to a lite music station. Make sure that floors do not squeak, or that loose floor beams do not cause displayed items to shake when you walk across a room. Once again, such details may seem trivial to someone with another Decision People Pattern, but if a non sounds right person refuses to play along, he may lose out on a major sale. We had an associate who was on the verge of selling his house when a train went by several hundred yards away, and the buyer backed out of the deal."

"I realize now that one of my best friends is a sounds right person. Until today, I could never understand how he decided to buy almost anything." I could now use this information in dealing with my own personal entourage, which pleased me greatly.

"What about the person with a feels right Decision Pattern? Unlike the sounds right person, he will not concentrate his attention on sounds. Unlike the looks right person, he will not be focused on how things look. On the contrary, a feels right buyer will want to literally feel comfortable in the home. Remember it specifically needs to feel right to him. What can he do to get that feeling? He will want to try out appliances, open/shut windows and doors, touch walls, turn on faucets, flush toilets, etc., anything that entails getting a feel for the house."

"My wife did that when we bought our home." I discovered with pleasure.

"Make sure that the temperature in the house is comfortable when showing it to feels right buyers. Try to find out in advance whether the person prefers temperatures on the cold or warm side. If your prospective buyer feels more comfortable in warm rooms, make certain that the thermostat is set appropriately. Likewise, if you are in the throes of a hot, sticky summer, be sure the air conditioning is on high. The reverse, obviously is true for one who prefers warmth."

"Yes. My wife would always remark about the temperature in the homes we would visit."

"That is typical of a feels right person. Also, keep the feels right buyer actively doing. For example, rather than show features off to the buyer through demonstration (which would work better with a looks right person), have him get involved and doing things. Have him turn buttons and switches, feel textures in and around the house — wood paneling, marble, drywall, wallpaper, carpeting, whatever. The feels right buyer is also usually fairly sensitive to odors. (One can't underestimate the power of the olfactory mode in most humans in general. Why do you think that fragrances translate into a multi billion dollar industry around the globe? Research has shown, meanwhile, that the positive smell of something associated with one's childhood acts as an indirect catalyzer of a decision. In the case of real estate, homes are sold more easily with the delicious odor of bread baking in the oven.) Make sure that things smell good. To entice a feels right buyer pop a loaf of bread in the oven, and offer him a cup of cider in an easy chair in front of a warm fireplace."

"All of this will probably seem insane and idiotic to the looks right person since I find it crazy." I added.

"You are correct. And it also seems insane and crazy to the sounds right person and particularly to the make sense person. It is hard to understand how something can feel right in the decision making context if you have another Decision Pattern. Meanwhile, for those in the feels right world of decision making, the visual aspect, the sounds associated with the home, or the make sense list are completely off track."

"All of this really does make sense, and as you are talking I have managed to create great pictures in my mind." I said with a smile.

"And, of course, you didn't consider the temperature in this room during all of this! For a looks right buyer like you comfort translates into a visual picture." Michael said with a change of tonality in his voice. "Although a secondary factor for those like you, comfort is the key for the feels right person. The whole thing just needs to feel right to him; and of, course, the elements which feel right will vary from one person to another. Again, one's Primary Interest Pattern will greatly affect what elements of the house and its surroundings are to take on significance for the prospective buyer."

"I can imagine this driving real estate agents with different Decision Patterns totally crazy!" I said.

"It really can be an amusing scenario. A real estate agent may be driven crazy by a feels right buyer. The agent will ask the buyer for a description of the house they want. The feels right buyer will describe the house. The real estate agent will take them to a house that matches their external description and they will stand in the living room or yard and say that it just does not feel right. A knowledgeable agent will, at this point, begin to focus on feelings and comfort, rather than on the usual appearance. What to a visual buyer may seem messy and tacky to a feels right buyer may seem comfortable and homey."

"I guess that leaves the most curious one of all: the makes sense buyer." I was anxious to hear about this type of person.

"Last but not least, the makes sense person takes again another totally different approach to buying a home. If the makes sense person does not place greatest emphasis on how the house looks, or sounds, or feels, how then does he make the decision to buy it or not? The makes sense person will make up a list of the characteristics that he wants in a house and will evaluate each house against this check list. He will want to know a lot of details concerning the house before he will make a purchase."

"It must be a challenge to deal with this type of buyer?" I asked.

"It certainly can be especially when the real estate agent has no clue as to the Decision Pattern in question. When dealing with a makes sense buyer, a real estate agent should be prepared to answer lots of questions, which may or may not seem relevant to a person with a different Decision People Pattern. The more knowledgeable you appear, the better the impression you will have on the makes sense buyer. Especially avoid asking them how it looks to them, or how they feel about the house. These are meaningless and often deadly questions to makes sense people. Instead, provide them with facts and reasons as to why buying the house is such a wonderful idea. Give them as many reasons as you can." Michael continued.

"It would be very helpful to know the kinds of issues of import to the makes sense buyer. Try to find out the list of criteria his ideal house must meet, and perhaps you can propose doing certain things to the house that may attract his interest. The makes sense buyer will love reading material about the house, so the more data that the agent can provide the better. Ironically, a house may not look so good in the eyes of a person with another Decision Pattern, but the purchase may make sense for whatever reasons in the mind of that makes sense person so he ends up buying it."

After all of this, I still did not know Michael's buying strategy. I figured that the revelation would come at some point.

INAPPROPRIATE BUYING STRATEGIES

I was ready for a quick review, and I got exactly what I asked for. Michael began.

"As we have emphasized, people buy for four different reasons. Some buying strategies are more appropriate for buying certain items than others. Obviously when buying visual, auditory or kinesthetic items it is more appropriate to evaluate them in terms of the corresponding criteria. There are many classic examples where this does not happen. Some buying decisions are quite amusing when analyzed in light of the Decision Pattern, and seem to make no sense at all!"

"Yes, like the way friends who don't have looks right patterns buy things!" I said jokingly.

"Take, for example the way people buy stereo equipment. As bizarre and extraordinary as it may seem, for most people, the bottom line reason that they bought their stereo was because it looked right. Imagine buying stereo equipment because of the way it looks rather than based on the sound quality of the equipment! Yet this is often the case. You certainly do not want looks right people to buy your sound systems for you, since they will be primarily concerned with the color of the equipment, the shape and how it fits in with the rest of the room."

"Like I want it to look right in the room and fit in with everything else." I said.

"Precisely. This is not the ideal strategy for such purchases, is it? Who cares how it sounds? Why should that matter as long as it works well in the context of the room? Actually, most visual people can't tell the difference between a high and medium fidelity stereo anyway, so the sound quality does not really matter that much. They may not have the best fidelity equipment (but if they can't hear it, it does not matter to them), but at least it looks good." I finally realized that he had the same Decision Pattern as I did.

"There are countless cases," he continued, "where people with one pattern apply it in all contexts and often inappropriately. It is well known that telephone sales operators are often hired on the basis of appearance rather than on their telephone voice. Also, people often buy clothes or furniture that are uncomfortable because they look good, or clothes or furniture that look terrible because they are comfortable. The list goes on and on."

"Now that we have spent so much time on buying strategies, let us discuss how this relates to product sales."

SALES

"Let us look more closely now at the implications of this Decision People Pattern in sales. How would you tailor your sales approach with each of the four Decision People Patterns: looks right, sounds right, feels right and makes sense." It was obvious that Michael knew what my pattern was in this realm, because everything was made to look tidy and coordinated in the room.

"First, let us go over the looks right sales presentation: Considering you will be face to face with a looks right person i.e., a person who will make his decision based on it looking right, it will be to your advantage to make sure that you look good for the sales presentation. Think about how many times, perhaps, you ended up not buying a product in a store, because you did not like the looks of the salesperson. The right look, of course, will vary for individual looks right buyers."

"I can tell you that this has happened more than once in my life." I quipped.

"More than you can probably count!" Michael said with a knowing glance at me.

"You won't have trouble putting yourself in the other person's shoes with this pattern. Remember that a seller needs to make a conscious effort to look more than presentable. The stereotypical car salesperson look is definitely out. Wear clean, pressed clothing and make sure your hair is clean and your shoes are polished. In short, your overall impression needs to be very good even before you begin your dialogue. If the looks right buyer has a favorable view from the start, you have enhanced your chances of selling them your product or service. A looks right buyer will certainly not look well upon a scruffy, unkempt salesperson. Even color coordination, or shall we say lack of it, trivial as it may seem to others, can mean the subtle difference between a sale or not with a looks right person."

"You have basically summarized what goes through my mind!" I revealed.

"All of these factors take on magnified significance in the realm of fashion. How many looks right buyers out there would be inspired to buy clothing from someone who himself is not put together very well. We call it the 'who did it and ran look'. Not only is the person's appearance consequential, but so is the environment in which he is selling as well. Try to arrange the meeting in pleasant surroundings that are colorful, neat and clean."

Since I had no comments, Michael continued.

"As for the actual sales approach, be sure to be equipped with photographs or visual descriptions of your product or service. Slides, videos, drawings, and whatever other graphic material you can put together will help you immeasurably with the looks right person. Without supporting graphic material you end up meeting the buyer just half way, if that much. Moreover, it would be to your advantage to have color material, rather than black and white, and to have clear, large photographs. Colors are also important to the visual buyer. The three favorite colors of people with incomes over $100,000.00 a year are IBM blue, hunter green (the color of money), and dove gray. Gold and silver are also good colors. There is a whole science to color which we will not get into right now. In any case, obviously someone up in the ranks at United Airlines knows something about this, as the company changed its colors from its traditional orange-red, white and blue to gray, blue, red, indigo and amber (the colors of the world according to United). They launched a whole new advertising campaign based on these 'bold new colors of the friendly skies' which are supposedly reminiscent of different places around the globe to which they fly ('the boundless blue of a Paris morning', 'the solid grey of Wall Street', 'the radiant reds of an Australian sunset', etc.) This type of bright, colorful sell is ideal for the looks right person."

I continued to be amazed at how accurate this information was, given what I knew about myself and others like me with a similar Decision Pattern, but I did not interrupt at this point.

"Visual buyers need to actually see the product or result of your service. Particularly if dealing with a service, let's say, wood refinishing, then take the potential buyer to see actual work done in person. If you are selling them clothing, then get them into the clothing. We have a friend who is one of the most successful clothing salespeople in the country. He gets the customer into a suit and then starts fantasizing situations where they will be effective in that suit. He calls this appeal to their looks right image 'romancing the cloth'. It works very well for looks right buyers."

"I would certainly fall into that trap!" I said with a puzzled look.

"If you are selling a product that can involve a real life demonstration," Michael added, "then do so. Show them how to use it. As you are describing the product, use visual language. Another twist would be to have them imagine themselves using the product or service. Guide them along, making a beautiful movie of them in the midst of enjoying your product. Also, if appropriate, show them pictures of other people using the product or service, and if possible, have other customers or clients come in and demonstrate its use and talk about their contentment with the product. Seeing others will have greater impact with looks right people with External Evaluation Patterns. If they have Internal Evaluation Patterns, it would be better to have the client visualizing himself using the product. The brighter and bigger the picture, the easier it will be for him to accept. Tell them stories which make them create vivid imagery in their minds. Avoid giving useless data. Finally, make sure you have eye contact with the looks right person a lot of the time. Remember he likes to see and be seen."

"Selling to someone like me is a piece of cake, then!" I said.

"Only if the salesperson has a grasp of People Patterns. If you are going to sell a product or service to a sounds right person, your sales approach will have to be in tune literally with how things sound to him. It would be helpful to play very pleasant background music, avoiding harsh Rap or Rock, or anything with a strong beat. Get them to talk to themselves about your service or product in the appropriate tone of voice in their head. A pleasant and agreeable voice tone is helpful. They will be paying more attention to your tone of voice than to the way you look, so be sure to speak in a melodious, even tone. Speak to them in a confident tone of voice about your product, avoiding wishy-washiness and doubt about its effectiveness and reliability. Tell them calmly and enthusiastically about your product and how to use it easily and efficiently. Talk about how they will enjoy using it. Stress that after buying it, they will be constantly telling themselves what a great decision that was. Bring tapes of others describing your product or service (again most useful with people who have external referential filters) or have them talk to product champions on the phone."

"From what I have learned thus far, it seems that sounds in the environment take on significance as well." I added with pride.

"Indeed. Be certain to have the meeting in a setting with minimal or no noise interference at all. Soft music might be appropriate. Avoid areas with people yelling or where you are within ears reach of others' conversation. Follow up phone calls are an especially useful idea with sounds right people, provided that you maintain your pleasant voice tone, and avoid extreme volume levels on either end. Why do you think voice is so important in hiring people for jobs in telemarketing?" Michael said with a markedly pleasant tonality. Since I had no questions, Michael went on to the feels right person.

"If you are preparing a sales presentation for a feels right person, start by making the person comfortable in the surroundings. Choose a meeting place with comfortable chairs. The visual impact of the milieu takes second place to the comfort level of the room. If it is your first one-on-one meeting, make a point of emphasizing the handshake. Your first physical contact with the feels right person will make a lasting impression. Remember that the feels right person likes physical contact, so what better way than by means of a handshake which is the accepted form of social greeting in our society. Moreover, shake his hand the same way he shakes yours. Doing so creates an unconscious link between the two of you that takes on added significance for the feels right person."

"Like the way each one of you shook my hand the very first time." I said.

"Yes, and you responded perfectly. In any case, smells and tastes can be very important to a feels right person. Offer them a cup of coffee or a piece of candy. Be careful about body odor. Do not overwhelm them with perfumes or colognes. Nowadays, lots of people find fragrances offensive and hazardous to their health. We recently heard about a group of people in California (where else!) who were trying to get legislation passed that would ban fragrances in public places. Where do we go from here? What about all the people in the world who have body odor because they do not bathe or else do not use deodorants? In any case, do not smoke around feels right people unless they do."

"How do you present the product?" I curiously asked.

"Describe your product from the point of view of it making the user feel really good and having him enjoy the product or service. Make sure the client or customer has physical contact with the product. Give him the opportunity to press buttons, shut it on/off, turn it, and feel textures and surfaces. Feels right decision makers need to touch or feel the product in question. If you are trying to sell a service and do not have products for perusal, you might suggest taking the person to a place where the service has been used so he may 1) move about and 2) have the opportunity to touch objects in an environment associated with your service. Have them physically move around during the presentation, since movement is important to feels right people. Many deals are closed on the golf course. Do your utmost to make the person feel good when using your product or service. Explain that he will feel great by using your product. In some cases, you may even want to loan the product for trial use for a few days or weeks. It might help to have minimal physical contact with him by touching his arm or hand at some important point in the conversation."

"I guess what you are saying is that the buyer needs to be made to feel good. Right?" I asked.

"Exactly. The bottom line in your sales approach should be to make the person feel good in connection with your product. After all,

Sales is the art of making the person feel good about giving you his money.

If you are dealing with a feels right person with an External Evaluation Pattern, it might be to your advantage to have other people besides you endorsing the product and interacting with him. You should also have both the endorsers and the prospective customers touch and use the product. Have the others there to contribute to making the buyers feel good about your product or service."

"What if a person has an Internal Evaluation Pattern?" I wanted to know.

"If you have a feels right filterer with an internal pattern, then tell him that you are sure that inside he will know for himself that the product is what he needs to feel good. In any case, with feels right people, avoid giving data and tons of information which this type of person does not like. Most importantly, leave him with a super positive feeling after having used your product and a super positive feeling about you. With a feels right buyer, your likability is critical. And end the meeting with either a handshake, pat on the back, or whatever is most appropriate given your familiarity with the buyer." I wanted to hear about make sense people so I kept quiet.

"Your approach with the make sense buyer will take on totally different nuances. First, the physical contact of the handshake is OK, but not crucial. Your goal should be to provide as many valid reasons as possible to buy your product or service. You will have to provide as much data and research as you can to support these reasons. In this case, you will definitely want to avoid asking how the person feels about the product or service. Doing so will probably steer the make sense person off course, and may sabotage your entire sales presentation."

"Of all the Decision Patterns, the makes sense buyer is the least into feelings. Talking to him about how he feels is like communicating with a brick wall. He wants to hear reasons and not nonsense about feelings. You will need to explain carefully and logically why this person should buy your product. Give him specific reasons. Be confident and knowledgeable and ready to answer questions. If you do not know an answer, simply say that you will come back with the information from a reliable source. Fudging it will simply make you look silly and more of an idiot. If you have any written material on the thing you are selling, make it available to the makes sense buyer. The more material for him to read and study the better. He will not usually care what it looks or sounds or feels like. He will, however, have a personal list of criteria to be met before he will consider purchasing the product or service. Remember words speak louder than pictures here. It would be helpful to find out what those criteria are before the meeting and to prepare your presentation in advance around them."

"It makes sense to me!" I said wryly. At least I got a slight smile this time.

"With that comment, I see that it is time to send you off to Beverly for a brief overview of how to relate the Decision Pattern to negotiations."

NEGOTIATIONS

Beverly was waiting and launched right in.

"Welcome back. Having talked with Michael in sales, you realize that much of what you learned from him is also applicable to negotiations. I will start by saying that I'll bet that so many negotiations are lost on a daily basis precisely because the person negotiating is unknowingly appealing to the wrong Decision Pattern. Once you understand how a person makes decisions, you have the tools needed to mold that decision so that it ideally ends up in a win/win agreement for all concerned. Many of the same principles discussed in the context of sales will be applicable here as well. Remember that people in general do not make sense, and that a very small number of negotiations are done on the basis of logic and reason."

"That fact was certainly an eye opener for me!" I exclaimed.

"Whether you realize it or not, you are negotiating every day with people in your daily entourage, children, spouse, friends, employer, etc. In essence, what you are doing is changing their pictures, sounds or feelings whether you realize it or not. The better and more proficient you are at transforming and modifying the other person's internal image, sound or internal sensation, the more likely you are to influence and inspire his decision to agree with you. In order to persuade effectively in any situation, you will need to understand the Decision People Pattern as the nucleus around which the other People Patterns revolve and mesh." Beverly went on.

"Many of the elements involved in sales presentations around the various Decision People Patterns apply to negotiations as well. With a looks right person at the other end of the negotiating table, you will once again need to be aware of how you look. A neat, clean appearance is crucial to your adversary who ultimately makes decisions based on things looking right. Find out about the other person's manner of dress beforehand, and be prepared to comment on it in passing. Be truthful".

"I know now that the setting is critical to the looks right person (like me)!" I said.

"Yes. As with sales, the physical surroundings are as important as personal appearance to the looks right negotiator. Choose a pleasant location for your meeting. Plants, flowers, overall nice decor will only enhance the effect of your negotiating. Next, bring as much appropriate graphic material as you can along with you in the form of photographs, videos, and slides to back up your position. Color is preferable to black and white."

"I can see that for sure." I said amusingly. "I really dislike drab colors or black and white presentations. They are so boring."

"Use visual language in your presentation. Make it colorful and make it come alive. Your goal is for the other person to see what you are saying. Have your adversary make a movie in his head (have him visualizing himself) about coming to a mutually beneficial agreement with you. If he has an Internal Evaluation Pattern, stress his deciding to reach the agreement in the picture. If he has an External Evaluation Pattern, then have him visualize others congratulating him on the agreement. The more vivid the picture in his mind, the better your chances at reaching an agreement of some kind. Use visual language and metaphors, when appropriate, which will pace his personal model of the world. Literally create in visual terms a future scenario which demonstrates an improvement in his existence as a result of your compromise together. Look him in the eye as much as possible. Lack of eye contact could make the looks right person uncomfortable."

"I can relate to that as well." I added before Beverly continued on.

"Negotiating with a sounds right person will use some rules similar to those used in sales, as discussed previously. Playing soft, background music will be in your favor. Avoid noisy places and keep interruptions to an absolute minimum. Speak in a pleasant tone of voice, using a lot of auditory language. Have them create an internal dialogue that is positive concerning your negotiating together. Talk about the advantages of coming to a mutually beneficial agreement and about how that will enhance both sides, still using a pleasant tone of voice. Stay clear of harsh or critical tones of voice. If dealing with a sounds right person with an External Evaluation Pattern, talk about what others are saying regarding the principal issues. If the opponent has an Internal Evaluation Pattern, then tell him you know that deep down inside he knows the agreement will be to everyone's benefit, and have him say that to himself."

"I can now see how these patterns really do work." I announced with pleasure.

"If you are face to face with a feels right person, your desired result is to make the opponent feel good about the negotiation in question. Choose a room comfortable to him. Remember the importance of the handshake from the start and at the finish. Introduce some form of physical contact — arm touching is usually easy and inoffensive — from time to time. If negotiating with a feels right person, move around, and have them move around. It may be appropriate in some cases to conduct the business while engaged in some activity like playing golf or racquetball. More and more these days, so much business gets taken care of out on the golf course. What an ideal place for the feels right negotiator. Get them involved in doing. That is so important to the feels right decision maker. Make them feel good about the agreement with you, have them create that feeling in themselves, so that they leave the room with an especially positive feeling about you and the entire negotiation."

"Now I have a better way of dealing with my own spouse who is a feels right person. Thanks a million!" I laughed.

"Any time. Meanwhile, steer away from long, drawn out, logical explanations with data overwhelm. Such a tactic will merely serve to alienate your opponent. Presenting a barrage of statistics to the feels right person will only make him ill at ease. Once you've come to a mutual agreement, follow it up with a handshake or appropriate manner of physical contact to cement the deal kinesthetically, i.e. in terms of the feels right person's internal sensory circuitry."

"Finally, with make sense decision makers, though, you will once again, as with sales, avoid emphasis on feelings. On the contrary, you will want to have a pile of data as ready fire ammunition. Be prepared to give them more than one good, logical reason as to why they should be acting in a given manner in the negotiation. More than anything, the reasons need to make sense to this type of opponent. Research in advance the goals of your opponent, and determine beforehand what standards and criteria are necessary for him to come to an agreement with you. Once you are aware of his personal guidelines for agreement, then you can have handy and ready the logical reasons for proceeding to that end."

"This is the type of person with whom I need practice, since I do not often meet people with the make sense pattern." I said.

"That's because there are so few of them in reality. In any case, keep your distance, literally, and avoid touching the makes sense person. Certainly avoid talking about his or your feelings in the course of the negotiation. He will not care about such matters. Be confident and know your material backwards and forwards. Answer questions intelligently and precisely. Words will import, not the images or sounds or feelings associated with them. In fact, if you use images, make sure that they are disassociated ones, i.e. pictures in which he is seeing himself, as though from the outside looking in, rather than bring in the actual experience. Explain each point clearly."

With that brief overview, Beverly politely escorted me over to Frank's office in the Training Department.

TRAINING

Frank was busy and looked up when I came in.

"I am glad to have you back. Obviously the Decision Pattern also applies to the domain of training and education. With so much needing to be done in this critical area in our country, an understanding of how we learn is particularly crucial at this time. The Decision Pattern affects how we learn and how we respond to training and education. Each Decision Pattern has its own preferred and efficient way of learning, which we shall now discuss."

"Looks right people - that's me." I blurted out.

"Well. People like you learn by making pictures in their heads. They learn best from graphic material such as pictures, movies, or books. In general, the more colorful, brighter, clearer and closer the pictures, the better they learn. If information is presented to them auditorially they translate it into pictures in their head. When they read they make pictures in their head of what they are reading. Because they store things in their mind visually, they are able to quickly access information."

"I had never thought about that, but I can see that you are right. That is fascinating." I said.

"The visual realm is the realm of space. Visual learners can juxtapose multiple pictures (like a split screen on television) to quickly pick out similarities and differences. This makes for rapid learning. Looks right learners tend to be good students and are appreciated by their trainers and teachers. In school they were good at reading, writing, arithmetic and spelling all of which are primarily visual activities."

"That is probably why my looks right child is so good in these subjects.!"

"Yes. Now on to the sounds right realm. With sounds right students we move from the realm of space to the realm of time. All visual distinctions are in space and all auditory distinctions are in time. They remember information like tape recorders. This involves playing an entire loop of information back in sequential order, unlike the simultaneous access of looks right people. Sounds right students learn best from lectures and from hearing the material. If the teacher shows a movie, this student will retain more information from the sounds and voices than from the pictorial images presented. They are sensitive to auditory distractions, and react most vehemently to the sound of chalk screeching across the blackboard. They are usually good at foreign languages and are good musicians."

Since I had no comments, Frank went on. "Feels right students learn best by doing, by actively participating in things. They are not usually the best students in the class, and have a tendency to become emotional. Their main emphasis is always on how they feel. If they have a teacher who makes them feel bad in any way, chances are they will not do well in school. How many of us can look back and think of instances when we thought our teachers or fellow students made us feel bad, and in so doing shut off the learning process for a time? Tragedy sets in when that learning process is shut off forever. If educators today only were aware of this all important People Pattern, we would at least be on the right road to improving our dis-educational system."

"It is quite discouraging when I think about the educational system in light of what I have been learning here at Success, Incorporated. You all here should consider doing something to improve the system and to enlighten educators and officials with decision making powers." I was quite serious.

"Actually, we have been working on a project for kids which I will tell you about another time. Speaking of decision making, let's go on with feels right kids. Feels right students enjoy recess and recreation immensely, since they like movement and physical activity. Feels right students are good at activities involving physical or manual dexterity. Often the football and other athletic stars at school come out of the Feels Right Decision Pattern."

Time was running out so I kept quiet once again.

"Makes sense students," Frank continued, " tend to be quite analytical. They like logical models and are good at abstract reasoning. This type of student also likes coming up with solutions to problems, deciphering puzzles, etc. They have a need to understand things from A to Z, and will ask all the questions necessary to come up with satisfactory answers. They are quite adept at analyzing, researching, examining, resolving, deciphering, interpreting, unraveling, and all the various mental operations available to the human mind."

"What about context with the Decision Pattern?" I asked.

FOUR WORLDS
Space - Visual
Time - Auditory
Sensation - Kinesthetic
Meaning - Sense

"As with the other People Patterns, the Decision Pattern can also be contextually determined, although most of us have a predominant, if not constant Decision People Pattern in all contexts of our lives. If you are one of the rare few whose Decision Pattern does vary a bit, begin to notice what your primary one is, and in what context it does differ. You may be surprised to find that your bottom line Decision Pattern is actually the same one after all."

After our session, Frank escorted me to the Personnel Department.

PERSONNEL SELECTION

Karen greeted me and we got right to the heart of the matter.

"The impact of the Decision People Pattern is evident in the realm of personnel and hiring as well. There are obviously jobs that will be best suited to looks right, sounds right, feels right or makes sense filterers due to the nature of tasks involved in them." Karen proceeded to talk without my interrupting.

"Let's start with the looks right person. This Decision Pattern will fit best in jobs where attention to the way things look is important. You should know this one well. What are some of these? Sales positions in department stores for cosmetics, clothing, skin treatment lines, etc. In short, any product that suggests its use will enhance one's appearance should be sold by someone with a Looks Right Decision Pattern. Why? Because, as we've said before, this kind of person will take great care to look good. Moreover, the looks right person will be more in tune to the visual aspect of people and things than the other Decision Pattern types, so he will be able to give a prospective buyer an opinion based on criteria relevant to the issue at hand. Hair professionals with a looks right pattern would be much better equipped to work on improving their clients' appearance that someone with the other Decision Patterns. The reasons for this should be obvious to all. The same goes for any service professional in the business of enhancing the looks of others, whether cosmetic surgeons, manicurists, seamstresses, fashion designers, make up artists, skin care estheticians, etc. As long as one's appearance comes into play, you'd be better off with one whose standards are those of a looks right person, since he will be most concerned with the way things look, hopefully the best way possible. Imagine having a makes sense person taking charge of enhancing the looks of stars for a movie. Or an average man or woman having his hair cut by one. What would the criteria for the end result be in that case? You can be sure that they will have nothing to do with looking right."

"People are not the only things we want to look right, I have learned today." I remarked.

"Exactly. It would also be preferable to have a looks right person in charge of the way things look in our homes and offices as well. Here, of course, we are referring to those service professionals whose expertise lies in the enhancement of physical space rather than the physical human body. Who are these specialists? They include the architects, space planners, set designers and interior designers of the world. Imagine having an architect build your home based on the Sounds Right Decision Pattern? What type of house would that turn out to be? All is, of course, relative. If your particular Decision Pattern happens to match this one, then you'll be in seventh heaven. The trades associated with the above such as upholsterers, painters and the like are supposedly around to make their part of the whole picture look right as well."

"Speaking of pictures, wouldn't it be helpful to have a professional photographer with a looks right filter?" I wanted to know.

"Yes. Of course. Wouldn't it be easier for him to know, for example, what angle of a person, place or thing looks right? Most people would like to have flattering photographs of themselves, whether it be wedding pictures, resume photos or just pictures taken for the family album. Even the more arcane professions such as umpiring or judging in which knowing when things look right or not, would be best realized with this type of Decision Pattern. Another domain where the looks right person would be right at home is in inspection and quality control. This looks right person will best be able to pick out defects in products before they get shipped to a disgruntled customer. A company could conceivably save a lot of money if it hired the right type of employee for quality control positions."

"I guess that is one of the reasons why I am dealing with quality issues here, isn't it?" I suddenly realized. That was no coincidence.

"That is for sure. So if you happen to be in a position of hiring someone in one of the above professions, it will be to your advantage to make sure you have someone with a Looks Right Pattern. Otherwise, you will end up complicating your life, and find yourself hiring and firing until you get the looks right person who will fit into the milieu much more naturally. Also, looks right people will be better at office jobs requiring paper work. They read and write faster and can digest large amounts of written material faster than any other type."

"If you are dealing with products or services in which sound imports over the other senses, it goes without saying that a sounds right person would best fit the bill. Think about the many times you have had a problem with your car. Often, there is some out of the ordinary sound that pops up when something is wrong. The sounds right person will be much better equipped to know what problem is associated with what sound. So it would be real helpful to have a sounds right mechanic fixing the car in those cases. In short, any job which entails the detection and recognition of various sounds to correct a malfunction would be ideal for a sounds right filterer. It may be anything from car repair to the tuning of pianos and other musical instruments. When it comes to the sound of music, you will obviously do well to deal with a sounds right person. For those companies out there that specialize in sound equipment of whatever sort, your ideal salesperson profile should include the sounds right person as a prerequisite for employment. Can you imagine having a feels right or looks right person selling you a CD system?"

"I touched on this with Michael in Sales. I can see what you mean." I said.

"In general, you will want to hire sounds right people for any kind of telephone work, whether it be telemarketing positions or else any of the catalogue phone sales. For any position involving people contact by means of the telephone or in person, hire a sounds right person because he is going to have a pleasant speaking voice. Also, this Decision Pattern type will be quite sensitive to the way in which people say things. In fact, he will pick up things about a person on the phone whom he does not even know, that will remain totally outside the reality of others with different Decision Pattern types. Companies with customer service departments would do well to hire sounds right people. How many of us have dialed a customer service line to either ask for information or to get a problem resolved, only to hear an extremely distasteful voice on the other end? The notion of customer service seems to be dwindling these days, and we have found that with certain stores, it is not simply abysmal, it is non existent! Alas! That is to be the subject of a future tome. How many of us have excitedly called some company to place an order for something for which we had been searching for ages, only to be totally turned off by the nasty voice on the other end of the line, so that we hung up and went elsewhere to buy the item? Sound familiar? Many companies lose volumes in business because they do not know about this People Pattern and end up hiring employees who are completely unqualified to handle a job involving telephone work." I simply continued to listen at this point.

"In having modeled top salespeople around the country, we have found that some of the best ones out there have sounds right patterns. And as such, they have very pleasant voice tones that put prospective customers at ease. Also, they happen to be real good at 'reading' others from the way they speak and respond to questions. Sounds right people 'hear' things from people's voices that escape others entirely."

"I know someone who fits that description to a tee, and he can be quite unnerving at times." I added.

"So do I, and it is extraordinary what these people do hear that escapes others. In any case, let us turn to the feels right domain. Feels right people would do best in jobs which entail a great deal of movement, activity and/or physical contact with machines. Assembly line jobs which involve the smooth running of complex machinery are ideal for feels right people. They will know from how things feel whether or not something is in proper position and operating well or not. If not machines, it may be simply working with tools, either to repair or service a machine, or building something with these implements."

"In fact, any job involving either fine or gross motor skills will be ideal for the feels right person. Truck drivers, gardeners, carpenters, handymen, typists, electricians, plumbers, telephone repair people or any repair service job (air conditioners, heaters, etc.) butchers, bus drivers, and any profession which entails use of hands to complete a task. If you think about it, the entire transportation industry revolves around the use of fine or gross motor skills, whether it be driving a bus or train, flying a plane, running a subway line, whatever. Each of these are suited to the feels right person to a tee, since the driver or pilot is responsible in essence for the smooth operation of a machine, albeit a huge one. Even astronauts in charge of a space shuttle!"

"Now with the makes sense person, what goes? I have met so few people in this category that it intrigues me greatly." I said.

"You are not in the minority. The makes sense person is best suited for jobs involving analyzing data. This sense pattern type does not do well in positions which demand attention to how things look, sound or feel. The sense person thrives on reasons and logic and data, and the more the merrier."

"So computer jobs are perfect for them!" I guessed out loud.

"You can bet on it. Computer jobs dealing with masses of information attract makes sense people. Often positions in some of the sciences—nuclear physics, engineering, chemistry among others—which revolve around theorizing, conceptualizing, analyzing, searching, investigating, postulating, hypothesizing, speculating, etc. are perfect for the makes sense person. Any time a job entails the amassing, comparing, analyzing of data and facts, and drawing conclusions based on them, you'd be better off hiring a makes sense person. Laboratory positions lend themselves to this type of person as well."

Karen looked at me and continued. "One word of caution. What I am giving you is a first order simplification relating to the People Patterns that you are learning. As I told you the first day, personnel selection is a highly complex art and it is never based on just one factor. People obviously have combinations of patterns and it is the combination that is the key. I have been teaching you the gross patterns. The refinement comes later. There is much more to learn."

SUMMARY

"There is much more to learn" was still echoing in my ears when I arrived back at Shana's office.

"How did the day go and what is the most important thing that you learned?" She inquired.

I reflected a minute and then answered. "I think that there have been two important lessons. The first is that logic and sense and reasons are not as important as I have always thought. The second and more important lesson is that most of my attempts to persuade people in the past have been on the wrong track. Now I realize that real persuasion has to do with getting people to change their pictures, internal voices, and feelings. I also realize that I need a lot of practice in this area, and somehow I think that I am going to get it here."

Shana smiled and nodded her head. "You just might be right. You just might be right."

KEY 6:

THE MOTIVATION PEOPLE PATTERN

I was anxious to get to work in order to learn the secrets of motivation. In our car pool we were stuck in traffic, and it seemed like it was taking for ever. Two of the men in my car pool were having a discussion about their children. One question was how to get one's kids to do their homework and their chores. The other was how to get them to turn down the volume on their music (which, by the way, was causing permanent hearing loss, unbeknownst to many parents). Dave was arguing that the best way to get your kids to behave was to reward them for being good. He had a rule in his house that if all homework and chores were completed on time every night, then his kids could stay up a half hour later. As a further reward for good behavior on that weekend, they would all go to a movie and visit the ice cream parlor afterwards.

Tom had a different approach to dealing with his kids. He said that he had tried Dave's approach with his kids, and that it didn't work. What he had discovered, instead, was that the best way to discipline his kids was by punishment for infractions and misbehavior. If his kids had not completed their homework and chores on time he would prevent them from watching television. For repeated offenses, he would deduct money from their weekly allowance. For extreme infractions he would even ground his kids for the weekend. Sue wondered who was being punished by making the kids stay home all weekend. She thought that there had to be a better way than having the kids bored in the house all weekend, making life miserable for everyone else. Dave and Tom seemed to be worlds apart, and the discussion continued while the traffic got worse.

Soon the discussion inevitably turned to politics. Dave was going to vote for a particular candidate, because he liked a lot of the things that the candidate had accomplished. Tom, on the other hand, was going to vote for the other candidate, because he disliked some of the things that Dave's candidate had done. Tom was not particularly excited about his own candidate, but he saw it as a matter of choosing the lesser of two evils.

While I was listening to them argue politics, I began to ask myself why I voted the way I did. In most cases I voted for candidates that I liked. But in some cases there were some candidates whom I really couldn't stand; and I honestly think that I would have voted for anyone who was running against those candidates. Suddenly I realized that we had reached my drop off point. I left the remains of the car pool to their discussion and hurried to Shana's office. She was there busily at work. She looked up with a smile and gestured for me to sit down. I reminded her that she had promised to teach me the secrets of motivation today. She came around and sat in the chair opposite me. What she said really got my attention.

CARROTS AND STICKS

"Here at Success, Incorporated we are focused on results." Shana began. "Results come from the coordination of the right actions at the right time. It is not enough just to know what to do and how to do it and to be capable of doing it. One must also be motivated and be allowed to do it."

"How do you know whether the right actions are going on?" I asked.

"I was getting to that." she responded. "At Success, Incorporated we know that when the correct actions are not occurring, that there are five probable explanations. These are: 1) Employees don't know what to do. 2) Employees don't know how to do it. 3) Employees don't want to do it. 4) Employees aren't capable of doing it. 5) Employees aren't allowed to do it. One is a management problem, two is a training problem, three is a motivation problem, four is a resource and personnel selection and staffing problem, and five is a systemic problem. At Success, Incorporated when the right action is not occurring at the right time, then the manager in charge must determine the reason and take the appropriate corrective action."

I did not gesture a question so Shana went on with her explanation.

PROBLEM AREAS REQUIRING MANAGEMENT ATTENTION
Employees don't know what to do - Management problem
Employees don't know how to do it - Training problem
Employees don't want to do it - Motivation problem
Employees aren't capable of doing it - Personnel problem
Employees aren't allowed to do it - Systemic problem

"When employees don't want to perform the activities, tasks, and objectives that are necessary to further the organization's mission, then there is a motivation problem which must be dealt with quickly and effectively. All workers must continually decide whether they will do one of four things. First and preferably, they will decide to fully support the organization's mission by channeling and directing their maximum effort toward its fulfillment. Second, they may decide to partially support the mission by channeling and directing some effort toward it. This may vary from high but not maximum effort, to the minimum effort with which they can get away. Third, workers may decide not to support the mission at all and to do nothing toward its fulfillment. They may or may not choose to direct their efforts elsewhere to accomplish something else that interests them more. Fourth and worst, they may decide to do what they can to thwart the mission. This happens more often than you realize in organizations which are poorly managed and where morale is low and resentment high. Obviously, how well an organization functions (and even whether it will survive) is directly dependent on the quality and the quantity of effort that its employees expend on the activities, tasks, and objectives which are critical to its mission." After a slight pause, Shana asked me for questions or comments. With a quick "no" non verbal cue, she continued.

MOTIVATION BAROMETER
Maximum effort
Less than maximum effort
Minimum effort
No effort
Sabotage

"The question for each worker" she added, "is always whether to do what he wants to do and what he feels like doing or to do what the organization needs him to do and what his manager wants him to do. The ideal is when the two come together. The ideal situation is one in which what each worker wants to do corresponds to what most furthers the organization's mission at that time. For a manager to make this happen, he has to have the right employees, the right support from the organization, and know the real secrets of motivation. The right employees have to be hired by personnel, the organization must be structured to foster motivation in its employees, and each manager needs to know how to combine all of the essential ingredients to ensure that each employee is constantly motivated to do what will support the mission of the organization. This is what you are going to learn today."

"It certainly sounds like a lot of really critical information not only for me but for the entire global work force!" I resounded.

"I am glad that you said global! Some people don't realize that these People Patterns apply to every human, no matter what creed, race or nationality." she stated quite emphatically. And with that she began with the basics.

"Motivation is critical to the success of any venture. Motivation is to provide a motive for a person. A motive is an urge, desire or reason that causes a person to act in a certain way or to do a certain thing. It drives, directs and selects his behaviors. Motives may be external (extrinsic) or internal (intrinsic). Extrinsic motivation is motivation which stems from positive or negative reinforcements which are external to the behavior itself rather than inherent in it. Intrinsic motivation is motivation which originates within the behavior itself rather than being external to it. People are motivated to do many things by both extrinsic and intrinsic motivators. It is usually not a problem to get people to do things that they find to be intrinsically rewarding and pleasurable. The challenge is to get employees to do things that are neither intrinsically rewarding nor pleasurable. This requires satisfying extrinsic motives."

INGREDIENTS FOR MOTIVATION
Employees with necessary inherent motives
Organization with necessary "satisfiers"
Managers to skillfully combine the two

"And that, I'm sure is a major challenge for corporations worldwide." I chimed in.

"Indeed. Motivation is directly connected with action or doing. As I have emphasized in any business it is necessary to channel and direct the employee's energy toward the activities, tasks, and objectives that further the organization's mission. It is necessary to take actions that enhance the three P's - performance, productivity, and profitability. Motivation provides the fuel or energy that drives action. Without motivation nothing gets done. Apathy is the state where one does not care what happens and where one is not motivated to do anything. Apathy is the worst state in which an employee can ever be".

"I have not seen that here at Success, Incorporated." I said, almost with surprise.

"That is because what I am explaining now is put into action here on a daily basis. Extrinsic motivation is basically pretty simple. You have known it all along, but you never really believed it or understood it. In essence, there are only two fundamental reasons why anybody ever does anything: One type of person will be motivated to do something because he wants to achieve or attain a particular goal or outcome or because he wants to get or obtain something. We call this kind of individual a *move toward* person. He is one who responds to carrots and is motivated like a donkey by having carrots dangled in front of him. The secret is to discover the right carrots. We will talk more about that tomorrow."

"I know many colleagues who don't fit that picture." I added.

"That's because they fall into the other category." Shana continued. "The second kind of person will be motivated to do something in order to avoid some particular thing or situation. We call this kind of individual a *move away from* person. A move away from person is motivated by sticks rather than by carrots. He is like the proverbial donkey that only moves when you beat him with a big stick. A move away from person only responds when he is threatened by sticks. The secret, once again, is to have the right sticks. More on that tomorrow."

"Does that mean that in motivation when it comes to brass tacks, that is all that there is - carrots and sticks." I asked.

"Precisely." she retorted. People either move toward or away from specific circumstances, situations, tasks, things, or other people. They will move toward things they desire and move away from things that they want to avoid. A 'normal person' will move toward something attractive and appealing to him, and this will often be associated with enjoyment, pleasure, or happiness. A 'normal person' will also move away from things that are unpleasant, painful, or repulsive. The more intense the pleasure, usually the stronger the move toward behavior will be. Likewise, the more intense the displeasure or aversion, the stronger the move away from behavior will be in response to it."

Shana went on. "Now, there are a few individuals in our society who, because of certain incidents in their childhood or for some other reason, have reversed toward/away from triggers. Instead of moving toward pleasure like 'normal people', they move toward pain, which translates reversely in their mind as pleasure. And instead of moving away from pain they seek it out and embrace it. Most people in our society, however, reflect the 'normal' pattern of 'toward' and 'away from' in their behaviors."

"I am familiar with the pain/pleasure notion from my studies." I said.

"That is not surprising." she responded. "This dichotomy of attraction/aversion is nothing new, and has been around for centuries, and is simply a part of what is called the human condition. If you use the wrong motivational trigger on someone, you are likely to get a negative reaction. Imagine trying to get a move toward person to act by threatening him with sticks. You'll end up provoking anger in him, and depending on what his threshold is, you may make him decide to seek revenge, whether covertly or overtly. It is totally inconceivable to a move toward person that anyone in his right mind would even consider threatening him. Such is the case with a strong move toward person whose major motivation in life is achievement. If you start beating him with sticks, rather than providing incentives and status oriented rewards such as a personal secretary, or a large office with a view, or a marked personal parking space in the company lot, you will end up losing a good employee."

"I have seen that happen in my former firm a number of times. Management there sure could have used your information." I said.

"Likewise with dangling carrots in front of a person with a strong move away from People Pattern. Such an individual will simply act with indifference. The incentive offered literally does not compute in his mind. 'So what? What do I care about this?' is a typical reaction from the move away from person presented with carrots. Verbal rewards will go in one ear and out the other. People who move away cannot compute incentives in their minds. To get them to move, you need to beat them with sticks. As with the other People Patterns, the ideal is balance, and being move toward or move away from in the appropriate situations."

"If I understand you correctly," I asked, "it is critical to understand that when a move toward person is beaten with sticks, this doesn't motivate him."

"You hit the nail on the head." she laughed. "It just makes the person angry and resentful, and he waits for a chance to get even. It is equally critical to understand that a move away from person will only move when threatened. He does not respond to carrots. One can wave carrots in his face all day, but he will not move until you light a fire under him. Meanwhile, each side obviously has trouble understanding the other. They also have trouble motivating the other. Move away from people keep threatening move toward people even when it does not work, and move toward people keep offering carrots to move away from people and wondering why they do not move. Granted, that if the fire is hot enough, most of us will move to avoid it. And if the pot of gold is within reach and bright and shiny enough, most of us will walk across the room to get it. Apart from the extremes, however, most people tend toward one pattern or the other."

"So balance is again the key, as with all of the People Patterns we have discussed thus far." I said.

Shana gestured agreement with her head, and then went on.

"Take the mafia. The mafia are masters of motivation. They call it 'making the person an offer that they can't refuse'. This practice began in Sicily during World War II when it was a capital offense to attempt to bribe a public official. Under such circumstances it was critical that the bribe offer be enough that one could not possibly refuse it. The mafia understand that people respond when you either offer them enough rewards or threaten them with enough pain. They do both until one works."

"Managers do that too. Right?" I asked in a doleful voice..

"Actually it is an erroneous idea that managers, or the mafia either for that matter, actually 'motivate' people. Motivation is not something that you do to people. As we have said, motives are internal states in a person that direct them toward certain goals and objectives. It is very difficult, if not impossible, to directly create or modify these internal states. Each person comes with these internal states already in place. So, you may be asking, if it is not possible to directly motivate people, then what can be done to influence their behavior?"

"You took the words right out of my mouth!" I said.

"The answer is that:

You cannot directly influence a person's internal state, but you can create expectations for the person that their motives will be satisfied by extrinsic rewards and punishments which you control.

These rewards and punishments only work because they correspond with motives already present in the person. Also, you have to have control over the rewards and punishments; and the person has to expect that they will receive them in exchange for the appropriate behavior which you want from them. In short, *to motivate someone is to satisfy a motive that they already have.* They have the motive and you must have the 'satisfier'. So extrinsic motivation reduces to three factors which are motive, satisfiers, and expectations. These are the keys that a manager must learn to utilize skillfully. They unlock both the doors to employee motivation and to organizational success."

THE KEYS TO MOTIVATION
Individual motives
External "satisfiers"
Expectations

"This is all so fascinating." I said.

"There is still more. So in summary, there are many possible 'satisfiers'. Tomorrow we will discuss specific kinds of satisfiers. All of these satisfiers, however, fall into the two broad classes which we are discussing today. These are the class of carrots and the class of sticks. For carrots and sticks to be motivators they must correspond with motives already present in the employee. To provide extrinsic motivation for move toward people, it is necessary to offer them carrots. To provide extrinsic motivation for move away from people, it is necessary to provide them with something to move away from. This usually takes the form of threatened sanctions and punishments. These people must know what the undesirable consequences of non compliance will be. For both move toward and move away from people, it is also necessary that they expect that the rewards and punishments will be determined by their actions."

"What you are saying applies to all kinds of organizations in all countries." I added.

"Quite so, and in each case certain factors need to be present. For an organization to manage motivation successfully three things have to be in place. First, it is necessary to hire people who have motives that can be satisfied by doing the organization's work. These motives may differ for each employee. Second, the organization has to provide a variety of rewards and sanctions that can satisfy the motives of each employee. Third, the manager must work with each employee to develop an equitable 'contract' with him that recognizes his particular desires and motives and creates conditions where these can be satisfied through activities, tasks, and objectives that further the organization's mission. So the key to it all is for the organization to provide the appropriate mixture of carrots and sticks that will match the motives of its employees so that they will be motivated to do the organization's work in order to satisfy their own particular motives. Also, the employees have to trust that their expectations will be fulfilled by the organization, and the organization has to monitor that the employees are indeed doing its work."

Shana stopped for a sip of water and then continued.

PRAYERS

"As always there are prayers for each type. Notice the move toward and move away from prayers on the wall. These provide a great deal of insight into the Motivation People Pattern. Heaven and hell were created for move toward and move away from people. The move Toward Prayer is:

Lord God, Maker of heaven and earth. Give me this day my daily motives from heaven. Provide me with all manner of good things for thou hast promised bountiful rewards for your followers. Let thy divine visions ever shine before me as a beacon of encouragement and hope. I am willing to work hard to reap my just rewards. I know that thou hast prepared a bountiful heaven for me and that my cup runneth over. Oh yes, Lord, could you arrange a little heaven on earth. I will work hard for rewards, but it would be nice to get them first in this life as well as in the hereafter. Amen.

"The Move Away From People Pattern Prayer is a little different."

God Almighty, deliver me from mine enemies and those things that make life unbearable. Protect me from temptation and evil. Remove my burdens and comfort me when I am afflicted. Please protect me from those who persecute me and remove me from pain and suffering. Also, Lord, protect me and rescue me from the tempter. I don't want to spend eternity in that horrible, hot place where evil doers perpetually live out their vices. I will do anything that Thou ask to avoid this place. I will work hard in any

way that Thou ask. Just save me from eternal damnation and suffering.
Things are bad enough here, Lord, and I would like to avoid more suffering
in the afterlife. Amen.

"You probably realize that religion has understood and effectively used rewards and punishments to shape human behavior from the beginning. It has emphasized both that righteousness is its own reward and that Heaven and its eternal rewards await those who follow the program. It has also emphasized that sin leads to suffering both in this life and eternally in the life to come. It can be a glorious world of abundance or a frightening world of scarcity. Which will you choose? Life provides both. The question is which to focus on."

DETECTING THE PATTERN

"I understand the pattern, but how do you tell which someone is? Are there target indicator questions?" I asked. Shana smiled, paused a moment to reflect on my question and then answered.

"How do you know whether someone moves toward or away from? There are several reliable indicators. One quick and easy way to determine whether someone is toward, away or balanced is to simply ask the following question: What do you want? For instance what do you want in a car, in a job, or in a relationship? You can fill in the blank with just about anything. Generally, a move toward person will answer the above question by telling you what he wants, and a move away from person will respond by telling you what he does not want." When I did not utter a sound, Shana proceeded to explain.

"For example, in asking the question 'What do you want in a car?', a person may say 'I want a car that corners well and that has excellent acceleration.' This person is characterized by a move toward People Pattern. He is telling you what he wants. He is specific about attaining a particular thing, in this case, good cornering ability and excellent acceleration. Remember that a move toward person is set on getting and obtaining something, or attaining or achieving some outcome or goal. They are motivated to do things precisely because they want to achieve or obtain whatever it is that they desire. Consequently, they are usually good at prioritizing and keeping track of their priorities. Once they have decided what they want, they manage to stay focused around attainment of that outcome. Move toward people are good at seeing the positive side of things and have faith in things working out."

"They can't be one hundred per cent perfect!" I said.

"Of course not. The downside of move toward people is that they are often blind to situations where things are going wrong. They often do not recognize failure and things that need to be eliminated or avoided. Because of their move toward perceptual filters that respond to incentives, rewards and carrots, they have a hard time understanding and getting along with those with different filters, i.e. individuals with a move away from People Pattern. They simply can't fathom that anyone could possibly be motivated by anything other than carrots. I will discuss the multiple implications of this misunderstanding of those unlike us later."

"A move away from person, on the other hand, is motivated by threats, punishments, and sticks. He will answer the 'What do you want?' question by explaining what he does not want. For example, in response to 'What do you want in a car?', he would say 'I do not want a car that will break down all the time, and I do not want a car that gets poor gas mileage.' These answers are move away from in that the person is focused on negative elements, i.e. on those things that he wants to avoid, to eliminate, to stay far away from or that repulse him. He concentrates on those elements he wants to keep out of the picture." Shana did not pause for questions at this point.

"The move away person does not know what he wants but only what he doesn't want. When asked what he really wants he often doesn't know. As long as he avoids the things that he is moving away from, this is all that matters to him. He feels no need to move toward anything. This often puts move away from people at a disadvantage, because to avoid something it is necessary to take some action that leads to something else instead. Move away from people are often so caught up in their avoiding actions that they fail to consider the merit of the actions in which they are engaging. Also, unlike move toward people, move away from individuals often have difficulty keeping priorities in line, and are less adept at staying focused on their outcomes or goals. They are always the first to see the drawbacks and negative consequences of situations and are often oblivious to the more positive side of events and circumstances."

I was about to say something when Shana went on with a decidedly firmer tone. "A word of caution is in order" she said, "about the question to determine if someone is toward or away. The responses to the 'What do you want?' question are not quite as cut and dry as they would seem to be on the surface. Often, you may need to delve a bit deeper, because some responses may appear superficially to be move toward answers, and are, in fact, really move away from answers in disguise. For example, if a person were to answer the above question with ' I want reliability in a car', one may jump the gun and assume that this is a move toward answer. Actually, it may be a move away from response in disguise, because the person's real motive may be to avoid the hassle caused by breakdowns. Having a vehicle that 'is reliable' really translates for the person into the desire to stay away from and eliminate potential problems. The implication of the word 'reliability' in this case is avoidance of negativity."

"That is like a false positive. Right?" I asked.

"Yes, and to detect false positives, it is always a good idea to ask a follow up question. After they have told you what they want in something, then ask them for each answer that they give you the following question: 'What will having that do for you?' For example, 'What will a reliable car do for you?' The move away from person will say that it will save him from the hassle and expense of continuous and costly repairs. A real move toward person might answer that it would provide him with safe and comfortable transportation. It is a good idea to use this follow up question even with obvious move toward responses as a confirmation of the pattern. Sometimes, a person will respond with a combination of both toward and away responses. He will tell you about things he wants and also about things that he does not want as well. This type of person is balanced in this context. They respond to a mixture of carrots and sticks."

"One further word of caution." Shana continued. "As always, the ultimate test of a person's People Patterns is behavioral. Pay attention to what people tell you, and pay even more attention to their behaviors. Do they respond to carrots or to sticks? This is the ultimate test. Also, pay close attention to how they try to get other people to do things. Do they offer other people things when they want something from them or do they threaten them? Most people project their own People Patterns onto other people and treat them accordingly. The observation of these projections can give you valuable insight into all of their People Patterns."

"Does contextuality also apply here as with the other People Patterns?" I asked.

"You are learning well. There are some people who always move toward, and there are some people who always move away. Other people will change their pattern when moving between different contexts of their life. It is always important to pay close attention to context and to note what the People Patterns are in each context. There are some people who are balanced in some or all contexts. They respond to both carrots and sticks." Shana sipped some water and went on quickly.

"Objectively speaking, there are some things that are worth having, and there are also certain things and situations that are best avoided. Perhaps the ideal is to be contextually balanced, that is, to move toward in situations where it would be beneficial to do so and to move away in other situations in which it would be more appropriate to avoid things. Statistically, about 40% of the population is toward, 40% is away from, and about 20% are both. Our experience in this area over the last several years has shown us that many people think that they move toward, when they really are move away in their orientation. So take heed when people tell you outright that they are move toward. The basic question is 'do they respond to carrots or sticks?' Do you have to bribe them to get them to do something or do you have to threaten them? This will tell from where they are really coming."

As she went on I was thinking about my conversation with those in my car pool.

"A good example is why you brush your teeth. Do you brush your teeth, because you like the look of clean, white teeth and because you like your mouth to feel clean and fresh? Or do you brush your teeth, because you want to avoid tooth decay and cavities and dental bills and the pain and inconvenience of a visit to the dentist? Many people fit in the latter category. Another helpful exercise to determine a person's Motivation People Pattern is to have him make two lists. The first list is of things he moves toward, and the second list is of things that he moves away from. Another way to do this is to have the person make one list of the things that he likes most and another list of the things that he really dislikes or can't stand. Next ask the person to prioritize his list of toward and away or likes and dislikes. Once he has done this, have him pick an item from each list, i.e. one toward and one away or one like and one dislike. Have him consider these two items, and then ask him to answer the following question. *'What would be worse, to have to live with the item which you want so much to avoid or which you so despise, or to have to live without the item that you want so badly or desire so much?'* Their response will be quite revelatory. We have been programmed in our society to learn to live without things we want. We learn this as kids when our parents either cannot or will not provide us with everything that we want. For most people, it is much more difficult to be forced to live under conditions that we do not want. Human nature is such that it is often more important to avoid certain things than to have the things that we desire. In fact, being forced to live with things that we don't want often leads to feelings of hopelessness and despair and often even to suicide. Most people, on the other hand, can stoically deny themselves things that they really want."

THE GETTING UP IN THE MORNING TEST

"So what do you think that you are in most contexts?" she asked me.

"I'm not still quite sure, but I think that I am move toward." I answered. At the same time I realized that one of my kids was definitely move away from in certain contexts. Shana went on.

"To find out what you are in one important context ask yourself the following question: *'How do you motivate yourself to get out of bed in the morning?'* Stop and think about this for a moment. What happened this morning when you woke up or when the alarm or something else woke you up? Did you want to get up, or did you want to stay in bed? If you did not want to get up or if you wanted to stay in bed, then how did you manage to force yourself to get up? This will tell you how you really motivate yourself in the morning." As I grinned, Shana proceeded to explain.

"Actually there are only two basic ways to motivate yourself to get up (each has several different versions) or to stay in bed. First let us talk about the move toward people. When they wake up, they either start making pictures in their head of all of the things that they want to do that day or they start talking to themselves about all of the things they want to do. Or else they get the feeling of being wide awake and energized. They get out of bed so that they can go do the things that are on their mind. Some of these people even explode out of bed, as amazing as that may seem. Some of them even sing to themselves in the morning and are actually cheerful and excited about the day ahead. Yes, as strange as it may seem to some people, there are actually people in the world like this. Does this describe the way that you get up in the morning? If this description doesn't fit you, then let us try another one."

"Actually, it does have a familiar look about it!" I said.

"How do the move away from people get out of bed? The alarm goes off, or they wake up. Their first reaction is 'oh God, is it morning already?' Then they lie there and feel how wonderful the bed feels and realize how tired they are. Next they ask themselves 'Do I really have to get up?'. That is the critical question. Then they start thinking to themselves about what will happen if they do not get out of bed. They may make a movie picture in their head of all the terrible things that might occur such as their being late for work, their boss yelling at them, their getting fired, their spouse and kids leaving them, their losing their house, their being thrown out on the street, etc. Each person has their own private nightmare fantasy sequence. When the movie gets bad enough, it is better to get up, however painful that may be, than to face the possibility of some or all of the possible negative repercussions coming about. Other move away from people start talking to themselves about all of the dreadful things that will happen if they do not get up. As they keep talking, their tonality gets worse and worse. Finally they can't stand to lay there and listen to themselves any longer, and they get up so that they will not have to listen to themselves further. Other people start imagining how bad they will feel if they do not get up. The feelings get worse and worse until they can't stand it, and they get up so that they wouldn't have to feel bad any longer. Do any of these scenarios sound familiar? If you still aren't sure how you motivate yourself to get out of bed, then pay careful attention tomorrow morning when you wake up to see what happens. Notice particularly the pictures that you make in your head and what you say to yourself. Also, notice the tonality in which you talk to yourself and note any feelings in your body." Shana quickly added another point.

"I should mention in passing that there are some strategies for not getting out of bed in the morning. One of my daughters is a master at this. I have done some research in this area to determine what her most effective methods are, and I will pass them on to you in case you desperately need to sleep in some morning. The most effective method that she uses is as follows. First do not drink liquids the night before, because you will have to get up to go to the bathroom. Second do not set the alarm. The critical moment is when you first wake up. At this moment it is important to totally clear your mind. Make sure that you are not making any pictures about the events of the day. Also, make sure that you are not talking to yourself about the day. Next feel how comfortable the bed is and how nice it is to lie there. Feel a feeling of warmth and total relaxation sweep over you. Direct your mind to some pleasant dream or picture such as a peaceful and serene landscape. With proper training you can be back asleep in no time, and with advanced training you can actually stay in bed all day. My daughter is a master of this."

"I think my daughter has mastered such a method already on school days, to my dismay!" I added.

"Well do you understand the basics of the Toward and Away People Pattern. If you are not sure what someone is, then provide him both carrots and sticks and observe which he responds to in life. Now that I have laid out all of this for you, do you have any questions at this point?" Shana wanted to know.

"Doesn't every toward have an away that is opposite to it and every away have a toward that is opposite to it? If so, then how do you know which way that they are really moving?" I asked.

"That is an excellent question, and I am glad that you brought it up because this often confuses people. It is true that when you move toward something that at the same time you will move away from something else. It is also true that in the process of moving away from something, you will actually end up moving toward something else. The confusion here is between the direction of travel and the motivation for the trip. Toward and away are spatial metaphors. In the Motivation People Pattern, we are referring to the source of energy behind the motive and not to the direction of travel. The basic question is are you moving because you are attracted to something or because you are repulsed by something else? Is the motive that moves you into action the desire to get, attain or acquire or is it the desire to avoid, get away from, or get rid of? So pay attention to the source of the propulsion or repulsion and not to the consequences of the action. Is this clear?"

"Yes. Thank you. This session has been such an eye opener on many levels. I am looking forward to (no pun intended) putting this valuable information to good use in all contexts of my life." I beamed.

"That is great." she said. "Now go on your rounds and come back as usual when you are done."

TOWARD AND AWAY FROM BEHAVIORS IN MANAGEMENT

Marvin was excited to see me. After shaking hands and inviting me to sit down he began talking.

"Today and tomorrow we will be learning the keys to motivation in management. This is obviously an important topic. The success of any manager is largely a function of his ability to create conditions in which the employees under him can be motivated, and the success of any organization is a function of how motivated its employees are. In so many organizations many of the employees are not motivated at all. They just do the minimum amount that is necessary to get by. They are sometimes referred to as 'deadwood'. At Success, Incorporated we work hard to insure that everyone is motivated. Would you like to know the keys to motivating any work force?" Marvin asked.

"Certainly." I responded.

"There is a great deal of discussion in business journals today about the changing roles of management and leadership. One of the functions of managers and leaders is to create conditions where both themselves and their employees can be inspired and motivated. To do this they have to have employees whose motives can be satisfied by doing the organization's work, they have to be able to manage expectations, and they have to manage both carrots and sticks. To do this they have to be able to design reward and punishment systems that work. A knowledge of the Motivation People Pattern is critical to performing this function. A great deal of wasted effort is spent by managers in a futile attempt to motivate employees with methods that do not work. Also, companies waste millions of dollars on incentive and reward packages that are ineffective. They do not have an inkling about behaviors. An understanding of the Motivation People Pattern and its applications and implications could save businesses not only in this country but companies worldwide from investing millions of dollars in incentives that don't work; and a failure to do so could result in businesses failing and managers losing their jobs."

When I did not ask any questions, Marvin went on.

"As you have learned, successful motivation is a real challenge. For managers it reduces to three things for each and every employee that they manage. The first is knowing the motives of each of their employees. The second is creating an atmosphere of trust in which each employee expects that his actions will be rewarded or punished. The third is being creative enough to work out ways with each employee in which his motives can be satisfied in the work setting. To do this it is necessary to provide the necessary carrots and sticks to satisfy each employee's needs. For each employee, the manager has to know whether to use carrots or sticks and in what proportions. The manager also needs to know which carrots or sticks will work and which will not. The manager needs to know this for each of his employees in all of the different contexts encountered in the work situation. It is not enough to know whether to use carrots or sticks, or which ones will work and which will not. If it is carrots that are required, one needs to know which carrots will work given a particular context. Likewise with sticks. There are as many possible combinations of carrot/stick choices relevant to different contexts as there are people in the world. Each of us has our own personal Motivation People Pattern Profile that, in turn, is nuanced by all of our other People Patterns."

"So how does a manager motivate a move toward or move away from employee?" I asked.

"To motivate employees who move toward, a manager has to provide them with the opportunity to acquire, achieve or accomplish things that they want. To deal with employees who move away from, a manager has to have available a series of punishments of increasing severity which are sufficiently undesirable to motivate an employee to do what is necessary to avoid them. For threats and sanctions to be effective, management has to possess the will to use them when necessary. Bluffs do not work." Marvin was firm.

MYTHS OF THE MOTIVATING MANAGER AND OF THE SELF MOTIVATED EMPLOYEE

"Most businesses operate out of the 80/20 rule. This says that 80% of the results in any business are produced by about 20% of the employees. That also means that 80% of the workers are only producing 20% of the results. What would happen if you could fire the 80% that only produce 20% of the results and replace them with people like those in the 20% that produce 80% of the results? If you could do this, then you could increase productivity by another 320%. Most businesses would be ecstatic to increase production by several percent. This is an indication of how important personnel selection is."

"I see and understand that oh so well here at Success, Incorporated." I added.

"Indeed. The moral is that *preselection always buys you more than training*. Businesses often operate under the erroneous belief that it is possible to train anyone to do anything. This only works if you have several life times in which to do so. In the real world this is not the case. It is critical to hire people with the necessary talent and innate ability from the start and to train them properly from the beginning. This is one of our fortes at Success, Incorporated. It is called 'modeling'. Our Success, Incorporated consultants are hired by a company to model their top performers and in so doing to determine what makes them so good at what they do. We then develop the ideal employee profile for hiring new workers, and simultaneously develop a training program to enhance the productivity of existing workers by teaching them the skills used successfully by the top performers that we modeled. It is important to hire people on the basis of attitude and learning ability, to train them properly, and to provide them with the proper rewards and sanctions to insure that they stay motivated. That is the ticket to success in any business."

"What about those motivation myths?" I asked.

"The first is the myth that 'managers motivate' workers. I think that Shana has already discussed this with you. I am sure that she told you that *nobody can motivate another person*. Motivation is an internal state in a person that directs them toward certain goals and objectives. What a manager can do is manage the motivation process. To do this it is necessary to follow a simple formula. This magic formula is: $W = M \times E \times S$. In this formula, W is the quantity and quality of work that furthers an organization's mission, M is the strength of the motive of the worker, E is the expectation of the worker that his efforts will be rewarded or punished, and S is the reward value that he expects to get to satisfy his motive. As I have emphasized, M is an internal state in the worker and E and S represent the worker's perception of the work environment. The skillful manager does not motivate workers, but he does manage the E's and S's so that they satisfy the worker's M's so that the worker will produce the W for the organization." It was obvious that silence was appropriate here.

THE MAGIC FORMULA
$$W = M \times E \times S$$

"The second myth is that of the 'self motivated' employee. Every business wants to hire self motivated employees who are self starters and cracker jack workers. When productivity falls, managers complain that they do not have dedicated, conscientious employees. This means that they either did not hire the right people to start with or that they did not train them properly or, more likely, that they failed to provide them with meaningful incentives in the way of a balanced and viable program of rewards and punishments. This is what the science of motivation is all about. Most people in positions of power and decision making will never admit that they failed in the hiring process or that they do not understand the behaviors of their employees. This is where honesty about one's limitations can make the difference between success and failure. As Freud said : 'Being entirely honest with oneself is a good exercise'."

Marvin proceeded. "Let us get back to *the myth of the 'self motivated' employee*. Let us state categorically that *no such employee now exists or ever has existed*. So the phrase 'self motivated' is an oxymoron. Everyone has certain motives. These are engaged when the person expects that he will be satisfied by certain carrots and sticks. When we say that an employee is 'self motivated', what really is the case is that the 'satisfiers', or carrots and sticks to which the particular employee happens to respond, are present in that job situation. It is not a case of the employee needing no motivation. It is, instead, a case of the things that motivate the employee (i.e., the 'satisfiers') already being present in that situation. The key is to match the motives of the employees to the carrots and sticks present in the situation."

MOTIVATIONAL THRESHOLDS

"There is one further key to motivation. This is that *a satisfied motive is no longer a motivator of behavior.* Beyond a certain point where the motive and its associated need are satisfied, additional rewards and punishments are of marginal motivational value. We call the point at which a motive is satisfied the 'threshold' for that motive. The higher that the threshold is, the more it takes to satisfy it. Likewise, the lower that the threshold is, the easier it is to satisfy it."

"Is it possible to have a really low threshold?" I asked.

"In fact, yes. We have found that some people have such low motivational thresholds that they are almost never motivated, because their needs are so easily satisfied. On the opposite end of the spectrum are people who have such high thresholds that they are almost always motivated, because it takes so much to satisfy their needs. For these people who have high thresholds and who are almost always motivated, it is simply necessary that the motivational satisfiers be constantly present in the situation."

"So I assume that businesses would like to hire only people with high motivational thresholds". I asked.

"That would be the ideal." Marvin said. "But there are not enough of those people out there. So what is a business to do? Does this mean that it will have to settle for mediocrity? The sad fact is that most do, and the sadder fact is that they do not have to do so. So, what is the answer? The answer is an understanding and proper application of the science of 'satisfiers' or the science of carrots and sticks. The first two lessons of this science are 1) that you can't get something for nothing and 2) that it is necessary to offer both rewards and punishments. The science of carrots and sticks reduces, as we keep emphasizing, to three things. The first is knowing whether to use carrots or sticks for a particular individual. The second is knowing what carrots and what sticks to use for that particular individual. And the third is determine which carrots or which sticks to use in different contexts for that individual. Carrot people often find it inhumane to use sticks, and stick people often find it demeaning to offer carrots. Both are necessary." Marvin took a second to answer a quick call and then resumed.

"A successful business has a proper mixture of carrots and sticks and managers who both know how and are willing to use them. If a business only offers carrots it will fail to motivate the move away from employees. This often happens when move toward managers project that everyone else is like they are. They design incentive programs that would motivate someone else like them and then wonder why these programs do not work on other people who are not like them. If a business only offers sticks, then it will be a sweatshop and the move toward employees will move toward a job elsewhere. So a business needs a balance of both."

"This reminds me of the so called Theory X and Theory Y argument." I interjected.

"In fact, there has been an ongoing debate in management circles between Theory X which uses sticks and Theory Y which uses carrots. Both are partially right and both are partially wrong. This is why the debate has gone on so long. The truth is that some people need to be managed like Theory X and other people need to be managed like Theory Y. Both are necessary for different employees. It is not a case of either/or but of both/and. There is a trend in corporate circles (promoted by well meaning but naive move toward people) to avoid using sticks. They have a hard time understanding that there are indeed people in the world who need threats and punishments to get them motivated. The end result is that a large percentage of the work force remains unmotivated."

"I have seen that time and time again in places I have worked before." I said.

"Managers can be trained in how to apply carrots and sticks. The bigger problem facing both American business and business worldwide today is the lack of appropriate carrots and sticks."

In fact let us state categorically that the biggest challenge faced by global business today is the creation of more powerful systems of 'satisfiers' to match the motives of the work force.

"This is the key to increased motivation and increased productivity. The problem is confounded by the fact that government regulations and the unions have removed more and more of the sticks from management's hands. It is impossible to motivate move away from people without the promise of punishment for non performance. Notice that we said promise and not threat - there is a difference. Threats may be bluffs whereas promises are kept. It is critical to have a graduated scale of punishments of increasing severity. The punishment hierarchy must correspond to the different motive thresholds of different workers. In many organizations, the only real, serious punishment is getting fired. And no one wants to go that far, so no employees are fired. This makes the punishment system worthless. I know people who work for or have worked for an organization in which gross incompetency was not considered grounds for dismissal. I can name quite a few. Bureaucracies are the worst. In them, it is practically impossible to fire anyone even though many people do little or nothing." Marvin said with an obvious tone of frustration regarding incompetency. My body language was aligned in agreement as he proceeded to explain.

"The government and unions rightfully sought to restrict the abuses of power used by managers in the past. Unfortunately, the situation has gone too far. The result is that managers do not have many sticks left. In a truly high performing organization neither management nor other employees are willing to tolerate slack performance. The time has come for government and the unions to return some sticks to the hands of management. Management, of course, will have to demonstrate that it can use this power in a responsible manner."

"Rewards are also needed, though." I said, obviously revealing my own preference.

"Of course. The other side of the coin is the need for more rewards. Management often has the attitude that high performance is the employee's responsibility. After all, this is what they are being paid to do. From this particular management point of view, it is okay to increase an employee's responsibilities without any increase in rewards. It is this power orientation that created the problem with the unions in the first place. What is needed is some fair form of pay for production or performance. When production and performance increase, then rewards increase accordingly and vice versa. With many jobs it is difficult to quantify performance. There is a pressing need for more effective means of performance appraisals that are tied to productivity. In any case, management has to give up expecting something for nothing. Management needs to provide incentives for move toward employees, and the incentives need to be ones that actually satisfy their motives. Remember it is not just carrots but the right kind of carrots that count. The challenge is to find or create carrots that work. We will talk more tomorrow about the different kinds of carrots and sticks."

PRAISE AND BLAME

"One of the most popular management books in recent times is *The One Minute Manager*. This is based on three principles. These are one minute goals, one minute praisings, and one minute reprimands. Praises are a carrot and reprimands are a stick. This book does a good job of covering the basics of three of the most critical elements of management communications. A manager needs to provide positive feedback when an employee is on track and negative feedback when an employee is off track. Both types of feedback are necessary and critical."

"An effective organization needs to cover both sides all the time." I said.

COMPLACENCY - THE BASIC PROBLEM OF THE GLOBAL WORK FORCE

"Would you like to understand the fundamental problem of motivation in the world work force?" Marvin asked.

"That's a loaded question. I really did know of a lot of organizations and businesses where lack of motivation and low morale were major problems. What, if anything, can be done about it?" I asked, paying careful attention to Marvin's answer.

"There are four types of workers in any work force. These are: 1) Those who move toward and who have not achieved what they want. 2) Those who move toward and who have achieved what they want. 3) Those who move away from and who have not succeeded in avoiding what they want to avoid. 4) Those who move away from and who have succeeded in avoiding what they want to avoid. Obviously the first and third types will behave quite differently than the second and fourth. The problem in any organization is when people don't move. The goal of management is to start productive movement, to keep it going, and to steer it in the right direction."

FOUR TYPES OF WORKERS
Move toward - Wants not successfully fulfilled
Move toward - Wants successfully fulfilled
Move away - Repulsions not successfully avoided
Move away - Repulsions successfully avoided

"The second and fourth types are the greatest challenge for a manager. These are people who are satisfied with what they already have and with their current position in life and who have no desire for anything else. In either case the result is the same. These people simply do not move any more than they have to!"

"I can name a whole number of friends and colleagues who fit into this category, sadly enough." I said.

"I'm sure of that." Marvin continued. "How many people do you know who live in a comfortable home and who are fairly content with their salary, spouse, children, and life in general? If they are move toward individuals and have more or less met their goals and have an acceptable lifestyle, then they are certainly not going to be motivated to go any further and to improve their status in life any more. They have somehow managed to reach their satisfaction threshold by achieving what little they desire, and they no longer find the inspiration or drive to go any further. Suddenly there is no more ambition. They did not have a lot of ambition to start with, and they have fulfilled it. So they just stay where they are."

"I assume that the same principle applies to the move away person in the same boat?" I asked.

"Yes. The same applies to a move away from person who has, in his way, managed to avoid most of those things he wants to avoid or eliminate from his life. The end result is the same. They have no need to move away from anything else, so they stagnate and do not move either. They have no more ambition. They had a low avoidance threshold to start with, and they have satisfied it. So they do not move at all." When I didn't say anything Marvin continued.

"Why do you think so many people lead such boring, dull and unexciting lives? Precisely because they've already gotten all of the carrots or sticks that they need to give them a basically acceptable lifestyle, so they no longer have the need or desire to move any further. Life is okay, nothing more, nothing less, yet that is sufficient for them to not budge at all. How boring! Human nature is such that if we are relatively content, we are not going to be motivated to do anything to change that comfort zone. So people end up staying in their jobs for years, and sometimes for entire careers if nothing changes that could trigger either a move toward or move away from behavior."

"So what is the key to motivating the work force?" I asked.

"There are only four reasons why people are not motivated." Marvin quickly retorted. "The first is people who move toward but who are not offered anything they want to move toward. To motivate them, find the right carrots and hold them out to them. The second is those who move away from but who are not given anything to move away from. To motivate them find the right sticks and threaten them with them. The third type are the move toward people, we have been discussing, who have attained their goals and who are already satisfied. And the fourth type are the move away from people, who we have also been discussing, who have succeeded in avoiding what they want to avoid. These latter two types are the bane of any work force. They are the great mass that do not move. They are the born sitters who are going nowhere. Moreover, they are mired in mediocrity and indifferent to change."

"So how do you motivate them?" I wanted to know.

"The answer is obvious but highly unpopular. To motivate them it is necessary to arrange conditions so that their need is no longer satisfied. One way to do this is to take away what they have! When you take away what the move toward person has, then his need is no longer satisfied and he has to do something to get it back. When you take away what the move away from person has and the wolf is at the door, then he now has something to avoid and he suddenly becomes motivated. Granted this is strong medicine, but it is the only thing that works for these people. And if business is really serious about finding solutions to their motivation problem, then they will take a hard look at these recommendations. The key, of course, is not to hire these people initially, but most businesses are already stuck with them and have to make do with the people that they have." Marvin went on.

"Part of the problem is that many businesses are what we might call 'entitlement cultures'. Both employees and managers think that they are owed a living whether they earn it or not. It is this attitude that is ruining society. The entitlement culture only works if it is the same entitlement culture everywhere, and then everything settles into mediocrity. The problem in the business world is that everything is not the same everywhere. We are moving into an age of global business competition where only the productive will survive. Organizations that operate out of entitlement cultures will not be able to compete with those that operate out of performance cultures. Entitlement cultures will have an easy ride in the short term and a rude awakening in the future. It is the age old story of the ants and the grasshopper all over again."

"That brings up a familiar scene in my mind." I added.

"It all comes back to the obvious which is that 'you can't get something for nothing,' and 'if you could, it would be worth nothing'. Every manager and employee needs to understand that only productive effort counts. The free ride is over. In a global market, motivated and productive employees are a necessity and not just a luxury."

SALES

I arrived in Michael's office a little early. As I looked around his office I noticed a number of pictures of advertisements on the wall. They had always been there, and I had not paid much attention to them. Suddenly some things in them began to catch my attention. I noticed that many of them contained scare tactics. In essence, they said buy our product or bad things will happen to you. Many of them stressed the necessity of reliability and the horrible things that can happen when things that we count on break down unexpectedly. Others of the advertisements did an excellent job of stressing various desirable features of different products.

"That is my favorite one." I heard Michael say over my shoulder. I had been so content studying the pictures that I had not heard him enter the room.

"Motivation is the key to sales." Michael said as he launched into the subject with his usual enthusiasm. "As I have emphasized to you, there are only certain reasons why people don't buy. These include no need, no desire, no value, no hurry and no trust. A top salesperson must first of all be motivated himself. He must have a passionate desire to sell. Second, a top salesperson must be able to assist his customers to be motivated to buy. Consultative selling involves finding out the customer's needs and matching them to a suitable product. When the prospect is sufficiently motivated, that is when he wants your product badly enough. Then he will buy it." Michael continued.

"Actually all sales, and, for that matter, all persuasion and all influence, all boil down to one question." Michael paused and smiled at me. I took the bait and asked what the question was. Michael went on.

"The question that all of the world revolves around is simply this."

What is in it for me?

"This is the most basic, the most fundamental, and also the most important question in the world. It is a question that we all ask unconsciously, and a question that many people ignore. Only when our society begins to seriously address this question do we have any hope of creating a world in which we can all live together in peace and harmony. In our daily dealings with people, only when we ask this question *from their perspective* do we have any chance of working out some viable agreement with them."

WHAT IS IN IT FOR ME?

"Let us get a few things straight." Michael went on. "Do you do things when there is nothing in it for you? Occasionally you may do things out of charity, because it makes you feel good. In that case, what is in it for you are good feelings. When it comes to brass tacks, we all operate out of a philosophy of 'enlightened self interest,' and for many of us we could probably drop the word 'enlightened'. In short, we do things, only because there is something in it for us."

"Be frank." Michael asked. "Do you do things that are not in your own self interest?"

"Usually not!" I responded.

"What would you call someone who consistently did things that were not in his own self interest? You would either think that he was a sadist or a saint or, more likely, you would think that he was either naive or stupid or both. So, in general, we do things that are in our self interest, and we consider people that do not, to be lacking in some way. Now this leads us to an interesting question. This is the single most important question that we as individuals and our nation (and other nations) as a whole need to face today. Do you want to know what it is? It is this:"

If we do not do things that are not in our own self interest, then why on earth should we expect other people to do things that are not in their self interest?

"Why should we expect other people to be naive, dumb or stupid? If we want something from other people, then we have to give them something in exchange for it that they want. There has to be something in it for them, or it is dumb and naive to expect that they will agree to an exchange. Zig Ziglar, who is one of the top sales trainers and motivational speakers in the world today, puts the essence of sales this way:

You can get everything in life that you want, if you will just help enough people get what they want.

Zig knows about that of which he speaks."

"It all sounds so one-sided, and I realize that it is true." I added.

"All of influence, persuasion, sales and negotiations reduces to this point. If you want something from someone, then you have to do two and only two things. These are: 1) Figure out from their perspective what it is that they want. In other words, what is in it for them from their perspective and not from your perspective. 2) You have to figure out something you have that they want and that you are willing to give up. You can't get something for nothing. You have to give in order to get. This is the golden rule on which all human interchange is based. It is amazing how often people expect to get something for nothing. It is amazing how often people think that they can threaten, flatter, cajole, or plead with people to give them something for nothing. If you do force someone to give you something without a reciprocal exchange (and this unfortunately is a common occurrence); then he will feel cheated, and he will unleash the dragons of remorse, recrimination and revenge upon you at the first opportunity."

RULES OF THE GAME
Determine what is in it for the customer from his perspective
Offer the customer something that he wants
in exchange for something that you want

"So what you are saying, Michael, is that the essence of sales is providing the customers with something that they want." I said.

"Precisely. This may be done by providing them with something that they want or by helping them to avoid something that they do not want. Both are critical in sales. Many salespeople think that all that they need to emphasize are the beneficial features of their product. But customers don't buy features. What they want to know is what the feature will do for them. What will it give them that they want or what will they avoid that they don't want by having it. In short, you need to know whether your customer is moving toward or away or both." With no remarks from me Michael continued.

"In sales, knowledge of the Motivational People Pattern will enable a salesperson to cater his sales presentation to his customer. This applies to both product and service sales. If you are selling to a move toward person, you then present your product or service in such a way so as to stress those things about it that will provide your client with what he wants. Remember that a move toward person is interested in obtaining, achieving, or getting certain things, and as the salesperson, you will have to show him that your product or service will allow him to have those things. *When the features of your product satisfy the customer's needs, then the they become benefits to that customer and the customer will be motivated to buy.*"

"With move toward buyers you should avoid talking about negative things or bad mouthing your competition. This is true even in casual social conversations not dealing specifically with the sales context, because on a subconscious level, the negativity will affect your prospective client and may even end up turning him off to you or to your product. Move toward people feel uncomfortable in general with negativity. If you have valid negative data about a competitor's product, then present it carefully to the move toward person, and reinforce your product in comparison by emphasizing all of its great qualities. Be honest above all else. Do all you can to toot the horn for your service or product, and be specific about how it will enable your customer to get what he wants and to make his life better."

Michael proceeded to explain.

"On the other hand, if you are selling to a person who is move away from in his orientation, your sales approach will be drastically different. First and foremost, you need to show how your product will allow the client to avoid problems or hassles. It is also prudent to have data ready for the customer to show how competitors' products will lead to problems galore. Move away from people will always have questions ready about what exactly might not work or might go wrong with your product. Make sure that you are aware of all of the potential problems, and that your company has considered how to respond to them. Emphasize this to your prospect." Michael drank some water and quickly continued.

"With a move away customer it is a waste of time to emphasize the positive features of your product or service. These same features which entice toward buyers will merely bore move way from buyers. What the move away from buyers care about is avoiding problems. Once they are satisfied about this, then they are ready to buy. At this point the salesperson should close. *Many sales are lost, because salespeople don't know when to shut up and ask for the sale.*"

"I must admit that I have seen that happen on more than one occasion." I said.

"It happens a lot more than you realize. One good way to find out what buyers want is simply to ask them what it is that they want in whatever context it is that you are selling. For instance 'what do you want in a car?'. See if they tell you what they want or what they don't want. To get more information ask the follow up question 'what will having that do for you?' for each of their previous answers. Another good strategy is to ask them about the same or a similar product that they already have. Find out if they liked it or not and why. The move toward buyers will stress features that they liked, and you should emphasize similar features of your product to them. The move away from buyers, on the other hand, will tell you about their dissatisfaction with what they had previously owned. In selling to them, all that is necessary is to emphasize how your product does not have the drawbacks which dissatisfied them in the products that they previously owned. Do not discuss other features of your product after you have assured them that your product will enable them to avoid the drawbacks and hassles that have plagued them in the past. This is what you need to close them on."

"And that works?" I asked almost knowingly.

"Need you even ask?. Because move away from people tend to focus on the negative, they will be thinking about all that could possibly go wrong, and will definitely want to know if there is a guarantee behind your product or service and for what period of time. Make sure you can provide some kind of guarantee and maintenance or service contract as well. Follow-up after the sale will be just as important to the move away from person as to the move toward person. Any questions?" Michael asked.

"I was thinking about some entire industries whose sales seem to be predominantly move away from in orientation." I said.

"That's an excellent observation on your part. There are many industries that rely heavily on move away from sales. Car and auto parts sales stress reliability and the danger of accidents and break downs. You do not want your tires to blow out or your battery to fail to start your car. Many of the advertisements for tires and batteries are prime time move away from pieces. The Michelin tire advertisement is a particularly good one. It is the one with the adorable baby playfully gurgling in a tire that is floating around a mock Earth. You certainly want to avoid a tire blowing out with your precious loved ones in it. You don't want your engine to overheat or carbon to build up on your cylinders. You don't want to risk your life or even worse the life of your family without air bags. You need a cellular phone or a CB in case you need to call for help. You need the club lest your car be stolen. You need a burglar alarm system in your house and business. You need a flak jacket and Gatling gun to survive in the inner city." Michael went on.

"The entire health insurance industry is built on move away from sales. People buy insurance, because they are afraid of what might happen if they do not have it. Investment and savings are also often sold as protection against an uncertain future. Consequently, most of the typical advertisements for house and auto insurance and many for investment plans are move away from in orientation. Most of them are put on the screen during evening hours when the potential buyer of these policies would be likely to be watching television. That is called pushing the right button at the right time. Just when the tired consumer is finally able to relax in his comfortable chair in his cozy little home surrounded by his loved ones is a great time to remind him of the horrors of what could go wrong to disrupt this peace and domestic tranquility."

"I'd say that was pretty darn clever." I chimed in.

"It's obviously no accident, yet I'll bet that the advertisers have no clue about this People Pattern. So let me summarize the keys to motivation in sales. Everyone has motives for wanting to buy something. Some of these motives involve wanting certain things, and other of the motives involve wanting to avoid certain things. It is up to good consultative salespeople to discover these motives. Next the salesperson has to match the features of his product to the toward and away motives of the customer. Finally, the customer has to expect that the product will enable him to satisfy his motives. For this expectation to occur, the customer has to trust the salesperson and know that the product will deliver what the salesperson promises. Trust is always critical in sales, and 'no trust' is one of the major reasons why a customer will not buy. A salesperson may have a product ideally suited to satisfy a customer's motives, but if the trust is not there, then the customer will not buy. You will learn more about how to develop trust is several months when you will take our basic training course on 'Essentials of Successful Selling'."

"I certainly have encountered a motivated work force at this company." I said.

"I know how obvious that is, I'm proud to say. I mentioned at the beginning that a good salesperson must himself be motivated. This happens when the company for whom he works provides the necessary carrots and sticks to satisfy his motives. Obviously, money can be a powerful carrot or stick, but it is not the only one. Tomorrow we will discuss some others."

MOTIVATIONAL SPEAKERS

"Before we leave the subject of the Motivation People Pattern in sales, let me say a few things about so called 'motivational speakers'. Many companies hire these people to come in on a regular basis to help their employees get 'fired up'. This temporary shot of adrenalin usually lasts from a few minutes to a few months. When the medicine wears off, the solution is another dose and usually from a different source. 'Motivational speakers' get paid a lot of money for their services, and many companies swear by them."

"I've heard my share with my former firm. And you are so right. The fire only lasts so long, or in many cases, so little. My response has in the past been 'so what!'" I stated.

"The question is exactly what do motivational speakers do? They usually do three things. First, they remind the people in the audience what their basic motives are and that they have failed to satisfy them to the extent possible. The reason that they have failed to satisfy them is usually diagnosed as either lack of effort or taking the wrong approach. Second, they get the people in the audience recommitted to the satisfaction of their motives. Third, and most important they assure the people in the audience that by following the motivational speaker's approach that they will now be able to succeed in satisfying their motives whereas they have failed in the past."

"Incredible! You have put it all in a simple nutshell!" I announced.

"Well, yes, and there is more. We have modeled several top motivational speakers and have discovered the three basic rules that they all follow. Rule number one is that they grossly oversimplify. They present no more than three points that the audience is exhorted to follow. There are no more than three, because this is all the complexity that the audience can handle. In essence, the problem is not that people lack motives, but that they lack a way to satisfy the motives. What they have done has only worked partially, and they have given up putting out further effort. The motivational speaker presents a new way to satisfy the motives." I sat in silence so Michael proceeded.

"The world is complex and solutions are usually not obvious. People's capacity to deal with complexity is quickly overloaded, and they become frozen and indecisive. The motivational speaker presents a grossly over simplified three step plan for action. People in the audience say to themselves: 'No wonder why I am unsuccessful. I thought the world was complicated. How stupid of me not to see that it is actually simple and that it all reduces to three things. How wonderful to finally learn the great secrets of the universe!' Now that people are operating out of a simple model, they suddenly become decisive and take action. Most of the time these actions are unsuccessful, but occasionally they are successful. These become the hero stories and the proof that the three step plan really works. The real truth is that the plan did inspire people to do something rather than nothing, and when you do something, there is an infinitely greater chance for success than when you are doing nothing." I maintained my silence since I was enthralled by this explanation.

"The motivational speaker needs to do more, however, than to just present a three step program. They need to present it congruently so that people in the audience will believe it and act on it. To do this, the motivational speaker needs to be able to do two more things. Rule number two is that the motivational speaker has to be able to lie congruently. He has to be congruent when he tells the audience that the world is not really complex but simple and that it all reduces to three things. If he is incongruent in any way in this lie, then the audience will detect it and will neither believe in nor follow the three step program." As I put on a huge grin, Richard made it known to wait before asking any questions.

"Rule number three is the secret of how motivational speakers are able to lie congruently. The secret is that they have to be able to lie to themselves first. When they can convince themselves that the world really is simple and reduces to three elements, then and only then will they be successful in lying to their audience. Each motivational speaker needs some rationale that makes sense to him and convinces him that the world really is as he says. This will differ with each speaker, of course."

"I said that the motivational speaker's medicine only lasts from several minutes to several months. The problem, of course, is that the world really is complex, and it really does not reduce to three elements. The problem with this complexity is that for most people it prevents them from taking decisive action. The motivational speaker's simplified three step plan did have the advantage of enabling decisive action. As I keep emphasizing, any action has a greater probability of success than no action. In any case, for most of the people who set out to follow the plan it may work for awhile or work a little, and then they begin to doubt it as reality sets in. Once they begin to lose faith in the plan, the downhill skid begins. Finally they say to themselves: 'How silly of me. How downright dumb. How could I have ever been so stupid as to believe that the world is really so simple and that it all reduces to three elements. Obviously, it is more complicated than that.'"

"So they move on to another motivational speaker. Right?" I jokingly asked.

"Well, yes, believe it or not. At this stage they are ready for another motivational speaker who will tell them something like this: 'The world really is simple. You had that right. The problem was that you had the wrong formula. You were doing the wrong things. The world does not reduce to A, B and C like you wrongly believed, but it actually reduces to X, Y and Z. Do this and you will be successful.' And, of course, the audience says to themselves: 'No wonder why I was having problems. I was following the wrong plan. Thank goodness that I have now finally had the real truth revealed to me.'"

"And so the cycle goes on and on. Here at Success, Incorporated we work hard to deal with complexity and to come up with complex solutions that work. To do this we have to consider large numbers of variables and to chart how these change with context and circumstance. Often we use computers to assist with modeling and with computations. Our solutions work more consistently than the simplistic models. *The key is to have employees who can deal with complexity and still take action. That is the real secret of success.* And it happens to be a major challenge, but more on that later. Well, enough of this for now. Do you have any questions about motivation in sales?"

"I'd rather study my notes and come back with any questions that come up." I said.

"Good. Tomorrow we will discuss values and a customer's principal motives in buying."

NEGOTIATIONS

I arrived at Beverly's office anxious to learn about negotiations. She was on the phone and waved for me to sit down. I overheard her telling the other person what was going to happen if they could not reach an agreement. It did not sound pleasant. She finished the call and said "I was just doing what we are going to talk about today."

"The Motivation People Pattern is critically important in negotiations. In any negotiation there are things that you want to happen and things that you don't want to happen. It is the rare person who knows what he wants and goes for it. More often people are not sure what they want. Some people don't even know this. They just know what they don't want to happen."

"In any negotiation it is important to start with a high goal. In negotiations in general, people have more power than they realize and tend to set their goals too low. This means that they usually settle for less than they could have gotten if they had set their goals higher in the first place, and if they had known the basics of negotiations." Beverly continued.

"If people just come into a negotiation knowing what they don't want, it will be difficult for them to set high goals or any goals at all for that matter. The problem with moving away is that to move away from something it is necessary to take some action which accomplishes something. To avoid getting something that you don't want, you have to get something else which you may or may not want either. There is nothing wrong with moving away; and there are many things and situations that are best avoided. As a practical matter in negotiations, if a person has a Move Away From People Pattern, he is best advised to consider the possible ways that he could avoid what he wants to avoid and to pick the one that is most advantageous and then go for it."

"Once you set a high goal for yourself in a negotiation, then you have to consider the person with whom you are negotiating. Ask yourself the question 'what is in it for him?'. Try to step into their model of the world and to view things from their perspective. Be aware of the constant danger of projection. Just because you value something does not mean that the other person will value it likewise. People have different needs and interests and you must take these into account and endeavor to understand things from their perspective. In negotiations you will need to give the other side something that they want in exchange for something that you want. You must be prepared to give up something of comparable value to get something of value. Any comments?"

I nodded no and Beverly proceeded.

"Next you need to consider the other side's Motivational People Pattern. If you are entering into a negotiation with a move toward person, from the start make it absolutely clear that you want to do all that you can to allow that person to achieve his goal or outcome - whatever it may be. Emphasize that in the process of negotiating, you will both be working together to ensure the attainment of goals that are mutually beneficial to you both. If you know in advance specific conditions that must be met for your opponent to reach his outcome, be prepared to state them in a positive, affirmative way to the move toward person. If you have difficulty identifying the People Pattern of the person with whom you are negotiating, remember that the move toward person will tell you about things, people, and criteria that they would like to include. Move toward people do not like to be threatened, so avoid threats and emphasizing the negative things that will happen if an agreement is not reached. In short, focus on the positive and upon things that are mutually beneficial."

"If you are negotiating with a move away from person, the main thing to remember is to emphasize that you are going to help him get rid of or avoid those things that he does not want to happen. The move away from person will go out of his way to tell you what things, conditions, people, and/or criteria that he wants excluded. With the move away from person you need to touch on and stress all of the negative repercussions of not reaching an agreement. Say 'If we do not come to an agreement, the following unwanted consequence will arise'. Stress all the hassles that can be avoided by reaching a fair agreement." Beverly continued the entire stretch without any interruptions.

"Also, if possible, find out ahead of time exactly what things your opponent would like to avoid, and be prepared to spell each condition out, stressing that none of it will come about. Certainly do not expect the move away from person to respond to incentives in your negotiation. In fact, offering him incentives is a mistake, since they will have no effect on him and you will have, in effect, given away something for nothing. Remember that the move away from person will have a list of potential problems and obstacles, so you will need to reassure him that such issues can and will be minimized or eliminated completely. With a move away person, help him to eliminate his problem and he will be happy."

"Finally, it may be necessary to threaten the move away from person. This is best done in the form of a warning as to what will happen if you do not reach an agreement. It should go without saying that physical threats are absolutely unacceptable in any professional negotiation. If you are a move toward person it will be a challenge to you to make threats, because it does not correspond to your model of the world. Nevertheless, threats may be absolutely necessary to motivate the move away from person to reach an agreement."

"It must be quite a scenario when there are two different motivational types negotiating together." I said.

"It certainly is. When a move toward person negotiates with a move away from person, the move toward person will often end up giving more away than necessary. All the move away from person is concerned about is that certain things will be avoided. The move toward person may interpret this as reluctance and keep offering more to try to reach an agreement. In the process he will make unnecessary concessions and still may not get an agreement, because he is searching in the wrong place. When the situation is reversed, the move away from person will often be making threats which will only de-motivate the toward person. To reach an agreement the move away from negotiator will have to be willing to offer the toward person something that he values."

TACTICS AND MANEUVERS

"Another area in which toward and away motivations come up in negotiations is in tactics and maneuvers. Tactics and maneuvers are efforts on the part of one party in a negotiation to gain unilateral concessions from the other side. Tactics may be move toward or move away or ambiguous. Toward tactics are often attempts to get one side to move toward something other than their own goals. Many tactics are move away from in their approach. The idea is to make things so unpleasant for the other party or persons that they will be willing to make concessions just to get the negotiation over with so that they can escape from the unpleasantness."

"I've been witness to some of those." I said.

"I'm sure of that." Beverly responded. "Examples of move away from tactics are all pressure tactics such as fait accompli, impasse, deadlock, stonewall, crunch, silence, limits and you need us. Obviously intimidation tactics are also move away from. Examples are anger, personal attacks, higher authority, experts, hot and cold, and threats." She went on.

"The most classic example of toward and away from in negotiations is the good guy and bad guy routine which is also the staple of grade B police movies. In the good guy and bad guy routine the bad guy makes exorbitant demands while the good guy seems reasonable and helpful. The bad guy then leaves the room and the good guy apologizes for the bad guy and invites the other side to quickly reach an agreement with him before the bad guy returns. It is not surprising that this often works. Of course you realize that there is no good guy but just a guy in cahoots with the bad guy who is masquerading as a good guy. Another version of this is the reasonable and unreasonable ploy."

"I've seen that scenario play out and work often!" I said.

"Delaying and harassment tactics are also often move away from in nature. Examples are rush, delays, waiting, confusion, linking, multiple objections and plain harassment. Also, many tactics designed to obtain concessions or get more are move away from. Classic examples are high initial demands and escalation." Beverly went on.

"All manipulative tactics ultimately rely on a major move away from strategy. The whole goal of manipulative tactics is to get the other side to introvert, to lose touch with its strengths, to focus on its weaknesses, to feel out of control, to lose confidence in its ability to achieve its objectives, to lower its aspirations and finally to feel that it must concede now or they will lose even more. This 'moving away from losing even more' is the state the tactics are designed to achieve."

"I know what you are about to say." Beverly quickly added. "Of course the tactic has not worked until the concession is actually made. Part of negotiation training is learning how to respond when people use these kind of tactics on you. The main thing to do is to shut up, to keep your cool, to dissociate from your negative feelings, to shift into a resourceful physiology and a mood of optimism, to reestablish touch with your strengths, and to make sure that when you do speak it is with a probe and not with a concession. You will learn more about this later when you take our basic in-house negotiation training."

"In summary, in all negotiations, whether with a business associate, a friend, your spouse, your children or your boss, you must learn to wear the perceptual filters of your opponent. If he is move away from and you are not, be prepared to look for the negative, which goes against your normal way of dealing with situations. Likewise, if he is move toward, and you are move away from, it will be strange suddenly for you to dwell on the positive and talk about what your opponent wants, rather than what he does not want, which is your habitual perspective on the world. Your customary sticks and threats simply will not work with your carrot and incentive drawn opponent nor will carrots work with your move away from opponent. Tomorrow we will discuss values and levels of negotiations. See you then."

TRAINING

Frank was sitting at his desk reviewing a stack of overheads when I arrived. He looked up and smiled as I entered. "I am here to learn about motivation in training. Is it important?" I asked and then laughed at the priceless look on Frank's face.

"Yes, it is critical." he said and laughed as he continued.

"Let me begin by telling you a little about the so called 'crisis in education' in our country. The fundamental question facing the world today is 'why should I?' This is a question to which we are going to have to find better and better answers, because many of the traditional answers are no longer compelling. Why should a child learn? This is a serious question. If learning is torture, as many students think it is, then they need compelling reasons to face this torture on a daily basis. If students believe that education is basically boring and irrelevant, then it is little wonder that dropout rates continue to rise while standardized test scores continue to plunge."

"We have all heard the maxim "spare the rod and spoil the child.""

"I have had quite a few discussions with fellow parents about this very thing." I said with an obvious air of frustration.

"This holds that if children do not learn, then they should be beaten or punished. This philosophy has gone out of vogue in modern education. It used to be that students were beaten with paddles, belts, or rulers for poor discipline or for failure to learn. Today most school districts have laws against teachers hitting students (but no laws to deter students from beating up or threatening their teachers it seems), and most teachers would fear some horrendous law suit from the parents anyway. In short, we have taken the threat of physical punishment out of education. What sticks does a teacher have left? They can complain to the parents in the hopes that they will discipline their own children, but this seldom works. About the only stick left to an educator is detention, and this is not much of a stick nowadays. The other stick is the threat that one will go through life stupid and unemployed. This stick is limited by the fact that it is quite possible to be highly intelligent and unemployed, and to be very dumb and still make an excellent living. In fact, this is often true. Many highly educated people earn lower salaries than less educated ones."

"So we come back to the basic question you mentioned." I said.

"Precisely. Why should I learn? Remember that is the basic issue. If there are no sticks, then what are the carrots? They are intrinsic and extrinsic. The intrinsic carrot is that learning is its own reward, because it is fun and challenging. Unfortunately, it can be but usually isn't. So this only provides motivation to a few learning junkies. The extrinsic carrot is that learning will enable one to get ahead in life and to make more money and to have a better lifestyle. Where's the guarantee? The problem is that there is none. It is evident that there are many educated people who are not well off, and many uneducated people who are very well off and living quite comfortably. Very few people today believe that more education is necessarily going to guarantee them an increased standard of living. Many blue collar workers with high school educations make more than college educated white collar workers. And then there are the kids who don't go to college because they get multi-million dollar contracts from major athletic teams." Frank obviously was deeply into this discussion so I remained quiet.

"Also, colleges and universities are being forced to become more employment oriented. People cannot afford the luxury of a liberal arts education - and more so at the high costs of education today. More and more students and parents expect college to prepare people to earn a living. More and more community colleges and trade schools offer courses designed to lead to employment in certain fields. It used to be that in liberal arts colleges and universities, more students majored in English than anything else with history second. This is certainly not true today. Who can afford a so called liberal arts education? For what they are paying to be 'educated', students want to major in some subject that will lead to a well paying job. The days of the well educated Renaissance person are over for all practical purposes."

"That is a real shame." I said.

"This is a whole other topic of discussion. Also, if you grow up on the streets, it is evident that the drug dealers have all of the money. This does not require a college education to figure out. Many of our more highly motivated youth are attracted to a life that promises rapid and lavish rewards - if you survive, that is. Why stay in school and slave away for an uncertain future, when you can drop out of school and have an uncertain future now? Why go to college to get an education to join the middle class when you can break the law and join the upper class now? When youngsters in the inner city see how well the other half lives with the spoils of drug wars, for example, how can we honestly expect them to joyfully accept work at the local fast food joint for a minimum wage? These are not just rhetorical questions. The tragedy is that our country does not take them seriously. *People today want to know what is in it for them now.* If there is nothing in it for them, then it is naive and unrealistic to expect that they will go along. Our educational system and our country need to address these issues before it is too late."

THE BIG WHY

"At Success, Incorporated we know that motivation is the front door to any training program. Training has to be relevant and to have a pay off. Remember when I told you that our training design process is based on a learning styles model. David Kolb developed an instrument to determine learning styles and Bernice McCarthy applied it to education. We have expanded on their work for our training design model. As I have told you, a training module must address four questions which are: why, what, how, and what if. So training begins with the question why."

"Why?" I asked. Frank laughed ever so slightly.

"There are two good reasons for this. The first is that about a third of all learners are 'why quadrant' learners. Kolb calls them 'divergers'. They will not learn until they get a satisfactory answer to their 'why' question. They will just sit there stuck until this question is satisfactorily answered for them. They operate out of a model that says first show me how it is relevant for me to learn this before I will engage my brain, my energy, and my attention to do so. Once the 'why' question is answered satisfactorily, then these people become excellent learners. So it is critical to address the issue of relevance at the very beginning of any training module, or a third of your students will be disinterested and will never get on board."

"Second, it is also important to answer the why question for the other learning styles. They may begin to learn without having this question answered, but they will not be as motivated and enthusiastic as they could be. A trainer needs to get buy-in at the beginning. People need to know what is in it for them. What will the skills that they develop in the training allow them to do that they cannot do now or to do better or faster. Also, what will be the consequences of not developing these skills. These are the questions that provide the propulsion system for the training. They are where the students' energy comes from. They are the difference between having to spoon feed someone and having that someone grab the spoon out of your hand and begin feeding themselves."

"So what about carrots and sticks?" I asked.

"Every good trainer has to be a master of carrots and sticks. They have to know when to praise and to provide rewards, and they also have to know when to prod and to push and, if necessary, provide punishment. Both are necessary, and the master trainer knows where each student is and just what is needed to motivate him to take the next step. As every trainer knows, the worst possible students are those who are only present because attendance is mandatory. The best situation is where attendance is voluntary and where the students in attendance are eager to learn. Every student enters the classroom with certain motives and expectations already in place. The trainer must immediately connect with the motives of the students and show them that by mastering and applying the course content, that they will be able to satisfy their motives."

Frank was on a roll (as a trainer) so I did not interrupt.

"The purpose of training in the workplace is to learn new skills or to upgrade existing skills. The focus is always on doing the job better and with less effort. There are only two ways to increase productivity. One is by working harder. The other is by working smarter. The former involves perspiration and the latter involves inspiration. The former involves either working longer or increasing effort and the latter involves working in a different and more efficient way. It should be evident that here at Success, Incorporated we favor the latter approach. We believe that training is one of the keys to a motivated work force. It is training that can provide each employee will the skills necessary to satisfy his motives. Without access to new skills, even successful employees stagnate over time and unsuccessful employees have no way to improve their situation. In short, any organization who wants alert, motivated employees had better give training and development a high priority."

"One final point is in order. Everyone wants to train alert, motivated students. And when students do not learn, then most trainers blame the students for lacking motivation. We understand that motivated students are not an accident. They do not just happen by chance. Student motivation must be managed. In fact, I might even go so far as to say that there are no students who are incapable of motivation, but there are just teachers and trainers who are uninspiring."

PERSONNEL SELECTION

They always seem busy in personnel. Because of its success, the company is growing rapidly, and personnel is always hiring new people and promoting existing people.

Karen delved right into the heart of the matter. "Everyone wants to hire highly motivated people. I am sure that you have learned about self motivated employees already or rather you have learned that they don't exist. Here at Success Incorporated we pride ourselves on hiring the right people. This is not always easy."

"You certainly make it look easy!" I exclaimed.

"Thanks. Obviously the conventional wisdom is as follows. Hire move toward people for jobs which align with their goals. To do this, you first have to find out what their goals and motives are and to see if they fit with those of the company. To motivate them to want to work for you, it is important to stress the benefits of working for you. Talk about perks and benefits, i.e. promotions, vacation packages, retirement, leave, profit sharing, and pay increases. Make sure that you offer perks and benefits that they want. This is why we have such a large variety of benefit packages that are geared toward different types of people and different lifestyles. It is also important to provide them every opportunity for advancement. As you well know, here at Success Incorporated pay and promotion are tied to performance, so everyone has a chance to earn a lot."

"Hire move away from people only when you have something for them to move away from. Realize that these people may only be working to avoid poverty. Do not expect initiative or high performance from them, unless you are willing to threaten them. When hiring them, stress the hassles avoided by a steady paycheck and emphasize the disadvantages of unemployment. Once you hire them, be prepared to provide a system of threats and sanctions if you expect to motivate them. Remember too, that the types of sticks will vary contextually."

"Contextuality again and again." I added.

"Nothing but. Obviously our benefit packages and our pay-for-performance strategy here at Success, Incorporated are designed to attract move toward people. We try to hire people who are both move toward and who have high aspirations. We don't want people who plateau easily or who are looking for a safe nest. In general, we avoid hiring people who move away from because they are too much trouble to motivate. Our move toward managers understand how to motivate move away from people, but they would rather not have to do so. There are a few highly motivated move away from people who are always afraid that the serpent is at the door, but they are uncommon. They can make good employees, and no matter how much they earn, they are afraid that it is not enough. We have hired a few people like this, and they have been successful here. Of course, they put themselves under a lot of stress, and we have to monitor their health."

"I see we are running over, so I'd rather wait to see if I have any questions once I have had a chance to review." I said.

"Tomorrow should not be such a busy day, and we will have more time to talk then. I will talk to you at that time about interviewing and how to determine a person's basic motives. As always, behavior is a better indicator than words. Our approach is based on observing behavioral preferences and not just on self report. I will see you then."

SUMMARY

I arrived back at Shana's office to find her talking to the company safety officer. She waved for me to set down. The safety officer was saying: "Statistics show that lost time accidents cost businesses millions of dollars a year. At the same time most accidents could have been prevented. Businesses are always stressing safety and looking for ways to prevent accidents. What is ironic is that in the process of trying to prevent accidents, they often end up inadvertently creating accidents." At this point I was curious as to how this could be the case. The safety officer continued.

"Almost all safety programs are move away from programs. Safety is viewed as accident prevention in most companies. The goal then becomes to avoid accidents rather than to work safely. In order to avoid accidents, these companies tell people what not to do. They educate their employees as to the various ways that accidents can happen, and then they tell them to 'not do this.' These programs have little effect on motivating move toward employees. They are primarily effective for move away from employees who want to avoid immediate pain or long term disability."

"These companies fail to understand several things. The first is that safety is more of an awareness and attention problem than a motivation problem. Hardly anyone is motivated to have accidents. Most accidents happen because people are not paying attention. Ironically, the second thing that these companies fail to realize is that their so called 'safety' programs often actually cause accidents." Once again, I wanted to know how this was possible.

"It is like this." the safety officer said. "One key component of most safety programs are warning signs. These signs tell you what not to do. They say things like 'do not slip' or 'don't stick your fingers in the machine' or 'do not cut yourself on the blade.' Often they have a graphic to accompany the text. For instance there may be a picture of a person slipping on a banana peel. The picture will be in a big red circle with the now familiar 'ghost buster x' through it. Guess what? These kinds of posters often actually create accidents rather than prevent them. How can this be? To understand this we have to understand three principles about the way that the mind operates."

Obviously I remained silent. "There is a fundamental principle that underlies all of human performance. This is that the mind/body will attempt to reproduce the last clear set of instructions it is given. There are two other principles, which, when combined with this one can lead to accidents. The second principle is that the unconscious mind cannot compute negation. Negation is only understood by the conscious mind. The unconscious mind only understands how to do. It does not understand how not to do. When the unconscious is told to not do something, it

,instead, forms a representation of doing it. The third and final principle is that to make sense of something, it is necessary to represent it in some way. So to make sense of 'do not trip' it is necessary to make a representation of yourself tripping. This usually takes the form of a picture of yourself tripping."

"The end result of all of this is that when you see a sign and a picture that says 'do not trip', you make a picture of yourself tripping and read the words 'don't trip'; and if you are not alert your mind/body will attempt to carry out the directions of this picture, and you will trip."

"I asked the agent who provides our company's insurance to let me look at the files on all of the tripping accident claims that he had settled. The insurance company always does a thorough investigation of the accident scene including taking many photographs. In 18 of the 20 tripping accident scenes there was a prominent sign that either said 'don't trip' or 'watch your step.'" How can anyone walk if you 'watch your step'? You can't."

I thought that the safety officer was right when he said "So many accidents are actually caused by the very signs that are intended to prevent them".

The safety officer went on to say: "The first thing that I did when I learned about People Patterns was to remove all signs that said 'do not .....' or that showed pictures of accidents with X's through them. I had them all replaced with signs saying what to do such as 'stay alert' or 'keep your fingers outside of the machine.' Our safety program stresses what to do and not what not to do. Also, our safety meetings stress being alert at all times and the benefits of health and well being. Move toward people are much more interested in this. As a result of the program that I have developed, our company's safety record is well above the national average. Well I have to go now. It was nice to meet you."

After she left my mentor, Shana, asked me how the day had gone and if I had any questions. I said that I was still reflecting on the question of 'what's in it for me?'. She laughed as she said: "This question has broad implications for individuals, for business and for society in general. Answering the question 'what's in it for me?' is a problem at every level of society."

"Tomorrow we will continue our discussion of motivation with the Motive People Pattern. This will expand the basic model and add some further refinements."

KEY 7:

THE MOTIVE PEOPLE PATTERN

OBSERVATIONS

The ride to work went more smoothly than normal. The discussion in the car pool was around downsizing and how to get ahead at work. Bill's company was about to downsize, and he was quite concerned. Normally he was a hard worker with a positive mental attitude. He was always listening to self improvement tapes and reading books on self improvement. The possibility of being laid off seemed to change him. His energy had seemed to change in the last week since he learned about the possible downsizing. He was more distracted and his sales volume was down. He seemed much more concerned about the immediate future than about his career. Then the discussion shifted.

An argument began about how to get ahead in the office and about who gets promoted. Dave was arguing that the secret of success was having a goal and working hard to achieve it. Sue said that she thought the real key to winning in the office was having the courage and tenacity to fight for whatever you think is right. Tom took a third approach. He said that the key to getting ahead at work was in your relationships with your colleagues. "Treat people right and fairly, and they will treat you right also" was his motto. Always smile, and be helpful to others. It is helpful people who get ahead. At this point I was dropped off, so I never got to hear how the discussion ended.

I arrived at work eager and excited to learn more about motivation. Shana was already at her desk and greeted me warmly. I told her about the discussion in the car pool and about my experiment with my kids. I said that last night I had tried using carrots and sticks to get my children to clean up their rooms, to do their homework and to behave in a reasonable fashion. I was a little confused, because when I had offered a monetary reward one of my children was excited by it, and the other two did not seem to respond. One of the two did, however, end up doing what I had asked, but she did not do it for the reward that I had offered. She simply said: "I am doing it for you daddy, I don't care about the money." My third child only responded when I threatened to take away his privileges. He wanted to argue, and it is always a power struggle to get him to do anything.

I turned to Shana and said: "I guess what confuses me is that not everyone seems to respond to the same carrots and sticks." She smiled and said: "You are right, and that is where we will begin today."

MOTIVES, NEEDS AND VALUES

"To understand the basis of motivation and why people respond to different carrots and sticks and also to understand what is happening to Bill in your car pool, we need to understand the relation between motivation and motives, needs and values. Yesterday, as you will recall, we said that there were three necessary ingredients for motivation to occur. What were they?" Shana asked.

I thought for a minute and said: "You said yesterday that the three ingredients were 1) employees with necessary inherent motives, 2) an organization with the necessary 'satisfiers', and 3) managers to skillfully combine the two."

"Correct." she said. "I am glad that you are learning and remembering what I have told you." and she continued.

Behavior is a function of a person and his environment.

"Motives exist in the person and 'satisfiers' exist in the environment. It is up to managers to skillfully combine the two so as to focus human energy toward the activities, tasks, and objectives that further the organization's mission."

"Are you with me thus far?" she asked.

"So far so good." I responded.

"Today we will begin with *motives*." Shana went on to say. "Motivation begins with human motives. Motives are the states within a person that energize and direct them toward a particular goal. Motives and needs are related. A need is a deficit. A motive is a need or desire coupled with an intention to attain an appropriate goal or value. In other words, we engage in actions that we expect will satisfy our needs. It follows from this that only unsatisfied needs are prime sources of motivation. Also, it follows that by studying a person's behaviors and values we can gain insight into his unsatisfied needs, and by studying his unsatisfied needs we can gain insight into his behaviors and values." After a quick phone call, Shana continued.

"A *need* is that which is necessary for a person's health and well being. Needs may be physical or psychological. Need deprivation in a person produces feelings of pain and discomfort, while need satisfaction in a person produces feelings of pleasure and well being. A need creates a pleasant or unpleasant tension, and the goal of the resultant behavior is the reduction of that tension or discomfort. Thus, need deprivation may lead a person to an attempt to satisfy his need, but this will only happen if the person expects that a specific action will satisfy the need. This assessment, like any judgement, may or may not prove to be accurate. The specific choices of actions a person takes to satisfy his needs are guided by his values."

"So what are values?" I wanted to know.

"*Values* are what individuals consider good or essential to their well being. They are a measure of the degree of worth or excellence assigned to or derived from an object. Values are acquired through experience whereas needs are innate. Values are those things that we move toward or away from. They are the things that we are willing to invest time, energy and resources to either achieve or avoid. They are the underlying forces that drive, direct and select our behaviors. They come from the affective domain."

"So where do values fit in with needs and actions?" I asked.

"Values are the link between needs and actions. Values allocate attention and effort to various needs by determining the relative worth of various goals or ends. Values are also the basis for emotions. Values may be either conscious or unconscious, and unconscious values may even conflict with conscious values and with each other." Shana explained quite clearly.

DEFINITION OF TERMS
"Motives" are the states within a person that energize and direct him toward a particular goal.
A "need" is that which is necessary for a person's health and well being.
"Values" are those things that we are willing to invest time, energy and resources to either achieve or avoid.

MASLOW'S HIERARCHY OF NEEDS
"Do you remember studying Maslow's hierarchy of needs?" she asked.

"That was a while ago, so I wouldn't mind a quick review." I responded.

"Maslow made three critical points." Shana proceeded. "They are the following."

MASLOW'S THREE THESES
Human needs can be viewed in a hierarchical fashion
Lower order needs must be partially satisfied before higher order needs
A satisfied need is no longer a motivator of behavior

"If you have no questions I will go on." she said. "Abraham Maslow proposed in 1943 that whatever needs a person is experiencing at the moment will have a major impact on his motivations, priorities and behaviors. As we have said, a need is a lack or deficit that creates tension or motivation to have it satisfied. Maslow identified five classes of human needs that he arranged in a hierarchy. Before one can move on to the next level, the level in which one finds oneself has to be at least partially satisfied."

"The first level of Maslow's hierarchy of needs which forms the base of the pyramid is basic physiological survival needs. These include the needs for food, water, clothing, shelter, sex and physical fitness. If a person does not have these, then all of their time, energy and attention will be directed toward obtaining them. They will live in a state of constant anxiety with a focus on the immediate present. Until these needs are met, they will have no energy left over to devote to other things. Once these needs are satisfied temporarily, the desire then emerges to have them permanently satisfied." Shana took a pause at which point I asked a question.

"If I recall correctly, that triggers a move to the next level." I remembered out loud.

"Yes." Shana responded. "This brings us to Maslow's second level which is that of safety and security. This is one step beyond survival. At this level a person is concerned for his own continued safety and security. This comes from permanent safe housing and an adequate income level to purchase food, clothing and adequate medical care. At these first two levels there is a short term time focus - from meal to meal and from payday to payday. Also, these are power levels in which one has to struggle and fight to move from bare survival to a safe and secure existence in which personal needs are satisfied. Christian charity as we know it does not exist at these levels."

"Is this where interactions come into play?" I asked.

"Precisely. Once one is at the safety/security level, then they have some energy left over to devote to relationships. They have affiliation needs, and these are met through interpersonal relationships. This brings us the Maslow's third level which is love, affection and belonging needs. At this level a person experiences a need for love, affection and affiliations. He needs to experience trust and caring relationships in which he can give and receive feedback and help others. These needs are met through family, friendships, and membership in business and social groups. At this point

Christian charity emerges as we know it. A person now has time and energy that can be spent in helping others. This level is concerned with affiliation needs." No pause. Shana simply continued her overview of Maslow.

"Once a person's social needs are met, he has excess time and energy to devote to getting ahead in life. At this level, achievement becomes important. A person wants to be perceived as worthy and to acquire status, privileges and prestige. Maslow calls this the level of ego/esteem/status needs where a person focuses on fulfilling his needs for esteem, mastery, competence, and prestige. At this level a person develops ambition and looks for ways to achieve and accomplish through both participation and independent thought and action. He seeks authority. He expects recognition from others and the environment. Depending on the situation, this may or may not be forthcoming. This dependence on external feedback makes the achievement level more difficult to fulfill."

"Now this is all coming back to me. We now move to the next level." I interjected.

"Yes. Once a person is successful and productive, Maslow says that the next and final level involves the need for self actualization. A person now has energy and attention available to channel into creativity and self expression. At this level he experiences the inherent needs for well-being, self-fulfillment, personal growth, development and the opportunity to actualize his potential and become his natural self. Maslow believed that the need for self actualization was a healthy man's prime motivation. He listed 13 characteristics of self actualization which I will not go into at this time. Later in his life, Maslow added another level beyond self actualization, which he called the need for self transformation. This involves an identity shift to another level of being."

MASLOW'S HIERARCHY OF NEEDS
One - Survival
Two - Safety and Security
Three - Love, Affection and Belonging
Four - Ego, Self-Esteem
Five - Self Actualization
Six - Self Transformation

"Maslow's hierarchy of needs and his description of self actualization were accepted by the white, liberal press of his day as a description of their basic experience; and he was anointed as a prophet of the new age. It turns out, however, that Maslow's description of self actualization does not apply to large numbers of people. To be more exact, Maslow's description is only one of eight views of self actualization. You will learn more about this in several months when you take our Success, Incorporated course on Value Cultures^{SM}."

"And read the book the founders of the company wrote on the subject!" I added.

"Maslow's hierarchy of needs is important for several reasons." Shana went on to say. "From wherever you are at on Maslow's hierarchy, the other levels are, in a certain sense, at worst criminal and demented and at best dull, boring and irrelevant. At each level we cannot understand the motives of those above us, and we quickly forget those of others below us."

"It is similar to having an entire different way of seeing the world, isn't it" I asked.

"Indeed it is." Shana proceeded. "The critical point is that circumstances beyond our control may cause any of us to drop back to lower levels on Maslow's hierarchy. If we are suddenly confronted with a mugger on the street, we may find ourselves at a survival level. If we suddenly lose our jobs we may find ourselves at the level of safety and security. If we have a major confrontation with a friend or relative we may be back to the love, affection and belonging level. In short, our basic motivation changes with context. When we are forced to downshift to a lower level, we will find that we behave in unexpected ways that we could not forecast or predict in advance. In emergencies and under stress people behave in ways that they would otherwise find inappropriate. Behaviors always have to be understood in context. As a manager it will be necessary whenever you encounter another person to understand his level on the hierarchy of needs in order to make sense of his behavior."

"So once again the notion of contextuality makes itself known." I interjected.

"You had best take that as a given." Shana responded and continued on. "Most managers and workers are at levels three or four on Maslow's model. When their jobs are threatened, however, they quickly revert to level two. Level two is a power level where one is focused on immediate individual survival and has no concern for the future survival of the organization. Also, when one drops from level four to level two, productivity declines dramatically. This is why job security is such an important issue. In a climate of downsizing, individuals and unions are focused at level two. Management may be at level four and focused on the organizations increased productivity while workers and unions are at level two focused on immediate safety and security. From the perspective of each, the behavior of the other is both criminal, unjust and outright crazy."

"I see exactly what you mean. No wonder why so many companies are stuck in a rut." I said.

"Businesses have to understand that whereas downsizing may be necessary, there will be a concomitant decline in productivity for anyone in the organization who feels threatened by this transition. This is one of the reasons that Japanese workers have been so productive. Until recently, a job in a Japanese company was a guarantee of cradle to grave security. One did not need to ever worry about safety and security; and Japanese workers could spend all of their time and energy at levels three and four focusing on belonging and achievement. It is no wonder that they could dramatically out produce their American counterparts who were constantly being dragged out of levels three and four back to level two by job security issues. Japan is experiencing economic problems now; and for the first time job security is becoming an issue for Japanese workers. This may result in a vicious spiral resulting in declining productivity by Japanese workers."

"I see job security as a major issue for companies around the globe." I said.

"That is an excellent observation. Forecasters are predicting that job security will become an increasing problem in coming decades. Downsizing does seem to be a wave of the future. Some predict a workplace in which everything is contracted out, and in which there is no job security. This does not bode well for future productivity given Maslow's model. If enough people find themselves at the security level, they will begin to put pressure on government to force companies to guarantee employment. This could lead to further vicious cycles. The matter is one that American business and government need to consider carefully. The bottom line is that workers are most productive at level four and most cooperative at level three; and anything that can be done to keep them there is good for business and the country."

VALUE CULTURES

"As I have indicated, another key to motives and motivation is values. I have also indicated that you will learn much more about this in several months when you take our Success, Incorporated course on Value Cultures. Here I will only be able to give you a brief preview of this incredibly powerful Value Culture Model^{SM}."

"As I have already indicated, values are the heart of motivation. They are what determines those elements toward which one moves or from which one moves away. The things that we as human beings either move toward or away from are our *values*. These are the things that control our behaviors. Values are those things, whether abstract or concrete, whether tangible or intangible, which a person invests energy, time, money and other resources either to achieve or to avoid. All of human behavior from the beginning of mankind on the planet to the present can be explained and understood from our values. Values, then, are the building blocks of the Motivational People Pattern." I did not dare interrupt this explication.

"Because each human being wears his own distinctive perceptual filters," Shana continued, "the combination of values, i.e. the components of the building blocks will vary from person to person, the end result being the diversity of personality types and behaviors associated with these personalities. We have found that certain personality types are highly move toward in their orientation, and other types definitely move away from. You will learn about these personality types in the Value Culture course."

"What you have been saying all along is that it is important to know not only whether a person is move toward or move away from, but also what they move toward or away from." I said.

"Exactly. This tells you what carrots or sticks to use. To motivate a move toward person you need to offer him the value that he wants. To motivate a move away from person you need to show him how he can avoid the value that he doesn't want. Each one of us has our own customized combination of different values which determine our behaviors. So in order to motivate a person, it is crucial to know his values - the specific things that he moves toward or away from. The Value Culture Model describes eight types of Value Cultures. We have discovered that the primary motive will be determined by the Value Culture from which the person is operating. You will learn this in great detail in the Value Culture course."

"Perhaps it would be appropriate to mention at this point" Shana went on to say, "that no one Value Culture is necessarily better or worse than another in the healthy manifestation of that Value Culture. One needs to remember that whatever values you have are not necessarily those of other people around you, and what motivates you, therefore, may not work for others. Motivation is a complex issue that becomes all the more nuanced as you move from one person to another, and likewise from one Value Culture to another."

"Here is where context comes in again. Right?" I added.

"What else is new! Our Motivation People Pattern must be contextually determined. Moreover, different circumstances and contexts may dictate different carrots and sticks. For example, a person may always be move toward in his life, and may have a whole series of varied carrots which motivate him in different situations. Similarly, a predominately move away from person may require different sticks for various life events and issues. The bottom line is that identifying a person's pattern is just half the picture, because to motivate effectively, you need to know precisely what carrots or sticks to use and which ones correspond to particular contexts in that individual's life. Choosing the wrong carrot or stick may produce a mitigated version of the desired result or may end up triggering the opposite behavior than the one you want to encourage."

"So values are a critical part of human behavior, something which I have seen in other firms is totally ignored or else misunderstood." I added.

"I cannot stress enough the importance of understanding the values which are the basis of all human behavior. Moreover, the decisions we make as a result of our values are often outside of our conscious awareness. If you were to ask yourself what your values are, the answers may not be as obvious to you as you might think." Shana asked me to continue listening for a bit more as she proceeded to discuss Value Cultures.

"With these points in mind, let me now briefly explain to you the eight Value Cultures or Worlds which comprise the Value Culture Model. Value Cultures are sets of coping mechanisms which we develop as a response to a changing environment. Each value culture reflects a new level of complexity regarding the problems of the environment and requires more sophisticated coping mechanisms with which to manage that complexity. The eight different Worlds and the Value Cultures associated with them are as follows:"

THE EIGHT VALUE CULTURES
World 1: The Human Herd
World 2: The Traditional Tribe
World 3:Tthe Socially Defiant
World 4: The Rigid Rule Makers
World 5: The Capitalist Achievers
World 6: The Societally Conscious
World 7: The Systemic Thinkers
World 8: The Wonder Wizards

"**WORLD ONE**: The first World is the level of the Human Herd. This involves a group or band of individuals coming together in order to meet their basic biological survival needs such as food, water and shelter. In World One, the focus of existence is on individual survival and on survival of the band. Any of us may revert to this very basic level of values if we are suddenly placed in a situation where we are denied food, water or shelter or in which our life is otherwise endangered. Under such circumstances, the acquisition of these basic necessities becomes our primary focus in life."

"**WORLD TWO**: The second World is the level of the Traditional Tribe. It is the level of chiefs, tribalistic rituals, ancestor worship and shamanistic figures who safeguard the members of the tribe from the evil forces found in the threatening world outside of the tribe. In World Two, the focus of existence is on the survival of the tribe which is locked in a perpetual struggle against the forces of nature and against other hostile tribes."

"**WORLD THREE**: The third World is that of the Socially Defiant. It is a World of hostility and hedonism in which only the strong and powerful survive. It is a World of 'haves' and 'have nots'. In World Three, everyone is competing for scarce and limited resources. The focus of the individual is toward his own immediate sensory gratification with no regard or concern for the needs or welfare of others. Individuals in this Value Culture have no sense of guilt or remorse for their actions. World Three is the World of many hard core criminals."

"**WORLD FOUR**: The fourth World is that of the Rigid Rule Makers. It is a World characterized by absolutistic thinking and rigid dichotomies (i.e., right/wrong, good/bad, sacred/evil, etc.). This is where the so-called 'silent majority' live. In World Four, the focus of existence is on obeying 'the rules' and working hard in order to obtain future rewards in both this life and the next. This is the first Value Culture at which the notion of 'delayed gratification' emerges. It is also the first Value Culture at which we experience guilt."

"**WORLD FIVE**: The fifth World is that of the Capitalist Achiever. This is the realm of business, materialism, science and technology. In World Five, the focus of the individual is on achieving the goal of 'the good life' now rather than putting it off for later. This means amassing as much wealth as possible. In World Five, 'he who dies with the best toys wins'. The materialist, however, prefers if possible to attain his goals in such a way that will not trigger reprisals or the indignation of others who may want to take away what he has amassed."

"**WORLD SIX**: The sixth World is that of the Societally Conscious. This is the domain of sensitivity to the needs of our fellow human beings in an effort to fill the dehumanizing void created by science and technology. In affiliative World Six, the focus of existence is aimed at establishing positive relationships with others and is directed toward working for the collective benefit of society. Among the Societally Conscious, feelings and bonding with our fellow man takes precedence over all else."

"**WORLD SEVEN**: The seventh World is that of the Systemic Thinker. In World Seven, the focus of existence is the attainment of knowledge and competency in order to deal with an ever changing and complex environment. The spotlight of attention for the Systemic Thinkers is the solving of interesting problems and the avoiding of unnecessary hassles. They prefer freedom and autonomy and resent regulations or structures that restrict their behavioral choices. This is a realm characterized by flexibility of behaviors to fit contextual needs and by systemic thinking marked by sophisticated distinctions."

"**WORLD EIGHT**: The eighth World is that of the Wonder Wizards. This is a World which combines both experiential and multi-level reality thinking. It is a Value Culture in which the physical and the metaphysical worlds come together. It is a Value Culture that is just barely manifest on the planet at this point in time. So if it does not make sense, then do not worry about it for now. World Eight is at the nascent stage and is in the process of emerging in response to problems of global coordination and survival. In this Value Culture, the focus of the individual lies in creating the necessary conditions for human growth and global survival and in eliminating threats to that survival."

"Each World or Value Culture corresponds to a particular set of coping strategies or 'Yang' elements, created in response to a particular class of life problems, or 'Yin' elements. Each Value Culture lies at the conjunction of a set of challenges posed by life and of mechanisms in the human mind activated to deal with these challenges. The following table is a brief overview of this process which is referred to as the 'Yin/Yang of Values[SM]'."

"YIN" ELEMENTS Challenges of the world	"YANG ELEMENTS" Responses of well adapted individuals
1) It is nature unbridled.	They survive like other animals do.
2) It is full of threatening natural and social conditions.	They unite for safety and appease menacing forces.
3) It is a survival of the fittest existence.	They exert power over others to survive.
4) It is hierarchal and structured.	They conform to absolute laws and to proper authority.
5) It is abundant in natural and other resources.	They compete to achieve material success.
6) It is dehumanized by science and technology.	They share and care for each other and collectivize.
7) It is complex and a constant search for meaningful and interesting preoccupations.	They seek autonomy and search for viable solutions.
8) It is chaotic and unbalanced.	They seek to restore equilibrium by neutralizing destructive forces in conjunction with others like themselves.

"Obviously, the Value Culture Model will give a person an incredible insight into peoples' values and motives." I chimed in.

"That is true and more. However, this session is not the time to go into detail about the Model. In the meantime, today I want to focus on another powerful model that is a half way house to the Value Culture Model. It is not as complex, and it will enable you to quickly select between three different classes of carrots and sticks. It is called the Motive People Pattern."

THE MOTIVE PEOPLE PATTERN

"You may be thinking that there are an infinite number of things that a person can move toward and away from, and there are. These values often cluster themselves, however, into groups. David McClelland the late Harvard psychologist was one of the leading authorities in the world on motivation. He says that people operate out of one of three basic motives. McClelland says that people are motivated by three things which are: 1) Power, 2) Affiliation and 3) Achievement. Everyone has one of these elements which is the fundamental driving force in their lives and another one that is secondary. One either moves toward or away in one of these three areas. There is nothing new about this model. These three motives correspond to the three temptations of Christ by Satan in the New Testament, i.e. power, fame, and wealth. Also, they originate from the three basic human instincts described by the Greeks before Christianity came into being. These are the self preservation instinct corresponding to power, the social instinct corresponding to affiliation, and the reproductive instinct corresponding to achievement."

"I can already think of friends and colleagues who may fit into these categories." I said.

"I would hold off until you hear the rest." suggested Shana. "*Power people* are concerned with accruing and maintaining power. They have a strong need to influence and lead others and to be in control of their environment. They view all human interactions as power struggles and contests of will. The issue of dominance and submission is of fundamental importance to them. They are motivated to power and domination and oppose any threat to their control, influence or leadership. They evaluate people as to whether they will support or oppose them. They enjoy competitive sports and like to be in leadership roles. McClelland sees power as being distributed along a continuum from positive or socially beneficial to negative or domineering. At the positive end of the continuum is 'socialized power' which is used for the benefit of others. At the negative end is 'personalized power' which is used to manipulate and dominate others."

"I can see some of my former managers as power people for sure." I was pleased to discover.

"*Affiliation people* have a need for friendly and close interpersonal relationships based on mutual understanding." Shana said. "They express their emotions readily, and they view all human interactions in terms of whether they create or destroy positive relationships. They value friendship. What people think about them and others is important to them. They like or dislike people. They are motivated to create or improve relationships and oppose those who threaten positive relationships. Issues of inclusion and exclusion are particularly important to them. They are maintenance oriented, and they evaluate people on the basis of whether they are nice to them or not. Affiliation people prefer cooperation to competition. McClelland also sees affiliation as distributed along a continuum. The positive end is 'affiliative interest' which emphasizes positive relationships or maintenance behavior, but not at the expense of task or goal oriented behavior. These people are able to give and accept negative feedback while maintaining the relationship and staying on purpose. The negative end is 'affiliative assurance' which emphasizes maintaining the relationship at all cost. These people move away from being disliked and so are conflict avoiding. They seek approval from others and are willing to sacrifice work goals to maintain relationships. Please let me finish before you interrupt."

"*Achievement people* are concerned with accomplishment and have a need to fulfill their goals, excel, and strive to continuously do things better. Success is the major factor in their lives. They are task or goal oriented and need feedback on how they are doing. They set challenging but realistic goals and succeed through good planning, decisiveness and their ability to prioritize tasks to meet their objectives. They are motivated to succeed and accomplish things, and they oppose anything that limits their success. They evaluate people on the basis of accomplishment and disapprove of people who are lazy or idle. Achievement people are excited to develop their skills and to invent or create new things. They like challenge and problems to be solved and will take moderate risks. Also, they are more interested in the process and outcome than the external rewards."

"Does a continuum also apply to achievement?" I asked.

"In fact it does. Achievement is also distributed along a continuum. The positive end is a genuine aspiration toward success. These people are positively attracted to goals and truly aspire to achieve. The negative end is the fear of failure. These people are concerned about avoiding failure and not about achieving success."

PEOPLE PATTERN	TOWARD	AWAY FROM	GOAL
Power	Control	Domination	Winning
Affiliation	Harmony	Discord	Popularity
Achievement	Success	Failure	Success

TEST

"Do you understand the Motive People Pattern?" Shana asked.

"I do and I would like now to find out how to tell what someone is. Are there target indicator questions?" I responded. Shana continued.

"To determine what the primary motive in a person's life is, pay careful attention to his behavior and to why he does what he does. Observe both the behavior and the motivation for the behavior. When you meet someone for the first time, engage him in polite conversation, and talk to him about his day. Listen for the themes in his conversation. Does the person tell you about what he accomplished, or about his relationships with the people involved, or about how he controlled the situation. Another good diagnostic trick is to observe some strangers engaged in an activity and get the person whose pattern you are eliciting to speculate on what he thinks that the strangers are doing. Once again pay careful attention to the theme(s) in his description."

"So power people will want control?" I guessed.

"On the mark. *Power people* will tell you about power struggles and about who is in control in the situation. They will describe efforts to control and regulate the behavior of other people. They will describe activities in which power is expressed and which involve strong, forceful actions. They will often describe how they or someone else provided unsolicited help or feedback to some other person. They will discuss status, position and reputation and how someone is impressing someone else. They will discuss efforts of one person to argue with, persuade, convince, influence or manipulate another person to take their view or side."

"Also, power people will often be confrontational and project these feelings onto others. In an argument they will equate victory or defeat to dominance and submission. They will value strong people and have contempt for the weak. They will be concerned about themselves. They will always view others in relation to themselves — as a superior, equal or inferior. They will expect you to lead, follow or get out of the way."

"I assume that there are positive and negative people for each motive type." I said.

"Fortunately the answer is yes." Shana said. "Positive power people will enjoy competitive sports and seek leadership roles in society. Negative power people lack inhibition and self control and are impulsive about dominating others. They tend to become nasty drunks and to exploit the opposite sex as chattels or objects of abuse and manipulation. They like to watch contact sports and violent shows. They also are attracted to prestige symbols but for different reasons than a positive power person."

"I know both kinds and I can see the difference immediately in the way they act." I said.

"*Affiliation people* will tell you about the people with whom they interact and to whom they were relating. They will tell you about people they and other individuals like and dislike. They will tell you about friendships and about positive emotional relations and they will talk to you about feelings. They also may discuss affiliative activities that they engage in. Also, they will be emotional in discussing these things. Affiliation people will be non-confrontive. They will not like to argue or compete. They will be maintenance oriented and concerned about means and about others. They will either like you, be indifferent toward you or dislike you."

"I'll bet that the affiliation people tend to get emotional." I said.

"Affiliation people will be friendly and display their emotions and feelings easily. They like to talk to people and will communicate more often than the other types. They also listen better and care what other people think. They will be the people in the organization who help to create a friendly and cooperative environment. They develop close relationships with others. They will engage in maintenance behaviors and strive to see that relationships are harmonious. They will dislike competition and contact sports. They will avoid violent programs."

"*Achievement people* will tell you about their goals and what they got done and about people who aided or assisted their accomplishments. They will tell you about goal directed activity and about the feedback that tells them what progress is occurring. They will also tell you about the standards that they use to evaluate performance. Listen carefully for comparative words that they use to evaluate performance."

"Achievement people are the competitors in life. Right?" I asked.

"Exactly. Achievement people will be competitive. They will be task or goal oriented and concerned about ends. They will believe that you are either part of the solution or part of the problem. If you can help them reach their goals, then they will value you. If you stand in the way of them reaching their goals, they will run over you or go around you in some way. Meanwhile, if you are neither an asset or a liability they will probably have little interest in you."

"Also, achievement people will engage in task behavior. They will always have clear goals and will be working toward them. They will set priorities and keep people on track. They will be concerned with accomplishment and achievement and will communicate only when needed to accomplish a task. They take responsibility and often work alone. They will seek ongoing feedback so that they can monitor progress toward the goal at hand." Shana took a brief pause.

PEOPLE PATTERN	INSTINCT	BEHAVIORAL ORIENTATION	ISSUE
Power	Self Preservation	Self	Control
Affiliation	Social	Maintenance	Inclusion
Achievement	Reproductive	Task	Expression

PRAYERS

"Do you have any questions? If not, I'll go on. Oh, I almost forgot about the prayers. Here they are. The Power Prayer is:"

Lord God Almighty, Source of all power, Ruler of all things. O Omnipotent One Who can do anything. Grant me this day the power to control my destiny. Give me the strength to oppose my adversaries. Grant me the cunning to defeat them. Grant me the wisdom to win over them. Allow me to crush them in defeat. Deliver me from those who would challenge my power and who would strive to control me. Amen.

"The Affiliation Prayer is:"

Lord God who created love and understanding. Eternal Friend to those in need. Always willing to lend a helping hand. Give me this day of Thy council, guidance and Love. Be as a loving Father unto me. Lead me into harmonious relationships. Let me serve as an agent of Thy love. Let my life be filled with caring and sharing. Surround me with positive people who are always concerned for the welfare of others. Allow me to live in charity and harmony with my neighbor all the days of my life. Deliver me from those who preach hate and intolerance. Deliver me from those who place might and success before love and compassion. Amen.

"And the Achievement Prayer is:"

Lord God, Maker of Heaven and earth. Thou art the Great Creator and the Great Builder. All that is, is the result of your creation. Grant me this day Thy spirit of creativity. Allow me to be a co-creator with Thou. Grant me the clarity to always have specific goals and the wisdom to select my goals carefully. Grant me the force of will to always act efficiently and effortlessly. Grant me the strength to work unceasingly. Make all of my labors fruitful. Help me to stay on task and on purpose. Help me in the task of building a heaven on earth. Deliver me from those who want to waste my time and who do not have clear aims and goals. Most of all, Lord, deliver me from those power mongers who resist progress and who block productivity. Amen.

"So everyone has a primary motive, and they may have a secondary one. Pay attention to what it is and to whether it is toward or away. This will tell you whether to use carrots or sticks and which kinds of carrots and sticks to use. Do you understand the Motive People Pattern? Good, then go on your rounds and see how this powerful pattern is used here at Success, Incorporated."

KINDS OF MANAGERS

Marvin was excited as always to see me. I was equally excited to find the specific applications of the Motive People Pattern. Marvin began. "Yesterday you learned the Motivation People Pattern, and today you have been taught the Motive People Pattern. These two patterns are the chief weapons in the managers' motivational arsenal. Also, they explain the psycho-dynamics involved in the internal politics of any organization, and they lie at the heart of the ongoing competition among various management approaches to be the flavor of the month. Let us begin with management styles."

"There are six kinds of managers based on the way that they motivate themselves and others. The six types either move toward or away from power, affiliation or achievement. Almost all organizational dynamics is a result of the interplay between these three powerful forces. In any organization they form a series of checks and balances that can either produce a high performance organization or bring productivity to a standstill. One job of leadership is to understand and direct the complex dynamics of the interaction of these three forces. A thorough grasp of *People Patterns* will facilitate this process."

"I think I have had my share of each somewhere along the line in my career. This information is clarifying so many incidents and interactions of the past, it's amazing." I blurted out.

"And we're still far from done. Power managers are the bosses of the world. What they want is control. They want to build empires and will fight anyone who comes on their turf. They tend to be theory X. They either move toward accruing more and more power or move away from powerlessness. For them what is most important is their place in the power hierarchy. They want total control over their domain. They expect obedience from those below them in the chain. Any disagreement from subordinates is seen as a threat to their power base and must be met with overwhelming force." Marvin went on.

"Those who move toward power are more aggressive than those who move away from powerlessness. Those who move toward power will invade another's territory in order to increase their power. They are constantly on the alert for opportunities to expand their sphere of influence and for potential weaknesses in others that can be exploited to their advantage. Those who move away will be relatively benign, until their power is threatened, at which time they fight like mad to protect it. They are less likely to aggressively try to usurp someone else's power unless that person poses a threat to their power base. As long as you leave them alone, they will usually leave you be."

"Power players are particularly prevalent in bureaucracies such as the federal, state and local governments and in hierarchical organizations such as the military and the Catholic Church. Obviously the power game is played with varying degrees of sophistication. The more sophisticated players are usually the more cunning and covert. They can be both positive and negative. The positive are the benevolent despots of the world and the negative are people like Saddam Hussein and the Colonel so aptly played by Jack Nicholson in the movie *A Few Good Men*."

"I can think of a few people in my own life like that!" I added.

"Research shows that many effective managers and leaders have a high need for power. Some argue that a manager needs a relatively high need for power to function effectively as a leader. In any case, although a power orientation may be a necessary condition for leadership, it is certainly not a sufficient condition. How effective a power person is as a leader will depend on other values. If the power person operates out of personalized power and if they are authoritarian and autocratic, then they will probably not be an effective leader except under certain special circumstances. On the other hand, if they come out of socialized power and if they use their influence skills to empower others, then they may be a very effective leader. Probably the ideal leader is one who is high in socialized power and who is also high in achievement and possesses good interpersonal skills."

"If you don't mind I will continue my discussion of the different types of managers." Marvin said. "The second type of managers are those that move toward achievement and those who move away from failure. What they want is to achieve success or to avoid failure. The goal of the game is achievement and accomplishment and the perks that go with it. They tend to be theory Y. They are the managers and leaders of the business world.

Success comes through setting high but realistic goals and through staying on task through hard work, careful planning and the skillful management of the situation."

"Those who move toward achievement are the more aggressive." Marvin went on to say. "They are more willing to take moderate risks to achieve success. They will try things in the hopes of success. They are looking for breakthroughs and changes that will lead to quantum leaps. Those who move away from failure tend to be more reactive. They do not take risks. Their main goal is not to mess up. They are cautious and conservative in their management style. They are content with the status quo and ever on the alert for problems that might have the potential for failure. If things are going okay, they believe that the best strategy is to do nothing rather than to do anything which might have the least risk of failure. Needless to say, these two approaches almost inevitably are in conflict. One wants to innovate and act now and the other wants to keep doing what has worked and to wait and see."

"Isn't business in general an achievement process?" I asked.

"Yes, by its very nature business is achievement oriented. Its goal is to increase productivity and profitability. The language of business is achievement language. We speak of missions, goals, objectives, plans, milestones, and budgets. Businesses are constantly torn between the desire for increased success and the fear of failure. Business has achievement as its aim or goal, but this does not necessarily mean that achievement is its means. It may use power, achievement or affiliation as a means to reach an achievement outcome."

Marvin continued. "Research shows that many effective upper level managers and leaders are not as high in achievement needs as in power needs. Research also shows that the most effective upper level managers have high needs for power and also a relatively high need for achievement. Effective middle-level and lower-level managers usually have a high need for both power and achievement. Although achievement managers are task oriented, they may not produce results because their tendency toward personal responsibility prevents them from delegating authority. Also, they prefer to work alone even when collaborative effort would be more advisable. In short they may be task oriented, but without power or affiliation skills they may find it difficult to enlist the help of others to accomplish the task. So high achievement by itself will usually not produce effective managers and leaders. It is interesting, however, that a high need for achievement does appear to be critical for entrepreneurs."

"I think I am beginning to see just where I fit in." I happily announced.

Marvin raised his eyebrows at me and proceeded to explain affiliation managers.

"The third type of managers are the affiliation managers. They either move toward harmonious relations or away from discord. They either go out of their way to make friends or to avoid making enemies. They want to build positive teamwork and cooperation or to avoid conflict. They manage by charm. People do things for them because they like them. They are the genuinely nice, concerned and caring people in an organization. This often brings out the best in others."

"Those who move toward affiliation actively pursue creating positive and beneficial relationships. They care about their employees and may adopt a fatherly attitude or a mother hen complex. They are well liked and respected. They tend to be a combination of theory Y and theory Z. Those who move away from disharmony are the conflict avoiders of the world. They are incredibly sensitive to conflict and make every effort to avoid it. They do not want their employees in conflict either and get very upset with anyone who introduces tension or discord. They feel we are all in the same boat, a boat we are better off not rocking. In their desire to avoid conflict and to be liked, they may fail to enforce the unpopular decisions of upper management. If they are forced to abide by and implement these unpopular decisions, they try to make it known that they do not support the decisions and that they have no choice but to go along."

"Who is the best manager?" I asked.

"Research shows that high affiliation needs alone do not make good leaders or managers. It is more common to find supervisors who are high in affiliation than upper level managers. Affiliative interest managers are more likely to be successful leaders because of their ability to balance goal-oriented behavior with interpersonal relationships. Affiliative assurance managers, on the other hand, make less successful leaders. Their need for approval and desire to avoid conflict interfere with their ability to make tough decisions and to achieve work goals." Marvin went on.

"Although high affiliation may not be sufficient for effective leadership and management, this does not mean that these skills are not necessary in a leader or organization. It is the affiliation people in any organization who often keep communication channels open and who are able to create the social networks that ensure collaboration. They frequently serve as a check against the misuse of personalized power and the over emphasis on productivity to the detriment of the maintenance of the health and well being of the employees. Please let me finish my train of thought." Marvin said.

"Also, it is precisely the lack of interpersonal skills that causes many mid and upper level managers to derail. The Center for Creative Leadership did an exhaustive study on managers who failed to successfully make the transition from middle to upper management. The one thing that they found that these managers most had in common was a lack of interpersonal skills. Power managers in general, and personalized power managers in particular, often failed because they reached a level where they required the cooperation of their colleagues and where they were unable to obtain it through the use of control, influence and manipulation. Also, achievement managers who had been successful through their own individual efforts suddenly required the combined efforts of others, and they lacked the affiliative skill to ensure this cooperation. And there is more." Marvin added.

"The study found that managers who were successful in transitioning to upper level positions had at least a minimum threshold of interpersonal skills. This enabled both the socialized power managers and the achievement managers to get the necessary cooperation and support of others. One of the more important courses we have developed here at Success, Incorporated is called Interpersonal Dynamics. It is in essence a charm school for power and affiliation managers."

MOTIVE	TYPE	ISSUE	TOWARD	AWAY
Power	Boss	Control	In charge	Domination
Affiliation	Friend	Respect	Being popular	Being unliked
Achievement	Manager	Success	Performance	Failure

ORGANIZATIONAL POLITICS

"In any organization", Marvin continued, "the power, achievement and affiliation people are locked in a constant struggle for control of the organization. The achievement people are production oriented and want to make the organization more effective and efficient. The affiliation people are maintenance oriented and want to make sure that the needs of the employees are safe guarded. The power people want to maintain control and to see that things are done their way."

"And the power people always want control. Right?" I said.

"Correct. The power people in an organization fight to maintain their control and to make sure that the achievement people do not achieve their goals at their expense, and that the affiliation people do not escape their domination. Power people are more concerned with maintaining their own power than with the productivity of the business or the maintenance of open and supportive relationships. Power players only believe in teams if they are in charge of the team and give all the orders. Negative power players are the curse of all bureaucracies and the primary reason that bureaucracies are so inefficient. In a bureaucracy, all the power players guard their territories at the expense of cooperation and production."

"Based on what you said before, aren't there nuances among the power players?" I asked.

"Indeed. You are learning well. The more sophisticated power players realize that they have to be more subtle and are constantly looking for ways to gain leverage and to shift blame. These can be very dangerous people to cross, since they are masters of stealthful maneuvering. Less sophisticated power players are willing to let the business flounder rather than sacrifice their power. Very sophisticated power players can be super manipulative either for the good of the company or for their own personal greed and ambition. The most successful power players combine power with an achievement orientation, and use their considerable skills to increase productivity. Power people are often found in line management and in accounting." Marvin did not take a break and went on to affiliation players.

"Affiliation players are always trying to promote harmony. To them positive teamwork is more important than wining or success. They are most often in conflict with the power people and are always trying to democratize their power base. Affiliation players come into conflict with the achievement people when productivity is bought at the expense of people. They are the humanists of the organization. They are the grease that keeps people working together and communication flowing. They are always looking to reach an accord and compromise with the power and achievement players. They argue that increased affiliation (i.e., teamwork and cooperation) will lead to greater achievement. They are often found in personnel and in the human resource department."

"Achievement players tend to be more into individual responsibility, accountability and rewards. They do not want to be lost in the collective. They are task oriented and are always looking for ways to increase productivity. Achievement is critical to business success. The challenge is to keep the power players in check so that productivity is not sacrificed upon the alter of their need for control. On the other side the achievement players have to temper the level of productivity with the legitimate needs of the employees. This is not always easy. In short, achievement players need the cooperation of the power and affiliation players if the organization itself is going to be successful."

THE CHANGING GLOBAL MANAGEMENT SCENE

Marvin then began a major discourse on the changing scene in corporate management, which applies to all of the major industrial giants of the world today.

"There has been a major shift in global business in the last fifty years away from a power orientation and toward an achievement orientation. Currently there is a shift toward an achievement through affiliation orientation. The sweatshops of the twenties where employees had no rights are a thing of the past. Today, most businesses are moving away from a power orientation, but this does not necessarily mean that they are heading toward achievement or affiliation. Many are tragically simply moving into the void." Marvin continued.

"The union movement in America sprang up as a response to a power management. Unchecked power can lead to tremendous misuse; and the abusive and inhumane treatment of employees led to a backlash. The unions came into being to protect employees against exploitation by a power management. This often led to violent power versus power confrontations. As management became more and more militant, the unions followed suit. Each polarized off of the other, and power players rose to the top. With the advent of the World Wars, government began to place restrictions on unrestrained capitalism. More and more government regulations were enacted to protect against the abuse of power. Many of these regulations came from a liberal congress more concerned with moving away from power than moving toward either success or cooperation. The regulations were frequently enforced by power bureaucrats which led to increasing conflict between government and business and unions."

"I see many companies today as achievement in orientation." I added.

"Yes. Today most successful businesses have moved on into an achievement mode, although there are still many power players in their upper management. Affiliation players are gaining a foothold. They argue that affiliation is good business and that teamwork leads to increased productivity. One of the greatest challenges facing this country today is for businesses and unions to transition from an adversarial power orientation to a more cooperative achievement/affiliation orientation. If business and the unions are going to survive, the achievement/affiliation oriented players in both are going to have to combine to take control away from the power players who will allow the ship to sink while they are engaged in constant warfare with each other."

Marvin went on to say: "The realities of the global economy make this crucial if the business of any country is going to remain competitive in world markets. We are increasingly being forced to compete with achievement oriented foreign competitors who have their own governments as partners. Our country is unique in having a power oriented federal bureaucracy that is in opposition to big business. This country needs to come to its senses and throw out the personalized power players in government, business and the unions. Only by a cooperative partnership of government, unions and management can we hope to compete against foreign companies who are in partnership with their employees and their governments. Until our nation either comes to its senses, the power players in business, unions and government will continue their constant struggle each blaming the other and each vainly attempting to control the other to the detriment of business and the country as a whole."

QUALITY

The discussion next turned to the question of quality in relation to the Motive Pattern, quality, of course, being a notion of utmost importance in today's global economy. As usual, Marvin jumped right into the topic.

"In any organization, as I have emphasized, there is an eternal conflict between the power, affiliation and achievement players. Each has different aims, and each uses different means to achieve those aims. In many organizations none has the power to control, and each can block the other. This can lead to cooperation and productivity or more frequently to stalemate, gridlock and stagnation."

"Every group is out for itself, though." I said.

"Well, yes." Marvin continued. "And each group is always looking for a banner to rally behind which they can use to conquer the other. The power players seize control when a temporary increase in production is critical and expediency becomes necessary. Usually this only lasts for awhile. The abuses of absolute power soon lead to a backlash, and things return to the status quo." Of course, I did not interrupt Marvin's train of thought; and he went on.

"There is a banner that is extremely in vogue today which the achievement players hope will allow them to win the war over their adversaries (i.e., the power and affiliation players). It is called total quality management (TQM). This all started interestingly enough with the public backlash at the Department of Defense (DOD). When the fraud, waste and abuse on the part of defense contractors was exposed, the public became very upset. The ever vigilant generals did not want to lose the good will of the people. They had battled back from Viet Nam and were all too aware of the need for public support. So DOD and some of the responsible government contractors got together and developed a brilliant stratagem to keep congress and the people off of their back."

"It was that American, oh, his name escapes me right now, who started the whole thing." I added.

"Indeed it was." said Marvin. DOD took a page from the Japanese who had learned it from an American named Edward Deming, who had taken it to Japan because American business would not listen to him. They decided that the solution was for the government to require quality. Quality by definition is quite simple. It is the best possible product at the lowest possible cost. How could the public argue with this? The government would require every defense contractor to provide quality and to have a program to guarantee and manage this quality."

Marvin asked if I had any questions or comments, and when I said that I had none he finished off this discussion.

"DOD even went a step further. Not only did they require every vendor who provided them material to have a TQM program but everyone who provided material to that vendor had to have one also. So the trickle down effect reached virtually every company in America. Almost anybody who makes anything, supplies it to someone who eventually supplies something to the government."

"So quality and TQM have become some of the hottest buzzwords in American management. The government gives an award for quality (The Malcolm Baldridge National Quality Award), and almost every major corporation in the country is applying for it."

"Is quality power, affiliation or achievement?" I asked.

"Great question." said Marvin. "Remember that by definition quality is the best possible product at the lowest possible price. This is the achievement bible! This is the achiever's dream come true. Their word has been made law. Now they have something with which to knock the power players off their pedestals. Now they can tell the affiliation players that they are just going to have to sacrifice, because quality is now king."

"I'll bet that the power and affiliation people are none too pleased." I said.

"That is for sure." Responded Marvin with a grin. "Of course, the pendulum is now swinging back the other way, and the backlash is coming. The power people are complaining that all of this concern for zero defects is hurting production, and the affiliation people are complaining that workers are being exploited in the name of efficiency. Many corporations are finding that TQM did not get them the savings that they expected and that it is causing more problems than it is worth. Even Florida Power and Light which was a Baldridge award winner is abandoning their program." Marvin went on.

"In defense of TQM, one of the problems has been that most companies did not follow the DOD guidelines in implementing their programs. The DOD manual on TQM clearly states that the greatest saving will come from a synergistic merging of technical and human solutions. Most technical managers are engineers and scientists who have been promoted into management positions. They distrust whatever they cannot understand and quantify, and they particularly distrust soft human skills. They invested millions in quality monitoring systems like statistical process control, and they invested nothing in the human systems required to make the technical systems work. They conducted mandatory training programs in quality and wondered why they didn't work. The answer is simple."

"Why didn't it work?" I pondered out loud as Marvin continued.

"Why don't people produce better quality? Is it because they don't know how to? Is it really true that all that is required to achieve quality is to train workers in the 'what' and the 'how' of quality? The answer is a resounding 'no'. But most TQM training programs are just that. They are nothing more than the 'what' and the 'how' of quality. This is the 'makes sense' brain at its worst. The reason that people do not produce quality is not because they do not know 'what' it is, nor is it because they do not know 'how' to achieve it."

"I would not have thought that." I piped in for what it was worth.

"It is because they do not want to! Pure and simple. There is nothing in it for them! In fact, they are afraid that it will mean working harder, and no one wants to work any harder than they already are. They are also afraid that it will lead to greater efficiency and the consequent loss of jobs. They would not do it just because it is mandated. There has to be something in it for them. A special type of training is required that leads to behavioral modification; but this requires the soft human skills that technical managers do not trust. So it is no surprise that TQM programs are only partially successful, if successful at all, in most companies. We have developed special programs here at Success, Incorporated that focus on the human dimension. To sell quality it is necessary to demonstrate to employees that it will make their jobs easier, that it will require less work, and that it will not lead to a reduction in the work force. In other words, it is necessary to actually demonstrate to employees that there is something in it for them. We have developed successful programs to do this."

"That has been obvious to me from the first day I walked in. The employees here really love what they do and do it well." I said.

SERVICE

"A second trend in international business impacts on the eternal triangle of power, affiliation and achievement." Marvin went on to say. "This has to do with the issue of service. As the business world becomes increasingly competitive, customers are becoming increasingly demanding. In a seller's market, customers have to take what they can get. But in a buyer's market, businesses have to compete for everything that they earn. In many areas of business we have entered into a buyer's market. In this market, customers are not requesting but demanding quality goods and services at a reasonable price. Customers expect service. If they do not get it, then they will go to someone who provides it."

"Service is so important around the globe." I said, and before I could say more Marvin began speaking again.

"Yes. In today's business climate, service is the order of the day. The customer is king. This is bad news to the power players and good news to the achievement and affiliation players. They preach finding out what the customer wants and providing it for them in an efficient and courteous fashion."

"Knowing how to provide service must be a real problem, though." I said.

"Bigger than you think. The problem, of course, is how to train power people who are used to a seller's market to suddenly be service oriented in a buyer's market. How do you teach an old dog new tricks? It isn't easy, as many businesses are finding out the hard way. Most businesses believe that the solution to this problem is training. They think that all you need to produce service oriented employees is to train them in service. They, of course, are running into the identical problem as the quality people. The problem is not that people do not know how to provide better service. The problem is that they do not want to! Service from their perspective means that they have to be nice to people and work harder, but they do not want to work any harder and they certainly do not want to have to pretend to be nice."

"That is definitely true, and more and more!" I said almost with a tinge of disgust.

"The service challenge cannot be solved by traditional training." Marvin continued. "It requires an attitudinal conversion. It requires people to change their values and beliefs and their attitudes toward other people. For this to happen, powerful carrots and sticks have to be carefully applied appropriately. This takes a special kind of training from someone who both understands People Patterns intimately and who is skilled in behavioral modification. It also requires a willingness on the part of the business to provide the necessary carrots and sticks. Unfortunately, these factors seldom come together, and we continue to face a crisis in service in this country and elsewhere around the globe."

Before I could utter a word Marvin said: "I'd like to finish up this discussion so that we can move on to another topic. I was talking to a manager of a large hotel not long ago who was concerned about service. His hotel chain had placed an emphasis on customer service, and he was anxious to be in the vanguard of the program. He conducted all sorts of trainings on how to provide service, and to his disappointment people seemed both bored and uninterested. They were courteous to the guests when managers were around but had relapses when they were not closely supervised. What distressed the hotel manager most was how they talked about the customers behind their backs. He was horrified by conversations that he had overheard in the halls, closets and break rooms. The hotel staff basically disliked the customers and merely tolerated their presence. He came to us for help. We told him that to correct the situation would require a multi-part program. First, it would be necessary to conduct a special behavioral modification training around employee motivation, values, beliefs and attitudes. Second, it would be necessary for the hotel to support the program with rewards for compliance and with heavy penalties for non compliance. About 80% of the staff could be changed and the rest would need to be let go or reassigned to non customer contact activities."

TEAMWORK
"Let us talk about another management buzzword that the affiliation people hope will enable them to win the war over their eternal enemies (the power and achievement players). It is called teamwork, and it often takes the form of so called self-directed work teams."

"At my last company they tried to bring it in and failed miserably, and I am not sure why." I said.

"I know you will understand what happened after our discussion. The affiliation players think that this is a wonderful concept. The idea is that if people work together as a team and set their own direction and direct their own work, then supervision and management will be virtually unnecessary. It will be possible to reduce the number of managers and let the workers work together in harmony. Productivity will increase, and there will be money saved by eliminating managers' salaries. A worker's paradise will finally emerge in the office and/or factory. This is the affiliation dream finally realized."

"Not so easy, though. What about the power people?" I asked.

"Of course, there are a few obstacles to this dream - predominantly composed of all the power and achievement people on the teams. Power people do not want to be part of a team, unless they are the boss. They do not believe in consensus decision making. They believe in individual responsibility. They believe that those who do not do their job should be fired. They certainly do not believe that they should have to do another team member's job. Also, they do not like management, and see this as a trick so that management can blame them for others on the team and get them to make up for the slackers whom management should get rid of anyway. If required to be on such a team, they exercise control behind the scenes through threat and intimidation and continually fight the process. They frequently disrupt productivity in an effort to force management to abandon the system."

"What do the achievement players think about all this?" I wanted to know.

"The achievement people do not like teams either unless they get to choose who is on their team and unless they are the leader who gets rewarded for its success. They want to get ahead and to achieve individual recognition. They do not want their achievement to be dependent on a team, and they want the credit themselves and not to have the credit go to the team. As individuals, they get ahead through hard work and skillful management of the situation. They need to distinguish themselves from their fellow employees. They do not want to have to help their fellow employees succeed. Only a few can achieve great success, and, furthermore, in the constant quest for individual accomplishment and recognition, it is not only important that you succeed but that others also fail."

"That last comment is certainly a curious twist I would have never thought about until you said it." I chimed in with a note of surprise as Marvin proceeded with his explanation.

"For self directed work teams to work, all of these forces have to be incredibly skillfully managed. If power people have been allowed to have their way in the past, then teams are not going to miraculously change this. Power people will continue to work behind the lines imposing their will, usually by manipulating the other team members. In order to have a high performance organization, it is necessary to first have a performing organization. This concept seems to escape a lot of managers and consultants. Many organizations think that self directed work teams are going to be a miracle solution to their management problems. What they fail to understand is that self directed work teams will not work at all unless these problems are dealt with first. Self directed work teams are difficult under the best of circumstances and require careful implementation and skillful supervision. Under the worst of circumstances they are impossible."

"It seems that there are so many companies trying to implement this notion of self directed work teams these days." I remarked.

"For sure." added Marvin. "Self directed work teams and teamwork in general appear to be the management flavor of the year. Many consultants have heavy affiliation filters and they are succeeding in selling management a pipe dream. As with quality and service, the pendulum will soon swing. After an initial euphoria, reality will set in, and the power and achievement players will rally to reclaim the field."

"Well, how can one have successful self directed teams within an organization?" I asked.

"Another great question." Marvin remarked. "There are two major keys to making self directed work teams work properly. The first is to create a viable process for group decision making and to get agreement that all members of the group will abide by the group's decisions whether they agree with them or not. The second is to create disciplinary procedures within the group which they will use to enforce cooperation and teamwork."

"The most important decision that any team ever makes is the decision as to how to make decisions, and this is frequently made unconsciously and without careful consideration. It is frequently the most important single element determining group cohesiveness and effectiveness. For this reason it is imperative that this matter be given careful consideration at the beginning by the team. What often happens is that this process is decided by fiat. This occurs when someone takes an action which goes unchallenged, and then this becomes the group team norm. Group decision making is far too important a matter to be left to accident or chance."

"I know for a fact that such a scenario occurs much more often than one would like in most organizations." I realized out loud.

"Any group or team goes through at least four stages of group process. The first is the initial stage of forming. This is where inclusion is the key issue and affiliation needs are most evident. The second is the dramatic stage of storming, in which a power struggle occurs for control of the group. At this point the power players bid to take control and engage in both an overt and a covert struggle with each other and with the other members of the group. This is the most critical stage in the life of a group, and many groups and teams never get beyond this point. For the work team to move beyond this stage, agreement on a decision process and the creation of a team disciplinary process are critical. If the team can move beyond storming, the final two stages are norming and performing. In these stages, group norms for process are agreed upon, and the group begins to perform. Obviously self directed work teams only work in a business environment if they reach the fourth and final stage. This is the achievement stage where the team becomes productive. Without very skillful implementation (usually by non affiliation consultants), this stage is often never reached."

"I never realized how much was involved in team dynamics." I said.

"And we are merely scratching the surface." Marvin added. "As emphasized, a group disciplinary process is critical to team success. As we keep stressing, carrots and sticks are always necessary in the real world. They do not mysteriously become unnecessary in self directed work teams. In fact, just the opposite is the case. Either management has to provide them or workers will have to create them. What happens when a team member does not want to carry his load or to go along with procedures that the group has agreed upon? Are other team members supposed to pick up his load also? If not, then what power do the team members have to force the worker to do his share."

"The teams need their share of appropriate carrots and sticks. Right?" I asked.

"Exactly." answered Marvin. "For self directed work teams to work, management has to provide the team with a viable mixture of carrots and sticks, and team members have to be willing to take responsibility for applying them. If management did not previously have available and actually use an adequate mix of carrots and sticks, then it is unlikely that they will be able to provide them to work teams. Self directed work teams are not going to be able to miraculously accomplish what management was incapable of doing from the start. Things have to be well managed in the first place for there to be any hope of self directed work teams working. Let me give you an example by describing an experience we had with this very issue." Marvin went on to explain.

"We recently had an opportunity to work with two plants in an organization that had hired another consultant to implement self directed work teams under the guise of what he called a high performance organization. It was an interesting study in contrasts. We were involved in creating skills training in both plants. The operations at one plant was run by an incredibly competent manager. He was an excellent learner and an excellent implementor. He quickly learned People Patterns from us along with many other things. He asked us for help in team building, since the other consultant was long on theory and short on practicality. We counseled him to come up with a list of carrots and sticks, which he did. We also counseled him on how to get the team decision process off on the right foot. At the initial meeting, he had the team reach certain agreements and then sign a covenant with each other, affirming that they would abide by them. He posted the covenants clearly on the wall, and whenever disagreement emerged, either he or other team members would point to the covenants and ask the team member in question if he no longer wanted to be part of the covenant. Because of his attention to process, he was able to dramatically increase productivity." Marvin proceeded to explain the scenario at the other plant.

"The other plant, unfortunately, was a study in contrast. We were involved with skills training design and implementation in the midst of a war zone around self directed work teams. Our first day in the plant we met with the other consultant who cautioned us that management was doing a poor job of implementing his proposals. So we found ourselves in the middle of a war between management and employees over self directed work teams."

"Sounds like a delightful situation, but at least a great learning place for you." I said.

"In fact, a great lesson was learned. The plant was a classic example of the conditions under which the implementation of self directed work teams is difficult if not impossible. Three factors exacerbated the situation. First, the management was starting with work teams at the top. The so called management team required consensus decision making which rendered them incapable of timely and proactive leadership and decision making."

"The next problem was that self directed work teams were presented as the solution to increased plant productivity. Workers had had their way for years, and management either wasn't given the necessary carrots or sticks or was afraid to use them. The result was a non performing organization. Once again, it is first necessary to have a performing organization before you can have a high performing organization. It is also necessary to first have plant discipline before you can have team discipline."

"If you don't have it at the top, you aren't going to have it below, as they say." I interjected.

"Yes, and there is more." continued Marvin. "The third problem was a lack of communication and a deep seated distrust of management. The whole effort at self directed work teams was seen by many workers as the latest management plot to get more from the workers and to give them less. From the workers' perspective, management had failed to discipline certain employees and had been arbitrary and capricious in enforcing regulations. They believed that self directed work teams was a clever idea concocted by management to shift the burden of management onto the workers so that management could do even less. It was also viewed as an attempt on the part of management to make the workers responsible for doing not only their own work, but the work of weak team members whom management should have fired or forced to do their job in the first place."

"Sounds like disaster city between management and workers." I said, happy that I had never been in such a situation.

"Some would call it a vipers nest." continued Marvin. "Once distrust emerges in an organization, communication becomes extremely difficult. To make matters worse, when management told the truth, workers did not believe it and adopted a wait and see attitude. Under such circumstances it is critical that management create ways to send clear signals to the workers in the form of direct actions that prove their intentions. Unfortunately, in this plant the opposite was happening. Management would give the teams authority to make decisions. When they exercised this authority and made decisions that management did not like, then they were told to make new decisions. In essence management was saying: 'We want you to run yourselves as long as we approve of what you are doing. We will tell you when we do not approve of what you are doing, but we will not tell you what to do. You will have to keep trying things until you find something of which we approve.'"

"In this atmosphere it is no small wonder that self directed work teams were not working." I said.

"Management pulled supervisors off of the floor and productivity dropped so they put the supervisors back on for awhile. Then they took them off again but kept them in a veto position." Marvin drank some coffee and then continued.

"Management was also trying to implement a program called pay for skills. The idea was that everyone would be trained to do everything. This is obviously another affiliation program. Achievement people believe in pay for performance and productivity. Of course, the pay for skills did not work out like the affiliation people envisioned that it would."

"Based on what I know now, that doesn't surprise me one bit." I said.

"There were only a limited number of the multi-skills positions, so immediately all of the achievement and most of the power people started in a race to get to the finish line first. The result of the program was massive dislocation with everyone learning other jobs than what they had been doing successfully for years. Not surprisingly productivity plummeted. Management would have to put the program on hold every other month and put people back in their old jobs until they could get productivity back up. Workers were concerned that management kept changing the rules to suit themselves and, as a result, distrust of management deepened even further."

"I can't even imagine having to put up with that day in and day out!" I said.

"Oh, but it gets better (or worse)." said Marvin. "Also, the achievement people said that if management were to pay them for performance they would get productivity up. Management in a foolish move said that this was an admission by the workers that they were not working as hard as they could, and that it was the workers' responsibility to increase productivity with no additional compensation. Not surprisingly, the situation continued to deteriorate. Management began to look for scapegoats to blame for their own gross incompetence. When we pointed out the problems to them they even accused us of sabotaging their program. Their reasoning was that we could not support the program if we were explaining to them how they had failed to implement it properly. Ironically, the workers who had gone through our behavioral and team work training said that as a result of the training they had begun to understand the issues involved. And moreover, it made them finally come on board to support the new HPO process, which until then they had been vehemently against. The last we heard, the situation was still going down hill fast."

"That should be no surprise." I added.

"The lesson is quite simple." Marvin went on to say. "Achievement people want pay for performance. They will increase performance, but you have to give them an incentive to do so. If management is arrogant and comes out of power (and often ego) and tells them that this is their job, then the battle is over and management has lost. Management has to learn that you cannot get something for nothing. You have to give to get. If management wants increased productivity, then they need to offer real incentives to the workers. And they also need to utilize sticks on the lazy and incompetent who only demoralize the producers. The only true idiots are the managers who are dumb enough to expect something for nothing and who fail to learn and apply the science of carrots and sticks because of their own egos that get in the way."

I left Marvin with my head reeling from what he had said. Suddenly many things made sense. I saw how all of my life as an achievement player with high power needs and some affiliation skills I had been frustrated at others for low productivity. I now knew why and, even more important, realized that the Motivation and Motive People Patterns would enable me both to understand and respond appropriately when I found myself in these situations in the future.

SALES

I was excited to find out if the Motive People Pattern was as important to sales as to management. Michael greeted me with his usual firm hand shake and launched right in.

"The University of Chicago did a study on the banking industry, and we find that the results apply to other industries as well. What the study found is that a third of the customers were rate oriented, a third were service oriented and a third were relationship oriented. Once again we have power, achievement and affiliation. There are several major implications of this study."

PEOPLE PATTERN	CUSTOMER ORIENTATION
Power	Rate or cost
Affiliation	Relationship
Achievement	Service

"At Success, Incorporated we have taught basic and advanced negotiation courses to bank loan officers around the country, and everywhere we have found that most of them behaved as if all of their customers were rate oriented. This had two unfortunate consequences. The first was that they gave away money needlessly. Service and relationship customers were not primarily concerned with rate. They would pay more if they thought that they were getting better service or if the relationship with the loan officer was positive. Also, customers who were rate oriented had no customer loyalty and would change banks as soon as someone else offered them a better rate. The second unfortunate consequence was that by focusing on rate, they ignored the service and relationships that two thirds of the customers were looking for at their banks."

"So once again, a knowledge of the Motive and Motivation People Patterns saves the day." I said.

"That would help a great deal. Every salesperson has to realize that both service and relationships are critical as well as good prices. The ideal salesperson is a master of all three, and tailors his approach to his clients' preferences. Traditionally, there are three types of salespeople. First, is the classic high pressure salesperson. He comes out of power, and his goal is to make the sale whether the customer needs it or not. This type of salesperson is largely responsible for the negative reputation that most salespeople have. The second kind of salesperson relies on charm. They are the people from whom you buy because you like them and enjoy doing business with them. They build positive relationships that last through generations. They live off of referrals and product champions. The third type of salesperson are the modern consultative salespeople. They view themselves as sales consultants. Their mission is to help the customer accomplish their goals in the best way possible. They find out what the customers needs are and satisfy them. If they don't have what the customer needs, then they refer the customer to someone who does. They provide excellent service. Their goal is to provide such an excellent product and service that the customer would never dream of going anywhere else."

PEOPLE PATTERN	SALES APPROACH	GOAL
Power	Pressure	Sale
Affiliation	Charm	Friendship
Achievement	Consultative	Satisfaction

"So power, affiliation and achievement have always been around in sales from what I understand." I said.

"Yes." responded Michael. "And today, most people who sell to businesses come out of the achievement orientation. They need to balance this with affiliation skills. In selling large ticket items to individuals such as automobiles and real estate, one finds all three kinds of salespeople. Some power people are successful, because they are pushy. Some affiliation people are successful, because people enjoy doing business with them and refer other people to them. And some achievement people are successful, because they provide better products and services. It takes all kinds. The more successful salespeople are able to balance all three. The most successful salespeople are those who have the flexibility to be any of the three when appropriate, and who have mastered the Motivation and Motive People Patterns so that they know what is appropriate with each customer."

"Obviously these two People Patterns complement each other and are both necessary to really understand what makes customers tick, so to speak." I added.

"Indeed." responded Michael. "The Motivation People Pattern tells whether the customer is buying to get something or to avoid something and the Motive People Pattern gives insight into what specific carrots and sticks to feed to the customer. As I have emphasized, the move toward person will want to know what your product or service will do for him. Obviously, to be most effective, it would be helpful to know the primary motive of the person to whom you are selling something. Is he moving toward power, affiliation or achievement? Let me take a specific example, such as car buying."

"If you are dealing with a person who moves toward power, you would position the car you sell accordingly. You would emphasize that having such a car will give him a lot of clout over people (say whatever is contextually appropriate and true, of course). Let the power person feel as though he is in charge of the sale. You want to make it known that he is not getting ripped off, and that he is definitely getting the best deal around. Ironically, with your knowledge of what motivates him and how to do so, you are the one in control of the situation; yet in dealing with the move toward power person appropriately, he will think that he is, and you will probably make your sale."

"That's great! If he only knew he would be furious!" I said.

"That is probably true. In any case, make sure you know in advance what your lowest price would be, and begin far above it in the initial sales presentation. Knowing what his other values are will be of enormous help to you in determining the kinds of things you need to be emphasizing in the presentation. For example, does he value a car that is a status symbol in the circles he frequents? If so, he will probably want a car that will render a certain aura of distinction and wealth, the *arriviste* mentality, 'I've made it, now that I am behind the wheels of this Bugatti, or Bentley or whatever', for all the world to see. He is likely to drive the car that translates into prestige, comfort and more prestige. The values are relative to one's social circles. The status symbol vehicle may be a Cherokee or Range Rover. If he values macho instead of status, then he will want a vehicle that expresses power and machismo, whether it be the top of the line Harley or the Stretch limo with dark tinted glass and the burly chauffeur."

"Obviously another approach entirely is needed for the affiliation person." I said. Even I knew that.

"Very definitely. If you are face to face with a person who moves toward affiliation, the sales presentation will most likely be a piece of cake. Remember that the most important thing to the affiliation person is relationships, so he will be most concerned with your relationship with him. If you show genuine interest in the prospective client and are pleasant, the customer will move toward you and the sale even more so. Affiliation people are going to buy from salespeople with whom they are comfortable and whom they trust. So make sure you go out of your way to make them feel at ease, and continue to stress how your product or service will provide them with what they want." Michael continued on to discuss the achievement sale.

"If you have to sell to a person who moves toward achievement, be certain to appear knowledgeable about your service or product. Stress how your product will help improve their life and enable them to achieve their goals. Make sure you provide excellent service now and mention that it will continue after the sale. Also, stress the fine quality of your product or service. The bottom line in sales is to determine what specific things the move toward person moves toward and to go for it."

"If I have learned my lessons well, it would be helpful to know your client's primary motive within the move away from framework also." I proudly stated.

"Great." Michael said. "If he is power oriented and is move away from, he will be moving away from anything he associates with weakness and lack of strength. If he is affiliation and move away from, he will be moving away from anyone and anything that creates or connotes disharmony. If he is achievement and move away from, he will be moving away from anything that can lead to failure or be associated with not succeeding. As with all of the People Patterns we have considered, remember that the Motive Pattern is highly contextual as well, so be sure to identify which your prospective client is in the context of your product or service."

"Is this clear?". asked Michael.

"So far so good. There is a lot for me to assimilate, and I am happy to say that I really do understand what you have been explaining to me. Thank you."

"I think that Beverly is waiting for you to discuss negotiations." With that, Michael wished me a good session and went into a sales meeting.

NEGOTIATIONS

Beverly was waiting and was obviously ready to delve into a discussion of the Motive People Pattern in negotiations.

"There are three principal approaches to negotiations in vogue today corresponding to the three Motive People Patterns. The oldest and most common is the power approach to negotiations. It is called 'hardball'. It views negotiations as a contest of will. The person who wins is the one who has the strongest will and who is most stubborn. In this approach, you get what you negotiate and not what you deserve. This approach often makes use of maneuvers and tactics in an effort to gain a one sided advantage over the other side. Less sophisticated forms of hardball may involve physical threats. There is always a high probability of deadlock with this approach. Each side becomes entrenched, and often the parties would rather spite the other side than reach an agreement that would be mutually beneficial."

PEOPLE PATTERN	NEGOTIATION APPROACH	GOAL
Power	Hardball	Unilateral gain
Affiliation	Softball	Appeasement
Achievement	Principled	Mutual gain

"I've never liked the hardball approach, and at least now I know why." I said with pleasure.

"So you are familiar with the rules." said Beverly as she continued on. "The rules of sophisticated hardball are well known. They are: 1) Set your goals in advance, and set them high. 2) Also, determine and be ruthlessly realistic about your minimums or maximums. 3) Try to get the other side to make the initial offer. 4) Always make your initial or counter offer beyond your goal. 5) Once the initial offer and the counter offer have been made, then concede slowly and in small increments, demanding something in exchange for every concession. I will go into these in more detail in the future when you take our Success, Incorporated course on negotiations."

"I'm sure that the affiliation game is much more pleasant!" I interjected.

"Quite so. The affiliation approach to negotiations is called 'softball'. In softball, maintaining the relationship is more important than reaching a favorable agreement. We all play softball with people with whom our relationship to them is of primary importance. These may include spouses, kids, parents, friends, relatives or bosses. The rules of softball are quite simple. They are: 1) Find out what the other side requires to be happy in the relationship. 2) Give them what they want. People with high affiliation needs usually hate to haggle, and they often get taken advantage of in negotiations. In softball you get what you are willing to give in order to maintain the relationship and not what you deserve."

"That still doesn't fit me." I said.

"Well, here it comes." she laughed. "The third approach to negotiations is the achievement approach. It is called principled or win-win negotiating. The idea behind it is that by cooperating, both sides may reach an agreement that benefits both. Instead of assuming that there is a fixed pie to be divided, both sides can work together to create a bigger pie which will benefit both. In win-win negotiating, an agreement is not even considered unless it benefits both parties. If it only benefits one party, then the other will feel exploited and either will renegotiate away from the table or will be looking for payback the next time around. In the modern business world where parties are going to do business over time, it is almost a necessity to negotiate in a win-win manner. In a win-win negotiation you get what will satisfy the other side and not necessarily what you deserve."

"Given what you have said, the possibilities of win-win must be endless!" I declared.

"Not quite, but almost." Beverly agreed. "There are many versions of win-win, and the basic rules are similar to those that follow. 1) Each side determines what it would like to get and what it is willing to give up to get it. 2) Each side shares its interests with the other side. 3) The two sides work together to brainstorm creative alternatives that will enable both sides to maximize gains. 4) Agreement is reached when both sides are satisfied with one of the solutions."

"I can certainly see how that works well." I stated.

"Our discussion would not be complete without mention of a particularly popular form of win-win negotiations. It is called 'principled negotiations'. It was developed by William Ury and Roger Fisher of the Harvard Negotiation Project and was originally presented in their little book called *Getting to Yes*. Principled negotiations is similar to the win-win rules we have discussed with an important change in the last rule. Instead of basing agreement on what satisfies both sides, agreement is based on fair, objective, impartial criteria. This is how 'principled' negotiations gets its name. Agreement is based on external principles and not on the interests of the parties involved. This insures that you get what is fair and not what you are capable of negotiating. The challenge to this approach is to find fair, objective, impartial criteria to apply to the options for mutual gain. This may end up as a 'makes sense' activity."

"Doesn't context come into play with these various approaches as well?" I asked, even though I already knew the answer.

"Of course." Beverly chuckled. "All the time. Besides, in the real world, negotiators may use all of these approaches or a combination of them. In a one time negotiations such as buying a house or a car, people are more likely to play hardball. In negotiations where the relationship is critical, people are more likely to play softball. In a professional situation where you need to continue to do business in the future with the other party, then you are most likely to take a principled approach. A principled approach is valuable in a situation where lack of trust and antagonism exists and in which a fair agreement would benefit both sides."

I realized that what Beverly had just said would benefit me greatly in negotiating the price of my next car lease as well as negotiating with other managers for in-house resources.

TRAINING

Frank was looking at a stack of overheads. He greeted me warmly, turned on the overhead projector, and then began his presentation.

"Why learn? What is in it for me?" he asked rhetorically. "We talked about this yesterday. People operating out of different motives have different needs to learn, and they learn different things. Power people view learning, like everything else in life, as a control issue. They created the classic Prussian educational system where the teacher's word is law, where students are taught to be obedient, and where strict discipline is the order of the day. The teacher is the authority and is not to be challenged. Teachers lecture and students pay strict attention, dutifully writing down and memorizing whatever the teacher says. There is a carefully laid out curriculum, students must pass rigorous examinations, and those who fail are punished severely. The maxim 'spare the rod and spoil the child' was invented here."

"No wonder why I've never been on that wavelength." I said.

"Obviously a system like I described is a heavy move away from power orientation. It is similar to a Theory X view of management. Times have changed and this approach has been challenged by the achievement and affiliation people of the world. In a democratic society, adults do not respond well to this kind of training approach. This approach is still used in many societies to educate children. Whether children respond well to this system today is also a matter of question. With standardized test scores dropping, educators continue to point the blame for the obvious failure of the 'dis-educational system,' and yet no one has the answer. Conservative power parents and elected officials are always calling for stricter discipline and for a return to the Prussian approach."

"I'm happy to say that I haven't seen that in my children's school." I said.

"In training adults today, the power approach is not in vogue. Every trainer knows that the toughest training assignment is to face a room of 'students' where attendance is mandatory and compulsory. When people are put into a training situation as a requirement rather than as a matter of choice, then problems are bound to arise. If, in fact, there is nothing in it for the student other than a negative move away from power, then learning will be a real challenge. The best that a trainer can do under such circumstances is to be entertaining and to work to convince the students that the material to be covered does have some relevance and value."

"Now that I know my own patterns, I can understand why I look at training from a totally different perspective." I declared.

"With reason. Achievement parents and students view training quite differently. They view education and training as a valuable way to develop skills that will enable them to be more successful and to accomplish more. For this to be the case, training has to be skill oriented. As we discussed yesterday, there is no evidence that more education leads to greater success in life. Blue collar workers often make more money and get more job satisfaction than higher educated white collar workers. So education will not necessarily be attractive to results oriented achievement people. In many cases they will view it as useless information and find it unattractive. For training to be attractive to achievement oriented people, the training itself has to have an achievement focus. Its goal must be to help the student develop skills and competencies that can be immediately applied to solving real world problems and to enabling the student to work more productively and efficiently."

"It is so vital for organizations to understand these issues." I said with an assertive tone of voice.

"Actually, business realizes more than anyone the limits of education. People come out of school largely unprepared for the work that they need to do. From a business perspective, much of what passes for education is simply filling students' heads with useless information instead of training them in hard skills. Training differs from education in that it is skill specific. More and more organizations are turning to so called 'competency based' instruction. This is indicative of the growing frustration around the lack of specific skills. 'Competency based' instruction is a step in the right direction, but it is not a panacea either. The first challenge is to define the necessary competencies at the appropriate gradient. Usually they are either too global or too specific. The second and greater challenge is how to train competencies. This requires special training methods."

"Competency based" training seems to be another buzzword around these days." I said.

"Yes, and I will talk about that later. Affiliation people have still another perspective on education. They view it as a social opportunity. For them it is not what you learn but the relationships that you develop that are important. They view what happens in the cafeteria and in extra curricular activities as what is most important. They reason that school should make you into a well rounded social personality who is well liked by everyone. Given this social bias they do not favor classrooms where only the teacher talks."

"Affiliation people want everyone to have his say. Right?" I asked knowingly.

"Of course." Frank continued. "In a training situation, affiliation people favor an experiential learning approach which features much social interaction and group work. Breaks are important to them as an additional opportunity to socialize. They prefer the trainer to be warm, open and approachable. They do not put a high value on expertise and are not impressed with credentials. They feel that the best way to learn is from each other through group activities and through collaboration."

MOTIVE IN THE "DIS-EDUCATIONAL" SYSTEM

"So there are three types of students with three different outcomes. The power people vary from the school leaders to the school bullies. They want control and influence and resist or subvert the system. The achievement people vary from the 'brains' to the 'grubs'. They want to get high grades and to get ahead. The affiliation students vary from the class president to the prom queen to cheerleaders. They want to be popular and to develop lasting friendships."

"I again see where I was at and still am!" I declared.

"There are also three kinds of educators. The power teachers believe in discipline and control. They are there to teach, and if students do not learn for learning sake, at least they will learn to obey. Homework is important as a means of control and to develop discipline. They are in a constant struggle with the power students whom they want to dominate, with the affiliation students whom they want to silence, and with the achievement students who think that knowledge is sufficient. They are viewed by the students as strict and often as mean." Frank proceeded to achievement.

"The achievement teachers are looking for high test scores as evidence that students are learning. They expect that students will be focused on learning. Homework is an opportunity for additional learning. They will struggle with the power students who are a discipline problem and will butt up against the affiliation students who view class as a social opportunity. Obviously, the achievement teachers will appreciate the brains and the grubs."

"That certainly brings back memories." I chimed in.

"The affiliation teachers want to be popular and to have a good time. They avoid discipline, since that would reduce their popularity. They want to be friends and surrogate parents to their students. Homework should be easy if there is any at all. They will let the power students disrupt to a point rather than enforce discipline. Meanwhile, the affiliation teachers want the brains of the class to learn the importance of developing social skills, too. They obviously get along well with the affiliation people who become their pets."

TRAINING STAGES

"Every trainer knows that people in any class will be coming out of these three basic motives. They further know that there are stages in the evolution of any training and that certain issues will emerge at each stage. If you have no questions I will continue on." Frank declared.

"The first stage is the beginning of any training. At this stage everyone asks the question 'Do I really want to be here?'. The affiliation people want an opportunity to meet their classmates as soon as possible. As they look around the room, the issues of inclusion and exclusion begin to emerge. When the trainer says to get into groups for an exercise, then the affiliation students either focus on those with whom they want to be in a group or on those with whom they do not want to be with in a group. A good trainer knows this and structures ice breaker activities for the students to have an opportunity to begin to interact."

"The next stage is the critical stage in any class. This is where the struggle begins for control. The power people will begin to demonstrate their need for control. This may be done overtly or covertly. They may struggle with each other or with the trainer. A good trainer knows that this stage is coming and is prepared for it. The good trainer must lay out what the class norms are to be, and he must be prepared to enforce those norms fairly and consistently. To do this he will need some carrots and sticks at his disposal. Trainers have to convince students that there is something in it for them. They also must be prepared to deal with overt or covert resistance. The most crucial time to do this is from the beginning, and the most effective way to do so is by getting buy-in from the class so that the class will become self-monitoring and self-disciplining. There are ways to do this which you will learn when you take our Train the Trainer Course."

"Still another one!" I laughed.

"The third stage" Frank went on, "in a class occurs when the class has developed norms for conduct and behavior. It is important that these norms be accepted by everyone. Only with accepted norms in place can the real work of training occur. Once the norms evolve from the power struggle phase and are accepted or at least acquiesced to by all, then the focus can shift to achievement and accomplishment. At this stage, the trainer manages the process to insure that all of the students develop the knowledge and skills that the training is designed to impart."

"The final stage is dissolution. At this stage the training ends and the students go back to their regular jobs. This is the point when the trainer must future pace all of the knowledge and skills to their actual job context and prepare the student to transition from learning to doing. The demonstration of the success of this stage is increased job performance as a result of the training. I have only outlined the process here, and you will have the opportunity to master it as I indicated in the Train the Trainer Course."

PERSONNEL

I arrived at personnel eager to learn how they used the Motive People Pattern. Karen shook hands with me firmly and motioned for me to sit down. I asked if they hired people with different motives for different jobs.

"You are certainly on track." she said. "Obviously you never hire anyone based on a single characteristic. The key is finding the right combination of characteristics. The conventional wisdom might be to hire power people for situations where you need a boss, fireman or lone wolf, to hire affiliation people for jobs requiring interpersonal skills, and to hire achievement people for management positions requiring accomplishment and success. Obviously a more sophisticated approach is in order."

"Wouldn't combinations be good to have?" I wanted to know.

"Actually, yes. The key ,of course, is balance. Research indicates that many successful leaders are high in power and also strong in achievement and that they also have good affiliation skills. Middle-level and lower-level managers should be high in achievement but also have strengths in power and affiliation. Other values are important as well." Karen continued.

"In general, when assessing power, we are more concerned with whether the individual is attracted to socialized power or to personalized power. We usually avoid people with a high need for personalized power. We look for socialized power people who are able to understand their need for power and to use it in creative and productive ways. We are particularly interested in socialized power managers who use a participative coaching style to empower their followers and who also have a high need for achievement coupled with good interpersonal skills."

"Sounds like a lot to ask." I said.

"There are some, but not a lot of these individuals around. In assessing achievement people, we are also looking for a moderate need for power and affiliation. It is important that they be able to delegate authority and enlist the support of their followers." Karen went on.

"Affiliation people serve an important function in any organization, and it is valuable to have some of them around. We look for people with affiliative interest and avoid people with a high need for affiliative assurance. In any case, their need for affiliation needs to be coupled with a moderate need for achievement."

PROMOTIONS

"Where the Motive People Pattern plays an interesting role is in the area of promotions, specifically with who gets promoted in an organization. This is something that we have had the opportunity to observe here in personnel since we maintain all of the employee records. We have made some interesting observations."

"Who is most likely to get promoted in an organization?" I asked.

"Good question. Power players tend to have an old boy network, and they often want to promote other power players who have been loyal to them. Achievement players get promoted because of their accomplishments and results. They have a work history of success to point to as a reference base. Affiliation people either get promoted because they are nice people whom everyone admires and respects or because other affiliation people control the appointments. In most businesses in the world today, there are many more power and achievement people in upper management than affiliation people."

"I have noticed." I say wryly.

"In many organizations there are a large number of high achievers. Often at promotion time there may be a large number of really high achievers vying for promotion. All are great, and none stand out above the others. So who gets promoted? In this case, when there is a tie, it is usually a secondary filter that determines who gets promoted, and this is usually affiliation. In an increasingly competitive business world, it is frequently the high achievers with either a secondary power or a secondary affiliation filter who get the advancement."

CASE STUDY - THE US POSTAL SERVICE

"Let me give you an example of this. One of our senior consultants here at Success, Incorporated spent several years teaching courses in interpersonal dynamics and in negotiations for the Advanced Management Program at the US Postal Service Management Academy. This was a great opportunity for him to interact with postal managers from all over the country. I had lunch with him the other day and he told me an interesting story."

"Which proved to be another good case study. Right?" I said.

"Precisely. In any case, like many organizations, the postal service has its challenges. The postal service is unique in that it is the only government agency that is expected to break even and to be self supporting. It is at the vanguard of the federal government. Most of the federal government is a power oriented bureaucracy. The postal service has to break even. This has forced it into an achievement orientation. It has many high achieving managers, and those getting promotions often have secondary affiliation skills."

"Most postal employees start off in operations. Their job is to move the mail. First line supervisors in the postal service are firemen. All they do is wage a never ending battle to do whatever it takes to move the mail. They are given an impossible challenge of enforcing government regulations and red tape, keeping the unions in check and getting the mail out. The people who frequently succeed best at this are power players. Often you have to be one tough, mean character just to survive under these circumstances. Do you follow?" Karen asked. When I nodded yes she continued.

"The next level of managers in the postal service is the managers of supervisors. They have to manage power oriented supervisors. Frequently they were power players promoted from operations. Suddenly they are told that they are managers and not supervisors. They are expected to be achievement oriented and to learn achievement skills. Some do, and some do not. The next level is the managers of managers. They are expected to be achievement oriented. They are promoted for their ability to be on plan and under budget. Many of them are highly skilled. About half are achievement oriented with forty percent power oriented and ten percent affiliation oriented."

"Human resources gets the affiliation people from what I remember." I said.

"Right." Karen affirmed. "The affiliation types gravitate to personnel and particularly to human resources. Many of the achievers go into marketing. Marketing views itself as the vanguard of achievement. Interestingly, the power people in operations often view marketing as affiliation, because they see them as trying to appease the customer rather than forcing the customer to go along. Finance and operations are viewed by the rest of the postal workers as power oriented. So the complex interdynamics continues to play itself out." Karen proceeded to finish the discussion.

"The final level of management in the postal service are the postal career executive service. They are the managers of managers. They are mostly high achievers with high affiliation abilities or power people who came up through the old boy network. There are a few rare affiliation people who got promoted because of likability and charm. So postal managers have to make several changes in management style as they move up. They probably start in power just to survive. They next have to develop achievement skills, and finally, they need to develop some affiliation skills to round things off. The postal service is probably typical of many organizations."

"This is interesting." I said. "Are things still the same way?" I wanted to know.

Karen smiled and said that she didn't know. "There is a footnote to the story which is also all too typical of bureaucracies." she went on. "The Advanced Management Program was achievement oriented, and was the best management training program in the government and one of the best in the country. Postal managers were extremely well trained. As often happens, it was too good to be true, and it was. A new power oriented Postmaster General was appointed with a mandate to cut spending. As usual, in a short sighted effort to save money, training is the first thing to be cut. Power people have little respect for achievement programs. The academy was closed on a month's notice, and the staff were reassigned. So the best management training program in the government is no more, and the postal service is headed for increasingly difficult times ahead. As frequently happens, that which is successful is somehow thrown out to the wayside by power managers in their mad rush for control."

I thanked Karen and hurried back to see Shana so that I would be on time for my car pool. She was busy at her computer and waved me in.

SUMMARY

"Do you have any questions on either the Motivation or Motive People Patterns? She asked.

"So far so good. I can see where I am going with the information. There is an incredible amount of material, all of which is so useful and helpful. I just wish I had known this before." I asserted.

"Better late than never. That is a start in any case. Now as a manager can you apply them to motivate your employees!" she declared.

"That depends." I said.

"It depends on what?" she responded with a semi puzzled look.

"It depends on three things." I declared with authority. "These are whether the employees have the necessary inherent motives to begin with, whether the organization that I work for provides me with the necessary mixture of carrots and sticks to serve as 'satisfiers,' and on my ability to skillfully combine the two."

She smiled. "You are obviously learning well."

KEY 8:

THE ACTIVITY PEOPLE PATTERN

I walked into Shana's office excited to find out what People Pattern I would learn about today. The power of these patterns continued to amaze me. If only I had learned these patterns earlier, my personal and professional life would have been easier and a lot more fun. Every night I eagerly discussed what I had learned that day with my wife, and we were beginning to understand things about each other and about our children that were amazing. Things that had annoyed us in the past about each other and the children now suddenly made sense. More important we were learning new ways to communicate more effectively. I was already applying the patterns with my children and getting results. I even got my son George to clean up his room, which was previously an unheard of possibility. I think that the ultimate test of any technology is whether it can work with your own children. It is one thing to get results with your boss and peers and the people who work for you. The real test is your children and perhaps your in-laws.

LIFE PUZZLES

When I arrived, Shana was involved in a spirited discussion with three of the secretaries. They had just upgraded to a new version of a word processing package and were encountering some difficulties in doing a mail merge. One of the secretaries, Sue, had the manual out on her desk and was assiduously following it line by line but seemingly to no avail. In utter frustration, she asked one of the other secretaries, Lori, to look over her shoulder to see if she was following the manual's instructions correctly and to make sure her fingers were in fact typing the right keys. Both concurred that she was doing what the manual said, complying with each and every direction. Nevertheless, they were stuck and very frustrated. As usual, the systems administrator was off learning some new program and was not immediately available. A third secretary, Nicole, who was considered a bit of a whiz with computers, was at another computer trying out various alternatives. Finally she announced triumphantly "I've got it. Let me show you how it works." Sue and Lori eagerly rushed to watch. Nicole demonstrated how to do the mail merge. Both Sue and Lori had the same reaction: Why wasn't Nicole following the instructions which were written as clear as day in the manual? What Nicole was doing did not go along with how the manual said to do it. Nicole responded that the manual did not work and that they could either keep doing what the manual said (which did not work and was obviously wrong) or they could do it her way which did work. At this point, the systems administrator arrived and was forced to admit that some of the documentation was wrong and was being revised. By now the secretaries were pretty mad about having wasted an hour and were about to roast the systems administrator. Shana intervened and the systems administrator beat a hasty retreat. Nicole was tasked to type up the procedure that worked, and Shana led me into her office.

Shana smiled and began to ask me some questions about what I had just observed. "Have you ever observed someone doing something over and over again when it obviously did not work, just like Sue and Lori did in their attempt to do a mail merge? "Have you ever wondered why some people repeatedly beat their heads against the wall to no avail and only end up more and more frustrated? Can you understand why some people waste countless time trying to do what doesn't work?"

I admitted that I found all this hard to conceive. In fact, such behavior seemed totally and completely alien to me.

"Is it because they are just stubborn or perhaps mentally deficient or is there something else involved here? On the other end of the spectrum, do you know people who go to incredible lengths to avoid following a simple set of instructions?" she continued.

"You must mean my youngest son," I said. "He could not follow a set of simple directions even if his life depended on it."

Shana laughed with a look that said she knew what I meant, and then she resumed talking.

"Have you ever been frustrated by the seeming inflexibility of some people who absolutely refuse to accommodate you, because they insist on following some stupid rules, regulations or procedures that you could care less about? Would you like to know what is really going on when you spend hours in vain trying to make a simple ticket change with an obstinate airlines agent on the other end of the phone, or even worse behind a ticket counter?" she queried with a tone of complicity.

"Definitely. I certainly can relate to that situation." I chimed in. "On my last trip it was a constant battle with the airlines and hotel desk clerks."

"On the other hand, do you know other people who are always changing their procedures in the hopes of finding a better way of doing things?"

"That sounds like my sister-in-law," I said. "Whenever we go to her house for dinner she is always changing the recipe. Just when some family members get used to her cooking she changes it. It is very frustrating to them." Shana smiled again.

"Today's People Pattern deals with what we call options and procedures, and it is the key to understanding and unraveling these mysteries. It will revolve around two types of people. One who can never do anything unless someone else shows him how to do it first, and the other who can never do it the way that he is shown."

WHAT ARE YOU?

"To begin to understand your own Options and Procedures People Pattern, ask yourself the following questions:"

"Have you ever been frustrated because there was something you wanted to do, but you did not know how to do it, and you felt stuck? Do you enjoy following routines? Have you ever entered an elevator, noticed that the button for your floor was already lit, and nevertheless felt compelled to automatically press it again? Come on. Be honest with yourself. If you need and enjoy procedures, then you are a procedures person." Shana grinned and resumed her expose.

"Or are you the type of person who is good at figuring out different ways to do things? Do you like to figure out ways to improve on things? Do you become annoyed when people want you to follow instructions or procedures? Or do you get angry when someone prevents you from violating a procedure? If you are good at creating procedures but hate to follow them, then you are an options person. "Would you like to know just what triggers such different responses from individuals in these situations?" Shana looked at me as though she expected me to say something.

"I can see from our discussion already that I am an options person and that this People Pattern will shed even more light on certain behaviors which have always irked me in others like those people you described who absolutely have to follow the rules no matter what." I said with some amazement on my part.

OVERVIEW

"Before I send you to some of our departmental managers to see how to apply this People Pattern, let me start by giving you a brief overview of it." First, this pattern deals with the way in which we engage in any activity. I have already said that some people cannot function in life, cannot do anything, or cannot learn anything new unless they are shown or told specifically how to do it. On the other hand, there are other people who get really upset if you start telling them how to do something. They get even more upset if you tell them that there is only one way of performing a task. The reason for this difference of approach is the Options and Procedures People Pattern. This pattern or filter deals with *how* people engage in activity. Since a person's day at the office comprises various activities, this filter will shine through in all that we do at our jobs on a daily basis. There are two ways in which people engage in activity. These are 1) *Sequential or linear activity and 2) Simultaneous or synchronous activity.*"

"The first type of person will view activity and learning, i.e. any task, as a sequential series of actions. These individuals are called *procedural people*, because they can only perform a task or engage in an activity by following a clear set of instructions and moreover by following them in a particular order. They can only engage in an activity by following a procedure. For procedural people, there is only one 'right way' of doing something."

"The second type of person views activity and learning, i.e. any task as a simultaneous grouping of different actions in no set, prescribed order. These individuals are called *options people*, because they prefer to have options and alternatives to deal with in any situation or activity. For them, there can be innumerable ways of doing any one task or learning any one thing. They do not like to limit themselves to the one 'right way' of the procedural person. In the case of the procedural person, we are dealing with linear processing of information and with the options person we enter the realm of simultaneous processing of information."

KEY QUESTION

"The key question behind this people pattern is: *How do I do this?* Do I stick to a procedure or do I find alternative ways of doing this? When faced with a set of instructions, i.e. a procedure, a person will react in one of two ways. He will either be delighted and feel secure, or he will throw up his arms in disgust and frustration. The former reaction is that of a procedural person. The latter reaction is that of an options person."

"From what I could gather, what you have just explained gives me a brief summary of this People Pattern." I said.

"Exactly." Shana responded and continued. "Before I send you off to our various departments to see how it is applied, I would like to elaborate a bit more on it and to give you some ways to identify this pattern in others."

"Procedural people are good at following procedures, but they do not know how to generate them. They are good at doing a task the 'right way'. When the procedure fails, however, or when they do not have a procedure to follow, they end up being stuck and do not know how to proceed. These individuals are motivated when they are following a procedure and have an almost compulsive need to complete the procedure."

"That definitely is the opposite of me." I said.

"Options people, on the other hand, are good at developing new procedures and at figuring out alternatives to a procedure, but they are very poor at following procedures more than once, if at all. Even if a procedure works, they will try to improve it or will feel compelled to alter it in some way."

"That's more like me." I figured out aloud.

"Wait. There is more." Shana added. "A procedural person will always want to do things the 'correct way,' i.e. the 'one right way' according to the procedure. For this kind of person there is usually only one way of completing a task. They tend to be quite inflexible in the context in which they are procedural, and options people view them as stubborn, mechanical, narrow-minded and set in their ways of doing things. Meanwhile, procedural people view their counterparts as erratic and unable to follow directions."

"That's actually quite amusing." I laughed out loud.

"Procedural people don't think so." said Shana. "They often like to carry through procedures from start to finish. Once they get involved in a procedure, heaven help you if you interrupt that procedure or try to change it. The quickest way to annoy a procedural person is by distracting him while he is ensconced in his precious procedure. Procedural people have great difficulty diluting their attention when they are concentrating on their procedures. Just as bad, if not worse, is when an age old procedure breaks down smack in the middle of things. We have been witness to many an irate procedural person caught in limbo whenever his procedure fails to work. In their intense desire to complete the procedure, procedural people become angry and frustrated when the world does not live up to their expectations. And in those situations in which they are faced with no procedures, procedural people are lost and sometimes too paralyzed to do anything at all. Or else they can get so carried away by a procedure that they forget what is happening around them."

"I have certainly seen that happen on more than one occasion, never realizing the dynamics involved." I said.

"This may or may not work to the advantage of the person or persons with whom they are dealing at that moment, as we saw earlier today when the secretaries were trying to figure out how to do the mail merge." Shana did not wait for comments and resumed her thoughts.

"If you do not believe that there are a lot of procedural people in the world, then just visit any book store in America and look at the large number of books that start with the two words in the title 'how to'. Also, the next time that you pick up the NY Times or the Washington Post, notice the separate weekly listing of best selling 'how to' books. Such books often sell like]hot cakes. They are simply 'how to' manuals written for procedural people who cannot do things unless they are taught 'how to' do them. There are procedural manuals for everything. How to lose weight. How to eat well. How to buy a house. How to live a healthy life. How to be an effective public speaker. How to study. How to behave on a date. How to be a parent. How to remodel your home. How to do table settings. How to get rich. How to invest your money wisely."

"Excuse me for interrupting" I said, "but I noticed a few of these so called 'how to' books on your bookshelf."

"Yes, indeed you did, but I do not read them to learn how to do things. Ironically these books have 'how to' titles but in actuality do not tell you *how* to do something but rather *what* to do. The *what* tells you the techniques to use, but it does not tell you *how* to use them. Frequently people know what to do, but they do not have a clue as to what changes they need to make in themselves to allow them to use the techniques. We touched on this topic the very first day."

Shana's response made perfect sense. She proceeded.

"Of course, all of these 'how to' manuals were written by options people. And, of course, they rarely bothered to check the procedures out to see if they work. And in some cases they don't work. This leaves the poor procedural person who is dependent on them stuck in nowhere land. Life for the procedural person is a constant search for procedures that work. And when the procedural person finds a procedure that works he will use it over and over again forever and ever in unending devotion. This, of course, leads to problems since the procedure may not work all the time or in all contexts."

"I could never put up with those procedures!" I declared.

"Now you know why." Shana smiled. "On the other side of the coin is the options person. He is one who prefers alternatives in any given situation, i.e. prefers to have options available to him and will even go out of his way to ignore or break any procedures presented to him. Even if an options person does manage to follow a procedure once, it is highly unlikely that he will repeat it if it is at all possible to avoid doing so. Moreover, if an options person sees that a given procedure does indeed work, he will somehow feel obligated to modify it in some way so as to avoid having to do it exactly as the procedure requires. Options people simply detest inflexible procedures and will always search for a way to get out of them. They tend to be less rigid and more open minded than procedural people (except about procedures) and are more willing to take risks, especially if it means getting something done. The more the possibilities abound, the happier the options person will be. Options people are great at coming up with new and interesting alternatives to a procedure."

"It sure sounds like options people and procedural people can really get at each others throats!" I said.

"Alas! There is an interesting twist to this People Pattern which is the symbiotic relation that exists between the two types. Options people are excellent at creating procedures, but they are incapable of following them. They need procedural people to follow the procedures created by them. The procedural person requires the options person to provide procedures and, hopefully, ones that work. It is the classic 'can't live with, can't live without syndrome' to the tee. Each often finds the other to be utterly impossible to deal with, yet together they keep the wheels of life running smoothly."

PRAYERS

"Notice the Procedural Prayer on the wall. Everyday the procedural person prays:"

Lord God, please make this day work. Give me this day my daily procedures. Lead me not into options or into new and strange situations. Let this day be filled with things that I know how to do. If I do not know how to do it, then, please God provide me with a procedures manual that tells me clearly and logically how to do it, or else with someone who can show me the procedure. Oh yes, dear and thoughtful Lord, P.S. please check out the procedures to ensure that they work. Amen.

"Hell is either not having a procedure or, even worse, having a procedure which does not work. Of course, the Options Prayer is a little different:"

God almighty, give me this day deliverance from procedures and especially from procedural people. Lead me not into procedures. Let this day allow me to peacefully go about my business without being required to follow any procedures. Also, open-minded Lord, please do not let me fall into the hands of any procedural people for they are truly stubborn and irascible. When I tell them that I do not want to follow their procedure, that I want an alternative, then they just want to explain the procedures to me all over again. Really Lord, as clever as you are, surely Thou could have created a world without procedures. Surely, Lord, that is an option worthy of your consideration. Amen.

"Hell is either being forced to follow procedures or else is other people - procedural people that is."

THE GREAT COMPUTER WAR

At this point, the systems administrator stuck her head in the office to thank Shana for having rescued her earlier from the wrath of the secretaries. Shana gestured her in and asked her to explain to me how options and procedures applied in the computer world.

She said: "Nowhere is the symbiotic relationship between options and procedures as evident as in the workplace. This is largely due to that amazing little machine that God arranged to have put on every desk in America. We, of course, are talking about one of the greatest technological advances of the past decade. It is called a computer. The machine is utterly magnificent to the procedural person. He is in absolute glory hacking away in front of his own personal picture screen."

I couldn't help but laugh out loud at the humor! Fortunately it was well received and the systems administrator continued her explanation of the great computer war.

"It isn't the procedural person who came up with this technological wonder, however. It is a creation of your friendly options person, and the programs that run it were written by an options person who is called a 'programmer'. It is much appreciated by the procedural people of the world who follow the procedures to do all sorts of neat things. The computer is perhaps the epitome of the procedural machine. It is accessible to anyone from the average John Doe to the wheelers and dealers in government and politics to the average technical wizard."

Then Shana interjected her own thoughts on the topic.

"Ironically," said Shana, "it is the options person who has created this amazing device which demands that one follow strict procedures in order to operate it. This all, of course, is utterly distasteful if not impossible to the typical options person. The problem is that the options people who like to write the programs truly loathe procedures. They can create them, but they hate to follow them. As soon as they know the solution, then the rest is 'trivial' as they like to say. Of course, the creators of the computer programs cannot stand to use them, because they hate the thought of following the same routine each and every time. That is why they write programs — so they can do it differently each time. Programs are just different ways of doing things. You have to follow them exactly, however. Even the most minor deviation from the procedure can really crash the computer as we saw with the mail merge earlier today." Shana then asked the systems administrator to mention the glitch.

"There is a problem here, however." said the systems person. "The friendly options people who designed the program weren't so friendly after all. What they failed to do (because of their natural distaste for following all of those boring procedures) was to check them out to see if they worked. They left that task to the poor user. They were even nice enough to create a name for their failure to finish their job. They call it a 'bug'. What an absolute pain to discover a 'bug' in the bloody computer! Of course, it is the poor helpless user who finds the 'bug', and he expects me to fix it. But the user can't believe that there is something wrong with the program, like what happened this morning. When a procedural person encounters a bug he thinks that something is wrong with him - that perhaps he can't read or type - since it never occurs to him that the program itself might be wrong. It would be far too frightening to envision a world in which the procedures fail."

"That must be so incredibly tragic for a procedural person!" I said, attempting a bit of humor.

"So the user assumes that it is he who has failed (to follow directions correctly, that is)." said the systems administrator. "So he just sits there repeating in vain the same procedure over and over again. Or else the user has someone look over his shoulder to make sure that his fingers are indeed typing the right keys or that he is indeed reading the manual correctly. The friendly options programmer, of course, is kind enough to provide the user with a set of encyclopedias called a reference manual to go along with the program. It is far too complicated to use so everyone wants me to explain how to do everything. Finally, the user may come to the realization that once again the programmer, being human and therefore fallible, has failed to provide procedures that work. And since the procedural person doesn't know how to program, he ends up stuck in limbo until I can get there or hopefully someone else can help bail him out."

"I'll bet these situations create a great deal of anxiety for some procedural people." I said based on what I had seen in the past.

"Indeed." responded the systems administrator. "This, of course, is one of the greatest causes of stress in the work place. I rate computer software according to the following scale. User vicious - user hostile -user belligerent - user neutral - user friendly - user helpful - user seductive. I have yet to find any software that fits into the last category, but I have found a lot that fit into the first three. What is needed is a new class of software called *userware*^{SM} which has been user proofed and which is user seductive. I keep challenging the options people who write programs to truly write them for procedural people and to develop userware that truly works. It would sure make my job much easier."

Shana and I were laughing in stitches when the systems administrator was beeped and had to run off to help yet another user in need of procedures that worked.

DETECTING THE PATTERN

"Now that you understand the pattern", Shana said, "the next question is how you can tell whether someone else is a procedural or options person. As always, the best way to determine a person's pattern is to observe his behaviors. A general rule of thumb for this People Pattern is as follows."

If the person is good at following routines and lost without a procedure, then he is a procedural person. If the person is good at creating procedures but never seems to be able to follow them, then he is an options person.

"The target indicator question for the Options and Procedures People Pattern deals with activity. What we are trying to determine is how the person engages in activity. Does he engage in activity sequentially or simultaneously? To determine this all you have to ask the person is why he did anything. So, for instance, a target indicator question would be: Why did you choose your present job? You can substitute anything for 'job'. For example: Why did you choose your current car, or your current bank, or your current house, or even your current pet? Another target indicator question would be: Why do you live where you do?"

"If you ask these questions you will get one of two kinds of answers: Either a person will give you reasons as to why he did what he did, or he will tell you a story about how he came to do what he did. The former is an options person and the latter is a procedural person." Shana did not stop for comments from me.

Reasons (WHY question - BECAUSE answer)
Or
A Story (WHY question - HOW TO answer)

"The options person" she continued, "will literally answer the 'why' question with a 'because' answer. He will tell you why he ended up doing what he did. Options people have reasons for doing things, and usually know specifically what these reasons are. They may even mention the options available to them in their response. Remember when the personnel interviewer asked you 'Why did you choose your current house?' you thought that it was a strange question to ask during a job interview. Well, your answer to this target indicator question revealed that you are an options person. An options person would give reasons as you did."

"Yes, I remember that well. I did think it was a strange question. I said that my house has just the right number of bedrooms and that it is well laid out and conveniently located in relation to my office. The school system is excellent in the area too. So how would a procedural person answer the question?" I wanted to know.

"The procedural person would answer the 'why' question as if it were a 'how' question. They will give you a 'how to' answer. The procedural person will end up telling you a story about how he came to make the choice. For example, when asked why he chose his present house, he would say 'Well, we were driving along one Sunday afternoon in the suburbs and came across a lovely wooded area with a little waterfall and beautiful brick homes. We stopped to get gas in the town and found out that the house we particularly liked was soon to be put up for sale. We got an appointment with the owner, looked around, and one thing led to another. Before long, we were drawing up papers for a mortgage.' Or he may simply give you facts, and will certainly not discuss alternatives that may have been open to him. Beware of short answers that appear on the surface to be reasons. By delving further, it becomes evident that the answer is a 'how to' answer, the sign of a procedural person and not an options person. The important thing to remember about a procedural person is that you get the impression that he did not have a choice in the matter, or that he was incapable of making a choice, or that his hands were tied, or that things just fell into place in a certain way. The bottom line is that his story is simply another way of explaining the procedure he went through to make the choice."

"Now I see why my procedural friends do not like my interrupting them in the middle of their how to ramblings." I said jokingly.

"Do you think that you can determine whether a person is options or procedures?" Shana asked.

When I responded affirmatively, she ended the discussion.

"This brings us to the next facet of today's lesson, that of sending you on your rounds to get first hand information and real life situations regarding the Options and Procedures People Pattern. When you finish with everyone come back to see me at the end of the day."

OPTIONS AND PROCEDURES IN MANAGEMENT

Marvin was setting at his desk when I arrived. After shaking my hand he asked me to sit down. He smiled at me and began talking.

"Welcome back for your eighth People Pattern in the context of management. Today we will talk about the implications of the Options and

Procedures People Pattern for management and supervision. Let me start by asking you to think about how often an employee considers his supervisor to be misguided, and vice versa. Remember that when we are with people who think a different way about things than we do, we tend to apply various derogatory names to them."

"I will refrain from mentioning them now." I chimed in.

"We all occasionally call someone else an idiot among other things." said Marvin. In any case, I remember years ago when I was working for another company. I was highly options and my manager was highly procedural. We used to drive each other nuts. My manager was constantly frustrated with me, both because I refused to follow the procedures that he had taught me and because I was continually coming to him with suggestions on how to improve upon the process. I remember that one day he screamed at me: 'Stop trying to change it. Just do it the way that you are supposed to!' I was frustrated with what I considered his stubborn and unreasonable attitude. I thought that he was too rigid and inflexible. Also, he was unable to accept better ways of doing things. I think that what irked me most was his unwillingness to recognize and appreciate my superior suggestions. He failed to appreciate that the procedures were mediocre and that he was lucky to have me around to improve on them."

"I can certainly relate to that kind of scenario!" I said.

"Later when I became a manager," Marvin went on to say, "I remember a situation where the situation was reversed. I was an options manager and I was given a developmental assignment in finance where all of the people who reported to me were procedural. It was a nightmare! They wanted me to provide procedures for everything. And when I did not, then they complained that they did not know how to do their jobs because I had not told them how. They said that either I did not give them a procedure, or even worse, that I would keep changing the procedures. They said that every time they learned to do the job one way, then I would come along and change the procedure. I was upset, of course, because they were always asking me for procedures on how to do their jobs. One day I even yelled at one of them 'can't you think for yourself? Do I always have to do your job for you?' I was frustrated, because whenever I came up with a better way of doing things, they would be resistant to change. Even worse, they did not appreciate my creativity and innovation. I was never happier than the day my developmental assignment ended, and I could finally move on." Marvin did not pause.

"Of course, now that I have become a P^3 Manager with People Pattern Power, I would handle these situations quite differently. (I can now refer to myself as a P^3 Manager because at this point in your training you now have a good idea what that means.) Now I know that if you are going to manage procedural employees, then you have to provide them with procedures. In other words, you have to teach them 'how to' do their job. Also, you have to check out the procedures to make sure that they work. If they break down, then you had better be around to fix them, because the employees will just stop work and wait for you to provide the solution. You will also need to understand that the procedural person will take what you say quite literally."

"As a P³ Manager, then, I would need to resist my natural tendency to be always changing the procedures." I said.

"Exactly. I had to do that very thing myself." Marvin responded. My advice is to develop the best procedures you can, and then leave well enough alone. Also, let the procedural people know that you appreciate their adherence to the procedures." Marvin suggested even more.

"If you are going to manage options employees, on the other hand, then it is unrealistic to assume that they will be good at following procedures. If you expect them to do so, you are only asking for built in stress and frustration. If it is absolutely necessary to follow procedures exactly, then do not hire options people. Or if they are already there, then reassign them to other work which does not involve following procedures. Options people will be great in situations where there are no procedures and in contexts where they have to figure out how to do things. They will also be good at figuring out new ways to do things. In managing options people, give them an assignment and let them go."

"That's what I like!" I piped in.

"No small wonder." laughed Marvin. "Listen to their suggestions and be prepared to give reasons if you disagree. They respond well to reasons but not to what they view as arbitrary and capricious dogmatism. Also, let them know that you appreciate their creativity. Usually we get along best with people who are most like us and who have the same People Patterns that we do. This applies to managers just like everyone else. All too often the people who are most appreciated and promoted in any organization are those who are most like their manager. Most managers, without realizing it, look for employees who are clones of themselves."

"Isn't that true!" I said.

"Let me elaborate on this. Remember the all important corollary of the People Pattern Creed:

> *We are most comfortable with those whom*
> *we perceive to be most like us.*

This applies quite appropriately to the employer/employee relationship. Most people feel that they themselves are doing a good job. In evaluating the work of other people, they usually compare that performance to their own. They apply the same barometer with which they measure their own work to evaluating the work of others. So it is not surprising that there is a tendency for supervisors to reward those of their employees who have similar patterns to themselves. This is usually a major source of discouragement to other employees who have different People Patterns. These employees end up resenting their supervisors for failing to appreciate their efforts."

"Then a P³ Manager knows how to handle rewards." I said as a declaration of sorts.

"Of course. A P³ Manager rewards employees for their contributions and not because they are clones of himself. He has a clear understanding of the complementarity of things in the world, in this case what our company calls the Yin/Yang of Management^{SM}. Good managers understand the need for balance in an organization and often look for people who complement their talents. Good managers understand that most situations require an ensemble of approaches and solutions in order to round out, to counteract, and to supplement their own talents. This is the key to achieving stability and harmony and, finally, success in any organization. By managing in this way, good managers are also able to reduce stress levels and minimize conflict in their organizations."

"I've seen both employees and managers be either overly procedural or overly options to the point of exaggeration." I said.

"That does happen quite a bit." responded Marvin. "Both managers and employees can be compulsive in their desire to be procedural or options oriented. This, as we have seen, can lead to incredibly amusing and complex scenarios. It is a good thing that the procedural person has the options person around when the procedures break down, and, likewise, that the procedural person is around to implement the creations of the options person. The two types are often at each other's throats in utter disgust; yet one can't flourish without the other."

"We have just scratched the surface on the subject of the Options and Procedures People Pattern in Management, but unfortunately our time is up. Do you have any pressing questions?" asked Marvin.

"For the moment I'm fine. Thank you for another great session." I said. "On to Michael who will tell you all about how this People Pattern is applied to the realm of sales." concluded Marvin.

SALES

Michael was a born salesperson. Or come to think of it, maybe he wasn't. Maybe he had used People Pattern Power to seem like a born salesperson. In any case, he greeted me like I was a close friend. He offered me a piece of candy and then popped one into his mouth. He looked at me a minute and then began.

"Come in and join me in the lucrative kingdom of buying and selling, a place made all the more profitable if you understand how to communicate with and influence your prospective buyers. You have already learned many fascinating and timely applications of the Options and Procedures People Pattern as it relates to management. With sales, you will see that many of the same principles that applied to these areas will also be germane to the realm of sales."

"Am I safe to assume that just as managers and negotiators with different Activity People Patterns will react differently to a given situation, that salespeople with different activity patterns will see the activity of buying and selling from two different points of view?" As I said this, I happily realized that I was actually beginning to understand and apply what I had learned to date.

"Precisely." grinned Michael. "You have learned well so far. In fact, the Options and Procedures People Pattern is so incredibly important in sales precisely because of the reason you just mentioned. It is critical to understand that options and procedures people buy differently and, hence, must be approached and sold to differently. Many successful sales campaigns are based unwittingly on this pattern in one way or another. An awareness of this People Pattern will make anyone a more effective salesperson. Also, the consumer needs to know his own buying style in order to avoid frustration and maybe even prevent being taken advantage of by the sharks of the world. We believe that an educated consumer is our best customer. The more that people can understand their own process, the easier it is for us to sell to them in the way they want salespeople to approach and deal with them."

"That is for sure. I will second that motion." I said as I nodded my head approvingly.

"First let's consider the procedural buyer. A procedural buyer often does not buy because he is either not sure how to go about it or else he is faced with too many options and cannot decide. If you are selling to a procedural person, be prepared to lay out up front the entire procedure for buying. As silly as it may sound, they want to know how to go about buying." Michael continued.

"When selling to a procedural buyer, the salesperson needs to proceed as follows. Remember that you need to provide the procedure as well as to lay out the sequential steps leading to the purchase and beyond. Start by saying something like this: 'Good morning Mr. Prospect. Let me explain to you the procedure for buying this car. It began when you discovered you needed a new car in the first place.' (This sets the stage and gets him immediately into the procedure.) 'The next step was when you drove by and saw our dealership. The next step was when you pulled into the lot and I greeted you. The next step is that you will tell me what you want. Then I will tell you how I can give you what you want. There are a lot of cars on the lot, and I will tell you which one is best for you. That way you will not have to worry about all the other ones that do not meet your needs.' (By saying this you limit the options and reduce the likelihood of confusion. This also unconsciously makes the procedural person comfortable with you.) ' After I show you the car that you want and you agree to the price, then you will sign this order form on this line.' (Notice that the signing or buying step is right smack in the middle of the procedure and not the last step!) 'Then we will prepare the car and get you plates for it. You can pick it up tomorrow. Of course, you will drive it home and be really pleased with it. Then in a couple of weeks when I call you, I expect to hear you say how much you are enjoying your new car. Of course, you will also give me the names of some of your friends who could use a new car as well.' (Here you get the best of two worlds. Not only do you have the buyer future paced into calling you, but you also have a way of increasing your client base by making that part of the entire procedure!)"

"You know, I would be annoyed at and even offended by this approach. Such a procedure would make me feel that the salesperson thinks that I'm some kind of an idiot to have to indicate all these steps!" I immediately declared in a rather piqued tone of voice.

"Precisely! Notice how frustrated and even angry you were when confronted with a specific, detailed procedure. Why such a reaction? Because you are an options person. The above scenario may seem silly and perhaps even outrageous to some people, that is, to our friendly options people. In fact, they would probably walk out of a sales appointment with this approach. However, you need to realize that once the procedural buyer is caught up in a procedure, they have difficulty stopping the procedure. Also, the procedural buyer is looking to find out *how to* rather than *why*. He will not give you reasons as to why he is buying, but will tell you a story as to how he came to be buying the product or service. It is exactly because of the delineated procedure presented to him that the procedural buyer feels comfortable with the sales presentation. Because they have a natural tendency to want to complete the procedure, procedural people may end up buying the product or service precisely because doing so comprises one of the steps in the procedure. Often this happens outside of their conscious awareness."

It was obvious that Michael wanted to say a few more things without being interrupted.

"There are several points that are important here which need elaboration." Michael continued. "First, the salesperson must explain the procedure up front. Second, when the salesperson begins his explanation, that point should already be several steps into the procedure so that the buyer realizes that the procedure has already begun and that he is already knee deep into it. Remember that for the procedural person, this represents the point of no return. Third, it is important that the actual close be several steps from the end of the procedure so that the buyer does not feel finished until after he has already purchased the product. Fourth, it is crucial not to present any options to the buyer, but instead limit choices at every point. Options will only confuse the procedural buyer and make it difficult for him to make a decision."

"Of course an options person like myself would go nuts if a salesperson used this approach in selling!" I exclaimed.

"Definitely!" Michael retorted. "Options people simply can't stand procedures, and they would probably have a similar reaction to yours when I presented this scenario to you."

"So what does one do when faced with an options person like me?" I asked quite curiously.

"I was just coming to that very point. In selling to an options person, the salesperson should stress that there are many options open to the buyer, and that there is no set way to go about buying. Better yet, make a point of saying that there is a customary procedure for buying, but the salesperson will violate it in this case, especially for you. It is music to the ears of the options buyer to know that procedures are being violated for them. In fact, the P^3 Salesperson would say the following to an options buyer: 'I want you to know that we normally have a set procedure we follow with our customers, but I have decided to go out of my way to bend the rules just for you.' The P^3 Salesperson would make the options buyer feel that he is going out of his way to accommodate him, and that the salesperson is deviating from the set procedure solely for him. The options buyer wants to feel that he is getting special treatment."

This was the first time Michael had referred to a P^3 Salesperson, and I was happy that I now knew what he meant by it. It was a sign that my initial training was about over, and that I was being accepted as one of the cognoscenti.

"Note too," Michael went on to say, "that the options buyer will, of course, want to know about all of the available options. He will want to choose between several products or services, and will expect reasons why he should buy them. Do not expect the options buyer to tell you a story as to why he bought the product or service. He will also want to know how the product or service can expand his possibilities. The wise salesperson will quickly get the options buyer focused on one model and then keep him busy deciding what options he wants on it. He will also stress the 'why' and give reasons for everything."

"I do not need to tell you," Michael continued, "that one of the best ways to increase sales is to identify and utilize your customers' Options and Procedures People Pattern. We have found that being able to identify whether a buyer is options or procedures and to sell to him accordingly will improve any salesperson's monthly sales figures. Many businesses lose sales because they fail to understand procedural buyers. Many buyers do not buy, as strange as it may seem, simply because they are not sure how to buy and do not want to go into an uncomfortable situation in which the responsibility and task of coming up with a procedure is put on their shoulders. Procedural buyers simply cannot and do not want to generate the required procedure. In such cases, more often than not, they just do not make a purchase."

"Could you give me a specific example of this?" I asked.

"You took the words right out of my mouth. Let's talk about bank accounts for example. Everyone has a bank account. Or do they? This will demonstrate the power of options and procedures in sales. As strange as it may seem, many people do not have bank accounts or fully utilize banking services, because they do not know how to open an account or how to use the services. To remedy this, the bank should place a sign in the window that says: *Procedures for opening a bank account with our bank.*"

"Again, this may seem silly to the options people out there in the world, but it is precisely what is needed by their procedural counterparts. The entire procedure needs to be clearly laid out. It would include things like: *Come into the bank and speak to one of the assistants who has a sign on his desk. He will explain to you exactly what to do to use our bank. He will help you fill out the forms and take your initial deposit. He will set up your account and get you checks. He will show you how to write checks and how to make deposits. Also, he will answer any questions you might have regarding your new account. Remember, the assistants are here to help you.*"

"Such an approach may seem just as weird to you, an options person, as did the other sales procedure I presented a few minutes ago. In fact, this approach may even seem ludicrous to some, but this is the way to help procedural buyers. Always remember that the main thing preventing procedural people from taking action is that they do not know how to proceed. Once the process is presented to them, then get out of the way and they will do fine."

"The two founders of Success, Incorporated have been studying top sales performers and doing research on sales for years here at Success, Incorporated. And they have found that some of the most successful sales programs and salespeople in the world are highly procedural. A case in point are the popular script books. Most successful sales forces would not survive without them. These books contain their most successful sales presentations, and effective salespeople memorize these presentations and deliver them verbatim. Canned presentations, if they are good, can be highly successful. They are most successful, however, if the salesperson has several different presentations and matches them to the type of person with whom they are dealing."

"Those script books are fine as long as I can change them when I need to." I asserted.

"Just like any good options person, I might add. There are still some other points I would like to make about the banking industry. In particular, they need to revamp their sales approach to incorporate the Options and Procedures People Pattern. They too, need to adopt the P^3 approach if they want to attract more customers. With the Savings and Loan fiasco, and with the constant possibility of a recession in our midst, many people are quite disillusioned with the banking industry in general. With continuous consolidations the banking industry is in turmoil, and the emerging regional banks are trying more than ever to attract new customers as well as to lure customers away from their competition. Promotional ploys are everywhere to be seen. Open a new account and get a free iron, or radio or other appliance depending on your initial deposit. Other banks guarantee free checking regardless of balance, or a bonus check with your first deposit."

"All such public relations maneuvers are fine and dandy especially for people who like having different options from which to choose. However, 40% of the market is being ignored when banks do not attempt to entice the procedural banking customer. Banking transactions are by nature procedural, but if you do not bother to show a procedural person how to carry out the procedure, he will stay out in the cold. So you need to do several basic things."

"Here we go again!" I added.

"First, you have to get the prospective customer into the bank. Most banks totally ignore this fact in their advertising and in their on site promotions. Why not get the attention of desired customers by laying out a procedure for drawing them into the bank in the first place? Once through the door, promptly determine if they are procedural and then provide them procedures. Tell them how to fill out the necessary forms. And remember that you need to tell them exactly what is involved in any given transaction. Provide no alternatives to these people. If they want to open a new account, then walk them through the different steps. Remember, that for procedural people there is only one way to fill out a form, and each transaction has its own separate form. The more specific and explicit the procedure, the more comfortable the procedural customer will be."

"Are you still with me? I have a few more points to make before moving on. In order to operate efficiently, banks must have a certain number of procedures. This provides for good service which is necessary to keep attracting business. Banks should remember that there are options people living alongside procedural people in this world, and when dealing with them it is necessary to bend the rules at times to provide alternatives for them. Try to deviate from procedure only in insignificant places, where doing so is neither illegal nor inefficient."

"Fortunately, there is one area in banking services that does appeal to the procedural customer. The great options person who came up with the convenient cash machine provided a major service to all those procedural people of the world."

"And if you press the wrong button, everything goes haywire!" I uttered in almost disgust.

"That's called deviating from a procedure." Michael said. "The entire process is clearly indicated to you on the screen. First you put in your card to get into the door. Then the card goes into the machine, where with each pressing of a button, you are led on the path to the next step in the procedure of getting the desired amount of cash. If you are an options person, and attempt to somehow deviate from the right procedure, you will not succeed at obtaining your money. So even the super stubborn options person has no choice but to follow the sequential steps of the procedure or otherwise he will be out of cash."

CREDIT CARDS

"I just thought of something. Don't banks try to attract customers through credit cards?" I asked.

"Very much so, and that brings me to yet another application of the Options and Procedures People Pattern to sales within the banking industry. How many applications for new credit card accounts do you get in the mail each week? I sometimes get as many as five in any given week from banks as far away as Timbuktu. What joy for the procedural person! For fun, pick up one of these forms and notice just how procedural the whole thing is! First, you are often told to carefully read the first section, then carefully turn the page to the next section which you are to systematically fill out. Then stop and open the attached little envelope for a surprise bonus. If you wish to continue you are told step by step how to proceed, even to the point of telling you to put down your pen at the end, and seal the form in the conveniently enclosed pre-stamped envelope."

My laughter did not keep Michael from going on.

"We have noticed an interesting thing regarding this. The interesting thing is that options people already have credit cards. They considered the various options available and selected the ones that made most sense to them. Who gets a credit card by mail? An options person may if it provides an interesting or practical alternative to the ones he has. Most mail order credit card acceptors are procedural. They do not already have credit cards, because they do not know how to go about getting them. And when the credit card companies conveniently outline the entire procedure for these procedural people, they are immediately hooked."

"If you are wondering what I am talking about," Michael went on to say, "I invite you to begin to notice the credit card applications you get in the mail. The banks that elicit credit card applicants through the mail must be marginally aware of two types of reactions (even though they do not know of this People Pattern distinction), since we have seen two different kinds of credit card applications. The one aimed at the procedural buyer starts with the words 'Before you turn the page, pick up a pen...' On the next page it says 'Got a pen? Good! First check out all the terrific benefits ... and then turn the page to apply.' At the bottom of the page it says 'Ready to apply? Wait a minute - there's more.' On the next page in the application it starts with 'select one' and then includes sections on 'please tell us about yourself,' 'important job information,' 'about your income,' 'important account information,' and 'please sign this authorization.' At the bottom it says 'Fold, moisten here, seal and mail. Please do not staple or tape. Return entire brochure.' A procedural person would love this application and it is probably very effective."

"I have seen an options version from the same bank. It is quite different. It begins with 'Consider the various options available to you.' It goes on to discuss clearly labeled options. The application says 'Select the options below' and it ends with 'Mail this now to make these options available.' This is also very effective for the options person. The bank was wise to send out two different forms even if they could not explain the two reactions. One appeals to procedural people and the other to their counterpart, options people. Between them they cover the entire market."

"What you said really does hit home, because I automatically place in the waste bin any application that arrives in the mail giving me a specific set of instructions to follow. In fact, the more procedural the form, the more likely I am to throw it away. The ones that I hate most are the ones from Publisher's Clearing House." I added.

"I have spent a lot of time on this example in banking, because it serves to elucidate the importance of the Options and Procedures People Pattern in sales in general. Before I send you off to Beverly in negotiations, I would like to talk about another aspect of sales and its application to this People Pattern. With our credit card example, we were dealing with sales through the mail. Now let us turn to another area of sales, that of phone sales or telemarketing."

TELEMARKETING

"Oh no! Not those pains who call just when I'm about to sit down and have dinner!" I grunted. "It never fails. Whenever I get home, ready to relax some telemarketer ends up calling like magic."

"Alas! Yes indeed. Obviously you have picked up the phone at times and found someone at the other end trying to sell you something that you did not need and certainly did not want! Who is this person who dares invade the privacy of your own home or of your office? Who is this pest?"

"Excuse me for interrupting, but how about 'Who is this public menace?'" I interjected.

"I'm sure many a disgruntled and tired John or Mary Doe would agree with that one! In any case, this 'person' or whatever designation you prefer, may be a representative of one of the many phone companies trying to get you to switch your long distance service or it may be someone trying to sell you on a vacation package or on travel insurance. The list of possibilities is endless. You know whom I am talking about. You find yourself on the other end of the line with - yes that is right - probably the most invasive and annoying pests in the world - your friendly telemarketer."

"I cannot think of anyone who is more of a pain than that voice on the other end of the phone always calling somehow at the most inopportune time imaginable for something I could not care less about. And then for me, an options person, to listen to their procedural spiel on who knows what irritates me beyond belief! So I really want to hear more." I implored with enthusiasm.

"Well, did you know that telemarketers are such a nuisance that Congress is always considering legislation to restrict them or outlaw them all together? Telemarketers have computers that dial for them automatically so that they never have to wait."

"I know the situation is bad, because I remember hearing on the news that during the 1991 San Francisco earthquake when the phones were out, the first time the rescue workers knew that the phones were back on, was when they heard a ring, reached under some rubble to find a phone, said hello and found themselves talking to - you guessed it - a telemarketer." I recounted.

"That is a great little anecdote! said Michael. "I hadn't heard that one, but your story serves to reinforce my point all the more. It is that our friendly telemarketer has become such an integral part of today's selling world and has not only managed to gain access to the one place where we are supposed to feel comfortable and secure and free - our own homes, but has also managed to reach otherwise inaccessible places in times of disaster when everyone else is literally unable to get through." I was laughing so hard I almost had tears in my eyes.

"We have gone off on a slight tangent," Michael said, "but at least you get the point. Let's talk a little about how telemarketing works and show how it relates to the Options and Procedures People Pattern. A company like MCI or Sprint wants to lure you away from ATT. Now if you are an options person, you have probably already decided what phone company you want with good reasons and have already called them first. If they call you, then you might switch if they can give you good enough reasons for doing so. Remember that options people give reasons for doing things. You will want to know what all of your options are, and then you will decide accordingly. You will probably ask questions that the person with whom you are talking can't answer. If you are a procedural person, however, you may not even know that you can switch telephone companies; and in any case you do not know how to go about it. You will listen to what they say - if you do not hang up first -and may decide to switch phone companies provided that you understand the procedure."

"I'm glad I wouldn't." I said.

"The phone companies know that a certain percentage of people are dissatisfied with their service for a variety of reasons, and if properly approached, they will switch. So the first thing that they do is have a sales script written. This script contains the sales presentation that their research shows is most effective. The script also contains answers to the most commonly asked questions, handles standard objections and presents a standard sales close. The phone company then spreads its business among several telemarketing firms, so as not to put all of its eggs in one basket. This also allows them to test the telemarketing firms against each other and to give more business to the more successful ones."

"I see what you mean since I have made calls in the past to several such firms." I said.

"Then you know that a telemarketing firm consists of a room full of cubicals with a phone and operator in each. The phones are hooked up to a computer which dials continually so that as soon as the operator finishes one call he can pick up another. The calls are monitored to make sure that the telemarketers are adhering to the script exactly. These firms are often located in rural areas like Oklahoma, Kansas or South Dakota where they can find an inexpensive and reliable work force. Telemarketers are usually not paid well and are often students, housewives or people moonlighting."

"The point of this little discourse" Michael said, "is to help you understand just how procedural the field of telemarketing is, from the sales script to the physical work environment itself. The entire telemarketing operation is totally procedural."

"I guess that is why I consider the process so utterly boring!" I grimaced.

"Just as any good options person like yourself would, but I will leave this part of the discussion to the Personnel Manager. In any case, the operator reads the prepared script but tries to make it sound like a normal conversation. In fact, the whole process is like a little game that works like this. You pick up the phone and realize that you are dealing with your friendly procedural telemarketer. You either immediately slam the phone down in disgust or..."

"That is what I do most of the time," I interjected.

"Or if you are too polite to hang up on the person, you listen further. At some point the telemarketer has to pause to breathe. This is the critical point at which you can interrupt and tell him that you are not interested. He knows this so he tries to say as much as possible in one breath. He also breathes quickly so as to continue his sales presentation."

"Those are the ones who have been doing it a while." I added.

"Yes, and if you let him get his first breath in, then you are in for the ride. He will mechanically ask you some closed questions (yes or no answers) and lead you through the procedure. If you happen to have questions, he will quickly locate the answer on his prepared script. If you ask questions that are not on his script, then he is lost and will not know what to do. He will probably ask you to speak to his supervisor. If you keep listening, then he will continue to take you through a complete procedure. You will probably wait for the close and then either say no to the service or product for sale, or else if you are hooked, you will say yes. If you say yes, then the operator will tell you that his supervisor has to confirm the order. They do not trust telemarketers very much in the business, and they are continuously supervised by someone usually slightly higher up on the managerial ladder."

"I know it seems as though we have been going at this for ages during your training sessions. It is just that the whole area of sales is so nuanced and multi-faceted that we could spend an entire week on this subject alone. Once you have been with the company for awhile, we will put you through our five day P^3 Sales Training which goes into more detail and even more applications of all of the People Patterns. Well, it looks as though you are already on your way to becoming one of our P^3 Managers!"

"I already am beginning to see myself as one!"

"That's great! You go to negotiations next, don't you? Sales and negotiations go hand in hand. Beverly really uses People Pattern Power effectively in negotiations, and I am sure that she will have some interesting insights into this pattern. She and I have discussed the connection between sales and negotiations often, and she has done an excellent job of integrating options and procedures into her negotiations training."

NEGOTIATIONS

Beverly was talking to a colleague when I arrived, and this gave me a few minutes to think about how options and procedures might apply to negotiations. Beverly greeted me and asked what I had learned so far. I gave her a brief summary, and then she jumped right in.

"First let me start by reminding you that negotiations are a fact of life. From the day we first met I have emphasized that we are all constantly engaged in a daily, ongoing process of negotiating with all of the people in our lives - our spouses, children, colleagues, managers, and the list goes on and on. Moreover, being able to negotiate effectively is going to be a crucial part of any manager's agenda if he is to succeed. Conflict is a growth industry in our society. No one ever does anything just because you ask. Everyone wants to know 'why'. As a manager, your ability to persuade and influence others is directly connected to your competency as a negotiator."

"At least I have that down already!" I said.

"You have already spent time with Marvin discussing management applications, so remember that managers negotiate all the time. What you will learn about formal negotiations with me applies just as readily to management. And all that you have learned thus far about Options and Procedures is a very critical component in all kinds of negotiations."

"Let me give you a brief summary of how the Options and Procedures People Pattern applies to negotiations. Let us begin with a few basic negotiations principles. It is important to realize that each negotiation is unique, yet all negotiations have certain processes in common. I am talking about the Yin/Yang of Negotiations^{SM}, about two contrary and equally important elements that complement each other. Which type of person do you think makes the best negotiator?"

I said: "Being an options person myself, I would think that another options person would make the best negotiator."

Beverly smiled and said: "I hope that you do not always use yourself as the barometer for competency in all areas. In this case, however, you are basically correct with a few qualifications. Our experience has shown that the best negotiator is probably an options person who is contextually balanced with the ability to follow procedures when necessary. The best negotiator is both able to generate a variety of options for mutual gain and choose wisely among those options and is also able to follow sound procedural principles when required. Such people are rare. The next best negotiator is a procedural person who has an excellent set of procedures to follow. The former usually come that way, whereas the latter can be trained. The worst negotiators are procedural people with poor procedures and options people who do not have a clue as to what they are doing. So obviously, being either procedures or options oriented does no good if you are a procedural person with bad procedures or an options persons working in ignorance."

Beverly excused herself to take an urgent call about a current negotiation and then resumed.

"We have been involved in both simple and complex negotiations over the years and have found certain things to be true. First, that negotiations is frequently counter-intuitive. When intuitions fail, then it helps to have a set of effective procedures to fall back on. Second, it is possible to teach someone the procedural principles of sound negotiations in a relatively short period of time. Success, Incorporated has been doing this with major corporations and organizations for years. Last, but certainly not least, getting someone to follow these principles, however, may take a lifetime. Good negotiations courses, of which there are not a lot around, teach sound procedural principles as well as options. None of these courses, however, incorporate People Patterns. This gives us a distinct advantage. The problem with most negotiations courses, and most other courses for that matter, is that they teach people *what* to do but not *how* to do it. This also works to our advantage."

"That is one of the things that attracted me initially to your company." I said. "You do not just tell people what to do, but you also show them how to make the necessary behavioral changes so that they can do the 'what'."

Beverly laughed and continued: "I am sure that Shana covered the basics of this pattern quite extensively this morning, so I will focus on how options and procedures applies to negotiations. The challenge in negotiations is to get options people to follow sound procedures when necessary and to get procedural people to deviate from procedures when necessary. The options person's creativity may be a disadvantage, and the procedural person's rigidity may be an equal disadvantage. Good negotiations training helps students to get in touch with what exactly it is inside of them that prevents them from following necessary procedures or that prevents them from abandoning those procedures when necessary. In order to assist students in dealing with their own internal resistance, a negotiations trainer needs a solid knowledge of this People Pattern."

"Based on what you have said thus far, it would seem to me that an options person would not see the negotiation the same way that a procedural person would. Using your P^3 analogy, then a procedural person would be looking at such an interaction through a different set of glasses. Right?" I asked.

"Yes." Beverly said "And there is more to it than that. Procedural people view negotiations as a process for reaching agreement. Now that you know this, here are some tips. If you are negotiating with a procedural person, then it will be critical to get agreement on the process at the very beginning. The procedural person will feel much more comfortable once the game is defined. This is a very important initial step in any negotiation. Most negotiations are won or lost in the first thirty seconds, because during this time it is usually determined what game you are going to play. There are three major games in negotiations. These are hardball, softball, and principled. Each game is different and has its own set of rules (i.e., its own set of procedures)."

THREE NEGOTIATION APPROACHES
Hardball
Softball
Principled

I had no comments so Beverly continued. "Procedural people need a procedure, and it is very frustrating to them to not know what the process is and, moreover, not to know where they are in it. Once they enter into the process they always desire to complete it. If they happen to get stuck in the middle of the negotiation, procedural people, as you know now from this morning, are in quite a quandary because they have an overwhelming need and compulsion to complete the procedure. When you are working with a procedural person, if you can get him into the procedure, he is going to want to complete it no matter what. It is almost like an inner drive that draws the person inevitably to concluding the process. If you are negotiating with a procedural person, then you want to provide him with an 'oh so cherished' procedure. Make sure that you provide him with a clear set of instructions which delineate very clearly not only what the procedure is, but the sequence of the steps. You may begin by telling him what the procedure is. For example, I was negotiating with a procedural person last week. I started the negotiation something like this: *The first thing I am going to do is to describe to you just how we are going to go about reaching an agreement. I do not want you to take advantage of me, and I do not want to take advantage of you. I want us to reach an agreement that meets both of our needs and that is based on fair, objective, impartial criteria. Do you agree? Good. Let me explain how we can do this. First, we will agree on this procedure. Second, we will share our interests with each other. Third, we will see where our interests overlap and find a couple of ways that satisfy both of our interests. Fourth, we will agree on fair, objective, impartial criteria. Fifth, we will apply the criteria to the ways that we selected in step three. Sixth, we will select the one that best fits the criteria. Is this procedure agreeable to you? Excellent. We have already completed step one. Let us move on to step two. Why don't you tell me about your interests.*"

"Basically, then, from what I have learned about this People Pattern, once you get them caught up in the procedure, procedural people have a natural tendency to follow the procedure as you have outlined it." I said.

"That is true." responded Beverly. "By quickly getting them into the procedure, you simply feed their inherent penchant to become so totally absorbed by it, that they can get lost in the procedure. This will work to your advantage. Certainly stay away from providing alternatives. Once in the procedure, continue to emphasize what is left to do in order to complete the negotiating procedure. Remember that the procedural person will always have a strong need to get to the end of the procedure, otherwise he feels totally disoriented. And if he finds himself perplexed or lost in the negotiation, your task is all the more difficult as far as reaching an agreement."

"I've found that some procedural people with whom I have had to negotiate can be quite stubborn." I added.

"That brings me to my next point." Beverly continued. "One drawback when negotiating with a highly procedural person is that he may deadlock. This happens because he is incapable of generating alternatives. If impasse is reached, his usual response is to follow the procedures even more rigorously rather than deviate from them. When his game plan breaks down, he does not have a procedure for generating a new one; and if an alternative game plan were to be proposed to him, he frequently would not accept it anyway."

"I've been in that unfortunate set of circumstances. If only I understood then what I know now!" I said.

"Here are some more rules of thumb when negotiating with procedural people. Remember that they will usually approach the negotiation in a mechanical fashion. They will follow a particular procedure to a tee. For example, they will have determined their bottom line and their goals in advance and will have a game plan for getting there. They will want the other side to make the first offer, and then they will make their counter offer beyond their goal. Moreover, they will concede slowly and in small increments, demanding something in exchange for every concession. Procedural people will be quite stubborn as well. All of this can often be quite effective. They frequently end up getting deals that are to their advantage. A procedural negotiator who has a good set of procedures can be tough."

Beverly saw that I had no questions so she continued her explanation.

"If procedural people use tactics, they will often be mechanical and obvious. They often view the negotiation like a chess game in which each side uses tactics to make moves and then waits for the other side to counter. Tactics may lead to escalation, however, and take one away from agreement. When procedural people do use tactics, they usually have a limited repertoire. Once their small arsenal has been countered, they may be at a disadvantage."

"Often procedural institutions like banks and insurance companies are highly inflexible in their approach to negotiations. They are used to following procedures and are frequently quite rigid and inflexible in their methods and strategies. They usually have already defined the game and expect the other side to follow their rules. If the other side refuses to do so, then they will usually deadlock rather than deviate from their initial game plan. If the person with whom the bank is negotiating also happens to be procedural, then the bank's rigidity will often be accepted. The other person will understand the importance of following procedures and that the bank, like every other institution in society, must have procedures which allow it to operate effectively and to provide the quality of service that is expected of it."

"What if the bank is dealing with an options person?" I asked, of course.

"If, on the other hand, the bank is negotiating with an options person there will probably be a problem. The options person does not want to hear about the bank's procedures. He absolutely detests procedures, and wants to know what other options the bank can provide him. He wants to know why the bank can't do this and that. He does not want to hear about policy. Options people would rather deviate from the accepted procedure. The fact that doing so means going against company policy will not be an adequate explanation for them."

"So my hunch was right." I said. "Options people do look at negotiations somewhat differently than their procedural counterparts."

"Indeed they do. Options people are frequently more focused on the outcome than on the process for getting there. They view negotiations as a way to discover the best option upon which both will agree. Options people hate rigid procedures and will want the negotiation process to be very flexible and perhaps even informal, usually too much so for the procedural person. They will be quite good at creating options either for mutual gain or for their own gain. Also, they will be highly flexible in going after their outcomes, and will usually be quite good at debating different points and coming up with a variety of arguments to defend their position."

"So how would I negotiate with an options person?" I asked.

"If you are negotiating with an options person, then stress options and reasons over processes and procedures. Let him know that you usually follow a set process, but that you are going out of your way to deviate from that procedure to make him happy. He will be good at generating options, so use his talent to your advantage. Make him aware of your requirements and let him do what he does best which is invent ways to satisfy you. Options people will respect reasons, so you need to be prepared to provide reasons for everything that you propose. For example, next week I have to negotiate with an options person. I intend to begin something like this: *I know that we are both busy so we will need to remain flexible in our process. I often follow a fixed process, but with you I know that it will not be necessary. Let me explain my situation to you. I need your help in discovering a variety of options that will satisfy both of our interests. I know that you are good at brain storming, and I view this negotiation more like a problem solving session than a confrontation. Shall we begin?"*

"So much of negotiating can be examined through the Options and Procedures People Pattern." Beverly went on to say. "Take tactics for example. What kind of person will feel more comfortable using different tactics?"

"Options people, I would think." I said.

"Options people can be quite ingenious in creating and utilizing tactics. Beverly continued. "After all, tactics in negotiations are just the collected wisdom of several thousand years of devious people figuring out one more way to get a one sided advantage over their neighbors. Devious options people can be quite a challenge in negotiations. They are continually creating new options that give them an advantage. Devious options people, when good, are the great peacemakers of the world and, when bad, are the great con artists of the world."

"To guard against such people requires strong medicine." I said.

"Fortunately it is available in one of the more popular approaches to negotiation." Beverly went on to explain. "This medicine is called *principled* negotiations. It was developed by William Ury and Roger Fisher of the Harvard Negotiations Project. I will simply mention it in passing again. It combines elements of both options and procedures, although they are obviously not identified as such. On the options side it stresses flexibility, problem solving, brain storming options for mutual gain, and discovering fair, objective criteria on which to base agreement. On the other side, it proposes a set of procedures which explain how to go about this."

"I would like to share with you now some other secrets we have learned over the years about negotiating. From having taught principled negotiation in a variety of contexts, we have discovered that two kinds of difficulties arise. The procedural students will painstakingly follow the procedures, but will be incapable of creating options for mutual gain. The options students, on the other hand, will be good at generating options but will quickly abandon the procedural process. They will skip steps, change the order or do anything to avoid following the process. To be an effective principled negotiator - or any other kind of negotiator for that matter - balance is required."

"You have probably realized by now that being a great negotiator means having flexibility of behavior. That means using procedures when appropriate, and deviating from them when appropriate. You can be a great negotiator by following procedures if warranted, and an even better one if you know when to provide alternatives to those procedures. Because each negotiation is unique and different, a good negotiator needs to be flexible. Sometimes, it may be necessary to abandon existing procedures and develop new ones. Therefore, balance is important. If you are overly procedural in your negotiating, you then become too mechanical in your behavior. You become like the person who presses the already lit button in the elevator. His gesture is purely a mechanical one. So it is with negotiations. You need to be flexible, but not too much so. You need to be both options oriented and to be able to follow procedures, each when contextually appropriate."

"Well this lesson was certainly an eye opener. Here I thought I had a good handle on negotiating techniques. Little did I know how ignorant I really was on the subject! You are absolutely right! Knowing a technique is almost useless if you do not understand how to communicate with the person on the other side of the negotiating table."

"Again, we have limited time and have only touched briefly on the subject of options and procedures in negotiations. We will put you through both our basic and advanced negotiations trainings in the near future, but now you are expected by Frank in the Training Department."

TRAINING

Frank greeted me cordially as usual.

"So you are here to learn about options and procedures in training. This particular People Pattern is one of the most critical in a training context. The battle over this pattern is fought every day in almost every classroom in this country. Most teachers and trainers are options people. They are primarily concerned with theoretical models and are less involved with the practical applications of these theories. They love to create procedures and love to generate options. This is precisely why they are teachers. Also, this ability is what is rewarded in academia. After all, isn't this what education is all about?"

"I had never really thought about it that way." I said.

"Of course, it goes without saying that the options teachers, in turn, hate to follow their own or anyone else's procedures for that matter. So along comes the poor unsuspecting procedural student. This scene is played out hundreds of times every day in high schools, community colleges, universities and business trainings all across America and around the world. For the procedural students, the function of education is to learn the procedures that will allow them to succeed in business and in life. It is the trainer's or teacher's job to provide the procedures and to check them out ahead of time to make sure that they work. After all, isn't this the essence of training and education? The procedural student wants to go to school so he can learn how to make a living. Making a living is a highly practical and indispensable activity. Success in achieving that goal is measured by one's ability to know and follow effective procedures."

"So the procedural student comes to class ready to devour the procedures supplied by the teacher or trainer?" I asked.

"Yes. Teachers can generate procedures. After all, that is why they are a teacher or trainer. Now the fun begins. The procedural student sits poised with paper and pencil in hand, ready to copy down the secret success procedures from the fountain of all knowledge. But much to the dismay of the procedural student, the teacher or trainer all too often refuses to provide the procedures, although he obviously knows them. The teacher or trainer simply does not want to supply procedures. He wants students to learn to generate their own procedures, and he encourages them to be creative. He wants the students to understand the subject so well that they can develop creative solutions to any problem that may arise."

"That makes me think of when I was back in school." I said.

"Trust me." Frank said. "You will have many an insight from now on, now that you have an understanding of these People Patterns. In any case, the teacher or trainer is in love with a magical thing, that *'je ne sais quoi'* which he calls 'understanding'. To him this is what training and education is all about. Training and education deal with 'understanding' which is the ability to generate procedures and not just to blindly follow them."

"For example, the teacher may say to the student: *I could give you procedures galore, but I would be doing you a tremendous disservice. Education is about you learning to create your own procedures and not about having somebody give them to you. If I provide you with ready made procedures, then you will never learn to create them yourself. And this means that I will have failed you. What will you do when I am not around to help you? You have to learn to think for yourself. And that is my goal in teaching you to generate your own procedures."*

"Of course at this point the poor procedural student throws up his hands in despair. He says: *I do not want understanding. I just want to learn the procedures that I will need to know in order to be successful in business and in life. I am not a scholar. I do not care why things work. I just want to know how they work. I came here to learn how. Please teach me the procedures that I need to get ahead in work and in life."*

"And so the battle goes on and on every day in training rooms and classrooms around the world. Trainers and teachers become more and more disillusioned about students. They secretly long for that ideal student who is interested in 'understanding' and who is like them. And, of course, the students wait for that ideal trainer or teacher who will just for once do what he is being paid to do, which is to provide students with a treasured 'how to' manual for business and life and success that really works."

"The implications of what you are saying are incredible." I added.

"This situation has far reaching implications for American education. It is no secret that the current 'dis-educational' establishment is failing miserably for a variety of reasons. And unfortunately, we in American business have to pay the price. We live in a world of increasing global economic competition. American business counts on the American 'dis-educational' system to provide it with a large pool of quality candidates for employment. Unfortunately, this often does not happen. Business leaders publicly and privately lament about the lack of preparation of the average American worker. What business wants is for teachers to provide students with the basic practical skills (i.e., procedures) that they need to be successful in the work place. In business there is a large need for practical people who can follow procedures and who know the procedures to follow. There is a smaller need for options people who can generate procedures. Awareness of this problem could begin to redress this appalling situation in the American classroom so that American business can remain competitive in the growing international economy."

"Here at Success, Incorporated you seem to have taken the middle of the road way." I said.

"Remember the importance of balance." Frank reminded me. "In our training department, we take a balanced approach to options and procedures in training, what we call the Yin/Yang of Training^{SM}. Our instructional design staff works hand in hand with each department for whom we train in order to develop the best procedures possible. In our trainings we focus on the best procedures and practices and on how to carry them out. All procedures are written out in order. We provide procedural students with what they need. We don't just stop there, however. After we give the procedure we discuss what to do if it breaks down. We then ask the options students for suggestions as to alternatives. We get many valuable suggestions this way. We have an active quality improvement program, and we encourage everyone to think of new ways to improve our effectiveness and efficiency. We find that often students who are new to an area will have new ideas that are helpful. After doing a job for awhile, people often lose sight of obvious ways to improve. So you see that training and education requires a balance of options and procedures. The best companies have developed and tested excellent procedures, but they are also constantly working to improve upon them. Do you have any questions?"

"No." I said. "But I am beginning to understand why my youngest son is having trouble this year in school. He is pretty procedural and his teacher is an off the wall options person. He is always complaining that she will never simply answer his questions. He wants one right answer and she is always providing him with alternatives. At the stage he is at now, doing this only confuses him. I think that I now know how I will be able to help him."

"Your last stop before you return to Shana is the Personnel Department. I have to go that way. I'll walk over there with you."

"Boy, it sure would have helped me then to know what I have learned during the course of this Training with all of you. I must admit that I really did not have a clue as to what was happening during my initial interview. I must have had the most ridiculous look of wonder on my face!" I said with a similar look.

"Obviously, you fit the bill, otherwise you would not be standing here with me now. Anyway, time to move on."

PERSONNEL SELECTION

Karen greeted me warmly, at the same time showing her characteristic no nonsense approach.

"I am sure that Frank has given you a thorough grounding in P^3 as it relates to training. By the way, I could not help but overhear your last comment to him as you were walking into my office. Yes, you did have a kind of queer look on your face when I was asking you what at that time appeared to you to be strange and unusual questions from extra-terrestrials. I will bet that things are finally falling into place for you regarding these patterns. I should tell you, if no one else has, that the purpose of this training is many fold. First and obviously, you are learning these various patterns from each of our top P^3 Managers. Second, you are observing throughout this ten day training any incidents or situations or conversations which arise that typify any of these patterns. And last, but certainly not least, you have already been assimilating on an unconscious level, many of these patterns in your responses to all of us and in your interactions with others. That is the crucial key which allows you to cross over from being a neophyte P^3 Manager to a practicing P^3 Manager. Once you have been here awhile and become fully versed and proficient in P^3 skills, you will then become a full fledged P^3 Manager. There is a test, by the way, which will measure your ability as a P^3 Manager. Once you have accomplished the task of opening the doors of perception using your People Pattern keys, this will not only facilitate your interactions with those around you, but will also be the larger, macro key to opening the door of success in business. I might add that you will even begin to notice a positive change in your personal interactions with your spouse, children, friends and others who cross your path of life."

"I would certainly like to take that step sooner than later! I assume that all of the handful of managers like yourself who have been training me in P³ skills are full fledged P³ Managers."

"Yes, and we learned our skills from the two principals of this company who created the P³ skills, the P³ Training Program and the P³ Test. They are the two P³ Masters not only because they created it, but unlike us who have been trained specifically in business contexts, the two P³ Masters apply People Patterns to all contexts and walks of life, both on the level of the individual and of society."

"Would it be possible to attend one of their P³ Trainings dealing with these other facets of life and society?" I wanted to know.

"Yes, I know that you will find it very informative and useful. By the way, you will be meeting them when they return from their latest project. Anyway, let's get back to applications of the Options and Procedures Pattern to Personnel and Hiring."

"Just before you walked in for our session together, I was talking to my assistants in Personnel about our need to hire two people in our travel branch to handle reservations. Most of us in this day and age have at one time or another picked up the phone to make a plane, train, car, hotel reservation or any kind of booking for that matter. As you will soon see, this is yet another area to which the Options and Procedures People Pattern is so appropriate and revelatory as far as understanding behaviors. Think a minute. Have you ever been confronted by a stubborn and unyielding voice at the other end of the phone who totally refuses your simple request to bend the rules regarding a reservation?"

"That has happened much more often than I would like!" I responded.

"You patiently explain to them what you want, and then they go on to say why you can't do it because of the rules and regulations. When you repeat your request, like a broken record they explain the ridiculous rules and regulations to you again. You feel like saying: 'You idiot. I understand the stupid rule. You do not have to repeat it again. What I want is for you to ignore the rules and do what I need done!'."

"This scenario sounds much too familiar for my comfort." I added.

"And, you know, of course, the reservation agents are not authorized to disobey the rules and may even get fired if they do. They were hired specifically to follow the procedures. If they violated the rules for everyone who asked them to do so, the airlines, rental car companies and hotels would not be able to function."

The look on my face gave away my thoughts as Karen continued.

"But, of course, this doesn't help you. You are probably cursing under your breath and wondering why you have to deal with such inflexible people. You wonder to yourself 'Why can't these stupid employees realize that alternatives do exist that would make life easier for so many?' The reason for their stubbornness is that they were hired for their jobs precisely because they are procedural people who can follow directions. They were hired because they manage to follow procedures oh so very well (in any case far too well for our liking) and because they are the very individuals who can't find the will or energy or desire to deviate from the procedures which they have been taught so efficiently. Their function is to make life miserable for the options people of the world who want to keep their alternatives open concerning their travel plans, particularly about when and where they will go and stay."

"I can certainly tell you how frustrating that is to me, an options person!" I chimed in.

"So it can be extremely upsetting for an options person who is trying to book a flight and who can't get the reservation clerk to budge an inch. The clerk is wedded to his computer screen and to following the procedures that he has been taught. Any modification of the procedure would only create stress and discomfort for him. So the tedious phone battle continues unceasingly. What can the options person do in such a case? He finds an alternative, of course! That option comes in the form of the savior supervisor."

"Well, thank God for the supervisor then!" I shouted with an amusing sigh of relief.

"You can say that again." Karen retorted. "Reservation agents are trained and required to follow procedures and obviously do not have the clout or the authority to make changes in them. But someone must have this authority. What happens when the clerk is not sure what to do? What is the second line of defense? The supervisors, of course. They are the only ones empowered to violate the procedures. The supervisor, if anyone, can generate other alternatives and solve the problem at hand. What would the options person do without this accommodating angel? Hang up the towel probably in dire frustration against a procedural world."

"So fortunately, there is an option available to all of us who choose to use it." I'd be lost without that cherished option!" I noted.

"The next time that you butt up against a procedural agent - whether it be at your local Hertz, Avis, Hilton, United, US Air or Delta counters or anywhere else - then quickly ask to speak with their supervisor, rather than wasting precious time and energy arguing in vain with someone you now understand is incapable of yielding in most cases!"

"Now I know why I always get along better with the supervisors who end up coming to my aid. If it weren't for them, I would probably avoid taking flights, renting cars or doing anything that forces me to deal with what are obviously highly procedural people. We certainly don't share the same filters here at all! I have been wearing blinders in my past dealings with procedural people. What you just related definitely sheds a new light on the matter. At least now I understand why I have experienced so much frustration and often anger and even dread whenever I had to make a flight reservation."

"You will find this scenario repeated in the realm of telemarketing." Karen went on to say. "I know that Michael has already covered this from a sales point of view, so I will simply make a few additional points in the context of personnel and hiring. As you know, the telemarketer is trained to read a prepared script verbatim. They are evaluated on total script adherence and can be fired for deviating from the script. The company hiring the telemarketing firm monitors the lines to ensure that their carefully worded scripts are being followed exactly. They also have names of their own employees randomly distributed on the list to further monitor adherence. Obviously, this is a job for a highly procedural person. An options person would quickly go nuts following the procedures. So telemarketing firms would do well to incorporate the P^3 Model and to carefully screen their applicants in light of this People Pattern."

"So what you are saying in effect is that an entire industry rides on the Options and Procedures People Pattern?" I stated in the form of a question.

"Yes. If the telemarketing firm can hire enough procedural people and develop the right procedures and have the right script, then it will be able to sell a certain percentage of procedural buyers and a far smaller percentage of options buyers. The key is procedures, procedures, and more procedures. Don't you just love it?" Karen asked with a tinge of irony in her voice.

"In this same vein, another thing comes to mind." she went on to say. "Have you ever had a problem with an order you placed? Recently I ordered an item that arrived defective, and the procedural phone order clerk could not and would not handle the problem, since that was outside of her set of instructions regarding orders. If a situation does not meet the usual criteria, then it is time to call upon - guess who - the friendly supervisor, who in the context of product and service sales is called the customer service representative. Just like the typical airlines reservations agent has to ask for a supervisor's intervention with issues that violate standard procedures, a telephone sales clerk often does likewise by calling upon the customer service person to deal with situations that do not fit the typical, ordered procedural mold."

"It's everywhere every day before our eyes, isn't it?" I said with a note of dismay almost.

"We live daily with options and procedures so it would really be great if others understood the dynamics involved here. In any case, as I told you, here at Success, Incorporated we now need to hire two people to handle reservations for us, so we will ideally have one who is a procedural person and one who is an options person. In fact, if we can find them, we would like to hire two people who are balanced in both areas. This is our Yin/Yang of Personnel Selection^{SM}, just as you learned about the Yin/Yang of Management, Sales and Negotiations. As you have been told time and time again, each and every day of your training, balance is the ideal."

"There is a very important lesson to be learned from these scenarios. Karen went on to say. "Employers would do well to know the orientation of their prospective employees before hiring them for positions requiring one pattern to be stronger than the other in the execution of a particular job. Besides telemarketers and reservations agents, there are other kinds of jobs in which procedural people are much better suited to work. These vary from assembly line positions where workers are required to put things together in a set way to auditors and accountants. Any job that is not procedural requires an options person. The two principals of our company, the P^3 Masters, as they are known, have come up with criteria using not just the Options and Procedures People Pattern, but all of the others as well, to help companies identify which applicants make the ideal employee to perform a particular job or task. This comes as a result of their work in performance enhancement, in particular, from modeling many varied skills and from their synthesis of many human typologies."

"Well, hiring and firing is serious business, so an understanding of these patterns is critical." I realized out loud.

"Indeed, and it is made even more sensitive at this time given the current economic conditions and the large number of government regulations. Employers need to be realistic about these things and to realize the importance of understanding People Patterns in the context of personnel selection. It is crucial to know what jobs require what skills, and then to determine the People Patterns which best fit the execution of those skills. For example, as I have just shown you, if you are hiring hotel desk clerks or airline reservation agents then hire procedural people. If you are hiring supervisors for these agents, then hire options people."

"If you are hiring people for jobs on machines, particularly assembly line type apparatus which, by their very nature, entail carefully following standard operating procedures, then you will want to place highly procedural people in those positions. Watch out when the machines falter, however, since procedural people are incapable of creating alternatives. They can only follow procedures, not create them. They sit there stuck, repeating over and over what doesn't work, because the procedure says that is the way it should be. For times when the machines do break down, employers should hire options personnel to deal with these problems. Such individuals are usually given the title of supervisor or shift manager. It is their job to understand and operate the machines using the standard operating procedures, but also to know how to handle problems and fix the machines when they do break down (and our performance enhancement projects in the manufacturing realm have shown just how often that does occur) or when the normal procedures fail. Remember it is options people who are the ones who generate new procedures when the standard ones break down."

"It's options people to the rescue again, thank goodness." I said as objectively as I could, given my own orientation.

"I need to remind you of balance, however." said Karen. "In any case, for every position in our company, we need to determine the People Patterns of the most successful incumbents and hire people who fit that profile. That is where our Profiling Plus^{SM} technology really comes in handy. You can train people to do many things, but it is unrealistic to believe that people will be able to change life-long behavioral patterns, particularly overnight. Well, that is enough for now. By the way could you give Shana this folder for me?"

SUMMARY

As I walked back into Shana's office she was just completing a phone call. "How are you doing? Did you learn a lot about how to apply the activity pattern?"

"That would be the understatement of the century!" I said half jokingly.

Shana adopted a more serious look. "Tomorrow the initial phase of your People Patterns Training Program will be over, and you are well on your way to becoming a P^3 Manager. There are three things that I need to reemphasize. The first is for you to always be on guard against projecting your People Patterns onto other people and assuming incorrectly that they filter the world the same way that you do. Second is to remember that no People Patterns are any better than or any worse than any other. Each allows us to pay attention to certain things and, at the same time, blinds us to other things. It is easy to begin to identify with your own People Patterns and to begin to think that they are what you are. They are a blessing and a curse. You must control them and not be controlled by them. Pride in your own patterns can be a dangerous thing. Pride must be balanced by awareness of your limitations and blind spots. This leads to my third and final point which is to seek balance in all that you do. We live in a world where people tend to focus on improving what they already do well and where people tend to ignore their weaknesses. I council a different approach. That is to seek balance not by further increasing your strengths, but by always striving to work on your blind spots and weaknesses. That is what real balance is all about."

KEY 9:

THE ORGANIZATION PEOPLE PATTERN

INTRODUCTION

The car pool was on time to pick me up, since it was Dave's turn to drive. He was always on time or early. You could count on him like clockwork. He always had gas in the car, and he checked the oil and tire pressure every week. Unfortunately, Tom was the last one to be picked up, and he never seemed to be on time. It was always frustrating to have a whole carload of people waiting for him. Being late never seemed to bother him. His apology always seemed perfunctory, and he had an endless series of excuses. This morning it was that his razor wasn't working right. It seemed like nothing ever worked for Tom. His car was always out of tune and breaking down. In general, both he and his car were a wreck. This used to really annoy me. Soon the conversation in the car turned to the weekend. Dave had his whole weekend planned and had had tickets to the game for months. Tom had no idea what he was going to do. He said that he would wait until the spirit moved him and then decide. The last weekend he had decided at the last minute to go to the game. He arrived twenty minutes late and it, of course, had been sold out for weeks anyway. Somehow Tom got lucky because someone had an extra ticket and somehow he got in. I never ceased to be amazed how he was able to pull things off at the last minute. He had a great time and was still talking about it. Then Tom started talking about his wife's birthday which was tomorrow. He still did not have a present for her. He had been asking for advice for two weeks and had made up his mind as to what gift to get six times and then changed it. He still had nothing, and I wondered if he would ever decide on anything. Fortunately, we arrived at my office and I was spared any more of Tom. I checked my watch and rushed to Shana's office. Luck had it that she was on the phone and did not seem to notice that I was five minutes late. I knew it, however, and still felt frustrated that Tom's irresponsibility should cause me to be late. While Shana was on the phone I looked at a brochure that Dave had given me for a time management seminar. I was thinking of getting the car pool to take up a collection to send Tom to it.

Shana finished her call and noticed the brochure. She smiled and began our introductory session with a question. "Would it be useful to know why time management courses are frequently just a waste of time?"

"Yes," I said with an incredulous look. "I have always wondered why some people are habitually late for appointments while other more responsible people are always on time. Being late really bothers me."

"I know." Shana answered. "That is also another of the reasons why we hired you at Success, Incorporated. We needed someone who was prompt and on time. Meanwhile, have you ever wondered why some individuals lead a very organized life with all of their activities planned in advance while other individuals seem to live their lives totally spontaneously with no planning whatsoever? How is it that some people seem to be totally oblivious to the consequences of their actions while other people cannot act until they determine what the consequences will be."

"I can already tell you which of the above descriptions fits me. I declared with pride. I can also tell you which friends and relatives fit these descriptions."

"So what is your usual reaction to anyone who behaves differently from you in this regard? If you like to always be on time, what do you think of people who are always late and who do not even seem sorry about it? You probably think that they are complete idiots, don't you." Shana said with a smile.

TIME AND SPACE DISTINCTIONS

I knew that this session would be particularly fascinating, so I did not want to break the flow of Shana's thoughts.

"The reason behind all of these differences is a fundamental People Pattern which has to do with the way in which each of us deals with *organization* and *structure*. People differ in the way that they organize and structure their time and space, and this affects the way that they make decisions. Some people prefer their lives to be organized. They want to schedule things in advance whenever possible. They need structure to guide their lives from one day to the next, and they like to be neat and organized. These individuals also tend to make up their minds easily and to be resistant to changing them. They are often viewed as judgmental by those who think differently. We call these people *structurists*."

"That's the perfect word to describe them. I like that." I said.

"On the other hand, there are other people who prefer to live their lives spontaneously. They do not like to follow schedules or to be committed to a timetable. They want to be free to do whatever they feel like at the time. These individuals tend to act impulsively. They have neither the time nor the inclination to be neat and organized. They have a hard time deciding on things and often change their minds once they do decide. They are often viewed as irresponsible by those who think in a different manner. We call these people *free spirits.*"

"Once again, the name really does conjure up the appropriate image of this type of person." I interjected.

"Obviously these two approaches to life are quite different. The structurist loves order, and the free spirit abhors it. Free spirits relish the idea of living every minute of every day in a spontaneous and carefree manner, and the structurist prefers to have a plan and to follow a schedule. The structurist makes up his mind and sticks to it, and the free spirit keeps changing his mind. The free spirit views the structurist as rigid and inflexible, and the structurist views the free spirit as quixotic and irresponsible. It is no great surprise, then, that so many relationships break up because these two divergent People Patterns have such a tremendous difficulty tolerating each other. Let us investigate each pattern in more detail and explore the consequences of these two radically different approaches to life." Shana took a pause.

ORGANIZATION PEOPLE PATTERN
Structurists
Free spirits

STRUCTURISTS

"Do you have any questions?" she asked.

"I'm ready to learn how to recognize these two patterns in people." I responded.

"That is what I was about to get into. Let's now delve into the heart of this all important People Pattern and begin to learn how to identify a person's organization pattern and understand the implications of being a structurist or free spirit in society today. First, a structurist is a person who organizes his life based on a set plan. He chooses to make life adapt to his personal preferences and desires, rather than accommodating himself to what life has in store. The structurist prefers to have a daily, weekly, or for that matter, a life's blueprint ready at all times. When some unforeseeable event or person disrupts his plans, the structurist feels a great deal of frustration and sometimes outright anger. He feels very uncomfortable with unexpected occurrences, because he may not be able to adjust his plans to accommodate them."

"Yes, those kinds of things are really annoying to me, a full fledged structurist." I said.

"That's because a structurist may not be able to control the circumstances or to predict the repercussions of the unexpected changes, and this may force him to modify or abandon his carefully laid plans. He is all too aware that 'the best laid plans of mice and men may often go astray' and does everything that he can to prevent this from happening. So surprises and haphazard events create tension for the structurist. He is locked in a constant struggle with the vicissitudes of life and fights a never ending battle to force circumstances to adapt to his plans."

After a pause for an urgent phone call, Shana continued.

"Going hand in hand with his need to plan is the structurist's high need for closure. He wants things nailed down and becomes very frustrated when events are left open ended. He wants 'yes' or 'no' answers, and the word that he detests most is 'maybe'. He is always looking for closure, and he has difficulty planning when things are not settled. He can be very impatient, and he often ends up paying more because he hates to haggle. He hates interruptions or to leave a job incomplete. He has a compulsive need to complete whatever he starts and believes that others should do likewise."

"It sounds like one of the structurist's fortes is his ability to plan and make decisions." I said.

"Precisely. You happen to know that very well, and again, this trait was instrumental in our deciding to hire you."   Shana declared to my contentment. "In making decisions, you, like all structurists, are especially aware of the future — of the consequences of your present decision on future events and situations. The structurist has an easy time making up his mind, and once his mind is made up, he usually sticks to his guns, unless newly acquired data necessitates a reevaluation of the factors leading to the original decision. In such cases, he will draw new conclusions based on the new information presented to him and will change his mind accordingly. Even though the newly acquired facts and findings may genuinely warrant a different conclusion, the solid structurist, nevertheless, experiences a tinge of annoyance or displeasure at having to shift his original position regarding the matter. He views indecisiveness and wishy-washiness as a sign of weakness of character."

"That's exactly how I view it!" I said.

"Not surprised at all!" she laughed as she went on. "The structurist believes that a firm grip on decisions allows one to more effectively dominate his environment, and structurists have an insatiable need to control their own reality, i.e., the circumstances and events that comprise the daily activities in their lives. 'Time waits for no man' is the structurist motto. The structurist maintains that one should know what one has to do and get on with it. Dawdling is a useless waste of the clock which continues to tick away no matter what. Things need to get done sooner rather than later. To facilitate time management, the structurists always has 'to do lists' and usually a schedule to accompany the lists. If you want them to do something, then it needs to be added to their list. As they complete the items on the list, they check them off and add others. The complexity of these lists depends on the degree to which the person is a structurist."

"There are times when my lists are lean, and other times when they are chock full." I declared with a question in my voice.

"Good point, since the degree to which one is a structurist may vary contextually. Structurists are the kind of people who love to be organized. Franklin Planners are usually bought by structurists, who, ironically need them least. (It's the free spirit person who needs them but doesn't buy them.) They attend time management seminars and are always shopping for things that will allow them to organize their space more efficiently. They want everything organized whether it is their desk, their closet, their day or their life. They believe that everything, and everyone for that matter, has its place and it should be in that place. This can lead to fastidious neatness and tidiness. The chain of 'Container Stores' that sells everything you can think of to organize elements of your life for every room of your home, and the 'Hold Everything' mail order catalogues with comparable items were created for the structurist consumer."

"My wife and I are probably some of their best customers!" I declared.

"And Structurists tend to be reliable. They plan their lives, and if they say they will do something, then they either do it or feel bad about it if they do not do it. When they are unable to carry out promises, it is usually due to circumstances beyond their control or the fact that they have bitten off too much. They generally keep their commitments and agreements and expect other people to do likewise. They can get very upset when other people break agreements or commitments. Such behavior interferes with their carefully made plans and forces them to recompute." Shana took another brief pause to see if I had any comments, then continued.

"A structurist likes to be on time or even early for appointments. It disturbs them immensely when others are late. Time is a precious commodity for the structurist. He expects to get every minute for his dollar and certainly does not appreciate inconsiderate people infringing upon his time. For example, if he is paying for a service, he expects to get the maximum time out of it, whether it be an office visit to the doctor, an appointment with the barber or hair stylist, a seminar, a therapy session, or any type of consultation for that matter. He expects the person performing the service to be on time and to be there ready for the scheduled period. He certainly looks down on thoughtless disrupters. If you deal with a structurist, be prepared to adhere to a schedule and then have a specific outcome or goal in mind, otherwise he will consider you to be a complete pest."

"As a structurist, I want everything around me to be organized." I said and before I could finish Shana went on.

"That is typical. The structurist's need for order goes beyond personal preferences. He also believes that society should be ordered. Trains should run on time or someone should be fired. The same goes for buses and subways. There needs to be rules and regulations to ensure the orderly conduct of society, and these rules need to be enforced. Structurists tend to be moralists. They believe they are responsible citizens and that others should be forced, if necessary, to be likewise. They support law and order and the need for punishment for lawbreakers."

She glanced at me with a look that said to continue to listen. "The business world and all bureaucracies are largely controlled by structurists. They create the systems and expect others to comply with them. They expect a day's work for a day's pay. People should be on time or early and stay until quitting time or later. Moreover, people should be held accountable. They should be able to plan their work schedule in order to meet deadlines. There is absolutely no excuse for failure to produce the required work on time. If people can't produce, then they should be replaced by those who can."

"That certainly reflects my way of thinking. Certain things would run much more smoothly if more people thought that way."

Shana laughed and reminded me how important balance is. "Remember that being too one-sided is not the ideal."

FREE SPIRITS

"Let us now turn our discussion to free spirits. First, a free spirit accommodates to life rather than having life accommodate to him. He takes things as they come and feels no need to plan things in advance. Experience has shown him that he can handle matters as they arise and that plans almost always go astray. Rather than plan, which is to invite disappointment, it is better to wait and see what happens and then respond accordingly. Free spirits prefer to be free to act spontaneously as the spirit moves them rather than to be tied down to some schedule or plan. Because of this spontaneity, free spirits do well in uncertain situations. Since they are good at rolling with the punches, they can handle unstructured situations well which involve unpredictability and change."

"I can think of some friends who fit that mold to the tee. As free spirits, they prefer to keep their options open." I said.

"Indeed. Much to the dismay of structurists. Free spirits do not like to be tied down and prefer openness to closure. They become frustrated when events are fixed. They do not like to be pinned down or committed. In fact, they avoid closure whenever possible. They do not mind interruptions or leaving a job undone until they get back to it. They like to haggle and often get good deals because of their patience in bargaining."

"But they can be so indecisive!" I added.

"That is certainly a great bone of contention for the structurist. One of the free spirit is Achilles heel is indecisiveness. Their desire to keep their options open makes it difficult for them to make decisions. They like one option one minute and another the next. They often have difficulty making up their mind and are likely to change it. This is why structurists consider free spirits to be Janus faced. Even when they do decide, they often change their mind or later regret their decision. They prefer open-endedness. They do not like closure. Unlike the structurist, free spirits prefer 'maybe' to 'yes' or 'no'."

I did not dare to interrupt the chain of thoughts. I realized how appropriate 'timing' was to our discussion. Shana continued in a timely manner.

"Another characteristic of free spirit decision making is a focus on the now. They are more concerned with achieving pleasure or avoiding pain now than worrying about the consequences of their present actions in some uncertain future. They prefer to take care of the future when it arrives rather than plan for it now. They are not concerned at the moment about future consequences. This interferes with spontaneity and impulsivity. Their forte is enjoying the now and letting the future come later."

"I could see where at times such an approach could come in handy, especially when I'm on vacation with my wife." I said.

"I'm delighted to see you are remembering balance. Again, there are times when contextually, a person would be better off acting out of the free spirit mode. In any case, the free spirit is usually totally involved with wherever they are at any given moment; and they easily loose track of time. They do not live by the clock. They prefer to get there when they get there and to do things when they get around to it. Unlike structurists, free spirits detest schedules and deadlines of any sort, since they restrict their freedom."

"It's no accident then, that I thrive on schedules and that you hired me, then" I asked knowingly.

"You've got it. There is no way you could be good at this job if you had a free spirit orientation. Timeliness with all of your appointments is critical here. Free spirits are almost always late, and they often cancel appointments at the last minute or simply fail to show up at all. They figure that they will get there when they get there. So what if someone is patiently awaiting their arrival (for their sake, hopefully not a structurist). Whatever they are doing now is more important than rushing off to be somewhere else doing something else." Shana chuckled at her own remark.

"God forbid I mention tardiness to my free spirit friends. They really detest that. In fact, now I realize why most of my friends are structurists." I concluded.

"Interestingly, one of the most common reasons for divorce in this country is based on the free spirit/structurist dichotomy. When one person is a structurist and the other is not, or just the opposite, then relationships (whether of a personal or a business nature) prove to be quite trying and challenging, and not just because of a different time orientation. Part of it is also due to a difference in space organization. Free spirits tend to be untidy."

"That makes such perfect sense! I can see that in my free spirit friends." I said.

"They have no need to arrange things neatly and orderly." Shana responded. "This takes too much time and effort. They leave things wherever it is convenient to do so. They do not believe that neatness is a particularly important notion. They believe that a cluttered desk is a sign of a creative mind. Spontaneity prevents organizing things in an orderly fashion. Free spirits in some way see order and structure as a barrier to sparks of creativity."

Shana did not wait for comments. "Free spirits also do not like rules and regulations. They view them as a nuisance or, at best, a necessary evil. They prefer to live in the midst of the moment and to have fun at whatever they are doing. They turn work into play. To them rules and regulations are meant to take the fun out of life. Free spirits prefer to get lost in life. They are easily distracted by whatever surrounds them. They like to explore the unknown and to wander off the beaten track. Their interest and attention is constantly moving, and they have difficulty staying on any one track. In conversation they are often jumping from one topic to another as things pop in and out of their mind and attention."

"This information is so incredibly helpful, since I can now understand some of the behaviors around me which I find so intolerable at times." I said.

"An understanding of the patterns should make you a bit more tolerant after all. In any case, free spirits do not like schedules and deadlines, because they restrict their freedom. They prefer to act spontaneously. For this reason they are often viewed as irresponsible by structurists who expect them to fit into their mold. Also, since they take a long time to decide and often change their minds, they are viewed as indecisive and even wishy-washy by structurists. They often miss deadlines, or if they do make them, it is usually due to a heroic effort at the last minute. This drives structurists crazy."

"I'll second that." I declared with obvious alignment.

"Also, because they are so enmeshed in the moment they often seem to be in a daze to structurists who are caught up in the passage of time. This is why some structurists view free spirits as outright flakes, if I may say so."

"Go right ahead. I know that you are not trying to demean when you say that."

"That's right. I'm simply telling it to you like it is in the real world of reactions among those who think and act in different ways." Shana explained.

DETECTING THE PATTERN

"So how do I detect the pattern. What are the target indicator questions?" I asked.

"There are several ways." Shana continued. "The most reliable is to observe their behavior. Are they always on time or early or are they habitually late.? Are they organized or do they take life as it comes? Do they make up their mind easily and stick to it or are they always changing their mind? Are they aware of what time it is or do they frequently lose all sense of what time it is? These are all reliable indicators. You could also simply ask them whether they prefer to live their life spontaneously or according to a plan or whether the are usually early or on time for appointments or whether they are usually late."

RELIABLE INDICATORS	
STRUCTURIST	*FREE SPIRIT*
Life is organized	*Life is spontaneous*
Organized	*Disorganized*
On time or early	*Habitually late*
Aware of time	*Loses track of time*
Decisive	*Indecisive*

PRAYERS

"Before you leave for your rounds, let me give you the prayers and you tell me which is which." Shana laughed. "The first prayer is as follows."

O Lord, Decisive God, who Thyself created a neatly structured and ordered Universe within a set time of seven days, please allow me to begin and end this day on time and in an orderly manner. Give me this day an organized agenda of activities which are part of my grand plan for life. Allow my entire existence on earth to be neatly structured and ordered so that there is no question as to what or when to do anything. Please give me the clarity of thought which leads to decisive action once and for all. If I somehow get caught up in the moment, please help me to move on quickly and expeditiously to a stable future. Deliver me at all times from those who might try to take me off track by their own scattered ways. Keep me far removed from those free spirits who live for the joy of the moment, and whose irresponsible behaviors create a heavy burden on those of us who are trying to create here on earth the orderliness of Thine Own Kingdom above. Amen.

"And the second prayer is as follows."

Eternal and ever present God, please let me live my life unfettered by the chains of time. Give me this day the freedom to do and to be as I choose in the moment. Lead me not into planned activities or into situations that might stifle my spontaneity. Deliver me from the rules and regulations of an invasive and rigidly structured society and especially from those who want me to fit into their neat plans and organized agendas of life. O, freedom loving God, please provide me with a world of free spirited joy, devoid of inflexible people and unyielding situations. Alas, my Lord, please keep me happy-go-lucky and spontaneous in whatever I do. And please allow me to change my mind when I feel like it. Amen.

"With this understanding of the Structurist/Free Spirit Organization People Pattern in mind, I will now send you off to your session with Marvin, who will explore the implications of the Organization People Pattern in the context of management."

"Thank you again for a fascinating journey into the world of time and space." I wasn't trying to be cute with my last comment, although it obviously came out that way to Shana who raised her eyebrows.

MANAGEMENT

"I hope you have your sleeves rolled up for this session," Marvin began, "since the work place is one of the main battlegrounds between the structurists and the free spirits. The structurists usually own the work place. The place of business is definitely structurist territory. They control it with time clocks, schedules, deadlines, plans, rules and regulations and all of the accompaniments of bureaucracy."

"Free spirits hate that, I'm sure." I stated with authority.

"You have learned well from Shana, I see. Yes. Free spirits are, to say the least, not comfortable in such surroundings. Free spirits survive by two strategies - adaptation and accommodation. If they have to, some free spirits are able to force themselves to play by the structurist's rules just enough to get by. They have no choice for basic survival in a structurist run world. They simply revert back to their free spirit mode whenever the situation allows. Other free spirits outsmart the system by finding places to hide out in it or by discovering ways to get around it. Creative people can be quite devious, and structurists who cannot imagine the worst are often fooled by these clever devils."

"So how would I manage structurists?" I wanted to know.

"If you are going to manage structurists, as every good bureaucrat knows, you need to tell them what to do in a logical, orderly and systematic fashion. It also helps to put it in writing. Carefully explain all of the rules and regulations and demand compliance with them. Lay out a schedule and require punctuality. Be decisive with structurists. They do not like things up in the air. Once they make up their minds they do not change them easily, so pay particular attention to their initial decisions. To get them to change their mind, present new data, and this still may not be enough. Expect rigidity of thought and action. Do not surprise them. Keep them abreast of the plan, mission, or program."

"Of course, structurists like me tend to like detailed plans."

"Yes. And they also like the work place organized and will not function well in a cluttered environment. Try to minimize interruptions while they are working. They expect structure in others and feel that transgressors should be punished. If they aren't, this will cause a decline in morale. Buffer them from free spirits, otherwise you are certainly asking for double trouble."

As Marvin was to begin discussing how to manage free spirits, he changed chairs and looked more relaxed.

"Managing free spirits, as every good bureaucrat also knows, can be an interesting challenge, to say the least. Free spirits do not like work in the humdrum structured sense and want to make it into fun and play. They will not like the rules, regulations, plans, schedules, deadlines, organization and time clocks so dear to the structurists."

I was really curious to learn how to deal with these free spirits, because I was always so frustrated by them. I continued to listen to Marvin quite attentively as he continued.

"In communicating with free spirits tell them what their options are. Stress alternatives. Provide them with multiple ways of doing things. Do not expect them to be on time or to stick to schedules. Anticipate irresponsibility. Expect them to put things off until the last minute. If you absolutely need something by a certain time, then give them false deadlines. Expect them to be indecisive. They will have a hard time making decisions so do not expect rapid evaluations. Expect that they will change their mind frequently so do not be surprised by it. On the other side of the coin, free spirits will often be quite creative and good at dealing with unstructured situations. If unforeseeable circumstances arise, the free spirit can usually handle them well. They may make excellent trouble shooters. Keep them from interrupting the structurists in the office." Marvin laughed as he said this.

"That's the perfect strategy." I chimed in. There are times when I feel like strangling them."

"That's a typical structurist reaction to free spirit behavior in the business world. So it is really a good idea to buffer them from the structurists who may want to hang them."

"I imagine that managers can be either type." I presumed.

"Of course. Managers, themselves, are obviously structurists and free spirits. Each type will find it a challenge to manage people of the opposite type just as employees have a hard time being managed by someone of the opposite type. Balance is obviously in order. If managers are too rigid and structured you may end up with a paramilitary organization. If, on the other hand, managers are too lax and free spirited, then nothing may ever get done. Many managers who are free spirits never make decisions, and things just seem to float along their merry way. They never plan and often just let events dictate what happens. Don't expect a free spirit manager to adhere to schedules and deadlines. All of this drives structurists absolutely crazy."

"I can certainly relate to that!" I beamed with agreement as Marvin proceeded.

"Management heroes are of two types. One type is the person who is in the right place at the right time. The fact that they are there is either due to luck, circumstances, or perceptive upper management. In different circumstances they might be a complete failure. The second type of management heroes are the ones who can adapt to any circumstances. They have the balance and the flexibility to do whatever is required in different situations. They are the people who can apply People Pattern Power to get the best from each of their employees."

"Marvin, I must say that I see you and the other P^3 Managers doing this all the time unconsciously, or is it!"

TIME MANAGEMENT SEMINARS

"I thought I would spend part of this session on so called 'Time Management Seminars'. They are largely a waste of time, because they were developed by structurists who do not need them for free spirits who do not want them. Structurists are already well organized. Time management seminars teach them to be even more organized. These seminars usually revolve around using some kind of planner or day timer. Such books, which become the structurist's bibles, are a sure indication of the type of individual with whom you are dealing."

Time management seminars are a waste of time,
because structurists don't need them
and free spirits don't want them.

"Now that makes perfect sense. Until now, I couldn't figure out for the life of me why these courses and tapes didn't work for so many." I said.

"Of course, structurists created time management to proselytize the free spirits of the world. Structurists assume, incorrectly, that free spirits are not organized because they do not know how to be organized. The structurists think that if the free spirits are only given a system and their very own time scheduling bible, then they will become good structurists. This could not be farther from the truth. Of course, free spirits are not organized, but it is because they do not want to be. It is a matter of personal preference and not of ignorance." Marvin said with a slight laugh.

"The free spirits I have met at various seminars really don't like them at all." I added.

"Precisely. They writhe in pain when it gets really too structured. When free spirits attend time management seminars, whether they are forced to or by accident, they shake their heads in despair at what they consider to be a deification of all that is basically wrong with the world in the first place. As for the lovely, little time scheduling books that are so reverently delivered into their hands, the free spirits dispose of them in two basic ways. The more brazen free spirits simply toss them into the nearest appropriate container whether it be a trash can or a desk drawer. The more caring free spirits pass them on to a structurist friend who will certainly appreciate them." It was obvious that Marvin was quite amused with his explanation.

SERVICE

"Now I would like to relate the Organization People Pattern to one of the major issues facing the corporate world today: service. The public expects and often demands it, that is, good service. As we have emphasized, people do not provide service because they do not want to and not because they do not know how. One place where service is a big issue is in the transportation industry."

"I have a whole series of complaints I could mention right away on that score!" I said.

"Join the throngs of others like us. One of the big gripes people have nowadays deals with increasingly poor airline service. Delays and cancellations seem to be more the rule than the exception. Imagine how frustrating that is to the good structurist! Fortunately, if one may say so, the delays are occasionally outside of the control even of the airlines. There are, however, some companies that win the tardiness game hands down. Haven't you ever noticed how some airlines over and over again, have late arrivals more than half the time? How is it that other airlines pride themselves on 'on time' arrivals and departures, even to the minute?" I could tell that Marvin was exasperated as he spoke about this issue. He went on.

"The well seasoned travelers among us can easily whip off the two lists in an instant. The epitome of a free spirit airline is Alitalia. Several years ago, Italian businessmen were up in arms with them, and the aviation board was actually considering revoking their license due to their disproportionately high rate of flight cancellations and unaccounted for delays. Whenever major cancellations occur on weekends (particularly Friday nights) this means frenzy on Italian roads - as if the situation were not already bordering on the chaotic. Hundreds of stranded airline passengers rush off to Avis or Hertz to pick up a car and head for their intended destination. The glut of customers is always too great to handle, with scores left with no vehicle and irate tempers."

"I won't even begin to tell you, Marvin, how many times we've had delays like that, whether on business trips or while on vacation." I said.

"Actually, my wife and I had a rather amusing incident which occurred while in Italy and Switzerland on business. Much to our dismay we found ourselves standing in a first class train car for which we had what we thought were firm seat reservations. Moreover, it had been decided to sample the picturesque train ride rather than take what one supposes to be a quick and easy flight from Milan to Geneva. Much to our surprise, the two gentlemen in our car, upon hearing our profusion of rather loud complaints, amusingly informed us that we were to consider ourselves fortunate to be on the train rather than the scheduled Alitalia flight to Geneva. For three consecutive weekends, the men had boarded flights in Milan which were then canceled minutes from departure time. The flights were on the runway and the passengers had to physically carry their baggage from the runway to the terminal where they were given a railroad ticket. To add insult to injury, they were not reimbursed for the difference between the rail and plane tickets, and to make matters even worse, they had to take an insane cab ride in bumper to bumper traffic to the railroad station. We were at the same time annoyed and relieved at this news."

Marvin proceeded to finish the story.

"Meanwhile, the free spirit Italian conductor not only had the nerve to allow the unpaying passengers to remain in our prepaid first class seats, but also wanted to charge us a supplement, because we were standing in first class without a seat. What happened to following rules? This was almost too much to bear! All we got was a smiling *non fa niente*, or 'it doesn't matter'. Well it did matter to us. So total chaos reigned. That apparently was par for the course on the Italian train, according to the veteran travelers in our compartment (and we had been forewarned but did not take heed)."

"Then, as though miraculously, as soon as we crossed over the border into Switzerland, the transformation which occurred was fit to be put on film for the record. At that point the very welcome structurist Swiss conductor took over, and immediately checked every single passenger standing or sitting, and quickly ousted all the offenders to the approving applause of the legitimate ticket holders."

"Thank goodness there are structurist airlines as well." I declared with relief.

"That is fortunate for all of us structurists. Just as there are free spirit oriented enterprises, we find their structurist counterparts competing in the same markets. On the other side of the fence from the free spirit airline we find the ultimate structurist airline to be Swiss Air, with Lufthansa a close second. When dealing with airlines such as these, you can be sure to depart and arrive on time to your destination, provided there is no unforeseen problem beyond their control. It is literally like clockwork with these companies. Service on board a plane will also be superior with a structurist-oriented airline; and baggage handling will be more efficient with such companies. Structurist oriented airlines, trains, etc, will be more cognizant of future consequences if they do not get to a destination on time, if they do not take care of your baggage, if they do not arrange feasible flight transfers, and the list goes on and on. Free spirit oriented airlines will be much more easy going in regards to these matters, and take the attitude that they'll just deal with problems as they come up."

MEETING ARRANGEMENTS

"All aspects of life are affected by this fundamental People Pattern. Even the way in which people arrange meetings indicates the type of person that they are. For example, at a recent conference which we attended, we ran into a friend who was a bit concerned, because he had told another friend who was driving him home (4 hrs away) to meet him at a general time on a certain floor of the conference area. After waiting over half an hour, he began to worry that perhaps they had missed each other in the crowd. When we asked him where the *rendez-vous* point was, the good free spirit that he is, he confidently told us that they had not specified where to meet on that particular floor, nor was a specific time mentioned."

"How people expect things to proceed smoothly when minimal planning is lacking is amazing!" I added.

"With such a large crowd of people it was fairly difficult if not impossible to run into someone even if you wanted to do so! Fortunately, it all worked out; and he got his ride back afterwards. Just another simple example where these patterns can so significantly affect us and be responsible for creating unwanted stress!"

"If they had been two structurists (or even one of them for that matter), a specific time to meet and specific location would have been indicated. In fact, the structurist might have given an auxiliary game plan in case the first did not work out, especially if he knew that his friend was a free spirit. How many times have you been in a similar situation in which you ended up somehow not meeting the intended person because of cross communication?" Marvin inquired.

"I won't even begin to count those times." I responded.

"More likely than not, one of the individuals was coming out of the free spirit mode."

MEETING MANAGEMENT

"Another area where this People Pattern plays an important role is in the area of meeting management." Marvin continued. "For meetings to be effective and efficient it is necessary to have an agenda and to stick to it. It is also necessary to develop and implement plans to make any changes that come out of the meeting. Do you suppose it makes a difference who is running the meeting?"

I smiled and said: "Yes, it makes a major difference."

Marvin continued. "Structurists hold meetings to accomplish things. They have schedules and agendas. The free spirits, on the other hand, will often call a meeting on the spot and not have a clear agenda. This can make for some interesting meetings."

"I can imagine."

"Here are some general structurist rules for efficient meetings" Marvin added. "Rule One is to only have meetings when necessary. Avoid regularly scheduled meetings if you don't have something specific to accomplish. Free spirits will always find something at these meetings to talk about. Rule Two is to schedule the meeting as far ahead as possible. Rule Three is to send out an agenda in advance and to tell people to be prepared to discuss the items on the agenda. This way the structurists will prepare and the free spirits may even by chance think about it before the meeting. Rule Four is to start and end the meeting on schedule and to use the relevancy challenge."

"Starting and ending on schedule must drive the free spirits crazy. Also, what is the relevancy challenge?"

"I am glad you asked." Marvin responded. "The relevancy challenge is the way to keep the free spirits in check. It works like this. At the beginning of the meeting the convener posts the agenda and says that this is what we are here to discuss. If anyone says anything that is not relevant to the item on the agenda that is being discussed, the convener or any other participant immediately invokes the relevancy challenge which is simply to ask the person who made the offending remark how it is relevant to the matter under discussion. If he can demonstrate relevancy, then it is accepted; and if he can't, then the remark is ignored."

I thought a minute and said that I thought that this would certainly expedite meetings. Marvin went on. "I have found that two or three unchallenged irrelevancies can completely side track an hour meeting."

Marvin looked at me briefly and continued. "These rules can help to keep things on track. Lest I denigrate the free spirits too much, in fairness I need to mention the important role that they can play in meetings. They are often quite good at brainstorming and at coming up with creative solutions. As long as you guide them and control their tangents when necessary, they can make invaluable contributions. Also, there are times when emergencies do arise and where it is necessary to drop everything and attack the problem. Free spirits find it easier to do this than the structurists who have a high need to follow their schedules. Are there any questions on this People Pattern?"

I reflected a moment and answered. "No I think that you have explained everything well."

"Good." Marvin said "Then I think as a structurist that it is time to send you off to see Michael in the Sales Department, otherwise as a free spirit we will go on for the rest of the day with examples. And you need to move on. Feel free to come back at any time to ask questions once you have had a chance to go over this material."

"Thank you, Marvin. As usual, your explanations have enlightened me tremendously."

SALES

Michael was busy preparing some viewgraphs when I arrived. He launched right in.

"As you can well imagine, awareness of the Structurist/Free Spirit Organization Pattern is critical in sales. As I keep emphasizing, the only way to increase sales is to work hard by seeing more prospects or to work smart by closing a higher percentage of the prospects that one sees. Working smart means adapting your approach to the type of person with whom you are dealing. In general, salespeople are much more comfortable with structurists, because they get either a 'yes' or a 'no'. They are less comfortable with free spirits where they usually get a 'maybe'."

Structurists say "yes" or "no"
Free spirits say "maybe"

"How would I sell to structurists?" I wanted to know.

"If you are selling to structurists, then present your product or service in a planned, organized and systematic fashion. Be on time and keep to any agreed upon schedule. Be neat and orderly. Focus on both immediate and future benefits. Also, explain the future consequences of not buying. Ask for a decision. Expect a 'yes' or 'no' answer. If you get a no, then do not expect it to change unless you present new information. Have some additional facts available for just such an occasion."

That explanation was extremely logical, and I could see how I was already doing that, given my personal orientation with this pattern. Michael went on.

"Free spirits are the bane of every salesperson for two reasons. Free spirits do not like to decide, and their favorite word is 'maybe'. Professional salespeople hate that word. They want to hear a definitive 'yes' or 'no'. Second, free spirits tend to change their minds. We live in the age of consultative selling where the professional salesperson strives to satisfy the needs of the client. The days of high pressure selling are a thing of the past (unless you indulge in the fast paced 'buy now while they last' sales of certain television shopping networks). The modern consultative salesperson wants satisfied customers who will provide referrals and become product champions. A wishy-washy person is not a good source of referrals, and his uncertainty is definitely not a good endorsement for your product. A consultative salesperson wants three things: 1) for the customer to be satisfied, 2) for the customer to be absolutely certain that he brought the right product, and 3) for the customer to not just be satisfied and feel certain now, but to be that way forever. This obviously poses problems when selling to free spirits."

"I would really need help selling to free spirits, because they think so differently than I do."

"Well, then, to sell to free spirits certain things are important. The salesperson should not appear to be too regimented. When dealing with free spirits, flexibility is the name of the game. The salesperson should not insist on schedules or punctuality. Greet the customer when he arrives and give no indication that he is late. Also, do not have an appointment you have to rush off to immediately afterwards, otherwise you'll be creating undue stress on yourself, since the free spirit will, more likely than not, be late. Moreover, the free spirit will not appreciate this. The free spirit wants to have fun, so be playful. Appear to be spontaneous."

I just had to interrupt Michael here. "I am sure that spontaneity is a huge stretch for staunch structurists."

"You had better believe it! Particularly for the really rigid ones. So do not adopt a rigid presentation style. The main thing is to expect indecision. Discuss how owning and using your product will provide the customer with more options. Free spirits may buy on impulse. Make sure that your product meets their needs. If it does, then do everything you can to force a decision. Realize that 'maybe' does not mean that your presentation is inadequate, but instead is a reflection of the free spirits' indecisiveness. You may have to come back many times in order to get the sale. Structurists have a hard time understanding this point. It may be necessary to close between eight and fifteen times, as frustrating as that may be."

"That must be absolutely excruciating for a structurist like me!" I said.

"That is probably a massive understatement of your reaction. Do not be discouraged as long as they seem interested. Once you do make the sale, then do everything possible to future pace the customer in order to avoid buyer's remorse. Get him on the road to thinking about using the product in a future context."

"I would say that I have my work cut out for me in this realm. I certainly need to do my homework here. Thank you for your insights."

"The information I have shared with you here will certainly provide the appropriate background for your next session on negotiations. Good luck."

NEGOTIATIONS

As usual, Beverly was in the middle of some important conversation, and she quickly finished up to begin our session together.

"I will briefly go over the major points to know about the Organization People Pattern in relation to negotiations. In any negotiation, structurists will have an advantage, because they are better prepared; and free spirits will have an advantage, because they can haggle forever and seemingly do not care if they ever reach agreement. Structurists often end up giving away more than they need to in negotiations because of their high need for closure. They want agreement and hate for things to drag on. They will often make unnecessary concessions simply to get things over with once and for all. Free spirits, on the other hand, may go on too long and pass up the opportunity for a settlement. Free spirits will do well in an unstructured situation and have an advantage if the structurist's plans fall through."

The structurist will make concessions to get closure
The free spirit will haggle forever

"As I found out in sales, free spirits can drive structurists mad. I now see that the same applies in the world of negotiations."

"More than you realize. In a professional negotiation the free spirit will often drive the structurist absolutely crazy. Let a free spirit do the actual negotiating, and have a structurist check in on him from time to time. When the structurist feels that the free spirit has gotten all that he can, then he accepts the deal. Otherwise, the free spirit could conceivably go on and on and on."

"If you are negotiating with a structurist and want to make him comfortable, then make sure that it appears that you have and follow a plan. Insist on setting a schedule and on following it. Start and stop meetings on time."

"Basically the same rules of organization apply here as they did in sales." I asked.

"Yes, indeed." Beverly responded with a laugh. "Appear to be organized. Keep the surroundings neat, clean and orderly. Emphasize the need to decide and to get closure. Be firm and decisive. Give reasons and focus on outcomes. Structurists will want to reach an agreement and may be willing to make concessions to do so. Be sure to discuss positive future consequences of reaching the agreement now."

"If you are negotiating with a free spirit and want to make him feel comfortable, then it is a totally different ball game. Appear to be flexible and spontaneous. Don't insist on schedules or fixed agendas or on following a rigid plan. Make the negotiation process light and fun. Figure that meetings will start late and end late. Pick a place with minimal distractions, since free spirits are distracted easily. Realize that the free spirits will want to keep their options open. So focus on options and on what the proposal will do for them now. Do not waste time talking about future consequences."

"Oh, that's right. There is no future for free spirits." My effort at being amusing was at least appreciated by Beverly.

"Focus on satisfying immediate needs. Expect discussions to drag on forever. Expect commitments to be painful and expect indecision. After an agreement expect some remorse. Free spirits want to avoid or delay agreement as long as possible and may never get one. Under such circumstances infinite patience is the order of the day."

"Unless you have any questions, I will now send you over to Frank in Training. I am sure you will need some time to digest the information learned thus far today."

"Thank you again. I'm sure I'll be back for more."

TRAINING

Frank was happy as always to see me. It was obvious that he really liked to train, and he launched right in.

"Obviously, another area of our lives touched by the Organization People Pattern is the field of education and training. Which are the students who fit best into the mold of our educational system that is geared to reward kids who are punctual and who get their homework and assignments done on time? Is it the free spirit kids who generally do their assignments on time? No, not usually. Normally, it is the structurists who are the conscientious little boys and girls who are rewarded for their good study habits, neatness and ability to follow schedules and orders! Free spirit children are the ones who often show up late (more so, if they happen to have free spirit parents), and are remiss with their tasks and homework."

"And the free spirit kids are often punished for being the way that they are. I see it with one of my own children." I said.

"Messy notebooks, by the way, are also a good indication of a free spirit child. A structurist child will often have a neat desk and neatly ordered papers and notebooks. He will know where he has placed items, and they will usually be arranged in a systematic way. I know one structurist child who has his notebooks arranged alphabetically and another structurist child who arranges them in the order of his classes. In both cases, the key operational word for the structurist behavior is *order*. One structurist child I know even organizes his pencils systematically with the sharpened ones on one side of the case and the unsharpened ones on the other."

"My eldest child is the most structurist of all our children. His desk is incredibly ordered, as is his school bag and even his lunch box." I just now realized why.

Frank was amused. "One of my own is a carbon copy of that." he retorted. If you think back to your own school days, to those seeming irresponsible, untidy, and lazy types or to that one, noisy kid who was constantly disrupting class, the chances are that they were the free spirits in the bunch. All in all, these disorderly children were probably the most interesting ones around, in spite of their disruptive nature. That is the irony once again. Although the structurist students are more organized and follow directions more readily, they often do not really 'enjoy' their time at school as do the free spirit kids who are totally into the 'now'. The free spirit kids make the best of the moment, whatever that entails for them. Free spirit kids have a good time in class, and often get reprimanded by their structurist teachers for having the audacity to try to make learning fun."

"What about the teachers and trainers?" I wanted to know.

"Obviously, the Structurist/Free Spirit People Pattern encompasses teachers and trainers as well as students. Teachers and trainers who are structurists expect the same orderliness, neatness and time consciousness from their pupils that they exhibit themselves. They tend to be very disciplinarian and require a great deal of order in their classrooms. Looking back at your childhood, you may remember that particular teacher with stick in hand ready to tap anyone who dared misbehave. It was just as much a crime to throw paper on the floor as to fail to complete a homework assignment."

"I had very strict structurist teachers throughout high school. Looking back, I can now understand why the free spirit students had such a hard time dealing with them." I chimed in.

"Heavy structurist teachers are usually viewed by free spirit children as mean and unyielding. They do not handle spontaneity in the classroom very well, and can get very upset when a pupil disrupts their planned curriculum in any way. They have their lesson plans carefully laid out and get very upset if they do not get through the amount that they planned to cover. Structurist teachers are also more punitive toward their pupils than their free spirit counterparts. Any questions?" Frank asked. When I shook my head no, he quickly proceeded.

"This scenario is particularly a challenge when such teachers work in ghetto schools or in those districts with so called 'tough kids'. Under these circumstances, schools often become battlegrounds; and it takes a particular type of tough love to maintain order without threats and punitive actions. Structurist teachers find it extremely difficult to put up with foolishness and with unruly, rowdy students. They tend to maintain a rigid classroom ambiance and prefer to establish the rules and make sure that they are obeyed."

"Free spirit teachers," Frank continued, "on the other hand, deal with unplanned events with ease and often with excitement. They would be the ones who would be most likely to turn an unpleasant incident into an enjoyable learning experience. They welcome openness and new options and are considered by students to be sympathetic and understanding. Classrooms run by free spirit teachers tend to be noisier and more fun. Their students are more likely to get away with outrageous behavior. Homework assignments will be given at more irregular intervals, with the various subjects assigned more arbitrarily than with structurist teachers. There will be less structure both within the context of the classroom and with activities outside the classroom."

"As with the other People Patterns I have been learning about, it sounds like it is a good idea to be flexible." I said.

"An excellent point. Contextuality always comes into play. With the Organization People Pattern, as with all of the others, balance is the key. Once a trainer or teacher develops the ability to mix both structurist and free spirit elements in his interaction with students, that leads to a more stable and effective interrelationship with his pupils. A trainer or teacher who is always exclusively in either a structurist or free spirit mode, at either extreme all of the time, is not going to be the ideal instructor. Excessive rigidity on either end of the Organization Pattern results in alienation of the corresponding opposite end of the Organization Pattern spectrum."

"There must be some ideal classroom scenario?" I queried.

"That is relative, of course. However, an ideal would be to have a certain amount of structure in the classroom relating to behavior and to getting work done on a timely basis and in a systematic manner. At the same time, the teacher or trainer needs to afford the students at least some spontaneity (the doses vary according to individual students) to encourage their creative spirits and to allow them to grow into healthy adults. Too much rigidity and discipline leads to programmed, robotic students. On the other hand, given the violent and rampant ambiance of many schools today, we need a good deal of restraint and correction to keep the unruly elements in check."

"In this day and age, free spirit teachers are often at a disadvantage within an educational system which caters primarily to the structurist teacher. Usually school boards and principals are structurists also. As long as you have structurists battling free spirits, whether it be teacher versus teacher, teachers versus school boards, or teachers versus students, then you are going to have a horde of problems with little room for negotiation and compromise. Once you begin to understand the behavioral subtleties involved, you get one step closer to establishing a more smoothly running system."

"What are the implications for training design and delivery?" I asked.

"That is a good question." Frank responded. "As you well know, there are two approaches to design and delivery that are popular in training circles today. At one extreme is the super structurist ISO 9000 approach. This analyzes every job into detailed tasks. Training then consists of training people to do these tasks. This approach may work well for highly routine jobs, but it becomes more problematic with many management jobs that require continual creativity and innovation and where part of the challenge is knowing what to do when. With many management positions, a half way house has been the effort to define competencies that all managers should have. The task for training then becomes to install these competencies. This may work well or be disaster depending on the level at which the competencies are defined. If they are defined too broadly, then they are often meaningless; and if they are defined too specifically, then they begin to approach matters of individual style. In short, too much structure can limit creativity and innovation; and too little structure can lead to chaos and anarchy."

"Balance again." I said.

Frank nodded his head. "Balance again. It is critical in training to distinguish between 'know what' and 'know how.' It is not just enough to specify 'what' to do. The real challenge is in 'how to' do something and most of all, in 'how to' do it well. As you already know, this is one of the things that makes our trainings unique here at Success, Incorporated."

I nodded and Frank continued.

"Let me mention one other approach to training that is often championed by free spirits. They call it 'experiential learning' and they call the instructors 'facilitators'. The idea behind 'experiential learning' is that human relation skills are best learned as a group through interactions with others. The role of the so called 'facilitator' is to manage the process and not the content. This approach is unstructured at the content level and partially structured at the process level. This approach works well with some groups in some situations for developing some human interaction skills. Obviously free spirits love it, and it drives structurists crazy. The problem is that this approach is based on the assumption that the group already possesses all the necessary skills and knowledge and that all that the facilitator has to do is draw these out. If the group is lacking in skills, then they need skills training and not facilitation."

Frank smiled and said that his time with me was up, and I went off to personnel.

PERSONNEL

With a constant flow of applicants coming through the door, it is surprising that Karen even has time to conduct a training session with me on a daily basis. Her ability to organize her time is quite apparent and her structurist orientation is what allows her to fit it all in so effectively. The result is a short, yet always informative session on the particular People Pattern application to personnel selection and hiring. Today was no different from the others from this perspective.

"Awareness of the Organization Pattern is critical in hiring."

As always, pre-selection is more important than training. People Patterns are mental habits developed over a lifetime. They can not be changed easily or rapidly, and they certainly cannot be changed by on-the-job training. It is naive and unrealistic to believe that people will be anything else than what they are. People can be trained to develop job skills, but they cannot be trained to develop People Patterns that are not part of their personality in the first place.

"I just had to add that it is really dumb to try to change these patterns. People are what they are, and if I have learned anything, it is that we need to understand this, even if I tend to joke about those who are different from me."

"That is so true. People may be able to adapt or accommodate, but this is always done at the price of stress and unhappiness. And what is the point of making people miserable. That affects productivity in a very negative way. People are happiest and most productive when their People Patterns match their job situation. With this said, the following guidelines will be helpful."

"Hire structurists for jobs requiring orderliness and decisiveness. Do not hire them for unstructured jobs. These employees are punctual and organized. They are responsible, meet deadlines and are the very backbone of many organizations. Be decisive and appear organized when interviewing and hiring them. Conduct the interview in neat surroundings. Be punctual with them. Explain their responsibilities in an organized and orderly manner and put it in writing. Keep commitments."

"Hire free spirits for jobs where punctuality and orderliness are not decisive factors. Hire them for unstructured jobs. Expect indecisiveness from them. They will not like routine, so make a point of emphasizing freedom and expanded options in hiring them. Stress that work is fun and that they will enjoy the job. Do not expect them to keep commitments or to meet deadlines, since this is not their forte."

"The above guidelines really do put the entire Organization Pattern into perspective. There is so much to know, and yet, I am actually taking it all in quite easily, thanks to the way in which all of you P³ Managers have been presenting the material. I can't express my gratitude enough for all of your help."

In her usual gracious way, Karen accepted the compliment.

SUMMARY

"Did you figure out which prayer goes with which?" Shana asked. I laughed, and Shana continued. "So which is best? To be a structurist or to be a free spirit?" "That depends." I said. "On what?" "On what behavior is most appropriate in that context." Shana smiled and said "You may make it here after all." Then she went on.

"Before you go let me tell you about some interesting research which we have been conducting. I have emphasized that People Patterns are life time habits, and that they are not easily changed. And this is usually the case. With the Structurist Free Spirit People Pattern, however, we have found a way to help an individual shift this pattern temporarily or even for extended periods of time. It involves changing the internal structure of the way the person experiences time. If you remember at your initial employment interview, there were several questions in which you were asked about the past, the future, and the now."

"Yes, I remember. Those were really strange questions to be asked at a job interview."

"They are highly revealing however." Shana continued. "They have to do with the way that you store and access your memories. We call the line connecting your past, present and future your 'time line'. It is possible by getting an individual to change aspects of his time line to assist him in switching back and forth between structurist and free spirit behavior. I have continually emphasized the importance of balance. The ideal situation is for a person to have enough control so that he can adjust his pattern to fit the circumstances in which he finds himself. With the Organization People Pattern and appropriate training this is possible. Sometime in the future I will teach you how to do this, if you are interested."

"I am very interested" I said "and would like to learn to do this at the earliest opportunity."

THE PEOPLE PATTERN PLEDGE

THE PEOPLE PATTERN PLEDGE

I was sitting in Shana's office after having just completed my two week orientation training in People Patterns. I had no more questions and was looking forward to the weekend to assimilate all that I had learned.

Shana looked at me and smiled. "There are two more things and then your initial orientation training in People Patterns will be complete."

"What are they?" I asked.

Shana smiled. "First, it is my privilege to present you with your very own People Pattern Power Cube as an indication of your beginning mastery of People Patterns." Shana handed me a People Pattern Power Cube like the one that I had seen on her desk the first morning of my training. It felt good to have it as a reminder of my experience. I could already imagine it in a prominent place on my desk. Then Shana continued.

"Also, it is my solemn responsibility to administer to you the People Pattern Pledge. Every manager here at Success, Incorporated takes the People Pattern Pledge as a symbol of his dedication to the ethical and professional use of People Patterns. It is a little ritual that helps to impress upon each of us the weighty responsibility that comes with our knowledge and mastery of such a powerful tool for human change. Please stand and raise your right hand, and while holding your People Pattern Power Cube in your left hand, repeat after me."

I stood up and raised my right hand as Shana had requested. I took the People Pattern Power Cube that she had just given me in my left hand and repeated the People Pattern Pledge after Shana. I have never forgotten it. It is as follows.

I believe in People Pattern Power. I also realize that with power comes responsibility. I promise to use my knowledge and skills with People Patterns in an ethical and professional manner. I will never use

them to intentionally exploit or to intentionally manipulate another
person in any way. I will use my knowledge of People Patterns to achieve
a win/win in my daily interactions with everyone. I will also use my
knowledge of People Patterns to enhance communication with others
and to understand and enter into their models of the world, which may be
different from my own. Finally, I will use People Patterns with integrity
and honor and wisdom in all of my interactions with my fellow man. This
I so pledge.

After repeating the pledge Shana congratulated me, and I departed.

POSTSCRIPT

As I look back, I reflect on how little I really knew about People
Patterns at that time. At the time it seemed like a lot, and I know it was. But
my knowledge of these powerful patterns and my skill in their use grew
tremendously in the days and weeks ahead. Now years later, I realize what
an impact they have had on my ability to relate to and influence other
people. They have also had an impact on my career, and I am now a Senior
P^3 Manager here at Success, Incorporated. I thank you for listening to my
story. It can be yours too, if you take the time and the effort to master
People Pattern Power and to become a People Pattern Person and a P^3
Manager yourself.

ABOUT THE AUTHORS

MARILYNE WOODSMALL, M.A.,M.Phil.

Ms. Woodsmall is the Founder and President of the International Research Institute for Human Typological Studies whose research focuses on the study of human difference. Her expertise and experience lies in the synthesis, classification and application of the various universal human typologies to a multitude of contexts in the corporate, public and athletic sectors. Ms. Woodsmall's work and interests revolve around the impact of typologies on performance, behavioral modification, gender issues and on cultural and social phenomena.

As an international, multi-lingual consultant, trainer and author, she applies her knowledge and practical skills to the domain of communication (advanced skills and cross cultural synthesis), management consulting, culture shaping, education, personnel selection, leadership, and performance enhancement with Olympic athletes and coaches and with clients in private industry. Ms. Woodsmall has concentrated recent work on using her synthetic typological approach to propose solutions to significant global challenges of today such as violence, crime and gender issues. She often addresses professional organizations on these topics.

Ms. Woodsmall is also Senior Vice-President of Advanced Behavioral Modeling, Inc. a consulting and training firm committed to increasing the performance and productivity of organizations and individuals. She is the co-creator of Advanced Behavioral Modeling^{SM} which is a powerful behavioral change technology. She was instrumental in pioneering the development and application of behavioral modeling technology in the corporate sector (in sales, manufacturing, management, personnel selection, and negotiations), in education (in learning and creativity) and in Olympic sports. In each case, she has developed models to increase and maintain high performance in high stress situations which enable clients to go beyond their potential in their given fields.

As a trainer, consultant and personal coach, the essence of her approach is the balancing of the intellectual, physical, emotional and spiritual aspects of the individual to engender elite performance in any context. Ms. Woodsmall is currently involved in projects that address this issue with athletes, corporate clients, professional women and children.

Ms. Woodsmall holds a Bachelor of Arts from Vassar, a Master of Arts and a Master of Philosophy from Columbia University and has studied at the Sorbonne. She is a certified Master Modeler and Trainer in

Neuro-Linguistic Programming. She has been practicing Feng Shui for over ten years, having studied with Grand Master Thomas Lin Yun.

Ms. Woodsmall is co-author of *People Pattern Power, Mind Coach* and *Our Vanishing Values: The Culture Crisis.* She is currently working on books dealing with values in business, women and power and is writing a book for children.

WYATT L. WOODSMALL, PH.D.

Dr. Woodsmall is the President of Advanced Behavioral Modeling, Inc., a consulting and training firm committed to increasing the performance and productivity of organizations and individuals through the use of advanced behavioral and learning technologies. Engaged in federal service and private practice for over twenty five years, he has provided training and management consulting expertise to the federal government, service and athletic industries, and the scientific community, with specific emphasis in culture shaping and in predicting and modifying behavior using specialized behavioral technologies. Dr. Woodsmall is also a Senior Vice President of the International Research Institute for Human Typological Studies which specializes in research on human typologies. His main emphasis is on the connection between human differences and performance and on the shaping of cultures to create high performance organizations. Dr. Woodsmall was instrumental in pioneering the concept and applications of behavioral modeling technology in the federal government, in private industry, and in the athletic sector.

Dr. Woodsmall's training programs include culture shaping, change management, leadership and management development, advanced interpersonal communication skills, values, negotiations, sales, training design, platform skills, and NLP. He has conducted training programs in 17 countries on five continents.

Dr. Woodsmall is a certified Master Trainer and Master Modeler in Neuro-Linguistic Programming. He is a former President and Board Member of the International Association of Neuro-Linguistic Programming. He is a co-founder and board member of the International Neuro-Linguistic Programming Trainers Association. He is internationally recognized as a leading expert on Neuro-Linguistic Programming and performance enhancement. He has conducted Neuro-Linguistic Programming Trainer's Trainings every year for over a decade. He is recognized as the trainer's trainer and has students on five continents in over twenty countries.

Dr. Woodsmall has a Doctor of Philosophy and Master of Philosophy from Columbia University in Philosophy, a Master of Divinity from Union Theological Seminary and a Bachelor of Science in Physics from the University of Virginia.

Dr. Woodsmall is the co-author of *People Pattern Power*, *Our Vanishing Values*, *Mind Coach*, and *Time Line Therapy and the Basis of Personality*. He is also the author of six monographs and of over fifty published articles on Advanced Behavioral Modeling[SM], Advanced Learning Technology[SM], and NLP.

THE INTERNATIONAL RESEARCH INSTITUTE FOR HUMAN TYPOLOGICAL STUDIES

INSTITUTE: *The International Research Institute for Human Typological Studies (IRIFHTS)* is an organization whose work and research focus on the study of human differences. The two principals of IRIFHTS, Marilyne Woodsmall and Wyatt Woodsmall, have been researching and applying a wide variety of human typologies to understanding and utilizing the diverse facets of human behavior in various contexts for several decades.

What distinguishes their work from that of others in their field is their ability to synthesize different typologies and to understand the interconnections of the various models, rather than to simply use a particular model as the one and only tool for understanding personality and human behavior. No one typology suffices to explain all behavior. In understanding human behavior, IRIFHTS emphasizes the study of a balanced model that incorporates the mental, physical, emotional and spiritual components involved. The different elements are, then, synthesized in a new and more powerful form that takes contextuality into account. IRIFHTS bases its approach on systems theory and the understanding that performance is improved not by building better parts but by optimizing the interactions of the parts.

RESEARCH: Marilyne and Wyatt use their own unique synthetic approach which is far more encompassing than any single model could ever be. They have incorporated and integrated many typologies in the work of IRIFHTS. These include psychological and educational typologies from Hippocrates, Jung, Freud, Adler, Erikson, Loevinger, Kohlberg, Horney, Montessori, Piaget, Assagioli, Bateson, Satir, Sheldon, Arieti,

Grof, Fromm, Cialdini, W. Lowen, A. Lowen, Maslow, Graves, McClelland, Kolb, Colby, Sullivan and Wilber. They also include spiritual models such as the Kabbalah, chakras, vijnanas, kosas, gunas, skandhas, zodiac, Chinese elements, and I Ching and spiritual teachers such as Gurdjieff, Mouravieff, Case, Fortune, Aurobindo, Da Free John, Castaneda, Sun Bear, Lin Yun and Ichazo. They have been using the Enneagram and Myers-Briggs since the early eighties long before these typologies even came into vogue.

SERVICES: IRIFHTS services include public and in-house training and consulting services in the public, private and athletic industries, the publication and distribution of books and tapes on personality differences, and the licensing of behavioral instruments. Trainings are available in People Patterns^{SM}, Value Cultures^{SM}, and the Enneagram. Coaching and consulting services include culture shaping, change management, leadership, negotiations, sales, training design, personnel selection (Profiling Plus^{SM}) team building, behavioral modeling, performance enhancement, and athletic performance coaching and managerial coaching under Mind Coach^{SM}.

IRIFHTS licenses two powerful behavioral instruments on People Patterns^{SM} and Value Cultures$^{\underline{SM}}$, created by Marilyne Woodsmall and Wyatt Woodsmall. Both of these instruments capture critical indicators of behavior and performance. IRIFHTS licenses trainings to qualified individuals who will, then, be authorized to administer the instruments.

CONTACTS: IRIFHTS may be contacted at 703 757-7945 or by fax at 703 757-7946 or at our web site at http://www.peoplepatterns.com.

NEXT STEP PRESS

Next Step Press came into being to fulfill a need for substantive publications in business and education. Next Step Press is a publishing firm dedicated to bringing selected knowledge and wisdom to individuals and organizations through the publishing of practical and relevant information that will enable them to take the next step in their personal and professional development.

THE MEEK SHALL INHERIT

*Detectives rush to stop a murder
in this gripping thriller*

JOHN DEAN

Paperback published by The Book Folks

London, 2025

© John Dean

ISBN 978-1-80462-302-2

www.thebookfolks.com

The Meek Shall Inherit is the twelfth standalone title in a series of British detective mysteries featuring Detective Chief Inspector John Blizzard. Information about the other novels and a list of characters can be found at the back of this book.

Chapter one

'It's your turn, Marjie,' said Louise Rylance as the front-desk staff watched the retired couple walk slowly up the drive towards the police station, stopping more than once to engage in animated conversation. 'What brings them here this morning, then?'

'Mmm, that's a tricky one,' said Marjie Craig. 'They don't look like the type of people who spend a lot of time in police stations, do they?'

'Appearances can be deceptive. You should have learnt that by now.'

Marjie nodded. The friends had been playing the game for years. It did not take her long to conclude that it was the woman's idea that she and her husband visit the collection of ageing portable buildings that comprised Abbey Road Police Station. The taller of the two pensioners, her hair greying, spectacles black and heavy-rimmed and clothes smart, had a body language suggesting a determined air which did not appear to be shared by her husband. Marjie guessed that they were both in their early to mid-seventies, although deciding that the man was three or four years older than his wife. He was slightly stooped, with thinning grey hair and clothes that looked like they had been purchased at a second-hand shop. As the couple finally approached the main entrance of the headquarters of the city's Western Division, the man's anxiety became clear to see and the couple hesitated for another vigorous discussion.

'They are here,' announced Marjie, 'because a neighbour has been parking his car across their drive. The husband doesn't want to cause trouble but things have got so bad that his wife has decided that something has to be done about it.'

'Good one, and you're right about the wife being the one who wants to make the complaint,' said Louise. 'And about the husband, too. She has dragged him along for moral support but he's an "anything for a quiet life" kind of guy and does not want to be here. However, I'm going for kids kicking a football against their house as the reason they are here.'

'Also a good one,' said Marjie. The automatic door slid open to admit the couple to the reception area and she smiled a welcome as they walked up to the desk. 'Good morning. How can I help you?'

'Someone wants to murder us,' said the woman, 'and we want to stop it happening.'

The words were delivered in such a calm voice that the reception staff stared at her for a few moments, searching her face for a sign that she was joking; in the long history of their game, no visitor to the police station had ever come to the front desk and said such a thing. However, the only emotion on display was an anxiety which seemed genuine and was mirrored in the worried features of her husband.

'I'm sorry,' said Marjie, 'did you say that someone wants to murder you?'

'I did, yes,' said the woman. 'It'll probably happen on Monday next week. We would like to see a senior officer before then because we don't want a re-run of last time.'

'Last time?' asked Marjie.

'I'd rather not explain it twice. Is there a senior officer who can talk to us?'

'I'll see who's available,' said Marjie. She looked at her colleague. 'Blizzard?'

Louise nodded. 'He's back from holiday today,' she said. 'I saw him earlier. He's in his office, I think.'

Marjie ran her finger down the list of extension numbers taped to the desk until she found the one for the head of Western Division CID, picked up the phone and looked at the couple.

'Can I have your names, please?' she asked.

'We'd rather tell Mr Blizzard,' said the woman. 'The fewer people that know we are here, the better. It's a very sensitive matter, as I am sure you can appreciate.'

'Of course,' said Marjie, increasingly intrigued by their conversation.

Having phoned John Blizzard, Marjie opened the security door and led the couple down the corridor to the detective chief inspector's office, where they found him sitting behind his desk. He smiled at his visitors as Marjie ushered them into the room. The inspector was pleased at the distraction from the paperwork that had accumulated during his holiday at Center Parcs with his girlfriend and young son the previous week and was also keen to learn more about the reason behind the couple's visit to the police station. He gestured for them to sit down but the woman did not do so until she had checked that Marjie had closed the door behind her when she left the office. Finally reassured, she sat down.

'Thank you for agreeing to see us, Chief Inspector,' she said. She nodded towards the documents piled up on his desk. 'I can see that you're busy.'

'It's amazing how it builds up,' said the inspector ruefully. 'However, your concern would appear to be somewhat more pressing. I don't think I know your names?'

'I am sorry to be so secretive. I am Jean Rawmarsh and this is my husband Robert.' Noting that the detective did not show any sign of recognition, she gave him a knowing smile. 'For some reason, people always seem to remember our nephew's name but not ours.'

'Your nephew?' murmured Blizzard. Understanding dawned. 'I take it that we are talking about Charlie Louden?'

'I am afraid we are,' said Jean. 'I'd rather we weren't but it wouldn't be the first time that he has tried to kill us.'

'No, indeed,' said Blizzard. 'He broke into your house in the middle of the night and attacked you in your bed, as I recall?'

'With a machete,' said Jean. She shuddered at the memory then glanced at her husband. 'Robert tried to fight him off, but Charlie was out of control. Like a wild animal. We're lucky to be alive, aren't we, love?'

Blizzard was struck by the affection that Jean showed her husband, who nodded, stared at the floor but said nothing.

'It was something about an inheritance, was it not?' asked the inspector.

'After his Aunt Margaret died, Charlie claimed that she had agreed to leave everything to him,' said Jean. 'As if my sister would do that for someone like him! When it emerged that the will said nothing of the sort and that he had been lying through his teeth, Charlie claimed that I had forced her to change it under duress in the days before her death.'

'A wicked suggestion,' said Robert. They were the first words that he had uttered since entering the police station and they were spoken with passion. 'Jean would never do anything like that. She hasn't got an evil bone in her body!'

Jean gave her husband a look of gratitude, then turned her attention back to the inspector.

'How much do you know about what happened that night?' she asked.

'Just what I heard at the time. I wasn't involved with the investigation.'

'Then this may help,' said Jean. She produced an envelope from her handbag, from which she extracted a yellowed newspaper cutting; she unfolded it and slid it across the desk towards the detective. It was a lead article on the front page of *The Daily Herald* newspaper. 'As I am sure you can appreciate, we do not like going into the details unless it's really necessary. It was a nightmarish experience and we would rather forget that it ever happened, but we think it is important that people know what kind of a man Charlie is.'

Blizzard nodded and looked at the date on the cutting.

'I was heading up the drugs squad on the east side of the city in 2009,' he said, 'but a couple of my pals were with Western CID at the time and they said that it was one of the most disturbing cases on which they have worked.'

'I am sure it was,' said Jean. 'No one is the same after coming into contact with Charlie Louden.'

She watched Blizzard over the rim of her glasses as the detective stared in silence for a few moments at the photograph of the fresh-faced young man which accompanied the article. Jean guessed what he was thinking.

'That picture has the same effect on everyone that sees it,' she said. 'If Charlie hadn't been disturbed, I am convinced that he would have kept going until we were dead, but it's difficult to believe that someone who looks that young and innocent could act like that, isn't it?'

Blizzard nodded and started to read the report.

> *Baby-faced nephew jailed after inheritance row led to frenzied attack.*
> *A Hafton man was jailed for twenty-one years yesterday after trying to murder his aunt and uncle with a machete as they slept in their beds.*
> *Charlie Louden, 17, hacked repeatedly at Jean Rawmarsh and her husband Robert during the bloodbath, which happened after he forced his way*

through the back door of their home in Marris Avenue in the middle of the night.

Barrister Angela Rouse QC, prosecuting at Hafton Crown Court, said that Louden, of Elmtree Avenue, carried out the attack in June last year because he believed that Mrs Rawmarsh had forced her sister to cut him out of her will, a claim which the family has always denied.

Mrs Rouse told the court that Louden hoped his attack would force Mrs Rawmarsh, 55, to give him the money. She was in Hafton General Hospital for six months following the incident, including five weeks in intensive care, having sustained thirteen injuries, the most serious of which happened when the machete hacked through the main artery on her wrist.

Her husband, 57, tried to fight Louden off and was in hospital for two months after sustaining seven wounds, mainly on his arms.

Doctors said that the couple were lucky to survive the onslaught, which only ended when a neighbour heard their screams and banged on the front door, causing Louden to flee through the back garden.

He was arrested following a four-hour manhunt which ended when two uniformed officers found him sitting in the bandstand in Alderman Riley Park.

The court heard that he launched his attack a year after the death of his aunt Margaret Kelleher, of Carmel Road, Hafton, from heart failure at the age of 52.

Gerald Morris QC, the defending barrister, told the court that Louden claimed that Mrs Kelleher, a widower with no children, had written a will in which she left her £175,000 estate to her nephew, including a terraced house on the edge of the city centre and more than £35,000 in savings.

Louden admitted two counts of attempted murder and Judge Edward Godfrey sentenced him to life on each charge, to run concurrently and be no less than twenty-one years in total.

The judge described him as 'deranged' at the time he carried out the attack, which was, he said, the kind of thing that would normally only be seen in a horror movie.

Describing Louden as one of the most dangerous men that he had ever sentenced, the judge said that 'great care' must be taken if he were ever to be considered for early release from prison.

Blizzard stopped reading and looked at Jean.

'Am I to assume that you are here because you believe that Charlie might be released early?' he asked. 'He had his parole hearing recently, I think.'

'He did and we don't *believe* it, we *know* it,' said Jean. 'We received a call from the assistant governor at Hafton Prison this morning, telling us that we should be prepared for the parole board to order his release when the outcome of the hearing is announced on Monday next week.'

'Are you sure about that?' said Blizzard in surprise. He glanced at the date on the newspaper again. 'He's still got five years to go, hasn't he? I'm surprised they decided to even consider him.'

'So were we,' said Jean. 'However, as I am sure you know, Chief Inspector, prisons like Hafton are releasing as many inmates early as they can, to ease the overcrowding. Apparently, they justify it in Charlie's case by saying that he has earned it because of his good behaviour.'

'Good behaviour!' exclaimed her husband with a snort of derision. He jabbed angrily at the newspaper cutting with a forefinger. 'Someone who is capable of doing something like that never changes. He's the same now as he was then, you mark my words.'

'So, do I take it that he has threatened to come after you again?' asked Blizzard.

'We have not heard anything from Charlie since the day the attack happened,' said Jean. 'But he doesn't need to say anything. We carry permanent reminders with us of what he is capable of doing.'

She rolled up her coat sleeve to reveal her forearm, across which the inspector could see a series of scars that were still livid despite the passage of time. Her husband did the same. Blizzard stared at the injuries in silence for a few moments. He had seen many serious wounds during his career, including more murders than he cared to count, but the sight shocked him. To his relief, the couple rolled their sleeves back down after a few seconds then stared expectantly at the detective, awaiting his response. For once, he was not quite sure what to say.

'So, what exactly do you want me to do?' he asked.

'We think that Charlie will try to force us to give him the money,' said Jean. 'We want you to make sure that they don't let him out.'

'That is way beyond my powers, I am afraid. And the force *did* send a letter saying that the situation had to be handled with care.'

'Typed by some secretary, I imagine,' said Jean. 'We want you to go and see him before they let him out. Let him know that he will be arrested if he comes anywhere near us.' The composure which Jean had maintained since she walked into the police station wavered – tears glistened in her eyes and her voice trembled. 'We can't go through all that again, Chief Inspector. We simply can't.'

'I understand–'

'No one can truly understand something like that unless they have experienced it,' said Jean sharply. She fixed him with a stare. 'Let's just hope that it never happens to you and your family.'

Images of his holiday with Fee and Mikey the previous week flashed into the inspector's mind and he found himself feeling resentful at the way Jean had tainted the memory. It felt like an intrusion into his private life and, as a man who prided himself on being in control of such situations, Blizzard was acutely conscious that it was Jean who had the upper hand. He felt the need to regain control.

'I appreciate that you are worried,' he said. 'But, in my experience, the parole board rarely get it wrong and they will not order your nephew's release unless they are sure that he no longer poses a threat. He's had a long time to think about what he did and, like you say, he hasn't tried to make contact with you since the day he was sent to prison, has he?'

'That doesn't mean that he hasn't thought about it,' said Jean. 'Who knows what goes on in the mind of a man like that?'

'True, but I imagine that one of the conditions of his release will be that he stays away from you, and it will be made clear to him that he will be sent back to prison if he breaches it. He'll never be released if he does – you don't get a second chance with the parole board, and they'll know if it happens because he will be closely supervised.'

'A somewhat naïve attitude, if I may say so, Chief Inspector,' said Robert. 'They'll know it has happened because we will be dead. They can supervise him as much as they want but they can't be with him every minute of the day, can they? Rage like that is always there with people like Charlie. It just needs something to trigger it and I have no doubt that he still thinks the money is his.'

'Yes, but–' began Blizzard.

'For God's sake, man, can you not see that this is our worst nightmare?' exclaimed Robert.

The vehemence of his response startled the detective, as did the way he reached across the desk and clasped Blizzard's hand. The inspector winced as Robert's nails dug into his flesh.

'Can you not imagine what it will be like for us if they let him out?' continued Robert; he was standing up and shouting now. 'Lying awake in our beds and listening for every sound in the middle of the night? Terrified that it's Charlie coming back to finish the job?'

As if suddenly aware of what he was doing, Robert let go of Blizzard's hand and slumped back in his chair.

'I'm sorry,' he said. 'I hope I didn't hurt you.'

Blizzard rubbed his hand ruefully.

'I'll live,' he said.

Silence settled on the room as he thought for a few moments. The couple awaited his response with hope written across their faces. Blizzard nodded, if reluctantly.

'I'll see if I can have a word with Charlie before the decision is announced,' he said. 'But I can't promise that I will be allowed to see him and, even if I do get to see him, there's no guarantee that he will take any notice of what I say.'

'At least you will have made an effort,' replied Jean. She folded up the newspaper cutting and slipped it back into the envelope. 'Then, if something awful does happen, you'll be able to tell yourself that you tried, won't you?'

Chapter two

Jean Rawmarsh's parting words weighed heavily on Blizzard's mind and, having seen the couple out of the police station, he headed back down the corridor in the direction of his boss's office. Now a detective superintendent, Arthur Ronald had started his career at the same time as Blizzard when they were rookies at Abbey Road. They were reunited at the station after Ronald was given responsibility for detectives in half the force's area and brought in Blizzard to improve the underperforming Western CID, the two men working well together despite their contrasting personalities. Ronald, a balding, smartly dressed man with ruddy cheeks, was the smooth-talking diplomat, whereas Blizzard, with his tie at its customary half-mast and tousled hair, was the outspoken one. He arrived at the superintendent's office to find Ronald engrossed in paperwork.

'Do you want to do mine as well?' asked the inspector as he sat down at the desk. 'I've got plenty to go round.'

'What, and deprive you of your favourite job of the day?' said Ronald. He did not look up but continued to scribble a note on one the documents. 'No, I couldn't do that. Anything happening?'

'I've just had a visit from the Rawmarshes.'

Ronald stopped writing and looked at his friend in surprise.

'What did they want?' he asked. 'As if I didn't know.'

'The prison has told them that the outcome of Charlie Louden's parole hearing will be announced on Monday next week. They seem convinced that he'll be released.'

'I can't help feeling that it'd be too early.'

'Good behaviour, apparently,' said Blizzard. 'The Rawmarshes are worried that he might go after them again.'

'I don't blame them,' said Ronald. 'I will take a lot of convincing that a man capable of violence like that can change his ways. That's certainly what we believed following his arrest. Our DCI at the time argued that Charlie should be admitted to a psychiatric hospital so that he could be kept in indefinitely, if needed.'

'How come no one listened?' Blizzard sat down at the desk. 'Surely, a DCI's opinion counts for something?'

'Clearly not. Worth remembering that, I'd say.'

'Yes, thank you for those kind words of support, Arthur, you can't imagine how comforting they are,' said Blizzard. He quickly turned serious again. 'You interviewed Charlie when he was brought in, I seem to recall you telling me once?'

'Several times. I was duty DI the day they brought him in.' Ronald gave a slight shake of the head as he recalled the experience. 'It was the most disturbing interview I have ever done. The Rawmarshes were fighting for their lives, we were trying to arrange counselling for officers who were in shock at what they had seen in the house, and there was Charlie acting like nothing had happened. I'm no shrink, but I reckon Charlie Louden is as dangerous now as the day he was arrested. Has he threatened the Rawmarshes?'

'No, but they're still frightened, and they want me to warn him off going anywhere near them. I thought I'd have a word with the prison governor, see what he thinks.'

'Be careful,' said Ronald sternly. 'I don't want you souring our relations. You know how hard we've worked to develop an understanding with him since he got the job. I don't want it thrown away for nothing.'

Blizzard thought of the scars on the arms of the Rawmarshes arms.

'It won't be for nothing,' he said, standing up. 'I can assure you of that.'

'You know what I mean – and don't waste too much time on it. We've got enough real crime to tackle without investigating one that does not exist.'

'Yet,' said Blizzard.

Ronald frowned but was not given the opportunity to respond because there was a knock on the office door and a middle-aged woman with short dark hair walked into the room. Jenny Carr had been recruited by Western CID when Blizzard requested an additional experienced officer following the arrival of several younger detectives. Having since been promoted, she was in her first week as a detective sergeant and looked like a woman with news to impart.

'Sorry to interrupt,' she said, 'but Control have just been on. The fire brigade have been called to a fire at the old carpet factory in Mounsey Street. It was only a small fire and after they put it out, they discovered a body.'

'Have they now?' said Blizzard. He rubbed his hands together in a satisfied manner. 'Everything comes to he who waits, eh, Arthur?'

'Yes, well, don't waste too much time on that, either!' said Ronald as his friend headed for the door. 'What happened in the past stays in the past when it comes to Mounsey Street. It's probably just some rough sleeper who drank too much cheap cider, anyway.'

Blizzard wafted a hand in the vague direction of the superintendent and disappeared into the corridor, followed by Jenny Carr, who scurried after Blizzard as he strode towards the door which led into the yard at the rear of the police station.

'Have I missed something, guv?' she asked as she fell into step with the inspector.

'Like what?' asked Blizzard.

'Like why would the super say that this could be a waste of time? I mean, it could be a murder, couldn't it?'

'It could be, yes, but it's more likely that it's a wino. Arthur is usually right about these things. Besides, he knows that I've got history with the Mounsey Street carpet factory.'

'Are we talking about the big fire a few years back?'

'The very same,' said Blizzard. He pushed his way through the door and led the way to his black BMW, which was parked at the far end of the yard. 'What do you know about it?'

'Not much, really. I was working uniform on the east side when it happened.'

'I'll give you all the details on the way.' Blizzard unlocked the doors to his car. 'You need to know about it, if you're going to be one of my team.'

As Blizzard drove them through a run-down industrial area on the edge of the city centre, he recounted a story that had stayed in his thoughts despite the passage of the years. In its heyday, Mounsey Street Carpets owned one of the largest factories in the northern city of Hafton but, like so many of the area's traditional industries, the firm went into decline until it was eventually purchased by Zhang Wei and Fu Li, two fresh-faced young businessmen from Singapore. The hope that they brought of a renaissance did not last long and they closed the firm within three months of completing the acquisition, after fire swept through the building one early November night. The building had stood derelict ever since and, although the incident happened before Blizzard returned to Abbey Road Police Station, he still yearned to solve the case. For him, it was a matter of principle.

'What principle?' asked Carr. 'Why are you so keen to solve it, given that it all happened before your time in charge of Western CID?'

'Because it's the oldest industrial building in Hafton, dating back to the mid-1700s – that's why it's Grade I listed – and every time I drive past it, not only am I annoyed by the fact that something which is such a big part of the city's industrial heritage has been left to ruin, I am also reminded of the bad old days of Western CID. It's an object lesson in how not to run an investigation.'

'Why, what did they do wrong?' asked Carr.

'What didn't they do wrong? For a start, the DCI, a chap called George Ramsdale – he's retired now – did not question the owners for two days, even though the fire brigade said that the blaze was suspicious and local people were openly speculating that it was an insurance job. By the time CID got round to them, Zhang Wei and Fu Li had disappeared. It was assumed that they had gone back to Singapore. I did hear suggestions that someone inside Western CID tipped them off that the police were going to bring them in for questioning but I never believed that. Western CID in those days was incompetent and lazy, but I don't think it was corrupt.'

'Could DCI Ramsdale not have followed the owners to Singapore?' said Carr. 'I mean, if everyone knew that they were responsible for the fire, it was worth pursuing, surely?'

'You'd think,' said Blizzard. He guided the vehicle past the first of a series of derelict warehouses. 'But Western Division was a very different animal back then and Ramsdale was approaching retirement; he was more interested in his new camper van than doing the job properly.'

'Did you discuss the case with him when you took over as head of CID?' asked Carr.

'I tried to, but he threatened to make a formal complaint about me. Said I was blackening his good name.'

'So, how come *you* haven't re-opened the case? I mean, you don't need George Ramsdale's permission, do you?' Carr noted a slight frown on the inspector's face and quickly added, 'Sorry, that came out wrong, guv. I didn't mean it to sound as if I was being judge–'

'No need to apologise, Sergeant,' said Blizzard as he turned the car into Mounsey Street. 'It's a perfectly reasonable thing to ask, but you heard the superintendent's comments back there. I did ask him to let me take another look when I was made up to DCI but he was already having to work hard to persuade some of the senior people at headquarters that I was the right man for the job, and he reckoned – probably rightly – that the last thing we needed was me picking a fight with George Ramsdale. Arthur felt that Mounsey Street should stay in the past – one that got away – and so it has remained.'

Blizzard guided the BMW past another couple of derelict warehouses and brought the vehicle to a halt outside the old Mounsey Street carpet factory with its skeletal roof timbers that clawed the air, its scorched walls and its shattered windows. The detectives got out and Blizzard gave a sad shake of the head.

'It was a wicked act, it really was,' he said. 'A lovely old building like that, but much as I would love to re-open the case, I have never been able to justify the large number of hours that it would require at a time when there is so much pressure on the budget.'

'I take it that no one has heard anything about Zhang Wei or Fu Li?' asked Carr.

'That's another problem. It's like they vanished into thin air and, without anything to suggest that they are still in Hafton, my argument for a cold case investigation is made even weaker.'

'Maybe this will present you with an opportunity,' said Carr.

'Maybe it will,' replied Blizzard. 'But don't hold your breath.'

The detectives walked over to the police vehicles parked outside the building. Uniformed officers had put up tape to keep the public out, and forensics officers in white overalls had already entered the factory to begin their inspection. A man in a dark suit approached them and, without realising that he had done it, Blizzard reached up to his tie, which was at half-mast, as usual. Detective Inspector Graham Ross, the head of Western Division's forensics service, noticed the gesture and chuckled; he represented the new breed of sharply dressed young officers and knew that Blizzard was acutely aware that he could not match their sartorial standards.

'What we got then, Versace?' asked Blizzard.

'Male, mid to late thirties,' said Ross. 'He's been there for a good five or six months, by the looks of him. The body is badly decomposed.'

Five minutes later, with the detectives now suitably clad in overalls, the forensics chief led them through the main entrance onto the empty factory floor and into an atmosphere redolent with the acrid smell of pigeon urine.

'The body is under those pallets,' said Ross. He pointed to a pile of timber stacked up in the far corner, around which were gathered a number of police officers in white overalls. 'Whoever killed him clearly tried to hide the body.'

'I assume the fire brigade found it?' asked Blizzard.

'That's right. The killer had made an attempt to burn the evidence and, even though the fire didn't fully take because the timber was too damp, it did enough damage to make identification very difficult.'

'Any clues as to ID?' asked Blizzard. He peered at the body, which lay face down, dressed in the rotting and scorched remains of the black trousers and jumper. 'Arthur's money is on a rough sleeper.'

'Ah, well, that's where it gets interesting,' said a voice.

The inspector turned to see an officer with short-cropped brown hair and also wearing white overalls approach them.

'Interesting, how?' asked Blizzard.

'Interesting in that we might be about to make your day,' said Detective Inspector Chris Ramsey, one of the Western CID team. 'From what's left of his hair, we're both pretty sure that he was Asian – and you know what that could mean.'

'That it could be a guy from Singapore,' said Blizzard. He rubbed his hands together enthusiastically. 'Splendid.'

'If nothing else, it's an intriguing coincidence,' said Ross. 'And everyone knows Blizzard's first law of homicide investigation. All together, boys and girls.'

'There's no such thing as coincidence on a murder inquiry,' chorused the other detectives.

'Exactly,' said Ross. 'You might finally get to re-open the investigation, after all, eh, guv?'

'It's certainly the nearest I have come,' said Blizzard. He turned to Ramsey. 'Chris, will you kick things off here and keep me informed of any developments, please?'

'Don't you want to run the investigation?' asked Ramsey with surprise.

'I do but I need to sort out a visit to see Charlie Louden first.' Blizzard turned and started walking back across the floor. 'It would seem that cold cases are the theme for the day…'

Chapter three

The next morning, Blizzard arrived at Abbey Road Police Station just before 7.30am to find Chris Ramsey already at work in his office.

'You're keen,' said Blizzard as he walked into the room. 'Couldn't sleep?'

'I wanted to see if our checks on the dead Asian chap brought anything in overnight,' said Ramsey. 'I don't like having John Does on our patch.'

'No, neither do I. Did they come up with anything?'

'Not yet,' said Ramsey. 'The guy I talked to at the Singapore High Commission last night was very helpful but he emailed me to say that they had no information on any nationals missing in the UK. Singapore Police were very unhelpful – I asked if they had anything that might prove if the body was one of the factory owners – but I got the distinct impression that they thought I was wasting their time.'

'Strange.'

'Yes, that's what I thought,' said Ramsey. 'And the less said about the Chinese Embassy the better. They couldn't get rid of me quickly enough.'

'There's a surprise,' asked Blizzard. 'Anything from Interpol or the National Crime Agency?'

'Nothing on their databases and our enquiries locally haven't thrown up anything, either.' Ramsey frowned. 'I know that we've only just started, guv, but this feels like a long drawn-out one. We're no nearer to confirming his identity.'

Blizzard nodded gloomily.

'It's certainly got the feel of it,' he said. 'Anything else I need to know?'

Ramsey removed a yellow Post-it note from his computer and handed it to the inspector.

'The Angel of Death wants to do the post-mortem on our John Doe at half past two,' he said.

'There's something to look forward to,' said Blizzard. He stood up. 'Tell him OK.'

'Will do. Where will you be if I need you this morning?'

'I'm going to get some paperwork out of the way then I'll be at the prison,' said Blizzard. 'Meeting the assistant governor to talk about Charlie Louden.'

'I thought you were going to see Louden himself?'

'That was the plan but the governor blocked us.'

'Why did he do that?' asked Ramsey. 'Surely, it can't do any harm?'

'The governor would beg to disagree,' said Blizzard. 'He thinks that he could be accused of allowing us to interfere with the parole process if we're seen to be talking to Louden. I'm not surprised, mind, the man's a stickler for the rules.'

'He certainly is,' said Ramsey. 'Remember the hoops he had us jumping through last year when we asked to see one of the inmates about that stabbing in Lord Lane? I was sorely tempted to give up. And I thought we were on the same side.'

'Ah, the naivety of youth,' said Blizzard and set off for his office.

Shortly after 9am, with his paperwork completed, Blizzard headed out to the car park behind Abbey Road Police Station, accompanied by fellow CID officer Detective Sergeant David Colley. Ten years younger than his boss, Colley was slim and clean-shaven with neatly combed short black hair. Another of the division's sharply turned-out young detectives, he was wearing a grey suit, his tie was fastened up and his shoes shone. Colley spotted Blizzard's interest in the suit.

'Do you like it?' he asked as they walked towards the inspector's BMW. He gave a mock curtsey. 'I got it at the weekend from that new menswear shop next to the post office. You'll know it well, I imagine?'

'Oh, aye,' said Blizzard. 'I'm never out of the place, me.'

'I'm sure,' said Colley. As the closest Western Division detective to Blizzard, apart from Arthur Ronald, he was one of the few officers able to get away with such banter. But he also knew when it was time to be serious. 'How do you want to play it with the governor? He's not exactly our biggest fan, is he?'

'I'm hoping that the fact we have taken the trouble to go and see his assistant might change his mind,' said the inspector, as they got into the car and he started the engine. 'I realise that it's a vain hope, but we owe it to the Rawmarshes to try.'

'Do we? They have nothing to suggest that Charlie is actually thinking of going after them, do they?'

'No, but I think we need to have a go.'

At least you will have made an effort. Then, if something awful does happen, you'll be able to tell yourself that you tried, won't you?

Colley looked at his boss intently.

'They have really got to you, haven't they?' he said.

'It's more the fact that Arthur is worried that's got to me,' said Blizzard.

'Arthur's always worried.'

'I know he is,' said Blizzard as he guided the car towards the exit. 'But this time, he's *really* worried.'

Just before they reached the road, the inspector's mobile phone rang and he brought the car to a halt to take the call.

'Control here, sir,' said a woman's voice. 'We've just had a woman called Janice Louden on. She wants to see you urgently.'

'I'll bet she does,' said Blizzard. 'You got an address?'

'Flat 69, Limetree House. It's on The Groves estate.'

'Tell her we'll be there in twenty minutes.' Blizzard ended the call and glanced at the sergeant. 'I wondered how long it would take her to come out of the woodwork.'

'What's she like?' asked Colley as the inspector took the vehicle out into the stream of morning traffic. 'Have you met her?'

'Before yesterday, I had not met any of them, but the word Arthur uses to describe Janice is "feckless". She does not appear to realise that she's no longer a teenager anymore. Still dresses up in low-cut tops, short skirts and high heels, even though she is in her mid-sixties.'

'And Charlie's father?' asked Colley. 'What do we know about him?'

'Baz died not long after Charlie was sent to prison. Had a heart attack in the office at his second-hand car showroom. Arthur reckons that he wasn't much better than his wife, still dressing up as Medallion Man long after it fell out of fashion; shirt open to the navel, hairy chest, false tan, sunglasses, the works.'

'Was Charlie their only child?' asked the sergeant.

'He was the only one that Baz and Janice had together but, all in all, she had five children by three different fathers,' said Blizzard. 'She had only just turned sixteen when the first one was born.'

'I take it that none of them received any of the money from the aunt's estate?'

'That was never going to happen. According to Arthur, Margaret was a God-fearing woman who regarded Janice's kids as the spawn of Beelzebub and was horrified at the thought of them squandering her estate. She left a note in her will saying that Jean was only to give anything to her nieces or nephews if she thought that they could be trusted to spend it wisely. As far as anyone knows, none of Janice's children has seen a single penny.'

'Cue Charlie at the end of Aunty Jean's bed with his machete,' said Colley. 'No wonder Arthur's worried.'

It did not take the detectives long to arrive at The Groves estate, which had become for many city residents another example of the problems that had afflicted post-boom Hafton. The estate's high-rise blocks of flats had been hurriedly built in the 1970s to cater for the influx of people reacting to the rapid growth of the city's heavy industry but the good times did not last – they never did in Hafton – and, one by one, the factories closed and the legacy of the developer's decision to use substandard concrete in the rush to construct the tower blocks became apparent. Several of the buildings had already been demolished, three more had been evacuated and stood dark, silent and vandalised as they awaited demolition, and although Limetree House was still occupied, the tenants were already beginning to move out.

The detectives got out of the inspector's vehicle and surveyed the bleak scene for a few moments; police officers in Western Division were no stranger to the estate. As they entered Limetree House, they were assailed by an acrid stench.

'Is that, perchance, the aroma of the lime tree wafting on the breeze?' asked the sergeant, wrinkling his nose.

'Somehow, I think not,' said Blizzard. He peered at the sign on the wall, struggling to read words which had been partially obscured by graffiti. 'Janice's flat would appear to be on the eighth floor.'

They walked over to the lifts only to see an Out of Order sign. Blizzard sighed and headed for the stairs. As the detectives began to climb, the inspector quickly fell behind his younger, and fitter, colleague, and by the time they arrived at the eighth floor, he was blowing hard. He leaned against the wall and gave Colley a sour look; a keen rugby player, the sergeant was not remotely out of breath and he grinned as they waited on the landing for a few moments to allow his boss to regain his equilibrium before knocking on the door to the flat.

Arthur Ronald's description of Janice Louden proved itself to be accurate, as the door was opened to reveal a woman wearing what was clearly a wig with luxuriant blonde hair trying hard to convey an image of youth at odds with the tell-tale lines on her face, which were only partially concealed by heavy make-up. Janice was wearing a tight red T-shirt that did nothing to hide the wrinkles on her scrawny neck, and a short skirt above thin legs encased in black tights which had several ladders.

'You must be Chief Inspector Blizzard,' said Janice. She watched him struggle to regain his breath. 'Stairs a bit much for you, lovey?'

'I'll be fine,' said the inspector grumpily. 'This is Detective Sergeant David Colley.'

'Can I see your warrant cards?' said Janice. 'You can't be too careful round here. You can't afford to let just anyone in.'

Blizzard scowled and, with their cards duly displayed, the officers followed Janice into a hallway whose walls were tainted yellow with years of nicotine. She led the way into the living room, which reeked of stale smoke, and sat down in an armchair, gesturing for the detectives to do the same on the grubby sofa. That she did not offer her visitors a cup of tea did not surprise them; everything about Janice Louden's demeanour suggested that, although she had requested the meeting, she would rather they were not in her living room. Blizzard was about to speak when he noticed Colley grimacing, having reached down to peel a lump of chewing gum off the jacket of his new suit. Blizzard gave the slightest of smiles and returned his attention to Janice.

'You wanted to see me, I think,' he said. 'Something about Charlie, I am guessing?'

'*Something about Charlie*,' said Janice, the words laced with contempt. 'Don't play the fool with me, Chief Inspector. You know exactly why I want to see you. Jean rang me to tell me that you're helping her, to stop Charlie being released from prison. Is that true?'

'No.'

'She thinks it is.' Janice took a cigarette from the box on the coffee table, lit it and took a deep draw before exhaling smoke. 'I asked to see you to tell you that it won't work. The poor lad has served his time.'

'Poor lad?' said Blizzard, unable to conceal the disapproval in his voice. 'Poor lad? Plenty of people will think that he's getting off lightly if they let him out. They think that he should never be released.'

'Yes, well, the psychiatrists disagreed,' said Janice. 'That's why he was sent to prison and not hospital. And there's nothing to say that he's planning to carry out another attack, either. Jean admits that she has not heard anything from him, and I've certainly not heard him say anything like that.'

'When did you last see him?' asked Colley.

Janice did not reply. For the first time since the detectives had walked into her flat, she seemed less sure of herself.

'It's a simple enough question,' said Blizzard. He gave her a questioning look as the silence lengthened. 'When did you last see your son?'

'Eight months ago,' she admitted reluctantly.

'Why so long?' asked Blizzard. 'Have you fallen out with him?'

'It's my new feller. He doesn't like the idea of having someone like Charlie in the family.'

'Get away,' said Blizzard.

'You're all the same,' said Janice. She gave a snort of derision. 'None of you give Charlie any credit. I told my feller that he's changed while he's been in prison, and that he explained at the parole hearing how sorry he is for what he did, but he refused to believe it.'

'He may be right,' said Blizzard. 'My guess is that your son still believes that his aunt's money is his by rights.'

'Well, Jean doesn't need it, does she?' said Janice vehemently. 'She's rolling in it but not one of my kids has received a single penny from her – and neither have I.'

She let her gaze roam round the room and scowled.

'You've seen how I live, while Jean and Robert rattle around in that big house of theirs,' she said. 'Can you really blame Charlie for feeling bitter?'

'Which is why Jean and Robert fear that he will have another go at getting his hands on the money,' said Blizzard. 'Be honest, Janice, can you *really* say, hand on heart, that he won't go after them if he is released?'

Janice did not reply immediately and when she did speak, her anger had been replaced by something more vulnerable and her voice was smaller, less certain than before.

'I have to believe it, don't I?' she said. 'I can't allow myself to believe anything else of Charlie.'

'It's not the most reassuring of answers, is it?' said Blizzard. He stood up. 'Let's just hope that you're right because if you're not, his release day could be a difficult one for all of us.'

At least you will have made an effort. Then, if something awful does happen, you'll be able to tell yourself that you tried, won't you?

Chapter four

After leaving The Groves estate, the detectives headed for
the dual carriageway which took them out of the western
district, bypassed the city centre and ran alongside the
River Haft towards the east side of Hafton. The journey
took the BMW through an area that, for many people,
acted as another symbol of Hafton's economic downturn.
Lined along the river were numerous wharves, jetties and
docks which had once bustled with life, the air filled with
the hollering of stevedores and the clank of heavy
machinery, but which had gradually been transformed into
an abandoned industrial wasteland on which scrubby
grasses forced their way through crumbling tarmac, and
buddleia plants seeded themselves in between rusting
railway tracks.

The poignance of such areas had always spoken to
Blizzard but never more so than now because, as a keen
student of the city's industrial and social history, he had
been commissioned to write a book on the subject by a
local publisher who attended one of his talks. At first, the
inspector was excited – the commission was a dream come
true – but the challenges of his job and the demands of a
young son meant that he had struggled to find time to

write and had already fallen behind. Not for the first time since the publisher made his offer, Blizzard's mind strayed onto the subject of early retirement as he drove along the riverbank that morning.

Hafton Prison was set back from the eastern bypass and, after the inspector parked his vehicle in the car park, he and Colley sat in silence for a few moments and surveyed the imposing red-brick building with little enthusiasm. Neither of them relished the prospect of a visit to a jail that had been constructed in the Victorian Age and had undergone little in the way of investment in the many decades that followed, as repeated government promises to modernise it came to nothing.

'It always amazes me why anyone would be a repeat offender,' said Colley, as the detectives got out of the car. 'Surely, anyone who has done time here can't forget what the place is like? I mean, Charlie Louden must know that if he attacks the Rawmarshes again, he'll be straight back in there and never get out. Mustn't he?'

'Ah, but criminals don't think like that, do they?' said Blizzard as they set off across the car park. 'They never think they'll be nicked.'

'I suppose so. Do you think that Charlie is *actually* planning something then?'

'Probably not.'

'So why are we here then?' asked the sergeant.

Blizzard thought of the scars on the arms of the Rawmarshes.

'We're just ticking the boxes,' he said.

Having undergone rigorous security checks carried out by unsmiling prison officers, the detectives were led by a taciturn warder into the main yard of the prison, where a group of inmates was engaged on a gardening detail, watched over by an officer accompanied by a mean-looking German shepherd. Colley eyed the animal warily; although he was a dog lover, and had been trying to persuade his girlfriend Jay to let them have one for a long time, the German shepherds had always been the thing that disturbed him most about his visits to Hafton Prison. There was something about their narrow eyes and curled lips that gave them a mean look that unnerved the sergeant.

At the end of the yard, the warder led them into the interior of the prison and along a cramped and dark corridor that took them onto overcrowded landings, pervaded by the fetid stench of stale sweat and fear. The detectives recognised a number of inmates because they were responsible for their incarceration at Hafton and the prisoners stared at them with undisguised hostility.

It all made for an oppressive atmosphere so it was with a sense of relief that the detectives arrived at the bright and airy staff canteen on the third floor. Now, a little more at ease, they sat at a corner table, sipping from mugs of tea and working their way through a plate of biscuits bought for them by Assistant Governor Maureen Rodgers, a bespectacled middle-aged woman, whose cheery demeanour was in sharp contrast to the bleak scenes not far away on the landings.

'So,' said Rodgers as she reached for a biscuit, 'what do you want to know about our Charlie?'

Blizzard frowned; he did not appreciate the familiar way in which she referred to a man who had tried to commit a double murder.

'Anything you can tell us,' he said. 'He's been out of circulation for a long time.'

'Some would say not long enough,' said Rodgers. 'I am sure you can appreciate that this is a sensitive issue for us, Chief Inspector. We're expecting a bad reaction from the public when people learn that he might be granted parole, especially when the media blow it up into a front-page story. I'm surprised that Jean Rawmarsh has not tipped off one of her tame journalist pals on the local rag already. She sure as hell will now.'

'Then why did you warn her?' asked Blizzard.

'I felt that we owed her at least that. Victims need to be kept up to date and we hoped that by taking her into our confidence, we might persuade her to be more reasonable and not go running to the media.' She sighed. 'Clearly, I was wrong. The media will probably run a campaign to keep him locked up. It's their kind of thing.'

A thought struck her.

'I take it that I can assume that Jean put you up to this?' she said. 'Rang you after I told her what's happening?'

Again, Blizzard frowned – Maureen Rodgers seemed to have a gift for coming up with an unfortunate turn of phrase.

'I'm not sure that I would say she "put us up" to it,' said the inspector. 'But, yes, she and Robert did come to see me after you rang them. They're very worried. You can't blame them, really.'

'I assume that they did their trick of showing you their scars?'

'I'm not sure I would call it a trick,' said Blizzard. 'Their fears seem reasonable to me.'

'I appreciate that you share their concerns,' said Rodgers. 'But I don't think that the Rawmarshes have reason to worry.'

'But how can you be sure?' asked Colley.

'The Charlie Louden of today is very different from the one who was sent here all those years ago.' Rodgers took a sip of tea. 'Jean does not believe me but it's true.'

'In what way is he different?' asked the sergeant.

'His behaviour has been impeccable from the moment he set foot in this place. I have worked here for thirteen years and he's never shown any signs of violence. That's why the parole board will probably let him go. That, and the fact that we need to free up some space because you lot keep sending us more punters. We're horribly overcrowded.' Rodgers gave the detectives a wry smile. 'If you want us to keep people like Charlie Louden in here, can I suggest that Western CID stops arresting criminals?'

In contrast to some of the assistant governor's other comments, Blizzard appreciated the quip. He was proud of his record since taking over as head of Western Division CID. Arrest rates and conviction levels had risen dramatically and crime in the area had fallen steadily. There were those who contended that, given the way Blizzard's outspoken approach infuriated some senior colleagues, it was the statistics that kept him in a job.

'Will that be all?' asked Rodgers, glancing at her watch. 'I have another meeting to go to.'

'Just one more thing,' said Blizzard. 'Has Charlie been particularly close to anyone during his time here?'

'He has, yes,' said Rodgers. 'But I don't think it's anything to worry the Rawmarshes. A chap called Martin Crumpsall.'

'I know that name,' said Blizzard. He furrowed his brow as he tried to summon the memory. He glanced at Colley. 'Why would I know that name, David?'

Colley shrugged.

'Dunno,' he said. 'I've never heard of him.'

'It was sometime in the past few months,' said Blizzard. 'Although now I come to think about it, I'm pretty sure that it was *Marty* Crumpsall, not Martin.'

'Same man, I suspect,' said Rodgers. 'He likes people to call him Marty because he thinks that it makes him sound more like a hardened villain.'

'Except he's still called Crumpsall,' said Colley. 'Perhaps he's one of the Crumpsall Mafia family. Capo dei Crumpsalli!'

He roared with laughter at his own joke and several prison officers sat at other tables looked in his direction.

'Sorry,' said the sergeant with a grin. 'I get carried away sometimes. I mean, it's not exactly Capone, is it?'

'Martin seems to have overlooked the irony,' said Rodgers. 'He likes to give the impression that he has links to organised crime.'

'And has he?' asked Colley.

'I very much doubt it.'

'What's he in for?' asked the sergeant.

'Fraud,' said Rodgers. 'He was a financial advisor who stole more than a hundred and fifty grand from his clients' pension funds and got three and a half years for his troubles. As far as we know, he operated alone. We've certainly heard nothing to suggest that he has links to anything organised. If you ask me, he's a bit of a fantasist.'

Rodgers looked at Blizzard.

'Unless you know different,' she said. 'Have you remembered where you heard his name?'

'I have,' said Blizzard. 'Our superintendent mentioned him. We'd been approached by the fraud investigation team at Hafton NHS. They wanted to know if we had anything on him because his name had cropped up in an investigation into a fake prescriptions racket.'

'That makes sense. Martin may be a fantasist but, boy, can he fake a document!' Rodgers chuckled. 'He almost got himself a weekend release from this place by forging a letter from our deputy governor. He was only rumbled when he waved at one of the reception staff as he was getting into a taxi. Were you able to help the NHS team?'

'We'd never heard of him, and it was an east-side case anyway, so we passed their enquiry onto our Economic Crime Unit. I have not heard anything further so it couldn't have been that big a deal.'

'When was this?' asked Rodgers.

'Five or six months ago.'

'Not long after he was released,' said Rodgers. She frowned. 'So much for rehabilitation.'

'He was close to Charlie, was he?' asked Blizzard.

'Very close. They shared a cell for Martin's last eleven months here and he has been back to see Charlie several times since he was released. He's the only person who has. His mother stopped coming several months ago and none of the rest of the family have ever been to see him. Sad, really.'

'That's what happens when you try to slice your aunt and uncle up with a machete,' said Blizzard. He glanced at Colley. 'However, I think we should consider the possibility that Charlie has adopted a different way of getting his hands on the Rawmarshes' money. Maybe he has asked Crumpsall to forge some documents for him.'

'It's certainly got to be worth a closer look,' said Colley.

'Now, hang on,' said Rodgers. An alarmed look had replaced her cheery demeanour. 'You're not going to start a new investigation into Charlie, are you?'

'We may well do,' said Blizzard. 'He and Crumpsall may be cooking something up.'

'This is out of order,' exclaimed the assistant governor. Several members of staff looked round from their conversations at other tables and her next words were uttered in a much lower voice. 'The governor only agreed that I talk to you on the grounds that you do nothing to disrupt Charlie's parole process. He'll regard this as well outside our agreement.'

'Actually, it was *his* agreement,' said Blizzard. '*We* didn't agree to anything.'

'If I didn't know better, I'd think that you already knew about Charlie's connection with Martin Crumpsall.' Rodgers looked at the inspector suspiciously, through narrowed eyes. 'I don't appreciate being played for a fool.'

'We didn't know anything about Crumpsall until you mentioned him,' said Blizzard. 'We have acted in good faith. We came here purely to satisfy ourselves that Charlie was not planning to attack the Rawmarshes again.'

'Well, you're going to get me into a lot of trouble when word of this gets out. It's a delicate enough situation without you stirring things up.' Rodgers drained the last of her tea, scowled as she discovered that it had gone cold and stood up. 'I think it's time that you left, don't you? I have another meeting to go to anyway.'

She led them back onto the landing where Blizzard noticed that he was being watched by a man whom he recognised among the hostile group of inmates gathered to watch the detectives depart, news of their presence in the building having spread quickly. The man who was staring at Blizzard was the only one who did not exude hostility; he rather preferred to watch the inspector with the faintest of smiles.

Blizzard had to look twice to confirm that the gaunt figure was indeed Charlie Louden; the years in Hafton Prison had not been kind to the man once dubbed by the media as a 'baby-faced' attacker. Gone was the fresh complexion to be replaced by something much older, the face lined, the skin sallow and marked with a couple of scars, one on the cheek, the other close to his right eye. Colley had recognised him as well and gave his boss a troubled look. Blizzard took a step towards Louden but Maureen Rodgers placed a restraining hand on the inspector's shoulder.

'Don't even think it,' she said. 'You've already done enough damage.'

Blizzard considered contesting the point but Arthur Ronald's warning of the previous day came to mind and he decided not to inflame the situation further. Instead, he allowed the assistant governor to lead the detectives back along the landings, her cheery demeanour of earlier, long since banished. When she had closed the front gate behind them, and once the detectives had breathed in welcome fresh air after the fetid stench of the landings, Colley looked at Blizzard.

'Did you see him?' he asked.

'Took me a while to recognise him,' said the inspector.

'I reckon that if they showed young tearaways a picture of Charlie Louden before he was sent to prison and one showing what he looks like now, a sizeable proportion of them would think twice about breaking the law. What do you think?'

'We've gone through this already,' said Blizzard as the detectives started walking towards the car. 'They never think that it's going to happen to them.'

'You're probably right,' said the sergeant. He gave a sigh. 'This is turning into a thoroughly depressing morning.'

'Maybe I can cheer you up then,' said Blizzard. He unlocked the car and got into the driver's seat. 'I've been talking to Arthur about making some changes to Western CID. It's time to freshen things up.'

'What kind of changes?' asked the sergeant suspiciously.

'Don't look so worried,' said Blizzard, starting up the BMW's engine. 'And keep this to yourself, for the moment, but Chris Ramsey is going to be promoted to DCI and be appointed to run the Criminal Intelligence Unit at headquarters.'

'A good choice,' said Colley. 'That's his kind of thing. He's just about the most thorough human being I know.'

'Everyone seems to think so. It does mean, of course, that we will need a new detective inspector at Western CID. We think that you would be ideal and it's high time you were promoted. Interested?'

'I don't fancy going back into uniform.'

'Arthur says that you can stay, if you want,' said Blizzard, reversing the BMW out of its parking spot. 'A straight replacement for Chris. So, do you fancy it?'

Colley beamed.

'I certainly do,' he said. 'Boy, that's improved my morning.'

'Thought it would,' said Blizzard.

Chapter five

The lighter mood that had been created by the detectives' discussion about promotions did not last long and Blizzard arrived back at Abbey Road Police Station to be greeted by a Post-it note stuck to his desk, which told him that Arthur Ronald wanted to see him immediately. Blizzard marvelled at the way his friend was able to communicate anger with a simple scrawl and, having guessed that a complaint from the prison governor was behind it, he sighed, scrunched up the note and viciously shied it towards the waste bin, cursing when it missed.

'Sometimes I wonder why I bother,' he muttered as he headed out of his office.

The inspector's irritation grew rapidly as he strode along the corridor, his mood darkened by the thought that, as someone who often deliberately stirred things up, he had genuinely tried to follow his friend's instruction not to cause friction with the governor. The extent to which he had failed was made clear by the baleful expression on Ronald's face as Blizzard entered his office. The inspector decided to ignore it.

'You wanted to see me?' he said as he sat down. He adopted a tone of voice which suggested that he was surprised to have been summoned. 'Is something amiss, perchance?'

'Don't play the innocent with me, John,' said Ronald irritably. 'What was the last thing I said yesterday?'

Blizzard produced his best puzzled look.

'Don't bollocks things up with the governor,' said the superintendent. 'That's what I said, and what happens? I get a call from him this morning, saying that you are deliberately trying to jeopardise Charlie Louden's parole process.'

'No, I'm not.'

'Well, he thinks you are.'

'I can't be responsible for what people think,' said Blizzard. 'I take it that he has submitted a complaint?'

'Not an official one, he hasn't,' said Ronald. 'Not yet anyway. He wants to keep things low-key if he can but, according to him, you are deliberately trying to scupper Charlie's release by concocting some fanciful story about that fellow the NHS fraud team were asking about a few months back. Martin something.'

'Capone,' said Blizzard, deadpan.

'What?'

'Sorry, I meant Crumpsall,' said Blizzard. 'I always get those two mixed up.'

'I hope you are not trying to be funny because this is not the time to be flippant. You've caused enough trouble as it is.'

'Hey, don't blame me,' protested Blizzard. 'It was the assistant governor who put us onto him. I don't think that there's anything to it but I'd like to look a bit deeper. Maybe talk to someone from the NHS Fraud Investigation Team. On the QT, of course. Nothing will get back to the governor. Trust me.'

'Why do I always fear the worst when you say that?' said Ronald. 'However, I'll put in a call to Ruth Stewart, if you want.'

'The east-side DCI? What's it got to do with her?'

'She has been appointed as the new head of the NHS Fraud Investigation Unit. I thought you knew? She got the call on the day of her retirement party last month. She's the seventh investigator they have taken on. All ex-job.'

'Nice work if you can get it,' said Blizzard. 'Retire on full pension then pick up thirty-odd grand a year.'

'Yes, well, you had better not be thinking of doing anything like that,' said Ronald, fixing his friend with a hard look.

'I'd never think any such thing,' said Blizzard. However, the comment had made him consider yet again the idea of early retirement and focusing instead on his new career as a writer. The fact that he had already fallen well behind on the writing for his new book had reminded him that he had drastically underestimated the amount of time it required.'

Ronald noted the inspector's reverie and gave him a suspicious look, but before he could say anything, there was a knock on the office door and David Colley entered the room.

'Sorry to disturb you, gents,' said the sergeant, 'but the Angel of Death has just been on the blower. He wants to know if we can bring the post-mortem on our Mounsey Street guy forward? He wants to do it in half an hour.'

'Why the rush?' asked Blizzard.

'He says to tell you that he's got something important to do at two thirty,' said the sergeant with a deadpan expression on his face.

Blizzard scowled and Colley tried to suppress a laugh. It was typical of the kind of comment which Home Office pathologist Peter Reynolds routinely uttered to irritate the inspector and, as usual, it had the desired effect.

'Cheeky bastard,' muttered Blizzard, getting to his feet. 'He'd better not try it on, though. I really am not in the mood for his nonsense today.'

'What's special about today?' asked Ronald.

Blizzard stalked out of the room and the superintendent and Colley exchanged amused looks. Blizzard's intense dislike of Peter Reynolds was well-known and their ill-tempered encounters had assumed legendary status over the years, the inspector doing little to conceal his loathing for the man and the pathologist taking every opportunity to provoke him.

Colley grinned at the thought of another encounter between them and looked forward to holding court in the canteen afterwards, as was his custom, recounting every sly look and provocative comment to colleagues eager to hear every utterance.

* * *

Post-mortems were held in the mortuary at the city's general hospital and Blizzard's mood was not improved when the detectives entered the room to be met by Reynolds with an expression of devilment on his face and a glint in his eyes. After terse pleasantries had been exchanged between the two men, silence settled on the room as, trying to ignore the stench from the rotting remains, the detectives watched the pathologist begin his examination.

A balding middle-aged man with piggy eyes that gleamed out of a chubby face, Reynolds hummed quietly to himself as he worked. Colley, who did not share Blizzard's antipathy for the pathologist, had always found himself fascinated by the sight of the pathologist's long fingers, encased in white gloves and flickering deftly cross the corpse, and now he assumed his usual position leaning against the wall to view proceedings.

Occasionally, Reynolds glanced across at Blizzard, smiling to himself as he noticed the inspector's impatience growing the longer the examination took.

'Well?' asked the inspector eventually.

'I wouldn't have said so,' said Reynolds. 'In fact, I'd say the opposite. Actually, I can't shake the nagging suspicion that the man you have brought me might be dead.' The pathologist winked at Colley. 'I had to go through seven years of medical school to be able to work that out, you know.'

Blizzard gave a sigh of exasperation then glowered at Colley when he heard the sergeant give a low laugh.

Colley tried to project a professional air as he waited for Blizzard to conduct the questioning of the medical examiner, as usually happened in post-mortems. This time, however, the inspector did not say anything and, as the silence lengthened, Colley found himself in the unusual position of taking the lead.

'We think he may be Asian,' he said as the pathologist returned to his examination of the body and the humming started up again. 'From the hair. What do you think?'

'I think that you're right,' said Reynolds. 'Chinese, or Malaysian, something like that. I doubt I'll be able to be more precise about his nationality from the examination alone but I'll send some samples off. The fire has caused a lot of damage to the fingerprints, leaving only partials, but, you never know, his DNA may be on record somewhere. We might get lucky.'

'Could he be from Singapore?' asked Colley.

'I take it that you are thinking of the two men who owned the factory?' said Reynolds.

'I am,' said Colley. He fished a notebook out of his jacket pocket and flicked over several pages. 'A couple of dodgy characters called Zhang Wei and Fu Li. They went missing a couple of days after the original fire and no one has seen them since. All very suspicious.'

'It is certainly possible that your man was from Singapore but I was talking to Graham Ross before you arrived and he can't find any record of their prints or DNA.' Reynolds gave Blizzard one of his sly looks. 'The Mounsey Street fire is one of your bugbears, is it not, Chief Inspector? Slapdash Western CID investigation at its piss-poor worst, as I recall.'

Blizzard did not reply but satisfied himself by glaring at the pathologist instead.

'Maybe your underling can make a better job of it,' said Reynolds. 'It's good to see the young ones taking over from the old fogeys, is it not? Are you taking things easy? Looking ahead to retirement, perhaps? Would you like me to get you a chair? Maybe you need a sit-down, a man of your age?'

Blizzard did not reply and Colley surreptitiously entered the comment in his notebook for later use; the post-mortem was living up to its promise as a vintage encounter.

Reynolds saw him making the note, chuckled and returned to his examination of the body, doing nothing to hide the fact that he was enjoying himself.

'Any idea on the cause of death?' asked Blizzard.

'It speaks!' exclaimed the pathologist. Noting Blizzard's thunderous expression, he held up his hands in a gesture of mock-surrender. 'I am sorry. It's just that I find that a touch of levity is useful in these kinds of circumstances.'

He beckoned the detectives to approach the examination table.

'And as it goes, I *do* have a good idea of cause of death, as it happens,' he said. 'Your chap was murdered.'

'What makes you say that?' asked Blizzard.

'It's not obvious to the untrained eye. You have to look very carefully to see it, but see those faint scoring marks on the bone? They suggest that he received a number of blows on his arms and one to his throat. I would suggest that it was the one to the throat that killed him. He probably bled to death.'

'What kind of weapon was used?' asked Blizzard.

'I'd say it was a large-bladed knife – or maybe a machete. I think a machete would be the more likely. They can cause an awful lot of damage, as I'm sure you can appreciate – this week of all weeks.'

A vivid image of the scarring on the Rawmarshes' ravaged arms came into Blizzard's mind and he frowned. Having always taught young detectives that there was no such thing as coincidence in murder inquiries, now here he was handling two cases involving the same weapon, having never previously investigated attacks with a machete in a career that stretched back more than twenty years. Blizzard knew that there was no way that the cases could be linked but it was a striking coincidence. Looking at Colley, he sensed that the sergeant had been struck by the same thought.

Blizzard lapsed into a distracted silence and the remainder of the post-mortem took place with little being said.

The pathologist sensed, to his disappointment, that there was little to be gained by trying to provoke a reaction from the inspector with his off-colour humour and lapsed instead into grudging silence.

With the examination complete, Blizzard left the mortuary, not waiting to hold the door open for Colley.

'Was that OK?' asked Reynolds as the sergeant walked towards the door. 'Enough juicy lines to enliven your performance in the canteen, I trust?'

'Very good,' said Colley. 'I particularly liked the "piss-poor investigation" line.'

'We aim to please,' said the pathologist. 'Although I do sometimes feel that my talents are wasted on your boss.'

As the sergeant followed Blizzard into the corridor, he heard the humming start up again. It did not take Colley long to catch up with the inspector and together they headed out of the hospital, appreciating for the second instance that day the fresh air, this time after the sickly atmosphere of the mortuary.

'What do you make of that then?' asked Colley as they approached the car. 'Given that Blizzard's first law of homicide investigation states that there is no such thing as a coincidence in murder inquiries, does that mean we're missing a connection between our dead guy and Charlie Louden?'

'I think we can safely say that this is the exception that proves the rule.'

'And how many times has that been the case?' asked the sergeant.

'Never,' admitted Blizzard. 'But I'm damned if I can see the link.'

* * *

Later that afternoon, Blizzard was sitting in his office, pondering on the problem, when his desk telephone rang.

'It's Ruth Stewart,' said a woman's voice. 'Arthur Ronald says that you want to talk to me about Martin Crumpsall and prescription fraud?'

'Yeah, we do,' said Blizzard. 'His name has cropped up in one of our investigations as well. I imagine it's a coincidence but I want to check it out just to be sure.'

'Actually, it could be a case of Blizzard's first law of homicide investigation,' said Stewart. 'I was going to ring you after I heard about your dead Asian chap anyway. I have this sneaking feeling that we may be investigating the same crime…'

Chapter six

Less than an hour later, an intrigued John Blizzard and Arthur Ronald were sitting in the superintendent's office in the company of Ruth Stewart, a slim woman whose short brown hair was showing the first streaks of grey as she passed into her fifties and whose dark suit with well-defined creases suggested someone who meant business. The Abbey Road officers had been eagerly awaiting the arrival of the former east-side detective chief inspector, keen to discover what linked Charlie Loudon and Martin Crumpsall with the man whose remains lay unclaimed in a hospital mortuary.

'I couldn't believe it when I heard that they are considering releasing Charlie Louden,' said Stewart. She took a sip of tea and looked at Ronald. 'It's way too early to be letting him out, isn't it, Arthur? *Once a psycho, always a psycho*, that's what we always said when we worked on the inquiry, didn't we?'

'We did,' said the superintendent. He glanced at Blizzard. 'As you might have noticed, John, police understanding of mental health has advanced a long way since those days.'

'Clearly,' said Blizzard, with a wry smile.

Stewart shook her head.

'I've never seen as much blood as there was in the Rawmarshes' house that day,' she said. 'And yet there was Charlie Louden sitting in our interview room and acting like nothing had happened.'

She fell silent as she struggled to drag her mind back to the present day. Ronald and Blizzard stayed silent.

'I'm sorry,' she said eventually. 'I have heard it said that no one who ever dealt with Charlie Louden is ever the same, that he is with you for ever. How come you're involved in this, anyway? It's purely a parole board matter, isn't it?'

'The Rawmarshes are worried that Charlie might attack them again,' said Blizzard. 'They want us to argue the case for keeping him inside.'

'Even though the decision is being taken without consulting you?'

'I'm not sure she's thinking things through,' said Blizzard. 'The problem with prison overcrowding has changed everything – and Charlie has not given anyone a reason for keeping him inside.'

'Nevertheless, I don't blame them for being worried,' said Stewart. '*I'd* be worried if I was in their shoes. And Martin Crumpsall, why the interest in him?'

'We are wondering if Charlie has asked him to help him get his hands on his aunt's money by fraudulent means,' said Blizzard. 'What do you think?'

'I've not heard anything like that but I doubt our guys would have taken much notice, anyway. Our unit's remit is very strict – we only deal with NHS cases. For what it's worth, I doubt if Crumpsall will be able to spare much time to help Charlie, given the scale of the scam in which he is involved.'

'The assistant governor at the prison thinks that he's a bit of a fantasist when it comes to his links with organised crime,' said Blizzard.

'That's because we haven't told them much,' said Stewart. She took another sip of tea. 'The place leaks like a colander and we are trying to keep it low-profile. The discovery of the body will change all that, if it's who we think it is.'

'We think it could be one of the guys from Singapore who owned the factory,' said Blizzard. 'I mean, how many Singapore businessmen can there be in Hafton?'

'More than you think,' said Stewart. 'We reckon it could be one of the two Singapore businessman involved in our investigation. How much do you know about them?'

'Only that they have something to do with fake prescriptions,' said Blizzard.

'That's right, and we're not talking about the odd prescription for cough mixture,' said Stewart. 'This is fraud on an industrial scale. It started when we received a tip-off that the GP's practice that had just opened on the new Morton Road housing estate was a front for criminal activity. Our informant reckoned that forty per cent of the prescriptions that they submit are fake. That turned out to be a conservative estimate. It's more like sixty per cent. It's a very lucrative business.'

'How lucrative?' asked Ronald.

'Half a million quid for Morton Road, rising to six mill if you take into account the other practices that the same three men have opened across the region in the past year and a half.'

'Impressive,' said Blizzard. 'And you think that our John Doe is one of them, do you? A falling out among thieves?'

'Something like that. It can't be Sean Gracey because he's Hafton born and bred. He's a genuine GP who went rogue after meeting the others at a medical conference in Amsterdam. Wei Ji Tan and Xavier Lim present themselves as respectable businessmen but they're villains with connections to organised crime in Singapore. They used to make regular visits to the UK but that stopped several months ago and nobody knew where they had gone, and the Singapore Police have not exactly fallen over themselves to help us find them.'

'That's been our experience as well,' said Blizzard.

'Anyway, we assumed that Wei Ji Tan and Xavier Lim had simply got wind of our investigation and gone to ground. Then we heard that Wei Ji Tan had been spotted in a wine bar in Singapore but without any sign of Xavier Lim, which is why we wonder if he might be the body in Mounsey Street.'

'Sounds feasible,' said Blizzard. 'Where does Martin Crumpsall fit into the story?'

'He's brilliant at producing fake documents. He's learned from the mistakes that got him banged up the first time around and now he's immaculate. We're not sure who put him in touch with Ji Tan and Lim but, clearly, someone did and he started working for them the moment he came out of prison. Whoever it was, they'd obviously been planning it for a while.'

'If you know all this, how come you haven't made any arrests?' asked Blizzard. 'Your team has been on the case long enough, surely?'

'Investigations like this take a lot of work,' said Stewart. Even though she had become familiar with Blizzard's direct manner during her years on the force, she still found herself bridling at the accusatory suggestion of his voice. 'Fraud cases are very complex.'

'Yes, but–'

'And I guess I could ask you why Western CID never arrested the guys who set fire to the carpet factory,' said Stewart.

There was a tense silence between the two of them for a few moments then Ronald, knowing that his friend was capable – as the superintendent often observed – of "starting a fight on his own in an empty room," intervened before an argument could flare up.

'What about Charlie Louden?' he asked Stewart. 'Is he anything to do with the scam or simply a friend of Martin Crumpsall?'

Aware why the superintendent had asked the question, Stewart shot him a look of gratitude.

'I'd go for the latter,' she said. 'A friend.'

'In which case, I'll ring the governor and let him know that we won't get in the way of Charlie's parole process. That should make his day.' Ronald gave Blizzard and Stewart a hard look. 'And you two, depending on the ID for our John Doe, you could end up working together, so might I suggest you forget your differences instead of acting like a couple of four-year-olds?'

'Yes, Dad,' said Blizzard.

'OK by me,' said Stewart. She reached into her jacket pocket and produced a photocopy, which she unfolded and placed on the desk, to reveal a photograph of a swarthy young Asian man. 'This is Xavier Lim. It's from his passport application.'

Blizzard looked at the man staring at him out of the page and thought of the decomposing corpse lying on the slab in Peter Reynolds' mortuary.

'He doesn't look like that now,' he said.

Chapter seven

Differences forgotten, Blizzard walked with Ruth Stewart to the front door of the police station then, when she had gone, he headed for Chris Ramsey's office to update the detective inspector on developments, after which he dropped in on the CID squad room where a number of detectives were working at their desks.

'Anything I need to know?' he asked.

'Missing Persons has still not turned anything up,' said a slim, dark-haired young woman in her twenties, who was sitting by the window; Detective Constable Sarah Allatt was the department's youngest, and most recent recruit. 'And we've been putting calls in to contacts in the local Asian community but nobody has given us a name yet.'

'Well, I may have one for you,' said Blizzard.

The comment was greeted with looks of surprise from the other officers.

'See, the old man can still do it,' said Blizzard. 'I have to go out so the DI will brief you on what we have. If anyone wants me, I'll be with the Rawmarshes.'

The inspector looked at Allatt.

'I seem to recall that you said that you know the Rawmarshes?' he said.

'Ever since I was a kid.'

'Do you fancy coming with me, then? I'm not exactly flavour of the month and a friendly face might prove useful.' Blizzard glanced at the wall clock. 'We might just make it, if we're lucky with the traffic.'

A few minutes later, the detectives were sitting in the inspector's car as he guided it on the journey that illustrated the dramatic difference between the two ends of Western Division. Having left behind bedsit-land on the edge of the city centre and passed soulless housing estates, the officers entered a world comprising the affluent tree-lined neighbourhoods that made up Hafton's western fringes. They travelled in awkward silence for a few minutes until Blizzard, who knew that his gruff demeanour could have an intimidating effect on less experienced officers, set out to engage the young detective constable in conversation.

'You've known the Rawmarshes since you were a child then?' he said. 'How come?'

'My mother and Jean go to the same church – St Margaret's on Beacon Lane,' said Allatt. She seemed relieved that her boss had broken the uncomfortable silence. 'Jean has run the youth fellowship for years, including when I was a member, and I still see her at church events. I don't know Robert that well. I'm not sure anyone does, really. He doesn't say much.'

'He doesn't need to,' said Blizzard; he felt a twinge from his hand, where Robert had grasped it.

'Guv?' asked Allatt as she noticed the inspector rubbing his hand.

'Nothing,' said Blizzard. 'Do you know Charlie then?'

'My mum reckons that he and I attended the same church events but I was too young to remember. I know Alec, though.'

'Alec?'

'The Rawmarshes' son. He's got a couple of kids in the youth fellowship.'

'What do they know about their Uncle Charlie?' asked Blizzard, slowing down for a mini-roundabout.

'Whatever it is, it won't have come from their father. As far as Alec is concerned, his cousin does not exist. Charlie has no time for Alec, either, not since Jean gave him a big chunk of the inheritance. I heard that it was thirty grand as a down payment on a house.'

'Very generous. Do you have the address?'

'I'm afraid not. Somewhere near the cricket ground, that's all I heard.'

'Is Alec their only child?'

'He is, and he's also the only one of the kids to have received any of the money. Charlie's always been furious about that. He doesn't talk to his half-brothers and sisters but he still thinks that they deserve something. The money is all he thinks about and his resentment has just kept on growing down the years, apparently.'

'Enough for him to attack the Rawmarshes again?'

'Never say never,' replied Allatt.

'I was afraid you would say that,' replied the inspector. He turned into a wide tree-lined road. 'This is Marris Avenue, isn't it?'

'It is. Their house is the one at the end. The big white one.'

'What's interesting,' said the inspector, 'is that the person that the assistant governor described when we went to see her at the prison this morning is not the person you describe. She said that Charlie's behaviour has been impeccable and that he is very different from when he was jailed. We've certainly heard nothing to suggest that he poses a threat.'

Allatt looked like she was about to say something but appeared to think twice before speaking.

'Is something troubling you?' asked the inspector. 'Spit it out. What are you thinking?'

'I am thinking that no one heard anything to suggest that Charlie would attack the Rawmarshes the first time around, either,' said Allatt.

Blizzard found it a troubling thought but did not offer a comment as he brought the car to a halt outside the detached Edwardian house with its immaculately managed flower beds, large vegetable patch complete with several greenhouses and extensive orchard populated by fruit trees. Having switched off the engine, the inspector sat and surveyed the house for a few moments.

'It's difficult to believe that an act so wicked happened in a place so peaceful, isn't it?' he said.

'It is,' said Allatt. She was not quite sure how to reply; she was not used to such circumspection from her boss. 'They considered moving after the attack. Jean would have gone – she says the house has never been the same – but Robert said that he was not prepared to let Charlie drive them out of their home.'

'It's certainly impressive,' said Blizzard as they got out of the car. He pushed his way through the wrought-iron gates and started walking along the gravel drive leading to the house. 'How come they were able to afford something like this before the inheritance?'

'You know the garden centre on the Mayfield Road Retail Park?'

Blizzard nodded; since the beginning of his relationship with former detective Fee Ellis, he had found himself being increasingly domesticated with weekend visits to garden centres part of his routine – not that he was about to share the information with a rookie detective constable. John Blizzard had a hard-earned reputation to protect.

'Robert started the business with a friend of his,' continued Allatt. 'They were bought out by a multinational which wanted to turn the site into the retail park. I heard that they shared more than a million quid between them.'

'Hence the immaculate garden.'

'Hence the immaculate everything,' said Allatt.

'What do you that mean?'

'You'll see when we go into the house. Original paintings, the best antique furniture, a home cinema, and Robert has three vintage sports cars in the garage out the back. They're not coy about showing off their wealth, either. Robert can often be seen on a Sunday afternoon driving his E-Type Jag around the area with Jean in the passenger seat. I did hear a suggestion that the car is worth more than £70,000.' Allatt noticed the curtain move in the living-room window and caught a glimpse of Jean watching the detectives make their way along the drive. 'We've been spotted.'

'It would appear so,' said Blizzard. 'I take it that Charlie knows about their wealth?'

'He certainly does, and it just infuriates him even more. There was him with nothing and a mother living in a crappy flat and an aunt who wouldn't give him any of her sister's inheritance, even though she didn't need the money.'

'I can see how that would play,' said Blizzard as they neared the house.

'It got even worse. Robert bought out his business partner and moved into timeshares in the Algarve, where he made another shedload of cash. Robert didn't need to work so he spent a lot of his time playing golf – until Charlie went for him with his machete, that is. He couldn't play after that. Nerve damage. Robert never forgave his nephew for taking it away from him.' Allatt noticed the curtain move again in the living room window. 'I don't think Jean minded. She thought he spent too much time on the golf course and wanted him where she could see him. That's what I heard, anyway.'

'You seem to hear a lot of things,' said Blizzard. 'Welcome to CID, Constable!'

Allatt grinned and Blizzard pressed the doorbell. The door was opened by Jean, who gave Allatt a welcoming smile which faded when she looked at Blizzard's solemn expression.

'I take it you've come with bad news?' she said.

'I'd rather not discuss it on the doorstep,' said Blizzard.

Jean led the way down the hallway into a large, sunlit lounge where her husband was sitting on one of the armchairs, reading the *Financial Times*. He ignored the detectives.

'I'll make us a pot of tea,' said Jean.

She went into the kitchen and they could hear the sound of crockery being removed from shelves. Blizzard looked round the living room and saw what Allatt meant about the couple having bought the very best for their home – everything was high quality. With Robert remaining silent behind his newspaper, conversation only resumed when Jean reappeared, carrying a tray of Royal Worcester bone china teacups, a teapot and a plate of biscuits.

'Have you seen Charlie yet?' she asked as she poured the tea and handed round the cups.

'Seen, yes,' said Blizzard as he and Allatt sat down on the sofa. 'Spoken to, no. The governor would not let us talk to him.'

'Did he say why?' asked Jean as she poured the last of the tea and sat down on an armchair. 'Although I can guess.'

'He's worried that we will try to prevent the release.'

'But I sense that you won't?'

'Not as it stands. We've heard nothing to suggest that Charlie plans to attack you and, without that, our argument is very weak. According to headquarters, sending a letter setting out our view that Charlie's release would have to be carefully handled is as far as we wish to go.'

'And I suspect it would achieve little if I still tried to persuade you otherwise?' she said through pursed lips. 'We'd just keep going round in circles, wouldn't we?'

'I imagine that you're right,' said the inspector.

With little more to say, the detectives finished their tea and left. Jean followed them into the hallway.

'You said you saw Charlie,' she said as she went past them and opened the front door. 'How did he look?'

'Old,' said the inspector.

'We all look old,' said Jean. She gave Allatt a hug. 'Nice to see you, dear.'

'And you,' said Allatt. 'I only wish it could be in happier circumstances.'

'At least you tried, love,' said Jean. 'Keep telling yourself that.'

The detectives had just walked through the gates when a car pulled up on the roadside and a smart, clean-shaven and casually dressed man with neatly cropped brown hair got out of the vehicle.

'Alec?' said Blizzard, glancing at Allatt.

She nodded.

'Chief Inspector,' said Alec as he walked over to them. 'I hope that you have been delivering some good news for my parents, although I suspect not?'

'We have no reason to intervene,' said Blizzard.

'But Charlie's as disturbed as the day he was sent to prison. Surely, you can see that?' Alec looked at Allatt. 'You've told him, haven't you, Sarah?'

'What either of us thinks is irrelevant,' said Blizzard. 'He has done nothing to send up the emergency flares.'

'Yes, well, as their son—'

'I have no intention of discussing this any further,' said Blizzard. 'I'm sorry, Alec, but the matter is closed.'

And with that, he walked towards his car. Once the detectives were in the vehicle, Allatt said, 'He's just worried about his parents. He's a decent lad.'

'I'm sure he is,' said Blizzard. 'But if I had to worry about every decent person…'

Chapter eight

Early the next afternoon, Blizzard was sitting at his desk, staring morosely at his computer screen as he tried to concentrate on completing the report that Arthur Ronald had asked him to produce about the reduction in burglaries in the Western CID area. Blizzard was proud about the turnaround of crime but detested writing reports, so he was relieved when the superintendent strode into his office. The relief did not last long as Ronald held up a copy of the local newspaper.

'You seen this?' he asked.

'Do I want to?'

'Not really,' said Ronald.

He laid the newspaper on the desk and Blizzard stared glumly at the front-page article, the main section of which broke the news that Charlie Louden was likely to be released, with the story published under a large 'exclusive' banner. The article drew the reader's attention to page 3 with the headline:

Why will no one listen to us? Victims' plaintive plea

Blizzard sighed and flicked to page 3 to see an article featuring an interview with Jean and Robert Rawmarsh, accompanied by a library picture of the couple in their garden, above another file picture of the prison governor and one of a curmudgeonly John Blizzard, who clearly did not want to be photographed.

'They only use that picture because they know that I hate it,' he said.

'Forget the picture,' said Ronald. 'Did Jean not mention that she had talked to the newspaper when you saw her?'

'No, she didn't.' Blizzard flicked back to the front page. 'There doesn't seem to be a quote from us?'

'There's not one from the prison or the parole board, either,' said Ronald. 'According to the press office, the editor was worried that since it's such a sensitive issue, one of us might try and get an injunction to stop them publishing the story, so decided not to ask us for a comment. Our legal people are talking to their lawyer and we can issue a rebuttal on your behalf, if you want?'

'What's the point?' said Blizzard. He looked at the front page again. 'It's true, isn't it? We *have* ignored their plea for help. The journalists are only doing their job.'

'OK, out with it,' said Ronald. 'What have you done with the real John Blizzard? I assume that you'll want us to pay a ransom for his return? Well, you can forget it because we don't want him back.'

Blizzard laughed and Ronald left the office, wondering how long his friend's good mood would last. Not long, as it turned out, because the inspector's state of mind darkened steadily throughout the afternoon as more and more colleagues called in to his office to draw his attention to the article. Each one received a shorter response than the last.

Not normally known as a nine-to-five man, Blizzard found himself increasingly frequently looking up from the burglary report in order to glance at the wall clock. The moment the hands ticked past 5pm, he switched off his laptop, reached his jacket down from its peg and rang Fee to tell her he was on his way home. Within a quarter of an hour of leaving Abbey Road Police Station, he was driving through the area in which the Rawmarshes lived. With the evening rush-hour traffic growing ever lighter as he approached Hafton's outer western fringes, the car left the city and entered the rural flatlands beyond.

It did not take the inspector long to enter the village where he lived with Fee and Mikey in a detached modern house. Fee, younger than Blizzard, a slim woman in her twenties with short blonde hair, had met the inspector when she was transferred to Western CID. Having taken maternity leave to have their son, she decided not to return and instead secured a post at a security company in the city, which offered the flexible hours that allowed her to take Mikey to and from nursery. She was in the kitchen preparing tea when Blizzard walked into the kitchen. Mikey, who was playing with his Thomas the Tank Engine toys on the floor, gave an excited squeal when he saw him.

'I bet you wish everyone was as pleased to see you,' said Fee with a smile as Blizzard hoisted the toddler into the air then brought him swooping back to the floor. Mikey held up his hands, demanding that his father do it again. 'I saw that Jean Rawmarsh had a go at you in the newspaper.'

She slid the pasta bake out of the oven, checked how much more time it required and put it back.

'A bit unfair, I thought,' she said.

'Yes, well, thankfully she's not my problem anymore,' said Blizzard. He knelt down, scooped up James the Red Engine and sent the toy careering towards Mikey, who laughed with delight when it collided with the table leg. Blizzard winced as his knee cracked when he straightened up. 'What kind of a day did you have, anyway?'

'Not too bad,' said Fee. She tipped carrots into a pan of water and turned up the heat. 'And I've got something that may well improve yours. Are you still trying to find out if the Singaporeans own the carpet factory in Mounsey Street?'

'We are, but we're not getting anywhere. I sent Jenny Carr to see the city council's estates department this afternoon but they didn't know who owns it.'

'Actually, they do know,' said Fee. 'From what I hear, it *is* the original owners from Singapore.'

'And how, pray, would you know that?'

'Before I tell you, you have to promise not to tell anyone where the information came from,' said Fee. 'It's highly confidential and you'll get me sacked if it gets back to me.'

'You have my word. So, what's happening?'

'A major redevelopment of the area,' said Fee. 'I knew that we had the contract to carry out night-time perimeter checks for a couple of derelict sites at the other end of Mounsey Street, but I did not know that the same man had bought them and that he's about to purchase the old carpet factory as well. I was in with our sales director this afternoon when he rang up, asking if he could extend our checks when the sale went through.'

'Why on earth would he want a load of derelict factories?'

'He's a property agent who is working with a developer who wants to create a retail park on the site; he's already signed an agreement with a supermarket and is in talks with a DIY chain. Once the carpet factory deal goes through, the developer will submit a planning application. It's a big project, John. Our sales director reckons the final budget will be north of five million.'

'It's about time somebody did something like that – as long as they respect the heritage of the area,' said Blizzard. 'I could do with talking to the agent. He could be very useful. I don't suppose he is from Singapore, by any chance?'

'I don't know the names of anyone involved, I am afraid, it's all very hush-hush, but our sales director says that he's local. I did not want to push it, in case it looked suspicious, but the city council's chief executive is handling this personally so I'd go to see her, rather than the estates department. Miranda is new in post and takes the view that the project will silence those male colleagues who keep saying that the job is too big for her. I am sure that she can put you in touch with the agent.'

'You'd have hoped that he would have approached us himself,' said Blizzard. He glanced down as Mikey, tired of being ignored by his father, tugged at his trouser leg and pointed to Gordon, the green railway engine. The inspector knelt down and pushed the toy towards his son, hard enough to make it veer off course and also plough into the table leg, bringing forth another squeal of delight from the toddler. His father stood up gingerly lest his knee protest again. 'Given that he's trying to buy a building where a murder victim was found.'

'He told our sales director that he knows that you will come knocking on his door sometime but that there's not much point in talking to you until he has bought the property.' Fee emptied a tin of sweetcorn into a pan. 'Of course, there is another possibility.'

'Which is?'

'That he has got something to hide.'

'Like what?' asked Blizzard.

'How about a motive for murder?' said Fee. 'Given everything that is riding on the plan, anyone who got in the way could well find themselves dead and buried at the bottom of a pile of wooden pallets, could they not?'

'Now there's a thought,' said Blizzard. 'Have you ever considered a career in CID?'

'I did,' said Fee, 'but I read in the paper that the guy who runs it is not very pleasant…'

Chapter nine

The evening passed by without event and the couple headed upstairs just after 10.30pm, where, after reading for a while, Fee fell asleep first, as was usually the case. Blizzard drifted off shortly before 11.30pm only for the insistent ringing of the bedside phone to wake him just before 1am. Always a light sleeper, he opened his eyes immediately. Next to him, Fee gave a groan of protest and pulled the covers up over her head.

'If this wakes Mikey up…' she said.

They listened for sounds from the toddler's bedroom but, to their relief, he did not stir. Blizzard reached for the phone on the bedside table, glancing at the digital clock's luminous readout as he did so. He sighed; a call at that time of night was going to be bad news.

'This had better be good,' he muttered grumpily into the receiver.

'I'm sorry to ring you at such an hour, sir,' said a woman's voice. 'This is Control. Inspector Sun asked us to contact you.'

'Why? What's happened?'

'The police have been called out to Marris Avenue,' said the control room operator. 'The Rawmarshes have reported an intruder in their garden and Inspector Sun thought that you might want to join him there, given your recent dealings with the family.'

'Tell him I'm on my way,' said Blizzard with a sigh.

A few minutes later, he was in his car and making a call as he began the journey back into the city.

'Hello, Hafton Prison,' said a man's voice. 'How can I help you?'

'This is DCI Blizzard, from Western CID. Can I check if one of your inmates is still with you, please?'

'And who exactly might that be?' asked the man suspiciously. 'Because we're not exactly in the habit of mislaying our inmates, you know.'

'My enquiry is about Charlie Louden.'

'If this is some sort of practical joke, I am pretty sure that Chief Inspector Blizzard will not be...'

'It's no practical joke,' said Blizzard. 'It's a genuine call.'

There was silence at the other end of the line for a few moments.

'Hang on a minute,' said the prison officer.

Blizzard could hear him talking in muffled tones to someone on what sounded like the radio, before he came back on the line.

'I am putting you through to Maureen Rodgers,' he said. 'She's the duty officer tonight.'

The assistant governor came onto the phone.

'Am I to assume that you have lost control of your senses, Chief Inspector?' she asked. Unlike the irritation displayed by her colleague, she sounded genuinely curious. 'I'm told that it happens to everyone who deals with Charlie Louden eventually.'

'You could well be right,' said Blizzard.

'Why would you want to know if we've still got him?' said Rodgers. 'Of course, we still have him. This is a prison, in case you hadn't noticed.'

'There's a flap on at the Rawmarshes' house. An intruder has been spotted in the garden and I wanted to check that the outcome of his parole hearing was not brought forward without anyone knowing.'

'I wish it had been – it would stop the press bombarding us with calls, but no, Charlie is still with us. In fact, I've just been checking his wing – that's where I was when you rang.'

'Sorry to have troubled you,' said Blizzard.

'It's alright, John. Hopefully, your intruder will turn out to be a false alarm.'

'Hopefully,' said Blizzard.

* * *

Twenty minutes later, the inspector brought his car to a halt outside the Rawmarshes' home in Marris Avenue. He got out of the vehicle and stood for a few moments as he watched the uniformed officers search the garden, illumination provided by a couple of spotlights attached to the house, which cast shadows where the inspector could easily believe someone might be hiding. Pinpricks of torchlight further down the road told Blizzard that a search of neighbouring gardens was also under way. As he started to walk up the drive towards the house, an officer in his mid-thirties headed towards him. Blizzard had not met Inspector Chen Sun since his arrival in Hafton several weeks previously but recognised him from the picture released by the press office. Sun had been the subject of intense interest from the local media following his recruitment as the force's first Asian officer in response to a report by the Inspectorate of Constabulary which had highlighted poor diversity among the local workforce.

'Pleased to meet you, sir,' said Sun as the two men shook hands. 'I'm sorry to call you out at this ungodly hour, but I thought you'd want to know what's been happening.'

'It's much appreciated,' said Blizzard as they walked towards the house. 'And what exactly has been happening?'

'Control received a call just before midnight from Robert Rawmarsh. He said that he's not been sleeping well and got up to make himself a cup of tea, which is when he looked out of the kitchen window and saw a figure all in black hiding in the pergola at the bottom of the garden.'

'Does he know who it was?'

Sun shook his head.

'Have you found anything to suggest that he actually did see someone?' asked Blizzard as the officers walked up the side path and into the back garden.

'Not so far. I've got officers checking the other houses in the road as well but they've not come up with anything. If you ask me' – Sun lowered his voice as they rounded the corner of the house and saw Robert standing on the back step, watching the officers conduct their search – 'all this stuff about the parole hearing has turned him twitchy and he imagined it. His wife looked out of the bedroom window when she heard him cry out but she didn't see anyone.'

'Charlie Louden gets to everyone sooner or later,' said Blizzard, recalling his conversation with Maureen Rodgers a few minutes previously. 'He gets into your head… or at least that's the myth that has grown up around him. It's what happens when someone notorious like him is not seen for sixteen years.'

'It's easily done,' said Sun. 'I'd be a bit nervy if I were him.'

Noticing the two officers deep in conversation, and guessing what they were saying about him, Robert walked over to them with the kind of expression on his face that suggested that he was prepared to argue the point.

'I didn't imagine it,' he said in a voice which dared them to defy him. 'There was definitely someone there.'

'That's why we are searching the area,' said Sun in a respectful voice – he was not about to let an argument begin. 'We take these things very seriously. It's better to be safe than sorry, is it not, Chief Inspector?'

'It is,' said Blizzard. 'Did you recognise the man, Robert?'

'No, but he was staring at the house. It gave me a right turn, I can tell you.'

'Well, it looks like he's not here now,' said Blizzard. 'But I'll send a couple of forensics officers up in the morning so they can do a check in daylight. Just to be sure.'

'And although my guys will be on their way now, I'll make sure that patrols go past the house as often as they can for the rest of the night,' said Sun. 'Hopefully, it might make you feel a bit more secure. You know how to get hold of us if you need to.'

Robert nodded and went back into the house, and they heard the sound of him triple-locking the back door. Sun accompanied Blizzard down the gravel path in the direction of the detective's car.

'How are you settling in?' asked Blizzard. 'I know that the force has not exactly proved itself to be a shining beacon when it comes to diversity.'

'Actually, it's not as bad as some people might think; it's more that some officers are stuck in the 1950s, particularly the older men. I've come from a force with officers from all over the world, where everyone gets along, but here?' Sun shook his head. 'Don't get me wrong, it's not out-and-out racist behaviour, just a case of not quite knowing how to work together.'

'Hopefully, it will improve,' said Blizzard as they arrived at his car. 'Actually, I'm glad I've met you. I was going to give you a bell anyway. Do you have any contacts in Singapore?'

'Oh, aye,' said Sun. 'Loads of them.'

'Really? That's great because I could really do with–'

'Of course I don't!' exclaimed Sun. 'What is this? Because we are foreign, everyone knows everyone? Well, for your information, I grew up in a small rural village where half the people have never even visited Beijing –

which is only five miles away – because it's too far for the goats to walk.'

'I'm sorry, I didn't mean it to sound like that,' said Blizzard quickly. He looked at him in horror. 'It's just that I thought…'

Sun burst out laughing.

'The look on your face,' he said. 'I'm just pulling your leg. It's one of the joys of coming to a force like this. Folks panic when they think they have said something racist. I do apologise, it was out of order.'

Blizzard gave a rueful smile.

'I guess we have much to learn,' he said.

'Maybe,' said Sun. 'Actually, I do have a contact in the Singapore police. He's a detective with the Organised Crime Unit over there. I met him when he came over to the UK to attend an inspectors' conference last year and we kept in touch. Why?'

'Because one of our investigations is pointing in the direction of Singapore but their police are not being particularly helpful. Someone with an *in* over there may come in handy.'

'I'm sure he'd be happy to help,' said Sun, 'when he's stopped trying to impress you, that is. He's absolutely desperate to land a job in the UK. He's got it into his head that it's some kind of utopia.'

'I've heard Hafton called many things, in my time, but never that,' said Blizzard.

Sun chuckled.

'I tried to tell him that but he wouldn't listen,' he said.

A car pulled up outside the house. Alec Rawmarsh got out and walked towards the officers.

'Mum rang me,' he explained. 'Have you found the intruder?'

'Not yet,' said Blizzard.

'It's not like Dad to imagine it,' said Alec. 'What do you think?'

'I'm saying nothing,' said Blizzard. 'The last thing I want is another story about me splashed all over the local rag.'

'Yes, I'm sorry about that,' said Alec. 'I told Mum that it wasn't a great idea but she has been under a lot of pressure since the news broke about the parole hearing. The same goes for Dad. It could be that he did see someone, mind.'

'Like who?' asked Sun.

'Maybe it's down to Charlie,' said Alec, 'getting one of his pals to scare my parents ahead of his release. He's always liked playing mind games, ever since he was a teenager. Getting someone to stand in the garden is the kind of thing he would do if he thought it might help him to get his hands on that blessed inheritance.'

'Maybe,' said Blizzard – and his thoughts turned to Martin Crumpsall.

Chapter ten

'So *was* there anyone in the Rawmarshes' garden?' asked Ronald as he looked across his desk at a bleary-eyed John Blizzard the next morning.

'Probably not,' said Blizzard. He took a sip of tea – extra-strong, plenty of sugar – in the hope that it would revive him. 'It certainly wasn't Charlie Louden. I checked with the prison last night and he's still an inmate.'

'Why would you do that?' said the superintendent in surprise. 'I thought if they decided to release him it wouldn't be until Monday?' Has it changed? It's a bit naughty if it was and no one told us.'

'No, the parole panel announcement is still scheduled for Monday.' Blizzard frowned. 'I just felt that it was something I had to do. To be honest, I can't explain it. In the cold light of day, it sounds ridiculous.'

'You don't need to explain it to me,' said Ronald. 'I'd be prepared to bet that there's no one who has had dealings with Charlie Louden who wouldn't say the same thing about him. Something happens and, suddenly, there he is, in your head again. And both Robert and his wife have been on edge since they heard about the hearing, haven't they? That can't exactly have helped. Hopefully, things will quieten down and we can–'

The superintendent was prevented from completing the sentence by the ringing of his desk phone.

'On the other hand…' said the inspector. He picked up the kettle as Ronald took the call. 'Top-up?'

'Please,' said Ronald. 'Hello, Detective Superintendent Ronald. Alison, long time no speak. How are you?'

Blizzard headed out to fill the kettle from the tap in the kitchen along the corridor and returned to make them both mugs of tea as Ronald continued to talk to the caller, his expression growing wearier the longer the conversation went on. Eventually, the superintendent replaced the receiver and sighed.

'Sorry, old son, but you'll not get the chance to drink your tea,' he said as Blizzard placed the mugs on the desk and sat down. 'Did you get the gist of that?'

'Something about the Rawmarshes staging a protest outside the prison?'

'That's right. That was Alison Marriott, one of the east-side uniform inspectors. The Rawmarshes and some of their supporters are holding a sit-down protest at the entrance to the car park. They've blocked the bypass and refuse to budge. Jean won't talk to any of the uniforms and things are getting ugly. Nothing has moved on the bypass for forty-five minutes and the traffic is backed up to the old Margrave Dock. There's a lot of angry drivers, apparently.'

'I'll bet there are,' said Blizzard. 'Why doesn't Alison get her lot to arrest them? It would make the others get out of the way pretty damn quick if they saw Jean being carted away in the back of a police van.'

'Headquarters think it would be bad PR, given that she is a victim. You know how sensitive the issue is, John, especially after the article yesterday. I'm already hearing on the QT that several senior officers are trying to make trouble for you over Jean's claim that you did not do enough to support her when she came in to see you.'

'The same people that are always trying to cause me problems, I assume? The same people, I'll wager, whose only response when they heard about the possibility of Charlie being granted parole was to send a crappy letter and are now looking for someone to blame? Well, as usual, they're not being fair, I did everything I...' Blizzard's voice tailed off and he gave Ronald a suspicious look. 'Hang on, what do you mean I won't be able to drink my tea?'

'Headquarters want you to try to persuade Jean to call her protest off before things get out of hand.'

'Why me?' protested Blizzard. 'She'll hardly give me the time of day. Besides, it's a problem for HQ, surely?'

'They beg to differ. They think that Jean might be more amenable to ending the protest if you show her that you are taking her complaint seriously. And it would be good PR for the force. Just have a go, will you?'

'I'll use my world-famous diplomatic skills, shall I?' said Blizzard, standing up and heading for the door. 'Sweet-talk her?'

'God forbid,' said Ronald. 'Just do your best.'

Blizzard gave a wry smile and headed out into the corridor where Graham Ross had just emerged from the CID squad room.

'The television is on, if you want to watch the Rawmarshes' protest,' said the forensics chief. 'Sky News are covering it live.'

'Never underestimate the resourcefulness of that woman,' said Blizzard. 'Did your people get a chance to examine her garden?'

'Yes, but they didn't find anything. I reckon you're right, guv. Robert's getting paranoid in his old age.'

'Aren't we all?' said Blizzard.

He continued on his way to the squad room, where he spent a few moments watching the television coverage of the protest then looked across at Sarah Allatt, who was sitting at her desk at the window, bringing her notes up to date.

'Do you fancy accompanying me on a job?' he asked. 'Give you a break from the dreaded paperwork?'

'Do I ever!' replied the young detective constable. She looked at the television. 'Is it to do with the protest?'

'It is, yes. I'd like you to take a run up to the prison with me. Headquarters want me to persuade Jean to stop all this silliness. I very much doubt that she will take much notice of me, but she might just listen to what you say. She clearly has a soft spot for you.'

'It's worth a try, I suppose,' said Allatt. She stood up and slipped into her coat. 'But I wouldn't hold out too much hope. From what I've heard, the nearer we get to the parole hearing announcement, the more she and Robert are losing their grip on things.'

'Charlie Louden certainly has a remarkable knack for causing trouble, for a man who has not actually done anything,' said Blizzard.

* * *

The inspector's BMW was two miles from the prison when the traffic on the bypass ground to a halt. Blizzard steered the car onto the hard shoulder and, after being waved through by a couple of traffic officers, his vehicle soon reached the protestors, who had spread out to block both lanes of the bypass.

Many of the people from the cars caught up in the action were out of their vehicles and several of them were shouting abuse at the protestors, of which there were more than fifty, most of whom appeared to be retired. Some were carrying placards, bearing the words *Why will they not listen to us?*, repeating the headline from the previous day's edition of the local newspaper, and the event was being recorded by press photographers and television film crews, whose attention was focused on a fierce argument between a resolute Jean Rawmarsh and an exasperated uniformed officer. It was immediately clear to Blizzard that Inspector

Alison Marriott was coming off second best in her attempts to calm the situation.

Blizzard sighed, brought the BMW to a halt close to the car park entrance and cut the engine. He was just about to get out of the vehicle when his mobile phone rang. Number unknown. He took the call.

'DCI Blizzard,' he said. 'Who is this, please?'

'I am the PA for Miranda Goldsworthy, the chief executive of the city council,' said a woman's voice. 'I have a message that you wish to talk to her? Something about Mounsey Street?'

'Thank you for ringing back so quickly,' said Blizzard. 'I am rather hoping that she can help us with our investigation into the death of the man in the old carpet factory. Can I fix a time to see her, please? As soon as possible.'

'You will have to wait your turn,' said the PA, in a tone of voice that suggested that the conversation was taking her away from more important matters. There was a brief pause, during which Blizzard could hear her fingers tapping on the keyboard. 'But if you insist, I can squeeze you in on the twenty-seventh. Would 3pm be OK?'

'The twenty-seventh!' exclaimed the inspector. 'That's ten days away! I was rather hoping to do it this afternoon.'

'Oh, no, that won't be possible.' The PA seemed horrified at the inspector's suggestion. 'That won't be possible, at all. The twenty-seventh is the first vacant slot in Ms Goldsworthy's diary. You're lucky she can do it then – it's only available because someone has cancelled.'

'You are aware that this is a murder inquiry, are you not?'

'I am, Chief Inspector, and I wish I could be more accommodating, I really do,' said the PA, who sounded like she didn't wish any such thing. 'However, as I am sure you can appreciate, council chief executives are extremely busy.'

'And detective chief inspectors aren't?' said Blizzard. 'I take it that she would be able to find time to appear in court if I charged her with obstructing our investigation?'

'What?'

'You heard me,' said the inspector.

As the PA considered his comment, he glanced at Allatt and rolled his eyes.

The young constable grinned.

Blizzard noticed that the uniformed inspector was still in conversation with Jean Rawmarsh.

'Well,' said Blizzard. 'What's it to be? And don't think that I won't do it, either, because I really am not in the mood to be mucked about. Unless I get to see the chief executive this afternoon, I *will* arrest her.'

Blizzard could hear the PA talking to someone in muffled tones.

'Two o'clock,' she said icily, having finished her conversation. 'Ask for her at City Hall reception and I will come down to get you.'

'Looking forward to it already,' said Blizzard. 'Get the kettle on.'

There was the sound of the PA angrily slamming the phone down.

'What's wrong with these people, Sarah?' said Blizzard. He looked at Allatt and shook his head. 'The whole world has gone stark raving mad!'

The constable grinned again.

Blizzard switched his attention to Jean Rawmarsh, who was still haranguing Alison Marriott, angrily jabbing a finger in the uniformed inspector's direction.

'Talking of which…' he said.

The detectives got out of the car and Marriott broke away from the argument with Jean and walked over to meet them, a look of relief on her face.

'Boy, am I glad to see you, sir,' she said. She lowered her voice so that Jean could not overhear what she was saying. 'The bloody woman is off her fucking head. She just won't listen to me.'

'I very much doubt that she'll listen to me either,' said Blizzard. He gestured towards the protestors. 'And, what's more, I've got the placards to prove it.'

As he was speaking, Robert Rawmarsh passed by.

'Can't you talk some sense into her?' asked Blizzard.

'Why should I?' replied Robert. 'We have as much a right as anyone to be heard. Those oil protestors do this kind of thing all the time, don't they?'

He walked away before Blizzard was able to reply. Blizzard looked at Allatt.

'See if Jean will talk to you, will you, Sarah?' he said. 'Tell her that I'm prepared to arrest her, if this carries on much longer. Her and her husband – and all the others, for that matter.'

'Hang on,' protested Marriott. 'The word from headquarters was very clear, that we should not, under any circum–'

'I know what the word was from headquarters, Alison, but if they want me to do a job, then they will have to let me do it my way,' said Blizzard.

'Yes, well I want nothing to do with it,' said Marriott flatly. 'You're on your own on this one, John.'

Blizzard noticed the anxious expression on Allatt's face.

'And you needn't look so worried,' he said. 'I'm the one who's given the order and you'll not get into trouble for doing what a senior officer tells you to do. Trust me.'

'If you're sure…' said Allatt.

'I am. Just go and talk to her, will you? Lay it on thick – the good cop, bad cop act, yeah?'

Allatt nodded unhappily and walked up to Jean, who tightened her grip on her placard and gave the young constable a disapproving look.

'Here to do Blizzard's dirty work for him, are you, Sarah?' she said. 'I thought better of you.'

'I'm just doing my job, Jean,' said Allatt. 'As is the chief inspector. He has been ordered to get the road cleared and wants you to know that if this carries on much longer, he'll arrest everyone here.'

'The other inspector didn't arrest us,' said Jean. 'She had been told that it will not look good.'

'Yes, well, John Blizzard is not like other officers. Surely, you've worked that out by now. Anyway, don't you think that you've made your point? It's even live on Sky News. What have you got to gain by carrying on?' There was a loud shout of profanities from a driver caught in the traffic jam. 'In fact, if this goes on any longer, you'll undo all your good work. You'll lose the public's sympathy. Can you not see that?'

Jean thought for a few moments and nodded.

'I suppose you're right,' she said.

* * *

Ten minutes later, the protestors had begun to disperse and the traffic was beginning to move again. Having stayed to make sure that the last of the group was leaving the area, Blizzard and Allatt headed for Abbey Road Police Station. As ever, bad news beat the inspector back and he walked into his office to find two Post-it notes placed on his computer by Arthur Ronald. Blizzard studied them for a few moments, sighed and walked down the corridor to his friend's office, where he held up the Post-its.

'Two?' he said affably. 'I mean, even for you, Arthur–'

'You've only been out for an hour and you've caused mayhem,' said the superintendent, ignoring his friend's attempt at levity. 'First, I get a complaint from the chief executive's PA at the city council saying that you threatened to arrest her boss and, no sooner had I put the phone down on her, than I get a call from Jean Rawmarsh, banging on about the European Court of Human Rights and complaining that you threatened to arrest her, when I thought that I had made it crystal clear that you were to do no such thing!'

Blizzard sat down.

'But apart from that, everyone's happy, are they?' he said.

Chapter eleven

It had often been John Blizzard's experience that people of influence tended to be more relaxed than the underlings who thought their job was to protect their employers. This was definitely the case with Miranda Goldsworthy, decided the inspector within moments of being ushered into the spacious first-floor office of the recently appointed city council chief executive. A slim, blonde, fashionably dressed woman, her rapid rise to the top job at the age of just thirty-one had, concluded the inspector, given her an inner strength that communicated itself clearly as she sat in one of the leather armchairs by the window and surveyed him with faint amusement over the top of her silver, thick-rimmed spectacles. For his part, Blizzard relished a challenge when it involved people who so obviously believed that they were in control of the situation. The inspector sensed that he was going to enjoy this.

'You have been upsetting my PA,' said Goldsworthy with a faint smile. 'You really do not want to do that, if you know what's good for you. They can be a fearsome proposition when they're upset, can PAs. You probably gathered that from the icy reception you received when you arrived.'

'I did get that impression,' said the inspector. 'It was difficult not to, really.'

'She means well.' Goldsworthy picked up the teapot from the low glass table between them, poured their drinks and handed the inspector his cup. 'I must apologise for not having any biscuits. The opposition objected to the cuts proposed in our budget and forced through a motion last week, demanding that we reduce the amount we spend on biscuits. A petty-minded thing to do, I am sure you will agree. I do rather like a custard cream. What about you?'

'I'm not sure I have an opinion.'

'And you did not come here to talk about biscuits, anyway,' said the chief executive. She still seemed to be amused by their encounter, which she appeared not to be taking at all seriously. 'You have much more important matters to talk about, I imagine.'

'I certainly don't have much time to waste on discussing biscuits,' said Blizzard, who had nevertheless decided to give her a little more time before he seized control of the conversation and revealed what he knew about the Mounsey Street redevelopment.

The chief executive changed his mind for him, by standing up and gesturing to the door.

'Well, I am afraid to say that you are wasting *my* time,' she said, in a clipped business-like tone of voice that made it clear that she had not appreciated his comment. 'As my PA told you on the phone, I am very busy, and the council does not have anything to do with Mounsey Street or know anything about the unfortunate man whose body was found in the carpet factory, so might I suggest that you finish your tea and leave so that we can both get on with our days?'

'You're probably right,' said Blizzard, draining his cup and standing up. His next words were delivered in a deliberately casual tone of voice, as if he did not fully appreciate the import of what he was saying; it was a tactic he had used for years to catch people off-guard. 'Although before I go, I suppose I should check if the businessman behind the redevelopment of the Mounsey Street site knows anything. Can you put me in touch with him, please?'

Goldsworthy looked at him in astonishment.

'How on earth do you know about that?' said exclaimed. 'It's supposed to be confidential.'

'Ah, now there's a word that tends not to feature in many police officers' vocabulary,' replied Blizzard; he was enjoying the impact that his revelation was having on her. 'Suffice to say that I know what's being proposed and where it's being proposed, but I don't know who is behind it.'

'And how, may ask, did you find out?'

'Let's worry about that another time, shall we?' said Blizzard. His voice had an edge. 'Sit down, please. For now, this is a murder investigation and I need to know who is behind the development.'

'Why?' she said, sitting down as instructed and trying to sound as if she was still in control but clearly, inwardly cursing herself for being so easily wrong-footed by the detective. 'I am sure that the body has nothing to do with the redevelopment. And as for the businessman, he is most insistent that his name should not be made public; at least, not until the time is right, and that will not be for several weeks, if not months.'

'Well, I need to know now,' said Blizzard.

'And I can't tell you. This project will create upwards of four hundred and fifty badly needed jobs for this city and I, for one, will not do anything to jeopardise that. I am sure you understand.'

'What I understand is that a man's body has been found on the site,' said Blizzard, his tone of voice hardening all the time. 'That he was very probably murdered there, and that he has a family somewhere, possibly in Singapore, who do not know what has happened to him.'

'What makes you think that he's from Singapore?' asked Goldsworthy.

'Because the last-known owners of the factory were a couple of sharp operators by the names of Zhang Wei and Fu Li, from Singapore. One of the theories we are investigating is that the body could be one of them.'

'I wouldn't have thought that to be the case. According to the businessman we have been talking to, they have not been seen in the UK for a long time.'

'I need to talk to him anyway. He has a lot of explaining to do. His name, please.'

Goldsworthy appeared as if she was going to continue to argue the point but the detective's stern expression persuaded her otherwise; she clearly knew when she was beaten. She had probably assumed that when Blizzard told her PA that morning that he was prepared to arrest her, it was purely for effect but, having now met him, she would no longer be sure.

'OK, OK,' she said with a sigh. 'He's called Alec Maynard.'

'And what do you know about him?'

'Not much, really. Mid to late thirties and his company is Maynard Associates but he was reluctant to give away any details about himself, the address on his business card is a PO box and the phone number is a mobile. In fact, Alec Maynard is a bit of a mystery man…'

* * *

'No, he's not,' said Sarah Allatt, when the inspector returned to Abbey Road Police Station and ran the name past the officers in the CID squad room. 'In fact, you've met him.'

'I have?' said Blizzard. 'Pray do tell, because the council's chief executive did not seem to know much. What do you know about him?'

'That he's another coincidence. Alec Maynard is the Rawmarshes' son.'

Blizzard stared at her.

'Are you sure?' he said.

'Maynard was Jean's maiden name. Alec used to work with his father in the property business but found that the name Rawmarsh was a distraction for some of their clients. Robert was not that bothered but Alec saw it differently. Apparently, it came to a head a few months after Robert retired and Alec took over the business full-time. He was closing in on a large property deal – it would have been the first he had signed since taking over, proof that anything his father could do, so could Alec – when the developer found about the link with Charlie Louden and decided it would be bad for his company's reputation if it became public knowledge. The deal collapsed, costing Alec a lot of money. He changed his surname by deed poll.'

Chris Ramsey walked into the room.

'Have you heard this?' said Blizzard. 'The businessman trying to broker the Mounsey Street carpet factory deal is the Rawmarshes' son.'

'The first law strikes again, eh, guv?' said Ramsey. Ever the organiser, the detective inspector walked over to the noticeboard that he had erected at one end of the squad room, on which he had started to pin slips of paper bearing the names of people the detectives had encountered during the investigation, alongside a number of their photographs of varying quality. 'In fact, there's far too many coincidences for my liking. Too many connections that don't seem to make sense. The Rawmarshes, Charlie Louden, Mounsey Street, Singapore, Martin Crumpsall, prescription fraud – they all link up in some way.'

'Well, having just lectured the city council chief executive about wasting time during murder investigations, I think it's high time that we started pulling this inquiry together,' said Blizzard. 'At the moment, we're going round in circles.'

'Do you want us to bring Alec in?' asked Ramsey.

'Not yet,' said Blizzard. 'We'll have a briefing first thing in the morning before we do anything. I think there's still plenty of things that we need to understand first.'

* * *

That evening, once Mikey had gone to bed, Blizzard settled down in his armchair in the living room with a pile of papers and a glass of whisky. Fee joined him a few minutes later, poured herself a red wine and sat down in the other armchair.

'Miranda Goldsworthy was not impressed that you knew about the redevelopment then?' she said.

'She certainly wasn't,' said Blizzard. 'I take it no one blamed you?'

'Not that I heard. Alec told our sales director that he thought someone in the council's estates had spilled the beans and Miranda's been stomping round, warning everyone to keep their mouths shut. What's your next move then?'

Blizzard yawned, the effects of his disrupted night beginning to catch up with him.

'A decent night's sleep,' he said, taking a sip of whisky. 'That's the next move.'

It was a comment that turned out to be too optimistic because the couple had only been asleep for an hour and half when the insistent ringing of the bedside phone woke them just after midnight.

'Not again,' groaned Fee. She rolled over and buried her head beneath her pillow. 'You need a new job.'

Blizzard listened for a sound from their son's bedroom but, as with the previous night, the toddler again slept through the ringing of the phone. Blizzard lifted the receiver.

'This had better be good,' he mumbled.

'I'm sorry to ring you again,' said the same control room operator as the previous night, 'but Inspector Sun asked us to contact you.'

'Not Marris Avenue again?'

'I'm afraid so.'

'Tell him I'm on my way.'

The same scene as on the previous night greeted Blizzard when he parked in the road outside the Rawmarshes' house. Uniformed officers were again searching the gardens and Inspector Chen Sun was again overseeing their activities. Seeing Blizzard walking up the drive towards the house, Sun went to meet him, an apologetic look on his face.

'Robert again?' asked Blizzard.

'He says that he got up to go to the toilet, looked out of an upstairs window and saw a figure in the garden. It wasn't in the pergola this time, though.' Sun pointed to the bottom of the garden, where there stood a wooden archway which was only vaguely visible in the shadows thrown by the lights fixed to the house. 'Robert reckons he was standing behind that.'

'What do you think?'

'He certainly seems very shaken up but, honestly? Honestly, no, I don't think he did see anyone. I think it's all in his imagination.'

'So do I,' said Blizzard. 'And I don't buy Alec's theory that Charlie is trying to scare them before he is released from prison, either. Charlie Louden is perfectly capable of doing his own scaring if he comes out.'

Sun nodded and the two officers walked round to the back of the house, where Robert and Jean were standing on the doorstep watching uniformed officers conduct the search of the darker recesses of the garden by torchlight. Robert caught sight of the new arrivals and walked over to them.

'I didn't imagine it,' said Robert before either officer could say anything. 'There was definitely someone there.'

'Did you recognise who it was?' asked Blizzard.

'It was too dark, but I'd say that it was definitely a man. He was staring at the house. Just like last night.'

'Well, we haven't found anything,' said Sun.

'My husband is not making it up,' said Jean vehemently. She gave Sun a hard look. 'If he says that he saw someone in the garden, then he saw someone in the garden, and I expect you to take it seriously!'

'We do take it seriously,' said Blizzard, 'despite what you might have told the newspaper. Do you have any theories about who Robert saw tonight? Clearly, it can't be Charlie because he's still in prison.'

'Then it's like Alec says,' replied Jean. 'Somebody trying to scare us on Charlie's behalf.'

'And why would he want to do that?' asked Blizzard. He did not try to conceal the scepticism in his voice. 'You have not heard from him for sixteen years.'

'It's the way Charlie's mind works,' said Robert. 'He likes playing games with people. Messing with their minds.'

Blizzard looked at Sun.

'I'm not sure there's much to be gained by staying here any longer, Inspector,' he said.

'I'll call our guys off then,' said Sun.

'I thought you said that you were taking it seriously!' said Jean, aghast at what she was hearing. 'What if we are in danger?'

'We've searched the gardens two nights running and seen nothing to suggest that you are,' said Blizzard. 'And I am sure that Inspector Sun can arrange for regular patrols to pass your house, like he did last night.'

Sun nodded but Jean scowled and went back into the house, followed by her husband.

'We could keep looking, I guess,' said Sun, when they had gone. 'I don't really want my name splashed all over the newspaper, like they did to you.'

'No, we've wasted too much time on this already,' said Blizzard, 'as I was telling the chief executive of the city council only yesterday…'

Chapter twelve

Blizzard's team began to gather for their briefing in the squad room at Abbey Road Police Station shortly before 7.45am the next morning. There was the low buzz of conversation as the detectives looked at the noticeboard, to which had been added more images and scrawled notes; it was clear to them that they faced a busy weekend. Standing next to the board, Blizzard let the conversation continue for a few minutes as he tried to ignore the thick-headed feeling that he had been struggling to shake off since getting up shortly after 6am. Having returned from the Rawmarshes' home, the inspector had lain wide-eyed in bed for the best part of an hour, turning the events of the night over in his mind before eventually drifting into slumber. He had only managed to grab an hour and a half hour of fitful sleep before being woken by the sound of his son calling his name from the next room.

With a groan, the inspector had carried Mikey downstairs to the living room where the toddler sat at a small plastic table, eating yoghurt and slices of kiwi as he watched Thomas the Tank Engine, and his father struggled to stay awake. Fee got up a short while later and, after a quick shower, Blizzard had left home, shaving with his electric razor as he drove into the city. Now, as the hands on the wall clock in the squad room ticked past 8am, he was preparing to begin his briefing when one of the reception staff ushered in Ruth Stewart, from the NHS Fraud Investigation Unit. She gave him an apologetic look as she took her seat.

'Sorry I'm late, John,' she said. 'I didn't expect to be attending an early morning CID briefing quite so soon after leaving the job. Bloody civvies, eh?'

Several officers chuckled at the comment.

'I'm sure you'll make up for it,' said Blizzard. He produced a marker pen from his jacket pocket and tapped the images and scraps of paper pinned onto the noticeboard. 'We need everyone to come up with ideas because in among this little lot may well be the connection that allows us to make sense of what has been happening. And those of you looking puzzled, you're right. At first glance, a lot of the links look like tenuous coincidences, but that does not mean that they are not important. Anyone fancy kicking us off?'

'It makes sense to start where we came in, doesn't it?' said Colley. The sergeant walked to the noticeboard and tapped the photograph of Charlie Louden that had been circulated to the media on the day he was jailed. He ran his finger slowly across the board, tracing a route to a picture of the Rawmarshes.

Blizzard drew a bold black line between them.

'Granted, it's the most obvious connection,' said Colley. He turned to look at the other detectives. 'But if you think about it, there are quite a few connections between Charlie and a number of the other people on the board.'

'Such as who?' asked Blizzard.

The sergeant tapped a black-and-white silhouette image with the name "Alec Rawmarsh/Maynard" scrawled beneath it.

'His cousin, for starters,' he said. 'And between them, they open up connections all over the board. Martin Crumpsall, for example.'

'Yes, we shouldn't forget the alleged stranger in the Rawmarshes' garden,' said Chris Ramsey, who was thoroughly enjoying the exercise. 'There is, after all, a suggestion that someone is trying to scare Jean and Robert on Charlie's behalf. Maybe it's Crumpsall. They shared a prison cell and have kept in touch since he was released.'

'Maybe,' said Blizzard, drawing the line.

Ramsey walked over to the noticeboard and pointed at the picture of Xavier Lim, next to which was pinned a silhouette bearing the name Wei Ji Tan.

'Crumpsall also opens up connections to Ruth's prescription fraudsters,' he said.

'And to organised crime,' said Ruth Stewart. She reached into her briefcase and produced a photocopy of a picture depicting a fleshy-faced man with short dark hair, which she pinned to the noticeboard. 'This is Crumpsall's passport picture, for those who want to know what he looks like.'

She produced a second photograph from her bag, which she also pinned to the board. This one showed a lean-faced man.

'And there is also a link to this guy,' she said. 'Sean Gracey. A dodgy GP who met Wei Ji Tan and Xavier Lim at a medical conference in Amsterdam and joined them in their fraudulent activities – he already had a long-standing relationship with Crumpsall.'

'Which is what?' asked Blizzard.

'There's only six months between them in age, and Gracey's Facebook page says that he attended Laneside Comprehensive School, so we rang the school and it turns out that the two lads were in the same year group.'

Blizzard drew the relevant line on the board.

'Interesting,' he said.

'And you can draw another line,' said Sarah Allatt. 'I happen to know that Alec Maynard went to Laneside Comp as well. He looks like he's a similar age to the other two, so there's a good chance that they knew each other. Maybe the prescriptions fraud is a crime made in Hafton, rather than Singapore.'

'Maybe it is,' said Blizzard, drawing another line. 'And there's also a link between Alec Maynard and the carpet factory because he's one of the businessmen trying to redevelop the site.'

The inspector stepped back to examine his handiwork.

'I'm not quite sure what all these connections mean, or even if they are all relevant,' he said, 'but I'm getting a feeling that there's something there, it's just that we're not seeing it yet.'

He turned round to face his team, a number of whom were nodding in agreement.

'One thing's certain,' he said, 'George Ramsdale and his team were never this thorough. It's a thought-provoking exercise, is it not? Perhaps they should have done something similar.'

'You could market it as a board game,' said Colley. '*Cluedo* – who killed John Doe? A N Other in the carpet factory with the machete.'

Laughter rippled round the room.

'Yes, and what about our John Doe?' asked Blizzard when the laughter had died away. 'Who does he connect to?'

'The two factory owners,' said Ramsey. He pointed to silhouettes bearing the names Fu Li and Zhang Wei. 'His body was found in their building – and we can also draw a line between them and the prescription fraudsters.'

'But we haven't turned up anything to say that they know each other, have we?' said Blizzard.

'We don't need to, guv,' said Ramsey. 'They're all from Singapore, all four of them are crooked, and all of them chose Hafton to carry out their dodgy activities. Blizzard's first law says that is worth a line, wouldn't you say?'

Blizzard nodded and drew it on the noticeboard, which was beginning to disappear beneath black ink.

'There should also be a line between Robert and Jean Rawmarsh and the John Doe,' said Jenny Carr. 'They were attacked with the same weapon.'

Blizzard drew a crude image of a machete on the board then stepped back to study the results of their work. He turned to face the team once again.

'So, where does that leave us?' he asked. 'Quite a few lines take in Martin Crumpsall, don't they? That's quite striking.'

'Do you want me to bring him in?' asked Colley.

'Not yet,' said Blizzard as Stewart opened her mouth to speak. 'We don't want to damage the NHS investigation. Ruth, are you happy to work with some of my people to see if we can dig up anything else?'

'Makes sense,' she said and gave a nod of the head in acknowledgment of the respect that Blizzard had shown for her team's inquiry.

'Anything else, folks?' asked the inspector.

Allatt opened her mouth to speak but thought better of it. Blizzard noticed her hesitation.

'You got something to say, Sarah?' he asked.

'I have, but it feels like a betrayal of a thoroughly decent man,' said the constable unhappily. 'I can't believe that he has done anything wrong, but a lot of the lines do seem to intersect with Alec Maynard, don't they?'

'They do,' said Blizzard. 'Time for that chat with him, I think.'

Chapter thirteen

With the briefing at an end, Blizzard and Sarah Allatt headed out to the Rawmarshes' home. Having struggled to find an address for Alec Maynard, the inspector had decided to go through his parents to track him down. He welcomed an excuse to discuss their son with them as he tried to work out if Alec was a credible suspect for the murder of the man in the old carpet factory. Little was said on the journey to Marris Avenue, with Allatt becoming increasingly uneasy about the encounter to come, an uneasiness that grew more visible as the BMW approached the Rawmarshes' house.

'Don't look so worried,' said Blizzard as he turned into the avenue. 'If Alec's innocent, he has nothing to worry about.'

'I'm sure he is innocent,' replied the young constable. 'Like I said, he's a decent man.'

'But we can't assume that, can we? Even decent people do bad things. It's worth always remembering that.'

Allatt nodded.

'I know,' she said. 'It's doesn't make it any easier, though.'

Blizzard did not reply but instead parked the vehicle, got out and headed for the gates, through which he saw two vehicles in front of the house. He recognised the Fiat as belonging to Alec Maynard.

'Now what on earth do you think he wants to talk to Mummy and Daddy about?' said Blizzard with a slight smile. The detectives started to walk up the drive. 'Any idea who owns the other car? Whoever it is, they are not short of money. Audis do not come cheap.'

'Too true,' said Allatt. 'My boyfriend was looking at buying a new car a couple of weeks ago and really fancied one like that but it would have cost more than £100,000.'

As the detectives neared the house, the front door swung open to reveal a stern-looking Jean Rawmarsh. Even the warmth that she usually displayed towards Allatt was missing and her attitude towards Blizzard was one of barely concealed hostility.

'Chief Inspector, what a surprise,' she said with little enthusiasm. 'Are you here to stand in the way of free speech again?'

'We gave you plenty of opportunity to have your say,' said Blizzard, 'but you were blocking the bypass and we couldn't let that continue.'

'Yes, you say—'

'I'm not here to talk about your protest anyway. Can we go inside, please?'

Blizzard expected Jean to allow the detectives into the house, but she didn't.

'You have news about Charlie then?' she said.

'It's not about him either.'

'Why are you here then?' she said, giving the inspector a suspicious look.

'It's a somewhat delicate matter concerning your son.'

'Alec? What do—'

'I'd rather not discuss it on the doorstep,' said Blizzard. Fatigue from lack of sleep sparked irritability and he scowled at her. 'Come on, Jean, stop playing silly buggers, I really am not in the mood.'

Still, Jean did not move.

'You're wasting your time,' she said. 'Alec is not here.'

'Except that's his car,' said Blizzard, gesturing at the Fiat. 'We're not going to give up, Jean. His name has cropped up in a murder investigation and we'll talk to him sooner or later, you know that. It's just a question of whether he does it voluntarily or is arrested. I am pretty sure that having your son taken out of your house in handcuffs won't impress the people who live round here. Well, most of them anyway – you've got your fair share of villains.'

Jean gave him a dark look and was about to reply when Alec walked out of the living room and into the hallway.

'He's right, Mum,' he said calmly. 'I've got to talk to them sometime. Let them in.'

'If you're sure, love,' said Jean with a worried expression on her face. Still, she seemed reluctant to stand aside.

'I'm sure,' he said. 'I've got nothing to hide.'

Finally, Jean stepped aside to allow the detectives into the house. She gave Allatt a withering look of disapproval as she did so.

'Just remember that none of us have done anything wrong,' she said to Blizzard as the detectives followed her down the hallway.

'I'm delighted to hear it,' said Blizzard. 'Although we tend to be the judges of such things.'

The detectives walked into the living room to find Robert sitting in his usual armchair. He ignored the detectives, as was his custom with visitors that had not been invited, which was just about everyone he encountered. Sitting on the sofa was Miranda Goldsworthy with a sick expression on her face.

'Well, well, well,' said Blizzard cheerfully; he loved it when people's deceit began to unravel, and to have caught the council chief executive out in a lie twice in such a short period of time, was too much to wish for. 'So much for not knowing where to find your mystery investor.'

The inspector nodded at the best china teacups laid out on the coffee table.

'In fact, your relationship would appear to be somewhat cosier than you led me to believe at our meeting,' he said.

'I've done nothing wrong,' said Goldsworthy but she sounded defensive and unconvinced.

'Are you sure?' said Blizzard. He sat down on the sofa and reached for a custard cream from the plate of biscuits. 'Do the opposition councillors know about these?'

Goldsworthy gave the inspector a wan smile, the extent to which she had underestimated him becoming ever more apparent. Allatt, who had moved to stand by the window where she stared out at the garden, sensed that Alec was looking at her and she turned back into the room towards him. Having sat down in one of the armchairs, he had noticed the young constable's discomfort and winked at her. She gave a smile of appreciation at his reassurance.

'This is not what it looks like, Chief Inspector,' said Alec, switching his attention back to Blizzard, his tone of voice clearly chosen to give the impression of someone who was relaxed and composed.

'And what do you think it looks like?' asked the inspector. 'Because, from where I am sitting, it looks like Miranda is reporting back to you on my meeting with her, which leads me to the unsavoury thought that you are trying to interfere with our murder investigation.'

'That's not fair!' protested Jean. 'Alec would never do a thing like that!'

'Then perhaps he would care to explain why he has tried to conceal from us the fact that he is negotiating to buy a building from a couple of crooks by the names of Fu Li and Zhang Wei?' said Blizzard. 'A building, oddly enough, where the body of a murder victim was found.

Some people with more suspicious minds than myself and the good constable here might even go as far as to suggest that such behaviour is a long way from the actions of an innocent man.'

For the first time since the detectives had entered the house, Alec Maynard's expression suggested unease. His mother gave the detective a deeply disapproving look and Robert lowered his newspaper and began to listen with a visible air of annoyance, although, for the moment, he said nothing.

'You must have realised that we would have found out about you sooner or later,' continued Blizzard, looking at Alec. 'It would have made things easier for everyone involved if you had come forward on your own volition, rather than us having to work it out ourselves. It would have looked a lot less suspicious. Surely, you got a sense that Fu Li and Zhang Wei were not on the level?'

'I have never met them,' said Alec. 'And no, I did not know that they were crooked.'

'But you must have heard the rumours at the time of the big fire?'

'There was a bit of local tittle-tattle, but they were never charged with starting the fire so I had no reason to mistrust them. Besides, I'm not in business with them. I'm just buying their building. As for the body, I was going to come and see you when the time was right. Its discovery has complicated matters, as I am sure you can imagine, and I had a few things to sort first.'

'And you knew nothing about the body?

'Nobody knew it was there,' said Alec. 'How could they? The newspaper said that it was under some old pallets. Well, no one had looked under them for years. You can be assured that if I had known about it, I'd have come to you immediately.'

'The way you did this week?' said Blizzard. He glanced at Allatt. 'He's been knocking our door off its hinges in the rush to help us, hasn't he, Constable?'

Allatt nodded her support for the comment; she knew whose side she needed to be on, and it was not the Rawmarsh family's.

'Like I said, I had things to sort,' said Alec. 'I wanted to get the purchase deal signed before the developer heard about the discovery and got cold feet over possible publicity.'

'But, surely, the developer must have known about it already?' said Allatt. She had an overwhelming desire to demonstrate to Blizzard that she was capable of being professional, rather than someone who was blinded to the truth because a friend was involved. 'It's been all over the press.'

'The *local* press,' said Maynard. 'But the developer is not from Hafton.'

'Where's he from then?' asked Allatt.

'Singapore.'

Blizzard and Allatt exchanged glances as they found themselves thinking back to the thick black lines snaking their way across the noticeboard in the CID squad room.

'And I don't deal directly with the company anyway,' said Alec. 'I go through a middleman, but he's in Singapore as well. Although he sometimes reads Hafton local news online, he's only really interested in property stories so I thought it made sense to get signatures on the contract before you started spooking folks over there with questions about the murder.'

'Very honourable,' said Blizzard. 'That must be what they mean by ethical investing, is it?'

Maynard frowned at the comment but his father produced a reaction that was far more vigorous – a re-run of the anger that he had displayed during his first encounter with Blizzard in the interview room at Abbey Road, when he had angrily grasped the detective's hand.

'How dare you talk like that!' he exclaimed. He jumped to his feet and jabbed a finger at Blizzard. 'My son is an honest man and an honourable businessman and I'd thank you not to come into our home and impugn his good name and that of this family! It's a disgrace!'

'Sit down,' said Blizzard; there was a harsh edge to his voice.

'I'll sit down when I want to!' exclaimed Robert; he was shouting now. 'How dare you…?'

'Oh, do sit down, Robert,' said Jean wearily. 'You're not helping things. This is a time for calm heads.'

Her husband remained standing for a few moments then nodded as his anger subsided as rapidly as it had exploded. Having sat down, he satisfied himself with glaring at the inspector.

Blizzard, for his part, returned his attention to Alec Maynard.

'This middleman in Singapore?' he asked. 'What's his name?'

'Do you really need to know?' asked Maynard. 'I don't really want him dragging into this. I can assure you that he is a perfectly respectable…'

'Yes, we need to know,' said Blizzard. 'You might as well tell us because we'll find out anyway. We normally do.'

'I don't doubt it,' said Maynard. 'You got to me quicker than I thought you would. How *did* you get to me, anyway?'

'Never mind that. What's your middleman's name?'

'Zayven Wen,' said Maynard. 'He works out of offices in the business district of Singapore, encouraging high-end investors from China and South East Asia to put their money into the UK, mostly northern cities like Hafton. He says that they are ripe for development because a lot of their sites are so run-down that they can be snapped up for virtually nothing. It's already happening in quite a few places.'

'It's true enough,' said Blizzard. He had heard his publisher voice similar sentiments on several occasions; the possibility that areas like Mounsey Street might undergo a revival was one of the main reasons he had commissioned the book. 'But why all the secrecy, Alec? Why get us thinking the worst of you?'

'It's the nature of the business,' said Alec. 'It's very competitive and Zayven plays things close to his chest. After a while, you become paranoid, just like the rest of them.'

'I told you,' said Jean. She gave Blizzard a triumphant look. 'He's done nothing wrong.'

'Tell us more about Zayven Wen, please, Alec,' said Blizzard, ignoring the comment. 'How does a property agent from Hafton end up working with someone at the high end of the Asian property market?'

'I met him at a conference in Leeds a year or so back. It was about investment opportunities in the north of England and we got talking in the bar after the evening session. The next thing I knew, he was on the phone asking if I was interested in the Mounsey Street carpet factory.'

'And you were?' said Blizzard.

'We certainly were. We'd been saying for years that it would be a good redevelopment site, hadn't we, Dad?'

Robert nodded.

'I asked Dad to come out of retirement to help me,' explained Alec. 'I'd never worked on anything that big. We could both see the potential, and the price that Fu Li and Zhang Wei were quoting for the carpet factory was very attractive. The timing was ideal as well, because Zayven had heard on the grapevine that the Singapore developer was looking for a UK retail opportunity and wanted someone to represent him over here. Perfect storm, really, and Miranda wouldn't be involved if it was dodgy.'

'And how exactly *has* the council helped?' asked Blizzard, turning his attention to the chief executive.

'We have offered them a grant to support the project,' said Goldsworthy. 'To pay for ground works, utilities, that sort of thing.'

'I've not heard anything about that,' said Blizzard. 'How big is this grant?'

'That's confidential,' said Goldsworthy.

'As I think I have told you before, when it comes to murder inquiries, we do not do confidential,' said Blizzard. 'How much?'

Goldsworthy looked at him uneasily.

'Three million,' she said.

'That's very generous of you,' said the inspector. He reached out for a custard cream. 'Particularly at a time when the council can't stretch to a few biscuits. I take it that there's a minute from a council meeting that confirms all this?'

'There isn't, no,' said Goldsworthy uncomfortably. 'But there will be. You needn't look like that, Chief Inspector. It's all above board. I haven't told the councillors yet but when I do, they'll back it, I'm sure. It's brilliant news for the city and means a lot of jobs at a time when they are desperately needed.'

'So, presumably you can now see why we are so concerned about something that might wreck the deal?' said Maynard, looking at Blizzard. 'Negotiations are at a delicate stage and, if they are not handled carefully, they could collapse, which would mean me and Dad could end up owing the bank a lot of money – and we're not the only ones with a lot invested in this project.'

'Yes, I can see that,' said Blizzard. He stood up. 'And I'm glad that you have explained everything to me. It's been very helpful.'

'Can I ask what you are going to do?' asked Alec, also standing up. 'Are you allowed to tell me?'

'I'm afraid not,' said Blizzard. He gave him a wry smile. 'It probably won't surprise you to discover that we have our own paranoia!'

'Whatever you do, I take it that it can't wait until we have signed the deal on the factory?'

'I think you already know the answer to that,' said the inspector. He looked at the chief executive. 'Good to see you again, Miranda. I suspect that we will need to speak to you again at some point.'

Goldsworthy did not look pleased at the thought of another encounter with the inspector.

Jean led the detectives into the hallway.

'Alec's a good lad, you know,' she said as she opened the front door. 'And I'm sorry about Robert's outburst. He's been very worried. We both have.'

'I imagine it's the last thing you want at a time like this,' said Blizzard. 'Are you ready for Monday?'

'We're as ready as we can be,' said Jean. 'Nice to see you again, Sarah.'

She closed the front door and the detectives started walking down the drive towards the inspector's car.

'That went well,' said Allatt; she seemed much happier. 'Alec's involvement is perfectly innocent. I told you that he was a decent bloke, didn't I?'

Blizzard did not reply.

'Are you still not sure about him?' asked Allatt.

'I'm not sure about anything, Sarah, and that includes your pal, I am afraid.'

'But, surely, he gave a plausible explanation of what he has been doing?'

'Ah, but did he?' said Blizzard. 'What do we always look for in any case? Motive. Find a motive and you are halfway there. So, what do we have we here? A couple of dodgy businessmen on the run after setting fire to their building, an ambitious young Hafton entrepreneur who would be deep in the shit if his deal collapses, a wheeler-dealer from Singapore about whom we know virtually nothing, and a John Doe who may well, for all we know, have been killed because he got in the way of some, or all, of them. Who knows?'

They had reached the bottom of the drive and the inspector stood aside to let Allatt go first, noting her disappointed expression as he did so.

'I'm sorry, Sarah,' he said, 'but we have to go where the evidence takes us.'

'You're right, of course,' she said glumly. 'So where will the evidence take us next, do you think?'

'The more I hear, the more I think that the answer is Singapore. I just have to find a way of persuading Arthur to pay for the trip, which is easier said than done given the parlous state of our budget.'

'Do you want me to ask Alec for Zayven Wen's contact details?' asked Allatt.

'It's better if we track him down ourselves. For the moment, I'd rather no one knew that I am thinking of going.'

The inspector had just unlocked his car when his mobile phone rang. He glanced at the caller ID and sighed before taking the call.

'John Blizzard,' growled a man's voice. 'George Ramsdale. I got your message saying that you want to talk to me.'

'I do, yes, I wanted to–'

'Actually, I'm glad you rang,' said Ramsdale, interrupting him. 'I hear that you've been bad-mouthing me again. I have warned you about this before. When do you want to come round?'

'Half an hour?'

'Don't be late,' said Ramsdale and the phone went dead.

'Who was that?' asked Allatt.

'That,' said Blizzard, getting into the car and reaching for his seatbelt, 'was the past catching up with me.'

Chapter fourteen

George Ramsdale lived in a sheltered housing complex on a quiet estate not far from Abbey Road Police Station. Although the door to the flat was opened by a stooped, grey-haired man wearing brown cords and a grey cardigan that had seen better days, Blizzard was immediately struck by the sense of someone who was still sharp of mind despite the passage of time. His predecessor's keenness of thought, and the fact that he retained friendships with a number of senior officers at headquarters, counselled a policy of caution for Blizzard. George Ramsdale was still capable of causing trouble and Blizzard knew it. Ramsdale gestured for his visitor towards one of the armchairs.

'Would you like a cup of tea?' he asked in a voice that lacked warmth.

Blizzard nodded and Ramsdale went into the kitchen and set about making the drinks, returning several minutes later with a tray. With the tea poured, and biscuits duly offered, an uncomfortable silence settled on the room for a few moments. The two men had never had a good relationship and the circumstances were doing little to improve the atmosphere.

'I read about the body in Mounsey Street in the newspaper,' said Ramsdale eventually. 'Any idea who it is?'

'Not yet,' said Blizzard. He took a sip of tea and reached for a biscuit. 'But he was definitely Asian.'

'One of the guys who owned the building?'

'I don't know. The inquiry is still in its early stages and I suspect that it's got a long way to run.'

'That's what I used to say when I hadn't got a clue what was happening,' said Ramsdale.

He gave the inspector a devilish look, challenging him to respond, but Blizzard said nothing; he had resolved not to let Ramsdale wind him up. There was no point in adding to the list of complaints being made to Arthur Ronald.

'I imagine,' said Ramsdale, 'that you will continue to rake up the past for a while then?'

'Meaning?'

'Meaning the fire,' said Ramsdale.

'That's why I wanted to talk to you. We have quite a few leads but nothing that is making any sense. However, the fire does keep cropping up. I wondered if you had any thoughts. Something that happened then and might be relevant today, maybe? Something I don't know about?'

'Do you not think that I would have made something of it at the time, if we did find anything? No, don't bother to answer that. You have made it abundantly clear to anyone who will listen what you think about the way I ran the inquiry.' Ramsdale was unable to conceal his irritation now and his voice had hardened. 'I had rather hoped that you had learnt your lesson but now I hear that you have started with the comments again. I have heard all sorts of words being used. Incompetent. Lazy. Complacent.'

Ramsdale paused for a few moments then fixed Blizzard with a keen stare.

'Corrupt,' he said.

The word hung in the air.

'I have never said you were corrupt,' said Blizzard.

'But you *have* suggested that someone from my team tipped off Fu Li and Zhang Wei that we were on our way to arrest them for arson. That's suggesting corruption in all but the word.'

'I might have said that there were those who believed it to be the case but I was not one of them. As for the other words, *mea culpa*, I did say that and I stand by them.'

'Yes, well, I very much hope that, after this, you will think twice before you use the investigation as an excuse to repeat your comments about me. I have a reputation to protect.'

'Not much of one,' said Blizzard. He cursed inwardly as the words came out; the response had been so instinctive that he almost did not realise that he had uttered them.

'And whose fault is that?' exclaimed Ramsdale furiously. 'Damn it, man, will you not let it go? You would do well to remember that I still have friends in the force and that if you continue to…'

Blizzard drained his mug and stood up.

'Thanks for the tea,' he said and walked out of the flat.

Chapter fifteen

The telephone call that Blizzard had been expecting came late on Monday morning after the inspector and his team had spent a frustrating weekend with little in the way of breakthroughs on the murder investigation. Although the Charlie Louden case had dominated the inspector's thoughts over recent days, his mind was on other matters as he sat in his office, scribbling notes on a notepad and tapping figures into his calculator. The reason was that he had that morning broached the idea of the trip to Singapore with Arthur Ronald, relieved to have discovered that George Ramsdale had not weakened his position by submitting a formal complaint against him. Although Ronald said that he viewed the premise as thin, he had not turned the request down but had challenged Blizzard to justify the expense.

The ringing of Blizzard's desk phone brought Charlie Louden back to the forefront of his mind. Glancing up at the wall clock, he was surprised to see that it was already noon but guessed immediately that the caller was Maureen Rodgers from the prison. He was right.

'Is he out?' he asked.

'As good as,' said the assistant governor. 'They have confirmed his release.'

'Presumably, with a warning not to chop up any of his relatives, if he can possibly avoid it?'

'Something like that,' said Rodgers. 'Although I'm not sure that's quite how they phrased it. Anyway, I thought you'd like to know that he's being released at three o'clock this afternoon.'

'That's quick, isn't it?'

'They need the cells,' said Rodgers. 'There's a lot of big trials coming to a close this week and the word is that thirteen bad lads will end up being sent here and we don't have room for them, unless we kick some of ours out. Charlie Louden is one of them. Are you still staying out of it?'

'I might pop down,' said Blizzard. 'I'm interested to see who meets him when he comes out of your gates.'

'Would I be right in thinking that you mean Martin Crumpsall?'

'Possibly.'

'Well, I think we can say that it is one hundred per cent certain he will be there,' said Rodgers.

'What makes you so sure?' asked Blizzard.

'Because the original plan was for Charlie to live in a hostel for the first few months after his release but Crumpsall has offered to let him share his flat instead.'

'Has he now?' said Blizzard. The inspector's mind went back to the noticeboard standing in the CID squad room and the black lines that now criss-crossed it. 'Life is full of connections, isn't it?'

'Isn't it just? And this one sure as hell alarmed the panel. They were worried about the idea of an ex-con playing the role of vouchsafe, when he's just as likely to be a bad influence.'

'A valid point, one would venture to suggest,' said Blizzard.

'Maybe so, but Charlie pointed out that just about everyone in the hostel was likely to be an ex-con. He'll be subject to a rigorous reporting regime for at least a year so they'll find out pretty quickly if he goes back to his bad old ways. Besides, I imagine that you will be keeping an eye on him.'

Blizzard could not be bothered to tell her that he had no intention of doing the probation service's job for them and, with the conversation having come to an end, he scooped up his notes relating to his proposed visit to Singapore and went to see Arthur Ronald.

'Charlie Louden's coming out,' said Blizzard, walking into the superintendent's office and sitting down. 'Three o'clock.'

'You going?'

'I think so. I'll only be there as an observer, though. I don't want to stand on Ruth Stewart's toes.'

Ronald gave a nod of approval.

'However, it might throw up something interesting,' said Blizzard. 'Particularly given his connections to Singapore. You never know.'

'I still need convincing that we have enough to justify the expense of going to Singapore,' said Ronald. 'It's all very well drawing pretty lines on a noticeboard, John, but it doesn't prove anything, and I'm not sure what one person can achieve, anyway.'

'Ah, well,' said Blizzard. He picked up his notes. 'I think we can afford to send three.'

'Three!' exclaimed Ronald. 'How much would three cost?'

'Well,' said Blizzard, glancing down at the scribbles on his notepad, 'working on the basis that we will probably need three or four days, and taking flights, hotels and other expenses into account, I reckon we can do it for less than six grand. Seven, if we have puddings.'

'Puddings?' said Ronald.

'Puddings,' said Blizzard solemnly.

'I take it that you have not forgotten the parlous state of the budget?' said Ronald.

Before Blizzard could reply, there was a knock on the office door and one of the reception staff ushered in Ruth Stewart. Ronald looked suspiciously at the head of the NHS Fraud Investigation Unit.

'And what are you doing here, might I ask?' he asked. He switched his attention back to Blizzard. 'And why do I sense that this is some kind of ambush?'

'Hardly,' said Stewart as she and Blizzard exchanged amused glances. 'Rather, I am your budget!'

'What do you mean?' asked the superintendent.

'After John's briefing yesterday, I went to see my line manager,' said Stewart. 'Even before your involvement, she had been agitating for us to close the prescription fraud inquiry unless we were ready to bring the guys in for questioning. It was the first thing she asked me about when I got the job. The problem has been that only Sean Gracey and Martin Crumpsall are over here. We're pretty sure that Xavier Lim and Wei Ji Tan are the main players and that they are back in Singapore, as are the people in whom John and his team are interested. The more we talked it over, Arthur, the more your idea that we work together made sense – and my manager really likes the idea of a joint trip.'

'And she would pay for it, would she?' asked Ronald.

'She'd pay seventy-five per cent.'

'Really?' Ronald looked at her in surprise.

'Really,' said Stewart. She gave him a wry smile. 'Let's just say that the NHS is somewhat less rigorous with its money than yourselves, shall we, Arthur? It hasn't taken me long in the job to discover that you can hide at lot of things in the middle-manager budgets.'

'Even puddings,' said Blizzard.

'Even puddings,' agreed Stewart.

'Well, this does change things somewhat,' said Ronald. 'I reckon I can swing twenty-five per cent. I take it that you would be one of those to go, Ruth?'

'I'd like to, yes,' she said.

Ronald turned his attention to Blizzard.

'And I take it that you quite fancy a nice trip abroad?' he asked.

Blizzard nodded.

'So who would be the third person?' asked the superintendent. 'An NHS investigator or one of ours? I assume that you are thinking of David Colley if it's one of ours, John?'

'That was my initial thought but when I thought some more, it became clear that Inspector Chen Sun, from Harrowby Street nick would be a much better choice,' said Blizzard. 'He's got a good contact over there who is willing to help us find our way around the city and liaise with their organised crime people. And Chen himself could be useful – if you ignore the fact that his goats have never been to Beijing, that is.'

Ronald gave Blizzard a bewildered look.

'What on earth have goats got to do with it?' he asked.

Blizzard responded with a mock-sigh, looked at Stewart and shook his head sadly.

'The Inspectorate of Constabulary is right, you know, Ruth,' he said. 'This force has such a long way to go when it comes to racial integration.'

The meeting broke up and Blizzard and Stewart went to the Abbey Road Police Station canteen to discuss the Singapore visit over lunch, after which the inspector returned to Ronald's office, just as the superintendent was replacing the desk phone receiver.

'That was George Ramsdale,' he said. The superintendent did not even try to conceal his exasperation. 'What's the plan, John, create a new record for hacking people off unnecessarily? The Rawmarshes, the prison governor, the council chief executive, her PA, now George Ramsdale.'

'What did he say?' asked Blizzard.

'That you are obsessed with him and are using the investigation into the murder as an excuse to keep repeating some of your claims about his time running Western CID.'

'And what did you say?'

'That it was your case and that it was up to you.'

'Is the right answer,' said Blizzard.

Chapter sixteen

That afternoon, as the time edged closer to 3pm, Blizzard and Colley headed back along the eastern bypass on their way to Hafton Prison. However, it was talk of Singapore that dominated the detectives' conversation, rather than Charlie Louden's long-awaited release.

'I can't believe the super has persuaded headquarters to approve the trip,' said Colley. 'I know Ruth's lot are going to foot most of the bill but I didn't think that even Arthur with his diplomatic skills would be able to swing that one. Last time I made a request for an overnight job, it was knocked back and we had to get the locals to lift him for us. You're one of the people going, I take it?'

'Yeah, with Ruth.'

'Any idea who the third person is?'

'I've recommended Chen Sun,' said Blizzard. 'I had hoped that I might be able to take you but the more I thought about it, the more it made sense to take Chen. Although the UK has a good extradition agreement with Singapore, we'll still need friends out there and Chen's links with their Organised Crime Unit will be invaluable. Sorry.'

'No need to apologise. From what I hear, Sun is impressing a lot of people. Who's going to run CID while you're away? Are they going to bring in another DCI?'

'Arthur's got permission for us to bump Chris Ramsey up to acting DCI. It'll be good practice for when he takes over the Intelligence Unit and Arthur will be there to help if he needs it.'

'Chris won't be able to run the Mounsey Street investigation as well as keeping an eye on everything else, will he?' asked Colley.

'No. We're bringing in some guy called Colley. He's got a nice line in suits, apparently.'

The sergeant looked surprised.

'Me?' he said.

'You,' said Blizzard. 'I had a chat with Arthur and we think that since you are going to be promoted to inspector sometime in the next few months anyway, you might as well have a run at acting DI now. Headquarters thinks it's a good idea so it's a question of whether or not you are OK with it. I take it you are?'

Colley grinned.

'Am I?' he said. 'I've always fancied running a murder inquiry. Thank you for showing faith in me. It's much appreciated.'

'No problem,' said Blizzard. 'There are two conditions, though, one being that when I get back, you remember who's boss.'

'I'm sure you can help me with that,' said Colley. 'What's the second condition?'

'That before you take on the role, you undergo a training session with me on marker pen technique. Those lines don't draw themselves on the noticeboard, you know.'

'Clearly, this job is more complicated than I thought,' said Colley.

The detectives arrived at Hafton Prison shortly after 2.45pm. Blizzard parked the BMW and they sat in silence for a few minutes. Rain clouds were gathering over the nearby Haft, a stiff breeze had sprung up to ripple the dark waters of the river and there was a heaviness to the air. A storm was blowing in from the east coast and both officers felt a sense of foreboding as they waited for Charlie Louden to emerge through the prison gate into a world that had undergone many changes since he was jailed.

'It must be a bewildering thing to happen to someone after so long,' said Colley. 'It must take a lot of adapting to.'

Before he was able to offer any further thoughts, a grubby red van caught the officers' attention as it pulled off the bypass and made its way slowly through the prison car park, until its driver squeezed into the only remaining space at the far end of one of the rows. The driver emerged from the vehicle and began to make his way towards the prison.

'I'm pretty sure that's Martin Crumpsall,' said Colley. He reached into the glove compartment and removed a photocopy of the photograph they had of him. 'Yup, that's him, alright.'

As Crumpsall neared the prison, the front gate swung open and a warder ushered Charlie Louden into freedom for the first time in sixteen years. He and the warder had a brief conversation then the gate closed behind the former inmate and he stood for a few moments, overwhelmed, it seemed to the watching detectives, by confusion, and not quite sure how to react after so long locked up. His confusion vanished when he spotted Crumpsall picking his way through the parked cars and he broke into a trot towards his friend. The two men gave each other a hug and began to make their way towards the van.

'Boy, but he's thin,' said Colley. He had more time to study the gaunt figure now, more than the glimpse the detectives had caught of him among the inmates on the landing during their previous visit. 'I know they're villains but I hate what places like this do to them.'

'Don't fall into the trap of sympathising with him,' cautioned Blizzard. He reached down to start the BMW's engine. 'Remember what he did to his aunt and uncle. Anyway, let's get out of here. We know that they're in touch with each other and there's nothing to be gained by being spotted.'

'I suspect it might be too late for that,' said Colley. The two men had changed direction and were now walking towards the detectives' vehicle. 'It looks like Charlie wants a word.'

Blizzard toyed with the idea of driving away to avoid confrontation but thought better of it, finding himself instead driven by intense curiosity for the man he had heard so much about over recent days. Personal contact, the inspector was constantly reminding younger officers, remained the best form of investigation in a world of email and social media; he had always believed, he would tell them, that you could not judge anyone without hearing their voice and looking into their eyes. Nevertheless, when Louden walked round to the driver's side window and knocked on the glass, a touch of devilment meant that the inspector did not react immediately but instead pretended not to have noticed him. Louden gestured for the inspector to wind down his window, and this time Blizzard complied.

'Sorry, Charlie, didn't see you there,' said the inspector.

'Yeah, likely,' said Louden. 'I knew that you wouldn't be able to resist making an appearance. Who sent you to warn me off, then? Aunt Jean or was it your boss Superintendent Ronald?'

'Nobody sent me,' said Blizzard curtly. Such comments always irritated him. 'And I would certainly not do anything just because Jean told me to do it.'

'Well, whoever it was, when you see my aunt, you can tell her that, under the terms of my release, I am not allowed within five hundred metres of their house and that

I plan to abide by that, so she and Uncle Robert need not worry.'

'It's all very well you saying that but it does not necessarily mean that you will actually–' began Blizzard, only to find himself interrupted by Martin Crumpsall.

'Charlie don't need you hassling him, pal,' he said.

Blizzard gave him a disdainful look. 'I'm sorry?' he said. 'You are?'

'You know who I am,' said Crumpsall. He did not seem to be affected by the inspector's hostile attitude. 'Charlie don't need no coppers cutting up funny when he's just had sixteen years in prison. Like he says, he ain't no danger to anyone.'

'Besides,' said Charlie Louden. 'You don't really have the powers to tell me what to do, do you?'

'I do if I think that you're going to commit a crime,' said Blizzard.

'Except I have done nothing to suggest that I am,' said Louden calmly. 'I mean, give me a break, Chief Inspector. I've only been out five minutes! Besides, I would not want to add to Aunt Jean's troubles at a time like this. She's got enough to worry about, has she not?'

'Like what?' asked Blizzard.

'Why, Alec, of course,' said Louden. He glanced at Crumpsall. 'She must be worried sick about him, mustn't she, Marty?'

Crumpsall nodded but it seemed to the detectives to be a reluctant gesture, one that suggested he would rather that Charlie Louden had not broached the subject.

'It's ironic, really,' continued Louden, seemingly not having noticed Crumpsall's discomfort and enjoying the freedom to say whatever he wished for the first time in sixteen years. 'There's my aunt banging on to the media about me when it turns out that the real villain of the family is actually her blue-eyed golden boy. Don't you think that's ironic, Chief Inspector? I do.'

'Will you stop talking in riddles?' said Blizzard. However, despite his irritation, the inspector found himself intrigued by the comment. 'Say what you want to say and we'll be on our way.'

'I am talking about Alec's close relationship with the guys who are selling the old carpet factory. I take it you know that it was them that torched the place all those years ago? Quite why your lot didn't nick them at the time, I don't know.'

'Can I suggest that you stop telling us things that we already know?' said Blizzard. He was in no mood for Charlie Louden's games and it was time to regain control of the situation. 'The question is, how come *you* know that they are selling the factory to your cousin? I assume that Alec told you?'

'Alec hasn't talked to me since I was locked up,' said Louden. 'He wouldn't be bothered with a low-life like me, and just imagine what dearest Aunty Jean would say if he did. However, there are no secrets in our world, are there, Marty?'

Crumpsall shook his head and again the detectives sensed that he was not enjoying the direction in which the conversation was going and would rather that Louden bring proceedings to an end.

'You see,' continued Louden, 'we cons, or I suppose I should say ex-cons now, get to hear everything and, from what I was told, the more Aunt Jean hears about Li and Wei, the more worried she becomes about Alec's involvement with them. They're a couple of nasty characters who are perfectly capable of turning violent, but then you, of all people, know that only too well.'

'Are you suggesting that they killed the man in the factory?' said Blizzard.

Louden glanced at Crumpsall, whose unease was growing by the second.

'What do you think, Marty?' he asked.

'I think we should go,' said Crumpsall. 'We don't want to hang around here all day, do we?'

'You're right,' said Louden and turned to go.

'Why have you told us all this, Charlie?' asked Blizzard. 'You're not exactly famed for your liking for the police.'

'You never know, I might need someone to vouch for me if I fall foul of the parole board,' said Louden.

'I wouldn't bet on it,' said the inspector.

'No,' said Louden with the thinnest of smiles. 'I'm not sure I would, either. Not that I've got any money to bet on anything, thanks to Aunt Jean's thieving ways. Still, she might have a change of heart, now that I'm out.'

'Why would she do that?' asked Blizzard as Louden started to follow Martin Crumpsall towards the van.

Louden turned round to give the inspector another of his quirky smiles.

'I'm just saying,' he said.

'Your aunt and uncle are worried about an intruder in their garden,' said Blizzard. 'They've had us out two nights in a row. We haven't found any evidence that anyone was there but your uncle swears that he's not imagining it. I don't suppose you know anything about it?'

'Now, how could I?' said Louden with yet another smile. 'I don't know if you heard, but I've been in prison for sixteen years. However, if Uncle Robert said he saw someone in their garden, then there was someone in their garden. Anyway, I've got to go. I've seen enough of the place to last me a lifetime!'

And with that, he turned and walked away to catch up with Martin Crumpsall.

'What do you make of that, then?' asked Colley, when he was out of earshot.

'It's another of his little games,' said Blizzard. 'Clearly, Charlie knows more than he's letting on. Most of it comes from Martin Crumpsall, I imagine.'

'Maybe our noticeboard is right and it all adds up to something much bigger than we thought.'

'Maybe it does,' said Blizzard. 'And I can't shake the feeling that Charlie Louden remains as dangerous as his Aunt Jean says he is, either.'

'Talking of which,' said Colley. He pointed to the other side of the car park where Jean and Robert Rawmarsh had appeared. 'This is turning into a real family affair.'

'Yeah, I didn't think she'd be able to stay away,' said Blizzard.

The detectives got out of the car and walked towards the Rawmarshes.

'You talked to him, after all, then?' said Jean.

'It's more accurate to say that he talked to us,' said Blizzard. 'And before you go blabbing to the media, I did not warn him off. He did point out, however, that he is under orders to steer clear of your house as part of the conditions of his parole and that you are not to be afraid.'

'Yes, well, Charlie would promise to stay away from us, wouldn't he?' said Jean with a snort of derision. 'But it's all words, isn't it?'

This time, her parting comment did not haunt the inspector as he went about his business in the days that followed; his mind was occupied with far too many other things for her words to find space. They only forced themselves to the front of his mind when it emerged that they were the last words that he ever heard her utter.

Chapter seventeen

The Boeing 787 dropped through the clouds and touched down at Singapore Changi Airport shortly before 8am, following its thirteen-hour flight. The first thing that struck the Hafton investigators as they emerged from the air-conditioned cool of the plane was the wall of stifling humidity that greeted them. None of them had slept much on the flight from the UK and the intense, cloying heat only added to their discomfort as they headed, bleary-eyed and thick-headed, towards the baggage carousel.

Having claimed their bags, John Blizzard, Ruth Stewart and Chen Sun walked towards the crowded main concourse of one of the world's busiest airports where they saw, much to their relief amid the sea of unfamiliar faces, a slim, well-groomed clean-shaven man standing by the barrier and holding up a board on which their surnames were written. Dressed in a grey suit with a neatly folded handkerchief in his breast pocket, he exuded a cheerful aura and bounded over to Chen Sun and vigorously shook his hand.

'It is good to see you again, my friend,' he said.

'You, too,' said Chen Sun. He turned round to the others. 'Guys, may I introduce Inspector Yeo?'

'But you can call me Andy,' said Yeo. He gave a slight bow and clasped his hands together. 'I'll be looking after you during your stay in our great city. My tours for aficionados of Singaporean organised crime are the talk of Asia! You can pay by cash or credit card.'

The visitors laughed at the joke; even though they had only just met their host, his welcoming demeanour was appreciated given the previous reluctance of the police in Singapore to assist their Hafton colleagues. Yeo gestured towards the exit.

'Let's get out of this madhouse,' he said.

The Hafton investigators nodded their agreement and followed him, wheeling their bags through the crowd that thronged the concourse until they left the terminal and emerged into the morning air, feeling their skin prickle once more as they were again assailed by the wall of heat.

'We assumed that you would wish to go to the hotel first to freshen up and maybe have some rest,' said Yeo as they entered the car park. 'I hope that's OK?'

'It's a good idea,' said Blizzard. He felt ragged after the flight and assumed that the others felt the same. 'I take it that there'll be some sort of briefing?'

'We've scheduled it for mid-afternoon,' replied Yeo. 'There's a lot of ground to cover and you'll want to be at your best to take it all in. Suffice to say that you have arrived at an opportune moment. If everything comes together, you should be in for a busy couple of days. I've booked a table for lunch at the hotel at one o'clock and we'll head off to our Organised Crime Unit after that. I'll tell you what's happening then.'

Yeo led them to a SUV and loaded their bags into the rear of the vehicle as Stewart and Chen Sun climbed into the back seats with Blizzard taking the passenger seat. Soon, they were heading along the busy highway into the city with its mix of modern high-rise towers, crowded apartment blocks and large, colonial houses set amid ornamental gardens that spoke of another age in the history of Singapore. Yeo talked constantly as he drove, mainly pointing out places of interest, and normally Blizzard would have been appreciative but he found himself struggling to keep his eyes open so he let the others engage in the conversation. The night before his departure for Singapore had been a disturbed one because Mikey had begun teething and neither he nor Fee had experienced much sleep. Now, the inspector drifted off, lulled by the motion of the vehicle.

Eventually, the SUV pulled up outside their city centre hotel and, after taking showers and resting, the Hafton investigators emerged for lunch, feeling, if not completely recovered then certainly considerably better than on their arrival. Their mood was improved by a feeling of anticipation about the contents of the afternoon's briefing. Andy Yeo had not given much away on the journey into the city but made enough cryptic comments to create the feeling that Blizzard could once more reach for his marker pen, this time to draw a line between a series of apparently unconnected events in Hafton and happenings on the other side of the world.

The overall impression for the visitors was of nervous energy, a thought that added to Blizzard's growing sense that he had overlooked something important that had been developing in Hafton. Just how big soon became clear as, with lunch completed, Andy Yeo drove them to a nearby police station in the city's suburbs where, after undergoing a rigorous security check which only served to heighten the charged atmosphere, the visitors were taken to a first-floor room. As they walked along the corridors, they caught glimpses through half-open doors of groups of officers engaged in their own briefings.

'What's happening, Andy?' asked Blizzard.

'You'll find out soon enough,' said Yeo. 'Suffice to say, this place is not like this every day!'

He ushered them into the next briefing room, at the front of which stood a noticeboard similar to the one in the CID squad room at Abbey Road Police Station. There were no black lines drawn on this one, but instead five photographs had been pinned up. Each image had clearly been taken by a surveillance officer and the Hafton investigators recognised Xavier Lim, the only one of their Singaporean suspects whose picture they had seen. As Yeo looked at the board, his demeanour changed, the cheeriness of earlier in the day replaced by something much more business-like.

'Before I start,' he said, 'I would like you to promise that nothing goes out of this room until we judge it safe to do so. As you can see, we are gearing up for a significant operation and the last thing we want is word getting out to the wrong people. It grieves me to say it, but bitter experience has taught us that not every Singaporean police officer can be trusted. It's made us very suspicious – some would even say paranoid. I take it that I can rely on your discretion?'

The Hafton investigators nodded their agreement.

'We have challenges of our own like that,' said Blizzard, thinking of his recent encounter with George Ramsdale.

'Much appreciated,' said Yeo. He reached onto a nearby table to pick up a pointer, after which he walked over to the noticeboard and tapped each picture in turn. 'You have given us some names over recent weeks. Well, here are their pictures – left to right, Xavier Lim, Fu Li, Wei Ji Tan, Zhang Wei and Zayven Wen. A right rogues' gallery.'

The visitors looked at them with interest. Apart from Xavier Lim, whose picture they were already familiar with, none of them presented the traditional image of a criminal. They were fresh-faced and appeared more like bookish students than violent gang members. The Hafton investigators appreciated the opportunity to see the pictures for the first time; it felt good to know what their suspects looked like, making the investigation feel more real and the potential perpetrators more human.

'It will not have escaped your attention that these pictures were taken on surveillance operations,' continued Yeo. 'That's because, as you may well have already suspected, all your guys have links to organised crime in Singapore.'

'It was certainly the way we have been thinking,' said Blizzard. 'That our guys were part of something larger.'

'You're right. All of them are middle-ranking members of The South Siders, one of the city's major gangs which was created about a year ago when two smaller gangs joined forces. The activity you are seeing here this afternoon is in preparation for raids that will be the culmination of twelve months' work. Our senior officers say that it's time we made some arrests because the investigation is costing too much, so we're going in tomorrow.'

'Your senior officers clearly work from the same playbook as our people,' said Stewart. 'What are you arresting them for?'

'Fraud, mainly.'

'Really?' said Blizzard. He thought back to his time heading up the drugs squad on Hafton's east side before he was promoted and took over at Western Division CID. 'I thought that most gangs from this part of the world were interested in drugs?'

'Normally you would be right,' said Yeo, 'but not The South Siders. As you can see from the pictures, they're a fairly academic lot. Fu Li and Zhang Wei knew each other from school and went on to university together, which is where they met Zayven Wen. Xavier Lim and Wei Ji Tan met at university as well. The somewhat esoteric challenges presented by fraud seemed to appeal to them. However, it's not the only reason they won't deal in drugs. They can make just as much money from fraud but it attracts lesser sentences if they are caught.'

'Which explains why Xavier Lim and Wei Ji Tan have placed such importance on the fake prescriptions scam,' said Stewart.

'Exactly,' replied Yeo. 'It makes them huge amounts of money and has global potential. They're already active in the United States and Canada, and you know about the UK, of course.'

'I can see why the potential for committing a crime like that on an industrial scale might appeal to a gang,' said Blizzard. He pointed to two of the pictures. 'But what about our guys? What about Fu Li and Zhang Wei? All they did was burn down a factory as part of an insurance scam. It's hardly a global crime, is it?'

'All crime is local when you get down to it,' said Yeo.

'Fair point,' said Blizzard; it was one of his mantras when talking to young detectives. 'But I still can't see it.'

'It rather depends on how many factories you burn down, does it not?' said Yeo, with a knowing smile.

'So, how many factories *have* they burnt down?' asked Blizzard.

'Thirty-seven,' replied Yeo.

'What?'

'Thirty-seven,' said Yeo. He was enjoying the impact that his words were having. 'All over Europe. They either buy businesses or create new ones, burn the factories down after a few months, claim their insurance and move onto the next one, and they use false names to make it more difficult for law enforcement to make the connection between fires. You may know them as Fu Li and Zhang Wei but we know them by half a dozen other names, and we're still not sure which ones are right. The last we heard, they had pocketed more than twenty million dollars from the scam.'

'And Zayven Wen is crooked as well, is he?' said Blizzard. 'Because we were talking to a businessman in Hafton just before we flew out here, and he swears blind that Wen's property agency is genuine and that he is working on a major development in Hafton which has the backing of the chief executive of our local council.'

'I take it the chief executive we are talking about is the fragrant Miranda Goldsworthy?' said Yeo.

'How the—' began Blizzard.

'I hate to be rude, Chief Inspector,' Yeo said and chuckled, 'but I am beginning to think that we may know more about what's happening in Hafton than you do.'

Chen Sun and Ruth Stewart held their breath for a moment. They were acutely aware of Blizzard's reputation for dealing harshly with officers who made the kind of comment that Andy Yeo had just made. They waited for the explosion but it did not come. Instead, Blizzard, who was becoming increasingly aware that he had missed something big, gave the Singaporean officer a rueful look.

'It would seem so,' he said. 'How come you know about Miranda Goldsworthy? She told us that she knows virtually nothing about the people in Singapore who are behind the project.'

'Well, that's a lie, for a start,' said Yeo. 'She has been out here twice in the past two months and met Zayven Wen on a number of occasions, including once in Hafton. I can probably root out a surveillance picture of her if you give me enough time. I seem to recall that there's a good one showing her with Zayven Wen, Fu Li and Zhang Wei at one of our nightclubs. They were with Alec Maynard. I assume that he's the businessman you mentioned?'

'That's him,' said Blizzard. 'And you're sure it was Miranda Goldsworthy, are you?'

'How could we forget?'

'What does that mean?' asked Blizzard.

'Like I said, she enjoys the nightlife. I take it that she's single?'

'I'm not sure,' said Blizzard. He gave Yeo a glum look. 'In fact, I'm not sure about anything anymore, Andy. So, where does Zayven Wen fit into the story?'

'His company is one of the businesses that the gang uses for its money laundering,' said Yeo.

'And Alec?' asked the inspector. 'Is he crooked as well?'

Before Yeo could reply, the door opened and an elegantly dressed woman entered the room.

'May I introduce Alya Goh,' said Yeo. 'The commander of our Organised Crime Unit.'

'I am sorry it has taken so long to get round to seeing you,' said Goh. She sat down at the table. 'As you can see, I have been rather busy. I assume that Andy has been keeping you entertained in his own inimitable style?'

'He has,' said Blizzard.

'They were just asking about Alec Maynard,' said Yeo. 'They want to know if he is crooked?'

'He's a major player within The South Siders,' said the commander. 'We think that his initial motive was genuine, that all he was interested in was the redevelopment plan on the carpet factory site in Hafton. However, at some stage, Zayven Wen seems to have suggested that he use his business for money laundering. The gang is making so much money that it needs as many crooked businesses as it can get their hands on, and it doesn't look as if Alec Maynard needed much persuading. Isn't that right, Andy?'

'It is, yes,' replied Yeo. 'I'll show you the annual accounts for his company if you want. Not the genuine ones but the real ones, where it's clear how much really went through his business. They're a work of pure fiction.'

'And what about Miranda Goldsworthy?' asked Blizzard. He was not sure that he wanted to hear the answer as embarrassing revelation followed embarrassing revelation. 'Does she know that she's dealing with criminals?'

'She must have her suspicions,' said the commander. 'We don't think she's crooked, though. In over her head, behaving in a foolish manner for someone her age, yes, but crooked, no.'

There was silence in the room as the Hafton investigators digested what they had been told. Blizzard's worst fears were coming true. He had, he realised, not paid enough attention to the signs that Hafton had been drawn into a large criminal conspiracy. He had ignored Blizzard's first law of homicide investigation for far too long; he should have asked more questions when the city's links with Singapore criminals first began to emerge. And, he concluded gloomily, he should have been more active over his suspicions about the fire at Mounsey Street when he took over as head of Western CID, instead of accusing his predecessors of complacency but doing nothing about it himself. He realised that the room had fallen silent as the others waited for him to speak.

'It's a lot to take in, isn't it?' said the commander with a knowing smile. 'How much of it did you know?'

'Not enough,' said Blizzard. 'Do you think Alec Maynard was involved in the murder of our John Doe? I guess it's difficult for you to say until we work out who he was.'

'We'd been thinking it's one of the prescription fraudsters,' said Stewart, trying, like Blizzard, to find a way of saving face. 'Xavier Lim hasn't been seen for months.'

'We thought that was a possibility when we heard about the body,' said Commander Goh. 'But we've had the gang under heavy surveillance over the past few days and one of our teams spotted Lim in a bar in the city last night.'

'So who *is* the dead man?' asked Chen Sun.

Commander Goh glanced at Yeo.

'Tell them,' she said.

'We suspect,' said Yeo sadly, reaching into his jacket pocket and producing a photograph of an unshaven Asian man, which he pinned to the noticeboard, 'that it's Mattias Chau. Or to be more precise, *Sergeant* Mattias Chau of the Singapore Police Surveillance Operations Unit. Hopefully, your forensics guys can help us confirm it.'

'A copper?' exclaimed Blizzard as all three of the Hafton investigators stared at Yeo in astonishment. 'You had a man working in our city?'

'An undercover officer, yes,' said Yeo.

The Hafton investigators examined the picture with intense interest; up until now, the dead man had been nameless and faceless – now it was possible that he had a name and a face and a job that it was reasonable to assume had cost him his life. Chastened by the volume of things he was learning about his own city, Blizzard saw an opportunity to regain some control of the situation.

'We really should have been told that one of your people was working in our area,' he said. There was an edge to his voice. 'We could have kept an eye on him. Who knows, we could maybe even have stopped him from being murdered?'

The comment led to a rapid change in the atmosphere in the room. Suddenly, there was tension in the air and, struggling to contain barely repressed irritation at being challenged in such a manner, the commander gave Blizzard a hard look.

'We would have told you that he was in Hafton, had we known,' she said in pinched tones.

'But he was your man,' said Chen Sun, also sensing that this was an opportunity for the Hafton officers to save face. 'You must have known he was there, surely?'

'Well, we didn't,' said the commander.

'Mattias was his own man,' explained Yeo. 'He played by his own rules and he didn't always tell us where he was. We assumed that he was in America because that is where he was when we lost track of him. His job was to stick close to Lim and Ji Tan. They were at a medical conference in San Diego. We talked to Mattias a couple of times when he was there but we didn't hear from him after that.'

'So do you think that Xavier Lim and Wei Ji Tan had something to do with your guy's death then?' asked Blizzard.

'It's not that simple,' said Yeo. 'We feared the worst, of course we did, but there was no body, and by the time the police in San Diego got themselves into gear, Lim and Ji Tan had moved on. They didn't show on our radar for seven weeks and that was in Florida, with Ji Tan on his own. Like you, Ruth, we had no idea where Xavier Lim was. Next thing we knew, a member of your team rang us to say that the two of them had been working in the UK.'

Commander Goh gave them a wry smile; her irritation had vanished and her guests sensed that she wished to banish the tension between them.

'You see, you're not the only ones who miss things,' she said. 'And to answer your question about Alec Maynard being responsible for the murder, we're not ruling anyone out at this stage.'

'How come you didn't tell us all this earlier?' asked Blizzard. 'The Singapore Police have been distinctly unhelpful.'

'That's been our experience as well,' said Ruth Stewart. 'The flow of information has all been one way, us to you, and you waited until we had flown halfway round the world to take us into your confidence. Why would you do that? We could have worked much better together.'

'I apologise,' said Goh. 'We were about to get in touch with Hafton Police, Chief Inspector, but your DI Ramsey beat us to it. If I am honest, Mattias's death has made everyone paranoid about security and we were not sure how much you could be trusted. Andy has probably mentioned that we have had a problem with officers leaking information and, clearly, someone betrayed Mattias.'

They heard loud voices in the corridor as a group of officers passed by the briefing room.

'When are you carrying out your raids?' asked Chen Sun.

'First light tomorrow,' said the commander. 'Seventeen addresses, including, I think I am right in saying, all your guys. That's right, isn't it, Andy?'

'It is,' said Yeo.

'Do you want me to ask our people to arrest Alec Maynard?' asked Blizzard.

'Not for the moment,' said the commander. 'We'll have enough to do with the ones we arrest here. You can bring him in later.'

'There's another name you might have heard,' said Stewart. 'Martin Crumpsall. He's from Hafton and he's been producing fake documents for Xavier Lim and Wei Ji Tan.'

'And not just for the prescription fraud,' said Yeo. 'He knocked up a load of stuff for Alec Maynard as well. Bank statements, investment certificates, the kind of thing that he needs to launder money through his business.'

'I'm happy to leave him for the moment,' said the commander. 'You can always pick the UK ones up as part of your investigations when the time is right.'

Blizzard and Stewart nodded and Goh stood up.

'I'll see you in the morning then,' she said.

Andy Yeo waited for her to leave the room.

'I told you that you had arrived at an interesting time!' he said when she had gone.

Chapter eighteen

A couple of hours later, John Blizzard, Chen Sun and Andy Yeo found themselves sitting in an unmarked police surveillance van parked in the city. It was still humid and the Hafton officers were sweating profusely in the cramped observation space behind the cabin as they studied a bank of screens. Even Andy Yeo, who was well used to Singapore's oppressive heat, frequently reached up to wipe away the glistening beads of sweat forming on his forehead with a handkerchief.

The vehicle had been parked for more than an hour, Yeo having selected a spot close to the city's most celebrated watering hole for their vigil. Taxis constantly pulled up outside the classically designed floodlit colonial building that housed the Raffles Hotel and the night air was full of chatter and laughter as the passengers spilled out, young men dressed in smart casual attire and women in expensive dresses.

Although one of the cameras took in a view of the Raffles, the watchers' main place of interest was a much smaller watering hole. Three men sat in the front window, deep in conversation as they drank their beer. The Hafton officers recognised factory owners Fu Li and Zhang Wei and money launderer Zayven Wen from the surveillance pictures. All three were smartly, but casually, dressed and Blizzard and Sun watched in fascination as their targets finally became real. They assumed that Ruth Stewart was experiencing similar thoughts as she sat with a couple of Singaporean officers in another surveillance van parked up in a narrow side street three miles away, close to a crowded bar with outside tables, at one of which sat fraudsters Xavier Lim and Wei Ji Tan. Chen Sun's attention wandered to the bar.

'Boy, how I could I do with a Singapore sling right now,' he said wistfully.

'You been to the Raffles before?' asked Yeo.

'I certainly have,' said Sun. 'I came here with my wife five years ago. We'd been to see family in China and spent three nights in Singapore on the way back.'

'I've never been here,' said Blizzard, adding ruefully. 'Perhaps I should make it a more regular stop so that I can keep an eye on Hafton's villains!'

'Don't beat yourself up about it,' said Yeo. 'It happens to us all.'

'I guess so,' said Blizzard. 'Anyway, going back to your question, Europe's more my thing really. Italy mainly.'

'I like Europe,' said Yeo.

Chen Sun winked at Blizzard; he had reminded the inspector before they left the hotel that Yeo would at some stage manoeuvre the conversation round to his desire to secure a job in Britain.

'Might there been a chance for me to work as a detective in Hafton, do you think?' asked Yeo tentatively. 'Do you take many people from foreign parts?'

'Oh, aye,' said Blizzard. 'Loads of them.'

Yeo glanced at Sun in confusion.

'Chen gave me the impression that you didn't,' he said.

'Why would you say a thing like that?' said Blizzard. He gave Sun a sharp look. 'Surely you know that we've even taken officers on from Lancashire?'

Yeo still looked uncertain and looked to Sun for an explanation.

'It's a joke,' said the inspector. 'He makes them from time to time. He'll probably do another one next year.'

Yeo relaxed, relieved that his dream had not evaporated.

'And in answer to your question,' said Blizzard, 'our force has been very poor when it comes to diversity but we are trying to change. Chen is our first Asian officer and we recently took on a couple of constables from the Caribbean and one from South Africa. I'm perfectly prepared to consider applications for a detective post from this part of the world. In fact, I've just made one of my sergeants an acting inspector so there may well be a vacancy there.'

'Excellent,' said Yeo. He took another look at the screens. 'I can't see the point of staying here much longer, guys. We just wanted to make sure that everyone was still in the city, and the longer we hang around the more chance there is that they'll begin to suspect that something's afoot. Shall we call it a night?'

The Hafton officers nodded with relief; the weariness brought on by their long day had begun to catch up with them.

'I know that you'll want to catch up on your sleep,' said Yeo, 'but how about a quick debrief at the hotel first?'

They returned to the hotel and Blizzard and Sun freshened up in their rooms before heading down to meet Yeo and Stewart in the lounge. As Blizzard emerged from the lift, one of the receptionists approached him, holding a piece of paper.

'I have a message for you,' she said and handed over the note. 'Can you please ring Acting Detective Inspector David Colley at Hafton Police? He says he tried your mobile but there was no answer.'

'It's charging in my room,' said Blizzard.

'No worries. I have jotted down the number. You can use the telephone at reception, if you wish.'

As Blizzard took a seat at reception and waited for the phone to be answered, he felt a powerful sense of foreboding; there was no way that this was going to be good news and, instinctively, his mind went to the Rawmarshes.

'Please, God, no,' he murmured as the phone was answered. 'David, it's Blizzard. Why do I have this awful feeling that this is not a social call?'

'Because it's not,' said Colley in a flat voice. 'We've had a murder.'

'Please don't tell me that it's Jean Rawmarsh.'

'I am afraid so.'

Blizzard swore so loudly that several guests sitting nearby turned to look at him. He mouthed an apology and his next words to Colley were quieter.

'What happened?' he asked.

'History repeating itself, guv. Jean's worst fear. Someone broke into their house and attacked her with a machete as she lay in bed. Unfortunately, this time he got it right. She was dead by the time the ambulance arrived.'

Blizzard closed his eyes and, sure enough, the last thing Jean Rawmarsh said to him returned to haunt the detective. *Charlie would promise to stay away from us, wouldn't he? But it's all words, isn't it?* She was right, he thought, opening his eyes, right like she always was when it came to Charlie Louden. It *was* all words. She had repeatedly warned him of the danger the couple were in, and he hadn't done enough to prevent it from happening. Blizzard sighed; this was turning into one of the worst weeks of his police career, he thought bleakly, and the ramifications were already playing out in his mind.

'You still there?' asked Colley.

'Unfortunately,' said Blizzard. A thought struck him. 'What about Robert? Was he there when it happened?'

'He's a bit of a hero. He heard the back door being kicked in and ran out onto the landing in time to see a masked man coming up the stairs, wielding the machete. Robert grabbed a lamp and tried to hit him but the guy caught him twice on the arm with his machete then slammed him against the wall. Robert lost consciousness and by the time he came to his senses, the intruder had gone and Jean was dead.'

Blizzard detected a slight tremble in Colley's voice, which was unusual for an officer known for his calmness in even the most difficult of situations.

'You OK?' asked the inspector.

'Not really,' replied Colley quietly. 'It was truly awful. Jean had half a dozen gashes on her arms but the blow that killed her sliced through her aorta. I've never seen so much blood. She had no chance. Absolutely no chance.'

He fell silent for a few moments and Blizzard gave him time to recover his composure.

'Sorry about that,' said Colley eventually. 'Very unprofessional.'

'No need to apologise, David. I take it that you have tried to arrest Charlie Louden?'

'Chris Ramsey and Jenny Carr went round to Martin Crumpsall's flat but there was no one there and Crumpsall's car has gone.'

'Did Robert ID Charlie as his attacker?'

'Not in a way that was particularly convincing. Sarah talked to him at the hospital and he told her that it was Charlie, but the guy had a mask on so he did not see his face. It was only a brief conversation, though. He took a nasty knock to the head and the doctors said that we would have to wait to talk to him properly. I saw Alec at the house and he said it had to be Charlie as well. It has to be him, hasn't it?'

'Maybe.'

'What do you mean maybe?'

'It's just that it's a bit too obvious, isn't it?' said Blizzard.

'Sometimes it *is* obvious.'

'Yeah, I know, but surely he would know that once his aunt had been attacked, we would be straight round to nick him, wouldn't he?'

'I dare say he would, but he knew that the first time he attacked them, and it didn't stop him then, did it? Maybe when the red mist comes down, he doesn't care what happens to him. Maybe, we have to face the unpalatable truth that Jean was right about him all along. He wouldn't be the first prisoner to con the experts in order to get out of prison, would he? It has to be Charlie. Who else could it be?'

'I find that such a question is always worth asking,' said Blizzard.

'What does that mean?' asked Colley; there was a hint of irritation in his voice at the way his judgement was being challenged.

'It means that when you are the officer in charge of a major inquiry like this, you have to consider all the options,' said Blizzard. 'I think it might be worth looking at Alec Maynard.'

'Surely, you don't think that he killed his mother?'

'I'm not sure I would go that far,' said Blizzard. 'However, I think it may be worth coming at Jean's death from another angle. Do you remember when Charlie told us that Jean was worried about Alec getting involved in criminal activity? Well, the cops over here reckon that she had good cause to be worried and that Alec is heavily involved with money laundering for our Singaporean guys.'

'So much for his father objecting when you impugned the good name of his family.'

'Indeed,' said Blizzard. 'I put Charlie's comment down to devilment at the time – he does have a record of trying to blacken the family's name, after all – but it would appear that he was right. What if – and I'm making this up as I go along, I have nothing to back it up – what if word gets back to the gang that Jean is panicking and is determined to help her son? Maybe they get it into their heads that she might try to do a deal with us – she tells us everything she knows in return for us going easy on Alec? Who knows what the gang would do to stop her spilling the beans?'

'It's certainly plausible.'

'And what's worse, it was unfolding in front of us and we did not see it,' said Blizzard. 'This could get very messy very quickly, David. It won't be long before the blame game starts.'

'It already has. The force has reported itself to the Independent Office for Police Conduct because of our previous contact with the family, and the chief has been onto Arthur three times, pressing him for assurances that we did everything we could have done to keep the Rawmarshes safe.'

'And what did Arthur say?'

'What can he say?' said Colley. 'Jean is in the morgue and her husband is in hospital. It's difficult to argue with that, isn't it? Arthur says that the media will have a field day and that the top brass will spend most of their time covering their backsides. He's going to try to ring you later. Anyway, enough of my problems. Anything interesting happening over there?'

'Plenty. Looks like our John Doe might have been an undercover cop.'

'Really?'

'Yeah, a guy called Mattias Chau. He was working for the Singapore police, keeping an eye on our suspects.'

'Nice of them to tell us.'

'The point has been made. Can you tell Versace that the cops will be emailing Chau's fingerprints over to him to check against our John Doe? They should be with him soon.'

'Will do,' said Colley. 'How come we didn't know about this undercover guy?'

'It's a long story,' said Blizzard.

After talking for a few more minutes, they finished the call and it was a pensive John Blizzard who walked into the bar where Sun, Stewart and Yeo were gathered at a corner table, drinks and snacks spread out in front of them.

'What do you fancy to drin…' began Andy Yeo, standing up then noticing inspector's grim expression. 'What's wrong?'

'Alec Maynard's mother was murdered last night,' said Blizzard. He sat down at the table. 'The attacker forced his way into the house and killed her with a machete.'

'So there *was* someone in their garden,' said Chen Sun. He frowned. 'I take it that you know what this means? There'll be a lot of questions. Were our searches of the street thorough enough? Did we miss anything? Should anyone face disciplinary action? Did we take Jean seriously enough?'

'The chief is already demanding answers,' said Blizzard gloomily.

'I'll bet he is, and it explains why I have two missed calls from my super on my mobile,' said Sun. He shook his head. 'I was about to ring him. What a mess.'

Chapter nineteen

It took John Blizzard a few moments to work out where he was when the ringing of the bedside telephone shook him roughly from sleep. After realising that he was in Singapore, he rolled over and looked at the digital clock in the bedside table, which told him that there was less than an hour to go before the Hafton investigators were due to meet Andy Yeo in the hotel lobby. Cursing as the insistent ringing of the phone continued to demand his attention, the inspector finally picked up the receiver.

'This had better be good,' he mumbled.

'You know it never is,' said Graham Ross's sombre voice. 'We have checked the partial fingerprints that the Singapore Police sent over and there's enough to say with reasonable confidence that our John Doe is indeed Mattias Chau. We've not told them yet. We thought you would prefer to do it face to face.'

'They'll appreciate that,' said Blizzard. His head was clearing rapidly. 'I think they'd pretty much guessed it was him but they weren't sure. Did you turn up any useful forensics from the Rawmarshes' house?'

'Not really. There's too much blood in the bedroom to extract anything there and the intruder must have worn gloves. There are no fingerprints either. I'm putting Dave back on to update you on the rest, such as it is.'

There was the sound of the phone being handed over.

'Morning, guv,' said Colley. 'Sad news about Mattias Chau but having his name has, at least, made things a little easier. You remember that I had Sarah Allatt checking flights from Singapore at around about the time we think he was murdered, just in case any of our Singaporean suspects were in the UK, but we drew a blank? Well, she went back to the passenger lists and checked for Mattias Chau and it turns out that he flew into the UK from the States on May 15. We don't recognise any of the other names but I've emailed the list over to you so that you can run it past the Singapore cops. We're trying to get hold of CCTV footage from the airport, as well. It may throw up a face that one of them recognises.'

'It may well do,' said Blizzard. 'How's it going on the Rawmarsh inquiry? Charlie Louden still missing?'

'He is, and so is Martin Crumpsall, but the more I thought about it, the more I liked your idea that it was the Singaporeans who had Jean silenced. I don't think Alec killed her. Sarah doesn't think that it was him either, and although I appreciate that she is close to the family, I tend to agree. However, I bet he knows who *did* kill her. It would be easy enough for the gang to bring in someone to do it, wouldn't it?'

'It would,' said Blizzard. 'Not as easy as it looks, this running a murder inquiry lark, is it?'

'What do you mean? It's child's play.'

'What?'

'Well,' said Colley, 'as far as I can see, you sit in your office drinking cups of tea and wait for someone else to solve your crime for you. Enjoy kicking some doors down. Talk later.'

* * *

138

Tears glistened in Andy Yeo's eyes as he sat at a corner table in the hotel lobby and listened to Blizzard breaking the news about the death of Mattias Chau.

'I guess, deep down, we always knew that he was dead,' said Yeo.

'I really am sorry, Andy,' said Blizzard. 'I wish I could tell you something different but our forensics guy says that there's little doubt that it's him.'

He wiped his eyes with the back of his hand and sighed. 'He was a difficult man to know, was Mattias, and absolutely infuriating to work with, but I counted him among my closest friends in the job and he didn't deserve this. You said that he flew into Manchester from the States?'

'That's right,' said Blizzard. 'On May 15.'

'Was he travelling alone?'

'We're not sure about that,' said Blizzard. He picked up his smartphone from the table and called up the passenger list that Colley had emailed over. 'We know that he only bought his own ticket – one-way – but we are wondering if someone was with him, maybe sitting separately on the plane. Or maybe following him.'

'It's always possible,' said Yeo. 'He walked a narrow line, did Mattias, and it was not really a surprise when he went missing. Do you have any idea who this mystery person might be?'

Blizzard held up the phone so that Yeo could read the passenger list.

'We were hoping that his name would be here,' he said. 'No one on the manifest is known to us.'

Yeo screwed up his eyes to decipher the small print as he scanned the list then gave a gentle exclamation and tapped the screen.

'You recognise a name?' asked Blizzard.

'Not just recognise it, but I also reckon that we can say with a degree of confidence that he is your murderer. You know I said that the factory guys used various names for their scams?' Blizzard nodded and Yeo tapped the screen again. 'Well, Caelum Lee is one of the names that Zayven Wen used – and he can be a nasty bastard, when he has to be.'

'But would Mattias not have seen him? They must have met during his time undercover.'

'Maybe they did but I am guessing that Zayven wore a disguise. He does have a sense of the theatrical about him. Anyway, whichever way you view it, you were looking for someone suspicious on the plane and you've found him, haven't you?'

Yeo glanced at the wall clock, looked across the lobby to where Ruth Stewart and Chen Sun were waiting for them, and stood up.

'We'd better get moving,' he said. 'The teams will be heading out on the raids soon and we don't want to miss out on the fun, do we?'

Chapter twenty

It was dark when the police minibus pulled into the car park in front of the apartment block on the fringes of Singapore city centre. The driver cut the engine and switched off the headlights and the officers, all of whom were armed, alighted from the vehicle and headed for the block. Most of the windows were still in darkness as the residents slept, unaware of the drama that was about to unfold. With the officers' way illuminated by the lights on their helmets, they approached the main entrance, followed by Blizzard, Andy Yeo and Chen Sun.

Amid the sound of tearing timber, the front door was ripped off its hinges with a single blow from a hydraulic ram, allowing the officers to make their way rapidly along the ground floor corridor until they reached Apartment 4. Once there, the door was again smashed open, this time accompanied by warning shouts as they entered the apartment. The first officers made for the bedroom, where a light had been switched on, and they burst in to be confronted by a startled and half-naked Zayven Wen, who was struggling out of bed.

'What the…?' he exclaimed.

Andy Yeo stepped forward, holding a set of handcuffs.

'Zayven Wen,' he said, 'you are under arrest on suspicion of involvement in fraud.'

'Fraud!' exclaimed Wen. He sat back on the bed and began to laugh. 'All these highly paid police officers for fraud, Andy? Talk about overkill, man. My lawyer will have me out by lunchtime. He did last time.'

'Yes, he did,' said Yeo, 'but last time we did not want to talk to you about murder, as well.'

Wen stared at him uneasily.

'Murder?' he said. 'What do you mean, murder? I don't know anything about a murder.'

Yeo gestured for Blizzard to step forward.

'Chief Inspector,' he said, passing the handcuffs to Blizzard, 'perhaps you would like to explain?'

The presence of a police officer that Wen did not recognise appeared to add to his unease, an unease which grew as the detective began to speak.

'I am Detective Chief Inspector John Blizzard of the British Police,' he said. 'And this is my colleague, Inspector Chen Sun. We wish to talk to you in connection with the murder in Hafton of Police Sergeant Mattias Chau, of the Singapore Police, earlier this year.'

'I've never heard of him,' said Wen. However, the flicker of concern on his face told another story. 'What's more, there's been nothing in the newspapers about a Singapore police officer being murdered.'

'That's because his body was only identified last night. We believe that he died shortly after May 15. You'll remember that date, Zayven, because it was the day you flew into Manchester on the same flight as the man you claim not to know,' said Blizzard. He held up the handcuffs. 'You, in the common parlance of the British police force, are nicked, my son!'

Chapter twenty-one

It took the best part of the morning for processing to be completed on all the arrested people – mostly men, but also half a dozen young women – and the police station buzzed with excited activity, as delighted detectives went about their business and shocked members of the gang tried to come to terms with what had happened to them. Following a meeting with the commander, it was agreed that the Hafton investigators could share some of the interviewing duties with members of the Singapore team.

With agreement reached, Blizzard and his colleagues spent some time in the custody suite.

'I don't see any lawyers,' said Blizzard as Andy Yeo came to join them.

Yeo gave a wry smile.

'The Singaporean justice system tends to – how can I put it? – "discourage" solicitors at this stage of the process,' he said. 'We find that they do rather get in the way.'

Ruth Stewart chuckled.

'John will think he has died and gone to heaven,' she said.

* * *

Early that afternoon, Blizzard and Andy Yeo found themselves sitting down with Zayven Wen in one of the stuffy little interview rooms. Wen had recovered much of his composure.

'Might I suggest that this is getting us nowhere?' he said. 'I have never heard of this Sergeant Chau and certainly had nothing to do with his murder. I am an innocent man.'

'But, surely, you can see what a remarkable coincidence it is that you and the sergeant were on the same plane taking you to the UK?' said Blizzard.

'Something you have pointed out repeatedly,' said Wen wearily. 'However, as I have said, what does it prove? I run a legitimate property agency and have visited the UK on a number of occasions, most recently in connection with the redevelopment of the Mounsey Street area in Hafton. From where I am sitting, you have nothing that links me with the unfortunate death of this police officer.'

'A police officer whose body was found in the building which lies at the heart of your redevelopment, might I remind you,' said Blizzard.

'I don't require to be reminded of the fact, or your pet theory on coincidences. It is just that, Chief Inspector, a coincidence. I do not own the building, I do not have access to it and it's not my redevelopment. You should really be talking to Fu Li and Zhang Wei.'

'We will be,' said Blizzard.

'In the meantime, might I suggest that it is time for you to release me then?'

There was silence in the room for a few moments as Blizzard made a point of appearing to consider the request. If he hoped, however, that a prolonged silence would increase the pressure on the suspect, he was wrong because Zayven produced a theatrical yawn and sat back in his chair, with his arms folded and a self-satisfied look on his face. Andy Yeo glanced at Blizzard, wondering how the inspector was planning to break the stalemate.

'Before I let you go,' said Blizzard eventually, 'can we talk about the murder of Jean Rawmarsh?'

Up until then, Zayven Wen had been drawing on his sense of theatre to display a range of facial expressions designed to convince the detectives that he was baffled as to why he had been arrested. However, at mention of Jean Rawmarsh's name, his puzzlement appeared to be genuine.

'Who's she?' he asked.

'Alec Maynard's mother,' said Blizzard. 'We know that you and Alec have worked closely together on the Mounsey Street development.'

'Our relationship is strictly professional and I have not met his mother.' Wen assumed a sympathetic expression. 'Murdered, you say? It's a tragic thing to happen but why ask me about it? Unless you are suggesting that I was somehow involved, which is ridiculous. Why on earth would I want to kill Alec's mother? Besides, in case you hadn't noticed, we're halfway round the world from Hafton.'

Blizzard had hoped against hope that the introduction of Jean Rawmarsh's death would throw Zayven Wen off-guard but the suspect's response was exactly what he had expected. Calm. Assured. Confident. The response of a man who knew that the inspector had nothing to back up his accusations – as did Andy Yeo. Suddenly, Blizzard felt a long way from home, but before he could try a new angle of attack for his questioning, there was a knock on the door and it opened to reveal Ruth Stewart. She had been in another interview room further along the corridor where she and a Singapore detective had been questioning Xavier Lim about the prescription fraud.

'Sorry to interrupt,' she said. 'Can I have a word?'

Blizzard and Yeo followed her into the corridor.

'I hope you have turned up something useful, Ruth,' said Blizzard, searching her features for an indication of hope but finding nothing. 'Andy's team may get some of the fraud stuff to stick to Wen but I'm sinking without trace in there when it comes to the murders. I'd hate to think that we've come all this way and spent all this money for nothing, but as it stands, all we have is a lot of guesswork and we'll only get a breakthrough if Zayven makes a mistake.'

'It doesn't look like he'll do that any time soon,' said Yeo. 'He's a smooth operator, is our Mr Wen. Always has been.'

'Maybe he doesn't need to make a mistake,' said Stewart enigmatically.

'You *have* turned something up, haven't you?' said Blizzard, still seeking something in her expression.

Stewart did not react.

'Remind me never to play poker with you,' said Blizzard.

The NHS investigator could contain her excitement no longer, she abandoned the deadpan act and her eyes gleamed.

'I certainly have turned something up,' she said. 'Xavier Lim has broken ranks. He wants to do a deal.'

'What kind of deal?' asked Blizzard.

'He won't give exact details until you are there as well,' replied Stewart. 'But from what he has said so far, it sounds like he knows enough to bring the whole lot crashing down!'

Chapter twenty-two

Even though Ruth Stewart was to be proved right about the importance of Xavier Lim's testimony, the early signs were not promising as Blizzard took a seat next to her, across the table from the suspect. Andy Yeo, having had a hurried discussion with his commander, leaned against the wall, and both he and Blizzard viewed Lim with profound scepticism; he did not convey the impression of someone who was about to strike a mortal blow to The South Siders. What struck Blizzard most of all was the stark contrast between the hunched frame of Xavier Lim and the assured way that Zayven Wen had conducted himself, exuding confidence and constantly making eye contact with his questioners in a gesture of defiance. Lim, however, did not look up and his hands shook. He was, to all intents, a broken man.

Blizzard glanced at Stewart. She gave him a knowing smile in return.

Sitting next to Lim, was a slim dark-haired woman in her thirties. Blizzard looked at Yeo and raised an eyebrow.

'We would not normally allow a lawyer in at this stage,' explained Andy Yeo. 'But these are somewhat extraordinary circumstances so we have made an exception.'

The lawyer viewed her client with growing concern.

'And I really would rather that we delayed this,' she said. 'I mean, just look at him.'

'No!' exclaimed Lim. He finally looked up. 'I want to get this done now. I want to do a deal.'

The lawyer shrugged and sat back in her chair.

'I've said what I think,' she said. 'If you ignore it, it's up to you.'

'What kind of deal do you have in mind, Xavier?' asked Blizzard.

Lim met the inspector's gaze with eyes that glistened with tears.

'It's my parents,' he mumbled in a voice that was so low it could hardly be heard. 'They're very old and very frail, and I am the only one who looks after them. If I am extradited to the UK, they'll have to go into a home and I could not bear the thought of them dying in there without me.'

He burst into tears, his body racked with sobs, and it was several minutes before he was ready to continue, during which time he rejected further attempts by his lawyer to delay proceedings.

'Let's say that I like the idea of a deal,' said Blizzard when Lim's tears had subsided. 'What are you offering? You're in a lot of trouble, Xavier, so whatever you are offering, it had better be good.'

'I'll tell you everything I know about The South Siders,' said Lim. He looked at Ruth Stewart. 'And in return, the only charge I face is a lesser one related to her investigation into the prescription frauds.'

Lim had started to gather his composure now and a more calculating man was beginning to emerge from behind the film of tears. Blizzard wondered if the detectives had been played all along, and whether or not the broken man in front of them was shrewder than the investigators had given him credit for. Blizzard concluded that it didn't really matter if Lim delivered on his promise. Nevertheless, he decided to not come over as too eager.

'I mean,' he said, 'it's all very well you offering your co-operation, but you are involved in the prescription fraud right up to your neck, Xavier. We can't just ignore that.'

Ruth Stewart nodded in agreement.

'It's not a victimless crime,' she said. 'And, at the end of the day, someone has to pay for it.'

'Yes, I know that,' said Lim. 'But I was really only a bit part player. Wei Ji Tan was the brains behind the scam and I can prove it. He has also hooked up with a brilliant forger called Martin Crumpsall, who a friend of his met in Hafton Prison. Crumpsall recently came out of prison and I have been sidelined more and more. I can give you what you need on both of them, not to mention other gang members who were involved, but it'll come at a higher price than a lesser charge. I'm not giving it away.'

Blizzard and Stewart exchanged looks which suggested that they were becoming increasingly interested. The inspector glanced over at Andy Yeo, who gave the slightest nod of the head.

'So what exactly do you want?' asked Stewart.

'I want a guaranteed suspended sentence from a Singapore court,' said Lim in a voice that was growing ever stronger and more assertive. 'I do not serve any jail time and I also want myself and my parents to be given new identities and admitted to the witness protection programme. The South Siders will come after me, and the last you want is for someone like Zayven Wen to catch up with you. You have got to keep us safe; it's part of the deal. Refuse to do that and everything is off.'

'We'd want more than a few snippets on Wei Ji Tan and Martin Crumpsall,' said Yeo. 'And since, by your own admission, you were a bit part player, how useful can you be, anyway? For all we know, you're just a mouth.'

'I've been with The South Siders from the start, so believe me when I say that I know everything about them,' said Lim. 'And I *mean* everything. Can you really afford to turn down this kind of an offer?'

'I'm prepared to go with it,' said Blizzard with a growing sense of anticipation at the possibilities before him. He looked at Stewart and Yeo, who both nodded their agreement. 'But before we say yes, put our minds at rest. Tell us something we don't know.'

'How about how The South Siders hacked into the computer systems of a couple of Singapore banks last year and got away with fifteen million dollars from each of them?' said Lim. 'I can give you it in detail. Chapter and verse. And I can tell you where to find the paperwork that proves it.'

Blizzard looked at Yeo, who nodded again, much more enthusiastically this time.

'We know nothing about any of that,' he said.

'That's because the banks have kept in quiet,' said Lim. 'It's not exactly good for business, is it?'

'It's certainly a good start,' said Blizzard. 'And the Singapore Police will be very interested in what you have to say, I'm sure, Xavier, but I'll need something specific to take back to my bosses in Hafton to justify dropping extradition proceedings. There's plenty of people back home who would like to see you standing in the dock at Hafton Crown Court. Isn't that right, Ruth?'

'There certainly is,' she said. 'There's few things that annoy people more than the thought of fraudsters robbing the NHS blind – particularly when they're not even from the UK.'

'Nasty old Johnny Foreigner, eh?' said Lim, giving her a wry smile. 'How about I give you Zayven Wen for the murder of Sergeant Chau in that factory in Hafton?'

'That's more like it,' said Blizzard.

He turned round to look at Andy Yeo; the Singaporean detective was leaning forward and listening intently. Lim clearly noticed his interest and there was a glint in his eyes;

he knew that he had their attention now and that the deal was there to be done.

'Chau presented himself as an expert in money laundering,' he said. 'That's why the gang accepted him without much in the way of questions. They were making so much money that they desperately needed people like him.'

'That sounds right,' said Yeo. 'Finance was Mattias's thing.'

'And he was very convincing,' said Lim. 'The thought that he was a police officer never crossed our minds but Zayven Wen found out. When Chau flew to the UK for a meeting with Fu Li and Zhang Wei about laundering money through the Mounsey Street development, Zayven followed him.'

'And he was the one who killed him, was he?' asked Andy Yeo. His voice trembled slightly but he managed to retain a professional demeanour.

'Under orders, yes. I'll sign a statement naming the gang members who told him to do it.' Lim gave Yeo a wicked look. 'He did it with a machete. He likes a machete, does Zayven.'

Yeo closed his eyes for a few moments, clearly struggling with his emotions as he relived his friend's final minutes of life. Blizzard's expression gave nothing away about what he was thinking but his emotions were probably very different to those of his Singaporean colleague. Deep down, the inspector was experiencing a powerful sense of satisfaction, overwhelmed by relief that a murder that had looked like it would be difficult to solve, and would cause him endless political problems at headquarters, was proving to be just the opposite. Sitting there, many miles from home as Lim revealed what he knew, Blizzard relished the thought of returning to Hafton and silencing his critics yet again, particularly George Ramsdale. He noticed that Yeo had opened his eyes and was looking at him expectantly, waiting for his next question.

'Why murder him in the factory?' asked Blizzard. 'Surely, he knew it would draw attention to The South Siders if the body was found?'

'It appealed to Zayven's sense of the theatrical,' said Lim. He gave a wry smile. 'He does like his theatrics, does Zayven. And when it was done, he said that it made more sense to leave the body there because nobody ever visited the factory. "Who would look under a pile of wood, anyway?" he said. He reckoned that it would be riskier to move it. He said that, if it looked like the Mounsey Street redevelopment was going to go ahead, he would hire someone to set fire to the corpse, making it difficult to identify, and no, I don't know who set the fire. There was nothing to suggest that the Singapore Police knew that their man was in Hafton, so Zayven assumed that the local officers would think that the dead man was a down-and-out, and everyone knows that the police don't spend much time on dead down-and-outs.'

'He had it all worked out, didn't he?' said Blizzard.

'Except he didn't take into account the fire not taking properly,' said Lim. 'And by the time he realised it, the fire brigade had found the body.'

Silence settled on the room as the investigators digested what they had been told. It was Andy Yeo who broke the silence.

'How come Zayven found out that Mattias was undercover?' he asked.

Lim gave him another wicked look.

'Because Zayven has a Singapore Police officer in his pocket,' he said. 'And no, I have no idea who it is, but wouldn't you like to know?'

Yeo closed his eyes again as his worst nightmare came true.

Lim chuckled – he was enjoying himself. He turned his attention back to Blizzard.

'And if your bosses want anything else,' he said, 'I will also make a statement saying that I heard Fu Li and Zhang

Wei discussing setting the first fire at the factory. It's an insurance scam that they have tried loads of times.'

'You have been a busy little bee, haven't you?' said Blizzard. As much as he valued the intelligence that was provided by informants, a part of him found their lack of loyalty to fellow criminals distasteful.

Lim probably guessed what he was thinking but said nothing; he had his own agenda to follow.

'One last thing,' said Blizzard. 'Alec Maynard's mother has been murdered. Do you know anything about that?'

'I know I told Zayven that killing someone like that crosses the line, that the police are not that bothered about dead down-and-outs but that they will throw everything they have at the murder of a respectable woman.' Lim shook his head. 'But he wouldn't listen. He said that there was no other option if she was determined to follow through on her plan to tell the police everything she knew in return for you letting Alec off lightly. And she knew a lot. According to Alec, he had told her everything. Silly boy.'

'Who did the actual murder?' asked Blizzard.

'I'm not sure, but I heard Zayven discussing it with Alec on the phone the day before it happened. Judging by their conversation, Alec was very reluctant to do it. I mean, you would be, wouldn't you? Your own mother?' Lim gave another of his knowing smiles. 'It's ironic really – if they had known that I was going to do this, there would be little point in murdering the old girl. Isn't life cruel? Anyway, I've told you enough. I'm not saying anything else until you say we have a deal. *Do* we have a deal, Chief Inspector?'

'It's a yes from me,' said Blizzard. He looked at Yeo. 'What about you, Andy?'

'I'll have to run it past my commander but I can't see a problem.'

Blizzard looked at Ruth Stewart.

'And what about you?' he asked.

Stewart nodded.

'There's enough in there for us,' she said. 'Somewhere along the line, we'll end up with someone going to court, and that's enough to keep my line manager happy.'

Lim beamed.

'In which case, it will be a pleasure to do business with you,' he said. 'Now, have you got some paper and a pen? I've got a lot of writing to do. And is there the chance of a cup of tea and some sandwiches? Ham would be ideal – but don't cut it too thick…'

Leaving another officer to oversee the taking of the statement, the three investigators walked out into the corridor and solemnly shook hands.

'I can't wait to see Zayven Wen's face when you tell him what's happened, John,' said Yeo.

'Actually, I thought you might like to do it,' said Blizzard. 'For Mattias.'

Yeo nodded.

'I would like that very much,' he said. 'Thank you. What will you be doing?'

'I have to lay my past to rest,' said Blizzard.

'Your arsonists?'

Blizzard nodded.

'Oh, yeah,' he said.

'That'll give you something to talk about the next time you pop round to George Ramsdale's for tea and biscuits,' said Stewart.

Blizzard's face broke into a rare grin as days of stress started to fall away.

'So it will,' he said. 'He'll like that, will George.'

Five minutes later, and still smiling at the joke, Blizzard strode down the corridor with Chen Sun, heading for the interview room that was holding Fu Li and Zhang Wei. They, like the other prisoners, were becoming increasingly apprehensive as they began to sense that something significant was happening, and looked uneasily at the Hafton officers as they entered the interview room.

'Sorry to keep you waiting, gentlemen,' said Blizzard. 'My name is Detective Chief Inspector John Blizzard, from Hafton Police, and my colleague Inspector Sun and I have travelled halfway round the world to have a nice, friendly chat with you. It's high time we talked about the fire at the Mounsey Street carpet factory, don't you think, Inspector?'

'It would be rude not to after coming all this way,' said Sun as the officers sat down.

'Unfortunately, DCI Ramsdale just missed you,' said Blizzard. 'He had to retire to spend more time with his camper van, but don't worry, we'll make the best of the situation without him. After all, we have so much to talk about, don't we?'

The prisoners looked even more worried. Something about the inspector's demeanour told them that the game was up.

Chapter twenty-three

Having left the Singaporean and British police legal teams to discuss the extradition process, the three weary, but exultant Hafton investigators boarded the Boeing 787 that would bring them home. On their arrival, they picked up their bags and headed for Chen Sun's car, where Blizzard lowered himself into the front passenger seat and rang Colley.

'The conquering heroes return,' said Colley. 'You'll be pleased to hear that Arthur told me that your critics at headquarters are struggling to come to terms with all the praise coming your way. They reckoned that you were in for a fall.'

'I'll bet they did,' said Blizzard. 'Did you put Alec Maynard under surveillance?'

'Your word is my command, Oh Great One. However, he's not shown any signs of doing a runner and he must know that something has been happening in Singapore.'

'Yes, but he may not know exactly what or how close we have got to him,' said Blizzard. 'Andy Yeo has been doing everything he can to stop word leaking out.'

'So, do you want me to arrest Maynard for when you get back?'

'No, leave him for now,' said Blizzard. 'I need to be sharp when we interview him and I hardly slept on the plane coming over. Tell the surveillance guys only to lift him if it looks like he's going to run, will you?'

'Sure,' said Colley. 'What time do you want to bring him in tomorrow?'

'Six?'

'Fine. I'll meet you at Abbey Road Nick at half-five then,' said Colley.

'Is his father still in hospital?'

'No, he came out yesterday. The cuts to his arms were superficial and the head injury was not as bad as the doctors feared. I went to see him with Sarah when he got home but he didn't give us anything in addition to what he has told us already, and that's not much.'

'How's Sarah taking it?' asked Blizzard. 'She's been struggling with everything that's coming out about Alec, I think.'

'She's trying to put a professional face on it. I was going to keep her out of it when we arrest Alec.'

'Fair enough,' said Blizzard.

* * *

Having gone into Abbey Road Police Station to check on developments, Blizzard finally headed for home and arrived shortly after 10.30pm. After a glass of whisky with Fee, he popped his head round Mikey's bedroom door – the toddler was sleeping peacefully – then headed for his bedroom. He fell asleep within seconds of his head hitting the pillow but was roused an hour later by a shaking of his shoulder.

'John,' hissed Fee's voice. 'Wake up.'

'What's wrong?' mumbled Blizzard, struggling to open his eyes.

Fee was standing at the window and staring down into the road through a crack in the curtain.

'I'm sure I saw someone in the street,' she said. 'I got up to go to the loo and looked out of the window on the way back and thought I saw him staring at our house.'

Blizzard snapped awake and joined her at the window to peer down into the road.

'I can't see anyone,' he said.

'I'm sure he was there, John.'

'Did you recognise him?'

'No, it was too dark,' she said. 'He was over near the street light. In the shadows. What should we do?'

'Well, we need to know if there really is someone there,' said Blizzard. 'I'll go down and ask him what he's up to.'

'What, just like that?' she said as he headed for the bedroom door. 'Do you want me to come with you?'

'No, you need to stay up here and make sure nothing happens to Mikey,' said the inspector as he walked out on the landing. 'Wish me luck.'

'Be careful,' said Fee.

Blizzard nodded and picked his way carefully down the stairs in the darkness – he had not switched on any lights so as not to alert the man in the street. At the bottom of the stairs, and now realising how foolhardy he was being, the inspector slipped on his shoes and looked round, wondering if there was anything that he could use as a weapon. Concluding that there was not – unless you counted Thomas the Tank Engine, and he didn't – he walked slowly along the hallway towards the front door where he quietly, and carefully, turned the catch and stepped onto his driveway. The street was deserted. Blizzard had expected it to be so; either the stranger had vanished or had not been there in the first place, but he was not about to start jumping to conclusions. He stood on the driveway for a few moments, watching for movement in the shadows, then Fee joined him and linked her arm into his.

'My hero,' she said, trying to sound like someone who was not worried. 'I take it you did not see him?'

'I am afraid not.'

'Do you think I imagined him?' she asked.

'After what happened to Jean Rawmarsh, I would not dare to even think it,' said Blizzard as they went back into the house.

'Who do you think it might have been?' asked Fee.

'There are two options, as I see it.'

'Which are?' asked Fee. She closed and locked the front door. 'And do I really want to know?'

'I'll tell you in a minute.'

He picked up the telephone from the hall table and dialled the number for the control room.

'It's DCI Blizzard,' he said. 'Can you let Acting Detective Inspector Colley know that we may have disturbed someone watching our house and can he rustle some troops to come out here, please? Apologise to him for waking him up.'

Call made, Blizzard and Fee walked into the kitchen where the inspector switched on the kettle.

'So what are these two options?' asked Fee. She opened a cupboard and produced a packet of biscuits.

'The first one is that it's Charlie Louden playing games,' said Blizzard. 'I think that Jean was right and that he's as crazy as the day he was sent to prison. That makes him extremely dangerous and I've not exactly endeared myself to him. Maybe I'm his new obsession.'

'Dear God, no,' said Fee. She looked increasingly worried. 'What if he goes for Mikey?'

'If it was him, it's me he's after.' Blizzard spooned coffee into Fee's mug and dropped a teabag into the mug that she had bought him for Christmas, which bore his photograph beneath the slogan *World's Best Cop*. 'But he can't stay on the run for ever. We'll nick him at some stage and, in the meantime, we can get some protection in place for the house and Mikey's nursery.'

'What's the other option?' asked Fee. 'A delivery man who is here to deliver a lovely fluffy teddy bear for Mikey?'

'You know that's not true.'

'A girl can hope,' she said. 'See, I have this nasty feeling that your second option is worse than your first one.'

'Well, it's certainly not much better,' said Blizzard. The kettle wheezed and he tested its warmth with the back of his hand. 'It's that we have spooked The South Siders so badly that they have decided to take action against us, starting with me.'

'So, who do you think was in our road tonight?' asked Fee.

She tipped the biscuits onto a plate.

'Might it have been Alec Maynard?'

'It could well have been,' said Blizzard. 'We have underestimated the man's propensity for criminal behaviour right from the start. Maybe The South Siders managed to get word to him despite Andy Yeo's lockdown. You should have seen the looks on their faces after they were arrested in Singapore, Fee. They thought that they were beyond the law, then suddenly they're all in handcuffs and facing long sentences after one of their own turned on them. Maybe they're hitting back.'

'So, what was the plan?' asked Fee. 'Come here tonight and try to scare you? If it was, he clearly does not know you very well.'

'I'm not sure about trying to intimidate me. We can't escape the fact that the gang has already killed two people in Hafton, one of whom was a detective.' Blizzard's hand hovered over the kettle's handle as the water approached boiling point. 'Maybe I'm number three.'

Fee gave him a sick look.

'I think I'll check that Mikey is OK,' she said and headed for the door into the hall.

Within half an hour, the road outside the house was a hive of police activity as uniformed officers arrived to search the village. Blizzard was in the kitchen with a worried-looking Arthur Ronald when Graham Ross walked into the room.

'Versace,' said Blizzard. 'Have you found anything?'

'I had a quick scout round but there's nothing useful,' said the forensics chief. 'It's exactly the same as happened at the Rawmarshes. Same for the officers searching the village, I believe. You may be off a few of your neighbours' Christmas card lists, though. They have not appreciated being woken up in the middle of the night by police officers tramping all over their gardens.'

'I don't imagine they have,' said Blizzard bleakly.

Colley walked into the kitchen, slipping his mobile phone into his coat pocket as he did so.

'Anything?' asked Blizzard.

'I am afraid not, guv. I've just been onto the surveillance team and they've got nothing. Alec has not left his home all night so whoever was outside your house, it wasn't him. They have been monitoring his mobile phone and ran a check to see if he got in touch with H for Hitman tonight, but he's had no calls in or out. Mind, they are pretty sure that he uses burner phones for the dodgy stuff so we'll not get anything there.'

'Like I keep saying,' replied Blizzard, 'we have underestimated our Mister Maynard.'

'I reckon you're right,' said Colley. 'Do you think that he killed his mother? It would make sense if your theory about her coming to tell us what she knew in return for us going easy on him is true.'

'It would indeed,' said Blizzard.

'So, what's the next move then?' asked Colley.

'Might I suggest that you take a few days off?' said Ronald, who had been listening intently to their conversation. 'Take Fee and Mikey and go away somewhere and leave us to wrap things up here?'

'Certainly not!' exclaimed Blizzard.

'No one will think any the worse of you,' said the superintendent.

'*I* will think the worse of me,' said Blizzard. 'I don't run away from things like this, Arthur. Surely, you know me well enough to know that's not my style. Besides, I want to be there when Alec Maynard realises that the game is up.'

Before Ronald could protest at the inspector's intransigence, Fee walked into the kitchen carrying Mikey, who was rubbing tired eyes. The toddler livened up when he saw his father, beamed and held out his arms.

'I'm sorry, John,' said Fee. 'He heard your voice and insisted that he see you.'

'No problem,' said Blizzard. He took his son in his arms. 'Always glad to see you, little man. And in answer to your question about the next move, David, I think it's high time that we disturbed Alec's beauty sleep. See how he likes it. Don't you?'

Chapter twenty-four

The clock on the dashboard in Blizzard's BMW had just ticked past 5.45am, and it was still dark as the inspector parked on the road outside Alec Maynard's Victorian villa, which stood in walled grounds in an affluent neighbourhood less than a mile from his parents' home. The inspector and Colley got out of the car and led the way up the drive. Following on behind him was Inspector Chen Sun, a couple of uniformed officers, one of whom was carrying a hydraulic ram, and two firearms specialists.

For Blizzard, it felt good to be carrying out a raid in the more familiar surroundings of Western District after his time in Singapore. He felt more in control of events than he had since the Rawmarshes walked into his office and, on arriving at the house, he rang several times on the doorbell and shouted 'Police!' a couple of times. However, the villa remained in darkness.

'Do you want me to smash the door in?' asked the officer with the hydraulic ram.

The inspector was about to give his approval when a light went on in the house. The officers heard movement and voices and the front door was opened by a bleary-eyed

Alec Maynard. He glowered at the officers for a few moments before anger replaced surprise.

'Do you know what time it is?' he protested.

There was the sound of crying children upstairs.

'I do,' said Blizzard, displaying no sympathy for any of the occupants of the house. 'Alec Maynard, you are under arrest on suspicion of money laundering and the murder of Jean Rawmarsh.'

'How dare you suggest that I killed my mother!' exclaimed Maynard. 'And with the woman not even in the ground!'

'We can discuss it when we get back to Abb—' began Blizzard.

'And why have you got them with you?' said Maynard, interrupting the inspector angrily as he noticed the armed officers. 'You'll terrify my kids!'

'We can't be too careful,' said Blizzard.

'Don't be ridiculous, man! I've never held a firearm in my life and I don't mind telling you that my family is sick and tired of your campaign of harassment and intimidation. If you had shown as much energy after my parents came to see you about Charlie, there's a good chance that my mother would still be alive.'

Maynard tried to close the door but Blizzard stepped forward and jammed it open with his foot.

'You're just making this worse,' he said.

A frightened-looking woman appeared in the hallway behind Maynard and the detectives caught a glimpse of two children on the stairs, peering nervously out from behind the banisters. One of them, a girl aged about seven, was crying.

'I'll give you five minutes to get dressed,' said Blizzard. 'Not a second more.'

Despite his growing sense of control, the inspector was keen to have the arrest completed as soon as possible and with the minimum of trouble; the last thing he wanted was newspaper headlines about the suspect being arrested at gunpoint in front of his distressed family – particularly *this* suspect and *this* family. For all that Blizzard had been receiving plaudits from senior officers at headquarters for the way he had handled the various strands of the investigation, he knew that one false move could cause all the good work to unravel.

Picking up on Blizzard's demeanour, which made it clear that the inspector would brook no more dissent, Maynard gave a snort of derision, turned back into the house and went upstairs to change, accompanied by Sun and Colley. Five minutes later, dressed in a suit, he left the house, ignoring the questions from his wife and instead instructing her to telephone their solicitor immediately as the officers led him down the drive. Having checked that he was out of earshot of his wife, who was now standing on the doorstep with the sobbing children, Maynard gave Blizzard a baleful look.

'I do hope, for your sake, that you know what you are doing, Chief Inspector,' he said. 'Because you will pay for the trauma you have caused to my family tonight. I'm no criminal, and you are going to look pretty foolish if you persist in saying that I am.'

'We'll see,' said Blizzard.

* * *

An hour later, having been processed in the custody suite at Abbey Road Police Station, Maynard found himself sitting next to his lawyer at the table in one of the interview rooms. Despite the early hour – the first wisp of daylight was yet to appear above the sleeping city – solicitor Edward Murray was clean-shaven and immaculately turned out in a dark suit complete with a neatly folded handkerchief in the top pocket of his jacket. How, thought Blizzard as he sat across the table from him, with his hair tousled and his tie at its customary half-mast, did these people manage always to look so smart, whatever the hour? Almost without realising he had done it, the inspector straightened his tie. Sitting next to him, David Colley, who was also neatly turned out as usual, noticed the gesture and gave the slightest of smiles. His boss returned it with an affectionate look. It was only a small moment but Blizzard found the familiar interaction between the two officers somehow reassuring after the disorientation of the globe-trotting of recent days. John Blizzard was ready to bring things to a conclusion.

For all the inspector's eagerness to resolve matters, and his anger at the way the stranger in the road had led Fee to fear for her son, he deliberately gave Maynard an easy ride for the first fifteen minutes of the interview, not showing his hand and allowing the suspect to grow increasingly confident in his belief that the police case against him was weak.

'Look, Chief Inspector,' said Maynard eventually, in a voice that suggested he was growing bored with proceedings, 'you can keep asking your questions, if it makes you feel better, but it won't change the fact that I know nothing about any of this and you have not presented us with any evidence to say otherwise.'

He glanced at his lawyer.

'I mean, money laundering, for God's sake, Edward,' he said. 'Have you ever heard anything so ludicrous?'

The solicitor shook his head.

'And that's before we get onto your crazy suggestion that I killed Mum,' said Maynard. 'We are all upset enough at her death without you adding to our distress with these false accusations. Everyone knows that Charlie killed her.'

Maynard looked accusingly at Colley.

'My father told you and Sarah Allatt when you came to the hospital on the night of the attack,' he said. 'And I told you when you came to the house later on. I mean, how many times do you need to be told?'

Colley was about to reply but Maynard did not give him the chance and instead turned his ire back on Blizzard.

'And, as for you,' he said, in a voice laced with contempt, 'not only do I fail to see why a detective with so much experience persists with this crazy notion, but I am also astonished that you should bring armed officers to my house in the middle of the night, terrifying my wife and kids!'

'I admit that it may have been a touch heavy-handed,' said Blizzard. He was still deliberately giving Maynard the sense that he was in control. 'And I can see why you would think that your mother was killed by Charlie Louden.'

'It hardly takes Sherlock Holmes to work it out, does it? As long as I have known him, Charlie has been obsessed with money. Even when we were kids, he was fixated on how much pocket money everyone got. My parents knew that, which is why they tried so hard to make you listen to them before he was released. But you just wouldn't listen, would you?' Maynard's words were coming in an angry torrent now. 'And now Mum's dead and my father is struggling with what's happened, even though he is putting on a brave face. And now, as if you needed any more reason to show you how wrong you have been about Charlie, he's gone on the run. Hardly the action of an innocent man, is it? If you ask me, you're the one who should be worried, not me.'

Apparently drained of emotion, he slumped back in his chair.

'He's right, Chief Inspector,' said Edward Murray. 'You really have made a terrible error of judgement. My client is a loving son and a respectable businessman, and anyone who has had dealings with him will tell you the same. However, we do not want to cause trouble for you; really, we don't. All we want is for my client to be released and for you to make a statement saying that he does not have a stain on his character. Just admit it, Chief Inspector, you've not been thinking straight and the time has come for you to make amends.'

'I blame the jet lag,' said Maynard.

'You may well be right,' said Blizzard. His voice sounded tired as he feigned weariness. 'I've not had much sleep in recent days.'

'Well, there you are then,' said Maynard. 'It's all a misunderstanding.'

He gave the detectives a look that was little short of triumph as his concerns about the confusing rumours coming out of Singapore faded and he began to contemplate the prospect of being released in time to have breakfast with the children. Alec Maynard did not know it at that moment, however, but it was to be a long time before he had breakfast with his children again. He did not notice the slight nod that Blizzard directed at Colley – the time had come to spring the trap.

'If we do release you,' said Blizzard, still sounding as if he acknowledged that he had been wrong, 'we will have to talk to people who know you. Just one or two and just so we can say that we have done it, you understand. We can't be seen to have just taken your word for it.'

'Of course, you can't,' said Maynard. 'I would be naïve to think that you could. Would it be helpful if I suggested some names?'

'Oh, I don't think that will be necessary,' said Blizzard. He glanced at Colley. 'I am sure that the acting inspector can come up with someone. Can't you, David?'

'One name does come to mind,' said Colley. 'How about Xavier Lim? Didn't you say that he had a lot to say about Alec when you met him in Singapore?'

'So he did,' said Blizzard, as if it had slipped his mind. 'He told me lots about organised crime, particularly The South Siders gang. It was very interesting.'

Maynard looked at him uneasily.

'In fact,' said Blizzard, and now there was an edge to his voice, 'one of the people he had a lot to say about was your pal Zayven Wen. Xavier had an awful lot to say about him.'

'What's Zayven got to do with it?' asked Maynard, clearly trying to conceal his growing concern at the change in the inspector's body language. 'Our companies have a legitimate working relationship and to insinuate anything else is indefensible.'

'Actually, it's you who may find things indefensible,' said Blizzard.

He reached under the table and produced his briefcase, from which he withdrew half a dozen sheets of paper filled with Xavier Lim's scrawl. The detectives could see that Maynard was increasingly nervous about the unexpected turn of events. His lawyer clearly noticed the transformation in his client too and viewed him with concern as Blizzard placed the papers on the table.

'What are they?' asked the solicitor. 'And who is Xavier Lim?'

'Xavier Lim is a member of The South Siders,' said Blizzard. He tapped the pieces of paper. 'And this is one of many statements that he has given over the past couple of days. This one is interesting because it confirms that your client has allowed his business to be used for money laundering, putting The South Siders' illegally obtained money through supposedly legitimate companies like his.'

'Well, he's wrong,' said Maynard but the look that had flickered across his face told a different story.

'Is he?' said Blizzard. He reached into his briefcase again and lifted out a much bulkier sheaf of papers, which he placed on the table with a hefty thud. 'I read this on the way over on the plane. Not the lightest of reads, if I'm honest, but very interesting, for all that. You probably recognise it, Alec. It's the audited accounts of your business for public consumption, which a good friend of mine in Singapore described as 'a work of pure fiction'. Beneath it is the real version, the one which shows how much dirty money has been flowing through your business. I am assured that a good forensic accountant would take about ten minutes to prove that you were money laundering on a grand scale, and that includes the time that it would take to make a cup of coffee.'

The inspector sat back in his chair and surveyed Maynard with a look of satisfaction.

'It's all over, Alec,' he said. 'Xavier Lim has stitched you up, good and proper. In fact, he's stitched the lot of you up. As we speak, twenty-three members of The South Siders are sitting in police cells in Singapore, awaiting court appearances. The gang is no more and you, my friend, are looking at a long prison sentence.'

Maynard had gone pale. He closed his eyes.

'I need some time with my client,' said Edward Murray. 'I knew nothing about any of this.'

'Well, when you talk to him,' said Blizzard, his eyes narrowing and his voice hardening, 'you may also want to discuss the fact that, as part of the deal to save his sorry hide, Xavier implicated Zayven in the murder of an undercover police officer whose body was found in the Mounsey Street carpet factory. He followed that up by signing a statement saying that your client and Zayven were involved in the murder of Alec's mother.'

'Why would they do that?' asked the solicitor.

'Apparently, her idea was that if she told us everything she knew about The South Siders, we would show our gratitude by promising a lighter charge and sentence for Alec,' said Blizzard. 'A show of loyalty to her son which subsequent events would seem to suggest he doesn't really deserve.'

It was this final comment that broke Alec Maynard's resolve. Emotion got the better of him and he doubled over the table, his body racked by sobs. The dispassionate detectives left him to talk to his solicitor and it was the best part of an hour before Edward Murray announced that his client was able to continue.

'Alec will admit to the money laundering offences,' said the solicitor, once they were all sitting in the interview room again. 'Apparently, you are correct when you say that the accounts tell you everything you need to know, so there is little point in him denying it. He wishes to say that he allowed himself to fall under the influence of criminals with whom he should not have been involved, and that he bitterly regrets the serious errors of judgement that followed. Greed is a terrible thing and it has cost him his good name.'

'Not to mention his mother her life,' said Blizzard acerbically. 'Talking of his mother–'

'Mum's death was nothing to do with me,' said Maynard. 'Xavier is wrong if he thinks that it was. Mum did not deserve to die like that, it was a wicked thing to do, but I did not do it. In fact, I did everything I could to persuade her not to come to see you. I told her that I'd be alright and warned her about the danger that she was putting herself in, but I don't think she believed me. Me and Dad even invented the stranger in the garden to scare her into keeping quiet but none of it worked. She always was a stubborn woman, was Mum.'

'And the murder itself?' asked Colley. 'Are you saying that Zayven carried it out?'

'I am saying that he planned it,' said Maynard enigmatically. His voice tailed off and he took a handkerchief out of his pocket as the tears started to flow again. He dabbed his eyes. 'That is all I am going to say.'

'But you haven't told us who killed your mum,' said Colley.

'You'll not get his name out of me.'

'Why not?' asked Blizzard. 'You've admitted everything else. I take it that it was him outside our house last night?'

'I assume so,' said Maynard. 'He said that he was going to check the area out. He's very careful, cautious you might even say, and he was furious when you spotted him. But you can take it from me that he'll be back, Chief Inspector. He'll keep coming back until he kills you.'

'But why kill me?' asked Blizzard. He tried to come over as calm; it was not his first death threat, far from it, but they were always difficult to deal with. 'I can understand why they decided that your mother had to die, but what would my death achieve? There will always be someone to step into my shoes.'

'The South Siders hope that killing a police officer will be so shocking that it will frighten other officers into keeping quiet,' said Maynard. 'Particularly if the one they kill is someone like yourself, who has a record of using the Proceeds of Crime Act to rob organised crime of its profits. The South Siders might look like a bunch of harmless students but they are absolutely ruthless. Just ask Mattias Chau. Anyone who is standing between the gang and their money is in danger – and you are standing between them and their money, as was my mother.'

'But you're not going to give us the name of the person that they have sent to do their dirty work?'

'Do you know, I think I'll leave you to work that one out for yourself,' said Maynard. He gave the inspector a devilish look. 'It'll be something to keep your mind active as you try not to succumb to jet lag. One thing I would say is that he won't kill you reluctantly, he's not being forced into it by The South Siders. He's always been obsessed with money and anyone that threatens to take it away from him is fair game, as far as he is concerned…'

Chapter twenty-five

Although every instinct in John Blizzard's body told him to finish work early and catch up on his sleep so that he was refreshed and ready to protect his family that evening, the inspector decided that the comment by Alec Maynard about the killer's cautious nature meant that he should stay at Abbey Road Police Station. He made it to 5pm, nodding off at his desk on several occasions but making sure that when he returned home, he had done nothing that might suggest a change in routine, should the murderer be watching the house.

The inspector's final words to Arthur Ronald before he left work were that they just had to hope that news of Alec Maynard's arrest would not deter the killer. However, Blizzard asserted confidently, Maynard's comment about the murderer's obsessive nature suggested that he would not be able to resist the opportunity to go ahead with his plan.

Ronald, who very much hoped that the killer would not appear, decided against one final attempt to persuade his stubborn friend to book himself and his family into a hotel for the night and leave fellow officers to deal with the evening's events. He knew that it would just be so much wasted breath.

So it was that John Blizzard arrived home at 5.30pm and crawled into bed half an hour later, Mikey having demanded playtime first. Fee woke the inspector up shortly before 9pm. After taking a shower, he dressed in jeans and a black T-shirt, looked in on Mikey, kissing the sleeping toddler on the forehead, then went downstairs to the living room, where he sat down in his usual armchair. The smell of his tea wafting in from the kitchen made the inspector realise how hungry he was, and he grinned when, just two minutes later, Fee emerged and handed him a plateful of shepherd's pie and assorted vegetables.

'Excellent,' he said. 'Thank you.'

'Did you get enough sleep?' she asked, sitting down in her armchair.

'Enough to keep me going.' Blizzard dug his fork into the pie. 'Boy, am I ready for this.'

'Did you look in on Mikey?' asked Fee. She tried to make the question sound casual, as if she did not have a care in the world, but she could not conceal her unease.

'Yeah, he's away with the fairies.' Blizzard looked at her when she did not reply. 'You OK?'

She could contain her composure no longer.

'Of course I'm not OK!' she exclaimed, her voice trembling with emotion. 'I still think that we should have sent him to my parents' for the night or taken Arthur up on his offer of a hotel.'

'I know you do, but everything has to look normal. This guy is very cautious and since there is every possibility that he may have been watching the house for a while, we can't do anything to spook him. We need to catch him in the act of trying to kill me. It's the only way we can prove that he's our murderer.'

'I know,' she said reluctantly. 'Have you come to any conclusions about who he is?'

'Alec was clearly trying to push me in the direction of Charlie Louden without actually naming him. Some kind of warped family loyalty, maybe.'

'But Charlie does not have much in the way of contact with The South Siders, does he?' said Fee.

'He doesn't, but Martin Crumpsall does, remember, and he and Charlie are thick as thieves,' said Blizzard. 'Perhaps they plan to kill me together.'

Fee shuddered.

'How can you be so matter-of-fact about it?' she said.

'Because I'm not worried,' said Blizzard. 'And there's no need for you to look so worried, either. There's no way we can come to any harm. We're well protected, you know that. And there's no way that Mikey will remember what happens here tonight – assuming that he even wakes up.'

'I know, I know,' said Fee. She looked at the clock on the wall and sighed. 'I just wish it was all over.'

'It will be soon enough,' said Blizzard and took another mouthful of shepherd's pie.

They spent the remainder of the evening trying, and failing, to concentrate on the television until, just after 11.15pm, there was a crackling sound from Blizzard's radio, which was on a side table next to his chair. It was Colley.

'It's past your bedtime, kiddywinks,' he said.

'Yes, Dad,' said Blizzard. 'Do I take it that he's here?'

'Yeah. One of our surveillance teams has just spotted him in a garden in the next road, heading towards your place. They couldn't make out his face, though.'

'Well, we won't have to wait long to find out who he is,' said Blizzard. He stood up and looked at Fee. 'Come on, let's get this done.'

They walked upstairs to the bedroom and lay on the bed. After twenty minutes, Blizzard leaned over and kissed Fee on the cheek.

'Sleep tight,' he said.

'Like that's going to happen,' she said.

They switched off their bedside lights and lay quietly in the shadows that were cast by the lamp on the landing, that was always left on at night for Mikey. They lay in silence for what felt like the longest hour of their lives, straining for any sound that would indicate the arrival of their man in the house. They didn't hear anything until, a few minutes after midnight, a faint noise downstairs told them that the intruder had forced the back door.

Blizzard and Fee tensed but neither spoke, trying instead to imagine the man's stealthy progress as he made his way across the kitchen floor and out into the hallway. They sensed that he stood and listened for a few moments before, having satisfied himself that everyone was asleep, he started to climb the stairs, his progress indicated by the characteristic creak of the fifth step. He reached the top of the stairs, where the glow from the lamp glinted off the machete in his hand, and was about to head towards the couple's bedroom when one of the other doors opened and two firearms officers appeared. Robert Rawmarsh stared at them in horror as they trained their guns on him.

'Drop the weapon,' said one of the officers.

Rawmarsh thought for a moment, unsure what to do, until another bedroom door swung open and John Blizzard emerged.

'You heard the man,' said the inspector. 'The game's up.'

Still, Robert Rawmarsh hesitated, then with a roar of fury, he lifted the machete above his head and lunged towards Blizzard, ready to bring the weapon slicing down on the detective's skull. He got no further because a single shot rang out. For a split second, his main reaction seemed to be surprise; then, without a sound, he slipped to his knees and pitched forwards to lie still. The firearms officer lowered his weapon.

'Sorry, John,' he said. 'I had no option.'

'You'll not find an argument from me,' said Blizzard.

Several police officers thundered up the stairs, led by Chen Sun and David Colley, and a shaken Fee emerged from the bedroom. The firearms officer glanced towards Mikey's bedroom and shook his head in disbelief.

'Your son will sleep through anything,' he said.

Fee gave a wan smile and went to check that the toddler was alright. Blizzard looked down at the body of Robert Rawmarsh.

At least you will have made an effort. Then, if something awful does happen, you'll be able to tell yourself that you tried, won't you?

Chapter twenty-six

Following the death of Robert Rawmarsh, a solemn Blizzard drove to Abbey Road Police Station, where he made his way immediately to Alec Maynard's cell. The businessman, who was due to appear before magistrates on money laundering charges later that morning, was awake and sitting up when the detective arrived. The expression on the inspector's face told the prisoner all he needed to know.

'He's dead, isn't he?' said Maynard.

'I'm afraid so,' said Blizzard. 'I'm sorry, Alec, I really am, but he went for me with a machete and one of the firearms officers shot him.'

Maynard shook his head sadly.

'It's the only way it was going to end,' he said.

'There'll be an inquiry, of course, but I'm not sure that our man had much choice. Your father clearly wanted me dead. Why would you not tell me that it was him who was coming for me?'

'I'm not sure,' said Maynard. He considered the question for a few moments. 'When you interviewed me yesterday, you said that I did not deserve my mother's loyalty. That hurt, it really did. Maybe, in some strange way, I wanted to show that I can be loyal. Not that my father deserved my loyalty, but I guess it's a families thing. For what it's worth, I'm glad that he did not kill you. The idea of your little lad without his father does not bear thinking about. I know that I've just lost my father but it's different for adults, isn't it? Particularly with a man like that.'

'I am getting the strong impression that you did not get on?' said Blizzard, walking over to him and sitting on the bench.

'That's the understatement of the year, Chief Inspector. I have not got on with him for a long time. He was always a domineering man, even when I was your little lad's age, and it got worse as the years passed. I really shouldn't have gone into business with him. I knew that it was a mistake. You know I told you that he was obsessed with money?'

Blizzard nodded.

'Well, it coloured his every waking thought,' said Maynard. 'When I told you that he came out of retirement because I needed his help on the Mounsey Street project, it wasn't true. I could have handled things, no problem. The real story is that my father just wanted to keep on making money. He didn't need any more of the stuff but it was like an illness, and the way he flaunted his wealth, driving his vintage car round the neighbourhood on a weekend, making sure that his friends knew how much he had spent on paintings and antiques, it was sickening. It's the same obsession that afflicts Charlie, it's just that my father could do something about it.'

'Surely, you could have got out of the business?' asked Blizzard.

'I was building up the courage to strike out on my own but then we got involved with The South Siders. After that, it was impossible to walk away. I saw what Zayven did to that poor undercover police officer and I was in no doubt that he would have done the same to me if I'd threatened to quit. I had to think of my kids. I did not want them losing their father.'

'I can understand that,' said Blizzard. 'How involved was your father with your criminal activities?'

'He was the one who pushed for it after Zayven pitched the Mounsey Street scam to us. I was keen, at first, but not for long. Pretty soon, I realised that I needed to get out but, like I say, then they murdered Mattias Chau, and there was no way I was going to do anything.'

'I assume that Jean knew what Robert was doing?'

'Of course she did,' said Maynard, 'and she hated it. Absolutely hated it. She was a very moral woman, was my mother. That's why Aunt Margaret asked her to look after her inheritance all those years ago. Mum was the only person in the family that she could trust.'

Blizzard thought about the family members he had met over recent days and nodded.

'Anyway,' said Maynard, 'she saw me getting more and more involved in crime and decided to do something to get me out of trouble. She said she did not want her grandchildren to have a father in prison.'

Tears started in Maynard's eyes; it was the first time he had shown emotion since Blizzard had walked into the cell. He rubbed his eyes with the back of his sleeve. Blizzard said nothing, giving him time to compose himself again.

'I told Mum that she should not do anything stupid,' Maynard continued, 'but she insisted that she was going to offer to tell you everything she knew in return for lenient treatment for me. She was not bothered about trying to save Dad – it had been a long time since she was bothered about him – and he was furious when he heard what she planned to do. I have never seen him so angry. Then Zayven said that we had to kill her.'

'And Robert did it?'

'He did it that night. He told me that he waited for her to fall asleep then attacked her with the machete. He'd bought it in a militaria shop. No questions asked, apparently.'

'Well, we'll be paying it a visit. I can assure you of that. And the injuries on him? I take it he inflicted them on himself?'

'He thought it would make it look even more likely that Charlie did it.' Maynard shook his head sadly. 'I am sure that Mum never thought that he would kill her. Neither did I. I mean, how could we think a thing like that?'

'And all this fuss over Charlie?' asked Blizzard. 'Did your parents genuinely believe that he might come for them when he was released?'

'I don't think Dad did but Mum definitely believed it. Charlie's crazy, always has been, and you know what happens to anyone who stands between a crazy member of my family and their money!'

'I certainly do,' said Blizzard. He stood up. 'Are you prepared to give us a statement saying what you have just told me?'

Maynard nodded.

'There's no loyalty owed to the dead, is there?' he said.

'I guess not. One more thing before I go. We've been going through your real accounts and there are monthly payments of £2,000 to a company called GD Limited but we don't know who owns it and what they are for.'

'And you'll not hear it from me,' said Maynard. He gave Blizzard a crooked smile. 'It's a loyalty to the living thing, Chief Inspector!'

With their conversation at an end, Blizzard returned to his office, sat down behind his desk and allowed himself to close his eyes. The inspector did not get to enjoy the luxury for long, however, because there came a knock on the door. He opened his eyes to see Sarah Allatt standing there, having returned to the police station after being among the many officers deployed to Blizzard's village ahead of the attack.

'I wondered when you would come to see me,' said the inspector, and gestured for her to take a seat.

'It took a lot of courage,' she said, sitting down. She appeared to be close to tears. 'I mean, I made a real hash of things, didn't I? I was the closest to the Rawmarshes and I didn't see any of it. I didn't see their money laundering and I had no idea that Robert could commit murder.'

'Don't beat yourself up over it. I'm not sure anyone comes out of this with much honour. We all reacted far too late.' Blizzard noticed that she was holding a sheet of paper. 'What's that then? Anything interesting?'

The young constable cheered up.

'It certainly is,' she said. 'You know that mention of GD Limited in Alec's accounts?'

Blizzard nodded.

'Well, a pal of mine works in bank security and he pulled a few strings to find out who's behind the company,' said Allatt. 'This email was waiting for me when I got back.' She slid the piece of paper across the desk.

Blizzard picked it up and a smile crept across his face.

'Well, well, who would have thought it?' he said. The inspector glanced up at the wall clock. 'It's a bit early to go calling on City Hall. Meet me back here at half eight and we can go and make ourselves feel better by ruining someone else's day!'

Chapter twenty-seven

Having made the short drive to City Hall, Blizzard and Allatt bypassed protests from the staff on the reception desk and climbed the stairs leading to the chief executive's first-floor office, where they found their way barred by Miranda Goldsworthy's stern-faced PA. She was about to object to their presence but Blizzard brushed past her and entered the office, followed by Allatt. Miranda Goldsworthy, who had been alerted by one of the reception staff, was standing in the middle of the room, arms crossed, awaiting their arrival.

'What on earth do you think you are doing?' she said.

'I think you know exactly what we are doing,' said Blizzard. He turned round and took the piece of paper from Allatt. 'Tell us about GD Limited. And perhaps you would also you care to explain why, as a paid employee of the city council, you are being paid a monthly fee by Alec Maynard's property company?'

'I don't know what you are talking about,' said Goldsworthy but she had gone pale and seemed unsteady on her feet.

'It's nothing to do with your regular trips to Singapore, then?' asked Blizzard. 'I understand you particularly like the nightclubs?'

The chief executive sat down heavily on her sofa.

'I hope you have a good answer,' said Blizzard, 'because from where I am standing, and given that Alec Maynard is due in court this morning on money laundering charges, you look like someone who has landed themself in a lot of trouble.'

Goldsworthy looked shocked at the news and took a few moments to compose herself.

'I am afraid that I have been rather foolish,' she said eventually.

'I know that,' said Blizzard. 'It's the word that was also used by Alya Goh. She said that you were in over your head.'

'Who's Alya Goh?'

'She's the commander of the Singapore Police Organised Crime Unit,' said Blizzard. 'She has taken a great deal of interest in your involvement with members of The South Siders gang, particularly Zayven Wen, Fu Li and Zhang Wei. I am told that there are some particularly good surveillance pictures of you with them at one of the city's nightclubs.'

Miranda Goldsworthy closed her eyes.

'For what it's worth,' continued Blizzard, 'the commander does not think that you have engaged in corruption.'

Goldsworthy opened her eyes and gave him a bleak look.

'And what do you think?' she asked.

'It does rather depend on what Alec Maynard was paying GD Limited all that money for.'

Goldsworthy sighed.

'I didn't do it for personal gain,' she said. 'None of the money came to me. You have to believe that. Alec was paying me to make sure that the Mounsey Street development went ahead. Listed building status was going to be awkward and he wanted me to, in his words, smooth the way.'

'Smooth the way, how?' asked the inspector. 'With financial inducements?'

Goldsworthy nodded.

'I know someone in the Department for Culture, Media and Sport, which is responsible for the National Heritage List,' she said. 'He's been helping me.'

'Did you not know that the whole thing was one big money laundering scheme?' asked Blizzard. 'Surely, you must have suspected something, especially after your visits to Singapore?'

'I did wonder, yes, but they seemed genuine about wanting to create the new retail park, and that was my only interest. I only ever acted for the good of the city.'

'We'll have to let a jury work that one out,' said Blizzard. 'Miranda Goldsworthy, I am arresting you on suspicion of bribery as set out in the Bribery Act 2010.'

He glanced at Allatt.

'And all before I've had my breakfast, Constable,' he said. 'That's some going!'

Allatt grinned; she was starting to enjoy working with John Blizzard.

The inspector had just led the chief executive out of her office, telling the stunned PA to 'hold Miranda's calls' on his way past, when his mobile phone rang. Leaving Allatt to accompany Goldsworthy down the stairs watched by shocked and silent staff, he took the call and walked a few paces behind her.

'Who is this?' he asked.

'Charlie Louden,' said a voice.

'How did you get my number?'

'Never mind how,' said Louden. 'I hear that it was my dear Uncle Robert who killed Aunt Jean and that one of your trigger-happy officers has shot him dead. Does that mean you will stop hassling me now?'

'Yes, you're in the clear,' said Blizzard. 'But my colleagues at the NHS Fraud Unit would very much like to talk to Martin. Is he with you?'

'He is, but I think you will find that he is somewhat disinclined to talk to you,' said Louden. 'Anyway, can't spend all day gossiping. We're going to lay low for a while until everything blows over. Somewhere foreign. I hear Singapore is nice at this time of year. Oh, one more thing before we go, now that Robert and Jean are dead and I imagine that Alec is going away for a long stretch, I reckon that I have a good chance of inheriting the remainder of Aunt Margaret's estate. What do you think?'

But before Blizzard could reply, the line went dead.

Chapter twenty-eight

Blizzard and Colley sat at the table in the inspector's kitchen, nursing mugs of tea and watching their children playing on the floor. It was a Saturday afternoon almost a year after the inspector's trip to Singapore. Fee and Jay had gone shopping so the fathers were looking after the children, before they all met up again for party tea. Mikey, as usual, was playing with his Thomas the Tank Engine toys and Colley's six-year-old daughter Laura with a couple of dolls. An earnest dark-haired girl, known as Looby to her friends, she would occasionally glance up at the two men and smile before returning her attention to Mikey.

'She's very good with him,' said Blizzard.

'Yeah, she is,' said Colley. 'She wants to be a teacher, after her mum.'

'I'm sure she'll do very well.'

'I reckon you're right,' said Colley. He reached for the A4 envelope that he had brought with him and which now lay on the table. 'Talking of teachers, I've been doing some maths for your jolly in Rome.'

'It's a working trip and well you know it,' said Blizzard.

'Oh, aye, an invite to address an Interpol conference that just so happens to be in your favourite city. A talk lasting one hour on how we successfully worked with the police in Singapore and the remaining time free for pizza and beer. Don't make me cry!'

Blizzard chuckled.

'Anyway,' said Colley, opening the envelope, 'I thought it would be useful if I totted up the number of years everyone was sentenced to.'

'Good idea,' said Blizzard. 'Who did you start with?'

'Alec Maynard,' said Colley. 'Pleaded guilty to twelve money laundering charges at Hafton Crown Court, sentenced to fifteen months in prison. Then you've got the Singapore nationals. Thirty-four members of The South Siders were charged with 211 offences, ranging from murder and arson to fraud. Jail sentences added up to 565 years in prison.'

'Does that total include those sentenced in courts over here after their extradition?' asked Blizzard.

'It does, yes.' Colley ran his down the sheet of paper. 'Fu Li and Zhang Wei pleaded guilty to arson at Hafton Crown Court and were each sentenced to three and a half years in prison, following which they will be sent back to Singapore to serve a four-year sentence for money laundering. Wei Ji Tan pleaded guilty to twenty-seven cases of prescription fraud at Hafton Crown Court and was sentenced to eight years.

'Zayven Wen pleaded guilty to the murder of Mattias Chau and was sentenced to life with a recommendation that he serve a minimum of twenty-eight years, and Xavier Lim pleaded guilty to three charges of prescription fraud at a Singapore court and was given a two-year suspended sentence. What's more, Sean Gracey pleaded guilty to seven charges of prescription fraud at Hafton Crown Court and was sentenced to three and a half years in prison, and Miranda Goldsworthy pleaded guilty to six charges of bribery and was given a two-year suspended sentence and was sacked from her job as council chief executive.'

'It's pretty impressive when you read it all out like that,' said Blizzard.

'It certainly is. Tot it all up and you have thirty-seven people dealt with, two hundred and thirty-six charges and prison sentences totalling six hundred years!' Colley frowned. 'The only black mark is that Martin Crumpsall is still wanted for questioning on prescription fraud charges.'

'We'll get him one day,' said Blizzard. 'After all, we'll go anywhere, won't we?'

'Speak for yourself,' said Colley.

'Next time, Inspector,' said Blizzard. 'Next time.'

List of characters

Other law enforcement officers:

Mattias Chau – plainclothes sergeant with Singapore police
Alya Goh – Commander, Singapore Police Organised Crime Unit
DCI George Ramsdale – retired Western Division CID detective chief inspector
Ruth Stewart – former east-side DCI, now head of Hafton NHS Fraud Investigation Unit
Andy Yeo – plainclothes inspector with Singapore Police

Rawmarsh/Louden Family:

Margaret Kelleher – Charlie Louden's deceased aunt
Janice Louden – sister of Margaret and Jean
Charlie Louden – Janice's son
Alec – Charlie Louden's cousin/Jean and Robert's son
Jean Rawmarsh – Charlie Louden's aunt/sister of Margaret Kelleher
Robert Rawmarsh – Charlie Louden's uncle/Jean's husband

Singapore nationals:

Fu Li – former owner, Mounsey Street Carpets
Xavier Lim – owner of GP practices
Wei Ji Tan – owner of GP practices
Zhang Wei – former owner, Mounsey Street Carpets
Zayven Wen – property agent

Others:

Laura (Looby) Colley – David Colley's daughter
Martin Crumpsall – fraudster/former inmate, Hafton Prison
Fee Ellis – Blizzard's girlfriend and mother of his son Michael (Mikey)
Sean Gracey – Hafton GP

Mikey – Blizzard's son
Miranda Goldsworthy – City Council Chief Executive
Maureen Rodgers – Assistant Governor, Hafton Prison
Edward Murray – solicitor
Peter Reynolds – Home Office pathologist

If you enjoyed this book, please let others know by leaving a quick review on Amazon. Also, if you spot anything untoward in the paperback, get in touch. We strive for the best quality and appreciate reader feedback.

editor@thebookfolks.com

www.thebookfolks.com

When a routine archaeological dig turns up bodies on the site of a WWII prisoner of war camp, it should be an open and shut case for detective John Blizzard. But forensics discover one of the deaths is more recent and the force have a murder investigation on their hands.

After a family is brutally murdered, one child is never found. It still troubles DCI John Blizzard to this day. But new clues emerge that will take him deep into the criminal underworld and into conflict with the powers that be. Cracking the case will take all of the detective's skills, and more. Coming out unscarred will be impossible.

Veteran crime-solver DCI John Blizzard is confronted with his hardest case yet when a boxer and wide boy is found dead in a railway signal box. Someone is determined to ruin the investigation and prepared to draw the residents of a local housing estate into a war with the police to get their way. Has the detective finally met his match?

While detective John Blizzard looks into a series of drug-related deaths, his nemesis, gangland thug Morrie Raynor, is released from prison. Blizzard becomes convinced Raynor is linked to a new crime spree, but with little evidence other than the ravings of a sick, delirious man, the detective's colleagues suspect his personal feelings are clouding his judgement.

A corrupt industrialist is found dead in his home. When his family shed crocodile tears, DCI John Blizzard turns the screw. But when their alibis check out, can his team track down the real killer among a long list of likely suspects?

An undercover detective is shot in his home. Later, police officers on a routine patrol are fired at. Someone has a big problem with law enforcement. DCI Blizzard starts a crackdown on his city's most notorious gangsters. But is he in danger of rubbing the wrong people up the wrong way? Or is he already on the killer's list?

Someone is starting deadly fires, but the only clue to their identity is the obscure poetry that DCI John Blizzard receives on his desk. Taunting the police is one thing. Taunting Blizzard another. He'll stop at nothing to crack the case and collar the arsonist.

No-nonsense detective John Blizzard faces a difficult case when the matriarch of a criminal family is found dead. He must act quick to stop the situation from escalating into a gangland war.

When a dangerous convicted felon is released from prison, DCI Blizzard makes it clear he is unwelcome on his patch. But when a local church takes the man in, Blizzard has to deal with the community uproar. When a local youth is killed it will take all of the detective's skills to right a wrong.

When a youth is scared out of his wits in the local church graveyard by a man dressed all in black, the police don't think much of his tales about a bogeyman, but they are forced to take them more seriously when a murder later takes place there. DCI John Blizzard will have to suspend disbelief and work out the identity of The Vengeance Man before he wreaks havoc in the neighbourhood.

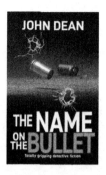

When a cop taking part in a reality TV show is shot dead, it is not the positive image the force was looking to convey. DCI John Blizzard, no media darling himself, sets to finding the killer. This leads him to lock horns with a renowned gangster who acts like he is above the law. Yet as Blizzard tries to balance the scales of justice, he is thrown a curve ball from his own side.

All these books are FREE with Kindle Unlimited and available in paperback!

Books 1-7 are also available in a box set exclusively on Kindle. They are great value for a binge-reading session.

Detective Chief Inspector Jack Harris is a former soldier
who, as a youth, fled his life in a remote North Pennines
valley when he began to get involved in crime. Having
joined the Army and then worked as a police officer in
Manchester, the northern hills drew him back, as he always
knew they would.

A man who would rather devote his time to walking the
dogs, he finds instead that his job running CID requires him
to deal with the effects of isolation on the community and
the impact of criminals who travel in from outside the area
to commit offences.

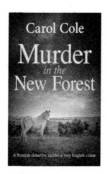

THAT CARE FORGOT by James Warren

Junior attorney Rebecca Holt isn't too happy when given the pro bono case of a convicted murderer. Yet Nick Malone isn't really interested in his parole hearing, rather he is obsessed with a serial killer who terrorized New Orleans in the 1990s. When Malone reveals his secrets, Rebecca is faced with a life-changing decision.

FREE with Kindle Unlimited and available in paperback!

Visit www.thebookfolks.com for more great titles like these!

Printed in Great Britain
by Amazon

57026106R10121